Fourth Edition

Career Counseling
Applied Concepts of Life Planning

Fourth Edition

Career Counseling
Applied Concepts of Life Planning

Vernon G. Zunker
Southwest Texas State University

Brooks/Cole Publishing Co.
Pacific Grove, California

I(T)P ™
The trademark ITP is used under license.

A CLAIREMONT BOOK

Brooks/Cole Publishing Company
A Division of Wadsworth, Inc.

Printed in the United States of America

10   9   8   7   6   5   4   3

Library of Congress Cataloging-in-Publication Data

Zunker, Vernon G., [date]
    Career counseling: applied concepts of life planning / by Vernon
G. Zunker. -- 4th ed.
        p. cm.
    Includes bibliographical references and index.
    ISBN 0-534-21205-0
    1. Vocational guidance.   I. Title.
HF5381.Z86   1993
371.4'25--dc20   93-31419
                                                                        CIP

Sponsoring Editor: Claire Verduin
Editorial Associate: Gay C. Bond
Production Editor: Nancy L. Shammas
Production Assistant: Tessa A. McGlasson
Manuscript Editor: Robin Witkin
Permissions Editor: Elaine Jones
Interior Design: Vernon T. Boes
Cover Photo: UNIPHOTO, Picture Agency, Inc.
Cover Design: Robert Taylor
Art Coordinator: Lisa Torri
Typesetting: Weimer Graphics
Cover Printing: Southeastern Color Graphics
Printing and Binding: Arcata Graphics/Fairfield

To Rosalie
For years of love, trust, and devotion

Contents

PART ONE
FOUNDATIONS AND RESOURCES

1

Chapter One ₳ᴸᴸ
Historical Development of Career Counseling

3

The Birth of the Career-Guidance Movement: 1850 to 1940   4
Growth of the Career-Guidance Movement: 1940 to the Present   9
A Glance into the Past and a Look into the Future   17
Summary   22
Supplementary Learning Exercises   24

Chapter Two ₙᴸᴸ
Theories of Career Development

25

Trait-and-Factor Theory   25
Developmental Theories   27
Ann Roe: A Needs Approach   42
John Holland: A Typology Approach   45
Social-Learning Theory of Career Choice   49
Career Development from a Cognitive
   Information-Processing Conceptual Perspective   52
Evolving Theories of Career Development   54
Other Theories of Career Development   56
Implications for Career Guidance   59
Summary   61
Supplementary Learning Exercises   62

Chapter Three   ɑʟ
Some Perspectives of Work   *64*

Work Motivation   64
Work Adjustment   69
Work Values   71
The American Work Ethic   72
Work Commitment   73
Stress at Work: Its Implications and How to Deal with It   76
Will There Be a Demand for Increased Quality of Work?   80
Summary   81
Supplementary Learning Exercises   82

Chapter Four   ɑʟ
Career Life Planning   *83*

Dimensions of Career Life Planning   84
Career Choice   85
Role of Leisure in Career Life Planning   86
Career Life Planning as a Promotion of Personal Competence   86
Dimensions of Lifestyle Orientation   88
Life-Planning Workshops   91
Other Prominent Career Life-Planning Programs   96
Career Life Planning in Perspective   99
Summary   100
Supplementary Learning Exercises   101

Chapter Five
The Dictionary of Occupational Titles, the Occupational Outlook Handbook, and Career Clusters   *102*

The Importance of Labor-Market Information   102
The Dictionary of Occupational Titles (DOT)   103
Definitions of Interests:
    The Guide for Occupational Exploration (GOE)   110
The Occupational Outlook Handbook (OOH)   114
Career Clusters   115
Summary   120
Supplementary Learning Exercises   121

Chapter Six ① Introduction
② advantage + disadvantages
Using Computers for Career Counseling   **123**

Some Implications of Research   124
Types of Computer-Assisted Career-Guidance Systems   126
The Development of Career Information Delivery Systems   127
Using DISCOVER   128
Steps in Using Computer-Assisted Career-Guidance Programs   133
Selecting a Computer-Assisted Career-Guidance System   134
Summary   135 only Occupational Handbook
Supplementary Learning Exercises   136

Chapter Seven not responsible 137-140
Using Standardized   146-153
Assessment in Career Counseling   **137**

Aptitude Tests   138
Achievement Tests   141
Interest Inventories   143
Personality Inventories   146
Values Inventory   150
Career-Maturity Inventories   153
Self-Assessment   155
Summary   156
Supplementary Learning Exercises   157

Chapter Eight
The Career Resource Center   **158**

The Purpose and Use of a CRC   159
Rationale   159
Organizational Procedures   160
Establishing an Advisory Committee   160
Developing Objectives   161
Location and Posture   162
Resource Components   163
Innovations in Dissemination of Career Information   173
Summary   175 only
Supplementary Learning Exercises   176

PART TWO
CAREER-GUIDANCE PROGRAMS IN EDUCATIONAL INSTITUTIONS   179

Chapter Nine
Implications of Developmental Patterns and Research for Career Guidance in Schools   181

Studies of Early Childhood Development   181
Stages of Development and Developmental
    Tasks for Elementary School Children   182
Stages of Development and Developmental
    Tasks for Junior and Senior High School Students   191
Career Development Concerns of Senior High School Students   198
Summary   203 only
Supplementary Learning Exercises   205

Chapter Ten
Career Guidance in Schools   206

Future Trends in Education   206
A Definition of Career Education   207
Current School Career-Guidance Programs   212
Strategies for Implementing Career-Development Guidelines   228
A Comprehensive School-Guidance Program   229
Integrating Academic and Vocational Education   230
Government-Sponsored Programs: Planning for the Future   232
Placement as Part of Career Planning   235
Summary   238
Supplementary Learning Exercises   238

Chapter Eleven
Career Guidance in Institutions of Higher Learning   239

The Psychosocial Development of College Students   239
NOICC Goals for a College Career-Guidance Program   243
Curricular Career-Information Service (CCIS): A Module Model   247
A Paraprofessional Model   251
Career Counseling at a Large University: A Metroplex Model   256
A Decision-Making Approach   259
Work and Experience-Based Programs   263

College Placement   264
Summary   274   only
Supplementary Learning Exercises   276

PART THREE
CAREER-GUIDANCE
PROGRAMS FOR ADULTS IN TRANSITION   277

Chapter Twelve
Career Development
of Adults in Organizations   279
The Organization As It Exists Today   280
Evolution of Career Development in Organizations   285
Changing Organizations and New Concepts in Career Development   299
Evaluating the Organization   304
Summary   307   only
Supplementary Learning Exercises   308

Chapter Thirteen
Career Counseling
for Adults in Career Transition   310
Issues Facing Adults in Career Transition   311
Midlife Crisis and Career Development   315
Basic Coping Skills for Managing Transitions   316
Career-Counseling Implications in Adult Developmental Models   316
Career-Counseling Components for Adults in Career Transition   325
Summary   336   only
Supplementary Learning Exercises   338

PART FOUR
CAREER-GUIDANCE PROGRAMS
FOR SPECIAL POPULATIONS   339

Chapter Fourteen   ALL
Special Issues in Career Counseling for Women   341
Career-Development Theories and Women   342
Identifying Special Needs of Women   345

Implications for Career Counseling   352
Components for Counseling Women   352
Counselor Bias   357
Gender Bias and Gender Fairness of Interest Assessment   358
Summary   361
Supplementary Learning Exercises   362

Chapter Fifteen
Special Issues in Career Counseling for Men   363
Influences on Gender-Role Development   363
Identifying Special Needs of Men   366
Implications for Career Counseling of Men   373
Components for Counseling Men   373
Summary   380
Supplementary Learning Exercises   381

Chapter Sixteen
Career Counseling for Various Ethnic Groups   382
Opinions of Ethnics About Preparing for Work   382
Asian Americans   383
African Americans   385
Hispanic Americans   388
Native Americans   389
The Poor   392
Barriers to Employment   394
Counseling Strategies for Ethnic Groups   395
A Prevocational Training Program for Ethnic Groups   400
Assessment of Ethnic Groups   405
Summary   408
Supplementary Learning Exercises   410

Chapter Seventeen
Career Counseling
for Individuals with Disabilities   411
The Americans with Disabilities Act   412
Special Problems and Needs of Individuals with Disabilities   414
Implications for Career Guidance   418
Rehabilitation Programs   418
Counseling Program: A Case Study   420
Career Education For Students with Disabilities   424

A Group-Counseling Program for Individuals with Disabilities 425
Assessment Instruments for Individuals with Disabilities 428
√*Summary* 434 *only*
Supplementary Learning Exercises 435

PART FIVE
TECHNIQUES FOR
THE CAREER-COUNSELING INTERVIEW 437

Chapter Eighteen *all*
Career-Counseling
Interview and Assessment Techniques 439

The Assessment Interview 439
A Suggested Sequence for an Interview 440
Techniques for Interviewing 441
Current Status Information 448
Discovering the Significance of Life Roles and Potential Conflicts 450
Interviewing Ethnic Minorities 455
Supplement to the Interview:
    Discovering Problems that Interfere with Career Development 457
Summary 465
Supplementary Learning Exercises 465

Chapter Nineteen *all*
Career-Counseling Interviews 467

Current Status Information 468
Discovering Problems that Interfere with Career Development 470
Discovering the Significance of Life Roles and Potential Conflicts 476
Developing Goals and Objectives 481
Summary 482
Supplementary Learning Exercises 483

Appendix 485
References 503
Name Index 539
Subject Index 549

Preface

This fourth edition brings back memories of how and why I wrote a book on career counseling. The research for the first edition took place soon after the career-education movement had run its course. There was a growing interest among professionals in the general field of counseling and particularly in psychotherapy. There also appeared to be a creditability gap between career counselors and psychotherapists; career counseling was perceived as not very challenging and rather dull. In fact, the career-counseling movement had lost its momentum and was once again cast to the side as a secondary field of counseling. However, the decade of the 1980s proved to be a period of rapid advances in career guidance through the development of innovative computer-assisted career-guidance programs and the growing needs of adults in career transition. More recently, and somewhat ironically, the recognition that career counselors must also deal with the psychological and sociological aspects of human behavior has drawn career counseling and psychotherapy closer together. It seemed to suddenly dawn on many in the counseling profession that some individuals are not able to make career decisions in their best interests because of psychological factors, their cultural background, or gender-role stereotyping. In addition, the increasing cultural diversity found in the work environment, the more inclusive and integrative approaches to career guidance, and the internationalization of the workplace, are causes for acknowledging the current broad scope of career counseling. In retrospect, the primary purpose of the first edition, and all the editions that followed, was to point out the relevance and pervasive nature of career guidance. The first edition has evolved into a more comprehensive textbook that has been buttressed by the research and innovative efforts of many professionals. As we move toward a greater emphasis on integrating all life roles in the career-counseling process, the subsequent challenges will require diverse intervention strategies to meet the needs of an ever-changing population of clients. I welcome these challenges!

The fourth edition contains two new chapters. One chapter covers the format and techniques for an assessment interview, from which career-intervention strategies are developed. The other illustrates the use of the assessment interview through case studies. In addition, every chapter has been revised and/or updated with more recent research and current programs. A greater emphasis has also been given to incorporating life roles in the career-counseling process.

A companion text, *Using Assessment Results for Career Development*, fourth edition, has been developed as a supplement to this book. The purpose of this ancillary text is to illustrate how assessment results can be used to increase self-awareness and rational career choices. Readers will find that this text provides detailed information on applying knowledge of tests and measurements in counseling encounters and using assessment results in a wide variety of counseling situations.

This book is divided into five parts. Part One—Foundations and Resources—covers historical developments, career-development theories, perspectives on work, career life-planning procedures, and career-counseling resources. The first chapter provides a historical perspective of the development of career counseling. Chapter 2 provides career counselors with a philosophical frame of reference. The third chapter discusses several work-related issues and prominent research concerning work motivation and how it relates to individual functioning in organizations. Chapter 4 covers several counseling programs promoting career life planning as a lifelong process. Chapter 5 discusses the use of occupational classification systems and provides the counselor with an understanding of occupational titles and job-information systems. Interactive and information-oriented computer programs designed to enhance the career-counseling process are the focus of Chapter 6. Chapter 7 discusses assessment techniques that emphasize the use of tests and inventories in career counseling. Chapter 8 provides a detailed discussion of career resource centers, including organizational structures and operational procedures, as well as comprehensive descriptions of career-information components and materials.

Part Two—Career-Guidance Programs in Educational Institutions—provides innovative counseling models and programs for elementary through senior high school and for postsecondary institutions of higher learning. Chapter 9 presents implications of human development and relevant research for career-guidance programs in schools. Chapter 10 explores a variety of approaches to career counseling for elementary, junior, and senior high schools; a comprehensive school-guidance program is also covered. The psychosocial development of youth in college and the development of career-guidance programs to help meet their varied needs are the subjects of Chapter 11.

Part Three—Career-Guidance Programs for Adults in Transition—is intended to build an understanding of career development of adults in organizations, stages and transitions in adult development, and career-counseling programs designed to meet their needs. Chapter 12 emphasizes how career development unfolds in organizations; the focus is on tasks and transitions of the stages of career development in organizations. Specific counseling components for adults in career transition are presented in Chapter 13.

Part Four—Career-Guidance Programs for Special Populations—includes a discussion of innovative counseling models and career-counseling programs for special populations. The special counseling needs of women are identified and discussed in Chapter 14. Chapter 15 reviews the socialization process that has shaped men's lives, influencing their perspectives of appropriate masculine roles. Career-counseling procedures designed to help men meet the needs of their career-life roles in a changing society are also discussed. Chapters 16 and 17 deal with career-counseling programs for ethnic minorities and persons with disabilities. Special-counseling components are suggested for meeting the unique needs of these populations.

In Part Five—Techniques for the Career-Counseling Interview—Chapter 18 includes the rationale for a career-counseling interview and some techniques for conducting the interview. A section of the chapter contains a supplement to the interview that covers problems that interfere with career development, such as behaviors that may lead to work maladjustment and a lack of cognitive clarity. Chapter 19 includes case studies that illustrate the use of the career-counseling interview.

I owe a special thanks to Howard Splete of Oakland University who has reviewed every edition of this text. His outstanding suggestions have been extremely helpful. I also want to recognize the help and suggestions of L. Sundal Hansen who continues to greatly enhance the career-guidance movement, as well as the following who reviewed chapters and offered helpful and constructive criticisms: Donna Bender, San Jose State University; Joanne Chenault, National University; Marianne Gillis, Georgia College; Carolyn Kern, University of North Texas; Robert Reardon, Florida State University.

I am indebted to Claire Verduin for having faith in the first edition and giving me the encouragement to continue. I also wish to thank Gay Bond and Nancy Shammas of Brooks/Cole who offered much-needed support and encouragement. I want to acknowledge the help of my typist, Amy Galle, who helped put this manuscript in final form. Finally, I want to acknowledge the companionship of my canine friend, Tani, who faithfully sat by my side through four editions but unfortunately will not be here to see this one in print.

Vernon G. Zunker

PART ONE

FOUNDATIONS AND RESOURCES

Chapter One
Historical Development of Career Counseling

Chapter Two
Theories of Career Development

Chapter Three
Some Perspectives of Work

Chapter Four
Career Life Planning

Chapter Five
The Dictionary of Occupational Titles, the Occupational Outlook Handbook, and Career Clusters

Chapter Six
Using Computers for Career Counseling

Chapter Seven
Using Standardized Assessment in Career Counseling

Chapter Eight
The Career Resource Center

Chapter One
Historical Development of Career Counseling

The career-guidance movement is a product of our development as a nation. It is the story of human progress in a nation founded on the principle of human rights. It touches all aspects of human life, for it has involved political, economic, educational, philosophical, and social progress and change. To think of the career-guidance movement as merely another educational event is a gross misinterpretation of its broader significance for social progress. It is, in fact, a movement that has had and will have a tremendous impact on the working lives of many individuals. Knowledge of the historical perspectives of this movement will provide a greater insight into the development of the career counselor's role in career guidance.

Many terms will be introduced and defined throughout this book. Some of the terminology that is briefly described in this chapter to clarify the theoretical concepts discussed will be explained in greater detail in succeeding chapters, within the context of the program descriptions and practical illustrations.

Career development, occupational development, and *vocational development* are used interchangeably. These terms refer to a lifelong process of developing beliefs and values, skills and aptitudes, interests, personality characteristics, and knowledge of the world of work (Tolbert, 1974). Specifically, the terms reflect individually developed needs and goals associated with stages of life and with tasks that affect career choices and subsequent fulfillment of purpose. *Vocation, occupation,* and *job* are also used interchangeably to indicate activities of employment and positions of employment. *Career* refers to the activities and positions involved in vocations, occupations, and jobs as well as related activities associated with an individual's lifetime of work.

Career counseling includes all counseling activities associated with career choices over a life span. In the career-counseling process, all aspects of individual needs (including family, work, and leisure) are recognized as integral parts of career decision making and planning.

Career guidance encompasses all components of services and activities in educational institutions, agencies, and other organizations that offer counseling and career-related educational programs.

This chapter is divided into three basic sections. The first section covers the period from 1850 to 1940, the second section discusses the period from 1940 to the present, and the third section offers some perspectives on the future. The content of these sections is devoted to a discussion of major events and important individuals that contributed to the development of the career-guidance movement during these periods.

The year 1850 was selected as a starting point because, at the time, the nation experienced the impact of the Industrial Revolution, which resulted in significant changes in social conditions and working environments. These changes contributed in no small way to the conditions that brought about the career-guidance movement.

THE BIRTH OF THE CAREER-GUIDANCE MOVEMENT

The discussion of the career-guidance movement during the period from 1850 to 1940 includes the following events: (1) the Industrial Revolution, (2) the study of individual differences, (3) World War I, (4) the National Conference on Vocational Guidance, (5) the measurement movement, and (6) significant federal acts. Individuals who made significant contributions during this period include: Francis Galton, Wilheim Wundt, James Cattell, Alfred Binet, Frank Parsons, Robert Yerkes, and E. K. Strong.

The Rise of Industrialism

The rise of industrialism in the late 1800s dramatically changed work environments and living conditions. Urban areas grew at tremendous rates, largely through immigration. In addition, the rapid growth and centralization of industry attracted many from rural areas who were in need of work. Many people found the long hours required by industrial establishments and the harsh and crowded living conditions in tenement houses to be undesirable. Perhaps even more significant was a loss of identity experienced by many in these crowded work and living environments. A spirit of reform emerged in reaction to the impersonal industrial systems and chaotic conditions of urban life in the United States and in Europe. As if in response to deteriorating social conditions, several outstanding scientists turned their attention to human behavior and to the study of individual differences.

The Study of Human Abilities

Francis Galton of England published his first and second books devoted to the origins of human abilities in 1874 and 1883. In 1879, Wilheim Wundt established an experimental laboratory in Leipzig, Germany, to study human behavior. In France, Alfred Binet and V. Henri published an article in 1896 describing mental measurement concepts (Borow, 1964). These studies of human differences turned our attention to the conditions of life and work in a society changed by the Industrial Revolution.

In the United States, G. Stanley Hall founded a psychological laboratory in 1883 to study and measure physical and mental characteristics of children. In 1890, James Cattell published an article in which he referred to mental tests as measures of individual differences. John Dewey called for a reform of the lock-step method of education to one in which more attention was given to individual motivations, interests, and development. The case for the individual was being carefully formulated.

Early Programs of Career Guidance

Near the turn of the century, isolated programs of career guidance were established in public schools. In San Francisco, George A. Merrill developed a plan for students to explore industrial arts courses. Merrill is given credit by Brewer (1918) as a forerunner of vocational guidance, but his primary interests were in vocational education (Picchioni & Bonk, 1983). Many of his innovations resemble the career-education movement of the 1970s (see Chapter 10).

In Central High School of Detroit, Jesse B. Davis served as counselor for 11th-grade students from 1898 to 1907 (Brewer, 1918). His major duties involved educational and vocational counseling. Later, as principal of this school, he required all 7th-grade students to write a weekly report on occupational interests for their English class. Davis emphasized the moral value of hard work as well as the benefits of occupational information.

These guidance activities and others were indeed innovative, but a logical and straightforward conceptualization of career guidance was needed to make it a viable movement. In the early 1900s, Frank Parsons provided a systematic plan for career guidance that has endured, with some modifications, to the present time. According to his philosophical orientation to social reform, there was to be equality and opportunity for all. The procedures he outlined for helping individuals select an occupation were to be primarily based on their interests and aptitudes and on occupational information.

Frank Parsons

The social reform movements and civic developments of the late 1800s captured the interest of young Frank Parsons, who had been educated as an engineer at Cornell University. He wrote several books on social-reform movements and articles on such topics as women's suffrage, taxation, and education for all. Parsons taught history, math, and French in public schools, worked as a railroad engineer, and passed the state bar examination for lawyers in Massachusetts in 1881 (Picchioni & Bonk, 1983). He also taught at Boston University's law school and at Kansas State Agricultural College, and he was academic dean of the extension division of Ruskin College in Trenton, Missouri. However, his real interests appeared to lie in social reform and in helping individuals make occupational choices. These interests surfaced when Parsons returned to Boston in the early 1900s.

In 1901, the Civic Service-House had been established in Boston for the purpose of providing educational programs for immigrants and young persons seeking work. In 1905, Parsons was named director of the Breadwinner's Institute, which was one of the Civic Service-House programs. Eventually, through Parsons's leadership, the Vocation Bureau of Boston was established on January 13, 1908.

On May 1, 1908, Parsons presented a lecture that had a tremendous impact on the career-guidance movement. His report described systematic guidance procedures used to counsel 80 men and women who had come to the vocational bureau for help. Parsons's major work, *Choosing a Vocation*, was posthumously published in May 1909. Frank Parsons died on September 26, 1908 (Picchioni & Bonk, 1983).

One of Parsons's important contributions to the career-guidance movement was his conceptual framework for helping an individual select a career. Parsons defined his three-part formulation as follows:

> First, a clear understanding of yourself, aptitudes, abilities, interests, resources, limitations, and other qualities.
> Second, a knowledge of the requirements and conditions of success, advantages and disadvantages, compensations, opportunities, and prospects in different lines of work.
> Third, true reasoning on the relations of these two groups of facts (Parsons, 1909, p. 5).

Edmund G. Williamson (1965) pointed out that, with some modification, Parsons's three-part formulation greatly influenced the procedures used in career counseling over a significant period of time. Parts of Parsons's three-part formulation are practices used in many career-counseling programs today. Moreover, Parsons's conceptual framework ignited a national interest in career guidance.

First National Conference on Vocational Guidance

In 1910, the First National Conference on Vocational Guidance was held in Boston. Several speakers, including Charles W. Elliott, president of Harvard, emphasized the need for school guidance personnel. Other speakers, including the superintendent of schools in Boston, strongly suggested that methods for determining each student's potential be an objective of future scientific investigations. Understandably, the spread of organized guidance in other cities was greatly influenced by this conference and the second national conference in New York City in 1912. At the third national conference in Grand Rapids, Michigan, in October 1913, the National Vocational Guidance Association, Incorporated, was founded. This organization, now called the National Career Development Association (NCDA), was most instrumental in providing the leadership to advance the career-guidance movement.

Industrial Psychology

An important related development that influenced the career-guidance movement was the work of the German psychologist Hugo Munsterberg. He joined the Harvard faculty in 1897 and introduced several methods of determining aptitudes and characteristics of men successfully employed in certain occupations in Germany. In his 1912 book, *Psychology and Industrial Efficiency*, Munsterberg reported several studies of occupational choice and worker performance. In this publication and in others, Munsterberg pointed out the utility of psychological-testing instruments and techniques for selection of industrial employees. Munsterberg was influential in establishing industrial psychology as a relevant field of applied psychology.

The Measurement Movement, 1900–1940

In many respects, the measurement and guidance movements coincided in development and shared many of the same roots. One of the early, influential individuals was Wilheim Wundt of Leipzig, Germany, who had established the first experimental laboratory in psychology. His work in measurement was confined to evaluation of reaction times to certain stimuli. However, Kraepelin and Ebbinghaus, two other German psychologists who were influenced by Wundt's work, became directly involved in constructing measuring devices and were among the pioneers of the measurement movement (Ross & Stanley, 1954). Wundt also contributed directly to the measurement movement by his standardization of procedures that became models for developing standardized tests.

James M. Cattell, who studied at Wundt's laboratory in Germany, became interested in individual differences. When Cattell returned to the United States, he became active in the measurement movement and first used the term *mental test* in an article written in 1890. He also studied the work of Galton, another pioneering force in the measurement movement, who had devised sensory-discrimination tests as measures of judgment and intelligence.

The credit for constructing the first intelligence test is generally given to Alfred Binet and Theophile Simon of France. This test, published in 1905, is administered individually and is known as the Binet-Simon scale or simply as the 1905 scale. In 1916, under the direction of L. M. Termen of Stanford University, the revised Binet-Simon scales were published as the Stanford-Binet. The introduction of the term *intelligence quotient* contributed to the popularity of this test and tests in general.

The need for testing the abilities of large groups became apparent at the beginning of World War I. Close to 1.5 million people were in need of classification and subsequent training for the armed services. Under the direction of Robert M. Yerkes, the first group intelligence tests were developed. Arthur S. Otis, who had constructed (but not published) an objective item test for group administration, contributed his work to the cause. The test developed for the army became known as the Army Alpha and Beta Tests. Unlike the more typical, verbal Alpha Test, the Beta Test contained a nonlanguage scale for illiterate and foreign recruits. After the war, these tests were made available to counselors of the general public.

The testing movement made rapid advances during the next two decades. Special aptitude tests were developed; Clark L. Hull published *Aptitude Testing* in 1928. This publication was devoted to the use of aptitude-test batteries in vocational guidance and emphasized his concept of matching human traits with job requirements. The idea of forecasting job satisfaction and success from standardized measures of aptitude succinctly linked the measurement and guidance movements.

Another direct link between the measurement and guidance movements was the development of interest assessment. In 1927, Edward K. Strong, Jr., of Stanford University published the first edition of an interest inventory, *The Strong Vocational Interest Blank*. This measure of interest, constructed from the responses of individuals in certain occupations, provided career counselors with a most important tool for linking assessment results with certain occupations.

Achievement testing in public schools made rapid progress during the 1920s. Personality testing began during World War I but was much slower in development. However, the testing movement also had its pitfalls for many career counselors. Too much reliance was placed on assessment results in the career-decision process; excessive dependence on testing provided little opportunity for considering many other aspects of human development and experience. Nevertheless, the testing tools developed during this period for measuring individual differences provided the much-needed standardized support materials for the career-guidance movement.

Significant Federal Acts and Contributions from the Private Sector

The federal government has played a significant role in the career-guidance movement. Relevant national legislative acts passed from 1917 to 1940 are summarized in this section, and other significant national legislation is reported in subsequent sections of this chapter.

In 1917, the Smith-Hughes Act established federal grants for support of a nationwide vocational educational program. This act was also influential in supporting the establishment of counselor-training departments at major universities. The George-Dean Act of 1936 continued the support of the vocational-education movement. In response to the Great Depression, the Wagner-Peyser Act of 1933 established the U.S. Employment Service. The Civilian Conservation Corps was created in 1933, and the Works Progress Administration was established in 1935. All of these legislative acts were designed to provide employment for the masses who could not find jobs during this period. In 1939, the first edition of the *Dictionary of Occupational Titles* was published by the U.S. Employment Service.

In the private sector, the B'nai B'rith Vocational Service Bureau was established in 1938. Its purpose was to offer group vocational-guidance programs in metropolitan areas. In 1939, the Jewish Occupational Council was established to conduct counseling, placement, and rehabilitation services for Jewish immigrants through the B'nai B'rith, other offices, and sheltered workshops. The efforts of the Jewish Occupational Council established models for delivery of career-guidance programs.

GROWTH OF THE CAREER-GUIDANCE MOVEMENT: 1940 TO THE PRESENT

Significant events covered during the period from 1940 to the present are as follows: (1) the appearance of major counseling publications, (2) World War II, (3) significant federal programs, (4) the formulation of theories of career development, (5) the development of career education, (6) the professionalism movement, and (7) the advances of technology. Individuals who made significant contributions to the career-guidance movement during this period are E. G. Williamson, Carl Rogers, Eli Ginzberg, Ann Roe, Donald Super, John Holland, David Tiedeman, and H. B. Gelatt.

Edmund G. Williamson's Directive Counseling

During the early 1940s, E. G. Williamson's publication, *How to Counsel Students* (1939), made a tremendous impact on the career-guidance movement. This comprehensive work was, in many respects, an extension of Parsons's formulations. However, his straightforward approach to counseling was thoroughly illustrated and contained six sequential steps: analysis, synthesis, diagnosis, prognosis, counseling, and follow-up. Williamson's approach to counseling became known as *directive counseling*. Williamson was one of the members of the Minnesota Employment Stability Research Institute who were influential in the development of vocational psychology at the University of Minnesota. This group was later identified with trait-and-factor approaches to career guidance as discussed in the next chapter.

Carl R. Rogers's Nondirective Counseling

In 1942, Carl R. Rogers's influential book, *Counseling and Psychotherapy*, was published. Although Rogers had primarily worked with emotionally distressed clients as a therapist, his method of *nondirective counseling* or *client-centered counseling* caused a complete reexamination of the early established assumptions in career counseling. The Rogerians attacked directive-counseling procedures and philosophical orientation in numerous articles and debates. First, according to opponents of directive counseling, the relatively straightforward concept of matching human traits with job requirements had to be revamped. The concepts of affective and motivational behavior were among other considerations to be included in the counseling process. Second, client self-acceptance and self-understanding were primary goals. Third, more attention was to be given to client-counselor interactions and to the verbalization of clients in the counseling process. In essence, the counseling relationship was to be one of mutual respect, directed toward the client's gaining an understanding of self and taking steps to control his or her destiny. The center of attention shifted to the client and counseling techniques, with less emphasis given to testing, cumulative records, and the counselor as an authority figure.

Rogerian theory was responsible for the first major breach from Parsons's straightforward approach. Many Rogerian concepts were later endorsed and integrated into directive counseling, resulting in an approach to career guidance that included a broader perspective of human development and life experience. However, the psychotherapy movement and the growing interest in expanding the professional role of counselors had to wait until after World War II.

World War II and Federal Programs

During World War II, the armed services were once again in need of testing procedures to classify recruits. In response to these needs, the army created a personnel and testing division in 1939. The Army General Classification Test (AGCT) was produced in 1940, and this instrument became the principal general-ability test used by the armed services during the World War II years. The points of influence here were the counseling programs established by the military. These programs were designed to maximize individual potential as measured by assessment results when placing recruits in various components of the armed services.

At the end of World War II, the armed services established separation-counseling programs. The major goal of these programs was to assist veterans returning to civilian life; counseling procedures introduced various options to veterans, including future educational and vocational planning suggestions. In 1944, the Veterans Administration established centers throughout the country for career guidance and other services. Many were established on college and university campuses; these counseling services became models for development of career-guidance programs at many institutions of higher learning.

In recognition of the general need for more guidance services, Congress passed the George-Barden Act in 1946. This act provided funds for establishing academic counselor-training programs and provided a more liberal method of distributing funds to states for maintaining vocational-guidance programs.

The Testing Movement After World War II

The growth of applied psychology after World War II contributed significantly to the growth of the measurement movement. Such branches of psychology as industrial psychology, counseling psychology, educational psychology, and school psychology were incorporated into formal training programs at many institutions of higher learning. Courses in testing principles and practices were major components of these training programs. A renewed interest in the use of tests in all branches of applied psychology had direct links with career-guidance practices. For example, the use of tests in counseling individuals for various life roles, including the work role, was recognized as a viable component of applied psychology. Moreover, the increased emphasis on the applied use of assessment results created a need to develop instruments that could be used as counseling support tools. This applied emphasis continues to motivate the development of instruments that are designed for use with individuals of both sexes and all age groups, ethnic minorities, and special populations. The use of assessment results in career counseling is discussed in Chapter 7.

After World War II, there was a significant increase in enrollment at colleges and universities. This increased enrollment and subsequent need for educational planning created a wider use of the College Entrance Examination Boards and the American College Testing Program (ACT). These tests, designed to predict success at the college level, are also used as one means for helping individuals select academic majors and/or careers. The ACT also contains an interest-inventory report that is directly related to jobs and college majors.

The passage of the National Defense Educational Act in 1958 greatly influenced the career-guidance movement in general and had special impact on the testing movement. In fact, this act endorsed the close relationship between testing and the career-guidance movement. The primary purpose of this act was to identify students of outstanding aptitude and ability early in their public secondary schooling and to provide them with counseling programs designed to help them make the best use of their talents. The specific use of tests mandated by this act significantly increased the opportunity to incorporate tests in public school counseling programs through federal funds that were made available to state departments of education.

Shortly before World War II and especially after the war, a significant number of books on the subject of testing were published. For example, the first *Mental Measurements Yearbook* was published in 1938 and has been followed by several editions. Books by F. B. Davis (1947), D. C. Adkins (1947), L. J. Cronbach (1949), F. L. Goodenough (1949), W. Stephenson (1949), D. E. Super (1949), R. L. Thorndike (1949), H. Gulliksen (1950), and A. Anastasi (1954) are other examples of significant publications on testing that appeared following World War II.

During the rapid growth of testing after 1945, there was a move toward centralizing the publication of tests. The Educational Testing Service was formed in 1948 by combining a number of specialized testing programs. The American College Testing Program was founded in 1959. Other commercial publishers merged into larger companies and corporations. The primary reason for these mergers was the need for financial and technical commitments to develop and maintain the variety of testing programs that are on the market today (Cronbach, 1984). Currently, the design, construction, and updating of tests requires sophisticated technical support systems.

The advances in technology that have led to rapid scoring procedures have made testing more attractive to career-guidance personnel. Computerized printouts of scores and narrative descriptions of assessment results have increased their utilization in career guidance. This immediate access to assessment results for career counselors and their counselees affords the use of a greater variety of testing instruments in the career-counseling process.

No doubt, the future use of assessment results in career counseling will be greatly influenced by advancements in technology. However, the use of assessment results in career counseling must be kept in perspective; assessment results should not dominate the decision-making process in career guidance. Skills developed through work and leisure experiences are examples of other considerations that are as important as assessment results in career decision making.

Theories of Career Development

In the early 1950s, Ginzberg, Roe, and Super published career-development and occupational-choice theories that have become landmarks in the development of the career-guidance movement. Understandably, these publications were instrumental in creating a greater interest in career-guidance practices and support materials used by practitioners. Their formulations have led to numerous research projects and subsequent methods for delivering career-guidance programs. Other theorists who followed were Holland, Tiedeman, Gelatt, Krumboltz, and Bordin, who have also contributed to career-development and/or choice theories. Theories of career development and choice have become enduring issues addressed by the counseling profession in important publications and professional meetings; several of the major theories are discussed in Chapter 2.

Theoretical perspectives on career development have contributed a great deal to career-guidance programs by providing insights into developmental stages and tasks associated with transitions between stages, identification of personality types and corresponding work environments, and decision-making techniques. In addition, these theories have delineated the effects of sex-role stereotyping, provided special insights into the career development of women, ethnic minorities, and other groups, and clarified aspects of social learning theory and its relationship to career development. For each new practitioner, theories serve as a starting point from which new ideas and practices can be generated and validated (Zunker, 1987).

The Career-Guidance Movement from the 1960s

At this point in our discussion, we have covered a period of over 100 years. During this period, the career-guidance movement made giant strides of progress. The counseling profession was provided with leadership through national and local organizations. Child labor laws prohibited the exploitation of the very young, and working conditions for most Americans generally improved. There was a growing interest in increasing and improving social services for all citizens at all age levels. At the end of the 1950s, the career-guidance movement had strong, organized leadership, but the 1960s were not destined to be peaceful times for the United States.

The turbulent 1960s have been described as a period of unrest that was precipitated by an awakened social conscience and the loss of a sense of meaning among the young. Several descriptions have been used to characterize the youth of the 1960s, including rebellious, militant, restless, and hippie. A questioning of all aspects of the American way of life erupted into overt acts of militant rioting in cities, protest marches on college campuses, and a general rebellion against many established social values. With these events came further challenges for the counseling profession in general and for career guidance specifically. For example, the role and meaning of work in society was seen as a major issue in the 1960s and 1970s. Other issues, such as the women's movement and guidance of the aged, were dominant forces in shaping the career-guidance movement.

In the last 20 years, the career-guidance movement has broadened its role and scope. There is a trend toward greater emphasis on a humanistic, existential orientation (Picchioni & Bonk, 1983). The humanistic approach, designed to expand one's awareness of life, brings greater meaning to all aspects of lifestyle. The philosophical rationale of an existential approach provides a greater recognition of individual significance in society. In essence, the more an individual is aware of his or her potential and experience, the greater the likelihood of self-assertion and direction. These philosophical orientations have set the patterns for career-guidance models now in vogue.

The federal government continued its support of programs that directly and indirectly affected career guidance. During the early 1960s, Congress passed manpower legislation designed to create new jobs through occupational-training programs. In addition, funds were made available for placement counseling in a variety of settings, including the establishment of agencies in communities. Other legislation under the Economic Opportunity Act funded such projects as Head Start, Job Corps, Neighborhood Youth Corps, and Community Action Programs. Many of these programs involved special counseling services like the Job Training Partnership Act (JTPA).

The Vocational Educational Act of 1963 deserves special recognition for its influence on the career-guidance movement. According to Picchioni and Bonk (1983), this act "provided individual job seekers the formal preparation through guidance and training necessary for occupational adjustment in an increasingly technical and sophisticated economy" (p. 81). Later amendments to the act provided funds for guidance services in elementary and secondary schools, public community colleges, and technical institutes.

Career Education

A new concept of education emerged in the early 1970s in reaction to the charge that current educational systems were not adequately preparing youth for work. In 1971, Commissioner of Education Sidney P. Marland proposed a plan that would specifically address career development, attitudes, and values in addition to traditional learning. This new educational philosophy—career education—was considered integral to the education process, from kindergarten through adulthood. The career-education programs that evolved during the 1970s have centered on such topics as career awareness, career exploration, value clarification, decision-making skills, career orientation, and career preparation. Understandably, career-education programs have focused more attention on the career-guidance movement. The concept of career education is discussed in Chapter 10, and the career counselor's role in delivering various components of career-education programs is also explored.

Vocational-Technical Education Changes

In the last decade, there have been significant changes in vocational education as we once knew it. The major thrust of current programs is centered around the goal of teaching students employable skills needed in the changing technological workplace. Students now face new technologies and business management systems that require high-level worker skills. As the result of vast technological changes, vocational education focuses more on technology than on vocational-educational perspectives. The growing interest in integrating academic and vocational education has primarily evolved from a need to encourage vocational-education students to take more rigorous academic courses. In fact, "Tech-Prep" programs are designed to offer vocational-education students more advanced academic courses that meet the admission requirements at some institutions of higher education. More information about the changing role of vocational education can be found in Chapter 10.

The National Occupational Information Coordinating Committee (NOICC)

In 1976, the National Occupational Information Coordinating Committee was established by an act of Congress. This committee is supported by four federal agencies: the Bureau of Labor Statistics, the Employment and Training Administration, the Office of Vocational and Adult Education, and the National Center for Educational Statistics. The NOICC has defined four basic functions: (1) to develop an occupational-information system that provides information on employment and training programs at federal, state, and local levels; (2) to assist in the organization and operation of state committees, referred to as State Occupational Information Coordinating Committees (SOICCs); (3) to assist all users of occupational information in sharing information; and (4) to provide labor-market information for the needs of youth (Flanders, 1980).

More recently, NOICC has sponsored a project to establish national career-counseling and development guidelines. The major purpose of the guidelines is to encourage the development of career-guidance standards at the state and local levels. Specifically, the guidelines are to be used to develop standards of client competencies, counselor competencies, and institutional capabilities at all

educational levels. Likewise, standards are to be developed for young adult and older adult career-guidance programming. The effectiveness of these programs will be evaluated in order to encourage program improvement.

The implementation of national guidelines by states and local communities should facilitate: (1) achievement of career development competencies by all students; (2) improved career-guidance and counseling programs that are comprehensive and integrated within the total guidance and counseling program; (3) clearly defined staff roles, increased teaming with teachers and other school and district staff, and improved counselor expertise; (4) greater program accountability; and (5) improved articulation of career-related programs across educational levels (NOICC, 1989, p. 30).

The steps for implementing national guidelines include developing a needs analysis, establishing local career-development standards, securing the resources and staff, conducting staff development, and designing and conducting program evaluations.

In 1992, NOICC established the National Career Development Training Institute (NCDTI) to design career-development training programs for states to use in training personnel who help students and adults acquire career-planning skills and make career decisions. Current plans call for this institute to be coordinated through the University of South Carolina, the Wisconsin Center on Education and Work at the University of Wisconsin at Madison, and the Continuum Center and Adult Career Counseling Center at Oakland University in Rochester, Michigan. All 56 SOICCs assisted the institute in designing and implementing the National Career Development Training agenda.

Professionalism

The focus of attention in the early 1970s shifted to standards of counselor preparation and to the general advancement of the counseling profession. In 1972, standards for entry preparation of counselors were approved by the Board of Directors of the American Personnel and Guidance Association (APGA). In 1977, APGA established guidelines for doctoral training programs in counselor education (Picchioni & Bonk, 1983). These actions were followed by a declared interest on the part of the APGA in state licensure of professionals. The APGA (now the American Counseling Association or ACA) has enhanced public recognition of all counseling efforts and has added support to counseling as a distinct social service. In 1984, the National Career Development Association set up procedures for the credentialing of career counselors, now carried out by the National Board of Certified Counselors (NBCC).

Advances in Technology

The development of computerized career information and interactive-guidance programs has greatly enhanced the career-guidance movement. The accessibility and immediate retrieval of vast amounts of information on specific occupations and educational programs has given the career counselor a most important supportive tool. Computerized, interactive career-guidance systems have provided additional supportive counseling programs.

Recent technological advancements have provided the necessary storage capacity to allow microcomputers to accommodate career-information files and interactive-guidance systems. The declining costs of microcomputers and software systems have increased the availability of computerized career-information systems for a wider range of users. Future advances in technology will surely continue to provide innovative programs for career guidance. Several computerized career-guidance systems are discussed in Chapter 6.

Comparing Career Counseling with Psychotherapy

According to Crites (1981), many in the counseling profession have abandoned career counseling in favor of psychotherapy. He singled out higher education counseling centers, which, he believed, ignore students' needs for career guidance in favor of concentrating their efforts on other counseling programs. No doubt there are numerous reasons for this phenomenon, but one of the primary reasons is the perception of many counseling professionals that career counseling is a rather mechanical, straightforward process with little room for creativity or reflection. This perception was challenged by Crites, among others, on the basis that comprehensive career-counseling programs incorporate many theories of counseling and psychotherapy. Moreover, Crites suggested:

1. The need for career counseling is greater than the need for psychotherapy (a view supported by several surveys).
2. Career counseling can be therapeutic (career and personal adjustment are interrelated).
3. Career counseling should follow psychotherapy (new directions in career development should follow personal adjustment).
4. Career counseling is more effective than psychotherapy (or at least career counseling carries greater expectancy of success than psychotherapy).
5. Career counseling is more difficult than psychotherapy (when career counselors use comprehensive approaches, they are perceived as being both psychotherapists and career counselors).

From this perspective, comprehensive career-counseling procedures require a wide range of expertise in counseling theory: Career-counseling approaches include trait-and-factor, client-centered, psychodynamic, developmental, and behavioral. In addition, the well-prepared career counselor has a working knowledge of personality, learning and decision theory, career and human development, and occupational information delivery systems.

Crites's position also implies that comprehensive career-counseling models are bringing psychotherapists and career counselors closer in terms of techniques and goals. A close relationship is welcomed, for counseling approaches typically endorse the "total-person" approach. In general, counseling strategies designed for personal and social adjustment should also include career adjustment.

A GLANCE INTO THE PAST
AND A LOOK INTO THE FUTURE

In the beginning of this discussion, several references were made to events and social conditions that determined the course of the career-guidance movement. The chronology of the career-guidance movement reflects the continuous influence of social, political, economic, and other changes in our nation. In the political arena, the career-guidance movement has found support. Federal legislation has provided funds for underwriting several career-counseling programs and training programs for counselors. The fact is that the federal government has played a significant role in the career-guidance movement.

We cannot overlook the foresight, dedication, and pioneering efforts of many individuals. Those who came forth with conceptualizations of career guidance that have endured for many decades provided the guidelines for contemporary practices. Other individuals concentrating on basic research in human development also contributed immeasurably to the career-guidance movement. The leaders in related branches of applied psychology and contributors to technological advancements all played a part in developing what has become the mainstream of this movement.

Career guidance was founded in order to help people choose vocations. The early, straightforward procedures used in helping individuals choose occupations have evolved into diverse strategies, incorporating career decision making and life planning. The development of career-guidance programs has been largely dictated by societal changes and subsequent needs of the society, and the future will no doubt provide changes and issues that we cannot fully anticipate at this time. It should be clear that career guidance is not a drab, static profession, but on the contrary provides vast opportunities for future leaders. The career counselors of today and tomorrow will become catalysts for an expanded guidance movement in this country.

The Need for Career Counseling

The results of several national surveys (see Chapters 9 and 10) show an overwhelming need for career-counseling assistance at all educational levels (Healy, 1982; Prediger & Sawyer, 1985; Herr & Cramer, 1992). An examination of objectives and strategies at these levels reveals how identified needs can be met. In elementary schools, programs are designed to provide students with an awareness of occupational roles, the role of work in society, social behavior, and responsible actions. In junior/middle schools, career-guidance programs are designed to help students develop concepts of basic skills, learn decision-making skills, and relate to the world of work. Continuing career exploration, exploring contingencies of occupational preference, and preparing for entry into work or further training are some of the major goals of senior high school career-guidance programs. In institutions of higher learning, students' needs are met through programs that help them reaffirm occupational choices, develop specific career skills, reevaluate interests and aptitudes, and plan for entry into a career field.

Extensive evidence also suggests the need for adult career-guidance programs (see Chapter 13). The number of adults in career transition has significantly increased over the last three decades (Arbeiter et al., 1978; Drucker, 1992). As they search for meaningful work, some adults have experienced a change in needs, a disparity between current work content and reformulated goals, a lack of conformity between personal goals and employer goals, a feeling of isolation in the work environment, despair about the future, and more recently a slow economy and downsizing of organizations. These new needs support the notion of career-guidance programs over the life span. In the following chapters, objectives and strategies of career-guidance programs in schools, in institutions of higher learning, for special groups, and for adults are presented and discussed in greater detail.

Some Future Perspectives of Current Industries

The 1990s are often referred to as "an age of transition." Significant changes in organizational structure and operational procedures in the work environment are forecast for this decade. Advances in technology will encourage a greater use of computers and robots in industry. Work conditions will change to accommodate the new technologies. Work itself will be different: many new jobs will be created and others will become obsolete. All of these forecasts have tremendous implications for career guidance and career counseling.

Computers and Data Processing
This industry employs about 2.5 million American workers and is growing by about 15% a year (Cetron & Davies, 1988). It is predicted that soon computers will be capable of taking dictation and transcribing flawlessly, and translating into many foreign languages. Eventually, robots will be able to do many menial jobs, such as cook meals, shovel snow, and clean house. Specific jobs in this industry that will be in demand are computer console and equipment operators, computer programmers, computer service technicians, and computer systems analysts.

Telecommunications
According to Cetron and Davies (1988), the telecommunications industry, now in its infancy, will grow rapidly. For example, by the year 2000 cellular car phones will be standard equipment in most cars. Most American households are now hooked up to cable television, which can also serve as a major data carrier for such events as polls and surveys.

Telemarketing is a major industry springing up from innovations in the telecommunications field. People can now shop for goods by viewing television and phoning in their orders. More efficient fiber optics technology will provide a more accessible and available telecommunications system.

Biotechnology

This field will have its greatest impact on medicine and agriculture. Synthetic versions of chemicals will revolutionize medical testing and treatment. In agriculture, bacteria have been developed to protect crop plants from frost damage, and many newly developed plants will be able to grow where they formerly could not. As a result, agriculture will become more productive on a worldwide scale.

Superconductivity

Superconductors are capable of delivering electricity without resistance or losses. Current high-voltage lines lose approximately 5 to 15% of the electricity sent through them. The superconductor transistor can operate more quickly and efficiently and will probably be an essential component of faster and more effective computers developed in the future (Cetron & Davies, 1988).

Advanced Material

The development of more durable and stronger synthetics, plastics, ceramics, and fiberglass will generate new manufacturing industries. The automobile and home-building industries will use more of the advanced materials as they become available. The use of diamond coatings, for example, on eyeglasses and household utensils will make them more durable and effective; and this will also produce different methods of manufacturing (Cetron & Davies, 1988).

Hazardous Waste Disposal

This field is predicted to be one of the largest new industries in the 1990s. The need for satisfactory hazardous waste disposal processes will create a tremendous demand for jobs such as hazardous waste technicians (Cetron & Davies, 1988).

Robots in the Work Force

In the early 1980s, there were approximately 15,000 robots in use throughout the world; about half were in Japan and one-fourth in the United States (Smith, 1981). The leading manufacturer of robots is Japan, but the United States will significantly increase production in the next 20 years. Clearly, there will be a significant increase in the use of robots during the 1990s, and robotic work quality should dramatically improve.

There are conflicting views regarding the effects that robots will have on the work force. Byrne (1983) suggested that robots will replace up to 25% of the factory work force, whereas Ogden (1982) more conservatively projected that less than 10% of all jobs will succumb. There does appear to be consensus that cost-effective robots will keep American industry competitive. The total effect of increased automation on the American labor force will undoubtedly occupy a large proportion of future industrial-research efforts.

One of the concerns of the career-counseling profession will be the impact of robotics on unemployment. Workers displaced by robots will need retraining and/or relocation assistance. Ogden (1982) contended that almost all displaced workers will be spared unemployment because of retraining or retirement. Furthermore, robots may have a positive effect on total employment by increasing economic growth and creating more available jobs. Byrne (1983) suggested that the problems faced by displaced workers are socioeconomic. Which group of workers will be displaced? Should it be women, minorities, or the entry-level worker? Will there be adequate retraining programs to meet the needs of displaced workers? What psychosocial effects will relocation have on individual workers? These questions are examples of issues to be addressed by the career-counseling profession.

Minorities in the Future Work Force

Recent studies in the labor market reveal that African American unemployment is about twice that of Caucasian unemployment. The difference is even greater among teenagers. However, African Americans have shown some employment gains in the acquisition of professional, technical, and clerical jobs. Nevertheless, they tend to have the less-prestigious and poorer-paying work. Most of the overall gain in minority white-collar employment has been in the public sector (Anderson, 1981). Factors helping minorities make employment gains are (1) the general economic conditions (when economic conditions are good, minorities have a better chance of getting better jobs); (2) the improvement in education (more minorities in high schools and colleges result in improved labor-market positions); and (3) protection of equal job opportunities (the Equal Opportunities Act has helped minorities obtain jobs).

These same factors will help job prospects for all minorities in the decades ahead. Long-term economic growth is projected to be slower through the 1990s. Through the 1990s the degree of change between African Americans and Caucasians who have higher-paying jobs is not expected to be significant. Minorities will continue to need counseling advocates and special assistance in educational planning and upgrading their career expectations.

Changes in the Work Force

A growing number of individuals (contract workers, temporaries, freelancers) are involved in part-time work. Well over half of these part-time workers are involved in clerical office jobs during peak periods in organizations (Worsnop, 1987). Multiple job holders, often referred to as "moonlighters," are steadily growing in number, spurred on by economic need, debt, and the desire to explore new career opportunities. Professional writers, editors, librarians, and accountants sometimes prefer part-time or contract work arrangements.

According to Naisbitt (1982), there will be an increasing demand for generalists who can adapt to different work environments and tasks, as opposed to

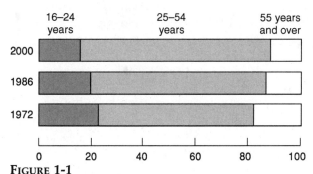

FIGURE 1-1
Proportion of workers by age group, 1972–2000. Adapted from U.S. Bureau of Labor Statistics, U.S. Department of Labor, 1988–1989.

specialists who have been prominent in the past. His conclusion is based on the necessity for continued retraining required by the changing "information society." The rapid changes of technology, especially in the use of computers, will make it necessary for organizations to retrain employees regularly. Individuals must be prepared to make adjustments to new and different work environments and sites.

Contrary to popular belief, there will be only a slight increase in older workers (age 55 and older) in the work force by the year 2000, according to the U.S. Bureau of Labor Statistics (see Figure 1–1). In fact, the Bureau predicts that the number of older workers will decline through the mid-1990s, and the increases thereafter will be offset by retirement of persons aged 65 and older and men 55 to 64. By the year 2000 about 73% of American workers will be in the age bracket 25–54 (U.S. Bureau of Labor Statistics, U.S. Department of Labor, 1988–1989).

Alternative Work Patterns

Future organizations are expected to provide greater flexibility in the hours employees will work. The 9-to-5 work schedule will probably still exist in the future, but there will be considerable variations. One of the variations, called *flex-time*, provides employees with their choice of daily work hours. For example, the work day is extended from 6:30 A.M. to 5:30 P.M., and employees choose blocks of hours they will work within this period. Workers may split the day into two- or three-hour work periods, or they may choose a straight eight-hour shift. Most flex-time schedules have designated core times when most employees are required to be present.

Contracted hours is another form of an alternative work pattern. In this plan, the individual contracts with the organization for a specific number of hours per month. Under the contractual conditions, there are usually limitations of choice of work hours.

Another variation of the altered work pattern is referred to as the *floating day*. In this plan, the worker negotiates the time he or she will arrive at work. The flexibility in this plan lies in the worker's choice of the hour of starting the work day, because the worker is required to put in an eight-hour shift after arriving at work.

Still another alternative work plan is labeled *variable hours*. The work hours in this plan are determined by demands of the job assignment. The plan is usually incorporated in industries that have seasonal-demand work loads.

Job sharing, another variation in alternative work patterns, is an arrangement in which two individuals have responsibility for one job. Wages are prorated according to the time each individual works. Olmsted (1981) contended that job sharing has distinct organizational benefits, such as reduced absenteeism and turnover, increased productivity, and flexible options for older workers.

Home telecommuting is another alternative work pattern appealing to a large segment of our society. Using personal computers or computer terminals connected to an employer's central computer, the worker performs assigned tasks at home. Some organizations refer to this arrangement as *homework*. The obvious benefit for the worker is more control of time, and the work can be combined with childcare. Telecommuting from the home can provide jobs for the disabled and elderly and can eliminate costs of transportation to work (Kingston, 1983).

Alternative work patterns do indeed provide flexible work schedules to suit individual needs. In dual-career families, household responsibilities are more easily shared, and individuals are given the opportunity for more appropriate time to spend with children and participate in leisure activities with their families. Alternative work patterns also provide flexible work schedules for single parents. Cohen and Gadon (1981) reported that the opportunity to make choices in various alternative work-pattern formats has mental-health benefits; workers that are given more autonomy tend to be happier and to have positive self-concepts.

The future nature of work will be greatly influenced by advances and growth in technology. More individuals will change careers. As some jobs become obsolete, new ones will have to be mastered. More than likely, changes in work will be accomplished by changes in values and orientation to work. Workers who want more than material gains from work will focus on more effective methods of cooperation, with greater family and community involvement (Coats, 1983; Maccoby & Terzi, 1981).

SUMMARY

1. The rise of industrialism in the late 1800s dramatically changed work environments and living conditions for many Americans. A spirit of reform

emerged in reaction to the impersonal industrial systems and chaotic conditions of urban life in the United States and in Europe.

2. Several outstanding scientists turned their attention to human behavior and to the study of individual differences. Francis Galton of England, Wilheim Wundt of Germany, and Alfred Binet and V. Henri of France published studies of human abilities and human differences.

3. In the United States, G. Stanley Hall became interested in mental characteristics of children, James Cattell published an article referring to mental tests, and John Dewey called for reforms in our educational system.

4. Frank Parsons developed a vocational bureau in Boston, in which he provided systematic guidance to 80 men and women. Parsons's major work, *Choosing a Vocation*, was posthumously published in May 1909. His three-part formulation of career guidance provided the foundation for early career-counseling procedures.

5. In 1910, the First National Conference on Vocational Guidance was held in Boston.

6. The measurement and guidance movements coincided in development and shared many of the same roots. In France, the first intelligence test was published in 1905. The Army Alpha and Beta Tests were made available to the public shortly after World War I. The first edition of *The Strong Vocational Interest Blank* was published in 1927.

7. The federal government played a major role in the career-guidance movement by passing significant national legislation between 1917 and 1940. These acts included the Smith-Hughes Act, George-Dean Act, Wagner-Peyser Act, Civilian Conservation Corps, and Works Progress Administration. The first edition of the *Dictionary of Occupational Titles* was published in 1939.

8. The private sector, through the Jewish Occupational Council, established counseling, placement, and rehabilitation services for Jewish immigrants.

9. Two books had a dramatic impact on the career-counseling movement: Williamson's book *How to Counsel Students* was published in 1939, and Rogers's influential *Counseling and Psychotherapy* was published in 1942. Rogerian theory was responsible for the first major break from Parsons's straightforward approach to career counseling.

10. At the end of World War II, the armed services established separation-counseling programs. The testing movement made rapid advances, and a number of significant books were published on testing.

11. In the early 1950s, career-development and occupational-choice theories were developed. The theories of career development and choice have become enduring issues addressed by the counseling profession, major publications, and professional meetings.

12. In the last 20 years, the career-guidance movement has broadened its role and scope. There is a trend toward greater emphasis on a humanistic and existential orientation.

13. Other developments that have influenced the career-guidance movement are the development of career education, the focus on professionalism, advances in technology, and the NOICC.

14. Growth jobs will include those in such industries as computers and data processing, telecommunications, biotechnology, superconductivity, advanced material, and hazardous waste disposal.

15. Robots will continue to increase in the work force. Workers displaced by robots will need retraining and/or relocation assistance.

16. Minorities in the future work force will continue to need counseling advocates and special assistance in educational planning and upgrading their career expectations.

17. There will be an increasing demand for worker generalists who can adapt to different work environments and tasks rather than specialists who have been prominent in the past.

18. Alternative work patterns include flex-time, contracted hours, the floating day, variable hours, job sharing, and home telecommuting.

19. The future nature of work will be greatly influenced by advances in growth and technology. Workers who want more than material gains from work will focus on more effective methods of cooperation.

SUPPLEMENTARY LEARNING EXERCISES

1. Defend or criticize the position that 1850 should be the beginning date for tracing the career-guidance movement.
2. Read Chapter 1 in the book listed below and write a summary of the contribution of the testing movement to career guidance since 1940.

   Anastasi, A. (1982). *Psychological testing* (6th ed.). New York: Macmillan.

3. Compare Parsons's three-part formulation of counseling procedures with Williamson's six sequential steps. Describe similarities and differences.
4. Read the article listed below and summarize your conclusions.

   Borow, H. (1984). The way we were: Reflections on the history of vocational guidance. *Vocational Guidance Quarterly*, 33 (1), 5–14.

5. Describe how the development of industrial psychology has aided the career-guidance movement.
6. Choose one of the tests mentioned in this chapter that you think has had the most direct influence on the career-guidance movement. Defend your choice by compiling a list of reasons.
7. Defend or criticize the following statement: The federal government should take an active role in supporting career-guidance activities in this country.
8. Choose either directive or nondirective methods of counseling as being the most influential to the career-guidance movement. Defend your choice in a debate or in writing.
9. Compile a list of consequences that robots will bring to the future work force. Using your list, develop at least two counseling components that would assist individuals in adjusting to the consequences.
10. Choose one of the alternative work patterns described in this chapter and write an essay on its benefits for workers and organizations.
11. Write to one of the National Career Training Institutes established by the NOICC and share with the class their plans for training.

Chapter Two
Theories of Career Development

In the beginning of any study, someone usually forms the shape, provides the model, establishes the pattern, and introduces the basic concepts. The theories discussed in this chapter have been most instrumental in providing the foundation for research in vocational behavior. To comprehend these theories is to understand the priorities in career counseling today. The conceptual shifts in career counseling, test format, work-satisfaction studies, and classification systems of occupations have primarily evolved from theories. Understandably, the study of career counseling should begin with them.

This chapter includes a brief discussion of several career-development theories and provides references for greater in-depth study of these theories. It serves as an introduction to trait-and-factor theory, several developmental theories, a needs-approach theory, a typology-approach theory, a social-learning theory, career development from a cognitive-information-process conceptual perspective, and evolving theories. Psychoanalytical, sociological, and learning approaches to career development are also summarized. References to the information contained in this chapter will be made throughout the book. However, the career-development theories discussed in this chapter have been for the most part developed from research on white males. This limitation severely limits generalizations drawn from these theories for many population groups, including women and minorities. In succeeding chapters, career programs for special populations are addressed.

TRAIT-AND-FACTOR THEORY

Among early theorists on vocational counseling, Parsons (1909) maintained that vocational guidance is accomplished first by studying the individual, second by surveying occupations, and finally by matching the individual with the occupation. This process, called trait-and-factor theory, became the foundation of many vocational-counseling programs such as those of the Veterans Administration, the YMCA, the Jewish vocational services, and colleges and universities (Super, 1972.)

The trait-and-factor approach has been the most durable of all theories of career guidance. Simply stated, it means matching the individual's traits with requirements of a specific occupation, subsequently solving the career-search problem. The trait-and-factor theory evolved from early studies of individual differences and developed closely with the testing, or *psychometric*, movement. This theory greatly influenced the study of job descriptions and job requirements in an attempt to predict future job success from the measurement of traits that are job related. The key characteristic of this theory is the assumption that individuals have unique patterns of ability or traits that can be objectively measured and correlated with the requirements of various types of jobs.

The development of assessment instruments and refinement of occupational information are closely associated with the trait-and-factor theory. The study of aptitudes in relation to job success has been an ongoing process. Occupational interests occupy no small part of the research literature on career development. The development of individual values in the career decision-making process is also a significant factor (Herr & Cramer, 1972). It has been suggested that the trait-and-factor theory may be more appropriately called *applied differential psychology* (Super, 1972).

Williamson (1939, 1949) was a prominent advocate of trait-and-factor counseling. Utilization of Williamson's counseling procedures maintained the early impetus of the trait-and-factor approach evolving from the work of Parsons. Even when integrated into other theories of career guidance, the trait-and-factor approach plays a very vital role. Its impact and influence on the development of assessment techniques and the utilization of career information have been of inestimable value (Zaccaria, 1970).

However, some of the basic assumptions of the trait-and-factor approach have been severely challenged over the last three decades. The limitations of testing have been made apparent from two widely quoted research projects. The first was by Thorndike and Hagen (1959), who followed the career patterns of 10,000 men who had taken tests in the armed forces during World War II. The results of this study suggest that tests given 12 years earlier did not accurately predict occupational success in that, for a variety of reasons, a significant number of individuals undertook occupations unrelated to their measured abilities. Another research project by Ghiselli (1966) suggests that predicting success by testing in occupational-training programs is only moderately reliable. The hazards of overreliance on test results as predictors of an individual's future career were made very clear by these research findings. In general, research efforts suggest that test results alone do not provide enough information to accurately predict future career success.

Brown and Brooks (1990) argued that trait-and-factor theory has never been fully understood. They suggested that advocates of trait-and-factor approaches never approved of excessive use of testing in career counseling. For example, Williamson (1939) suggested that test results are but one means of evaluating individual differences. Other data, such as work experience and general background, are as important in the career-counseling process.

Recently, Sharf (1992) summarized the advantages and disadvantages of trait-and-factor theory and suggested that it is a static theory rather than a developmental one. Furthermore, it focuses on identifying individual traits and factors but does not account for how interests, values, aptitudes, achievement, and personalities grow and change. The major point is that clients can benefit from dialogue that is directed toward continually evolving personal traits and how changes affect career decision making.

The following assumptions of the trait-and-factor approach also raise concerns about this theory: (1) there is a single career goal for everyone, and (2) career decisions are primarily based on measured abilities (Herr & Cramer, 1992). These assumptions severely restrict the range of factors that can be considered in the career-development process. In essence, the trait-and-factor approach is far too narrow in scope to be considered a major theory of career development. However, we should recognize that standardized assessment and occupational analysis procedures stressed in trait-and-factor approaches are useful in career counseling.

DEVELOPMENTAL THEORIES

The developmental theories discussed in this section are based on assumptions similar to those of the trait-and-factor approach, but the primary assumption is that career development is a process that takes place over the life span. Because career development is viewed as a life-long process, career guidance programs should be designed to meet the needs of individuals at all stages of life. Thus, stages of career development are important points of reference for the career development theorists. Indeed, among other points of reference, the theorists have focused on developmental stages that are somewhat related to age: the process of career maturity, the development of self-concept as one relates it to a career, and the development of sex-role orientation. Adult developmental models have received particular attention in the last two decades.

Ginzberg and Associates

Ginzberg, Ginsburg, Axelrad, and Herma (1951) are generally considered to be the first to approach a theory of occupational choice from a developmental standpoint. This team, consisting of an economist, a psychiatrist, a sociologist, and a psychologist, set out to test and develop a theory of occupational choice. Their original study was part of a more comprehensive study of the world of work.

In developing their theory, Ginzberg and associates undertook an empirical investigation of a carefully selected sample of individuals who would have reasonable freedom of choice in selecting an occupation. Their sample was comprised of males from upper-middle-class, urban, Protestant or Catholic families of Anglo-Saxon origin, whose educational level ranged from sixth grade to graduate school. Because of the highly selective nature of the sample, the conclusions of the study have limited application (Osipow, 1983). Specifically, female and ethnic minority career-developmental patterns were not considered. Nor were the rural or urban poor. Therefore, be aware that the conclusions reached by this study do not necessarily apply to other than the identified sample.

The Ginzberg group concluded that occupational choice is indeed a developmental process, which generally covers a period of six to ten years, beginning around age 11 and ending shortly after age 17 or in young adulthood. There are three distinct periods or stages in the occupational-choice process entitled *fantasy*, *tentative*, and *realistic*. Table 2-1 outlines these steps.

According to Ginzberg and associates, during the fantasy period play gradually becomes work oriented and reflects initial preferences for certain kinds of activities. Various occupational roles are assumed in play, resulting in initial value judgments on the world of work. The tentative period is divided into four stages. First is the *interest* stage, during which the individual makes more definite decisions concerning likes and dislikes. Next is the *capacity* stage of becoming aware of one's ability as related to vocational aspirations. Third is the *value* stage, a time when clearer perceptions of occupational styles emerge. During the final *transition* stage, the individual becomes aware of the decision for vocational choice and the subsequent responsibilities accompanying a career choice.

The realistic period is divided into three stages. The first stage is the *exploration* stage, which, for the group studied by Ginzberg and associates, centered on college entrance. During this stage, the individual narrows the career choice to two or three possibilities but is generally in a stage of ambivalence and indecisiveness. However, the career focus is much narrower in scope. The second stage, *crystallization*, is when the commitment to a specific career field is made. Change of direction for some—even at this stage—is referred to as pseudo-crystallization. The final stage, *specification*, is when the individual selects a job or professional training for a specific career.

The Ginzberg group recognized individual variations in the career-decision process. Individual patterns of career development that lacked conformity with

TABLE 2-1
Stages or Periods in the Ginzberg Study

Period	Age	Characteristics
Fantasy	Childhood (before age 11)	Purely play orientation in the initial stage; near end of this stage, play becomes work oriented
Tentative	Early adolescence (ages 11–17)	Transitional process marked by gradual recognition of work requirements; recognition of interests, abilities, work rewards, values, and time perspectives
Realistic	Middle adolescence (ages 17 to young adult)	Integration of capacities and interests; further development of values; specification of occupational choice; crystallization of occupational patterns

age-mates were identified as deviant—that is, deviant from the highly selected sample comprised of white males from upper-middle-class, urban families. Two primary causes for individual variations in career development were suggested: (1) early, well-developed occupational skills often result in early career patterns, deviant from the normal development; and (2) timing of the realistic stage of development may be significantly delayed due to such variables as emotional instability, various personal problems, and financial affluence.

From this study emerged a distinctive, systematic process based primarily on adolescent adjustment patterns that lead individuals to occupational choice. More specifically, the occupational-choice process was the gradually developed precept of occupations subjectively appraised by the individual in the sociocultural milieu from childhood to early adulthood. As one progresses through the stages outlined by this study, vocational choice is being formulated. As tentative occupational decisions are made, other potential choices are eliminated.

In the original study, Ginzberg and associates stated that the developmental process of occupational decision making was irreversible in that the individual could not return chronologically or psychologically to the point where earlier decisions could be repeated. This conclusion was later modified to refute the earlier stand that occupational decision making is an irreversible process; however, Ginzberg (1972) continued to stress the importance of early choices in the career-decision process. The work of Ginzberg and associates has greatly influenced occupational research, particularly in dealing with developmental tasks as related to career development.

In a review of his theory, Ginzberg (1984) reemphasized that occupational choice is lifelong and coextensive with a person's working life:

> Occupational choice is a lifelong process of decision making for those who seek major satisfaction from their work. This leads them to reassess repeatedly how they can improve the fit between their changing career goals and the realities of the world of work (p. 180).

There has been some evidence to support the major theoretical tenets of this theory. O'Hara and Tiedeman (1959) investigated the four stages of the tentative period (interests, capacity, value, and transition) and found that they do occur in the order theorized, but at earlier ages. Studies by Davis, Hagan, and Strouf (1962) and Hollender (1967) tend to support the concepts of vocational development postulated, although the timing and sequence of the stages have not been completely supported.

The developmental conceptualization of the process of career decision making is quite a departure from the trait-and-factor approach. Although not fully tested, the theory provides a description of a developmental process for normal and deviant patterns of vocational development. The theory is more descriptive than explanatory in that it does not provide strategies for facilitating career development or explanations of the developmental process. It appears that the major usefulness of this theory is in providing a framework for the study of career development (Osipow, 1983).

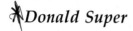Donald Super

Donald Super (1972) thought that he had often been mislabeled as a theorist. In fact, Super did not believe that he had developed a theory that could be labeled specifically at that time. On the contrary, he looked on his work as the development of segments of possible theories of the future. He indicated that if he is to carry a label, it should be broad such as Differential-Developmental-Social-Phenomenological Psychologist. His multiple approach to career development is reflected first of all in his interest in differential psychology or the trait-and-factor theory as a medium through which testing instruments and subsequent norms for assessment are developed. He thought that differential psychology is of utmost importance in the continuing attempt to furnish data on occupational differences related to personality, aptitude, and interests. This he viewed as an ongoing process as we learn more about the world of work.

Self-concept theory is a very vital part of Super's approach to vocational behavior. This approach has generated a number of research projects aimed at determining how the self-concept is implemented in vocational behavior (Norrell & Grater, 1960; Englander, 1960; Stephenson, 1961; Kibrick & Tiedeman, 1961; Schutz & Blocher, 1961; Anderson & Olsen, 1965). The research projects have focused more attention on the significance of self-concept in the career-development process. Specifically, the research has indicated that the vocational self-concept develops through physical and mental growth, observations of work, identification with working adults, general environment, and general experiences. Ultimately, differences and similarities between self and others are assimilated. As experiences become broader in relation to awareness of the world of work, the more sophisticated vocational self-concept is formed. Although the vocational self-concept is only a part of the total self-concept, it is the driving force that establishes a career pattern one will follow throughout life. Thus, individuals implement their self-concepts into careers that will provide the most efficient means of self-expression.

Another of Super's important contributions has been his formalization of vocational developmental stages. These stages are as follows:

1. *Growth* (birth–age 14 or 15), characterized by development of capacity, attitudes, interests, and needs associated with self-concepts;
2. *Exploratory* (ages 15–24), characterized by a tentative phase in which choices are narrowed but not finalized;
3. *Establishment* (ages 25–44), characterized by trial and stabilization through work experiences;
4. *Maintenance* (ages 45–64), characterized by a continual adjustment process to improve working position and situation; and
5. *Decline* (ages 65+), characterized by preretirement considerations, reduced work output, and eventual retirement (Issacson, 1985, pp. 51–53).

These stages of vocational development provide the framework for vocational behavior and attitudes, which are evidenced through five activities known as vocational developmental tasks. These five developmental tasks are shown in

Table 2-2, delineated by typical age ranges (tasks *can* occur at other age levels) and by their general characteristics.

The *crystallization* task is the forming of a preferred career plan and considering how it might be implemented. Pertinent information is studied with the goal of becoming more aware of the preferred choice and the wisdom of the preference. The *specification* task follows, in which the individual feels the need to specify the career plan through more specific resources and explicit awareness of cogent variables of the preferred choice. The *implementation* task is accomplished by the completion of training and entry into the career. The *stabilization* task is reached when the individual is firmly established in a career and develops a feeling of security in the career position. Finally, the *consolidation* task follows with advancement and seniority in a career (Super et al., 1963).

More recently, Super (1990) has modified developmental tasks through the life span, as shown in Table 2-3. He uses the terms *cycling* and *recycling* through developmental tasks. This formulation clarifies Super's position, which may have been misunderstood in the past; that is, he views ages and transitions as very flexible and as not occurring in a well-ordered sequence. A person can recycle through one or more stages, which refers to a *minicycle*. For example, an individual who experiences disestablishment in a particular job may undergo new growth and become ready to change occupations. In this instance, the individual has reached the point of maintenance but now recycles through exploration in search of a new and different position.

The concept of career patterns was an early interest of Super (1957) and his colleagues. He was particularly interested in the determinants of career patterns

TABLE 2-2
Super's Vocational Developmental Tasks

Vocational Developmental Tasks	Ages	General Characteristics
Crystallization	14–18	A cognitive-process period of formulating a general vocational goal through awareness of resources, contingencies, interests, values, and planning for the preferred occupation
Specification	18–21	A period of moving from tentative vocational preferences toward a specific vocational preference
Implementation	21–24	A period of completing training for vocational preference and entering employment
Stabilization	24–35	A period of confirming a preferred career by actual work experience and use of talents to demonstrate career choice as an appropriate one
Consolidation	35+	A period of establishment in a career by advancement, status, and seniority

TABLE 2-3

The Cycling and Recycling of Developmental Tasks Through the Life Span

Life Stage	Adolescence 14–25	Early Adulthood 25–45	Middle Adulthood 45–65	Late Adulthood over 65
			Age	
Decline	Giving less time to hobbies	Reducing sports participation	Focusing on essential activities	Reducing working hours
Maintenance	Verifying current occupational choice	Making occupational position secure	Holding own against competition	Keeping up what is still enjoyed
Establishment	Getting started in a chosen field	Settling down in a permanent position	Developing new skills	Doing things one has always wanted to do
Exploration	Learning more about more opportunities	Finding opportunity to do desired work	Identifying new problems to work on	Finding a good retirement spot
Growth	Developing a realistic self-concept	Learning to relate to others	Accepting one's limitations	Developing nonoccupational roles

SOURCE: From "A Life-Span, Life-Space Approach to Career Development," by D. E. Super in *Career Choice and Development: Applying Contemporary Theories to Practice,* 2nd ed., by Duane Brown, Linda Brooks, and Associates, p. 206. © 1990 by Jossey-Bass, Inc., Publishers. Reprinted by permission.

revealed by the research of Davidson and Anderson (1937) and Miller and Form (1951). He modified the six classifications used by Miller and Form in their study of career patterns for men into four classifications, which are outlined in Table 2-4.

Super also classified career patterns for women into seven categories ranging from a stable homemaking career pattern to a multiple-trial career pattern. Recently, he suggested that these classifications were no longer valid for women in modern society and has applied the principles of his theory to both genders (Super, 1990).

One of Super's best-known studies, launched in 1951, was designed to follow the vocational development of ninth-grade boys in Middletown, New York (Super & Overstreet, 1960). One of the major considerations of this study was to identify and validate the vocational developmental tasks relevant to each stage of development. Super thought that the completion of the appropriate tasks at each level was an indication of what he termed *vocational maturity.* The findings suggest that the ninth-grade boys in this study had not reached a level of understanding of the world of work or of themselves sufficient to make adequate career decisions. Vocational maturity seemed to be related more to intelligence than to age.

TABLE 2-4
Super's Career Patterns for Men

Classification of Pattern	Classification of Typical Career	Characteristics
Stable career pattern	Professional, managerial, skilled workers	Early entry into career with little or no trial work period
Conventional career pattern	Managerial, skilled workers, clerical workers	Trial work periods followed by entry into a stable pattern
Unstable career pattern	Semi-skilled workers, clerical and domestic workers	A number of trial jobs that may lead to temporary stable jobs, followed by further trial jobs
Multiple-trial career pattern	Domestic workers and semi-skilled workers	Nonestablishment of career marked by continual change of employment

Various traits of vocational maturity (such as planning, accepting responsibility, and awareness of various aspects of a preferred vocation) proved to be irregular and unstable during a three-year period in high school. However, those individuals who were seen as vocationally mature in the ninth grade (based on their knowledge of an occupation, planning, and interest) were significantly more successful as young adults. This suggests that there is a relationship between career maturity and adolescent achievement of a significant degree of self-awareness, knowledge of occupations, and developed planning capability. Thus, ninth-grade vocational behavior does have some predictive validity for the future. In other words, boys who successfully accomplish developmental tasks at periodic stages tend to achieve greater maturity later in life.

The career-maturity concepts developed by Super have far-reaching implications for career education and career-counseling programs. The critical phases of career-maturity development provide points of reference from which the desired attitudes and competencies related to effective career growth can be identified and subsequently assessed. Moreover, the delineation of desired attitudes and competencies within each stage affords the specification of objectives for instructional and counseling projects designed to foster career-maturity development. Super (1974, p. 13) identified six dimensions that he thought were relevant and appropriate for adolescents:

1. *Orientation to vocational choice* (an attitudinal dimension determining if the individual is concerned with the eventual vocational choice to be made);
2. *Information and planning* (a competence dimension concerning specificity of information individuals have concerning future career decisions and past planning accomplished);
3. *Consistency of vocational preferences* (individuals' consistencies of preferences);
4. *Crystallization of traits* (individual progress toward forming a self-concept);

5. *Vocational independence* (independence of work experience); and
6. *Wisdom of vocational preferences* (dimension concerned with individual's ability to make realistic preferences consistent with personal tasks).

The translation of these dimensions into occupational terms provides clarity for program considerations. For example, the attitudinal dimension of orientation to vocational choice may translate for one individual to mean "I don't know what I'm going to do and haven't thought about it"; for another, "I really want to decide, but I don't know how to go about it." The difference in levels of career maturity development are apparent from these remarks, providing clues from which the counselor may stimulate the growth of both individuals.

The dimensions of career maturity developed by Super support the concept that education and counseling can provide the stimulus for career development. The index of career maturity may be assessed by standardized inventories, which are discussed in Chapter 7. Career maturity is concerned not only with individually accomplished developmental tasks but also with the behavior manifested in coping with the tasks of a given period of development. The readiness of individuals to enter certain career-related activities is of inestimable value in the career-counseling process.

The phenomenology of decision making and career development, according to Super, is indeed the combined complexities and variables of differential psychology, self-concept theory, developmental tasks, and sociology of life stages. Primarily, Super took a multisided approach to the career-development process. His theory of vocational development is considered the most comprehensive of all developmental theories (Bailey & Stadt, 1973, p. 88) and offers valid explanations of developmental concepts that have been generally supported by numerous research projects (Osipow, 1983). The theory is highly systematic and is useful for developing objectives and strategies for career-counseling and career-education programs. The developmental aspects of Super's theory provide explanations of the various factors that influence the career-choice process. The following two major tenets of his theory give credence to developmental theories in general: (1) career development is a lifelong process occurring through defined developmental periods, and (2) the self-concept is being shaped as each phase of life exerts its influence on human behavior. More recently, Super (1984) clarified his position on self-concept theory as "essentially a matching theory in which individuals consider both their own attributes and the attributes required by an occupation" (p. 208). Super saw self-concept theory as divided into two components: (1) personal or psychological, which focuses on how individuals choose and adapt to their choices; and (2) social, which focuses on the personal assessment individuals make of their socioeconomic situations and current social structure in which they work and live. The relationship of self-concept to career development is one of the major contributions of Super's theory.

Super's concept of vocational maturity should also be considered a major contribution to career-developmental theories. Conceptually, career maturity is acquired through successfully accomplishing developmental tasks within a continuous series of life stages. Career maturity on this continuum is described in terms of attitudinal and competence dimensions. Points of reference from this continuum provide relevant information for career-counseling and career-education objectives and strategies.

In a more recent classification of stage transitions, Super (1990) illustrated a life-stage model by using a "life rainbow." This two-dimensional graphic schema presents a longitudinal dimension of the life span, referred to as a "maxicycle," and corresponding major life stages, labeled "minicycles." A second dimension is "life space," or the roles played by individuals as they progress through developmental stages, such as child, student, "leisurite," citizen, worker, spouse, homemaker, parent, and pensioner. These roles are experienced in the following theaters: home, community, school (college and university), and workplace.

This conceptual model leads to some interesting observations: (1) because people are involved in several roles simultaneously within several theaters, success in one role facilitates success in another; and (2) all roles affect one another in the various theaters.

In the early 1990s, Super created an "archway model" to delineate the changing diversity of life roles experienced by individuals over the life span. This model is used to clarify how biographical, psychological, and socioeconomic determinants influence career development. Figure 2-1 illustrates the archway model. One base stone in the arch supports the person and his or her psychological characteristics, while the other base stone supports societal aspects such as economic resources, community, school, family, and so on. The point is that societal factors interact with the person's biological and psychological characteristics as he or she functions and grows.

The column that extends from the biological base encompasses the person's needs, intelligence, values, aptitudes, and interests—those factors that constitute personality variables and lead to achievement. The column rising from the geographical base stone includes environmental influences such as family, school, peer group, and labor markets—factors that affect social policy and employment practices.

The arch joining the columns is made up of conceptual components, including developmental stages from childhood to adulthood and developed role self-concepts. The keystone of the archway is the self or person who has experienced the personal and social forces that are major determinants of self-concept formation and active life roles in society.

In essence, interactive learning is the fundamental concept that forms the keystone (self) of the archway as the individual encounters people, ideas, facts, and objects in personal development. The relationship of all the model's segments highlights the profound interactional influences in the career-development process. The integration of life activities and developmental stages is a prime example of perceiving career development as a pervasive part of life. Career-guidance programs that incorporate developmental concepts must address a broad range of counseling techniques and intervention strategies. This seems to be the message that Super has promoted for several decades.

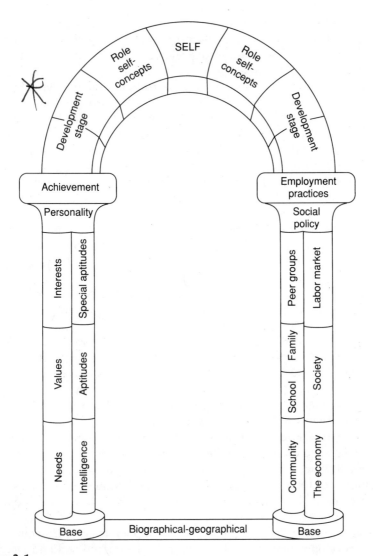

FIGURE 2-1

A Segmental Model of Career Development

SOURCE: From "A Life-Span, Life-Space Approach to Career Development" by D. E. Super in *Career Choice and Development: Applying Contemporary Theories to Practice*, Second Edition by Duane Brown, Linda Brooks, and Associates, pp. 206–208. ©1990 by Jossey-Bass, Inc., Publishers. Reprinted by permission.

David Tiedeman

The key concept of Tiedeman's approach to career development is self-development in the broadest sense (Tiedeman & O'Hara, 1963). The total cognitive development of the individual and the subsequent process of decision making have been its main focus. According to Tiedeman, career development unfolds within the general process of cognitive development as one resolves ego-relevant crises. He believed the evolving ego identity is of central importance in the career-development process. He referred to the evolving self-in-situation from the earliest awareness of self to the point at which the individual becomes capable of evaluating experiences, anticipating and imagining future goals and storing experiences in memory for future reference.

Within this context, the path of career development parallels stages of development drawn from the theoretical orientation of Erikson's (1950) eight psychosocial crises as follows: (1) trust, (2) autonomy, (3) initiative, (4) industry, (5) identity, (6) intimacy, (7) generativity, and (8) ego integrity. Self-in-situation, self-in-world, and the orientation of work evolve as one resolves the psychosocial crises of life. As the ego identity develops, career-relevant decision-making possibilities also develop; one can contemplate broad career fields and specific occupations, taking all possible situations into consideration.

Eventually in career decision making, one reaches the point that Tiedeman referred to as *differentiation and integration*. Differentiation is the process of evaluating self or self-in-world through identification and study of various aspects of occupations. The process is complex and yet unique for each individual, depending on biological potential and the social structure of the individual's milieu. Influences are both internally and externally generated. As the individual's cognitive structure develops, impetus for differentiation may be internally provided either physiologically or psychologically. Activities within the individual's environment, including formal education, provide external stimulation.

One of the major goals of differentiation is to resolve the trust-mistrust crisis (Erikson, 1950) as it relates to the world of work. Tiedeman and O'Hara (1963) postulated that society and the individual continually strive toward a common goal: to establish what meaning each has for the other. In essence, the individual is striving to integrate within society—more specifically, within a career—searching for acceptance by members of a career field yet retaining some individuality. If the uniqueness of the individual finds congruency with the uniqueness of the world of work, integration, synthesis, success, and satisfaction will follow. According to Tiedeman, theories of occupational choice and vocational development have not explored how the evolutionary process of differentiation and integration could apply to career development. He has, therefore, conceptualized a pattern or paradigm of problem solving as the mechanism of career decision making. His paradigm covers four aspects of *anticipation* or *preoccupation* (exploration, crystallization, choice, and clarification) and three aspects of *implementation* or *adjustment* (induction, reformation, and integration), which are summarized in Table 2-5.

Tiedeman viewed decision making as a continuous process in which individuals will change their courses of career action, generally by leaving a particular setting or environment. The departure from a particular setting may be caused by external forces (such as the call of the armed service, an economic crisis, the work setting itself) or by broad internal psychological drives (such as unmet needs, changing aspirations, role diffusion). A new decision unfolds and

TABLE 2-5
Aspects of Anticipation, Preoccupation, Implementation, and Adjustment

Aspects of Anticipation or Preoccupation	Characteristics	Aspects of Implementation or Adjustment	Characteristics
Exploration	1. Thinking is rather temporary and evanescent in nature. 2. There is consideration and reconsideration of possible courses of action. 3. Through imagination, one experiences numerous activities by relating feelings of self within certain structures or premises. 4. There is searching through projection into tentative goals. 5. There is a focus on future behavior with alternative courses of action. 6. There is reflection upon aspirations, abilities, interests, and future societal implications related to career choice.	Induction	1. This period begins the social interaction experience with career identification. 2. There is a further identification of self and defense of self within the career social system. 2. As acceptance is experienced within the career, part of self is merged with the accepting group. 3. There is further progression of the individualized goal but within the framework of the totality of a career concerning social purpose.
Crystallization	1. There is a continued assessment of alternatives. 2. Fewer alternatives are under consideration. 3. There is an emergence of tentative choices. 4. Tentative choices may be reevaluated in the process of valuing and ordering. 5. Goals become more definite and formed but are not irreversible. 6. There is a definite move toward stability of thought.	Reformation	1. The career group offers acknowledgment of acceptance as a group member. 2. There is assertive action on the part of the individual within the career group and outside the career group, spawned by the newfound conditions. 3. Assertive action takes the form of convincing others to conform to the self-view held by the individual and toward greater acceptance of modified goals.

TABLE 2-5
(continued)

Aspects of Anticipation or Preoccupation	Characteristics	Aspects of Implementation or Adjustment	Characteristics
Choice	1. A definite goal is chosen. 2. There is focus on the particular behavior necessary to reach the chosen goal.	Integration	1. A compromise of intentions of goals is achieved by the individual as he or she interacts with the career group. 2. Objectivity of self and the career group is attained. 3. Identification of a working member within the total system of the career field emerges. 4. Satisfaction of a committed cause or action is at least temporarily attained.
Clarification	1. This period is marked by further clarification of self in the chosen position. 2. Further consideration of the anticipated position lessens the doubts of the career decision. 3. A stronger conviction about the career decision is developed. 4. This ends the anticipatory or preoccupational stage.		

SOURCE: Adapted from Tiedeman and O'Hara, 1963.

must be made according to the prescribed sequence, beginning with exploration and eventually reaching integration. If integration is not reached once again, the individual may adapt to a career environment or simply withdraw and begin a new search for eventual integration.

The duration and timing of developmental stages is of major importance in career development, according to Tiedeman. The individual's self-awareness and total combined activities make up a part of the time that must be spent in career decision making. But how much of the individual's time, awareness, and activities are concerned with considerations of the world of work? Is there a time-occupancy framework pertinent to work per se within personal development patterns?

Tiedeman suggested that time occupancy is preempted by biological requirements (such as sleeping and eating), expectations of independence (at work, in the community, and so on), and the quest for identity (as a citizen, parent, worker, and other roles). These particular aspects of human time commitment are assigned stages of timing within the overall pattern of human development. As individuals fit their careers into life plans, the study of the time invested in this activity as well as its particular time staging may yield information of inestimable value for the study of career-development patterns as well as personal-development patterns.

Tiedeman and others (Dudley & Tiedeman, 1977; Peatling & Tiedeman, 1977; Miller-Tiedeman & Tiedeman, 1990) have recently focused on ego development as a major component for the career-decision process. Their position was that each person has I-power or potential for self-improvement. Clarifying one's current status and projecting oneself into anticipated career environments are examples of self-development. Understanding of one's belief system is a product of the decision-making process and allows one to live a decision-guided life. Moreover, in viewing life as a career, individuals should be guided to become more self-directed. As Miller-Tiedeman (1988) stated, "One is essentially a scientist applying and observing the results of moving to one's own inner wisdom" (p. 34). While theorists have generally focused on the decision-making process itself, Tiedeman and Miller-Tiedeman have researched individual processes in decision making. Individual experiences and understanding of the decision-making process are important outcomes for career development and selection.

In sum, career development was conceptualized by Tiedeman within a framework of time stages. The process is one of continuously differentiating one's ego identity, processing developmental tasks, and resolving psychosocial crises. Career decisions are reached through a systematic problem-solving pattern requiring the individual's total cognitive abilities, and combining both the uniqueness of the individual and the uniqueness of the world of work.

Miller-Tiedeman and Tiedeman (1990) currently advocate a "lifecareer theory." Based on self-organizing systems, process, and decision theory, lifecareer theory views career choices as a "shift and focus to one's internal frame of reference" (p. 31). Following this logic, one searches from within to find career direction and then applies the strategies of career development for a career decision. However, to find career direction, one must view life as a learning process, recognizing that one should be flexible in using various methods to solve problems and meeting one's needs as life unfolds. In reviewing the theory, Wrenn (1988) observed: "Don't push life in *your* direction (or what you assume this direction to be), life has a direction for you to learn; learn from life, and let life teach you" (p. 340).

A major contribution of Tiedeman's and O'Hara's (1963) theory is the focus on increased self-awareness as important and necessary in the decision-making process. Attention is directed toward effecting change and growth through adjustment to the mores of existing career social systems. Adaptation to a working environment for meaningful peer group affiliation and work performance is stressed. While this theory has had an important impact on the career-decision process, it is limited by lack of empirical data. It was theoretically formulated in accord with Erikson's stages on the basis of the vocationally relevant experiences of five white males.

Circumscription and Compromise: A Developmental Theory of Occupational Aspirations

The development of occupational aspirations is the main theme of Gottfredson's (1981) theory. Incorporating a developmental approach similar to Super's developmental stages, her theory describes how people become attracted to certain occupations. Self-concept in vocational development is a key factor to career selection, according to Gottfredson, because people want jobs that are compatible with their self-images. Yet self-concept development in terms of vocational choice theory needs further definition, argued Gottfredson: key determinants of self-concept development are one's social class, level of intelligence, and experiences with sex-typing. According to Gottfredson, individual development progresses through four stages:

1. *Orientation to size and power (ages 3–5)*
   Thought process is concrete; children develop some sense of what it means to be an adult.
2. *Orientation to sex roles (ages 6–8)*
   Self-concept is influenced by gender development.
3. *Orientation to social valuation (ages 9–13)*
   Development of concepts of social class contributes to the awareness of self-in-situation. Preferences for level of work develop.
4. *Orientation to the internal, unique self (beginning at age 14)*
   Introspective thinking promotes greater self-awareness and perceptions of others. Individual achieves greater perception of vocational aspirations in the context of self, sex-role, and social class.

In this model of development, occupational preferences emerge within the complexities that accompany physical and mental growth. A major determinant of occupational preferences is the progressive circumscription of aspirations during self-concept development; that is, from the rather simplistic and concrete view of life as a child to the more comprehensive, complex, abstract thinking of the adolescent and adult. For example, in stage 1 the child has a positive view of occupations based on concrete thinking. In stage 2 the child makes more critical assessments of preferences, some of which are based on sex-typing. In stage 3 the child adds more criteria to evaluate preferences. In stage 4 the adolescent develops greater awareness of self, sex-typing, and social class, all of which are used with other criteria in evaluating occupational preferences.

Gottfredson suggested that socioeconomic background and intellectual level greatly influence individuals' self-concept in the dominant society. As people project into the work world, they choose occupations that are appropriate to their "social space," intellectual level, and sex-typing. In the Gottfredson model, social class and intelligence are incorporated in the self-concept theory of vocational choice.

Another unique factor in this theory is the concept of compromise in decision making. According to Gottfredson, compromises are primarily based on generalizations formed about occupations or "cognitive maps" of occupations. Although each person develops a unique map, each uses common methods of evaluating similarities and differences, namely through sex-typing, level of work, and field of work. In this way, individuals create boundaries or tolerable limits of acceptable jobs. Gottfredson suggested that people may compromise their occupational choices because of the accessibility of an occupation or even give up vocational interests to take a job that has an appropriate level of prestige and is an appropriate sex-typing. In general, individuals are less willing to compromise job level and sex-type because these factors are more closely associated with self-concept and social identity.

Although the various components of Gottfredson's theory have not been fully evaluated, she has outlined some possibilities for evaluation. Recently, Hesketh, Elmslie, and Kaldor (1990) evaluated Gottfredson's theory of compromise with 90 high school students and 73 adults who were dissatisfied with their careers. The results suggested that interests were more important in career choice than either sex-type or prestige. Meanwhile, we can only speculate on the degree of influence sex-type, intelligence, and social class have on occupational aspirations. The hierarchy of priorities in compromising goals needs further specification and validation, as does her conclusion that most individuals circumscribe their aspirations according to sex-type and prestige by the age of 13.

ANN ROE: A NEEDS APPROACH

Early relations within the family and their subsequent effects on career direction have been the main focus of Ann Roe's work (1956). The analysis of differences in personality, aptitude, intelligence, and background as related to career choice was the main thrust of her research. She studied several outstanding physical, biological, and social scientists to determine if vocational direction were highly related to early personality development.

Roe (1956) emphasized that early childhood experiences play an important role in finding satisfaction in one's chosen field. Her research led her to investigate how parental styles affect need hierarchy and the relationships of these needs to later adult lifestyles. She drew heavily from Maslow's hierarchy of needs in the development of her theory. The need structure of the individual, according to Roe, would be greatly influenced by early childhood frustrations and satisfactions. For example, individuals who desire to work in contact with people are primarily drawn in this direction because of their strong needs for affection and belongingness. Those who choose the nonperson-type jobs would be meeting lower-level needs for safety and security. Roe hypothesized that individuals who enjoy working with people were reared by warm and accepting parents and those who avoid contact with others were reared by cold and/or rejecting parents.

Roe (1956) classified occupations into two major categories: *person-oriented* and *nonperson-oriented*. Examples of person-oriented occupations are: (1) service (concerned with service to other people); (2) business contact (person-to-person contact, primarily in sales); (3) managerial (management in business, industry, and government); (4) general culture (teaching, ministry, and journalism); and (5) arts and entertainment (performing in creative arts). Examples of nonperson-oriented jobs are in the arenas of: (1) technology (production, maintenance, and transportation); (2) the outdoors (agriculture, forestry, mining, and so on); and (3) science (scientific theory and application).

Within each occupational classification are progressively higher levels of functioning. Roe (1956) contended that the selection of an occupational category was primarily a function of the individual's need structure but that the level of attainment within the category was more dependent on the individual's level of ability and socioeconomic background. The climate of the relationship between child and parent was the main generating force of needs, interests, and attitudes that were later reflected in vocational choice.

When thinking back on how she developed the classification system, Roe says she was greatly influenced by research on interests and the development of interest inventories (Roe & Lunneborg, 1990). Nevertheless, six studies reported by Roe and Lunneborg (1990) support the validity of the classification system in that approximately two-thirds of job changes by the individuals studied occurred within the same occupational classification group.

Roe modified her theory after several studies refuted her claim that different parent-child interactions result in different vocational choices (Powell, 1957; Green & Parker, 1965). She currently takes the position that the early orientation of an individual is related to later major decisions—particularly in occupational choice—but that other variables not accounted for in her theory are also important factors. The following statements by Roe (1972) express her own viewpoint on career development:

1. The life history of any man and many women, written in terms of or around the occupational history, can give the essence of the person more fully than can any other approach.

2. Situations relevant to this history begin with the birth of the individual into a particular family at a particular place and time and continue throughout his or her life.

3. There may be differences in the relative weights carried by different factors, but the process of vocational decision and behavior do not differ in essence from any others.

4. The extent to which vocational decisions and behaviors are under the voluntary control of the individual is variable, but it could be more than it sometimes seems to be. Deliberate consideration of the factors involved seems to be rare.

5. The occupational life affects all other aspects of the life pattern.

6. An appropriate and satisfying vocation can be a bulwark against neurotic ills or a refuge from them. An inappropriate or unsatisfying vocation can be sharply deleterious.

7. Since the goodness of life in any social group is compounded of and also determines that of its individual members, the efforts of any society to maintain stability and at the same time advance in desired ways can perhaps be most usefully directed toward developing satisfying vocational situations for its members. But unless the vocation is adequately integrated into the total life pattern, it cannot help much.

8. There is no single specific occupational slot which is a one-and-only perfect one for any individual. Conversely, there is no single person who is the only one for a particular occupational slot. Within any occupation there is a considerable range in a number of variables specifying the requirements.[1]

Roe's theory is usually referred to as a *need-theory approach* to career choice (Zaccaria, 1970; Bailey & Stadt, 1973). According to Roe, combinations of early parent-child relations, environmental experiences, and genetic features determine the development of a need structure. The individual then learns to satisfy these developed needs primarily through interactions with people or through activities that do not involve people. Thus, Roe postulated that occupational choice primarily involves choosing occupations that are person-oriented, such as service occupations, or nonperson-oriented, such as scientific occupations. The intensity of needs is the major determinant that motivates the individual to the level hierarchy within an occupational structure (Zaccaria, 1970).

There have been several practical applications of Roe's classification system (Lunneborg, 1984). For example, both dimensions of the system were used to construct the *Occupational Preference Inventory* (Knapp & Knapp, 1977), the *Vocational Interest Inventory* (Lunneborg, 1981), and an interest inventory used in the fourth edition of the *Dictionary of Occupational Titles* (U.S. Department of Labor, 1977).

[1] From "Perspectives on Vocational Development," by A. Roe. In J. M. Whiteley and A. Resnikoff (Eds.), *Perspectives on Vocational Development*. Copyright 1972 American Personnel and Guidance Association. Reprinted by permission.

Roe's theory has generated considerable research but little support for her theoretical model (Osipow, 1983). The effect postulated by Roe of the parent-child interactions on later vocational choices is difficult to validate. Differing parental attitudes and subsequent interactions within families present such an overwhelming number of variables that no study could be sufficiently controlled to be considered empirical. The longitudinal requirements necessary to validate the theory present another deterring factor. Notwithstanding, Roe made a great contribution to career counseling in having directed considerable attention to the developmental period of early childhood.

JOHN HOLLAND: A TYPOLOGY APPROACH

According to John Holland (1985), individuals are attracted to a given career by their particular personalities and numerous variables that constitute their backgrounds. First of all, career choice is an expression of, or an extension of, personality into the world of work followed by subsequent identification with specific occupational stereotypes. A comparison of self with the perception of an occupation and subsequent acceptance or rejection is a major determinant in career choice. Congruence of one's view of self with occupational preference establishes what Holland refers to as the *modal personal style*.

Modal personal orientation is a developmental process established through heredity and the individual's life history of reacting to environmental demands. Central to Holland's theory is the concept that one chooses a career to satisfy one's preferred modal personal orientation. If the individual has developed a strong dominant orientation, satisfaction is probable in a corresponding occupational environment. If, however, the orientation is one of indecision, the likelihood of satisfaction diminishes. The strength or dominance of the developed modal personal orientation as compared to career environments will be critical to the individual's selection of a preferred lifestyle. Again, the key concept behind Holland's environmental models and environmental influences is that individuals are attracted to a particular role demand of an occupational environment that meets their personal needs and provides them with satisfaction.

For example, a socially oriented individual prefers to work in an environment that provides interaction with others, such as a teaching position. On the other hand, a mechanically inclined individual would seek out an environment where trade could be quietly practiced and would avoid socializing to a great extent. Occupational homogeneity provides the best route to self-fulfillment and a consistent career pattern. Individuals out of their element who have conflicting occupational environmental roles and goals will have inconsistent and divergent career patterns. Holland stressed the importance of self-knowledge in the search for vocational satisfaction and stability.

From this frame of reference, Holland proposed six kinds of modal occupational environments and six matching modal personal orientations. These are summarized in Table 2-6, which also offers representative examples of occupations and themes associated with each personal style.

Holland proposed that personality types can be arranged in a coded system following his modal-personal-orientation themes such as R (realistic occupation), I (investigative), A (artistic), S (social), E (enterprising), and C (conventional). In this way, personality types can be arranged according to dominant combinations. For example, a code of CRI would mean that an individual is very much like people in conventional occupations, and somewhat like those in realistic and investigative occupations. Holland's Occupational Classification (HOC) system

TABLE 2-6
Holland's Modal Personal Styles and Occupational Environments

Personal Styles	Themes	Occupational Environments
Aggressive, prefers concrete vs. abstract work tasks, basically less sociable, poor interpersonal interactions	Realistic	Skilled trades such as plumber, electrician, and machine operator; technician skills such as airplane mechanic, photographer, draftsperson, and some service occupations
Intellectual, abstract, analytical, independent, sometimes radical and task-oriented	Investigative	Scientific such as chemist, physicist, and mathematician; technician such as laboratory technician, computer programmer, and electronics worker
Imaginative, values aesthetics, prefers self-expression through the arts, rather independent and extroverted	Artistic	Artistic such as sculptor, artist, and designer; musical such as music teacher, orchestra leader, and musician; literary such as editor, writer, and critic
Prefers social interaction, social presence, concerned with social problems, religious, community-service-oriented, and interested in educational activities	Social	Educational such as teacher, educational administrator, and college professor; social welfare such as social worker, sociologist, rehabilitation counselor, and professional nurse.
Extroverted, aggressive, adventurous, prefers leadership roles, dominant, persuasive, and makes use of good verbal skills	Enterprising	Managerial such as personnel, production, and sales manager; various sales positions, such as life insurance, real estate, and car salesperson
Practical, well-controlled, sociable, rather conservative, prefers structured tasks and prefers conformity sanctioned by society	Conventional	Office and clerical worker such as timekeeper, file clerk, teller, accountant, keypunch operator, secretary, bookkeeper, receptionist, and credit manager

SOURCE: Adapted from Holland, 1985.

has corresponding *Dictionary of Occupational Titles (DOT)* numbers for cross-reference purposes.

The four basic assumptions underlying Holland's (1985) theory are as follows:

1. In our culture, most persons can be categorized as one of six types: realistic, investigative, artistic, social, enterprising, or conventional (p. 2).
2. There are six kinds of environments: realistic, investigative, artistic, social, enterprising, or conventional (p. 3).
3. People search for environments that will let them exercise their skills and abilities, express their attitudes and values, and take on agreeable problems and roles (p. 4).
4. A person's behavior is determined by an interaction between his personality and the characteristics of his environment (p. 4).

The relationships between Holland's personality types are illustrated in Figure 2-2. The hexagonal model provides a visual presentation of the inner relationship of personality styles and occupational environment coefficients of correlation. For example, adjacent categories on the hexagon such as realistic and investigative are most alike, but opposites such as artistic and conventional are most unlike. Those of intermediate distance such as realistic and enterprising are somewhat unlike.

According to Holland, the hexagonal model introduces five key concepts. The first, *consistency,* relates to personality as well as environment. Some of the types have more in common than others; for instance, artistic and social types have

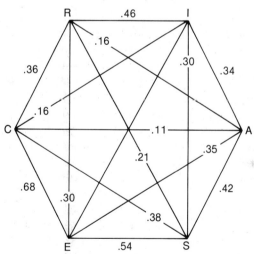

FIGURE 2-2

Holland's model of personality types and occupational environments

SOURCE: From *An Empirical Occupational Classification Derived from a Theory of Personality and Intended for Practice and Research,* by J. L. Holland, D. R. Whitney, N. S. Cole, and J. M. Richards, Jr., ACT Research Report No. 29, The American College Testing Program, 1969. Copyright 1969 by the American College Testing Program. Reprinted by permission.

more in common than investigative and enterprising types. The closer the types are on the hexagon, the more consistent the individual will be. Therefore, high consistency is seen when an individual expresses a preference for adjoining codes such as ESA or RIC. Less consistency would be indicated by codes RAE or CAS.

The second concept is *differentiation*. Individuals who fit a pure personality type will express little resemblance to other types. Conversely, those individuals who fit several personality types have poorly defined personality styles and are considered undifferentiated or poorly defined.

Identity, the third concept describes those individuals who have a clear and stable picture of their goals, interests, and talents. In the case of environments, identity refers to the degree to which a workplace has clarity, stability, and integration of goals, tasks, and rewards. For example, individuals who have many occupational goals, as opposed to a few, have low identity.

The fourth concept, *congruence*, occurs when an individual's personality type matches the work environment. Social personality types, for example, prefer environments that provide social interaction, concerns with social problems, and interest in educational activities. In reviewing the major studies investigating this concept, Spokane (1985) concluded that the research did support the theory that congruence is highly related to academic performance and persistence, job satisfaction, and stability of choice.

Finally, Holland's model provides a calculus for his theory. Holland proposed that the theoretical relationships between types of occupational environments lend themselves to empirical research techniques. The practical application of further research will provide counselors and clients with a better understanding of Holland's theory.

As important as the individual's self-knowledge is occupational knowledge. Holland believed critical career judgments are partially drawn from the individual's occupational information. The importance of identification with an occupational environment underscores the significance of occupational knowledge in the process of appropriate career choice. Knowledge of both occupational environment and corresponding modal personal orientations is, according to Holland, critical to appropriate career decision making.

In the process of career decision making, Holland postulated that the level hierarchy or level of attainment in a career is primarily determined by individual self-evaluations. Intelligence is considered less important than personality and interest (Holland, 1966). Furthermore, the factor of intelligence is subsumed in the classification of personality types; for example, individuals who resemble the investigative type of modal personal orientation are generally intelligent and naturally have skills such as analytical and abstract reasoning.

Extensive testing of Holland's theory suggests that his constructs are valid (Osipow, 1983; Assouline & Meir, 1987; Spokane, 1987; Latona, 1989). According to Holland, the stability of career choice depends primarily on the dominance of personal orientation. Putting it another way, individuals are products of their environment, which greatly influences their personal orientations and eventual career choices. Personality development is a primary consideration in Holland's career-typology theory of vocational behavior.

Holland's theory is primarily descriptive, with little emphasis on explaining the causes and the timing of the development of hierarchies of the personal modal styles. He concentrated on the factors that influence career choice rather than on the developmental process that leads to career choice. Holland's early theory was developed from observations made on a population of National Merit Scholarship finalists. He later expanded the database to include a wider sample of the general population. His research has been extensive and longitudinal. Recently, Holland (1987a) compared his theories with developmental positions:

> I find experience for a learning theory perspective to be more persuasive (than developmental views). In my scheme, different types are the outcomes of different learning histories. Stability of type is a common occurrence because career (types) tend to snowball over the life course. The reciprocal interaction of person and successive jobs usually leads to a series of success and satisfaction cycles (p. 26).

There is some evidence to suggest that Holland's theory is applicable to male and female nonprofessional workers (Salomone & Slaney, 1978). However, the widely used *Self-Directed Search (SDS)* and Holland's theory in general have been attacked as being gender-biased. The major criticism has centered on the claim that the *SDS* limits the career considerations for women and that most females tend to score in three personality types (artistic, social, and conventional) (Weinrach, 1984, p. 69). In defense of the *SDS*, Holland suggested that in our sexist society, females will display a greater interest in female-dominated occupations.

Holland's theory places emphasis on the accuracy of self-knowledge and career information necessary for career decision making. It has had a tremendous impact on interest-assessment and career-counseling procedures; a number of interest inventories present results using the Holland classification format. Its implications for counseling are apparent; a major counseling objective would be to develop strategies to enhance knowledge of self, occupational requirements, and differing occupational environments.

SOCIAL-LEARNING THEORY OF CAREER CHOICE

A social-learning theory approach to career selection was first proposed by Krumboltz, Mitchell, and Gelatt (1975) and more recently by Mitchell and Krumboltz (1990). The theory is an attempt to simplify the process of career selection and is primarily based on life events that are influential in determining career selection. In this theory, the process of career development involves four factors: (1) genetic endowments and special abilities, (2) environmental conditions and events, (3) learning experiences, and (4) task approach skills.

Genetic endowments and special abilities include inherited qualities that may set limits on the individual's career opportunities. The authors do not attempt to explain the interaction of the genetic characteristics and special abilities but emphasize that these factors should be recognized as influences in the career decision-making process.

Environmental conditions and events are considered factors of influence that are often beyond the control of the individual. What is emphasized here is that certain events and circumstances in the individual's environment influence skills development, activities, and career preferences. For example, governmental policies regulating certain occupations and the availability of certain natural resources in the individual's environment may determine to a large extent the opportunities and experiences available. Natural disasters, such as droughts and floods, that affect economic conditions are further examples of influences beyond the control of the individuals affected.

The third factor, *learning experiences*, includes instrumental learning experiences and associative learning experiences. *Instrumental learning experiences* are those the individual learns through reactions to consequences, through direct observable results of actions, and through the reactions of others. The consequences of learning activities and their later influence on career planning and development are primarily determined by the reinforcement or nonreinforcement of the activity, the genetic endowment of the individual, special abilities and skills, and the task itself.

Associative learning experiences include negative and positive reactions to pairs of previously neutral situations. For example, the statements "all politicians are dishonest" and "bankers are all rich" influence the individual's perceptions of these occupations. These associations may also be learned through observations, written materials, and films.

The fourth factor, *task approach skills*, includes the sets of skills the individual has developed, such as problem-solving skills, work habits, mental sets, emotional responses, and cognitive responses. These sets of developed skills determine to a large extent the outcome of problems and tasks faced by the individual.

Task approach skills are often modified as a result of desirable or undesirable experiences. For example, Sue, a high school senior, occasionally takes and studies class notes. Although she was able to make good grades in high school she may find that this same practice in college may result in failure, thus causing her to modify note-taking practices and study habits.

Krumboltz and associates stressed that each individual's unique learning experiences over the life span develop the primary influences that lead to career choice. These influences include (1) generalization of self derived from experiences and performance in relation to learned standards, (2) sets of developed skills used in coping with the environment, and (3) career-entry behavior such as applying for a job or selecting an educational or training institution.

The social-learning model emphasizes the importance of learning experiences and their effect on occupational selection. Genetic endowment is considered primarily as a factor that may limit learning experiences and subsequent career choice. Career decision making is considered to be a lifelong process and a very important skill to be taught in education and career-counseling programs. In the teaching of decision-making skills, it is recommended that the identified factors that influence career choice be stressed.

The factors that influence preferences in the social-learning model are composed of numerous cognitive processes, interactions in the environment, and inherited personal characteristics and traits. For example, educational and occupational preferences are a direct, observable result of actions (referred to as self-observation generalizations) and of learning experiences involved with career tasks. If an individual has been positively reinforced while engaging in the activities of a course of study or occupation, the individual is more likely to express a preference for the course of study or the field of work. In this way, the consequence of each learning experience, in school or on a job, increases the probability that the individual will have a similar learning experience in the future. However, an individual can become proficient in a field of work by developing skills, but even this fact does not ensure that an individual will remain in the field of work over a life span. An economic crisis or negative feedback may initiate a change of career direction.

Genetic and environmental factors are also involved in the development of preferences. For example, a basketball coach might reinforce his players for their skills, but the coach will more likely reinforce tall players than ones smaller in stature.

Other positive factors influencing preferences are valued models who advocate engaging in a field of work or an educational course, or who are observed doing so. Finally, positive words and images, such as a booklet describing an occupation in glamorous terms, will lead to positive reactions to that occupation. In social-learning theory, learning takes place through observations as well as through direct experiences.

The determination of an individual's problematic beliefs and generalizations is of major importance in the social-learning model (Mitchell & Krumboltz, 1984). For example, the identification of content from which certain beliefs and generalizations have evolved is a key ingredient for developing counseling strategies for individuals who have career decision-making problems. The counselor's role is to probe assumptions and presuppositions of expressed beliefs and to explore alternative beliefs and courses of action. Assisting individuals to fully understand the validity of their beliefs is a major component of the social-learning model. Specifically, the counselor should address the following problems:

1. Persons may fail to recognize that a remediable problem exists (individuals assume that most problems are a normal part of life and cannot be altered).
2. Persons may fail to exert the effort needed to make a decision or solve a problem (individuals exert little effort to explore alternatives; they take the familiar way out).
3. Persons may eliminate a potentially satisfying alternative for inappropriate reasons (individuals overgeneralize from false assumptions and overlook potentially worthwhile alternatives).

4. Persons may choose poor alternatives for inappropriate reasons (the individuals are unable to realistically evaluate potential careers because of false beliefs and unrealistic expectations).

5. Persons may suffer anguish and anxiety over perceived inability to achieve goals (individual goals may be unrealistic or in conflict with other goals) (Krumboltz, 1983).

This theory is both descriptive and explanatory because the process of career choice is described and examples of factors that influence choice are given. Although the authors have attempted to simplify the process of career development and career choice, the many variables introduced in this theory make the process of validation extremely complex. Meanwhile, the authors should be commended for specifying counseling objectives based on this theory and for providing strategies designed to accomplish these objectives. They also provided several observations for career counseling (Krumboltz, Mitchell, & Gelatt, 1975, pp. 11–13):

1. Career decision making is a learned skill.
2. Persons who claim to have made a career choice need help too (career choice may have been made from inaccurate information and faulty alternatives).
3. Success is measured by students' demonstrated skill in decision making (evaluations of decision-making skills are needed).
4. Clients come from a wide array of groups.
5. Clients need not feel guilty if they are not sure of a career to enter.
6. No one occupation is seen as the best for any one individual.

CAREER DEVELOPMENT FROM A COGNITIVE INFORMATION PROCESSING CONCEPTUAL PERSPECTIVE

This career-development theory is based on the cognitive information processing (CIP) theory and was developed by Peterson, Sampson, and Reardon (1991). CIP theory is applied to career development in terms of how individuals make a career decision and use information in career problem solving and decision making. CIP's major premise is based on the ten assumptions shown in Table 2–7. Using these assumptions as a focal point, the major strategy of career intervention is to provide learning events that are designed to develop the individual's processing abilities. In this way, clients develop capabilities as career problem solvers to meet immediate, as well as future, problems.

The stages of processing information begin with screening, translating, and encoding input in short-term memory, then storing it in long-term memory, and later activating, retrieving, and transforming the input into working memory to arrive at a solution. The principle function of the counselor in CIP theory is to identify the client's needs and develop interventions to help the client acquire the knowledge and skills to address those needs.

TABLE 2-7
**Assumptions Underlying the Cognitive Information
Processing (CIP) Perspective of Career Development**

Assumption	Explanation
1. Career choice results from an interaction of cognitive and affective processes.	CIP emphasizes the cognitive domain in career decision making; but it also acknowledges the presence of an affective source of information in the process (Heppner & Krauskopf, 1987; Zajonc, 1980). Ultimately, commitment to a career goal involves an interaction between affective and cognitive processes.
2. Making career choices is a problem-solving activity.	Individuals can learn to solve career problems (that is, to choose careers) just as they can learn to solve math, physics, or chemistry problems. The major differences between career problems and math or science problems lie in the complexity and ambiguity of the stimulus and the greater uncertainty as to the correctness of the solution.
3. The capabilities of career problem solvers depend on the availability of cognitive operations as well as knowledge.	One's capability as a career problem solver depends on one's self-knowledge and on one's knowledge of occupations. It also depends on the cognitive operations one can draw on to derive relationships between these two domains.
4. Career problem solving is a high-memory-load task.	The realm of self-knowledge is complex; so is the world of work. The drawing of relationships between these two domains entails attending to both domains simultaneously. Such a task may easily overload the working memory store.
5. Motivation	The motivation to become a better career problem solver stems from the desire to make satisfying career choices through a better understanding of oneself and the occupational world.

(continued)

The authors stress that career problem solving is primarily a cognitive process that can be improved through a sequential procedure known as CASVE, which includes the following generic processing skills: communication (receiving, encoding, and sending out queries), analysis (identifying and placing problems in a conceptual framework), synthesis (formulating courses of action), valuing (judging each action as to its likelihood of success and failure and its impact on others), and execution (implementing strategies to carry out plans). Table 2-8 describes the CASVE cycle in terms of its phases by using career information and media.

This model emphasizes the notion that career-information counseling is a learning event. This is consistent with other theories that make this same assumption and present procedures for developing decision-making skills. However, one major difference between CIP theory and other theories dis-

TABLE 2-7
(continued)

Assumption	Explanation
6. Career development involves continual growth and change in knowledge structures.	Self-knowledge and occupational knowledge consist of sets of organized memory structures called *schemata* that evolve over the person's life span. Both the occupational world and we ourselves are ever-changing. Thus, the need to develop and integrate these domains never ceases.
7. Career identity depends on self-knowledge.	In CIP terms, career identity is defined as the level of development of self-knowledge memory structures. Career identity is a function of the complexity, integration, and stability of the schemata comprising the self-knowledge domain.
8. Career maturity depends on one's ability to solve career problems.	From a CIP perspective, career maturity is defined as the ability to make independent and responsible career decisions based on the thoughtful integration of the best information available about oneself and the occupational world.
9. The ultimate goal of career counseling is achieved by facilitating the growth of information-processing skills.	From a CIP perspective, the goal of career counseling is therefore to provide the conditions of learning that facilitate the growth of memory structures and cognitive skills so as to improve the client's capacity for processing information.
10. The ultimate aim of career counseling is to enhance the client's capabilities as a career problem solver and a decision maker.	From a CIP perspective, the aim of career counseling is to enhance the client's career decision-making capabilities through the development of information-processing skills.

SOURCE: *Career Development and Services: A Cognitive Approach,* by Gary Peterson, James Sampson, and Robert Reardon, pp. 7–9. Copyright 1991 by Brooks/Cole Publishing Company. Reprinted by permission.

cussed in this chapter is the role of cognition as a mediating force that leads individuals to greater power and control in determining their own destiny. As we learn more about CIP theory, the CASVE approach will be further delineated for the counseling profession.

EVOLVING THEORIES OF CAREER DEVELOPMENT

In one of the most recent and comprehensive reviews of career-choice and development theories, Brown and Brooks, (1990) have devoted a chapter to evolving theories. Currently recognized theories have been criticized, in part, because of their failure to address the vocational behavior of groups such as

TABLE 2-8
Career Information and the CASVE Cycle

Phase of the CASVE Cycle	Example of Career Information and Media
Communication (identifying a need)	A description of the personal and family issues that women typically face in returning to work (information) in a videotaped interview of currently employed women (medium)
Analysis (interrelating problem components)	Explanations of the basic education requirements for degree programs (information) in community college catalogues (medium)
Synthesis (creating likely alternatives)	A presentation of emerging nontraditional career options for women (information) at a seminar on career development for women (medium)
Valuing (prioritizing alternatives)	An exploration of how the roles of parent, spouse, citizen, "leisurite," and homemaker would be affected by the assumption of the worker role (information) in an adult version of a computer-assisted career guidance system (medium)
Execution (forming means-ends strategies)	A description of a functional résumé emphasizing transferable skills, followed by the creation of a résumé (information) presented on a computer-assisted employability skills system (medium)

SOURCE: Career Development and Services: A Cognitive Approach, by Gary Peterson, James Sampson, and Robert Reardon, p. 200. Copyright 1991 by Brooks/Cole Publishing Company. Reprinted by permission.

women and racial and ethnic minorities. Other criticism has been directed at limited definitions of human behavior, and some criticism has suggested that current theories have focused on the young and neglected adults. Others may argue that another population has been ignored: individuals with disabilities.

Most of the early career-development theories were devoted to explaining the career development of men. Only recently has there been an attempt to explain gender differences. Some research has noted that women underutilize abilities and talents, while other research has pointed out differences in the developmental processes of women and men (Betz & Fitzgerald, 1987). But currently we do not have a definitive career-development theory for women.

Among the evolving theories discussed were a self-efficacy theory, a need-based sociopsychological model, relational identity, multidimensional models, life-span/life-role approaches, and promising research on racial and ethnic minorities. Much of the research done on these theories involves gender differences, while less seems to be directed toward racial and ethnic minorities.

One of the most promising theories that may lend itself to addressing gender differences is Hackett and Betz's (1981) self-efficacy theory. The brief explanation that follows only summarizes this theory. More information can be found in the above-mentioned reference.

To explain the essence of this theory, the term *career self-efficacy* is defined as "the possibility that low expectations of efficacy with respect to some aspect of career behavior may serve as a detriment to optimal career choice and the development of the individual" (Betz, 1992, p. 24). Further delineation of this theory involves the author's reference to career-choice content (content domains such as math, science, or writing) and career-choice process (behavioral domains that enhance the implementation of a career). From this frame of reference, an individual may avoid areas of course work surrounding a career because of low self-efficacy. Likewise, self-efficacy deficits may lead to procrastination in or avoidance of a career decision.

Hackett and Betz (1981) suggested that social beliefs and expectations are the mechanisms through which self-efficacy deficits are developed, particularly for women. They cite a restricted range of options and underutilization of abilities as important factors in hindering women's career development. Using this logic, women's vocational behavior can at least be partially explained. This theory, as with many of the others mentioned in this section, will undoubtedly be further developed to guidelines for career-development counseling and intervention strategies to meet the needs of clientele.

OTHER THEORIES OF CAREER DEVELOPMENT

In this section three general theories of career development—psychoanalytical, sociological, and learning—will be briefly reviewed. Although elements of these theories are contained in many of the specific theories discussed earlier, their unique contributions to the understanding of career development warrant additional emphasis. More detailed information for each theory can be obtained by using the references cited in this section and in the supplementary exercises at the end of this chapter.

Psychoanalytical Theory

Psychoanalytical approaches have primarily treated work as a method of satisfying impulses and providing outlets for sublimated wishes (Osipow, 1983). Bordin, Nachmann, and Segal (1963) have proposed a framework of vocational development from psychoanalytically developed need dimensions. Like Roe, they emphasized the importance of early parent-child interactions that subsequently result in the establishment of a need hierarchy. Of major significance are the early developmental processes; the authors postulated that needs are established by the age of six. Within this framework, occupational choice is primarily made to satisfy these early established needs and is, therefore, a function of early experiences. Bordin, Nachmann, and Segal (1963, p. 113) would have individuals consider occupations in terms of psychoanalytical need dimensions they satisfy, as follows:

Oral aggressive dimension:
1. Cutting, biting, devouring—satisfaction is related to the use of the teeth in chewing and biting. Activities range from use of cutting tools to employing cutting, or "biting," words.

Manipulative dimension:
1. Physical—using physical strength or machines to exert power.
2. Psychological—influencing or controlling others by psychological means.

In the manipulative dimension, the assumption is that the individual who finds gratification in manipulating or controlling others would seek out jobs that provide an outlet for these needs. Likewise, in the oral aggressive dimension, the individual achieves gratification from using tools that cut objects.

A severe limitation of this theory is that it does not take into consideration the external influences that individuals experience over their life span, such as those described earlier in the social-learning theory model. Second, career choice is regarded as less important than personality development, and little or no emphasis is placed on developmental tasks or concepts of vocational maturity. Third, the theory excludes individuals whose occupational choices are affected by cultural influences or financial limitations and those who cannot experience gratification from work. Finally, there has been little evidence from research to validate psychoanalytical views of occupational choice (Osipow, 1983; Herr & Cramer, 1988, p. 87). The major contribution of this theory is that it directs attention to the importance of early developmental processes and early parent-child relationships.

Sociological or Situational Approach

The Blau-Gustad-Jessor-Parnes-and-Wilcox (1956) paradigm, *Relationships of process of choice and process of selection,* is a synthesis of the effects of social institutions on career choice and development. This model emphasizes the interrelationship of psychological, economic, and sociological determinants of occupational choice and development. The authors suggested that the individual characteristics that are responsible for choice are biologically determined and socially conditioned through family influences, social position and relations, and developed social-role characteristics. Eventually, the individual reaches a preference hierarchy from which choices are made.

The process of selection evolves because of socially related influences and physical conditions such as resources, topography, and climate. For example, an individual reared in a rural environment whose family has limited financial means may tend to select an agricultural occupation, which is related to the climate (long growing season) and topography (rich, flat land).

These factors are considered beyond the control of an individual but are determinants in the process of selection. It is the combination of choice factors and selection factors that determines a series of choices eventually leading to occupational entry. Other basic assumptions in this approach include the following: (1) a social structure exists that imparts patterns of activities, identification with models, and aspirations among various social groups; (2) career development is a continuous process; and (3) situational conditions also exert influences on career-development patterns.

This model is effective for clarifying situational elements in the career-development process. Career choice is seen as a series of interrelated decisions involving the individual's biological endowment, social milieu, and environmental conditions. The model is primarily descriptive in that individually developed preferences, ideals, and expectancies are not explained. This model importantly points out the biological and social complexities of career development and situations that influence this development.

Sociological research continues to focus on situational variables, such as technological changes in local and national economic conditions. Moreover, sociologists have been more concerned with social roles, influence of institutional life, and status attainment as opposed to how and why individuals select careers. Nevertheless, their research continues to provide career counselors with variables that are most important for understanding career development and choice. Examples of relevant issues are status barriers to occupational mobility, racial and sexual discrimination, occupational structure as a social hierarchy, occupational socialization process, work and leisure, work alienation, and career status aspirations (Hall, 1975; Krause, 1971; Hall, 1983).

Learning-Theory Approaches

The applications of learning-theory principles to career development in general and decision making specifically are apparent in a number of theories previously discussed. However, a review of the theoretical principles postulated by O'Hara (1968) and A. W. Miller (1968) should amplify the contribution of learning theory to career development and career decision making. Both authors stressed learning principles as the basis for effective vocational decisions.

O'Hara postulated that career development is primarily a learning process. O'Hara believed most theoretical approaches do not sufficiently emphasize that career-development skills must be learned. For example, we *learn* to associate patterns of behavior and stereotyped roles with various occupations such as electrician, teacher, and lawyer. Because the decision-making process involves what the individual has learned about careers, the degree of learning will determine the effectiveness of choices.

According to O'Hara, vocational goals are best established when academic training requirements are closely linked to vocational requirements. That is, formal learning experiences should be related to occupational requirements so that they may be integrated into subsequent career decisions. In the career-development process, adolescents should be encouraged to compare their personal aptitudes, interests, and values to vocational requirements.

In sum, the individual should learn to vicariously explore the world of work by learning the occupational vocabulary and symbols that characterize particular products or jobs. In this way, the individual may learn to differentiate and integrate occupational information. According to O'Hara, familiarity with an occupation's terminology and orientation will do much to ensure more adequate vocational responses.

A. W. Miller (1968) also believed learning theory should be applied in career decision making. He concentrated on the relationships of behaviors that are consistently and significantly related to occupational choice. Four such categories of behavior were suggested: (1) overt physical activities, (2) overt verbal statements, (3) covert emotional or physiological changes, and (4) covert verbal responses, or thoughts. The functions of a career decision-making theory are to predict, explain, and control decision behaviors.

In Miller's approach, the counselor attempts to identify those behaviors involved in decision making. The identified behaviors provide clues about the events that have motivated the behavior. Once these events are isolated, it is possible to exercise some control over the behaviors that generate decisions. Through application of learning and behavior-modification principles, predictable changes in behavior are possible. In essence, given adequate information about an individual, there is potential for controlling behaviors that constitute decisions. To Miller, this is the major strength of a learning-theory approach.

IMPLICATIONS FOR CAREER GUIDANCE

Theories of career development are conceptual systems designed to delineate apparent relationships between a concomitance of events that leads to causes and effects. Although the theories described in this chapter have a variety of labels, all emphasize the relationships between the unique traits of individuals and the characteristics of society in which development occurs. The major difference among the theories is the nature of the influential factors involved in the career-decision process, but all the theories have common implications for career guidance.

1. Career development takes place in stages that are somewhat related to age but are influenced by many factors in the sociocultural milieu. Because career development is a lifelong process, career-guidance programs must be designed to meet the needs of individuals over the life span.

2. The tasks associated with stages of career development involve transitions requiring individuals to cope with each stage of life. Helping individuals cope with transitions is a key concept to remember while promoting development.

3. Career maturity is acquired through successfully accomplishing developmental tasks within a continuous series of life stages. Points of reference from this continuum provide relevant information for career-guidance program development.

4. Each person should be considered unique. This uniqueness is a product of many sources, including sociocultural background, genetic endowment, personal and educational experiences, family relationships, and community resources. In this context, values, interests, abilities, and behavioral tendencies are important in shaping career development.

5. Self-concept affects career decisions. Self-concept is not a static phenomenon but rather an ongoing process that may gradually or abruptly change as people and situations change. Accurate self-concepts contribute to career maturity.

6. The stability of career choice depends primarily on the strength and dominance of one's personal orientation of personality characteristics, preferences, abilities, and traits. Work environments that match personal orientations provide appropriate outlets for personal and work satisfaction. Finding congruence between personality traits and work environments is a key objective of career development.

7. Individual characteristics and traits can be assessed through standardized assessment instruments. Identified traits are used to predict future outcomes of probable adjustments. Matching job requirements with personal characteristics may not dominate career-counseling strategies but remains a viable part of some programs.

8. Social learning emphasizes the importance of learning experiences and their effect on occupational selection. Learning takes place through observations as well as through direct experiences. Identifying the content of individual beliefs and generalizations is a key ingredient in developing counseling strategies.

9. Introducing occupational information resources and developing skills for their proper use is a relevant goal for all educational institutions. Moreover, this need persists over the life span.

10. Career development involves a lifelong series of choices. Assistance in making appropriate choices is accomplished through the teaching of decision-making and problem-solving skills. Understanding individual processes involved in choices enables counselors to be of better assistance during the decision-making process.

11. The concept of human freedom is implied in all career-development theories. This concept implies that career counselors should provide avenues of freedom for individuals to explore options within the social, political, and economic milieu. The limits of personal freedom are often external (for example, economic conditions, discrimination, and environmental conditions), but freedom may also be constrained from such internal sources as fear, lack of confidence, faulty attitudes, poor self-concept development, and behavioral deficits. Within this context, the career counselor should be concerned not only with career development but with all facets of human development. Counseling strategies must be designed to meet a wide range of needs.

12. The importance of cognitive development and its relationship to self-concept and subsequent occupational aspirations are receiving greater attention. This focus is primarily concerned with the role of cognitive development

in terms of appropriate gender roles, occupational roles, and other generalizations that directly affect career development. This fine-tuning of relationships between human and career development implies that counselors must develop a greater sensitivity to both.

SUMMARY

1. The trait-and-factor theory evolved from early studies of individual differences and developed closely with the psychometric movement. The key characteristic of the trait-and-factor theory is the assumption that individuals have unique patterns of ability or traits that can be objectively measured and subsequently matched with requirements of jobs.

2. Ginzberg, Ginsburg, Axelrad, and Herma are considered the first to approach a theory of occupational choice from a developmental standpoint. They suggested that occupational choice is a developmental process that generally covers a period of six to ten years, beginning at around the age of 11 and ending shortly after age 17. The three periods or stages of development are called fantasy, tentative, and realistic.

3. Super has made many contributions to the study of vocational behavior, including his formalization of developmental stages: growth, exploratory, establishment, maintenance, and decline. Super considered self-concept as the vital force that establishes a career pattern one will follow throughout life. In 1951 he designed a study to follow the vocational development of ninth-grade boys in Middletown, New York. Those individuals who were seen as vocationally mature in the ninth grade (based on their knowledge of occupations, planning, and interests) were significantly more successful as young adults. His conclusions suggest that there is a relationship between career maturity and adolescent achievement of a significant degree of self-awareness, knowledge of occupations, and developed planning ability. Super's theory on the career-development process takes a primarily multisided approach.

4. Tiedeman conceptualized career development as a process of continuously differentiating one's ego identity, processing developmental tasks, and resolving psychosocial crises. These ongoing activities are perceived within a framework of time stages. According to Tiedeman, career decisions are reached through a systematic problem-solving pattern that includes seven steps: (a) exploration, (b) crystallization, (c) choice, (d) clarification, (e) induction, (f) reformation, and (g) integration.

5. In Gottfredson's model, occupational preferences emerge from the complexities that accompany physical and mental growth. A major determinant of occupational preferences is the progressive circumscription of aspirations during self-concept development. Gottfredson suggested that socioeconomic background and intellectual level greatly influence self-concept development.

6. Roe's theory focuses on early relations within the family and their subsequent effects on career direction. Roe emphasized that early childhood experiences were important factors in the satisfaction of one's chosen occupation.

She classified occupations into two major categories: person-oriented and nonperson-oriented.

7. Holland considered career choice as an expression or extension of personality into the world of work, followed by subsequent identification with specific occupational stereotypes. Holland considered modal personal orientation as the key to individual occupational choice. Central to Holland's theory is the concept that individuals choose careers to satisfy their developed preferred personal modal orientations. Holland developed six modal personal styles and six matching work environments: realistic, investigative, artistic, social, enterprising, and conventional.

8. Krumboltz, Mitchell, and Gelatt postulated that career selection is significantly influenced by life events. Four such factors are (a) genetic endowments and special abilities, (b) environmental conditions and events, (c) learning experiences, and (d) task approach skills. Decision making is considered to be a continuous process extending over the life span.

9. Cognitive information theory has been applied to career development in terms of how one makes a career decision. A sequential procedure has been developed to help individuals process information in order to make career decisions in their own best interests.

10. Several evolving theories of career development will undoubtedly be developed further to provide us with guidelines for career-development counseling and intervention strategies in the future.

11. Psychoanalytical approaches to career development have considered work as a method of satisfying impulses and providing outlets for sublimated wishes. Sociological or situational approaches emphasize the interrelationship of psychological, economic, and sociological determinants of occupational choice and development. The learning-theory approaches see career development primarily as a learning process. For example, skills and work roles are learned and are directly applied to the decision-making process.

SUPPLEMENTARY LEARNING EXERCISES

1. Why is the trait-and-factor approach considered the most durable theory? Give examples of the use of the trait-and-factor theory in current career-counseling programs.
2. Defend the statement: Career development is a continuous process.
3. Write your own definition of career development and career counseling.
4. Using the following references, write a comprehensive report on Super's Career Pattern Study conducted in Middletown, New York. Identify the dimensions of vocational maturity used, the procedures, and the conclusions.

   Brown, D., Brooks, L., and Associates (1990). *Career choice and development* (2nd ed.). San Francisco: Jossey-Bass Publishers.

5. Compare Holland's approach to career development with Roe's. Summarize the similarities and differences.
6. Using the following reference, explain the principles behind Holland's theory of vocational choice. Defend and/or criticize his thesis that vocational interests are not independent of personality.

Holland, J. L. (1985). *Making vocational choices* (2nd. ed.). Englewood Cliffs, NJ: Prentice-Hall.

7. Compare Tiedeman's aspects of anticipation and preoccupation with those he outlines for implementation and adjustment. What are the major counseling considerations for both sets of aspects?

8. Apply a career-development theory to your own career development. Using Super's developmental stages, identify your current stage of development and the ages at which you accomplished other stages.

9. Outline the factor that you consider most important in the career development of an adult you know or one you interview.

10. Develop your own theory of career development. Identify the components of other theories you agree with and why you agree with them.

Chapter Three

Some Perspectives of Work

Work is at the heart of our concerns as professionals and individuals fortunate enough to live in a free society. Work can involve the most simple step-by-step procedures or be physically and mentally demanding, complex, interesting, boring, creative, or menial; or it can involve all of the descriptions listed and many more. Throughout our history, work has fascinated researchers who have attempted to delineate the complexities of the labor itself and the problems of individuals who do it. Today, work has prevailed as a most viable subject with the scientific community and has occupied the thoughts of scholars from a variety of disciplines who dared venture into the complex arena associated with work. Work in America has a fascinating, extensive history.

This discussion of work focuses on several issues that are important to career counseling. The first part of the chapter presents prominent research on work motivation and its relationship to individual functioning in the workplace. The second part is devoted to a discussion of work adjustment, work values, work ethic, work commitment, stress at work, career burnout, healthy work, and the quality of work.

WORK MOTIVATION

Work motivation is one of the content areas encompassed by the broader concept of organizational behavior (Korman, 1977). Organizational behavior has been researched within a variety of disciplines, including psychology, sociology, and anthropology. In our discussion of work motivation in the organization, we will also consider a variety of theories that integrate the behavioral sciences. Our discussion centers on prominent representative research in work motivation. We wish especially to provide the counselor with a frame of reference concerning how organizational management has researched human behavior in the organization.

The research cited should aid the counselor in helping others (1) develop and clarify motivational needs and ways they may be fulfilled in an organization, (2) develop awareness of potential organizational support in meeting identified needs, (3) develop awareness of potential obstacles in organizations that may prevent need fulfillment, (4) develop an awareness of why people behave the way they do in organizations, (5) develop an awareness of the dynamics of work motivation, (6) develop an awareness of how organizational management evaluates work motivation, and (7) develop a plan to promote career development within the organization.

Human behavior has long been a topic of discussion among personality theorists. Voluminous amounts of literature have been published exploring human behavior patterns in various environments. The question of what causes men and women to behave the way they do has remained controversial and has resulted in a wide range of theories and postulates. The *psychoanalytical theorists* led by Freud (1953) consider that the human being is motivated by internal conflicts and that the individual is attempting to direct inherited drives toward satisfaction and subsequent achievement in a socially accepted manner. The *behaviorists* have postulated that motivation is learned from the environment through a set of reinforcement contingencies by which one is able to determine those behaviors that are appropriate. The basic assumption of behaviorists is that human desires and needs are learned via internal and external rewards. *Humanists* Maslow (1943), Rogers (1961), White (1959), and Adler (1929) have theorized that motivation is derived from a need for self-fulfillment and a search for a feeling of competence and accomplishment that would be followed by the ultimate experience of self-actualization. The *field theorists* led by Lewin (1951) consider that behavior is a function of a combination of inherited motives and their interaction with contemporary situations in the environment. In this context, behavior is a function of the individual's interaction with all factors in a contemporary field (Snodgrass, 1975).

These theorists and others consider the etiology of an individual's behavior in terms of motivation; that is, motivation is seen as the prime moving force to satisfy a set of goals or needs. For example, Maslow (1943) identified a hierarchy of needs that the individual strives to accomplish. Herzberg (1966) postulated that individuals are motivated by two categories of needs: one category consists of extrinsic compensation (materials, status, security), and the other category is intrinsic in nature (achievement, recognition). Need for affiliation, achievement, and power has been the center of McClelland's (1961) research on why individuals behave the way they do. Finally, the individual's need to be consistent with beliefs, attitudes, and perceptions is derived from Festinger's (1957) *cognitive-dissonance* theories. The remainder of this section is devoted to exploring these four theorists' ideas in further detail.

It is apparent that theorists have basic disagreements as to what motivates behavior, but there are two common elements that are important to our consideration of the individual in the organization. First of all, individuals develop a unique set of needs either genetically and/or through individual experiences that, to a large extent, determine what motivates and satisfies the individual. Second, needs or motivators in some way originate either behaviorally or through environmental interactions. These two issues are our concern.

Maslow's Hierarchy of Needs

Maslow (1943) developed a model of human needs, which are arranged in a hierarchical structure as follows:

1. *Physiological needs*—these are basic needs satisfied by food, water, sleep, and so on;
2. *Safety needs*—these needs involve protection from danger and are met by a secure environment;
3. *Social needs*—these needs are met through friendship and love and through acceptance by peers;
4. *Ego needs*—these needs involve concern for self-esteem, feelings of independence, achievement, and a feeling of a position of status; and
5. *Self-actualization needs*—this level involves self-fulfillment and recognition of one's unique characteristics and potential.

As lower-level needs are satisfied, motivation generated to meet the next level in the hierarchy becomes the center of influence on behavior. In this scheme, the individual strives to fulfill basic needs first, before concentrating on higher-level needs.

The theory has two basic assumptions: (1) needs that have not been satisfied tend to motivate behavior; and (2) as lower-level needs are satisfied, the next level becomes the primary motivator. In the context of our discussion, work performance is thought of as a means of self-actualization. In an organizational setting, opportunities for fulfillment of needs can come through a variety of interactions, including the work setting and job opportunities. Even though there are some questions concerning the validity of Maslow's theory (Korman, 1977, p. 79), opportunities for meeting individually developed needs in a work setting are important considerations in the career search. For some individuals, the higher-order needs are a major motivating force and must be considered in the career-exploration process.

Herzberg's Two-Factor Theory

The two-factor theory, as introduced by Herzberg (1966), was quite a departure from earlier research on work motivation. Previous research had primarily focused on bipolar and unidimensional aspects of job satisfaction and job dissatisfaction; at one end of the scale was job satisfaction while at the opposite end was job dissatisfaction. Following this logic, one would simply have to remove those variables that cause dissatisfaction and job satisfaction would result. Herzberg disputed this concept by considering job satisfaction and job dissatisfaction as two separate dimensions. He considered one distinct group of variables as contributing to job satisfaction and a separate group as causing job dissatisfaction. Herzberg labeled sources of job satisfaction as *motivators*, elements within the context of the job such as recognition, achievement, responsibility, and the work itself. Sources of dissatisfaction were considered to be related to the job context or the work environment. For example, negative perceptions of company policy, administration, supervision, salary, and so on were contributing factors of job dissatisfaction; these sources were called *hygienes.*

The focal point of Herzberg's two-factor theory, that job satisfaction and dissatisfaction are the result of different types of factors in an occupational milieu, contends that an individual can be both satisfied and dissatisfied with an occupation at the same time. Furthermore, Herzberg suggested that satisfaction can only be increased with motivators (recognition, achievement, responsibility). His work has led to the growth of the well-known job enrichment programs found in many organizations.

The two-factor theory (motivators-hygienes) created a great deal of controversy and speculation concerning motivation theory. Herzberg's work was followed by a number of research projects that suggested his conclusions could not be entirely supported. A study by Dunnette, Campbell, and Hakel (1967) suggested that both job content (motivators) and job context (hygienes) contribute to job satisfaction or dissatisfaction. However, there was also evidence that Herzberg's motivators (achievement, responsibility, recognition, and so on) had greater overall influence on satisfaction and dissatisfaction than the so-called hygienes (Korman, 1977, p. 143). Even though there are questions concerning the validity of the theory, Herzberg has provided us with the concept of evaluating job satisfaction and dissatisfaction as two distinct entities.

McClelland's Need-to-Achieve Theory

The research of McClelland, Atkinson, Clark, and Lowell (1953) has provided us with a unique approach to motivation, which they labeled *n ACH.* According to this theory (based on research on male subjects), some individuals strive for accomplishment simply because they enjoy it, are highly motivated to do well, and strive to do their best. The n ACH individuals are characterized as highly ambitious, setting high personal standards, enjoying surpassing previous achievement, and ultimately finding high levels of achievement a great source of pleasure. Their satisfaction comes primarily from intrinsic rewards associated with achievement, and monetary gains are considered as secondary.

Korman (1977, p. 53) characterized the n ACH person when he discussed McClelland's hypothesis as follows:

1. Individuals differ in the degree to which they find achievement a satisfying experience.
2. Individuals with high n ACH tend to prefer the specific work situations and will work harder than individuals with low n ACH.
   a. In situations of moderate risk, feelings of achievement will be minimal; achievement will probably not occur in cases of great risk.
   b. In situations where knowledge of results is provided, a person with a high achievement motive will want to know whether he or she has achieved or not.

c. In situations where individual responsibility is provided, a person who is oriented toward achievement will want to make sure that he (or she) and not somebody else gets the credit for it.

3. Since these three types of situations are found in the business entrepreneurial role, individuals with high n ACH will be attracted to the entrepreneurial role as a lifetime occupation.

The second hypothesis provides some clues that one may use to evaluate working situations in which the n ACH person is likely to perform better. In the third hypothesis, the n ACH person will eventually be attracted to an entrepreneurial role. Implications for immediate and future career plans are implied. If one is to aspire for a leadership role in an organization, several questions should be answered. Will the organization provide opportunities for advancement? Will the available entry-level position provide mobility and/or flexibility for movement up the career ladder within the organization? Will the skills developed by an individual enhance opportunities for upward mobility in the organization? Answers to questions such as these should be beneficial in evaluating the organization under consideration. The achievement-related concerns expressed by individuals, made much clearer to us through McClelland's work with the n ACH, are viable considerations in career exploration.

Cognitive-Dissonance Theory

In studying organizational behavior, cognitive dissonance is often referred to as a *consistency theory of behavior* (Korman, 1977, pp. 58–77). The theory was developed by Festinger (1957) and is based on the assumption that when a person has contradictory thoughts or ideas that are inconsistent with an established behavior pattern, dissonance occurs.[1] Festinger postulated that individuals attempt to maintain consistency among various beliefs, attitudes, and self-perceptions within their cognitive structure. However, when there is awareness of a discrepancy between self-perception and behavior, for example, the individual experiences dissonance. This state of disequilibrium produces tension and a state of psychological discomfort; thus the individual is motivated to gain balance and consistency.

A number of studies in organizational settings support the consistency theory. Most of the studies have related self-esteem with occupational choice and performance. Korman (1967) found that individuals who have high self-esteem usually choose occupations that they view as requiring a great deal of ability. M. C. Shaw (1968) found that academic achievement is related to a positive self-concept. Another study revealed that those individuals with high self-perceived competence at a work task tend to work at the task more productively (Korman, 1977, p. 69). Finkelman's (1969) study was reviewed by Korman (1977, p. 69), who concluded that individuals with high self-esteem

---

[1] We will not attempt to fully cover the antecedents of this theory but will apply the principle of the theory to organizational behavior.

perform tasks more successfully when their work requirements are challenging than do individuals with low self-esteem.

These studies provide evidence that self-esteem and achievement are highly related. Following this logic, one who locates a work setting that is consistent with achievement goals should find a greater chance for satisfaction in that work setting. Furthermore, an organization evaluated from the standpoint of its goals, products, or outcomes would provide the individual with a means of determining consistency with his or her own value structure. Finally, consistency with the organizational social structure (formal and informal) should also be considered of major importance in the selection process.

WORK ADJUSTMENT

The theory of work adjustment by Dawis and Lofquist (1984) emphasizes that work is more than step-by-step task-oriented procedures. Work includes human interaction and sources of satisfaction, dissatisfaction, rewards, stress, and many other psychological reinforcements. The basic assumption of work-adjustment theory is that individuals seek to achieve and maintain a positive relationship within their work environment. According to Dawis and Lofquist, individuals bring their requirements to a work environment, and the work environment makes its requirements of individuals. To survive, the individual and the work environment must achieve some degree of correspondence.

To achieve this consonance or agreement, the individual must successfully meet the job requirements, and the work environment must fulfill the requirements of the individual. Stability on the job, which can lead to tenure, is a function of correspondence between the individual and the work environment. The process of achieving and maintaining correspondence with a work environment is referred to as *work adjustment*.

Four key points of Dawis and Lofquist's theory are summarized as follows: (1) work personality and work environment should be amenable, (2) individual needs are most important in determining an individual's fit into the work environment, (3) individual needs and the reinforcer system that characterizes the work setting are important aspects of stability and tenure, and (4) job placement is best accomplished through a match of worker traits with the requirements of a work environment.

Dawis and Lofquist (1984) have identified occupational reinforcers found in the work environment as being vital to an individual's work adjustment. They have evaluated work settings to derive potential reinforcers of individual behavior. In the career-counseling process, individual needs are matched with occupational reinforcers to determine an individual's fit into a work environment. Some examples of occupational reinforcers are achievement, advancement, authority, co-workers, activity, security, social service, social status, and variety.

In related research, Lofquist and Dawis (1984) found a strong relationship between job satisfaction and work adjustment. Job satisfaction was evaluated from outcomes (results or consequences) of work experience, such as tenure, job involvement, productivity, work alienation, and morale. They found that satisfaction is negatively related to job turnover, withdrawal behavior (such as absenteeism and lateness), and worker alienation. On the other hand, satisfaction is positively related to job involvement, morale, and overall life situations, or nonwork satisfaction. In general, satisfaction is only minimally correlated with job performance and productivity (pp. 228–229).

The research reviewed by Lofquist and Dawis (1984) strongly suggests that job satisfaction is a significant indicator of work adjustment. For example, job satisfaction is an indicator of the individual's perception of work and the work environment and is highly related to tenure in a work situation. The theory of work adjustment has the following implications for career counselors:

1. Job satisfaction should be evaluated according to several factors, including satisfaction with co-workers and supervisors, type of work, autonomy, responsibility, and opportunities for self-expression of ability and for serving others.

2. Job satisfaction is an important career-counseling concern but does not alone measure work adjustment. Work adjustment includes other variables, such as the individual's ability to perform tasks required of work.

3. Job satisfaction is an important predictor of job tenure, and the factors associated with job satisfaction should be recognized in career counseling. An individual's abilities and how they relate to work requirements are not the only career-counseling components of work adjustment.

4. Individual needs and values are significant components of job satisfaction. These factors should be delineated in career-counseling programs designed to enhance work adjustment.

5. Individuals differ significantly in terms of specific reinforcers of career satisfaction. Therefore, career counseling must be individualized when exploring interests, values, and needs.

6. Career counselors should consider the reinforcers available in work environments and compare them to the individual needs of clients.

In this conceptual framework, career counselors should consider clients' job satisfaction needs in order to help them find an amenable work environment. Job satisfaction is a significant variable in determining productivity, job involvement, and career tenure. Career counselors should use occupational information to assist clients in matching individual needs, interests, and abilities with patterns and levels of different reinforcers in the work environment. For example, the reinforcer of "achievement" is related to experiences of accomplishment in the work situation. Social service is related to the opportunities that a work situation offers for performing tasks that will help other people.

Lofquist and Dawis warned that career counselors may have difficulty identifying occupational reinforcers because of the lack of relevant research, the vast variety of jobs in the current labor force, and emerging jobs in the future. Meanwhile, the theory of work adjustment has focused more attention on the importance of worker satisfaction. In the future, workers may have to adjust to satisfaction in a variety of jobs that use their individual skills rather than in one job setting.

WORK VALUES

Cultural values can sometimes be difficult to separate from work values. As Rosenberg (1957) noted several decades ago, occupational choice is made on the basis of values, which are the principles that guide individuals in making decisions and developing behavior patterns. Values are influential in determining individual goals and lifestyles and influencing work motivation, behavior, and satisfaction.

Attitudes toward work are also reflected in changing cultural values. Spindler (1955), who studied changing values in American mainstream culture after World War II, found significant changes from traditional values to what he called "emergent values." For example, the traditional value of future-time orientation or working toward future goals was contrasted with the emergent value of hedonistic, present-time orientation, which reflected a new focus on living for the present because the future is unknown. Following this logic, all work is perceived as temporary with little value placed on longevity of the job, job identity, or the value of work itself.

Pine and Innis (1987) suggested that individual work values are influenced by a number of factors including ethnicity, subcultures, historical cohorts, socioeconomic status, significant others, society, and economic conditions. Work values are influenced by changing conditions in our society, as illustrated by Schnall's (1981) study of longitudinal value shifts. The researcher found that basic belief systems in our society had shifted in stages over a half-century: (1) during the period from the 1930s through the 1950s, more attention was paid to the welfare of others than self; (2) during the 1960s, the focus changed to self-indulgence and instant gratification with little regard for others; (3) during the 1970s, distrust for others was manifested in a strong movement toward self-reliance; and (4) during the 1980s, there was a shift back to concern for others with the growing need for individuals to experience self-fulfillment (Pine & Innis, 1987). Schnall's study clearly suggests that we have returned to some of the dominant values of the 1950s.

In a related study of value changes of college students, Astin (1984) suggested that students in the 1980s had value orientation similar to students in the 1950s: they wanted security, jobs that were indicators of success, and a home in the suburbs. However, Wall (1984) indicated that value orientations of college students in the 1950s and 1980s differed significantly because the possibility of moving up the career ladder, a foregone conclusion in the 1950s, was uncertain in the economically unstable 1980s.

The uncertain economic forecast changed the process of choosing careers from idealism to pragmatism—"where do I have the best chance of being employed" and "how can I best market myself for that occupation." Economic realities influence not only career choice but also how individuals work at jobs they otherwise may not have chosen. Self-fulfillment, which Schnall mentioned as a prevalent goal in the 1980s and yet not fully attainable in the uncertain economic conditions, may cause some people to withhold a firm emotional involvement in their work (Yankelovich, 1979).

The implications of observing work values in the context of changing cultural values and economic patterns in our society are profound. For example, career counseling should focus more on available opportunities than individual psychology. This shift in emphasis implies that career counseling must become more realistic to be most effective. Finally, individual perceptions of work and commitment to work are inextricably connected with economic and societal forces. How these factors influence individual value systems must always be considered when evaluating work values (Pine & Innis, 1987).

THE AMERICAN WORK ETHIC

The American work ethic has been a focus of writers and researchers since our early history. Weber (1958) claimed that the work ethic was at the heart of the Protestant Reformation, which exalted labor as a religious imperative, performed for the common good and the greater glory of God. Puritans of New England and Quakers of Pennsylvania came to this country to establish a godly civilization, and they viewed work as a moral obligation. The Puritans especially considered work a spiritual calling, and their teachings emphasized the dangers of idleness.

Maccoby and Terzi (1981) suggested that there are four work ethics, representative of the social and economic stages in the changing American character: (1) the Protestant ethic, (2) the craft ethic, (3) the entrepreneurial ethic, and (4) the career ethic. They also suggested that a fifth ethic, a self-development ethic, is now emerging.

The Protestant work ethic was gradually secularized to a craft ethic when 80% of the work force in preindustrial America was self-employed as farmers and craftspersons. This new perception of the American work role was not seen as a religious calling but as a social obligation that benefited the individual. The craft work ethic represents an orientation toward self-sufficiency, a desire for control of work standards, and independence from entrepreneurs and industrial organizations.

The entrepreneurial ethic evolved when technology made it feasible to hire groups of people and to organize and build businesses. For example, when machines capable of mass production were invented, the craftsperson who did his or her work by hand became obsolete. Trained machine operators could process more items at less cost and greater profit for the entrepreneur, who, favoring free enterprise and individual initiative, sought economic independence. The entrepreneurial ethic represents an orientation toward risk taking, striving to get ahead, and exploiting opportunities.

The career ethic emerged as the opportunity for self-employment decreased. From 1800 to 1970, the number of self-employed in America decreased from 80% to 8% of the labor force (Maccoby & Terzi, 1981). Large corporations with complex organizational hierarchies sought individuals who were trained as career managers. Schools of business responded by training professional managers and technicians, who set out to establish careers within organizations. The professional manager expects to earn success and promotion within organizations through his or her developed expertise to solve problems; to apply the latest information; and to manage people. The career ethic represents an orientation toward ambition, financial success, movement up the career ladder, and loyalty to an organization.

The emerging self-development ethic represents an orientation toward greater concern for self-fulfillment, personal growth, enjoyment of work, and a lifestyle that provides more opportunities for leisure. There appears to be a growing concern among Americans that successful careerism is achieved at the expense of one's personal health, family, and friends. Although most Americans want employment (Yankelovich, 1981), they do not want work to be all-absorbing; yet they want jobs that are challenging and that provide opportunities for self-expression and personal development.

WORK COMMITMENT

The American worker has recently been charged with having poor work habits and little commitment to work. The question often asked is, "Do American workers really want to work?" According to Hackman and Oldham (1981), most employees have indicated that they would continue working even if given the opportunity to retire to a comfortable living. It seems clear that most Americans believe in the value of work and have a strong commitment to it. Most Americans expect to and want to work, yet indications of disenchantment and dissatisfaction exist in the work force. For example, Hackman and Oldham (1981) reported that there are increasing unscheduled absences (primarily sick leave) from work among the nation's work force. Employees also continue to strike against a variety of private and public organizations. Both situations cover many issues but are indicative of worker dissatisfaction.

There is growing evidence that work conditions are the source of employee dissatisfaction. Hackman and Oldham (1981) suggested that a crisis exists in what they referred to as *person-job relationships*. They proposed the following:

1. Many people are underutilized and underchallenged at work. Because many jobs have become routinized and simplified in organizations, work is no longer challenging or fulfilling.

2. People are more adaptable than we realize. Thus, some workers perceived as satisfied and comfortable and who appear to be settled in their work may have merely resigned themselves to job requirements. Indeed, many of these workers have devised ways of dealing with work monotony, turning their

attentions to outside interests. The long-term effects of their adaptation processes may give the impression that these individuals are unmotivated, not
wanting to be considered for advancement. However, these workers are being
judged superficially on the basis of what they have become through adaptation
rather than what they may be capable of doing.

3. Self-reports of job satisfaction are suspect. The authors suggest that surveys can be misleading because some workers who have adapted to the work
environment and have indicated satisfaction are actually not satisfied. It is
difficult to determine the degree of satisfaction or dissatisfaction attributable to
such individuals.

4. Changes often will be resisted, even when beneficial. Resistance to change
is often related to anxieties over learning new procedures and facing problems
associated with adaptation to a different work environment. Even the thought of
change resurrects anxieties long since put aside by a worker who has gone
through the adaptation process associated with other work environments.

According to Maccoby and Terzi (1981), there is a crisis of leadership, and
many workers are dissatisfied with management that blocks the opportunity for
self-fulfillment on the job. There appears to be a growing lack of confidence in
management and a negative reaction to the nature of supervision in the work
environment. The most dissatisfied group of workers is under 30, is African
American, and has an income under $10,000; the most satisfied is over 50, pro-
fessional, and either in management or self-employed (Maccoby & Terzi, 1981).

Dissatisfaction among workers may not be with work per se but with the
nature of leadership in the workplace. O'Toole (1981) pointed out that managers often create institutional structures, prohibiting workers from assuming
responsibility for the quality of their work. He added, however, that managers
who are also employees may be given little incentive from their own chief
executives to foster responsible behavior among their subordinates. The vicious
cycle of poor management can have devastating effects on everyone in the
work force.

It would be misleading to leave the impression that all management in our
organizations is poor and is the primary cause of worker dissatisfaction. On the
contrary, American management has been innovative and quite concerned
about the welfare of the workers. In Chapter 12, several types of management
leadership styles are discussed.

A Synthesis of Opinion
About Work Commitment and Work Ethics

There is growing evidence to suggest that causes of job satisfaction and dissatisfaction are indeed complex issues. Just as intricate are the issues surrounding
work commitment and work ethics. Some researchers have suggested that there
is a common bond connecting these issues that is rooted in our society. O'Toole
(1981), among others, has postulated that low productivity is a cultural prob-

lem rather than a result of national economic policy. Yankelovich (1981) suggested that our work ethic is an inextricable part of social issues. Both positions have common themes that are related to our national social development.

According to O'Toole (1981), there is overwhelming evidence that culture is a fundamental determinant of our economic performance. He cited the economic superiority of Germany and Japan as examples of cultures that encourage efficiency and productivity. He suggested that the Japanese especially have adopted managerial policies compatible with their culture. The answer is not simply to adopt another country's philosophy and orientation toward work but to develop policies that are compatible with our own culture. Furthermore, the major problem in the American workplace today is that most of our current managerial and organizational policies and practices were developed in the 1940s and 1950s. These policies were compatible with American culture at the time, but in the last 30 years there have been dramatic social shifts. The rules for work commitment have been altered, and Americans simply are unwilling to do work under outdated mandates. The new work values are congruent with changes in the broader culture.

Yankelovich (1981b), in search of answers for self-fulfillment in work, has suggested that we are in need of an ethic of commitment. He, like O'Toole, also addressed the changes of values in our culture. He particularly attacked the self-psychology practices promoting the idea that sacredness lies within self. According to Yankelovich, the impact of the "duty-to-self" ethic has led to development of selfishness and hedonistic values. These self-indulgent values have subverted self-fulfillment. Yankelovich suggested that what is now needed is a new ethic that promotes a more cooperative attitude among workers and places less emphasis on competitiveness for personal gain.

Yankelovich contended that an ethic of commitment would emerge slowly over the next several decades. Changes in self-concept and attitude are key ingredients for self-fulfillment under the ethic of commitment. The first step is to discard the goals of the duty-to-self ethic and to concentrate on sharing, showing more concern for others, being cooperative, and striving to develop closer and deeper personal relationships. Relationships with others are to be simple, direct, and unencumbered by pursuit of status or financial rewards. Ultimately, more satisfying personal achievements will come from *sacred expressive values*. Sacred values include increased concern and dedication to improving community and country. Expressive values are personal, but they do not originate from me-first attitudes; they are broader in concept and allow for greater self-involvement and a closer connection to others.

Following the logic of Yankelovich (1981b), the shift in attitudes and values associated with the ethic of commitment will change workers' perspectives of their jobs and work environment. The primary motivation to work will not be based on moving up the career ladder at all costs. Commitment to work will be a sharing of producing, creating, and mutually expressive accomplishments. The work environment is to be one in which direct, honest, and straightforward communications are exchanged. The organization is to adopt leadership policies that are conducive to openness of communication between workers and supervisors and involve a caring interest in each worker. Work will continue to be an important commitment but will not be all-absorbing. Sufficient time to enjoy leisure and develop family relationships will be emphasized. Self-fulfillment is achieved when "one understands that the self must be fulfilled within the shared meanings of psychoculture" (p. 242).

STRESS AT WORK: ITS IMPLICATIONS AND HOW TO DEAL WITH IT

One factor inherent in modern working life is stress, induced by work and the work environment. Stress in this context has been defined as a psychophysical response to various stimuli. Work-related stressor sources have been studied by a number of researchers (Kasl, 1978; Ivancevich & Matteson, 1980; Shostak, 1980; Levi, 1984). Sources of stress compiled by these researchers dramatize the complexity and variety of potentially stressful conditions faced by most workers:

1. conditions of work (unpleasant work environment, necessity to work fast, excessive and inconvenient hours);
2. work itself (perception of job as uninteresting, repetitious, overloaded, and demanding);
3. shift work (rotating shifts affecting bodily functions and role behaviors);
4. supervision (unclear job demands, close supervision with no autonomy, scant feedback from supervisors);
5. wage and promotion (inadequate income);
6. role ambiguity (lack of clarity about one's job and scope of responsibilities);
7. career development stressors (little job security, impending obsolescence, dissatisfaction over career aspirations and current level of attainment);
8. group stressors (insufficient group cohesiveness, poor group identity in the organization);
9. organizational climate (impersonally structured organizational policies); and
10. organizational structure (too bureaucratic or too autocratic).

Job-Related Stress Is a Global Phenomenon

Job-related stress afflicts British miners, French nurses, and Australian government workers as well as American executives. Blue-collar workers also experience job stress, perhaps because they have less control over their jobs and lives than do higher-paid white-collar workers. An international survey conducted by the United Nation's International Labor Organization found that women suffer as much or more job-related stress than men (*San Antonio Express-News,* 1993).

One reason suggested for the increase in job stress is that many workers are involved in a sort of electronic assembly line, which allows supervisors to evaluate them constantly during the workday. Perhaps more important are job demands that do not match a worker's current abilities, needs, or expectations. That is, there is a poor fit between workers and their work environments and subsequent requirements. Job-related stress has many roots and causes, but among the important ones are organizational management and work environment.

Magnuson (1990) has suggested the following indicators of job-related stress:

- Low self-esteem;
- Low motivation to work;
- Poor concentration on work tasks;
- Poor work relationships with peers and supervisors;
- Poor communications with others on the job site;
- Feelings of inadequacy and resentment;
- Depression; and
- Excessive tardiness and absenteeism.

The effects of stress are pervasive; work performance and interpersonal relationships are often affected. Stress has been linked to numerous physical problems, including cardiovascular diseases. Stress exists at all levels of the work force, extending from executives to blue-collar workers (Shostak, 1980). As organizations grow in complexity, potential stressor sources will multiply.

Career Burnout

In the early 1970s, the term *burnout* emerged in career-counseling articles and in the popular media. Freudenberger (1974) is generally given credit for first using the term to describe certain kinds of career behavior (Herr & Cramer, 1992). More recently, Freudenberger and Richelson (1980) defined burnout as the depletion of an individual's physical and mental resources caused by excessive attempts to meet self-imposed, unrealistic goals. A number of symptoms have been identified with burnout, including depression, fatigue, irritability, sleeplessness, and uncontrollable anger. Important to our discussion is the fact that Freudenberger identified the work environment and work situation as precipitating factors that lead to symptoms of burnout.

A more precise explanation of burnout was discussed by Cherniss (1980), who concentrated on workers in the "helping" professions. Conceptually, Cherniss perceived burnout within the helping professions in three stages: (1) workers experience stress due to demands of job, (2) workers experience strain due to emotional responses of anxiety and tension, and (3) workers attempt to cope defensively by changing their attitude toward commitment to their job. For example, they may treat clients in a manner that reflects an attitude of little concern for them. He observed that when helping professionals experience burnout, devotion to helping others is no longer a strong commitment. Cherniss suggested that in response to work-related stress and strain, helping-profession workers will actually disengage from their work. Other writers, such as Maslach, have come to similar conclusions concerning mental-health workers (Maslach, 1976, 1981; Maslach & Jackson, 1981; Pines & Maslach, 1979).

Burnout is used to describe a number of work-related behaviors. For example, burnout is used to describe individuals who hold occupations in which they do not make full use of their education and training and consider their jobs to be less than challenging (Howard, 1975). Similarly, the terms *burnout* and *stagnation* are used interchangeably to describe individuals who have lost enthusiasm for work (Edelwich & Brodsky, 1980). Another interchangeable term is *plateauing*, which is used to describe individuals who have reached their highest level in an organization (Ference, Stoner, & Warren, 1977). In essence, burnout has not been clearly delineated and has received only preliminary and small-scale research validation (Herr & Cramer, 1992). Therefore, the correlates of burnout described in the next paragraph should be considered as preliminary observations in lieu of further research and delineation of the term.

There appears to be general agreement among investigators that burnout is not a single event but a process of gradual change in behavior, eventually reaching intense reactions and leading to crisis if left unresolved. Burnout has been associated with work overload, repetitive work tasks, boredom, ambiguity, lack of advancement opportunities, and time pressures (Forney, Wallace-Schultzman, & Wiggens, 1982). Schwab (1981) contended that burnout is highly related to role conflict. Farber and Heifetz (1981) and Emener and Rubin (1980) suggested that excessive work with very disturbed people is highly correlated with burnout. Other researchers suggested that off-the-job stress should also be evaluated when counseling individuals who exhibit symptoms of burnout (Pardine et al., 1981).

There appears to be a high degree of relationship between work-associated stress and burnout. Perhaps one strategy to use in dealing with individuals who exhibit symptoms of burnout is to evaluate work-related stressor sources as outlined earlier. Support groups designed to foster self-acceptance and coping skills through the use of relaxation techniques and biofeedback are also recommended (Argeropoulos, 1981). Leisure therapy has been suggested by Garte and Rosenblum (1978). The variety of strategies suggests that burnout is a viable counseling consideration for individuals throughout the life span.

Pine and Aronson (1988) suggested a four-step plan for dealing with career burnout: (1) recognize the symptoms of burnout, (2) activate a plan for solving the causes of burnout, (3) distinguish between what can be changed and what cannot be changed, and (4) develop new coping skills and refine old ones. The first step is intended to promote awareness of stressors that cause individuals to feel they are helpless. Some, for example, may feel that burnout is "life's course" and little can be done to change that course. Others try to ignore existing problems. Even though awareness may increase anxiety, it is a necessary first step in solving career burnout problems. When individuals become aware of problems, they are usually willing to take action. For example, a

worker who receives poor feedback on job performance from a supervisor may elect to confront the supervisor or transfer to another work environment.

In many work environments, it is difficult to assess the causes of burnout, but to make progress toward change the individual must carefully evaluate the underlying causes. Pine and Aronson (1988) pointed out that some bureaucracies cannot change their unresponsiveness to individuals; the system simply does not provide for it. For example, the work of a rehabilitation counselor is demanding and has many frustrating aspects. Even when success is attained, the counselor may only receive an increased client load as a reward. In this case, the counselor views the organizational changes to make the job more fulfilling as overwhelming. However, the counselor at least recognizes that the source of the problem is in the system rather than in himself or herself. In this scenario, the fourth step, developing coping skills, might include teaching the rehabilitation counselors to reinforce each other's work. This method promotes appreciation and respect for peers.

Other coping skills involve a careful evaluation of individual needs to solve a specific problem. Individuals may accomplish this through self-introspection or through professional help.

In conclusion, Pine and Aronson (1988) suggested that career counselors can help clients who may be experiencing burnout by (1) clarifying symptoms of burnout, (2) helping them develop the ability to distinguish sources of stress that they can control and those that are inherent in the work itself, and (3) developing tools for coping with stress by teaching how to focus on positive work aspects and develop positive attitudes.

Healthful Work

In the last decade, a number of publications have addressed the sources of job-related stress while others have suggested methods of dealing with it. The relationship between job stress and disease has also been exposed as an ongoing problem that has been ignored in many workplaces. Recently, however, the connection between work and health has focused attention on designing more healthful workplaces. The physical, psychological, and psychosocial consequences of work are significantly related to job design (Karasek & Theorell, 1990). For example, bad job design fosters social isolation, little feeling of the social value of work, unrestrained job competion, sex-role conflicts, little or no freedom or independence, long periods of intense time pressures, and little autonomy for workers.

Jobs designed for the future and considered healthful work—that is, beyond the material rewards of work—are described by Karasek & Theorell (1990, pp. 316–317) as follows:

1. More jobs are to be designed to make maximum use of every worker's skill and provide opportunities to improve and increase skills.
2. More work freedom exists when workers are able to select their work routines and peer affiliates. Some work may be done in the home.

3. Workers are given equal status in making decisions as far as work demands are concerned. Jobs may require routine tasks, but they also provide new learning challenges.
4. Social contacts are encouraged to promote new learning and prevent work isolation. Advanced technologies are made available to encourage new learning.
5. Democratic procedures are prevalent in the workplace. Grievance procedures protect workers from arbitrary authority.
6. Workers receive feedback from customers, and in fact, customers and workers are encouraged to work together to customize products.
7. All workers are to share in family responsibilities and tasks, especially in two-earner homes. Time is set aside for family activities.

In sum, healthful work reduces the sources of job stress prevalent in current work environments primarily by giving the worker more freedom and autonomy. Social interactions are encouraged to reduce threats associated with job competition. New learning is encouraged by making new technologies accessible to workers. Finally, more freedom of choice concerning work roles and greater autonomy in the workplace are recommended as key ingredients for designing jobs for the future.

WILL THERE BE A DEMAND FOR INCREASED QUALITY OF WORK?

As we become more involved with global economics and multinational work forces, the quality of our products will become increasingly important. A quality product has been defined as one that is without defects or mistakes and is delivered on time. There have been significant signs that an international standard for certain products may be in the making. The International Organization for Standardization (ISO) in Switzerland may provide the framework from which quality is assured (*CHEMICALWEEK*, 1992). The ISO 9000 standard series explains fundamental quality concepts and guides organizations in tailoring and designing production systems to ensure quality. Other countries, including the United States (National Institute of Standards and Technology), also have organizations for standards.

Does this movement mean that there will be global supervision of products, and will these products only be exported and imported if they are registered under some system of standards? That question has yet to be answered, but changes in the workplace may follow adoptions of some system of standardization. Some U.S. chemicals and associated products are registered under the ISO 9000. Currently, few changes affect workers and management, but there has been some concern that this kind of standardization approach could evolve into a rating system affecting job security.

Workers' welfare and mental health will continue to be our concern as counselors, and we will always be faced with ongoing changes that make our

job a challenge. No doubt situations will continue to occur that create the need to develop new intervention strategies to assist individuals in making career decisions and adjusting to fast-paced changes in the workplace. The ISO 9000 approach to standardization may be a method of creating satisfaction among workers or a situation of change that creates more job-related stress. Within the next 10 to 20 years, we should have some answers.

SUMMARY

1. Research on human behavior in organizations should aid the counselor in helping clients choose working climates. Maslow identified a hierarchy of needs, from physiological to self-actualization. Herzberg postulated two basic needs: extrinsic compensation (materials, status, security) and intrinsic needs (achievement, recognition). McClelland identified needs for affiliation, achievement, and the power to explain individual behavior. The individual's need for consistency of beliefs, attitudes, and perceptions is derived from Festinger's cognitive-dissonance theory.

2. The theory of work adjustment emphasizes that work is more than a step-by-step procedure; it includes human interaction, sources of satisfaction and dissatisfaction, rewards, stress, and many other psychological reinforcements. The basic assumption is that an individual seeks to achieve and maintain a positive relationship within his or her work environment.

3. Work values are influenced by a number of factors, including changing cultural values and economic patterns in our society. Career counselors should focus more on opportunities and choices that individuals perceive as available to them; career counseling must be realistic to be most effective. Individual perceptions of work and commitment to work are inextricably connected with economic and societal forces.

4. The American work ethic has been a major subject for writers and researchers throughout the nation's history. Some researchers have claimed that the work ethic was at the heart of the Protestant Reformation. Maccoby and Terzi suggested that there are actually four work ethics, representative of the social and economic stages in the changing American character: the Protestant ethic, the craft ethic, the entrepreneurial ethic, and the career ethic. A fifth work ethic—a self-development ethic—is now emerging.

5. Stress, defined as a psychophysical response to various stimuli, is inherent in modern working life. The effects of stress are pervasive: work performance and interpersonal relationships are often affected. Stress affects all levels of workers, from executives to blue-collar workers.

6. The term *burnout* is used to describe a number of work-related behaviors. Burnout is a gradual process of behavioral change. Burnout is associated with stress caused by work overload, boredom, repetitious work tasks, time pressures, and other work-related stressor sources.

7. Healthful work reduces the sources of job stress by giving workers more freedom of choice for work roles and autonomy.

8. The International Organization for Standardization (ISO) may provide the framework used in organizations to ensure quality of work. The effects of change in the workplace may create opportunities for greater work-related satisfaction and/or change that creates job-related stress.

SUPPLEMENTARY LEARNING EXERCISES

1. Describe your own work ethic and how it developed. Compare your description with a classmate's.
2. Develop a counseling component that is designed to help individuals overcome job stress.
3. Defend or criticize the following statement in writing and/or in a debate: Work ethics change because society changes.
4. Using the list of occupational reinforcers developed by Dawis and Lofquist, identify specific occupations in which these reinforcers would be prevalent. Explain your results.
5. Write a review of Chapters 23 and 24 (pp. 234–264) in the book listed below.

   Yankelovich, D. (1981). *New rules*. New York: Random House.

6. Explain how cognitive-dissonance theory could be applied to career-counseling programs that assist individuals in evaluating an organization. When considering consistency between individual values and organizational goals, what would be some major issues?
7. Using Maslow's hierarchy of needs, explain how an individual could become dissatisfied with the position currently held in an organization. What alternatives would you suggest as a counselor?
8. Select at least two of Herzberg's sources of job satisfaction labeled as motivators and describe how each is a source of job satisfaction.
9. Assume you have identified an individual who is highly ambitious, striving, and has a strong need to achieve. What would be your strategy in assisting this individual to choose an organization?
10. Using the reference below, write an essay on the changes we will experience in the workplace by the year 2000.

    McDaniels, Carl. (1990). *The changing workplace*. San Francisco: Jossey-Bass Publishers.

Chapter Four
Career Life Planning

Throughout this book, constant references will be made to individual needs associated with work, leisure, and home. Individual lifestyle will be the focal point of our discussion whenever career-counseling programs are considered. We will only segregate individual needs when considering how each facet of individuality contributes to the concept of the *total person*; we have the total person in mind as we counsel, offer guidance, and provide direction toward career life planning. What will be communicated is that career counseling is a vital part of life planning. We will not consider an individual's work in isolation; rather, work is conceptualized as a major commitment in life planning that must be integrated into an individual's style of life. Because career life planning can affect individual lifestyle tremendously, it should be considered an ongoing process that must allow for change of individual needs and/or situational circumstances. We cannot imply that career utopia is possible for everyone, but we can stress that those career-counseling programs that emphasize career life-planning concepts and cope with change provide the best avenues to fulfillment in life.

In this chapter, we will consider several counseling programs designed to promote career life planning as a lifelong process. Each program considers career life planning as a developmental process that must encompass needs generated from work, family, home, and leisure. Each program focuses on strategies that assist individuals in meeting these needs and adjusting to changes that are both internally and externally caused. The first program is designed to present career life planning as a promotion of personal competence, introducing skills that are helpful in meeting future events. The second program introduces methods of identifying dimensions of lifestyle associated with work, family, home, and leisure. More specifically, this program focuses on such factors as place of residence, marital status, levels of education and income, leisure-time activities, family status, leadership needs, social opportunities, and major goals in life. Lifestyle dimensions are compared with potential career choices in an attempt to determine lifestyle congruence with certain careers. Clarification of lifestyle dimensions can be accomplished through group and/or individual counseling.

We will review other prominent career life-planning programs, such as Shepard's (1965) planning-for-living workshops and the life/work planning programs developed by Bolles (1982) and Crystal and Bolles (1974). Shepard's programs focus on integrating all aspects of life in the planning process, whereas the Crystal/Bolles programs emphasize individual research efforts as one of the most effective means to successful living. A representative list of other career life-planning programs is also provided.

DIMENSIONS OF CAREER LIFE PLANNING

In the process of career life planning, the individual uses a variety of skills. One of the primary purposes of career life planning is to develop skills through which individuals learn to control their futures. For example, we learn to identify our skills and plan how we can continue to upgrade them through life-learning programs. We learn how to develop options and alternatives and effectively decide which to follow. We learn to identify our personal needs and the needs of our closest associates and how to integrate those needs into our life plans. We learn to make plans that we can change and revise as we ourselves change or as circumstances necessitate change. Thus, our planning must be flexible and include realistic options from which effective decisions can be made to promote a fuller and more satisfying life.

Humanity has long searched for fulfillment and satisfaction. Recent generations are no exception. In fact, their search has been perhaps as intense as any ever experienced in American society. Many traditional beliefs have recently been challenged; even our working role and the organizations in which we work have been questioned (McDaniels, 1990). The prevailing question of the current generation is, "How do I find fulfillment in life?" We have stressed that fulfillment or satisfaction with what we do and how we live changes as we ourselves change. Thus, the fulfillment we seek is an ongoing challenge all of us must face as we work and live. As we pass through various stages of life and as situational changes occur, we set goals, choose from options and alternatives, and make decisions. For many, the process of change is difficult and threatening, particularly for those who haphazardly chart their course only to find frustration and dissatisfaction. Through career life planning, we learn to center our attention on carefully laid plans and on those variables over which we have some control.

There are many variables to be considered in career life-planning programs. One is how we judge success. This is a crucial decision consciously or subconsciously faced by everyone. As career counselors, our concerns are centered on the success criteria with which we evaluate our lives and others evaluate us. These success criteria are based, to a great extent, on the kind or quality of work we do. What motivates us to work is a key question. According to McClelland (1961), people have a driving need for achievement and subsequent power over others. Other work motivators are the security and symbols of success that come from earning money, identification with prestigious organizations or peer affiliates, and status associated with certain occupations and professions (O'Toole, 1981). Central to our concerns, however, are the intrinsic satisfactions from which individuals judge their success in life and work. We should recognize that these judgments may change as individuals' needs change over their life spans. We should set a goal of providing flexible career life planning that can help individuals identify their changing needs and set realistic goals to meet them.

Obsolescence is insidious to all of us, and it not only threatens our ability to perform in our chosen occupation but also can hinder our effectiveness and the subsequent satisfaction that comes from staying up-to-date in what we do. A number of authors have suggested that educational programs should be developed to support the ongoing life-learning needs of today's individuals (Drucker, 1992; Bolles, 1993). More and more educational institutions offer flexible, continuing education programs (Cetron & Gayle, 1991), and career-development programs are also sponsored by organizations. Through career life-planning programs, we not only provide sources of education and training, but we assist individuals in determining their needs for programs and in understanding the reasons for adopting a life-learning concept.

As we project into the future, our major effort should be to identify those variables in our lives over which we can exert some control. Our lives can be charted more effectively through the maze of changes that we experience, both individually and situationally, by planning programs that place these variables in perspective.

CAREER CHOICE

Career life planning focuses on a significant number of factors that influence career choice. Setting priorities and goals for career life planning, developing ultimate life designs, and setting long-range and short-term goals are major choice objectives. In career life planning, values, interests, abilities, achievement, and work-life experiences are viable factors to discuss, evaluate, and clarify in order to make career life-planning determinations. Decision-making models also provide a framework from which career-choice counseling objectives are derived (Gelatt, 1989). Clearly defined steps in decision-making strategies provide sequences designed to assist individuals in making a career choice.

One problem-solving approach for career choice was suggested by Tiedeman and O'Hara (1963). Career choice involves the processing of developmental tasks and resolving of psychosocial crises. All theories, systems, and strategies underscore the inclusive and complex nature of the career-choice process. Because individuals experience periods of indecision and indiscriminateness, career choice is not considered wholly continuous (Crites, 1969).

Super (1990), among others, considered indecisiveness as a period in the developmental process when interests have not been fully crystallized. Uncertainty about future career goals may lead some individuals to make indiscriminate choices of two or more occupational objectives. As individuals become more aware of the developing character of the career process itself, they are more willing to make changes and to alter or redefine a decision (Miller-Tiedeman & Tiedeman, 1990; Healy, 1982). The process of deciding is complex and unique for each individual, depending on cognitive factors and the social structure of the individual's milieu. In essence, individuals evaluate their choices internally by considering values, interest, achievement, and experiences and externally by seeking acceptance and approval within the working environment.

In career life-planning programs, career choices are tentative from the standpoint that practically every choice involves some doubt about the credibility of the chosen career and the possibility that it can be successfully carried out over a lifetime. The individual's uncertainty is compounded by the career possibilities that have disappeared because of changing economic conditions and the career uncertainties and unknowns forecast by vast imminent technological changes. Moreover, career choice is a process in which one not only chooses but also eliminates and consequently stifles some interests and talents. Parts of us are left to go to seed when a career choice is made, because eventually we must give up a chance to develop talents and interests as we limit ourselves on the narrow pathway leading to a career. Career choice is also clouded by the search all of us experience for self-identity and meaning in a world society that is drawing closer together. Fortunately, career life-planning programs provide for a regular reevaluation of where we have been and where we are going. Opportunities are provided to reconsider choices of the past and to realign them with new values and interests. Those talents and interests that have remained latent can be nurtured and developed in career life-planning programs.

ROLE OF LEISURE IN CAREER LIFE PLANNING

The role of leisure in career life planning can easily be overlooked because leisure activities are often taken for granted. However, in recent decades, the role of leisure has taken on new meaning in terms of self-expression (Kelly, 1981) and counseling responsibility (McDaniels, 1984).

According to McDaniels (1990), who has written extensively on leisure as a counseling objective, career planning involves a work-leisure connection. In this conceptualization of a career, work and leisure are seen as inseparable counseling objectives that should be addressed in a holistic framework. Wilson (1981) suggested that leisure should not be viewed as an activity that one does if and when time permits, but instead as an endeavor that requires active planning and definite time commitments. In this framework, leisure is considered an essential ingredient in life. In essence, career life planning must include planning for leisure activities that provide for relaxation with family and friends.

CAREER LIFE PLANNING AS A PROMOTION OF PERSONAL COMPETENCE

The concept of career life planning as discussed in this chapter suggests that career programs should be constructed from a broad-based framework of life events, conditions, and situations over the life span. The major goal of career life planning is to help individuals cope with changing events and accomplish the tasks and transitions of developmental stages successfully.

Although the experiences of life teach us how to cope with certain events, the future is always challenging and unpredictable. Lazarus (1980) suggested that past experiences, however, can help one cope with future events. Calling this process "anticipatory coping," he proposed that the skills learned through successfully coping with experiences can help when encountering future events, and unsuccessful experiences can provide a basis for identifying behaviors that should be modified. Though all experiences are useful for future encounters, successful experiences tend to have a snowball effect by providing indexes to appropriate behaviors. The purpose of career life planning is to provide skills that may be applied in coping effectively with a variety of future events. Teaching skills that are helpful in meeting future events is one of the developmental goals of career life planning.

The model in *Life-Development Intervention* (Danish & D'Augelli, 1983) provided a framework for teaching skills for career life planning:

1. Identify levels of skill development

    a. problem-solving skills
    b. decision-making skills
    c. planning skills
    d. goal-setting procedures
    e. career resources and how to use them

2. Decision-making skills

    a. knowledge of personal characteristics
    b. steps in decision making and applying them to a variety of life encounters

3. Identifying assistance systems

    a. public and private career-counseling locations
    b. sources of career counseling in organizations and institutions
    c. educational and training assistance programs
    d. social support systems

4. Identifying and using job market projections

    a. sources and use of job market projections
    b. potential future work roles

5. Identifying career and life-coping skills

    a. job satisfaction variables
    b. sources of stress
    c. methods of modifying behavior
    d. coping skill in work and life

The first step requires a careful analysis of individual skills in specific areas related to problem solving, decision making, goal setting, and using resources. From this baseline, individual needs determine the objectives for developing skills in these vital areas. Danish (1977) has suggested a method of teaching skills as follows: (1) skills are defined in behavioral terms, (2) the purpose for learning a skill is presented, (3) a criterion for measuring skill attainment is discussed, (4) a model of effective and ineffective skills is presented, (5) skills are practiced and supervised, (6) skills are practiced in assigned sites, and (7) skill levels are evaluated.

The second component recommends that individual skills be assessed and projected into work environments. The rationale for decision making is presented in terms of its use in both career decisions and other life decisions, such as purchasing a home or automobile. The second component reinforces the skills learned in the first component while emphasizing the probable necessity of making several career decisions over the life span. Coping with increasing family obligations and changing values and interests is also stressed.

The third component is designed to assist individuals in locating support systems that may be helpful in the future. Although every community is different in this regard, the skills learned in locating systems in one community should help in locating systems in others.

The evidence suggests that major shifts will occur in the labor market, as well as in the creation of new occupations (Cetron & Davies, 1988). Individuals will have to cope with these changes, probably through retraining. Coping with career changes and refocusing training efforts can be assisted by anticipating and planning such changes through appropriate interpretations of future projections.

The final component focuses on developing personal competencies and methods of modifying behavior to cope with stress. By building individual strengths and increasing learning skills, supplemented by assistance systems, individuals are better able to adjust to adverse circumstances that may be encountered in the future. This component focuses on preventing stress through the development of coping skills that may be transferred to other life situations.

The next section describes a method of helping college students project into future lifestyle dimensions by exploring the variety of choices available through career life planning.

DIMENSIONS OF LIFESTYLE ORIENTATION

The emergence of career life-planning programs and their subsequent popularity clearly established the need for career-counseling programs that clarify the individual's lifestyle orientation (Super, 1990). Programs that incorporate dimensions of lifestyle address important career-planning factors that might otherwise be ignored. For example, the individual's orientation toward such factors as job, leisure, membership in organizations, home, and family is an important consideration in career life planning. In addition, attention must be directed to choices of residence and work locations as well as to other individual lifestyle aspirations. More specifically, individual aspirations for social status, a particular work climate, education, mobility, and financial security are key factors in determining life plans.

A Dimensions of Life-Style Orientation Survey (DLOS) (Zunker, 1994), still in an experimental stage, was incorporated into ongoing career-counseling programs at Southwest Texas State University. The survey is designed to assist students in determining individual lifestyle dimensions. From a list of 80 phrases, students are asked to select those phrases that they feel are important to their lifestyles. They are also asked to answer several questions concerning desired geographical location, and given the option to write an essay. Part I, the phrase selection component of the survey, is outlined below.

> *Directions:* This is not a test but an inventory to help you think in terms of lifestyle after graduation from college. Your lifestyle preferences are important to consider when making future decisions about your life. In this first part of the inventory you are asked to rate your preferences from a list of statements concerning such matters as job style, leisure style, membership style, home style, and family style.
>
> Examples of the phrase-selection part are as follows:
>
> 43. Be comfortable, but not rich
> 48. Strive to be outstanding in my work
> 68. Have a job from 8–5, five days a week
> 82. Be a recognized authority in my field

To complete the DLOS, students are asked to select those phrases that are "unimportant," "moderately important," or "of greatest importance" to their lifestyle. The student assigns a value on a 3-point scale to each phrase to indicate its importance.

In Part II, the individual chooses a place of residence, indicating preference for a community, state, or foreign country from lists provided. In each case, the individual can indicate "undecided" or "no preference." The counselor may also opt to have the student write an essay envisioning his or her lifestyle in ten years, from a list of ten selected topics.

The DLOS was designed primarily as a counseling tool for assisting individuals in determining their lifestyle orientations and preferences in regard to career, family, leisure, place of residence, work climate, and overall style of life. The survey may be used for a variety of counseling programs, but it is most useful as a facilitator for discussion in groups and/or individual counseling programs where important decisions for career life planning are determined.

Individual items marked "of greatest importance" provide relevant materials for discussion. For example, lifestyle preferences such as "Like to live in different parts of the country" or "Have a job that is easygoing with little or no pressure" can be clarified and considered in the decision-making process. Likewise, other items provide stimulus for discussion groups and assist individuals in clarifying their individual needs through group interaction.

A varimax factor analysis of the 80 items extracted 11 dimensions common to males and females. The scores are reported on a profile that shows the degree of importance the student has rated each dimension as compared to students in the normative sample. The 11 dimensions of lifestyle are identified as follows:

1. *Financial Orientation*—an orientation toward financial independence and social prominence.
2. *Community-Involvement Orientation*—an orientation toward participation in community activities and community services.
3. *Family Orientation*—an orientation toward family life.
4. *Work-Achievement Orientation*—an orientation toward career development and commitment.
5. *Work-Leadership Orientation*—an orientation toward a leadership role in the workplace.
6. *Educational Orientation*—an orientation toward self-improvement through educational attainment.
7. *Structured Work-Environment Orientation*—an orientation toward regularly scheduled work hours.
8. *Leisure Orientation*—an orientation toward leisure activities.
9. *Mobility Orientation*—an orientation toward diversification and change.
10. *Moderate-Secure Orientation*—an orientation toward moderation.
11. *Outdoor-Work-Leisure Orientation*—an orientation toward work and leisure activities in the out-of-doors.

As mentioned, the dimensional factors can be used as a stimulus for discussion in either group or individual counseling programs. Take, for example, a strong orientation toward factor 1, the financial dimension. In the clarification process, the individual considers this need with potential financial compensation from identified careers. If there are significant differences between individual financial needs and potential careers under consideration, the individual is required to prioritize preferences for lifestyle. For one individual, need fulfillment associated with a career may be more important than the financial potential. For another individual, the opposite may be true. Through this process priorities are clarified, and realistic alternatives and options are developed for future planning.

A summary of lifestyle dimensions also provides an index to overall lifestyle preferences that focuses on important considerations in career life planning. A comparison of lifestyle factors with other individual characteristics, such as skills identification and interests, can point up congruences and/or striking differences. For example, if an individual has strong orientations toward factor 3, the family dimension, and factor 8, the leisure dimension, but is considering careers that are highly pressured and require long hours and considerable dedication, these differences are identified and discussed. The approach is not to discourage any of the identified needs associated with lifestyle or career, but to promote an understanding of current potential conflicts that could cause serious future problems. When striking conflicts are evident, further clarification of lifestyle orientations and career interests is encouraged. Thus lifestyle factors assist in the setting of priorities and goals for career life planning.

LIFE-PLANNING WORKSHOPS

Since the early 1970s, life-planning workshops for college students have been conducted at Colorado State University (Birney, Thomas, & Hinkle, 1970). These workshops are primarily designed to actively involve individuals in developing life plans through highly structured step-by-step programs. The workshop format was adapted from Shepard's (1965) planning-for-living programs to meet the specific needs of college students (Johnson, 1977). These programs especially promote self-awareness and the recognition that each individual has certain responsibilities in the development of his or her future.

The life-planning workshops are usually conducted in one-day sessions lasting approximately seven hours. Groups of four persons are formed with a facilitator for each group. The program is highly structured, but each group may progress at its own pace. Because the structure of the program is set, facilitators need only minimal training. Group members remain together through the session.

The workshop format consists of eight structured exercises as follows. Each exercise is shared in the group, and interaction is strongly emphasized. The first exercise, *life line*, requires an individual to draw a line from birth to death (life line) and to indicate on it key life experiences and present position. These exercises are designed to actively involve the participants in concentrating on future tasks and life planning.

Exercise	*Purpose*
1. Life line	To identify past and current situations in life
2. Identifying and stripping of roles	To identify individual roles in life and share individual feelings as one strips roles
3. Fantasy time	To develop more self-awareness when free of identified roles
4. Typical day and a special day of the future	To further crystallize self-awareness and individual needs for the future when free of identified roles
5. Life inventory	To identify specific needs and goals with emphasis on identification of each individual's positive characteristics
6. News release	To further clarify specific interests and future accomplishments desired
7. Reassume roles	To clarify or reformulate goals while reassuming originally identified roles
8. Goal-setting	To set realistic short-term and long-term goals

Identifying and stripping of roles, the second exercise, requires each individual to identify and to rank in importance five different roles currently occupying his or her life. Each participant is encouraged to identify positive as well as negative roles. The next step is to start with the least important role and "strip" that role (no longer assume the role) and express feelings associated with freedom from that role. In this manner, each role is "stripped" until the person is role-free and subsequently able to express "freely" personal life-planning needs.

The third exercise, *fantasy time*, is a continuation of the second exercise, in which the individual is encouraged toward further introspection while being role-free. More specifically, the individual considers the influence of roles when developing future plans.

Now that roles have been stripped, in the fourth exercise, the individual is to outline a *typical day and a special day of the future*. Now that the individual is able to visualize his or her life without the restrictions of roles, he or she can subsequently better consider ideal circumstances. This exercise is designed to provide an opportunity to consider how identified roles influence or actually block present and future need fulfillment.

The fifth exercise requires each individual to fill out a *life inventory* and includes questions asking for greatest experiences, things done well and poorly, and desired future accomplishments. Each individual is directed toward developing specific needs and values while focusing attention on desired changes in the future. This exercise is designed to be a rebuilding process through identification of specific needs.

During the sixth exercise, *news release*, each individual considers his or her life line, as drawn in an earlier exercise, in relation to what the future should be. Each person writes a sketch of his or her life, projecting into the future while focusing on accomplishment and predominant roles. The major purpose is to promote the development of realistic future needs.

In the seventh exercise, *reassume roles*, the focus is on reassuming the roles that were stripped in earlier exercises. Each individual now must decide which roles should be kept and which should be discarded in order to reach his or her life goals. Reassumed roles may be rearranged in priority or replaced with new roles that provide greater opportunity for meeting goals. The emphasis is on the factors that can be changed in order to gain greater control of future life planning.

The final exercise, *goal-setting*, requires each individual to describe specific behaviors that can bring about desired changes in his or her life. Again, the emphasis is on the individual's ability to make changes in order to meet life-planning goals.

An Example of Life-Planning Workshop Exercises

The following illustration demonstrates the more specific activities involved in this program. Dot has been married for six years, has two children, and is currently employed as a high school biology teacher. Her family life has been stable for most of her marriage, but she has recently felt a need to change her career and life direction. As she stated to her counselor, "I'm not sure of what's happened—I just feel frustrated. I love my husband and children, but I am unhappy." After several counseling sessions, the counselor recommended that Dot participate in a life-planning workshop.

After being introduced to staff and members of the group, she heard an explanation of the purpose and goals of the exercises. The first exercise required Dot to construct a life line in which she included the results of important decisions and events, such as the birth of her brother, death of her father, meeting her husband, marriage, the birth of her children, and so on. She jotted down her age at the time of each event and drew an arrow next to the more significant decisions. Valleys and peaks indicated the ups and downs of life.

Then Dot shared her life line with Chris, another participant.

Dot: We have some similar experiences, I see.

Chris: Yes, but you have more work experiences than I have. I wish I had more experiences so I could figure out what to do.

Dot: I have worked since I was married and before, and yet I am confused. Come to think of it, I guess working helps you figure out some things.

Chris: Yeah, I would hope so.

Dot: Mainly, what you learn is what you don't want to do.

Chris: Oh look, the major events in your life line are like mine; they center around family.

A general discussion of the purpose of a life line was led by the group leader. Her major focus was the value of previous experience in determining future goals.

The next exercise, identifying and stripping of roles, created considerable tension for Dot because she was not prepared to strip her roles as parent, spouse, teacher, homemaker, and friend.

Dot: I don't want to dump my husband and children—it's hard for me to think of myself without them.

Chris: I know, but remember, this is make-believe.

Dot: That's so, but I still feel it is difficult.

Chris: Go on, tell me what you would do.

Dot: Well, I've always wanted a higher degree, but with the children, I don't have time for college.

Chris: Go on. I bet you would like a different job too!

Dot: This sounds like bragging, but my college profs encouraged me to consider college teaching.

As Dot and Chris continued to strip away roles, they recognized the ambiguities associated with the exercise as well as the benefits of imagined freedom.

Dot: I've wound up with quite a different lifestyle, and you have too.

Chris: If only I could do it. How many jobs do you have listed?

Dot: Let me see. College professor, model, business owner, chief executive officer. Oh yeah, I want to live on the West Coast! But really, how could I realistically accomplish any of these?

After the third exercise, fantasy time, Dot outlined a "typical day" and a "special day" in the future.

Typical day

> Breakfast between 8:00 and 9:00
>
> Go to campus for class preparation 9–11
>
> Teach classes 11–12
>
> Have lunch at faculty lounge 12–1:30
>
> Office hours 2–3
>
> Play tennis 3–5
>
> Shop 5–6
>
> Dinner 7–8
>
> Attend play 8–10
>
> Bedtime

Special day (no time commitments)

> Wake up whenever I want in a plush room in a resort hotel
>
> Breakfast in bed
>
> Hike in the mountains
>
> Go skiing
>
> Meet friends around the fireplace at Happy Hour
>
> Dine and dance

As Dot fantasized a role-free lifestyle, she also recognized the meaningfulness of her current roles. She deeply cared for her husband and children and did not want to give them up under any circumstances, but she also came to the conclusion that something was missing from her life. Perhaps, she thought, it was the desire for more freedom with fewer time commitments. But everyone likes that, she mused, so what's new?

As she filled out the life inventory for Exercise 5, she was now faced with having to make significant decisions about the future. As she listed her greatest experiences and things she had done well and poorly, the items seemed to center around academic achievements and her family. Surprisingly, after considerable thought, Dot listed some of her teaching activities under tasks done poorly. "This is awful," she almost stated out loud, but it was true. She had to face it. Her heart had not been in it. What a mess—she loved her students, and yet, she was not giving them her best.

When Dot focused on changes for the future, she came to the conclusion that a career change was necessary, but accompanying this thought was the chilling reality of what this would mean. Her entire lifestyle and routine would have to be changed, she concluded. Is it worth it? How would her husband react? Dot's list of specific needs included the following:

- a greater commitment to my work;
- a change to pursue my interest of more academic training;
- a higher-level job in education; and
- more and better communication with my family—let my family know how *I* feel

During this exercise, Dot heard the following exchange in her group.

Fred: What's the sense of all this? These needs I have would disrupt my current life-style tremendously.

Jim: It might take that, Fred.

Ted: It's not that simple. I would like to follow through on my needs, but I have to consider the needs of my family too. I think we gotta negotiate.

As Dot listened to the members discuss the problems of implementing their needs list, she realized that she was not the only one experiencing frustration. It was comforting to know she was not alone in wanting something different, but she also realized that different personal situations required personal solutions. The conversation in the group continued.

Jean: I never thought of getting older as an advantage, but my perspective of the future has fewer complications since my children left home.

Dot: Would you follow through on your need list if your children still lived at home?

Jean: Yes, I think so; in fact, I know I would, but everyone's situation is different.

Dot performed the sixth exercise, news release, while observing her life line. By looking at her life as a series of peaks and valleys, she realized that it was more important now to live a more directed life with a balance between life roles. She recognized that it was her choice to devote the major part of life to her family, but she also wanted more out of life at this point. Perhaps, she thought, there would be fewer valleys and more peaks in the future for everyone in the family.

As the group continued this discussion, Jean made another point.

Jean: Being older also makes you realize that life goes by quickly. Just look at your life line—if it tells you anything at all, it is that opportunities are there for the taking. But if you don't, well, the line just keeps on moving.

As Dot began Exercise 7, she felt no aversion to reassuming roles, and in fact, realized that she wanted to retain her current life roles.

Dot: There is no way I would give up my family. Through all of this, they still come first.

Jean: I don't see that as a negative; in fact, I think it's great.

In the final exercise, goal setting, Dot felt that she had gained the confidence to follow through on some specific goals. It would take courage, she thought, to change career direction. It would disrupt everyone's lifestyles to do it, but the chances were that it would be worth it in the future. She would use negotiation as a means of restructuring family life while she attended the university. Putting some money aside each month for the next year would help finance graduate school, and meanwhile she could attend evening classes.

Dot: I have decided that going back to the university is best for me and my family!

Fred: That's not good enough, Dot. You're supposed to give specific behaviors to change things.

Jean: Yes, that's too general.

Dot: OK, let me see. I will have a meeting with my husband on Monday at 6:30. We will discuss the following topics: advantages of going to graduate school, financial arrangements, family arrangements, sharing household duties, and options for time of enrollment.

Dot's case points out the value of delineating and specifying the consequences of life roles. Individuals may become so involved in fulfillment of a particular role that other roles are ignored, and frustrations and stressful conditions that evolve are often left unidentified and unresolved. The interaction of group members often provides support for individuals to discover their own needs for career development.

The effectiveness of the life-planning workshops has been evaluated by a number of researchers. L. E. Thomas (1972) found that 80% of the participants in a series of workshops considered their experience "helpful or very helpful." In addition, she found individual participants felt they had significantly greater control over their lives as a result of their workshop experience. Because the participants consider themselves more capable of directing and planning their lives, the primary purpose of the workshops is substantiated (Johnson, 1977).

Birney, Thomas, and Hinkle (1970) found that the life-planning workshops had an impact on participants' self-perceptions and perceptions of others; that is, the participants became increasingly aware of self and others. Aigaki (1970) found that low-income group participants had changed perceptions of life-planning principles and increased skills in establishing behavioral goals. Through a post-workshop questionnaire, Delworth (1972) found general client satisfaction among workshop participants. These results suggest that life-planning workshops are an effective method of initiating life planning.

OTHER PROMINENT CAREER LIFE-PLANNING PROGRAMS

A very well-received job hunter's manual, *What Color Is Your Parachute?* by Richard Bolles, was first published in 1978 and revised most recently in 1993. The informal and straightforward writing style and clever illustrations have made this manual a phenomenal success. Two other manuals, written in the same style and more directly related to life planning, have also been published. *Where Do I Go from Here with My Life?*, coauthored by Bolles and John C. Crystal, was published in 1974. Bolles's *The Three Boxes of Life* (1978) introduces life/work-planning concepts. Bolles and Crystal successfully communicated the steps they consider necessary to career selection and life planning. Their publications have removed much of the drabness and boredom associated with career exploration and have turned it into an exciting adventure—a process they visualized as not only continuous and complex but also interesting and challenging.

In *What Color Is Your Parachute?* Bolles attacked current methods of job hunting and suggested steps he found more effective. Examples of useful methods of locating job openings and the advantages and disadvantages of each are given. A list of resources for career-counseling help is also provided. The process of deciding on a career is approached from a career- and life-planning perspective; that is, while he considered decisions that meet immediate needs, he also pointed out how planning should include long-term future goals. He suggested that life-planning programs consider the possibility of several careers. His prescription for successful planning includes the following objectives: (1) establish goals, (2) identify skills, (3) establish time lines (when goals are to be accomplished), and (4) establish who's in control (the individual should take control of his or her own life).

In the book's final section, Bolles provided information on the job market and offered practical suggestions for finding job openings. He suggested that deciding where one wants to work is a key factor in the career-decision process. More specifically, he advised that each individual consider geographical location, work climate, organizational structure, and the purpose of each organization as relevant to career/work planning.

Practical exercises are offered throughout the manual on such subjects as resume preparation, interview skills development, skills identification, achievement identification, and the process of finding occupations of interest. The Quick Job-Hunting Map (Bolles, 1993), adapted from Holland's (1985) six modal personal styles and matching work environments, is a basic tool for career decision making.

Where Do I Go from Here with My Life? is a life/work-planning manual for (1) trainers who are teaching future instructors in career- and life-planning methods, (2) instructors who are working with groups or individuals, and (3) individuals who are working on their own. Three sets of highly structured and systematically ordered instructions are provided for the three specific groups of users. The manual suggests the course be given in 16 sessions with a 3-week interval between the first and second sessions and 2-week intervals between the remaining sessions. The topics covered in the 16 sessions are listed in Table 4-1.

The manual assists individuals in finding fulfillment in work and life by teaching them how to develop alternative career paths, learn effective decision-making techniques and job-hunting skills, and develop alternatives for life planning. *What Color Is Your Parachute?* is the text used to accompany this manual.

In *The Three Boxes of Life*, the individual life span is seen as consisting of "three boxes"—education, work, and retirement. Retirement and education are seen as relatively shorter periods in our life span. Bolles suggested that the "boxes of life" should not be mutually exclusive or isolated from one another but, on the contrary, should be coordinated through life/work planning in such a way as to build a better balance in life. He suggested that there are four major issues to promote in life/work planning that he calls (1) *what's happening?* (current, relevant issues), (2) *survival* (family issues such as physical, emotional, spiritual, and financial), (3) *meaning or mission* (individual goals, purpose, targets, ambitions, and so on), and (4) *effectiveness* (for accomplishing goals)

TABLE 4-1
Topics Covered in Course from *Where Do I Go from Here with My Life?*

Session	Topics
1	Your work autobiography
2	Your most important achievements, reading assignments, professional skills, job hunt, distasteful living and working conditions
3	Your educational background, typical working day, practice field survey
4	Your geographical preference and your contacts list
5	Targeting, people environments, your philosophy of life
6	Your ideal job specifications and your personal economic survey
7 & 8	Skills identification and skills list
9	Clustering of your skills, your talking papers, your ten top clusters
10	What would you like to accomplish, how much are you worth, and what needs doing?
11	Your ultimate life goal, your immediate job objective
12	Systematic targeting, your personal operations plan
13	Your functional summary, where you are going, the active job search
14	How to meet your individual targets, interview, and campaign actively
15	How to survive after you get the job
16	Postscript: Full career/life planning and professional development, a solution-finding tool, your estimate of the situation

SOURCE: *Where Do I Go from Here with My Life?* by J.C. Crystal and R.N. Bolles, 1974, New York: Seabury Press. Copyright 1974 by Seabury Press. Reprinted by permission.

(Bolles, 1982, p. 11–28). Bolles postulated that the first three issues must be tackled in order to reach the fourth issue of effectiveness. How we get out of the "boxes" and into a more balanced life is his focal point.

Helpful suggestions for developing life/work plans are given throughout the text along with impressive lists of resources for further reading. Numerous exercises are provided to assist the individual in reaching a better understanding of the life/work-planning programs suggested by Bolles.

A number of other career life-planning programs are available today. Some representative examples are listed below.

> *Career Planning: Search for a Future*
> Gerald P. Cosgrave, Consultant
> Guidance Centre
> Faculty of Education
> University of Toronto
> Toronto, Ontario M5S 1A1
>
> *Life Work Planning*
> Arthur G. Kirn and Marie O'Donahoe Kirn
> McGraw-Hill Book Company
> 1221 Avenue of the Americas
> New York, NY 10036

This Isn't Quite What I Had in Mind: A Career Planning Program for College Students
John W. Loughary, Ph.D., and Teresa M. Ripley, Ph.D.
United Learning Corporation
P.O. Box 5351
Eugene, OR 97405

You CAN Change Your Future: A Program for Career Life Planning
Patrick J. Montana
AMACOM
A Division of American Management Associations
135 West 50th Street
New York, NY 10020

Training for Life
Fred J. Hecklinger and B. M. Curtin
Kendall/Hunt Publishing Company
Dubuque, IA 52001

Take Hold of Your Future
Jo Ann Harris-Bowlsbey, James D. Spivack, and Ruth S. Lisensky
The American College Testing Program
Iowa City, IA 52240

Full Potential
Robert J. Radin
McGraw-Hill Book Company
1221 Avenue of the Americas
New York, NY 10036

CAREER LIFE PLANNING IN PERSPECTIVE

In this chapter, we have emphasized numerous components of career life planning that when integrated into future plans can effectively pinpoint and meet individual needs. We have discovered that career life planning includes continuous learning; that is, some education or training will more than likely be necessary throughout the life span. Critical to career life planning are decision-making techniques that are useful in making not only an initial choice but many subsequent decisions as well. Career life-planning programs give significant consideration to dimensions of lifestyle preference; a major goal of career life planning is to identify those dimensions that provide meaning and purpose and that sustain our efforts toward self-fulfillment.

Finally, it is the individual who must chart his or her life course and decide on the direction that course will take in this ever-changing society. A positive outlook on life and the realization that factors important to career/life success can be controlled are good attitudes to cultivate. Our challenge is to help others and ourselves by remaining optimistic throughout various changes we experience individually and situationally. We must recognize that there are options to pursue if we learn to plan effectively and keep our alternatives in proper perspective. Ideally, through career life planning we become better prepared to meet life's challenges. Ultimately, we hope to be as confident of our choices and actions as was expressed so succinctly over 400 years ago: "If I knew the world was coming to an end tomorrow, I would pay my debts and plant the apple tree" (attributed to Martin Luther [1483–1546] in a speech by Martin L. Cole, 1963).

SUMMARY

1. Career life planning is an ongoing process that allows for change of direction as individuals' needs change and/or as situational circumstances cause change. Career life planning provides the means to manage changes and thus allows greater opportunity for fulfillment in life. Career life planning is a developmental process encompassing needs generated from work, family, home, and leisure.

2. One of the main purposes of career life planning is to develop skills with which individuals can learn to control their futures. Through career life planning, individuals learn to center their attention on carefully laid plans and on those variables over which they have control.

3. There is a need for career life planning and career-counseling programs that clarify individuals' lifestyle orientation. Programs that incorporate dimensions of lifestyle address important career-planning factors.

4. The DLOS, currently in experimental stages, was developed to measure dimensions of lifestyle orientation. The DLOS is used as a counseling tool to assist individuals in determining their lifestyle preferences for career, family, leisure, place of residence, work climate, and overall style of life. The dimensions of lifestyle orientation, found through factor analysis, can also assist in arranging priorities and setting goals of career life planning.

5. Life-planning workshops for college students have been conducted at Colorado State University since the early 1970s. The workshops are primarily designed to help students develop a life plan. Life-planning workshops (usually one-day sessions) consist of highly structured, step-by-step exercises. Several research projects have concluded that life-planning workshops are effective in initiating life planning.

6. Richard Bolles attacked commonly advocated methods of job hunting in his book *What Color Is Your Parachute?* Practical exercises are also offered on such topics as résumé preparation, interview-skills development, skills identification, achievement identification, and the location of occupations of interest.

7. The life/work-planning manual *Where Do I Go from Here with My Life?* was designed for three groups of users: (a) trainers who teach future instructors, (b) instructors who are working with groups or individuals, and (c) individuals who are working on their own. The manual provides detailed instruction for 16 life/work-planning sessions.

8. In *The Three Boxes of Life*, the life span is compartmentalized into three boxes: education, work, and retirement. Emphasis is placed on considering and coordinating all three with the objective of building a better balance in life. The manual gives many helpful suggestions for developing life plans and provides impressive lists of resources for additional reading.

9. A number of other career life-planning programs are also on the market today.

SUPPLEMENTARY LEARNING EXERCISES

Using the DLOS (Dimensions of Life-Style Orientation Survey), answer the following questions and complete the projects listed below.

1. Select the dimensions of lifestyle that describe you. How can these dimensions be incorporated into your career life plans?
2. Select three lifestyle dimensions and develop a list of careers that correspond to each.
3. Select two lifestyle dimensions and write a description of each, projecting future family, leisure, and career orientations.
4. Form a discussion group and have each member select a different lifestyle dimension. Discuss careers, family, leisure, and place of residence associated with each lifestyle dimension.

Using the description on pages 91–96 of the Life-Planning Workshops developed at Colorado State University, answer questions 5, 6, and 7.

5. Complete Exercises 1 and 2 and describe their significance for career life planning.
6. Form a group and complete Exercises 2, 3, and 4. What is the significance of being free of roles in career life planning?
7. Describe what you consider to be the major advantages of life-planning workshops.
8. Review the suggested career life-planning strategies outlined in Richard Bolles's text *What Color Is Your Parachute?* (Berkeley, CA: Ten Speed Press, 1993). Summarize your reactions.
9. Explain the concept of the three boxes of life as expressed in Bolles's *The Three Boxes of Life* (Berkeley, CA: Ten Speed Press, 1978). What is the significance of these boxes in career life planning?
10. What do you consider the major goals of career life planning? Describe the major principles and components that you feel should be integral to career life-planning programs.

Chapter Five

The Dictionary of Occupational Titles, the Occupational Outlook Handbook, and Career Clusters

The U.S. Department of Labor generates and publishes a vast amount of career-related information that is used primarily by a number of federal and state agencies for research, job placement, and career-counseling programs. Many of the career-related materials are free, and others may be purchased for a nominal fee. Of all career-related materials published by the Department of Labor, the *Dictionary of Occupational Titles (DOT)*, now in its revised fourth edition, is as widely known as any and has been in use for over 40 years. The *DOT* is an occupational classification system developed by the Department of Labor. The format used in describing occupations is highly technical. Because of this technical style, the voluminous amounts of information, and the complexity of accessing the information, career counselors have had difficulty making the most effective use of the *DOT* in career-counseling programs.

In this chapter, we briefly discuss the development of the *DOT*, explain it's numerical classification system, and emphasize the usefulness of these volumes in career-counseling programs. The recently published *Guide for Occupational Exploration (GOE)* will be highlighted as providing a career-counseling approach to the occupational information in the *DOT* and other related publications.

In the second section of this chapter, the *Occupational Outlook Handbook (OOH)* is reviewed. This is another Department of Labor publication, written in a nontechnical, narrative style. In contrast to the *DOT*, the *OOH's* format is straightforward, and the occupational information is easily accessed. The major sections of the *OOH* are described and the usefulness of this volume for career-counseling programs is emphasized.

The third section of the chapter consists of a discussion of career clusters and other career-classification systems, including two-dimensional ones.

THE IMPORTANCE OF LABOR-MARKET INFORMATION

To assist in the career decision-making process, the counselor should be alert to the most relevant labor-market information available. The availability of resources has grown tremendously in the last 20 years. Thus, counselors must assist clients in sorting out the most relevant information, monitoring the process of collection, and eventually integrating the information with other resources such as test data. Among other purposes, labor-market information is most helpful in evaluating how certain careers can meet the individual client's needs, discovering available options, and considering occupational alternatives.

Throughout this text, references will be made to the changing workplace, economics, downsizing of organizations, the internationalization of workplaces, and the changing job market. Current labor-market information is therefore a viable part of each client's career search. Our goal as counselors should be to help clients understand and effectively use the occupational information available. An impressive program for integrating occupational information and guidance was compiled by Ettinger (1991) with the assistance of several contributing authors and resource groups. The Improved Career Decision-Making Program (ICDM) was developed to train career-development facilitators to help students and clients (1) understand labor-market information, (2) use information to make career decisions, (3) improve decision-making skills, and (4) develop an action plan to make more effective use of information in career decision making. To accomplish these goals, ten modules were developed for clients and training materials were prepared for counselors.

A good example is module 3, "Demographic Trends that Impact Career Decision Making." Demographic trends point out the maturation of America and the effects this trend will have on the labor market. For example, there will be a greater need for training and retraining entry-level workers from new sources. A second trend is the predicted increased diversity of our population and the special programs that will be needed to fully utilize ethnic minorities in the workplace. These are national trends, but they could differ significantly in local situations. Nevertheless, the ICDM helps the informed client interpret this information in terms of entrepreneurial opportunities or the impact on tentative career choices. Relating available opportunities in the world of work to self-knowledge in the career decision-making process is an important step to understanding the significance of the changing world of work. The resources discussed in this chapter are only examples of career-information and labor-market information projections. Computer-assisted career guidance programs are discussed in Chapter 6, and a career resource center is covered in Chapter 8.

The Dictionary of Occupational Titles (DOT)

The first edition of the *DOT* was published in 1939. It contained 17,500 alphabetical listings of occupational titles and coded each definition according to an occupational classification system developed for this volume. Each occupation was assigned a five- or six-digit code, according to 550 occupational groups. In addition, each occupation was classified as skilled, semi-skilled, or unskilled.

The *DOT* was updated in 1949 when the second edition was published. This edition combined the material in the first edition and the supplements published between 1939 and 1945 into one volume. More than 6,100 new occupations were added to the second edition, which reflected the newly created occupations of the World War II era. Several new manufacturing industries developed during this period, and subsequent occupations were added to the second edition.

Rapid changes in technology accompanied by new and different occupations brought forth the third edition of the *DOT* in 1965. This edition reflects the industrial development and occupational changes experienced during the 1960s and earlier. Volume I of the third edition, like the earlier editions, contains an alphabetical listing of occupations consisting of 21,741 separate occupations and 13,809 alternate titles.

Volume II of the third edition (also published in 1965) groups the occupations contained in Volume I. The groupings were determined by code numbers assigned to each occupation in Volume I. A six-digit coding arrangement was devised for each occupation in this volume. The first digit specifies the occupational category, the second digit the occupational division, and the third digit the occupational group. The last three digits provide information concerning the activities involved in each occupation according to worker-function arrangements. More specifically, the last three digits express the relationship the worker would have with data, people, and things. The worker-function hierarchy of data, people, and things will be discussed later in this chapter.

Two supplements were added to Volumes I and II, and the complete *DOT* system before 1977 consisted of four publications:

- *Volume I, Definitions of Titles*
- *Volume II, Occupational Classifications*
- *A Supplement to the DOT, Selected Characteristics of Occupations*
- *Supplement 2 to the DOT, Selected Characteristics of Occupations by Worker Traits and Physical Strength*

These publications have made a significant contribution to the job-information system developed by the Department of Labor. However, rapid changes of industrial technology since the 1960s and subsequent changes in occupational requirements brought about a need for the *DOT* fourth edition, published in 1977.

The DOT *Fourth Edition*

During the years from 1965 to the mid-1970s, the Department of Labor State Occupational Analysis Field Center staffs conducted 75,000 on-site analyses of a variety of jobs in numerous industries. The major purpose of these on-site visitations was to provide an up-to-date definition of occupations and to identify new ones. This study resulted not only in identifying 2,100 new occupational definitions but also in deleting 3,500 that were in the third edition.

One of the major changes in the fourth edition is in the listing and definitions of occupational titles. In the previous editions, occupational titles were listed in alphabetical order, but in the fourth edition, occupational titles are listed in ascending order according to their assigned nine-digit code numbers. However, an alphabetical index of occupational titles with their respective industrial designation and occupational codes is provided. This change is significant because it focuses more attention on the occupational codes.

The DOT *Fourth Edition Revised*

The fourth edition of the *DOT* was revised in 1991 and is contained in two volumes. The occupational definitions in the 1982 and 1986 supplements were incorporated in this edition, which contains three different arrangements of occupational titles: (1) occupational group arrangement (occupations listed in ascending order by nine-digit code numbers), (2) alphabetical order of titles (an alphabetical list of titles followed by the nine-digit code numbers and industry designations), and (3) occupational titles arranged by industry designation. Table 5-1 summarizes the uses of these three arrangements.

The nine-digit occupational code incorporated in the revised fourth edition warrants special consideration. Each digit in the code has important occupational meaning. An example of an actual occupational code for an automobile upholsterer, 780.381–010, will be used to illustrate the code structure. The nine digits will be divided into three groups to make it easier to identify the significance of each digit in the occupational-code structure.

In this example, the first three digits of the occupational code are identified. The first digit identifies the occupational category from nine divisions used in the *DOT*. The second digit is used to identify one of 97 occupational divisions. The third digit specifies the location of the occupational group within an occupational division.

7—Occupational Category

This category is based on nine broad categories as follows:

0/1. Professional, Technical, and Managerial Occupations
   2. Clerical and Sales Occupations
   3. Service Occupations
   4. Agricultural, Fishery, Forestry, and Related Occupations
   5. Processing Occupations
   6. Machine Trade Occupations
   7. Bench Work Occupations
   8. Structural Work Occupations
   9. Miscellaneous Occupations

8—Occupational Division

There are 97 occupational divisions listed in the *DOT*. This particular code is within the Bench Work occupational category and in the occupational division of occupations in fabrication and repair of textile, leather, and related products.

0—Occupational Group

The third digit specifies the location of the occupation within the occupational division. In this case, the occupational group is occupations in upholstering and in fabrication and repair of stuffed furniture, mattresses, and related products.

TABLE 5-1
Arrangements of Occupational Titles in the *DOT*, Fourth Edition

Use . . .	If you . . .
The Occupational Group Arrangement	have sufficient information about the job tasks.
	want to know about other closely related occupations.
	want to be sure you have chosen the most appropriate classification using the other arrangements.
Occupational Titles Arranged by Industry Designation	know only the industry in which the job is located.
	want to know about other jobs in an industry.
	want to work in a specific industry.
The Alphabetical Index of Occupational Titles	know only the job title and cannot obtain better information.

SOURCE: From the U.S. Department of Labor, 1991a, p. xxvii.

Thus, for the automobile upholsterer the *occupational category* (7) is Bench Work. The *occupational division* (78) is occupations in fabrication and repair of textile, leather, and related products. The *occupational group* (780) is occupations in upholstering and in fabrication and repair of stuffed furniture, mattresses, and related products.

The middle three digits (381) of the nine-digit system are used to identify the relationship the worker has with three worker-function groupings of data, people, and things. The following worker functions form a hierarchical structure, in that the functions become progressively more complex as one ascends the scale. For example, under the data/worker function, *comparing* is less demanding in nature and worker performance than *copying, computing,* and others on the scale. Conversely, *mentoring* under the people/worker function is at the highest level of complexity for that group. The definitions of all the worker function terms are provided in the appendix (pp. 485–502).

3—Data	*8—People*	*1—Things*
0 Synthesizing	0 Mentoring	0 Setting-Up
1 Coordination	1 Negotiating	1 Precision Work
2 Analyzing	2 Instructing	2 Operating/Controlling
3 Compiling	3 Supervising	
4 Computing	4 Diverting	3 Driving/Operating
5 Copying	5 Persuading	4 Manipulating
6 Comparing	6 Speaking/Signaling	5 Tending
	7 Serving	6 Feeding/Offbearing
	8 Taking Instructions/Helping	7 Handling

The automobile upholsterer is near the top of the scale for things/worker function, having to do precision work to accomplish the job. The work is somewhat less demanding in the data/worker function, which requires compiling, and significantly less complex in the people/worker function of taking instructions/ helping. The worker-function scheme provides a means of analyzing each occupation from the basis of a hierarchical structure that may be used to determine specific demands of a job from three distinct dimensions. In the case of the automobile upholsterer, it is essential that the individual be able to work well with his or her hands, use tools or work aids, and follow established standards. The other worker functions are of less importance.

The last three digits (010) of the occupational code are used to further identify a particular occupation within an occupational group. For example, some occupations have the same first six digits; therefore, the last three digits are used to differentiate these occupations. Thus, one can expect to find occupations in the *DOT* with the same first six digits, but none will have the same nine digits. The distinction between similar occupations is determined by alphabetical position within occupational groups. In the example of the automobile upholsterer, this occupation takes the first position within its occupational group and is assigned the digits 010. Each occupation in the group thereafter is assigned a different number by adding 4. More specifically, each occupational group begins with 010 and continues with 014, 018, 022, and so on. The example that follows illustrates this format (U.S. Department of Labor, 1991a, p.808):

780.381–010 Automobile Upholsterer
　　　　　014 Automobile Upholsterer Apprentice
　　　　　018 Furniture Upholsterer
　　　　　022 Furniture Upholsterer Apprentice
　　　　　026 Hearse Upholsterer
　　　　　030 Pad Hand
　　　　　034 Slipcover Cutter

Automobile upholsterer appears in the *DOT* (U.S. Department of Labor, 1991a, p. 808) as follows:

780.381-010   AUTOMOBILE UPHOLSTERER (automotive ser.)
　　　Repairs or replaces upholstery in automobiles, buses, and trucks: Removes old upholstery from seats and door panels of vehicle. Measures new padding and covering materials, and cuts them to required dimensions, using knife or shears. Adjusts or replaces seat springs and ties them in place. Sews covering material together, using sewing machine. Fits covering to seat frame and secures it with glue and tacks. Repairs or replaces convertible tops. Refurbishes interiors of streetcars and buses by replacing cushions, drapes, and floor coverings. May be designated according to specialty as Body Trimmer (automotive ser.); Bus Upholsterer (automotive ser.); Top Installer (automotive ser.).
　　　GOE: 05.05.15 STRENGTH: M GED: R3 M2 L3 SVP: 6 DLU: 77

Of particular interest to the counselor are the so-called components of the definition trailer found immediately following the description of the occupation:

- *GOE* is the *Guide to Occupational Exploration* (U.S. Department of Labor, 1979), which is discussed in the following pages.

- The code assigned to occupations provides an index to interests, aptitudes, adaptability requirements, and other descriptors found in the *GOE*.
- The strength rating is expressed in five categories—Sedentary, Light, Medium, Heavy, and Very Heavy—and is defined in Appendix C of Volume II of the *DOT*.
- GED (General Education Development) ratings are made within six levels (1–6) and explained by reasoning, mathematical, and language development in Appendix C of Volume II of the *DOT*.
- SPV (Specific Vocational) is the amount ot time required to learn an occupation's techniques and requirements. For the automobile upholsterer, the number 6 suggests that the preparation time is over one year and up to and including two years.
- DLU (Date of Last Update) indicates the last year in which the descriptive material was obtained.

Using the DOT

Many counselors have found the overwhelming amount of information contained in the *DOT* system insurmountable and too difficult to manage for practical use. Before the fourth edition, two volumes and two supplements were used conjointly, which contributed to the apprehension of critics. The revised fourth edition combines the information contained in previous publications into two volumes to provide easier access to useful information for the career counselor. This section will provide suggestions for making this publication useful for career counseling.

Knowledge of occupations. The *DOT* is most useful in providing relevant information on a majority of occupations found in the U.S. economy. Each occupation is thoroughly defined, providing the counselor and client a resource for learning facts about occupations to incorporate in the counseling process. Let us return to the example of the automobile upholsterer to make this point clear.

During the process of career exploration, specific information about an occupation becomes relevant. Certain questions are usually considered in the information-seeking sequence. Examples of key questions and answers found in the *DOT* revised fourth edition are as follows:

Question	Answer
1. What are the typical work activities performed on this job?	1. Repair, replace, remove, measure, cut, and tack upholstery. Adjust and replace seat springs. Refurbish interiors of streetcars and buses.
2. What are the specific skills needed to perform the required work?	2. Use body members, tools, and work aids. Measure

Question	*Answer*
	according to required dimensions. Use knife or shears. Sew covering material together.
3. What is the typical industry(s) in which the job is performed?	3. Automobile service.
4. What are the work aids typically used on this job?	4. Knife, shears, hammer, and sewing machine.

In summary, the *DOT* system can be used most effectively to determine the following: (1) the specific tasks and skills required of occupations; (2) the purpose of the occupation; (3) the machine, tools, equipment, or work aids used; (4) the service, products, materials, and academic subject matter included; (5) the industries with which the occupation is typically identified; (6) the worker/function requirements; and (7) the location (indoors, outdoors, water, and so on) of work for each occupation.

Using the Military Career Guide *with the* DOT

The *Military Career Guide*, covering all branches of the armed forces (Army, Navy, Air Force, Marine Corps, and Coast Guard), describes military career paths for enlisted personnel and officers. The enlisted and officer occupations are grouped in clusters. For example, the enlisted category of "Transportation and Material Handling Occupation" includes air crew members, air craft launch and recovery specialists, boat operators, cargo specialists, construction equipment operators, flight engineers, petroleum supply specialists, quartermasters, seamen, and truck drivers.

Each military occupation is described by eight factors: (1) function, (2) special qualifications, (3) helpful attributes, (4) physical demands, (5) training provided, (6) work environment, (7) civilian counterparts, and (8) opportunities. Under the civilian counterpart subheading, comparable civilian occupations are listed. For example, under Flight Operations Specialist for enlisted personnel, the civilian counterparts section states: "Civilian career operations specialists work for commercial and private airlines and air transport companies. They perform duties similar to military flight operations specialist" (*Military Career Guide*, 1989, p. 103). The reader is then referred to a *DOT* index by occupations. Under the Flight Operations Specialist, the following is listed:

DOT #248.367–010 Airplane Dispatch Clerk
248.387–010 Flight Operations Specialist
912.367–010 Flight-Information Expediter

Using the *DOT* codes, the reader can find more specific information on related civilian occupations in the *DOT* and the *OOH*.

Another interesting feature is the use of the *Armed Services Vocational Aptitude Battery Results* (see Chapter 7). The results of the test battery are used to help individuals identify military and civilian occupations. By using the score report, individuals are directed to consider occupations on the basis of scores and experience for both military and civilian occupations.

DEFINITIONS OF INTERESTS: THE GUIDE FOR OCCUPATIONAL EXPLORATION

Supplement to the DOT *Fourth Edition.* A supplement to the *DOT* is entitled *Guide for Occupational Exploration (GOE).* It was primarily designed to be used by career counselors and by individuals working on their own career exploration. The *GOE* is to be used with a recently developed United States Employment Service (USES) interest inventory and a revised interest checklist. In fact, the data in the *GOE* (all jobs in the United States) are organized to coincide with the twelve interest areas measured by the USES inventory. The USES interest areas in turn are arranged to coincide with Holland's (1985) six modal personal styles and corresponding work environments as shown in Table 5-2 (U.S. Department of Labor, 1979, appendix).

The *GOE* data are keyed to the interest areas as shown in Table 5-2. An interest area is identified by a two-digit code number accompanied by a brief description as follows (U.S. Department of Labor, 1979):

TABLE 5-2
Holland and the USES Interest Areas

Holland Occupational Categories	*USES Occupational Interest Areas*
Artistic	Artistic
Investigative	Scientific
Realistic	Plants and Animals Protective Mechanical Industrial
Conventional	Business Detail
Enterprising	Selling
Social	Accommodating[1] Humanitarian Leading-Influencing[2] Physical Performing

[1]This is a relatively narrow area, but it includes a few occupations covered by Holland's enterprising and realistic categories in addition to those covered by the social category.

[2]This is a broad area. It includes, in addition to those covered by the Holland social category, business management and law/politics occupations covered by the enterprising category, and social science occupations covered by the investigating category.

1. *Artistic*—Interest in creative expression of feelings or ideas.
2. *Scientific*—Interest in discovering, collecting, and analyzing information about the natural world and in applying scientific research findings to problems in medicine, life sciences, and natural sciences.
3. *Plants and Animals*—Interest in activities involving plants and animals, usually in an outdoor setting.
4. *Protective*—Interest in using authority to protect people and property.
5. *Mechanical*—Interest in applying mechanical principles to practical situations, using machines, hand tools, or instruments.
6. *Industrial*—Interest in repetitive, concrete, organized activities in a factory setting.
7. *Business Detail*—Interest in organized, clearly defined activities requiring accuracy and attention to details, primarily in an office setting.
8. *Selling*—Interest in bringing others to a point of view through personal persuasion, using sales and promotion techniques.
9. *Accommodating*—Interest in catering to and serving the desires of others, usually on a one-to-one basis.
10. *Humanitarian*—Interest in helping others with their mental, spiritual, social, physical, or vocational goals.
11. *Leading-Influencing*—Interest in leading and influencing others through activities involving high-level verbal or numerical ability.
12. *Physical Performing*—Interest in physical activities performed before an audience (p. 8).

General Educational Development Work Groups were allocated to each of the 12 interest areas, primarily based on capabilities (levels, skills, physical requirements, job knowledge) and adaptability (tolerance of work-group situations) required of workers as judged by a group of occupational analysts. A four-digit code and title are assigned to each work group. Each work group is further divided into subgroups that are assigned six-digit codes and titles accompanied by the nine-digit *DOT* codes. The following example illustrates the six-digit code and the title arrangement:

01 Artistic
01.01 Literary Arts
01.01–01 Editing
01.02–02 Creative Writing
01.03–03 Critiquing

Each work group is described in a nontechnical narrative form accompanied by lists of jobs and profiles of worker requirements. The nontechnical approach was adopted to provide a more useful guide for career-counseling programs. For example, specific suggestions are given in the guide for (1) identifying occupational areas to be considered, (2) exploring work groups, (3) exploring subgroups and specific occupations, (4) selecting occupational goals, (5) developing a plan for attaining the selected goals, and (6) assigning appropriate occupational classifications.

Using the Guide for Occupational Exploration (GOE)

The *GOE* primarily provides a counseling approach for aiding individuals in determining occupational goals and accessing the vast data bank of occupational information compiled by the U.S. Department of Labor. In other words, it can be used both as a counseling tool and as a reference tool. The career-counseling program evolving from USES through the *GOE* will be welcomed by career counselors and should provide guidelines for greater use of related government publications and assessment instruments.

The *GOE* describes career exploration in five steps. The first of these steps has the individual *relate interests to job titles.* For example, if one is interested in 01 Artistic, as shown in the above example, all job titles under that work group would be evaluated.

Step 2, *select one or more work groups to explore,* directs the individual to investigate each work group selected in Step 1, evaluating specific job titles by level of skills, training, and work requirements. In most cases, work groups that require the most education, training, and experience are listed first. For example, under the fifth work group, 01 Industrial Supervision and Instruction and Production Technology, 06.01–01, requires more training and experience than Wrapping and Packing, 06.04–38. An overview of a complete work group also provides a career-ladder approach to evaluating related occupational opportunities.

In Step 3, *explore the work group selected,* the individual is directed toward the *GOE* section providing a description of each work group. For example, Medical Services (U.S. Department of Labor, 1991a), 02.03 is described as follows:

> 02.03 Medical Services
> Workers in this group are involved in the prevention, diagnosis, and treatment of human and animal diseases, disorders, or injuries. It is common to specialize in specific kinds of illnesses, or special areas or organs of the body. Workers who prefer to be more general may become general practitioners, family practitioners, or may learn to deal with groups of related medical problems. A wide variety of work environments is available to medical workers ranging from large city hospitals and clinics, to home offices in rural areas, to field clinics in the military or in underdeveloped countries.
>
> What kind of work would you do?
> Your work activities would depend upon your specific job. For example, you might:
>
> - perform surgery to correct deformities, repair injuries, or remove diseased organs
> - diagnose and treat diseases of the ear, nose, and throat
> - diagnose and treat mental illnesses
> - remove teeth and perform other mouth surgery
> - examine patients to determine causes of speech defects
> - oversee all medical activities of a hospital
> - examine and treat patients for all physical problems, referring them to specialists when necessary

What skills and abilities do you need for this kind of work?

To do this kind of work, you must be able to:

- use logic and scientific thinking to diagnose and treat human or animal injuries and illnesses
- deal with people or animals when they are in pain or under stress
- stay calm and keep your head in emergencies
- use eyes, hands, and fingers with great skill and accuracy
- deal both with things that are known and obvious and with things which frequently are not easy to recognize or understand
- make important decisions using your own judgment
- make decisions based on information you can measure or verify

How do you know if you would like to or could learn to do this kind of work?

The following questions may give you clues about yourself as you consider this group of jobs.

- Have you taken courses in biology, physiology, or anatomy? Can you understand scientific concepts?
- Have you had any training in first-aid techniques? Have you treated an accident victim? Can you work well with people in emotionally upsetting situations?
- Have you dissected an animal? Can you skillfully handle small instruments such as scalpels, syringes, or tweezers?
- Have you watched medical shows on television? Do you enjoy these programs? Can you understand the technical terms used?
- Have you been a medical corpsman in the armed services? Did you learn techniques and terminology that would be helpful in medical school?

How can you prepare for and enter this kind of work?

Occupations in this group usually require education and/or training extending from four years to over ten years, depending upon the specific kind of work. Academic courses helpful in preparing for the medical sciences are: algebra, geometry, advanced math, chemistry, biological sciences, English, and Latin. Two to four years of undergraduate study followed by four years of advanced study is considered the minimum preparation. Most doctors serve a one- or two-year internship in an approved hospital after graduation from medical school.

Some physicians spend several additional years in study and training as a resident or intern to specialize. Dentists who specialize, teach, or perform research must have post-graduate courses or complete a residency in a hospital or clinic. Medical doctors, dentists, and veterinarians must have a license to practice.

What else should you consider about these jobs?

The training time and cost involved are significant. Workers must adjust to irregular hours, weekend and holiday work, and 24-hour on-call duties.

Workers should update their knowledge and professional skills through periodic courses and continuous study.

If you think you would like to do this kind of work, look at the job titles listed on the following pages. Select those that interest you, and read their definitions in the *Dictionary of Occupational Titles* (pp. 43–44).

The work-group description and questions provided in the *GOE* offer rich sources of counseling material. The working situation requirements, skills, and training of each work group are potential sources of discussion for further exploration. Interests, aptitudes, skills, traits, and occupationally significant information provide a basis for integrating relevant material and personal characteristics into career exploration.

Step 4, *explore subgroups in specific occupations*, refers the individual to the *DOT*. Specific occupations in each work group are given a *DOT* code (such as Veterinary Meat-Inspector [GOV, SER.] 073.264–010) easily referenced in the *DOT*.

In Step 5, *get it all together*, the individual establishes goals and plans, selecting specific occupations to be evaluated for immediate employment and/or training required. The requirements for upward movement in a work group are concisely illustrated in the *GOE* steps for career exploration.

THE OCCUPATIONAL OUTLOOK HANDBOOK (*OOH*)

The *OOH* is prepared by the Bureau of Labor Statistics, Division of Occupational Outlook, of the U.S. Department of Labor and published every two years. The 1992–1993 handbook contains employment projections, 250 occupational descriptions grouped in 13 clusters, 125 additional occupational classifications, *DOT* codes, and information on how employment projections are made. Explicit instructions for using this handbook are provided in the introductory section.

A major section of the *OOH* covers employment trends and projections. Because the current job market is so competitive, many individuals turn immediately to this section, particularly readers who will soon be entering the labor force. The 1992–1993 edition provides several interesting graphs of employment shifts and projections, such as those shown in Figure 5-1. Other graphs in this section project total labor-force growth, percentage of employment in certain occupations, and so on.

Detailed descriptions of the 250 occupations are also provided. Each occupation is assigned to one of the following 13 occupational clusters:

Executive, Administrative, and Managerial Occupations
Professional Specialty Occupations
Technicians and Related Support Occupations
Marketing and Sales Occupations
Administrative Support Occupations, Including Clerical
Service Occupations
Agriculture, Forestry, Fishing, and Related Occupations
Mechanics, Installers, and Repairers
Construction Trades and Extractive Occupations
Production Occupations
Transportation and Material Moving Occupations
Handlers, Equipment Cleaners, Helpers, and Laborers
Job Opportunities in the Armed Forces

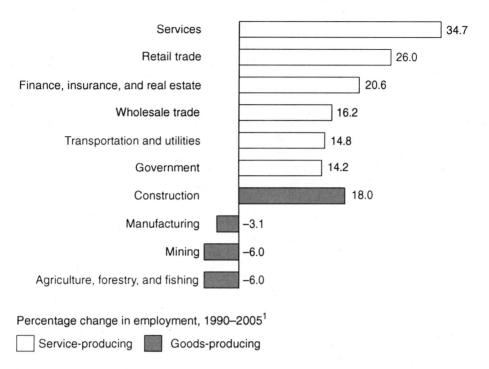

Percentage change in employment, 1990–2005[1]

☐ Service-producing   ◼ Goods-producing

[1]Wage and salary employment, except for agriculture, forestry, and fishing, which includes self-employed and unpaid family workers.

FIGURE 5-1
Employment growth will vary widely by broad occupational group.
SOURCE: Occupational Outlook Handbook, U.S. Department of Labor, 1992–1993. p. 110.

Each occupation is described in concise, straightforward, nontechnical language, covering the following information: (1) nature of work, (2) working conditions, (3) employment, (4) training and other qualifications and advancement, (5) job outlook, (6) earnings, (7) related occupations, and (8) sources of additional information. The *DOT* code is also listed.

The value of the *OOH* for the career counselor is apparent. Its nontechnical format makes the *OOH* attractive to many readers. The overview of national job prospects and the long-term job outlooks are important resources and are receiving increasing attention from individuals who are planning their education and career.

Another government publication, the *Standard Occupational Classification Manual* (U.S. Executive Office of the President, 1977), was created to develop a classification system that standardized occupational data collection. The format and structure of this manual are included in the appendix.

CAREER CLUSTERS

The idea of career clusters is not new to the field of career counseling. On the contrary, one may consider the *DOT* system and the census classification system as career clusters. For our discussion, let us consider *career clusters* as a method of grouping occupations according to commonalities. As our discussion of career clusters progresses, we will develop the rationale for a variety of cluster systems, emphasizing their usefulness for career-related instructional programs and career guidance.

The attraction of a career-cluster arrangement is the provision of a broad overview of occupational fields from which the commonalities of specific and related occupations within the field may be explored. For example, the common training, experience, and other requirements associated with the career cluster are easily identified. Specifically, career-cluster systems provide for (1) information concerning methods and levels of entry into an occupational field, (2) related job skills, (3) information concerning commonalities of work requirements and worker functions, and (4) information concerning training requirements for mobility within the occupational field. In this section, we will first consider several forms of cluster organizations in order to better understand the patterns and structure of cluster systems. In addition, two cluster systems will be presented and discussed.

The first format to be considered is clustering occupations by their products. In this format, the center of attention is on the production aspect of an occupational field and the occupations that form productive units. The illustration that follows is taken from an agricultural component developed by the Maryland State Department of Education (Maley, 1975, p. 87).

Agricultural production:
Animal science
Plant science
Farm mechanics
Farm business management

Agricultural supply and service:
Agricultural chemicals
Feeds
Seeds
Fertilizers

Agricultural mechanical services:
Agricultural power and machinery
Agricultural structures and conveniences
Soil management
Water management
Agricultural mechanics skills
Agricultural construction and maintenance
Agricultural electrification

This form of clustering is most helpful for an individual who wants to evaluate specific jobs based on products of an occupational field. The format would also be useful to the individual who is interested in the field of agriculture but is not sure about the specific jobs available. Clustering jobs by their products provides a unique and interesting way of considering an occupational field.

In most discussions concerning career-cluster systems, the term *ladder approach* is used. As the term implies, occupations are placed in ascending order within a cluster, usually by level of training or skills necessary to qualify for a particular occupation. The rationale of this approach is that as individuals are exposed to a career field, they are also exposed to the hierarchy of occupations within the field. Table 5-3 illustrates this concept. A major argument for using this format is that occupational exploration of a career field is greatly enhanced when the skills and other requirements of upward mobility are identified. In addition, the individual is much better prepared to make career decisions when exposed to the commonalities of a career field.

U.S. Office of Education (USOE) Career Clusters

The USOE has prepared 15 occupational clusters to illustrate for students and teachers the career opportunities available in the United States and also to provide a standard method for classifying occupations in career-education programs. This system is primarily designed to provide a national format for career-related instructional projects and career-guidance programs. By using one classification system, the USOE hopes to provide a basis for designing career-related materials in most educational institutions.

The USOE clusters have a career-ladder format, which emphasizes possibilities of upward mobility within each cluster. Each of the clusters is broken down into occupational fields similar to the transportation cluster shown in Table 5-3. The 15 USOE major occupational clusters are as follows:

Agribusiness and Natural Resources
Business and Office
Communications and Media
Construction
Consumer and Homemaking
Environmental
Fine Arts and Humanities

Health
Hospitality and Recreation
Manufacturing
Marketing and Distribution
Marine Science
Personal Service
Public Service
Transportation

Holland Occupational Classification System (HOC)

Holland's six modal personal styles and corresponding work environments (discussed in Chapter 2) form the structure for the HOC (Holland, 1985). Holland's cluster system is divided into six broad occupational areas:

R—*Realistic* (skilled trades; technical and service occupations)
I—*Investigative* (scientific and some technical occupations)
A—*Artistic* (artistic, musical, and literary occupations)
S—*Social* (educational and social-welfare occupations)
E—*Enterprising* (managerial and sales occupations)
C—*Conventional* (office and clerical occupations)

TABLE 5.3
Transportation Clusters

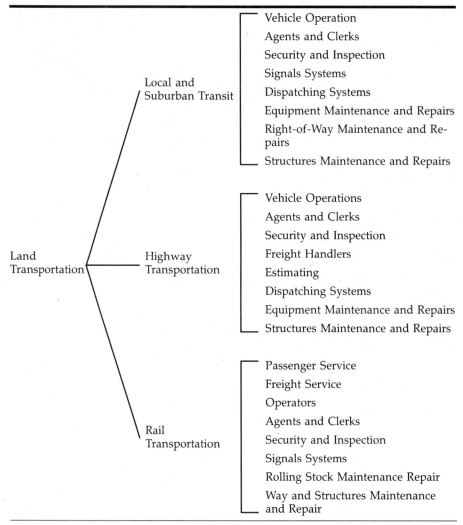

SOURCE: Taken from Career Information Center, Career Education Occupational Cluster, Austin Independent School District, Austin, Texas, 1981. Reprinted by permission.

The use of the classification system is illustrated with the *Self-Directed Search (SDS)* (Holland, 1987b), a self-administered and self-interpreted instrument designed for educational and vocational planning. For example, the results of the *SDS* provide the three most dominant modal personal styles within the HOC. These three dominant styles form a combination of code letters (primary, secondary, and tertiary) for which occupations are provided in the *Occupations Finder* (Holland, 1987c). In the example that follows, several combinations of codes illustrate cluster groups used in this system. In addition to the specific occupations listed, the third edition *DOT* codes and the general educational level for each occupation are provided (Holland, 1987c, pp. 3–5).

	ED
Code: RIA	
Landscape Architect (019.081)	5
Architectural Drafter (017.281)	4
Dental Technician (712.381)	4
All-Around Darkroom Technician (976.381)	4
Code: IAS	
Economist (050.088)	6
Mathematician, Statistician (020.088)	6
Marketing Research Worker (050.088)	5
Code: ASE	
Drama Coach (150.028)	5
English Teacher (091.228)	5
Journalist/Reporter (132.268)	5
Drama Teacher (150.028)	5
Dancing Teacher (151.028)	5
Foreign Language Interpreter (137.268)	5

This system has the distinction of being derived from a research base of personality styles and corresponding work environments. The specific occupations suggested in each cluster are based on a number of factors, including values, personality traits, role preferences, and preferred activities. The clusters' emphasis is on the congruence of one's personality type with the suggested work environment. It is quite likely that other classification systems developed in the future will be derived from a research base.

Two-Dimensional Classifications

In our consideration of the form and structure of career clusters, the vertical dimension (*ladder concept*) of upward mobility was emphasized. You will recall that the vertical dimension provides information on requirements, background, and experience necessary to move up the occupational ladder. Let us now consider a two-dimensional system that employs a horizontal *activity dimension* as well. The two-dimensional system simplifies career exploration by combining occupational groups with their primary activities. The two-dimensional system designed by Roe (1956) is an excellent example.

The first dimension of Roe's system (the horizontal dimension) provides a classification of occupations by field as follows: (1) service, (2) business contact, (3) organization, (4) technology, (5) outdoor, (6) science, (7) general culture, and (8) arts and entertainment. The second dimension describes occupations within the field according to the following levels: (1) professional and management—independent responsibility, (2) professional and managerial—other, (3) semiprofessional and small business, (4) skilled, (5) semiskilled, and (6) unskilled. Thus for each of the occupational groups, a hierarchy of occupations is provided. For example, a skilled job in the science occupational group could be technical assistant, while the professional and managerial positions in the same occupational group may include scientists, nurses, pharmacists, and veterinarians.

One can readily see the advantage of a two-dimensional classification for both the counselor and the counselee. We live in a world consisting of an overwhelming number of possible job opportunities. Adolescents and adults both are often confused and sometimes frustrated when attempting to find their way through the maze of occupational structure and the vast amount of career-related material available today. By combining occupational groups with training, skills, and other job-function demands, the career-exploration process is simplified. Finally, the major value of the two-dimensional classification system is that it succinctly illustrates the relationship of educational training and occupational mobility.

A more recent two-dimensional classification system, the World-of-Work Map, was developed by the American College Testing Program (ACT). This system is used in conjunction with the ACT national testing program, the ACT Career-Planning Program, and the computerized career information system, DISCOVER. Most of the occupations used in this system require postsecondary training, as the ACT program is designed for students seeking admission to postsecondary institutions.

The first dimension of this system is the 12 regions of work that represent general areas of work or job families. The second dimension is derived from bipolar work dimensions—data/ideas and people/things. These dimensions provide information on the required work tasks associated with the job family. For example, Region 7 is designated as engineering and other applied technologies and consists of major tasks involved with things (machines/materials).

The usefulness of this system, as in Roe's two-dimensional system, stems from the presentation of broad occupational areas along with corresponding work tasks. In the ACT system, however, the work dimensions are given in terms of data/ideas and people/things. Thus, the individual is not provided only with a system of exploring an occupation within a job family structure but also with the work tasks and the work dimensions associated with that job family.

SUMMARY

1. The *DOT* is an occupational classification system developed by the U.S. Department of Labor. The complete *DOT* consists of the following publications: Volume I—*Definitions of Titles*, Volume II—*Occupational Classifications*, Supplement 1—*Selected Characteristics of Occupations*, Supplement 2—*Selected Characteristics of Occupations by Worker Traits and Physical Strength*, the *DOT*

fourth edition, fourth edition revised, and the supplement to the *DOT* fourth edition—*Guide for Occupational Exploration (GOE)*.

2. The *DOT* is most useful in providing information on the majority of occupations found in the United States. Each occupation is defined and described by the typical industry in which the job is performed, and the specific skills needed to perform the required work are delineated.

3. The supplement to the *DOT* fourth edition, the *GOE*, is primarily designed to be used by career counselors and individuals in career exploration. All jobs in the U.S. economy are organized to coincide with 12 interest areas used in the USES interest inventory. The *GOE* provides a counseling approach for determining occupational goals and accessing the vast data bank of occupational information compiled by the U.S. Department of Labor.

4. The *Military Career Guide* describes career paths for all branches of the armed forces and references the *DOT* codes and comparable civilian occupations.

5. The *OOH* is also prepared by the Department of Labor and is published every two years. The handbook contains employment projections, occupational descriptions, industrial briefs, and an index of job titles by *DOT* code. An overview of national job prospects and long-term job outlooks contained in the *OOH* makes this publication a valuable resource for career-counseling programs.

6. Clustering or grouping occupations according to some scheme, such as commonalities of work content, is another method of classifying occupations. The primary attraction of the career-cluster arrangement is the provision of a broad overview of occupational fields from which the commonalities of specific and related occupations within the field may be explored.

7. The USOE has prepared 15 occupational clusters to illustrate to students and teachers the career opportunities available in the United States. This system provides a standardized method of classifying occupations for career-education programs.

8. Holland's Occupational Classification System is based on six modal personal styles and corresponding work environments. The specific occupations suggested in each cluster are based on a number of factors, including values, personality traits, role preferences, and preferred activities.

9. Two-dimensional classification systems are designed to simplify career exploration by combining occupational groups with their primary activities. Roe's two-dimensional classification of occupations is a good example. More recently, the American College Testing Program developed a two-dimensional classification system combining occupational groups with their primary activities.

SUPPLEMENTARY LEARNING EXERCISES

1. Identify the hierarchical components of the worker functions data, people, and things as described in the *DOT*. List ten separate jobs and describe each job in terms of the coded worker functions of the *DOT*.
2. List and describe at least five ways a counselor can use the *DOT* publications in career-counseling programs. Document your suggestions with examples.

3. Using the list of occupations below, choose two or more and do the following:
   a. Define the occupation according to the *DOT*.
   b. Describe the worker-function traits and qualifications.
   c. Identify the industry in which the occupation is found.

1. Podiatrist	11. Printing-press operator
2. Surveyor	12. Over-the-road truckdrivers
3. Industrial traffic manager	13. Lather
4. Chemist	14. Blacksmith or farrier
5. Commercial artist	15. Furniture upholsterer
6. Newspaper reporter	16. Brakeman
7. Librarian	17. Bank teller
8. Civil engineer	18. Ovenman
9. Architect	19. Pipe-layer helper
10. Pharmacist	20. Welding-machine operator

4. Choose two or more of the occupations listed and consult the *OOH*. Write a review of each occupation. Include the nature of the work, places of employment, training, employment outlook, earnings, and work conditions.
5. Consult the section of the *OOH* that reviews the outlook for industries. Choose two or more industries and summarize the nature of the industry, occupations in the industry, and the employment outlook.
6. Using the "Additional Sources of Information" section for any occupation described in the *OOH*, write to one of the recommended resources for additional information. Compare the information obtained with that included in the *OOH*. Summarize the similarities and differences.
7. Using the *DOT* section "Occupations in Fabrication and Repair of Musical Instruments," locate and describe three occupations associated with a piano.
8. An individual who has had some experience in working with jewelry is interested in reviewing related jobs. Locate the occupational category in the *DOT* and compile a list of jobs with *DOT* titles for review.
9. Describe the advantages of a two-dimensional classification system. Describe how this type of classification system will aid students in career exploration.
10. Develop a list of advantages and disadvantages of using cluster systems in career-counseling programs for junior and senior high school students and college juniors and seniors.

Chapter Six

Using Computers for Career Counseling

New technology, automation, computer science, and increased specialization have brought about numerous changes in occupational structure and job demand in the last three decades. The pace of change is ever increasing; jobs that existed a few years ago no longer exist. The career counselor has traditionally been faced with an overwhelming amount of career information that must be organized to be useful—always requiring an enormous time commitment. An attempt to keep abreast with basic occupational information itself is very time-consuming. In addition, career counseling has broadened in scope as more emphasis is focused on the variables involved in career life planning. The traditional primary role of occupational information provider is now only part of most career-counseling programs. By necessity, the time once allocated to organizing, editing, and classifying occupational information has been reduced by the increasing demand for the development of broad-scope career-related programs. Nevertheless, the effective career counselor must be provided with current occupational information and resources reflecting the ever-changing labor market.

Today's sophisticated student demands up-to-date projections on the work force and uses this information as a major factor in making career decisions. Current job-search strategies must include projections of the labor market as well as current job descriptions. Therefore, keeping abreast with changing occupational trends remains a very important part of the career-counseling program.

It is not surprising that career counselors are constantly searching for new methods of providing up-to-date occupational information. Counselors have been slow in using computerized information, partly because they are not familiar with computer languages, logic, and hardware. Most career counselors lack the necessary training to fully utilize computer-produced systems. The challenge of designing computer systems for counselors who have minimal computer training has been addressed since the early 1960s. There is no doubt that the needs of the counseling profession would be well served by the unique capabilities of the computer.

The first section of this chapter presents some relevant research about computer-assisted career-guidance systems, including a discussion of the advantages and disadvantages of using these systems. The second section describes system components. In the third section, the development of Career Information Delivery Systems (CIDS) is described, including the names and addresses of systems currently being used. The fourth section illustrates how DISCOVER (the college and adult version) might be used to counsel a college student. Finally, the last sections describe how to use and select a computer-assisted career-guidance system.

SOME IMPLICATIONS OF RESEARCH

Evaluating the effectiveness of computer-assisted career-guidance systems is an ongoing process undertaken by many counseling professionals, including the Center for the Study of Technology in Counseling and Career Development at Florida State University. The purpose of this center is to provide continuing support for the improved professional use of computer applications in counseling and career guidance. In recent years, the center has contributed a great deal of research for this effort.

In a study comparing the effectiveness of three computer-assisted career-guidance systems, DISCOVER (1984), System of Interactive Guidance and Information (SIGI) (Katz, 1975), and SIGI PLUS, the center found that clients who used these systems responded favorably to the career options generated (Peterson et al., 1987). In a related study, Kapes, Borman, Garcia, and Compton (1985) compared user reactions to DISCOVER and SIGI. Specifically, they evaluated the reactions (ease of use, quality of information provided, and total effectiveness) of undergraduate and graduate students and found no significant differences among the ratings of the two systems. Perhaps more important, both systems were rated as highly useful.

In a study of general satisfaction of computer-assisted career guidance among undergraduate students at a medium-sized Southern university, Miller and Springer (1986) found that students rated DISCOVER as a worthwhile counseling intervention that helped them meet their career-exploration needs. In another study analyzing the effectiveness of SIGI, Maze and Cummings (1982) found that the users needed very little assistance with various components. Splete, Elliott, and Borders (1985) have successfully used DISCOVER II and SIGI in their Adult Career Counseling Center at Oakland University.

A study by Roselle and Hummel (1988) compared the effectiveness of using DISCOVER II with two groups of college students, who were separated according to levels (high versus low) of intellectual development as measured by a standardized instrument. To evaluate how effectively they used the system, the students were observed and audiotaped as they interacted with DISCOVER II. The evaluation criteria included how well they learned about career possibilities, integrated career information, reached a career decision, and took appropriate action. The results supported the hypothesis that effective interaction with DISCOVER II is related to intellectual development. These results may not be surprising, but they did suggest that students with low intellectual development need more structure and opportunities for discussion with a counselor during and after their interaction with computer-assisted career-guidance systems.

The uses of the Guidance Information System Guide (1978) in schools and in human service agencies were evaluated by Ryan, Drummond, and Shannon (1980). They found that most users rated the system as helpful in increasing career awareness. The information-retrieval module was considered especially useful.

In general, these studies indicate that users react positively to computer-assisted career-guidance systems. Moreover, the results suggest that these systems are worthwhile counseling tools that can help clients meet career-exploration needs. Therefore, career counselors should be computer literate in terms of understanding the development, rationale, and purpose of computer-assisted career-guidance systems and being able to use them on a daily basis.

Disadvantages of Computer-Assisted Career-Guidance Systems

Some disadvantages of computer-assisted career-guidance systems have also emerged from the research. Maze (1985) pointed out that hardware and software equipment can be very expensive and may require personnel commitments, calling into question the feasibility or even necessity of computerized systems, since career guidance can be accomplished in more traditional ways.

A more serious concern is that of confidentiality (Sampson, 1983). Confidentiality abuses are more likely with electronic data storage systems than with traditional approaches. Velasquez and Lynch (1981) maintained that this problem can be solved with identification codes, passwords, and general restrictions on individuals who may access client information, but career counselors must assure each client of the specific methods used to maintain confidentiality.

The fear among some career-counseling professionals is that computerized systems will be the sole source of career-guidance programming. Computer-assisted career-guidance systems should supplement, but not replace, the counselor. Although software programs are becoming more user-friendly, the career counselor must structure and sustain the client throughout the career-guidance sequence. Computers do allow for independent and individualized courses of action but do not remove the career counselor's responsibility for direction and structure.

Finally, the counselor must address the problem of user anxiety. Inadequately prepared users may easily become discouraged with computerized systems. Personnel must be available to instruct the user during the initial stages, assist users through various phases of the system, and follow up users who have experienced the system (Sampson & Pyle, 1983).

Advantages of Computer-Assisted Career-Guidance Systems

The interactive capability of computerized systems allows users to become more actively involved in the career-guidance process. It is hoped that this active involvement will encourage users to ask more questions of the process itself. Second, user motivation is sustained through the unique use of immediate feedback. Third, the opportunity to individualize the career-exploration process provides opportunities to personalize career-search strategies. Fourth, computer-assisted career-guidance systems provide systematic career-exploration and career-decision programs that may be accessed at any given time. Finally, access to large databases of up-to-date information is immediately available.

TYPES OF COMPUTER-ASSISTED CAREER-GUIDANCE SYSTEMS

The most common types of computer-assisted career-guidance systems are information systems and guidance systems. Information systems provide users with direct access to large databases on such subject areas as occupational characteristics (work tasks, required abilities, work settings, salary) and lists of occupations, educational and training institutions, military information, and financial aid.

Guidance systems are typically much broader in scope. They contain a variety of available modules, such as instruction in the career-decision process, assessment, prediction of future success, assistance with planning, and development of strategies for future plans. Many computer-assisted career-guidance systems contain an information system as well as a guidance system. Many systems are directed toward certain populations such as students in junior high school, high school, and college; some systems are for people who work in organizations; and some address the needs of retirees.

Computer-assisted career-guidance systems have undergone vast changes in the last decade. Future modifications could come even more quickly as these systems are designed to meet the needs of an ever-changing work environment and the skills associated with rapid technical change.

Understandably, many of the computer-assisted career-guidance systems have similar components and are accessed through menus that provide some flexibility for individual needs. The following components are found in most systems:

1. Occupational information
2. Armed service information
3. Information about postsecondary institutions of higher learning
4. Information on technical and specialized schools
5. Financial aid information

6. Interest inventories
7. Decision-making skills

Other common components include:

1. Local job information files
2. Ability measures
3. Value inventories
4. Prediction of success in college
5. Job-search strategies
6. How to prepare a résumé
7. Information on job interviews
8. Components for adults

THE DEVELOPMENT OF CAREER INFORMATION DELIVERY SYSTEMS

The growth of the Career Information Delivery Systems (CIDS) was a direct result of funding from the National Occupational Information Coordinating Committee (NOICC) through its State Occupational Information Coordinating Committees (SOICCs). Improved microcomputer technology in the 1980s resulted in a movement away from mainframe delivery systems and significantly reduced the cost of implementing a system. Career information is organized in most systems on a national and state basis. Some of the national commercial systems include options to develop state and local information (McCormac, 1988).

The advantage of state and local information is illustrated by the following example of the Colorado Career Information System (COCIS). This system, developed at the University of Colorado at Boulder, is a modification of the Oregon Career Information System. The occupational information component of COCIS includes 250 selected occupational fields, which represent about 90% of Colorado's labor market. Each occupation is described in terms of its function, related occupations, conditions of work, requirements, salary, and employment outlook. The occupational information also includes hiring policies, special programs, and future employment trends, as shown in the following sample teletype printout:

```
***COMPANY PROFILE***


AMPEX CORPORATION
DIVISION OF AUDIO-VISUAL SYSTEMS
600 WOOTEN ROAD
COLORADO SPRINGS, COLORADO
AN INTERNATIONAL CORPORATION WITH HEADQUARTERS IN
CALIFORNIA, AMPEX CORPORATION, A SIGNAL-OWNED COMPANY,
HAS 11,000 EMPLOYEES WORLDWIDE. THE COLORADO SPRINGS
FACILITY, PART OF THE AUDIO-VIDEO EQUIPMENT DIVISION,
WAS OPENED FOR MARKETING TO THE PROFESSIONAL BROAD-
```

CASTING INDUSTRY. THE COMPANY MANUFACTURES COMPUTER
MEMORIES AND DATA HANDLING PRODUCTS, AS WELL AS MAG-
NETIC TAPE, AT OTHER LOCATIONS.

EMPLOYMENT PROFILE

THERE ARE 1,470 EMPLOYEES AT THE COLORADO SPRINGS AMPEX
PLANT, WORKING TWO SHIFTS. THE CATEGORIES OF EMPLOYEES
RANGE FROM CLERICAL AND ADMINISTRATIVE EMPLOYEES IN
OFFICE JOBS TO SKILLED FABRICATION WORKERS SUCH AS
SHEET METAL WORKERS AND MACHINISTS, TO ELECTRONIC
ASSEMBLERS AND TECHNICIANS, TO MATERIAL DISPATCHERS
AND PLANNERS, TO MANUFACTURING ENGINEERS.

GENERAL HIRING POLICY

AMPEX ADVERTISES JOB OPENINGS IN THE LOCAL COLORADO
SPRINGS NEWSPAPERS AND THROUGH COLORADO JOB SERVICE.
THE COMPANY IS AN AFFIRMATIVE ACTION, EQUAL OPPORTUNITY
EMPLOYER. IT GOES OUTSIDE THE COMPANY TO HIRE EMPLOYEES
ONLY WHEN OPENINGS CANNOT BE FILLED THROUGH INTERNAL
PROMOTIONS AND TRANSFER.

SPECIAL PROGRAMS

AMPEX PROVIDES ON-THE-JOB TRAINING FOR MOST OF ITS
EMPLOYEES, AND HAS SOME FORMAL TRAINING PROGRAMS. MOST
OF THE JOBS ARE GROUPED IN JOB FAMILIES. FOR INSTANCE,
THE JOB OF PRODUCTION OPERATOR LEADS TO PRODUCTION
OPERATOR SPECIALIST. THUS, THE JOB FAMILY IS THE AVENUE
BY WHICH EMPLOYEES RECEIVE PROMOTIONS. AMPEX HAS AN
INTERNAL BIDDING SYSTEM AND CONDUCTS SALARY REVIEWS
EVERY SIX MONTHS.

PROJECTED JOB OPENINGS

A HIRING FREEZE IS IN EFFECT FOR THE FORESEEABLE FUTURE.
IT IS ANTICIPATED THAT IT WILL BE LIFTED WHEN THE BUSINESS
CLIMATE IMPROVES.[1]

The commercial systems used in the state CIDS are listed in Table 6-1. However, we should expect these systems to change rapidly and new systems to be adopted as technology for other systems continues to evolve. Also the content may change as well.

USING DISCOVER

The original DISCOVER system, designed for high school and college students, assisted them in making career choices. DISCOVER for colleges and adults,

[1] From the *Career Information System*. Copyright 1984, Colorado State Dept. of Education. Reprinted by permission.

TABLE 6-1
Currently Used Computer Systems

System	Developer
Career Information Delivery Systems (CIDS)	National CIS University of Oregon Eugene, OR 97403
Choices	Canada Systems Group Federal Services Div. 955 Green Valley Crescent Ottawa, Ontario K2C 3V4
Coordinate Occupational Information Network (COIN)	Dr. Rodney Durgin COIN Career Guidance Products 3361 Executive Parkway Suite 302 Toledo, OH 43606
DISCOVER	DISCOVER Center Schilling Plaza South 230 Schilling Circle Hunt Valley, MD 21030
Guidance Information System (GIS)	Houghton Mifflin Co. Educational Software Div. P.O. Box 683 Hanover, NH 03755
KANSAS CAREERS	KANSAS CAREERS College of Education Bluemont Hall Manhattan, KS 66506
System of Interactive Guidance and Information (SIGI)	SIGI Office Educational Testing Serv. Princeton, NJ 08541

SOURCE: From McCormac, 1988.

published by the American College Testing Program (1987), contains the following modules:

1. Beginning the career journey
2. Learning about the world of work
3. Learning about yourself
4. Finding occupations
5. Learning about occupations
6. Making educational choices
7. Planning next steps
8. Planning your career
9. Making transitions

Although users are advised to proceed through the modules in a sequential order, certain modules can be accessed on demand. For example, an individual seeking information about educational institutions can access two-year or four-year college lists. In the case of Jill, a freshman who is undecided about a major or a career, the sequential order is most desirable.

Jill: In high school, I never gave too much thought to a career, even though my parents tried to persuade me to make up my mind. I guess I just didn't get around to it. I hope you can help me decide.

Counselor: We have several ways to help you. First I'll explain the various materials we have, the usual sequence students go through, and the time involved.

After the counselor informed Jill of the career-guidance programs, he obtained a time commitment from her.

Counselor: I want you to understand that you will have to spend considerable effort and time to find the answers to your questions. If you agree to that, I believe we can help you make a good decision about your future.

Jill chose the DISCOVER program from the range of options offered by the counselor.

Jill: I actually like to work with computers. In high school, we used computers in several of our courses.

The counselor informed Jill of the various components of DISCOVER, their purpose, and how to access them. Jill began with Module I. She was asked to respond to questions as follows:

3 = I already know this
2 = I know something about this, but not enough
1 = I don't know this at all[2]

The first group of questions concerned the world of work. For example, Jill was asked whether she knew that academic majors can be grouped in a logical way, and how choices of academic majors are related to occupations. In the second group of questions, she was asked about herself; that is, if she had knowledge about her abilities, interests, or work-related values. In the third section, she was asked to explore occupations in terms of how they related to her interests, abilities, values, and experiences. Other questions dealt with learning about occupations, making decisions about education, planning next steps, planning a career, and coping with transitions.

After Jill completed these questions and the computer compiled the information, the counselor requested a printout to determine what direction Jill should take. In Jill's case, the greatest needs seemed to involve knowing about the world of work, herself, and which occupations to explore. From this list, the counselor and Jill decided that she would take the ability, interest, and value inventory offered in the system.

[2] This and the following computerized material in this section are from the DISCOVER programs, college and adult version. American College Testing Program, Iowa City, Iowa. Reprinted by permission.

Jill began with the interest inventory offered in Career Planning Task Two. She received the following instructions: Consider whether you would like or dislike doing each of the activities listed, not your ability to do it. For each of the 90 activities, use the following key. Circle your choice.

L = If you LIKE the activity
I = If you are INDIFFERENT (don't care one way or the other about the activity)
D = If you DISLIKE the activity

Then Jill moved on to the abilities inventory, where she was asked to rate herself in comparison to other persons her own age. She was instructed to use the following scale:

5 = High (top 10% of persons my age)
4 = Above average (upper 25%)
3 = Average (middle 50%)
2 = Below average (lower 25%)
1 = Low (bottom 10%)

Jill was asked to rate her ability in meeting people and helping others; that is, whether she was good in sales, leadership, organization, and clerical or mechanical tasks. She was asked about her manual dexterity and her numerical, scientific, creative/artistic, creative/literary, reading, language usage, and spatial abilities.

On the values inventory, she was instructed to read each value carefully, mark one of the choices provided, and rank-order the values from 1 through 9. An example of one value is listed below.

Priority   *Value*

1. *Creativity in a job means:*
   • discovering, designing, or developing new things, and/or
   • being inventive in your job, and/or
   • finding new ways to make or do things

   What opportunity for creativity do you want in a job?
   4 = High
   3 = Medium to high
   2 = Medium
   1 = Skip this value

After completing this module, Jill made an appointment to see the counselor.

Meanwhile, Jill could investigate science careers on her own. The combination of her scores on the inventories suggested that she was interested in ideas and things as opposed to people and data. (The DISCOVER World-of-Work Map depicts 12 regions of work represented by general areas of work or job families, and a second dimension of work by Data/Ideas and People/Things. A third dimension refers users to Business Contact, Business Operations, Technical, Science, Arts, or Social Services.) Jill was directed toward Region 9, Natural

Science and Mathematics, and Region 8, Medical Specialties, Technologies, Engineering, and Related Techniques. Her second dimension was Ideas and Things, and the third dimension was in Science. At the next counseling session, the following exchange took place.

Counselor: You seem to have a definite interest in the sciences and medical special-
              ties, Jill. What do you think?
Jill: All I can say is, I did well in biology, chemistry, and math in school.
              Maybe that's the reason I ended up in this area.

As the conversation continued, it became clear that Jill needed more information about occupations since her work experience was very limited. She decided to go to Career Planning Task 6: Selecting Occupations. In this module, she was asked to select desirable characteristics of occupations. For example, in selection of a work setting she responded to the following:

Work Setting (where you'd work)—I want to work:
   a. Indoors in an office
   b. Indoors other than in an office
   c. Outdoors
   d. Combination of indoors and outdoors

Other characteristics evaluated by Jill were "employment outlook," "work hours," "supervision of others," "travel required," "unusual pressure," "beginning income," and "educational level."

Jill wanted a job projected to have openings by 1995. She also preferred working indoors as opposed to outdoors and wanted a regular shift of seven to eight hours a day. Jill also indicated that she would be willing to earn a bachelor's degree or continue with graduate work, if necessary, to meet her goal. She was interested in a starting salary of about $20,000 per year.

After providing the program with a measure of interests, abilities, values, and characteristics of desired occupations, Jill was presented with a list of occupations for consideration. She asked the counselor to assist her in evaluating these findings.

Jill: I have a long list of occupations here, and I'm not sure what to do with
              all of them.
Counselor: Well, follow the instructions and you can get more information about
              each of them. Perhaps you might want to think about or explore several
              of them further. Remember, you can get a printout for the ones you
              select.

Jill then selected some occupations from the list. One of her selections was Medical Technologist. She requested a detailed printout that included a description of the work tasks, work settings, tools and materials used, related civilian occupations, related military occupations, education or training possibilities, special requirements, personal qualities needed, the career ladder, salary potential, projected demand for new workers, the advantages and disadvantages, and where to get more information. In addition, the code for the *Dictionary of*

Occupational Titles was given along with the code for the *Standard Occupational Classification* and the *Guide for Occupational Exploration.*

In subsequent counseling sessions, Jill concluded that medical technology was of great interest, and she decided to further explore this field. To gain more information, she visited a local hospital where medical technologists were employed. In the course of considering this career, Jill discovered that medical technology matched her interests, values, abilities, work tasks, and desired work setting. She was also pleased to discover that the starting salaries for medical technologists generally met her financial requirements. Jill later returned to the computer for more information concerning training sites and financial aid.

DISCOVER provided meaningful interactive tasks and information modules to help Jill make a career decision. The on-line assessment program provided an effective method of evaluating interests, abilities, and values. The flexibility of this program made it possible to access relevant tasks and data as needed, such as job descriptions and education-training information. Using the job description, the counselor encouraged Jill to seek more information from other materials and from an on-site visit.

STEPS IN USING COMPUTER-ASSISTED CAREER-GUIDANCE PROGRAMS

Throughout this chapter, several direct references have been made to the use of computer-assisted career-guidance programs. The primary purpose has been to emphasize the computer's role in meeting the career-exploration needs of individuals and groups. Structured procedures that utilize components of computerized programs as a career-counseling assistant are a major advantage. Computer-assisted career-guidance programs are one of the major components of a total career-guidance program. As such, they are coordinated with other components, materials, and procedures; they are not the *sole* delivery system. Individual needs may dictate the use of several components including computerized systems; or in some cases, computerized systems alone may meet client needs. Within this framework, the following steps for using computer-assisted career-guidance programs are offered.

1. *Assessment of needs.* Individualized needs of each student should determine the direction of program use and the components accessed. For example, one student may only need information on financial aid programs. A student moving to a distant state may be seeking information on two-year and four-year colleges within driving distance of his or her future residence. Others, like Jill, can be helped in determining their career direction.

2. *Orientation.* Each student or group of students should be given a thorough orientation on the purpose, goals, and demonstrated use of computerized systems.

3. *Individualized programs.* Each individual should follow a preconceived plan based on needs. This plan can be modified as needed; the flexibility of computerized programs can be a distinct advantage when plans change.

4. *Counselor intervention.* The individualized plan should provide for counselor intervention. For example, an appropriate point may be a discussion of the results of one of the inventories. Providing sources of additional occupational information and discussing tentative occupational choices are good strategies in the career-exploration process. The point is that individuals should not be "turned over to the computer" without any planned intervention from a counselor.

5. *On-line assistance.* Provisions should be made to assist individuals in various stages of career exploration. How to return to the main menu or how to access various components can be frustrating experiences for the computer novice. Questions that can be anticipated are "How can I get this printed?" "I need to stop now and go to class—what should I do?" "I hit the wrong key, can you help me?"

6. *Follow-up.* As in all phases of career exploration, individual progress should be monitored. Career counselors should help individuals sustain their motivation, evaluate their progress, and evaluate the effectiveness of programs.

These activities are designed to develop the individual's decision-making skills. The counselor should assist the student at various stages, including helping the student and accessing different areas of the system. Most important, the counselor should make use of the information obtained from the computer for more effective career counseling.

SELECTING A COMPUTER-ASSISTED CAREER-GUIDANCE SYSTEM

The process of selecting a computer-assisted career-guidance system will become more complex as additional software programs become available. However, regardless of the variety and number of systems, the first step in the selection process is to determine career-counseling needs through a thorough analysis of current program-service effectiveness. Maze (1984) suggested the following steps in selecting a computer-guidance system:

1. *Obtain input from staff.* Use a brainstorming process to determine how a computer-assisted career-guidance system will improve existing counseling services. Determine specific information about services that are considered weak, and obtain opinions on how a computerized program might provide more efficiency.

2. *Obtain relevant information about computerized programs under consideration.* Evaluate each component of software packages, costs, hardware requirements, and recommended user populations. Harris-Bowlsbey (1984) suggested that current computer-based information systems provide adequate delivery

programs for vocational choice. Guidance-emphasis systems are helpful in meeting career-development theoretical positions.

3. *Obtain a demonstration of software programs.* Preview all software components personally and/or buy a "potential user" program.

4. *Obtain samples of the system's output.* Evaluate sample printouts of each module contained in the system.

5. *Obtain the cost of the system.* Calculate the cost of both software and hardware systems under consideration.

6. *Obtain cost per user.* Calculate both maximum and minimum user estimates to help determine the system's cost effectiveness.

7. *Obtain one-time charges and ongoing charges.* Systems used in microcomputers require one-time charges for the printer and telephone-line adapter. Ongoing charges include the fee for renewing software packages, equipment maintenance, and such items as printer paper, ribbons, and backup disks. Mainframe or centralized systems include one-time terminal and printer costs. Ongoing charges include telephone lines, time-sharing computer service, maintenance contracts, and incidentals such as printer paper and ribbons.

Selection of software systems should precede hardware selection, making possible the most effective accommodation of user needs. Moreover, selection of software will usually limit hardware choices. Finally, it will be necessary to reevaluate software systems every two to three years, anticipating software and hardware system revisions and improvement.

SUMMARY

1. The rationale for computerized career counseling stems from the need for up-to-date information and the unique capabilities of the computer to satisfy this need. A number of computerized counseling systems with different combinations of computer hardware and software and different sets of objectives have been developed.

2. Recent research indicates a positive reaction to computer-assisted guidance systems by users. Moreover, the results suggest that the systems evaluated are worthwhile for counseling intervention and help individuals meet career-exploration needs.

3. The most common types of computer-assisted career-guidance systems are information systems and guidance systems.

4. Career Information Delivery Systems (CIDS) were developed with the assistance of NOICC and the SOICCs. One of the major purposes was to give states the opportunity to develop state and local data.

5. The Colorado Career Information System (COCIS) includes a component of 250 occupational fields that represent 90% of Colorado's labor market.

6. The DISCOVER program for colleges and adults is an example of a system that includes on-line assessment programs, job descriptions, and educational information, all of which are easily accessed.

7. When selecting a computerized career-guidance system, the software should be chosen before the hardware, to accommodate the user's needs most effectively.

SUPPLEMENTARY LEARNING EXERCISES

1. Visit a school, college, or agency that has a computer-based career-information system. Request to preview the system, and identify the major components in a written report.
2. Outline and discuss the advantages of having a computer-assisted career-guidance system in one or more of the following: a high school, a community college, a four-year college, or a community agency providing career counseling to adults.
3. Form two groups and debate the issues relating to the following statement: Computer-assisted career-guidance systems will replace the career counselor.
4. Develop a local-visit file (individuals in selected occupations who agree to visits by students) that could be included as a component in a computer-assisted career-guidance system. Describe the advantages of a visit file.
5. Interview a career counselor who has substantial experience in using computer-assisted career-guidance systems. Write a report on the systems used and summarize the counselor's evaluation of the systems.
6. Describe the advantages of having a statewide occupational information data bank of job openings and labor forecasts. How could you incorporate this information in career-counseling programs in high schools, community colleges, four-year colleges or universities, and community programs for adults?
7. Decide what is meant by an interactive computer-assisted career-guidance system. Illustrate your description with your own version of an example script.
8. What do you consider to be the major components of a computer-assisted program for adults? Defend your choices.
9. Compare the DISCOVER subsystems with the SIGI-PLUS subsystems. What are the major differences? What would you adopt for a community college? Give your reasons.
10. Explain your conception of the future role of computer-assisted career-guidance systems in educational settings and community programs.

Chapter Seven

Using Standardized Assessment in Career Counseling

The development of standardized tests and assessment inventories has been closely associated with the vocational-counseling movement.[1] As early as 1883, the U. S. Civil Service Commission used competitive examinations for job placement (Kavruck, 1956). Multiple aptitude-test batteries developed during the mid-1940s have been widely used in educational and vocational counseling (Anastasi, 1988). Scholastic aptitude tests used as admission criteria for educational institutions were implemented through the Educational Testing Service (ETS) established in 1947 and the American College Testing Program (ACT) established in 1959.

The use of aptitude tests in career counseling—specifically using assessment instruments to predict success in an occupation or in an educational/ training program—has generated considerable controversy. The results of two widely quoted studies challenged the value of tests as predictors of future success; that is, in predicting how one will perform on a job or in a training program. A longitudinal study by Thorndike and Hagen (1959) followed the career patterns of 10,000 men who had taken tests during World War II to determine if these test results were valid predictors of their job success. The study suggested that tests given 12 years earlier did not accurately predict occupational success. A study by Ghiselli (1966) suggested that predicting success in occupational-training programs on the basis of test results is only moderately reliable. These widely quoted studies and other issues—including the use of tests for special populations (ethnic groups and women)—have brought confusion concerning the proper uses of assessment instruments in career-counseling programs.

Currently, more emphasis has been placed on skills identification through informal techniques (Holland, 1985; Bolles, 1993; Zunker, 1990). The growing popularity of informal methods of identifying skills strongly suggests that some assessment of individual aptitudes, skills, and other individual characteristics is of vital importance in the career-decision process, despite the controversy surrounding standardized aptitude tests and job-success predictions. Healy (1990)

---

[1] The terms *vocational* and *occupational counseling* are now incorporated in the more widely used term *career counseling*.

has also suggested encouraging clients to develop self-assessment skills. These skills would help them focus on their choices rather than on those suggested by a standardized measure. What seems to be the major issue is how assessment results can be most effectively used in career-counseling programs. A good approach considers assessment results as only one facet of individuality to be evaluated in the career-decision process.

More specifically, career decision making is seen as a continuous counseling process within which all aspects of individuality receive consideration. Skills, aptitudes, interests, values, achievements, personality characteristics, and maturity are among the more important aspects that might be evaluated by assessment measures. Thus, assessment results constitute counseling information that can provide the individual with an awareness of increased options and alternatives, and encourage greater individual exploration in the career-decision process.

Prediger (1974) recommended that the role of assessment in career counseling be threefold: "(1) to stimulate, broaden, and provide focus to career exploration; (2) to stimulate exploration of self in relation to career; and (3) to provide what-if information with respect to various career choice options" (p. 338). Many researchers suggest that all relevant information be included in the career-decision process to encourage greater individual participation and consideration of a wider range of career options. Furthermore, the more knowledge we have of individual characteristics, the greater assurance we have of a balance of considerations in career decision making. Career-counseling programs that are designed to incorporate all relevant information should lessen the chances that career decision making could be dominated by any one factor.

In this chapter, we focus on the use of standardized assessment results in career counseling. We consider assessment results as information that is used with other materials to stimulate and enhance career exploration. The discussion of assessment results includes aptitude and achievement tests and interest, personality, values, and career-maturity inventories. Brief examples of applications of assessment results are included to help clarify the use of specific tests or inventories. These examples provide only brief descriptions of anonymous individuals and do not describe other materials and program considerations involved with a specific test or inventory.[2] With the exception of achievement tests (major publishers listed only), representative examples of tests and inventories are provided.[3]

APTITUDE TESTS

Aptitude tests primarily measure specific skills and proficiencies or the ability to acquire a certain proficiency (Cronbach, 1984). More specifically, aptitude-test scores provide an index of measured skills that is intended to predict how

---

[2] The brief descriptions may appear to oversimplify the career-counseling process and ignore other data and materials.

[3] The use of assessment results of the culturally different and individuals with disabilities is covered in Chapters 16 and 17. The issues of gender bias and gender fairness in career-interest measurement are discussed in Chapter 14.

well an individual may perform on a job or in an educational and/or training program. In addition, they indicate an individual's cognitive strengths and weaknesses; that is, differential abilities that provide an index to specific skills. For example, a measure of scholastic aptitude tells us the probability of success in educational programs. A clerical aptitude-test score provides an index of ability to perform clerical duties. In the former example, we are informed on combinations of aptitudes that predict scholastic success, whereas in the latter, we are provided with more specific measures of skills needed to perform well on a specific job.

Aptitude tests may be purchased as batteries measuring a number of aptitudes and skills or as single tests measuring specific aptitudes. Combinations of battery scores provide prediction indexes for certain educational and/or training criteria as well as performance criteria on certain occupations that require combinations of skills. An example of an aptitude battery is the *General Aptitude Test Battery (GATB)* published by the U.S. Department of Labor. This test was originally developed by the U.S. Employment Service for state employment counselors. The *GATB* measures the following nine aptitudes: intelligence, verbal, numerical, spatial, form perception, clerical perception, motor coordination, finger dexterity, and manual dexterity.

Other aptitude tests published as single-test booklets measure a wide range of specific skills including dexterity, mechanical comprehension, occupational attitude, clerical aptitude, design judgment, art aptitude, and measures of musical talent.

Although aptitude tests primarily provide a basis for predicting success in an occupation or in training programs, they may also be used as counseling tools for career exploration. In this approach, measured individual traits provide a good frame of reference for evaluating potential careers. The following sample cases illustrate the use of aptitude-test batteries.

> Jim, a college freshman, reports to the Career Resource Center that he is interested in architecture. While his father owns an architectural firm, Jim is not sure of his own aptitude for architectural work. The career counselor explains that there are a number of skills needed for this particular profession and suggests that Jim should attempt to identify those skills from resources in the career library. After identifying several required skills, Jim's past academic record and work experiences are evaluated to determine if he has used any of these skills in the past. Eventually, it is decided that two skills, space relations and form perception, would be best evaluated through standardized aptitude tests. Measurement of these particular skills was considered the most important information to be included in the career decision-making process.
>
> Susan is a senior in high school and does not plan to attend college. She is interested in obtaining work after graduation from high school. Her academic record indicates she is an average student with no particular strengths evidenced by academic grades. Her interests have not crystallized to the point at which she would be able to specify a particular occupational interest. Several assessment inventories were administered including a complete battery of aptitude tests. These scores were used to discover areas of specific strengths and weaknesses for inclusion in Susan's career-exploration program. Identification

of specific aptitudes was seen as a stimulus for discovering potential career considerations.

Ron is returning to the work force after a serious head injury received in a car accident. During several months of recovery, his previous job in construction work was terminated. He is now interested in "looking for other kinds of work." An aptitude battery was administered to determine possible deficits resulting from the head injury. As the counselor suspected, the test scores indicated poor finger and manual dexterity. Jobs requiring fine visual-motor coordination had to be eliminated from consideration in career exploration.

In Jim's case, the aptitude test was used to verify or to check the feasibility of a particular career choice. That is, Jim had decided on a career and wanted to determine if he had the aptitude requirements of that career. In Susan's case, aptitude scores provided stimulus for the discussion of measured aptitudes along with other materials used in career counseling. Susan was provided with specific focus in career exploration. In the final example, Ron's deficiencies were found and considerable time in career exploration was saved.

Representative examples of multiple aptitude-test batteries available on the market today are:

The Differential Aptitude Test (DAT)
G. K. Bennet, H. G. Seashore, and A. G. Wesman
The Psychological Corporation
555 Academic Court
San Antonio, Texas 78204-2498

This test consists of eight subtests: verbal reasoning, numerical ability, abstract reasoning, space relations, mechanical reasoning, clerical speed and accuracy, spelling, and language usage. The entire battery takes over three hours to administer. This battery was designed primarily for use with high school and college students. When verbal and numerical scores are combined, a scholastic aptitude score is created. Other subtests are used for vocational and educational planning.

The General Aptitude Test Battery (GATB)
United States Employment Service
Washington, DC 20210

This battery is composed of 8 paper-and-pencil tests and 4 apparatus tests. Nine abilities are measured by the 12 tests: intelligence, verbal aptitude, numerical aptitude, spatial aptitude, form perception, clerical perception, motor coordination, finger dexterity, and manual dexterity. This test is administered to senior high school students and adults. Testing time is two and a half hours. Test results may be used for vocational and educational counseling and placement.

Flanagan Aptitude Classification Tests (FACT)
J. C. Flanagan
Science Research Associates
155 Wacker Drive
Chicago, IL 60606

This test consists of 16 subtests: inspection, coding, memory, precision, assembly, scales, coordination, judgment/comprehension, arithmetic, patterns, components, tables, mechanics, expression, reasoning, and ingenuity. Each test measures behaviors considered critical to job performance. Selected groups of tests may be administered. The entire battery takes several hours. This test is primarily designed for use with high school students and adults.

> *Armed Services Vocational Aptitude Battery (ASVAB)*
> U.S. Department of Defense
> Washington, DC 20402

The *ASVAB* form 19 consists of 9 tests: coding speed, word knowledge, arithmetic reasoning, tool knowledge, space relations, mechanical comprehension, shop information, automotive information, and electronics information. These tests combine to yield three academic scales: academic ability (word knowledge, paragraph comprehension, and arithmetic reasoning), verbal (word knowledge, paragraph comprehension, and general science), and mathematical (math knowledge and arithmetic reasoning). Four occupational scales are also checked: mechanical and crafts (arithmetic reasoning, mechanical comprehension, and auto, shop, and electronics information); business and clerical (word knowledge, paragraph comprehension, mathematics knowledge, and coding speed); electronics and electrical (arithmetic reasoning, mathematical knowledge, electronics information, and general science); and health, social, and technical (word knowledge and paragraph meaning, arithmetic reasoning, and mechanical comprehension).

ACHIEVEMENT TESTS

Achievement tests are primarily designed to assess present levels of developed abilities. Current functioning and basic academic skills such as arithmetic, reading, and language usage are relevant to planning for educational and/or training programs. Academic proficiency has long been a key factor in career planning for individuals considering higher education. However, basic academic competencies are also major determinants in qualifying for certain occupations. For example, identified academic competencies and deficiencies are major considerations for placement or training of school dropouts. Achievement-test results provide important information to be included in programs for adults who are entering, returning to, or recycling through the work force. Changing technology and economic conditions will force many workers to enter programs to upgrade their skills or to train for completely different positions. Assessment of present levels of abilities will be needed to determine the possible scope of career exploration for these individuals.

For our use in career-counseling programs, we will consider achievement tests in three categories: (1) general survey battery; (2) single-subject tests; and (3) diagnostic batteries. The general survey battery measures knowledge of most subjects taught in school and is standardized on the same population. The single-subject test, as the name implies, measures knowledge of only one subject/content area. Diagnostic batteries measure knowledge of specific proficiencies such as reading, spelling, and arithmetic achievement.

The use of achievement tests in career counseling is illustrated in the three cases that follow. In the first example, a general survey battery is used to assist a student in determining a college major and minor. In the second example, the achievement-test results are used for the same purpose, but single-subject achievement tests are used instead of a general survey battery. In the final example, a diagnostic battery is used to assist a woman who is returning to the work force after several years of being a homemaker.

> Ana is interested in determining her most proficient subject matter area for the purpose of choosing a major and/or minor in a liberal arts college. At this point in her life, she is not interested in career selection (deferring this to later) but is more interested in educational planning. The counselor chooses to administer a general survey battery, which provides meaningful comparisons of all subjects tested since the battery was standardized on the same population group. A single profile will provide Ana with an overview of comparative ability on all subjects tested.
>
> Juan is a senior in high school who is considering college, but he cannot decide between biology and chemistry as a major. All other factors being equal as far as career opportunities are concerned, the decision is made to determine which is Juan's strongest subject area. The counselor chooses to administer the single-subject tests in biology and chemistry, as these tests are relatively more thorough and precise as compared to the general survey battery and the diagnostic battery. Thus, single-subject achievement tests provide a more thorough evaluation of specific subject abilities for Juan's consideration.
>
> Betty quit school when she was in the sixth grade. After several years of marriage, she was deserted by her husband and is seeking employment. Other test data reveal that she is of at least average intelligence. A part of the evaluation for this woman includes a diagnostic battery for the specific purpose of determining basic arithmetic skills and reading and spelling levels. The counselor is especially interested in determining academic deficiencies for educational planning; that is, consideration should be given to upgrading basic skills for eventual training for a high school equivalency. This information is seen as essential for both educational and career planning.

Because of the wide range of achievement tests on the market today, individual tests will not be listed. Instead, representative major publishers of achievement tests are provided:

CTB-MacMillan-McGraw-Hill
Publishers Test Service
20 Ryan Ranch Rd.
Monterey, CA 93940

Educational Testing Service
Princeton, NJ 08540

Houghton Mifflin Company
One Beacon Street
Boston, MA 02108

The Psychological Corporation
555 Academic Court
San Antonio, Texas 78204-2498

Science Research Associates, Inc.
155 North Wacker Dr.
Chicago, IL 60606

INTEREST INVENTORIES

In recent years, a considerable body of literature has concerned itself with gender bias and unfairness in career-interest measurement. A number of the most relevant articles have been compiled by Diamond (1975) under the sponsorship of the National Institute of Education (NIE). The NIE publishes guidelines that identify gender bias as "any factor that might influence a person to limit—or might cause others to limit—his or her consideration of a career solely on the basis of gender" (Diamond, 1975, p. xxiii).

According to Diamond (1975), the guidelines have led to some progress in reducing gender bias in interest inventories by calling for fairness in the construction of item pools ("Items such as statements, questions, and names of occupations used in the inventory should be designed so as not to limit the consideration of a career solely on the basis of gender"), fairness in the presentation of technical information ("Technical information should include evidence that the inventory provides career options for both males and females"), and fairness in interpretive procedures ("Interpretive procedures should provide methods of equal treatment of results for both sexes" [p.xxiii]). Generally, the guidelines are aimed at encouraging both sexes to consider all career and educational opportunities, and at eliminating sex-role stereotyping by those using interest-inventory results in the career-counseling process.

Interest inventories have long been associated with career counseling. Two of the most widely used are the *Strong Interest Inventory (SII)*, originally developed by E. K. Strong (1983), and the Kuder interest inventories, developed by G. F. Kuder (1963). More recently, Holland's (1985) approach to interest identification (as discussed in Chapter 2) has received considerable attention. For example, a number of interest inventories including the *SII*, the American College Testing Program Interest Inventory, and the *Self-Directed Search* (Holland, 1987a) are constructed to correspond with Holland's personality types and corresponding work environments. In most inventories, interests are primarily designated by responses to compiled lists of occupations and lists of activities associated with occupations. The rationale is that individuals having similar interest patterns to those found in an occupational group would probably find satisfaction in that particular group.

Two methods commonly used for reporting results are direct comparison (likes and dislikes) with specific occupations and comparisons with themes or clusters of occupations. Interest inventories that provide direct comparisons with specific occupations usually include a numerical index for comparative purposes.

For example, the *Kuder Occupational Interest Survey* (Kuder, 1966) provides a coefficient of correlation as an index for comparing an individual's response with an occupational group—that is, higher correlations indicate similar interest patterns to certain occupational groups (Kuder, 1963). The *SII* provides a standard score for this purpose. In addition, a number of inventories provide profiles that indicate whether interests are similar or dissimilar to those of occupational criterion groups. For example, an individual may give interest responses very similar to those of accountants and very dissimilar to those of social workers.

Clusters of occupations are presented in a variety of schemes. Some clusters are based on the *DOT* models of people, data, and things (see the appendix, p. 485). The *Kuder General Interest Survey* (Kuder, 1964) yields ten interest scales as follows: outdoor, mechanical, computational, scientific, persuasive, artistic, literary, musical, social service, and clerical. The *SII* yields six general occupational theme scales taken from Holland's (1985) six modal personal styles and matching work environments. The cluster systems index a group of occupations rather than a single occupation, although the individual can derive specific occupations from the clusters.

For the nonreader, picture interest inventories are used to determine occupational interests. These inventories depict occupational environments, individuals at work, and a variety of job-related activities. Individual response is recorded by circling numbers or pictures or by pointing to pictures. Picture interest inventories also provide a basis for discussion about career exploration.

Representative examples of interest inventories are as follows:

Kuder Occupational Interest Survey
Publisher Test Service
CTB-MacMillan-McGraw-Hill
20 Ryan Ranch Road
Monterey, CA 93940

This survey is computer-scored and consists of 77 occupational scales and 29 college-major scales for men and of 57 occupational scales and 27 college-major scales for women. Recommended uses of the inventory include selection, placement, and career exploration. The survey is untimed, usually taking 30 to 40 minutes. Norms are based on samples of data from college seniors.

Ohio Vocational Interest Survey (OVIS)
The Psychological Corporation
555 Academic Court
San Antonio, TX 78204-2498

This survey is used by students in grades 8 through 12 and takes between 60 and 90 minutes to complete. The score results yield 24 general-interest scales that are related to people, data, and things. This survey primarily measures general-interest areas.

Self-Directed Search (SDS)
Psychological Assessment Resources
P.O. Box 998
Odessa, FL 33556

This interest inventory is based on Holland's (1985) theory of career development. It is self-administered and self-scored, as well as self-interpreted, and takes approximately 30 to 40 minutes to complete. The scores are organized to reveal an occupational code or a summary code of three letters representing the personality types and environmental models from Holland's typology: realistic, investigative, artistic, social, enterprising, and conventional. This inventory is used with high school and college students and with adults.

Strong Interest Inventory
Stanford University Press
Stanford, CA 94305

This inventory combines the male and female versions of the *Strong Vocational Interest Blank* into one survey. The interpretation of scores is based on Holland's typology. The interpretation format includes six general occupational themes, 23 basic-interest scales, and 124 occupational scales. Administrative indexes include an academic-orientation index and an introversion-extroversion index. Time to complete: 30 to 40 minutes. Both male and female occupational-scale scores are available.

Brainard Occupational Preference Inventory
P. O. Brainard and R. F. Brainard
The Psychological Corporation
555 Academic Court
San Antonio, TX 78204-2498

This inventory is designed for use in grades 8 through 12 and requires approximately 30 minutes to complete. Scores are expressed in percentiles for males and females and are used as guidelines for career exploration. Scores yield individual preference for six broad fields: commercial, mechanical, professional, aesthetic, scientific, agricultural (males only), and personal service (females only).

Career Assessment Inventory (CAI)
C. B. Johansson
National Computer Systems
P.O. Box 1416
Minneapolis, MN 55440

This is a computer-scored inventory that can be administered in approximately 45 minutes. It is designed for eighth-grade students through adults. Three types of scales reported are general occupational-theme scales, basic-interest scales, and occupational scales. This inventory is primarily used with noncollege-bound individuals.

Geist Picture Interest Inventory
Harold Geist, Ph.D.
Western Psychological Services
12031 Wilshire Blvd.
Los Angeles, CA 90025

This inventory is for nonreaders. Examinees are required to circle one of three pictures depicting a work or leisure activity. Separate editions are available for males and females. The male edition assesses 11 general-interest areas: persuasive, clerical, mechanical, musical, scientific, outdoor, literary, computational, artistic, social service, and dramatic. The female edition assesses these same 11 general-interest areas and one other—personal service. Norms for various occupational groups are also provided.

> *Wide Range Interest and Opinion Test*
> Guidance Associates of Delaware, Inc.
> 1526 Gilpin Avenue
> Wilmington, DE 19806

This test consists of 150 sets of three pictures from which the individual is asked to indicate likes and dislikes. The pictures depict activities ranging from unskilled labor to the highest levels of technical, managerial, and professional training. The test evaluates educational and vocational interests of a wide range of individuals, including the educationally disadvantaged and the developmentally disabled.

> *The Campbell Interest and Skill Survey (CISS)*
> NCS Assessments
> P.O. Box 1416
> Minneapolis, MN 55440

This instrument is a part of a new integrated battery of psychological surveys that currently includes the *CISS*, an attitude-satisfaction survey, and a measure of leadership characteristics. Two other instruments, a team development survey and a community survey, are being developed and will complete this integrated battery. The *CISS*, developed for individuals 15 years and older with a sixth-grade reading level, has 200 interest and 120 skill items on a 6-point response scale. The results yield parallel interest and skill scores: orientation scales (influencing, organizing, helping, creating, analyzing, producing, and adventuring); basic scales (29 basic scales, such as leadership, supervision, counseling, and international activities); occupational scales (58 scales, such as financial planner, translator/interpreter, and landscape architect). Special scales measure academic comfort and extroversion.

PERSONALITY INVENTORIES

Major career theorists have emphasized personality development as a major factor to be considered in career development. For example, Roe (1956) postulated that early personality development associated with family interactions influences vocational direction. Super (1990) devoted considerable attention to self-concept development. Tiedeman and O'Hara (1963) considered total cognitive development in decision making. Holland's (1985) system of career selection was directly related to personality types and styles. The case for the use of personality inventories in career-counseling programs seems well established. However, there is a lack of evidence that personality inventories are being widely utilized in career-counseling programs.

The development of the *Sixteen Personality Factor Questionnaire (16 PF)* by Cattell, Eber, and Tatsuoka (1970) led the way for integrating personality inventories into career-counseling programs. Vocational personality patterns and occupational fitness are considered major components of this questionnaire. The 16 factors measured by the *16 PF* are "source" traits or factors, which are derived from distinct combinations of an individual's personality traits (Cattell, Eber, & Tatsuoka, 1970). These traits are compared with occupational profiles and provide vocational observations and occupational-fitness projections. *Vocational observations* include information concerning the individual's potential for leadership and interpersonal skills and potential benefits from academic training. *Occupational-fitness projections* rank how the individual compares with specific occupational profiles as being extremely high to extremely low. Specific source traits are recorded for each occupational profile available (currently there are 24), providing a comparison of characteristic traits common to individuals employed in certain occupations. The *16 PF* is singled out because a major portion of the development of the inventory was devoted to vocational personality patterns and occupational-fitness projections.

Throughout this text, references are made to the importance of satisfying individual needs associated with work, family, and leisure. As we assist individuals in career exploration, we must consider the individuality of each person we counsel. Within this frame of reference, individual personality patterns greatly assist in the task of identifying and clarifying each individual's needs. As needs change over the life span, our goal is to help individuals clarify their needs for effective planning and goal achievement. Personality inventories provide valuable information for identifying needs and providing a stimulus for career exploration.

The following examples demonstrate the use of personality inventories in career-counseling programs.

> Al reports that he is quite frustrated in his present working environment and is considering changing jobs. His unhappiness has caused family problems and social problems in general. His performance ratings by his superiors were high until the last two years, when they dropped to average. Assessment results indicate that he is interested in his current job as accountant. A personality inventory indicated a strong need for achievement. Group discussions that followed brought about a consensus that Al was still interested in the field of accounting, but in his current position, he was not able to meet his needs to achieve. Earlier these needs were apparently met from positive reinforcement received from high ratings by his superiors. At this point in his life, he is searching for something more than "just doing a good job of bookkeeping." Recognizing his source of frustration, he decided to stay in accounting but moved to another division in the firm.
>
> Wendy had definitely decided that she was interested in an occupation that would provide her with an opportunity to help people. A personality

inventory indicated that she was very reserved and nonassertive, and deferred to others. She agreed with the results of the personality inventory and further agreed that these characteristics would make it difficult for her to accomplish her occupational goal. Wendy became convinced that she would have to modify these personality characteristics through a variety of programs, including self-discovery groups and assertiveness training.

In these cases, personality-inventory results provided the impetus and stimulation for action to meet individual career needs. In the first example, Al recognized as the major source of his frustrations a motivational drive that he had repressed for years. Fortunately, he was able to meet his needs to achieve in another division of the firm in which he was employed. In the second example, Wendy chose to keep her career goal but increased her chances of success in that career with further training. These examples provide only two illustrations of the use of personality inventories in career counseling but clearly establish their potential usefulness. Personality inventories provide important information that can be incorporated into group and/or individual counseling programs to assist individuals with career-related problems.

Representative examples of personality inventories follow:

California Test of Personality
CTB-MacMillan-McGraw-Hill
20 Ryan Ranch Rd.
Monterey, CA 93940

Five levels of the test are available: primary, elementary, intermediate, secondary, and adult. The test assesses personal and social adjustment. Subscale scores are provided for the two major categories. The test is primarily used in career counseling to assess measures of personal worth and of family and school relations.

Edwards Personal Preference Schedule (EPPS)
The Psychological Corporation
555 Academic Court
San Antonio, TX 78204-2498

This inventory is designed to measure the following 15 personality variables related to needs: achievement, dominance, endurance, order, intraception, nurturance, affiliation, heterosexuality, exhibition, autonomy, aggression, change, succorance, abasement, and deference. In addition, a consistency score indicates the reliability of the responses. These scores provide an index for determining dominant individual needs to be considered in career exploration. The inventory is untimed and is hand- or machine-scored. Norms are based on data taken from college students' responses.

Guilford-Zimmerman Temperament Survey
Sheridan Psychological Services
P.O. Box 6101
Orange, CA 92667

This survey measures the following 10 traits: general activity, restraint, ascendance, sociability, emotional stability, objectivity, friendliness, thoughtfulness, personal relations, and masculinity. Norms were derived primarily from college samples. Single-trait scores and total profiles may be used to determine personality traits to be considered in career decision making.

Minnesota Counseling Inventory
The Psychological Corporation
555 Academic Court
San Antonio, TX 78204-2498

This inventory was designed to measure adjustment of boys and girls in grades 9 through 12. Scores yield criterion-related scales as follows: family relationship, social relationship, emotional stability, conformity, adjustment to reality, mood, and leadership. Scales are normed separately for boys and girls. These scores provide indexes to important relationships and personal characteristics to be considered in career counseling.

Sixteen Personality Factor (16 PF)
Institute for Personality and Ability Testing
1602 Coronado Drive
Champaign, IL 61820

This instrument measures 16 personality factors of individuals 16 years or older. A major part of this questionnaire has been devoted to identifying personality patterns related to occupational-fitness projections. These projections provide a comparison of the individual's profile with samples of occupational profiles. The instrument is hand-scored or computer-scored. Four forms have an average adult vocabulary; two forms are available for low-literacy groups.

Temperament and Values Inventory
Charles B. Johansson
Interpretive Scoring Systems
A Division of National Computer Systems, Inc.
P.O. Box 1416
Minneapolis, MN 55440

This inventory has two parts: (1) temperament dimensions of personality related to career choice, and (2) values related to work rewards. The inventory has an eighth-grade reading level and is not recommended for use below the ninth grade. The inventory is untimed and computer-scored. Scores help determine congruence or incongruence with an individual's career aspirations.

Myers-Briggs Type Indicator
Consulting Psychologists Press, Inc.
3803 East Bayshore Road
Palo Alto, CA 94303

This inventory measures individual preferences by personality types: extroversion or introversion; sensing or intuition; thinking or feeling; and judging or perceiving. Scores are determined according to the four categories. The publisher's manual provides descriptions of the 16 possible types (combinations). Occupations that are attractive to each type are presented in the appendixes. This inventory provides direct references to occupational considerations based on one's personality type.

VALUES INVENTORIES

In the last two decades, much has been written about beliefs and values. Some argue that we have experienced significant changes in our value systems over the last 20 years. There is the ongoing debate about differences in values between the so-called establishment and the younger generation. Much of the concern has centered on lifestyle and the work role. Questioning the social worth of one's work has motivated many to reformulate their life goals. As career counselors, we must be concerned with individual beliefs and values in the career decision-making process. An important function is to act as agents who provide methods for clarifying values. In this frame of reference, we are concerned not only with work values but also with values per se as we help others find congruence with the inseparables—work and life.

For counseling purposes, we classify values inventories into two types: (1) inventories that primarily measure work values, and (2) inventories that measure values associated with broader aspects of lifestyle. Work value inventories, as the name implies, are designed to measure values associated with job success and satisfaction (achievement, prestige, security, and creativity). Values found to be high priorities for the individual provide another dimension of information that may be used in career exploration. In our second category, values are considered in much broader terms but can be related to needs and satisfactions associated with life and work. Thus, both types of inventories provide information that can be especially helpful for clarifying individual needs associated with work, home, family, and leisure.

Two examples of the use of a value measure follow.

> Don, a middle-aged, married man with five children, was employed for five years as a salesman in a local furniture store. He is currently seeking a change in employment, and sought out a state agency for assistance. As part of the assessment program, he took the *Survey of Personal Values* (Gordon, 1967). The results of the inventory clearly indicated that Don was very goal-oriented; that is, he preferred to have definite goals and plan precisely for the future. However, he felt that he had no real control over his life, particularly since in his past job as a salesman his commissions had fluctuated greatly from month to month. He expressed frustration and despair. The major focus of the group discussions that followed centered on identifying those variables through which individuals can exert control over their lives. Don was encouraged to recognize his past experiences as assets for his future in the job market. Exploring potential careers by identifying skills from previous work experiences gave him the confidence he lacked in the past. More important,

Don learned of several jobs for which he was qualified that gave him the opportunity to set goals and plan for the future.

Rosa was considered an outstanding student in high school and was very active as a member of the student council. She expressed a deep concern to the career counselor about her inability to identify a working environment in which she felt she could find satisfaction. There were no particular role models, organizations, or occupations that seemed to have the potential to satisfy her needs. In the *Work Values Inventory (WVI)* (Super, 1970) administered to her, she rated intellectual stimulus, creativity, and job placement very high. These values were incorporated into further discussions that provided her with a starting point from which she was able to launch a career exploration. Potential occupations were partially evaluated to determine how they could satisfy her work values identified by the *WVI*.

In the first example, a values inventory identified Don's major difficulty in career planning as stemming from a need to identify sources of discontentment with his past job. Once the unsatisfied value was revealed—a desire to have control over his life—Don was encouraged to identify past job skills that were applicable to new jobs over which he could have more control. In the second example, the identified work values served as a stimulus in launching a study of careers from the perspective of finding a career that could meet Rosa's needs. Once one is able to consider careers from an individual viewpoint, more realistic decisions usually follow.

Representative examples of work-values inventories follow:

Work Environment Preference Schedule
The Psychological Corporation
555 Academic Court
San Antonio, TX 78204-2498

This inventory measures an individual's adaptability to a bureaucratic organization. It is untimed and self-administered. A total score reflects the individual's commitment to the sets of attitudes, values, and behaviors found in bureaucratic organizations. Separate norms by sex are available for high school, college, and Army ROTC students.

Work Values Inventory (WVI)
Houghton Mifflin
One Beacon Street
Boston, MA 02108

This inventory measures sources of satisfaction individuals seek from their work environment. Scores yield measures of altruism, aesthetics, creativity, intellectual stimulation, independence, prestige, management, economic returns, security, surroundings, supervisory relations, value of relationship with associates, way of life, and variety. Norms are provided by grade and sex for students in grades 7 through 12. The scores provide dimensions of work values that can be combined with other considerations in career counseling.

Representative examples of broader values inventories include the following:

Study of Values
Houghton Mifflin
One Beacon Street
Boston, MA 02108

This is a self-administered inventory that measures individual values in six categories: theoretical, economic, esthetic, social, political, and religious. Norms are provided by sex for high school, college, and various occupational groups. The measured strength of values (indicated as high, average, or low) provides points of reference for individual and group counseling programs.

Survey of Interpersonal Values
Science Research Associates
155 North Wacker Drive
Chicago, IL 60606

This inventory measures values considered important in relationships with other people: support, conformity, recognition, independence, benevolence, and leadership. These measures assist in evaluating the individual's personal, social, marital, and occupational adjustment. Norms are available for high school and college students and adults.

Survey of Personal Values
Science Research Associates
155 North Wacker Drive
Chicago, IL 60606

This inventory measures values that influence how individuals cope with daily problems. Scores yield measures of practical-mindedness, achievement, variety, decisiveness, orderliness, and goal orientation. The inventory is self-administered. National percentile norms are available for college students, while regional norms are available for high school students.

The Values Scale
Consulting Psychologists Press, Inc.
3803 East Bayshore Road
Palo Alto, CA 94303

This scale measures 21 values: ability utilization, achievement, advancement, aesthetics, altruism, authority, autonomy, creativity, economic rewards, lifestyle, personal development, physical activity, prestige, risk, social interaction, social relations, variety, working conditions, cultural identity, physical prowess, and economic security. The measures are designed to help individuals understand values in relation to life roles and evaluate the importance of the work role with other life roles. Scores are interpreted by using percentile equivalents. Norms are available for high school and university students and adults.

The Campbell Organizational Survey
NCS Assessments
P.O. Box 1416
Minneapolis, MN 55440

This instrument provides a measure of an overall index for the individual's satisfaction with the working environment. It is part of an integrated battery that includes several other surveys, such as the *Campbell Interest and Skill Survey*. Some of the scales include measures of the following: the work itself, working conditions, level of stress, co-workers, supervision, and job security.

CAREER-MATURITY INVENTORIES

Career-maturity inventories measure vocational development in terms of specified dimensions from which one is judged to be vocationally mature. The dimensions of career maturity are derived from career development concepts. That is, vocational maturity, like career choice, is a continuous development process that can be segmented into a series of stages and tasks (Super, 1957; Crites, 1973, pp. 5–7). Super put the process of career choice on a continuum, with "exploration" and "decline" as endpoints (as discussed in Chapter 2). Career maturity is considered the degree of vocational development measurable within this continuum. Super measured career maturity within several dimensions: orientation toward work (attitudinal dimension), planning (competency dimension), consistency of vocational preferences (consistency dimension), and wisdom of vocational preferences (realistic dimension). These dimensions identify progressive steps of vocational development and determine the degree of development relative to normative age levels.

Thus, career-maturity inventories are primarily measures of individual career development. For example, attitudinal dimensions reveal individual problems associated with career choice. Competence dimensions provide measures of an individual's knowledge of occupations and planning skills. Career-maturity inventories provide a focus for individual and/or group programs. They also evaluate the effectiveness of career-education programs and curricula and help identify other career-guidance program needs.

Following is a list of representative career-maturity inventories.

Career Development Inventory
D. E. Super, A. S. Thompson, R. H. Lindenman,
J. P. Jordaan, and R. A. Myers
Consulting Psychologists Press, Inc.
3853 East Bayshore Road
Palo Alto, CA 94303

This inventory is a diagnostic tool for the development of individual or group counseling procedures; it can also be used to evaluate career-development programs. Scores yield measures of planning orientation, readiness for exploration, information, and decision making. The reading level is sixth grade, and the inventory is applicable to both sexes. Both cognitive and attitudinal scales are provided.

Career Maturity Inventory (CMI)
John O. Crites
CTB-MacMillan-McGraw-Hill
20 Ryan Ranch Rd.
Monterey, CA 93940

This inventory is divided into two parts: an attitude scale and a competence scale. The attitude scale measures decisiveness, involvement, independence, orientation, and compromise in decision making. The competence scale measures self-appraisal, occupational information, goal selection, planning, and problem solving. Both scales can be hand-scored or computer-scored. Both scales are applicable to males, females, minorities, and other special groups. The standardization sample is derived from scores of students in grades 6 through 12.

Cognitive Vocational Maturity Test (CVMT)
B. W. Westbrook
Center for Occupational Education
North Carolina State University
Raleigh, NC 27607

This test is primarily a cognitive measure of an individual's knowledge of occupational information. Scores yield measures of knowledge of fields of work available, job-selection procedures, work conditions, educational requirements, specific requirements for a wide range of occupations, and actual duties performed in a variety of occupations. This inventory provides important information about career-choice abilities and can be used as a diagnostic tool for curricula and guidance needs.

New Mexico Career Education Test
C. C. Healy and S. P. Klein
Monitor Book Co., Inc.
195 S. Beverly Drive
Beverly Hills, CA 90212

This test primarily assesses specific learner objectives of career-education programs for grades 9 through 12. Six criterion-referenced tests yield measures of specific learner outcomes for attitude toward work, career planning, career-oriented activities, knowledge of occupations, job-application procedures, and career development. Norms for the test are based completely on samples of students from the public schools in New Mexico.

Career Beliefs Inventory
Consulting Psychologists Press, Inc.
3803 East Bayshore Road
Palo Alto, CA 94303

This inventory is used as a counseling tool to help clients identify career beliefs that may inhibit their ability to make career decisions that are in their best interest. The results are computed for 25 scales under the following five headings: My Current Career Situation, What Seems Necessary for My Happiness, Factors that Influence My Decisions, Changes I Am Willing to Make, and Effort I Am Willing to Initiate. Norms are available for junior high school students as well as for separate norms for male and female employed adults. Scores can be interpreted in percentile ranks for each scale.

> *Adult Career Concerns Inventory*
> Consulting Psychologists Press, Inc.
> 3803 East Bayshore Road
> Palo Alto, CA 94303

There are three major purposes listed for this inventory: career counseling and planning, needs analysis, and a measure of relationships between adult capability and previous, concurrent socioeconomic and psychological characteristics. Scores are related to career-development tasks at various life stages as follows: exploration, establishment, maintenance, disengagement, retirement planning, and retirement living. Norms are available by age, starting at 25 to 45 and up, by combined sexes, and by age groups and sex.

> *The Salience Inventory*
> Consulting Psychologists Press, Inc.
> 3803 East Bayshore Road
> Palo Alto, CA 94303

This instrument, a research edition in developmental stage, is designed to measure five major life roles: student, worker, homemaker, leisurite, and citizen. Use of inventory results provides counselors with an evaluation of an individual's readiness for career decisions and exposure to work and occupations.

SELF-ASSESSMENT

As Prediger (1974) pointed out, a greater emphasis has been placed on using assessment results to stimulate exploration of self in relation to career decision making. One of the major advantages of self-assessment techniques is that individuals are not required to judge the strength of specified traits, subsequently allowing them more freedom in expressing their individuality (Tyler, 1961). Bolles (1993) employed self-assessment in his widely used *What Color Is Your Parachute?* and Figler (1975) used self-assessment of abilities in his *PATH* workbook. Tyler (1961) used a card-sort method in an attempt to further clarify individuality among clients in search of a career. She asked each client to sort the names of 100 occupations, printed separately on small cards, into the categories Would Not Choose, Would Choose, or No Opinion. Clients were then asked to give reasons for rejecting or choosing certain occupations. These discussions were designed to enhance self-understanding. Dolliver (1982) reviewed the development of card sorts, and Zunker (1990) gave examples of their use.

Jones's (1981) *OCC-U-SORT* is a good example of a currently used self-assessment instrument.

OCC-U-SORT
Publishers Test Service
CTB-MacMillan-McGraw-Hill
20 Ryan Ranch Rd.
Monterey, CA 93940

This instrument is designed to encourage career exploration by stimulating thinking about motives for making occupational choices. The reasons for rejecting
certain occupations as well as the reasons for making selections are discussed.
The cards may be used by eighth-graders through adults. The front side of each
card contains the occupational title, *DOT* number, general educational level, and
a two-letter Holland occupational code. On the back side of the card, the occupational description is given along with card identification material. A self-guided
booklet, in which the individual writes down the reasons for choosing and rejecting occupations, may also be used. One of the distinct advantages, according to
the author, is the sex-fairness of this approach in career decision making.

SUMMARY

1. Standardized tests and assessment inventories have been closely associated with career counseling. Skills, aptitudes, interests, values, achievements,
personality characteristics, and vocational maturity are among the assessment
objectives of career counseling.

2. The use of standardized assessment procedures in career counseling
provides the counselee with increased options and alternatives, subsequently
encouraging greater individual involvement in the career-decision process. In
career-counseling programs, assessment scores are used with other materials to
stimulate and enhance career exploration.

3. Aptitude tests primarily measure specific skills and proficiencies or the
ability to acquire a certain proficiency. Measured aptitudes provide a good
frame of reference for evaluating potential careers.

4. Achievement tests primarily assess present levels of developed abilities.
The basic academic skills such as arithmetic, reading, and language usage are
relevant information to be included in planning for educational and/or training
programs.

5. Interest inventories are relevant counseling tools because individuals
having interest patterns similar to those of people in certain occupations will
probably find satisfaction in that occupation. Interest inventories can effectively stimulate career exploration.

6. Personality development is a major factor in career development since
the individuality of each counselee must be considered. Personality patterns are
integral in identifying and clarifying the needs of each individual.

7. Assessment and clarification of beliefs and values are important components of career counseling. Two types of values inventories are (a) inventories
that primarily measure work values and (b) inventories that measure dimensions of values associated with broader aspects of lifestyles.

8. Career-maturity inventories measure the dimensions from which one is judged to be vocationally mature. Super identified dimensions of career maturity as orientation toward work, planning, consistency of vocational preferences, and wisdom of vocational preferences. Career-maturity inventories have two basic purposes: (a) to measure an individual's career development and (b) to evaluate the effectiveness of career-education programs.

9. Self-assessment instruments are designed to stimulate exploration of self in relation to career decision making. Discussions of reasons for choosing and rejecting certain occupations are designed to enhance self-understanding.

SUPPLEMENTARY LEARNING EXERCISES

1. Visit a state rehabilitation office to determine the assessment programs used for rehabilitation programs. Summarize the purpose of assessment in this context.
2. Administer and interpret one or more of the tests and inventories discussed in this chapter. Summarize the results and discuss strategies for using the results in career counseling.
3. Interview a personnel director of an industrial company and discuss the company's assessment program for placement counseling. Identify the rationale for each assessment instrument used.
4. Review APA's *Standard for Educational and Psychological Tests*. Present your review to the class.
5. Interview a high school and/or a college counselor concerning their assessment programs for career counseling. Identify the counseling strategies underlying the use of assessment instruments.
6. Request permission from a university counseling center to take (or self-administer and interpret) their battery of tests and inventories used in career counseling. Summarize the results.
7. Review the evaluations of an aptitude test, an achievement test, and one interest, values, personality, and career-maturity inventory in the *Mental Measurements Yearbook*.
8. Write an essay defending this statement: Assessment results can be effectively used in career-counseling programs.
9. Choose one or more of the following situations and develop an assessment battery that can be incorporated in career-exploration programs.

   a. a middle school in a socioeconomically deprived neighborhood
   b. a senior high school from which 70% of the graduates enter college
   c. a community college in a large city
   d. a small four-year college
   e. a large university
   f. a community agency providing career counseling for adults
   g. a rehabilitation agency
   h. a private practice in career counseling

10. Using the following reference, describe a model for using assessment results for career-development counseling.

    Zunker, Vernon G. (1994). *Using assessment results for career development* (4th ed.). Pacific Grove, CA: Brooks/Cole.

Chapter Eight

The Career Resource Center

Until recently, the counselor's career resources typically consisted of a few volumes and a file of career-related materials. A nearby book room or a conveniently located closet served as the storage area for the meager and rather drab-appearing materials available to counselors. Little consideration had been given for developing a centrally located facility for organizing and displaying the materials, mainly because up-to-date materials that appealed to students were difficult to find. Career-related media components were almost nonexistent. In the last decade, this pattern has been drastically reversed due primarily to the career-education movement and a competitive job market, which has focused renewed attention on career guidance. An abundance of career-related materials are on the market today for students at practically all educational levels and including materials for special populations such as older adults, disabled persons, and minority groups. Career resource materials have now been elevated to a position of central importance. The nearby closet and storage room are no longer sufficient, because the attractive career-related materials available today are designed to be openly displayed. In addition to space allotments for traditional printed materials, consideration must also be given to recently developed audiovisual materials and computer-assisted programs. Understandably, considerable attention has been focused on providing a facility that will encourage the use of these materials by students and faculty. In the 1970s, quite a few centrally located facilities for collecting and displaying career-related materials were developed in educational institutions at all levels (Reardon, Zunker, & Dyal, 1979) and in government-sponsored agencies (Vandergoot, 1982). This trend appears to continue in the 1990s (Herr & Cramer, 1992).

The centrally located centers are often referred to as Career Resource Centers (CRCs), Career Information Centers (CICs), or Career Development Resource Centers (CDRCs). In this chapter, we will refer to this type of facility as a CRC. The development of the CRC has paralleled the recent development of a variety of career-counseling and career-education programs. In many respects, the CRC has become the focal point of career-planning and placement programs. The facilities are highly visible and attractive; in effect, they are designed to attract students to make use of career resources and programs.

This chapter covers (1) the purpose and use of a CRC, (2) the rationale for developing a CRC, (3) organizational procedure, (4) functions of an advisory committee, (5) developing objectives, (6) location and posture, (7) resource components, and (8) innovations in the dissemination of career information.

THE PURPOSE AND USE OF A CRC

CRCs have been developed as a major component of career-guidance programs. The management of programs and the use of occupational-information material are major responsibilities of the career counselor. The counselor's understanding of how to use occupational information is highly related to the effectiveness of the CRC. Counselors must also be well acquainted with the content of the various sources of career information. Program development for individual and group use of the center must be carefully planned.

Presentation of materials will vary according to the differing needs of groups and individuals. For example, a senior high school freshman class may be given an overview demonstration of the various resources in the center, while a group of high school juniors are presented with specific resources needed for a class project. Or a group of college students may be given the assignment of researching the various careers in their declared majors.

Individual use of career information is highly personalized, and the counselor must recognize that different learning styles among counselees call for flexibility in the use of career-information resources. Moreover, Sharf (1984) pointed out that information-seeking behavior will vary from counselor to counselor. As counselors help individuals sort and assimilate information, they must also provide direction by generating questions concerning specific information that can be obtained from available resources. Just as career decision making is an individualized process, so too is the use and assimilation of career information.

In sum, the CRC is used by individuals who are in various phases of career decision making; some are seeking information to narrow down choices, while others are searching for answers in the beginning phases of decision making. It is also a place where instructors can meet with groups of students or entire classes for a variety of career-guidance objectives. Finally, the entire professional staff is encouraged to use the center as a resource for ongoing projects.

RATIONALE

Several advantages of a CRC are worthy of consideration. First, a centralized location provides the opportunity to systematically organize all career materials into more efficient and workable units. The centralized facility also provides the opportunity to monitor materials on hand and simplifies the task of maintaining and selecting additional materials.

Second, students and faculty are attracted to centrally displayed materials that are easily accessed. Thus, a wider use of materials is usually assured, and in addition, attention is directed to programs offered by the CRC. In essence, the CRC brings into focus the career-related programs and the career resources offered by an institution.

A third consideration is the methods of promoting coordination and acceptance of career-related programs among faculty, staff, administration, students, and the community. A well-organized and well-operated CRC will encourage a variety of members of an institution to participate in development, programming, and evaluation of CRC materials and facilities. A commitment from a cross section of individuals will greatly enhance the career-guidance efforts offered by an educational institution.

A final consideration is programming innovations for the use of career materials and outreach activities, which are usually generated within the CRC and/or sponsored by the CRC. A well-planned facility can become the focal point in planning new programs and innovative activities for career guidance and career education. In essence, the CRC should facilitate a wide variety of program-development opportunities among staff and faculty.

ORGANIZATIONAL PROCEDURES

In this section, we consider organizational procedures for founding a CRC. The National Career Information Center has published guidelines for establishing a CRC in secondary schools (Burnett, 1977). The following steps have been adapted from these suggestions:

1. Access existing career-guidance service.
2. Create an advisory committee.
3. Determine objectives and the space and budget needed to meet the objectives.
4. Identify the individuals in the school system and the community who are actively involved in disseminating occupational and educational information.
5. Locate and request space, furniture, and equipment.
6. Develop methods of identifying and filing career-related materials.
7. Collect all existing career-related materials.
8. Establish operational procedures.
9. Plan for periodic evaluations.
10. Have a grand opening.

ESTABLISHING AN ADVISORY COMMITTEE

Special attention should be given to creating an advisory committee. Establishing an advisory group is a valuable and effective way to assure early involvement from a cross section of individuals within the institution and community. This procedure is considered an effective strategy for promoting acceptance and support from faculty and community leaders. The membership of this committee may consist of student users, teachers, administrators, counselors, and community members. Representatives of local businesses and industrial complexes should also be part of the advisory group.

At all educational levels where any advisory committee is formed, it is important to include representatives from both the formal academic programs and vocational/technical training segments. At the postsecondary level, alumni are a valuable resource.

In general, the advisory committee establishes guidelines for developing the CRC, initiates early planning programs, sets policy, and eventually acts as a governing body for the appointed director. The following recommendations are for functions of a CRC advisory committee at the secondary level.[1]

1. Develop long- and short-term objectives for a Career Information Center.
2. Establish contacts with local businesses, industrial complexes, manufacturing firms, and labor unions.
3. Review, evaluate, and recommend occupational materials and equipment for purchase.
4. Advise on the establishment of an adequate budget to maintain the center.
5. Initiate and encourage follow-up studies of graduates.
6. Assist in promoting career-education programs within the district.
7. Encourage teachers and counselors to become familiar with industries and businesses in the community via tours. Write entry-level job descriptions for the elementary reading level.
8. Develop a research design for the evaluation of a center.
9. Assist in identifying sources of funding for centers.

The advisory committee is a very important part of a CRC. This committee will greatly determine the direction of the center in developing objectives and budgets and in purchasing occupational materials. As the CRC becomes operational, the committee will also become actively engaged in evaluating programs and revising objectives for future development. A governing board of this type will be able to promote greater acceptance and wider use of a CRC in educational institutions and in government-sponsored agencies. Such a board is particularly important for developing a stronger commitment from the local business community.

DEVELOPING OBJECTIVES

Establishing objectives for a CRC provides a framework for the selection and utilization of materials to meet the career-guidance needs of the institution. Staffing requirements may also be determined by the objectives. Developing objectives will to a large extent depend on local needs and available resources. Therefore, consideration should be given to developing a needs assessment to

---

[1] From Alameda County School Department, *Guidelines for the Establishment of Career Information Centers*, 1972, p. 1.

document specific material and program needs, as well as needs for available resources such as innovative career-related programs and materials being used in academic departments and by individual instructors. An effective needs assessment can help clarify the CRC's goals and objectives and identify available career materials as well as ongoing career-related programs. Criteria that should be included in the assessment are (1) the existing resources; (2) how current the materials are, and how much they are being used; (3) the career-guidance services currently available; (4) any support services for career guidance; (5) the personnel providing career-guidance services; (6) the scope and sequence of career-education programs; (7) the career-related materials used in career-education programs; (8) available community resources; and (9) other related career-guidance programs.

Although educational institutions and governmental agencies may develop similar objectives, they may differ significantly in organizational structure and programming needs. Therefore, consideration of the following objectives—developed for a CRC by Dittenhafer and Lewis (1973, p. 1)—must take into account the specific programs, functions, and related activities that are necessary to meet the needs identified by an assessment.

1. To collect, evaluate, and disseminate accurate and relevant career information;
2. To provide assistance to the center's clientele in locating, evaluating, and using career information;
3. To help students integrate self-knowledge with relevant career information by providing counseling services;
4. To assist the faculty in integrating information into the instructional activities to support students' career development;
5. To assist parents in becoming active, concerned, and understanding participants in the career development of their children; and
6. To utilize community resources in fostering a better understanding of the relationship of education to work.

In summary, objectives can be developed after the institution's needs have been assessed and evaluated. Objectives should be developed with the help of a cross section of professional personnel and user groups. The objectives should communicate the CRC's purpose, programs, user groups, and materials collected. A well-developed, clearly stated set of objectives will set the pattern for staffing, space, equipment, and materials needed, as well as establish lines of communication with students, instructors, administrators, alumni, and the community.

LOCATION AND POSTURE

Once the CRC's objectives have been determined, its space requirements are more easily identified. In most instances, the CRC will be viewed as a multipurpose center from which a number of career-related programs and activities will evolve. The CRC may be a focal place for all career-related programs, providing a setting in which all interested parties may browse through materials. Thus, it will become a central meeting place for students, instructors, counselors, and administrators. In essence, the CRC becomes the hub of activities from which a variety of programs may be launched and to which a variety of programs may be directed. In view of the potential activities, the considerations of space and location are of major importance. Ideally, elaborate plans for constructing a new facility or for extensive remodeling would be recommended. However, in view of the increasing demand for reduced expenditures in education and in state agencies, one may have to settle for something less than ideal.

The location of the CRC should be in a high-traffic area of the campus. The importance of exposure and accessibility for students and faculty should be among the primary considerations in determining location. Existing classrooms are considered good prospective locations, and in some cases only minor modifications are necessary. In many secondary schools, existing counseling centers can be modified or adjacent classrooms converted to accommodate a CRC. Locating the CRC within or adjacent to the counseling center enables the most effective use of existing staff and administration. In addition, students are usually accustomed to going to counseling centers for assistance, and the CRC programs can be easily incorporated into other services offered within the center.

At postsecondary institutions, most CRCs are organized and supervised by the Career Planning and Placement Center (Reardon, Zunker, & Dyal, 1979). In some instances, the counseling center has incorporated a CRC within its program structure. (The floor plans for a CRC located within a career planning and placement office for a university and community college are shown in Chapter 11.) The CRC may also be placed within the library facility or within existing learning resource centers. In both these cases, local conditions would determine the feasibility of these locations. The major considerations include the possibility of using existing equipment, materials, and space, and the accessibility to both students and staff.

The CRC should not take on an institutional look but rather should communicate just the opposite atmosphere. The rationale is that the physical arrangement should be student-oriented and appear rather casual and relaxed. Students should feel welcome to browse through the attractively displayed materials.

Various media components should also be considered in the floor plans. Places for viewing filmstrips, television, and microfilm and listening to audio components such as cassettes will be needed. Placement of computer terminals also requires careful planning. Most of the media components may be used for individual study as well as for group programs.

RESOURCE COMPONENTS

This section describes resource components that may be selected for a CRC. The component categories were arbitrarily chosen and should not necessarily be considered as a format for a filing system. The categories are logical divisions of currently available career-related materials and recently developed career-counseling programs, however, and at least suggest ways to organize materials and program units to meet local needs.

All of the resource components discussed are designed to provide information for career-counseling programs and career-education instructional units. Most of them provide specific information for educational and vocational planning, while a few provide techniques and strategies for developing skills needed for career planning. A list of applicable publications is provided for each component. Each list is representative but not exhaustive.

Access to the CRC's resources is a primary consideration. Instructions on how to use various resources may be given through individual or group orientation sessions or modules. An effective entry system can provide the user with a review of the resources available and the most direct means of making use of these resources.

A number of specific information-resource components should be considered, including (1) occupational descriptions, (2) occupational-outlook projections, (3) postsecondary education and training information, (4) military information, (5) apprenticeship and internship information, (6) information for special populations (for example, minorities and individuals with disabilities), (7) a resource-persons file, and (8) financial aid information. (All of these resource components are included in the computer-assisted career-guidance systems discussed in Chapter 6.) In addition, to help students assimilate all this information, components that promote effective career planning should be considered as well. And finally, a wide variety of audiovisual materials are available to augment information and career-planning resources.

Occupational Descriptions

Occupational descriptions are one of the CRC's major information components. They may be found in a wide variety of attractively designed materials. There are publications that describe occupations in a straightforward and nontechnical narrative form, while others like the *Dictionary of Occupational Titles (DOT)* provide very technical descriptions. Occupational information that can generally be retrieved includes (1) salary, (2) work activities, (3) working conditions, (4) physical demands of the occupation, (5) employment locations, (6) employment outlook, and (7) sources of additional information. The following list provides examples of the range of materials available.

> *Dictionary of Occupational Titles*
> Superintendent of Documents
> U.S. Government Printing Office
> Washington, DC 20402
>
> *Encyclopedia of Careers and Vocational Guidance*
> Doubleday and Company, Inc.
> 501 Franklin Avenue
> Garden City, NY 11530

Occupational Briefs
Chronicle Guidance Publications, Inc.
Moravia, NY 13118

Occupational-Outlook Projections

The competitive job market has not only increased the concern for job-outlook information but also for technical and industrial developments. As a result, many individuals are at least partially basing their career decisions on projections of future job needs. This component has become increasingly popular. In addition to the following sources listed, the CRC staff should investigate local, state, and regional sources of labor forecasts. State employment agencies and other state and federal agencies are active in developing job-forecast information and provide excellent resources for this component.

Occupational Outlook Handbook
Superintendent of Documents
U.S. Government Printing Office
Washington, DC 20402

Occupational Outlook for College Graduates
Superintendent of Documents
U.S. Government Printing Office
Washington, DC 20402

Modern Vocational Trends Reference Handbook
Juvenal L. Angel
Monarch Press
Division of Simon and Schuster, Inc.
12th Floor, 1320 Avenue of the Americas
New York, NY 10020

Postsecondary Education and Training

This component provides information about education and training program opportunities and the entry requirements of specific occupations. For ease of access, this component may be subdivided into three categories: (1) two- and four-year colleges, (2) technical-school programs, and (3) continuing-education opportunities.

College program information may be organized into one component for secondary students who are selecting a two- or four-year institution, or one for currently enrolled and graduating students seeking transfer and graduate school information. The college information desired usually includes (1) geographical locations, (2) tuition, (3) financial aid, (4) type of institution, (5) accreditation, (6) special programs, (7) college calendars, (8) campus life, (9) cultural activities, (10) residence policies, (11) social organizations, (12) religious services, (13) academic characteristics of the student body, (14) median freshman entrance test scores, (15) freshmen attrition, (16) faculty, (17) campus activities, and (18) athletic programs. In addition to the catalogs published by most institutions, a number of independent publications provide general information about most accredited institutions in the United States. Representative examples are listed later on in this section.

Vocational, trade, and technical-school information should include a listing of postsecondary programs and private and public schools that offer specific entry-level trade and technical training. In particular, a listing of local, regional, and statewide programs would be most appropriate. This file may be augmented with national publications to provide general information about the trade and technical programs, and with a compilation of brochures that are usually disseminated free of charge by individual schools.

In most areas of the country, a number of outreach continuing-education programs provide entry-level and advanced occupational training. A file of information about local continuing-education programs can make the CRC more flexible in meeting a wide range of needs. Periodic announcements to interested individuals through available community media will increase the use of this information. Nationally published resources provide examples of the type of programs in continuing education. A few of these are listed as follows:

College Information Publications

American Universities and Colleges
Otis A. Singletary and Jane P. Newman, Eds.
American Council on Education
1 Dupont Circle
Washington, DC 20036

The College Blue Book
Macmillan Information Corporation
866 Third Avenue
New York, NY 10022

American Junior Colleges
Edmund J. Gleazer, Ed.
American Council on Education
1 Dupont Circle
Washington, DC 20036

Vocational, Trade, and Technical-School Publications

Lovejoy's Career and Vocational School Guide—A Handbook of Job-Training Opportunities
Clarence E. Lovejoy
Simon and Schuster, Inc.
1230 Avenue of the Americas
New York, NY 10020

Continuing-Education Publications

Guide to Continuing Education in America
College Entrance Examination Board
Quadrangle Books, Inc.
330 Madison Avenue
New York, NY 10017

So You Want to Go Back to School—Facing the Realities of Reentry
Elinor Lenz and Mar Hansen Shaevitz
McGraw-Hill Book Company
1221 Avenue of the Americas
New York, NY 10036

Military Information

Another component provides information about military careers. Students generally find this component of interest because all branches of the military provide information covering special training programs. This component may provide job descriptions found in the military and related civilian jobs. The local addresses of the recruiting centers should be included. The U.S. military provides the following publications on career-related subjects:

Military Career Guide
U.S. Military Entrance Processing Command
2500 Green Bay Road
North Chicago, IL 60064

The U.S. Army Career and Education Guide
Available in three editions: Student Edition; Audio/Visual
Edition; and Counselor Edition
Army Careers
U.S. Army Recruiting Command
Hampton, VA 23369

Navy Career Guide
Chief of Naval Personnel
Dept. of the Navy
Washington, DC 20370

Air Force Information
Headquarters, U.S. Air Force Recruiting Service
Attn: Director of Advertising and Publicity
Wright Patterson Air Force Base, OH 45433

Apprenticeship and Internship Information

There is a recognized need for students to gain firsthand experience with occupations they are considering. Moreover, on-the-job training is still a very viable part of our occupational education system, and for many occupations, apprenticeship training is required. The current work-experience programs found in many educational institutions have brought a renewed interest in apprenticeship and experiential training programs. The CRC staff will want to investigate state agencies and local business and industry to compile a localized list of these programs. The following publications are examples of this type of resource:

> *Directory of Internships, Work Experience Programs*
> *and On-the-Job Training Opportunities*
> Ready References Press
> Specialized Indexes, Inc.
> 100 East Thousand Oaks Blvd., Suite 224
> Thousand Oaks, CA 91360

> *First Supplement to the Directory: On-the-Job Training*
> *and Where to Get It*
> Robert Liston and Julian Messner
> Simon and Schuster
> 1230 Avenue of the Americas
> New York, NY 10020

> *Alternative to College*
> Miriam Hecht and Lillian Traub
> Macmillan Information
> 866 Third Avenue
> New York, NY 10022

Information for Special Populations

In recent years a considerable amount of material has been published to facilitate employment of minorities, individuals with disabilities, and women. Sources of material for minorities and individuals with disabilities include the U.S. Department of Labor and other federal, state, and local agencies. The target populations reached through this component are provided with a means to increase their career options. Publications generally focus on issues faced by racial and ethnic minorities and individuals with disabilities in job-placement situations. However, a substantial segment of the material discusses available training, education programs, and special financial aid programs to assist these groups.

Information about opportunities for women should contrast traditional and nontraditional jobs open to women and cover state, local, and private agencies and organizations especially designed to help women. The following national publications address special population groups:

Individuals with Disabilities

Your Handicap—Don't Let It Handicap You
Sarah Splauver, Ed., and Julian Messner
Simon and Schuster
1230 Avenue of the Americas
New York, NY 10020

Directory for Exceptional Children
Porter Sargent Publishers, Inc.
11 Beacon Street
Boston, MA 02108

Minorities

Equal Employment Opportunities for Minority Group College Graduates: Locating, Recruiting, Employing
Robert Calvert, Jr.
Garrett Park Press
Garrett Park, MD 20766

Placing Minority Women in Professional Jobs
Superintendent of Documents
U.S. Government Printing Office
Washington, DC 20402

Women

Five Hundred Back-to-Work Ideas for Housewives
Barbara Prentice and Peter Sandman
Macmillan Publishing Co., Inc.
Riverside, NJ 08075

Career Guidance for Young Women: Considerations in Planning
Professional Careers
John G. Cull and Richard F. Hardy
Charles C. Thomas, Publisher
301-327 E. Lawrence Avenue
Springfield, IL 62717

I Can Be Anything: Careers and Colleges for Young Women
Joyce Slayton Mitchell
Bantam Books, Inc.
414 E. Golf Road
Des Plaines, IL 60016

Resource-Persons File

This component lists individuals from various types of occupations who volunteer to serve as resource persons. Using this resource, personal visits arranged by the CRC allow the student to make on-site investigations of a particular occupation. The name, address, telephone number, occupational field, and appointment instructions are recorded for each resource person in the file. Recorded interviews of resource persons can provide another means of personalizing occupational information. Local industrial and business directories and employment surveys of former students can serve as a valuable resource for developing a resource-persons file. At the higher education level, college alumni associations may be of great assistance in locating volunteers for the file.

Financial Aid Information

This component should include the usual types of financial aid such as loans, grants, and scholarships from federal, state, private, and local sources. Emphasis is most often placed on both local and statewide sources. A selective list of financial aid officers may also prove to be helpful. The following publications offer information on financial aid:

Scholarships, Fellowships and Loans
Bellman Publishing Co.
P.O. Box 164
Arlington, MA 02174

Financial Aids for Higher Education
William C. Brown Co., Publisher
2460 Kerper Blvd.
Dubuque, IA 52001

How to Get Money for: Education, Fellowships and Scholarships
Chilton Book Co.
School Library Services
201 King of Prussia Rd.
Radnor, PA 19089

Career-Planning Resources

To assist students in the most efficient use of career-information resources, components that promote effective career-planning skills should be considered for inclusion in the CRC. These components may be designed for independent use but will probably be more effective if used in conjunction with ongoing career counseling. Career-planning resource components may include (1) career decision making, (2) vocational assessment, (3) job-search skills, and (4) job simulation.

Career Decision Making

The purpose of this component is to provide resources for teaching career decision-making techniques and self-help materials. The materials collected for this component may be used in seminars for a variety of group sessions, including seminars for older adults. A wide range of material is also available for individual study of career decision-making techniques. The following publications represent a small sample of a wide range of available materials on this topic.

Effective Personal and Career Decision Making
Karl Bartsch, Elizabeth B. Yost, and Kristen W. Girrell
Westinghouse Learning Corporation
100 Park Avenue
New York, NY 10017

Career Skills Assessment Program
The College Board
888 Seventh Avenue
New York, NY 10019

Decision Making for Career Development
Donald H. Parker, Shelby W. Parker, and William H. Tryback
Science Research Associates, Inc.
Order Department
155 North Wacker Drive
Chicago, IL 60606

Guided Career Exploration
Donald E. Super and JoAnn Bowlsbey
The Psychological Corporation
555 Academic Court
San Antonio, TX 78204-2498

Vocational Assessment

A variety of tests and inventories are available for this component, including standardized cognitive measures of intelligence, achievement, aptitudes, and career maturity as well as noncognitive inventories (some of which are self-administered) of interests and other personal characteristics. While most of these measures should be used in conjunction with a counseling program, self-administered personal-assessment devices can be designed to promote self-awareness for career-decision purposes. Representative examples of tests and inventories are listed in Chapter 7.

Job-Search Skills

This component primarily provides self-help materials that assist individuals in developing interviewing skills, writing a résumé, and locating sources of job openings. There are numerous outstanding publications covering these topics. The following list is representative of the materials available.

What Color Is Your Parachute? (A Practical Manual for Job Hunters and Career Changers)
Richard Nelson Bolles
Ten Speed Press
P.O. Box 7123
Berkeley, CA 94707

How to Get a Better Job Quicker
Taplinger Publishing Co., Inc.
200 Park Avenue South
New York, NY 10003

Job-Simulation Component

Career counselors have long recognized the value of experiential-learning activities in helping individuals make realistic career decisions. Job-simulation exercises provide real-life experiences. The resources listed provide learning experiences that simulate working-world reality. Individuals are provided with learning experiences in exploring career fields and life and leisure activities, and they are given feedback on decisions made in the process.

Life Career Game
Sarane S. Boocock
Sage Publications, Inc.
211 W. Hillcrest Drive
Newbury Park, CA 91320

Job Experience Kit
Science Research Associates, Inc.
Order Department
155 North Wacker Drive
Chicago, IL 60606

Audiovisual Materials

Many types of audiovisual materials (including filmstrips, cassettes, microfiche, films, and videotapes) are available to augment CRC information and career-planning resources. Career-related information communicated via audiovisual media can often provide a refreshing break from traditional resource materials. Locally prepared audiovisual materials may be developed in addition to commercially prepared media aids. The following list gives examples of publishers of career-related audiovisual material.

A/V Media in Career Development
College Placement Council, Inc.
P.O. Box 2263
Bethlehem, PA 18001

The Multi-Media Catalog
American Personnel and Guidance Association
Subscription Department
1607 New Hampshire Avenue, N.W.
Washington, DC 20009

Audio Visual Market Place; a Multimedia Guide
R. R. Bowker Order Dept.
P.O. Box 1807
Ann Arbor, MI 48106

INNOVATIONS IN DISSEMINATION OF CAREER INFORMATION

The increasing attention focused on labor forecasts and occupational data has created a genuine concern among career-guidance professionals that career information be made more flexible, accessible, and attractive. Career-resource materials in their traditional form can be restructured and creatively combined with nontraditional sources of material for innovative dissemination. Currently, a number of CRCs throughout the country have developed innovative means of disseminating and calling attention to their available resources. Career monographs, newsletters, posters, and other media are used to enhance access to information. These publications usually contain the employment outlook for various careers, the nature of the work, and the job status of recent graduates.

Using Past Job-Order Requests

Career-planning and placement centers use past job-order requests as a means of locating prospective employers for individuals seeking placement. This material is collected by compiling the job-order requests received during the previous year in a notebook according to the date they were processed. Students are directed to scan this file for locating prospective employers who have hired individuals with qualifications similar to their own. For example, by identifying several companies that have recently hired tax accountants, the accounting major is provided with a list of prospective employers. In addition, the job-order file provides information on (1) careers available in the community, (2) actual requirements of a particular occupation, (3) realistic job descriptions, and (4) organizations that were hiring at the time the job order was processed.

Audiotapes of Major Fields of Study

Career-counseling centers are developing audiotapes that describe major fields of study offered by an institution. The taped interviews usually include the department chairperson outlining areas of specialization available to students in each major field. The tapes may be structured in a variety of formats but usually contain the following information: (1) occupational forecasts for graduates in each major, (2) the occupations and graduate programs selected by previous graduates, (3) aspects of personal satisfaction experienced by others in each major field of study, and (4) special considerations for each department such as student/faculty ratio, strength of the department, research opportunities available, and other special considerations.

Videotape File

The use of videotaped presentations of individuals representing certain career fields is another innovative delivery system currently being used in some centers. These tapes may be in the form of an interview, lecture, question-and-answer format, or a combination of all three. They are often taped during career awareness week when presentations are being made to student groups. In this way, the center builds a videotape library of individuals discussing their field of work. Through these videotapes, students are able to obtain firsthand accounts of job descriptions and current requirements of particular jobs in a given career field. The videotapes appear to be an attractive method of communicating current job requirements.

Career Resource Centers in Industrial Organizations

This chapter has been primarily devoted to the discussion of CRCs in educational institutions and in state agencies; however, industrial organizations are also interested in supporting CRCs for their employees (Moir, 1981). The purpose is to assist employees in their career development through a variety of resource components similar to those found in educational institutions. A good example of a CRC in an industry is the one established in 1976 by the University of California's Lawrence Livermore National Laboratory (LLNL) in Livermore. The LLNL is an organization devoted to applied research consisting of several thousand employees, including scientists, engineers, technicians, administrators, and clerical personnel. The CRC was established to provide information to interested employees about educational opportunities, career development, reference material for on-site training courses, and resources for training managers and supervisors (Moir, 1981).

The resource components in the LLNL CRC consist of the following: (1) educational information (catalogs of all colleges within 100 miles and other educational programs); (2) career planning (occupational references, methods for job seeking, career guides, and career-planning theory); (3) world of work (resources for job opportunities and training requirements); (4) personal growth (books and cassettes containing such topics as adult development, alcoholism, employee development, assertiveness training, retirement, stress and time management, and women's issues); (5) management/supervision (resources for improving leadership effectiveness, interviewing, and managerial behavior); (6) computerized career-information system (*The Guidance Information System [GIS]* as discussed in Chapter 6 is used); (7) periodicals (professional journals and newsletters); (8) self-study (resources for personal improvement, including in-house programs on employee development, and several courses of study, including English grammar); and (9) off-site training (resources on seminars and conventions).

The LLNL CRC has been used for educational information (25% of inquiries), management supervision (15%), job-finding skills (10%), off-site training (5%), and self-study (5%) (Moir, 1981). In the first five years of its existence, the LLNL CRC received the endorsement of management and was used by a wide range of employees, including senior scientists as well as individuals in entry-level positions. Moir (1981) suggested that the career development of employees is a good rationale for maintaining interest and creativity in industrial organizations. CRCs also provide supervisors and managers with a referral source in support of career-path and developmental programs as discussed in Chapter 12.

The reported innovations for using career information are only representative examples of methods in use today. We have merely scratched the surface of methodology for making the working world a relevant and meaningful part of our educational programs. It is only a matter of time before teachers and counselors build a vast volume of techniques and programs that will improve the understanding of the relatively unknown working world. The examples of innovations discussed verify that the study of occupational data can be interesting and certainly informative!

SUMMARY

1. In the past decade, centrally located facilities for collecting and displaying career-related materials have been developed in educational institutions at all levels. The centrally located centers have often been referred to as Career Resource Centers (CRCs).

2. A CRC provides the opportunity to systematically organize all career materials into more efficient and workable units.

3. Organizational procedures include the establishment of an advisory committee consisting of a cross section of faculty members and the local business community.

4. Objectives and operational procedures for the CRC will, to a large extent, depend on local needs and available resources.

5. The ideal location for a CRC is in high-traffic areas of the campus. Existing classrooms and counseling centers may be modified to accommodate a CRC. Ideally the CRC consists of space for individual study, group meetings, browsing, displays, audiovisual equipment, and computer programs.

6. A number of specific information-resource components considered for the CRC include (a) occupational descriptions, (b) occupational-outlook projec-

tions, (c) postsecondary educational and training information, (d) military information, (e) apprenticeship and internship information, (f) information for special
populations, (g) a resource-persons file, and (h) financial aid information.

7. Resource components that promote effective career-planning skills
include (a) career decision making, (b) vocational assessment, (c) job-search
skills, and (d) job simulation.

8. Innovative programs for dissemination of career information include
career monographs that provide information to college students on employment outlook, nature of work, and job status of recent graduates, by major
fields of study. Past job-order requests in placement centers are used in career-
counseling programs to provide information on careers available in the community, actual requirements of a particular occupation, realistic job descriptions, and organizations that were hiring at the time the job order was
processed. University placement centers are also collecting audiotapes that
describe major fields of study offered at the university. Videotape files of individuals representing certain career fields are another innovative delivery system being used in career-planning and placement offices. Industrial
organizations are interested in supporting CRCs for employee use.

SUPPLEMENTARY LEARNING EXERCISES

1. Visit a CRC and report on the following:

   a. resource-component classification system used
   b. square footage and floor plan
   c. programs serviced by the CRC
   d. resource materials used
   e. filing system
   f. organizational structure

2. Design and rationalize a floor plan for a CRC for one or more of the following:

   a. middle school
   b. senior high school
   c. community two-year college
   d. four-year college
   e. community center offering career counseling to adults

3. Select and name the resource components that you consider are most needed by a
   community college and a four-year college. Rank the components in order and
   defend your choices.

4. Select and name the resource components that you feel are essential for a middle
   school, high school, and community agency providing career counseling to adults.
   Defend your choices.

5. Assume that you were selected as a career counselor in a local high school and
   were asked to establish a CRC. Develop the goals, objectives, organizational structure, and rationale.

6. Describe the strategies you would use for improving the use of a CRC for career-
   education programs in a middle school.

PART TWO

CAREER–GUIDANCE PROGRAMS IN EDUCATIONAL INSTITUTIONS

Chapter Nine
Implications of Developmental Patterns and Research for Career Guidance in Schools

Chapter Ten
Career Guidance in Schools

Chapter Eleven
Career Guidance in Institutions of Higher Learning

Chapter Nine

Implications of Developmental Patterns and Research for Career Guidance in Schools

Human development is not an isolated, detached, or unrelated series of events in life, but rather a blend of diverse elements including psychosocial and economic variables. These interacting elements formulate life stages and cover the entire life span. Understanding human development is one of the essential ingredients leading to a greater comprehension and interpretation of career-development stages and tasks.

Selected models of human development and related research are discussed in this chapter. The discussion focuses on issues that may be used to develop career-guidance programs for elementary school children and adolescents in junior and senior high schools.

The vast number and variety of human development studies include many research models and theoretical orientations from several academic disciplines, including developmental psychology. Understandably, there are differences of opinion about how to interpret this accumulated wealth of information and how to apply it to programs and practices in career guidance. However, the interrelationships between human and career development are becoming more clear as investigators carry out more complete and sophisticated experiments and apply their results to more comprehensive sets of principles. Of course, more research is still needed to provide definitive evidence of relationships between career and human developmental models, but meanwhile human developmental models and selected research provide career counselors with a greater understanding of their task of building goals and developing career-guidance programs.

This chapter is divided into three sections that explore the developmental patterns of and selected research on elementary school children, junior high school students, and senior high school students. At the end of each section, implications for career-guidance programs are presented.

STUDIES OF EARLY CHILDHOOD DEVELOPMENT

Early childhood, especially the first three years, has been previously designated as the most formative years in human development (White, 1959). Before the

1970s, child development specialists seemed convinced that the first three years greatly determined a person's future motives, drives, and behavior. More recently, this viewpoint has gradually shifted to a more adaptive view of human development over the life span. Moreover, each stage of development has its own set of unique tasks to be accomplished for a smooth transition.

In studying human development over the life span, Biehler and Hudson (1986) reviewed several longitudinal studies:

1. Early personality tendencies may be diverted by the experiences one has during subsequent stages of development.
2. Predictions of adult adjustment based on child behavior were often found to be inaccurate. Individuals have a profound adaptive capacity at various stages of development.
3. Even the negative impact of infant deprivation does not have a permanent negative effect for all children.

These results suggest that *all* stages of human development are important. Infancy may better be viewed as a very important and sensitive period in an individual's development rather than one necessarily having a permanent impact on later behavior. Moreover, the impressive adaptive capacity found in human development longitudinal studies illustrates the importance of developmental tasks at different stages of the life span.

STAGES OF DEVELOPMENT AND DEVELOPMENTAL TASKS FOR ELEMENTARY SCHOOL CHILDREN

Stage theorists have concentrated on developmental patterns that take the form of accomplishments, events, and psychological, physiological, and sociological changes in human development. During the transition process from one stage to another, developmental tasks provide a description of requirements or actions that are necessary to pass successfully through a stage of development. This perspective suggests a foundation for building effective career-guidance programs. Only selected theories and research are summarized here; more in-depth coverage of these subjects can be found in developmental psychology textbooks.

Tables 9-1 through 9-3 summarize the continuity of development by stages, ages, grades in school, and the developmental tasks assigned to stages. Erikson's (1963) developmental stages have been selected as a good example of the stage theorists' approach; Piaget's (1929) research has been selected to illustrate cognitive development; and Havighurst's (1972) well-known work is a good example of developmental tasks over the life span. Other developmental stages and tasks will be discussed when relevant.

According to Havighurst, the developmental tasks expected of students before leaving the sixth grade reveal a set of physical and academic skills, social role development, and personalized values. Practically all of these tasks can be related to Super's (1990) concept of career-development tasks (see Chapter 2). For example, during the growth stage (ages 0 to 14), according to Super's scheme

TABLE 9-1
Havighurst's Developmental Stages

Developmental tasks of infancy and early childhood
1. Learning to walk
2. Learning to take solid foods
3. Learning to talk
4. Learning to control the elimination of body wastes
5. Learning sex differences and sexual modesty
6. Forming concepts and learning language to describe social and physical reality
7. Preparing to read
8. Learning to distinguish right and wrong, and the beginning of conscience development

Developmental tasks of middle childhood (ages 6 to 12 years)
1. Learning physical skills necessary for ordinary games
2. Building wholesome attitudes toward oneself as a growing organism
3. Learning to get along with peers
4. Learning an appropriate masculine or feminine social role
5. Developing fundamental skills in reading, writing, and calculating
6. Developing concepts necessary for everyday living
7. Developing morality, a conscience, and a scale of values
8. Achieving personal independence
9. Developing attitudes toward social groups and institutions

Developmental tasks of adolescence (ages 12 to 18 years)
1. Achieving new and more mature relations with peers of both sexes
2. Achieving a masculine or feminine role in society
3. Accepting one's physique and using the body effectively
4. Achieving emotional independence from parents and other adults
5. Preparing for marriage and family life
6. Preparing for an economic career
7. Acquiring a set of values and an ethical system as a guide to behavior—developing an ideology
8. Desiring and achieving socially responsible behavior

Developmental tasks of early adulthood (ages 19 to 30 years)
1. Selecting a mate
2. Learning to live with a marriage partner
3. Starting a family
4. Rearing a family
5. Managing a home
6. Getting started in an occupation
7. Taking on civic responsibility
8. Finding a congenial social group

Developmental tasks of middle age (ages 30 to 60 years)
1. Assisting teenage children to become responsible and happy adults
2. Achieving adult social and civic responsibility
3. Reaching and maintaining satisfactory performance in one's occupational career
4. Developing adult leisure-time activities
5. Relating to one's spouse as a person
6. Accepting and adjusting to the physiological changes of middle age
7. Adjusting to aging parents

TABLE 9-1
(continued)

Developmental tasks of later maturity (ages over 60 years)
1. Adjusting to decreasing physical strength and health
2. Death of a spouse
3. Adjusting to retirement and reduced income
4. Establishing an explicit affiliation with one's age group
5. Adopting and adapting social roles in a flexible way
6. Establishing satisfactory physical living arrangements

SOURCE: *Developmental Tasks and Education*, 3rd edition (pp. 9–113) by Robert J. Havighurst. ©1972 by Longman Inc. Reprinted by permission of Longman Inc., New York.

TABLE 9-2
Piaget's Stages of Cognitive Development

Sensorimotor stage (0 to 2 years)
Individuals develop schemes through senses and motor actions.

Preoperational stage (2 to 5 years)
During this stage, individuals develop symbolic images but have little ability to perceptualize viewpoints other than their own.

Concrete operational stage (6 to 12 years)
This is the beginning phase of understanding differences by means of stimuli. Children solve problems only by generalizing from concrete experiences.

Formal operational stage (adolescence)
At this stage, the ability to utilize hypothetical/deductive thinking provides many solutions to a problem rather than a single answer. Individuals are able to deal with abstractions and engage in mental manipulations.

SOURCE: Adapted from Piaget, 1929.

of developmental stages and tasks, individuals go through numerous experiential learning activities while developing greater self-awareness. Directed experiences in the elementary school that promote physical and academic growth, interpersonal relationships with members of the same and the opposite sex, and self-concept development are important components of career development. Students who fail to achieve the developmental tasks in both Havighurst's and Super's steps may require special attention and direction.

In related studies of children's development in elementary school, Kagan and Moss (1962) concluded that the first four years of school are critical in terms of long-term influences on future lifestyle. These researchers reviewed longitudinal research projects conducted at the Fels Institute in which children were followed into adulthood. The results suggest that well-established behavioral tendencies in elementary school children show up in young adults.

Erikson suggested that the stage of development from ages 6 to 11 emphasizes industriousness; that is, children learn that productivity brings recognition and reward. In Erikson's view, children develop a sense of industriousness

TABLE 9-3
Stages of Psychosocial Development

Trust versus mistrust (0 to 1 years)
Order in the environment and consistency in the quality of care lead to trust. Inconsistency and unpredictable care lead to mistrust.

Autonomy versus doubt (1 to 3 years)
Opportunities to explore or try out skills provide a sense of autonomy. Excessive rejection and lack of support lead to doubt.

Initiative versus guilt (3 to 5 years)
Freedom to express self through activities and language creates a sense of initiative, while some restrictions create a sense of guilt.

Industry versus inferiority (6 to 11 years)
Freedom to make things and to organize them leads to a sense of being industrious. Persistent failure to produce or to perform valued activities leads to a sense of inferiority.

Identity versus role confusion (11 to 18 years)
Through a multitude of experiences in different environments, the individual seeks continuity and sameness of self in search of an identity. Confusion may lead to a negative identity, perhaps a socially unacceptable one.

Intimacy versus isolation (young adulthood)
Commitment in terms of reaching out to others for a lasting relationship leads to intimacy. Isolation and a lack of close personal relationships is a result of competitive and combative behavior.

Generativity versus stagnation (middle age)
During this stage one concentrates on guiding and preparing the next generation. Focusing primarily on self creates a sense of stagnation.

Integrity versus despair (old age)
A sense of integrity is developed from acceptance of one's life and satisfaction with past achievements and accomplishments. Despair comes from the perception that life has been unsatisfying and misdirected.

SOURCE: Adapted from Erikson, 1963.

through accomplishments but may be intimidated by the requirements of success and develop a sense of inferiority. Expressing success through academic achievement, for example, is a major contributor to establishing industriousness in terms of work-role and self-concept development. A sense of inferiority at this stage of development calls for intervention strategies of an individualized nature.

Learning Through Concrete Experiences and Observations

Piaget (1929), noted for his work in cognitive development, has provided a description of how humans think and what the characteristics are of their thinking at different stages of development. In early development, children cultivate "schemes" through their senses and motor activities. During the years 2 through 5, children begin to develop conceptual levels but do not yet have the ability to think logically or abstractly. By the time children reach elementary school age, they have developed the ability to apply logic to thinking and can understand simple concepts. Through concrete experiences children learn to make consistent generalizations. For example, children learn to classify persons or objects in more than one category (the Little League coach can also be a police officer).

Encouraging and directing concrete experiences to promote increasingly abstract conceptual operations during this stage of development is a vital part of educational and career-guidance programming in elementary schools. An example of an exercise illustrating this process would be asking students to identify one type of skill necessary for good schoolwork and then asking them to identify a job that requires a specific school subject.

Observation is also a contributing element to early cognitive development. The social-learning model discussed in Chapter 2 emphasizes the importance of observation learning, attributed to reactions to consequences, observable results of actions, and reactions to others (Mitchell and Krumboltz, 1990). Children are particularly prone to adopting the behavior of models they observe (Thelen et al., 1981). According to Bandura (1977), there are five stages of observable learning: (1) paying attention, (2) remembering what is observed, (3) reproducing actions, (4) becoming motivated (to reproduce what is observed), and (5) perfecting an imitation according to what was observed. Within this frame of reference, parents, teachers, teachers' aides, and classmates are potential models that elementary school children will imitate. Of course, models may come from other sources, such as television, movies, and books. The potential benefits of observational learning for career development of elementary school children are of major importance. Directed observable learning experiences involving work roles are an important component of early career-guidance programs.

Self-Concept Development

In Chapter 2, brief mention was made of Super's self-concept theory and its pervasive nature (Super, Starishesky, Matlin, & Jordaan, 1963). In a later publication, Super (1990) clarified his position on the nature and scope of self-concept in career development. Individuals, in Super's view, have constellations of self-concepts or "self-concept systems" that denote sets or constellations of traits. In an elementary school setting, for example, an individual may have a different view of self as a student and as a member of a peer group. An individual may see himself or herself as gregarious while also being a weak student or not very intelligent. Elementary students are formulating sets of self-concepts as they focus on class requirements, interrelationships with peers, teachers, and important adults, and the social structure in which they live and function.

Self-concept development is not a static phenomenon, but an ongoing process, which changes sometimes gradually and sometimes abruptly as people and situations change. In elementary school, children experience for the first time many aspects of existence in an adult world, such as competition and expectations of productive performance. In play, they interact with peers and also assume roles in supervised and unsupervised situations. Self-esteem for some will be enhanced through academic achievement, while others will experience both positive and negative feedback in peer-socialization activities. Enhanced self-esteem encourages development of personal ideas and opinions of a positive nature; accurate self-concepts contribute to career maturity.

Play as a Factor in Career Development

Examining the period of childhood before age 11, Ginzburg and associates (1951) theorized that various occupational roles are assumed in play, resulting in initial value judgments of the world of work. Engaging in such activities is intrinsically rewarding for children, but their expressed occupational choices are made with little regard for reality. However, by the middle of the elementary school years, work orientation displaces play orientation. Similarly, Elkind (1971) and Gibson, Mitchell, and Basile (1993) suggested that children in the upper elementary grades have developed a more realistic view of the adult world—that is, a sense of independence and self-reliance.

Self-attributes become more prominent among children in upper elementary grades, causing them to intensify their focus on personal likes and dislikes.

Physical Development of Elementary School Children

Physical growth and maturation during the elementary school years play a major role in psychosocial development. Of particular significance is the noticeable difference in growth rate between boys and girls. At 6 years of age, girls are on the average slightly shorter than boys, but by age 10, they are as tall or taller. The average age of puberty for girls is 12.5; for boys, 14 (Tanner, 1972). Many American girls reach puberty before they finish the sixth grade.

Differences in growth and physiological changes between girls and boys in elementary school greatly influence social relationships and emerging self-perceptions. Learning appropriate masculine or feminine roles, according to Havighurst (1972), precludes greater equality between sexes, especially in occupational behavior. Of particular importance are perceptions of appropriate behavior patterns; that is, patterns regarded as acceptable for a given sex. Sex-role stereotyping is fostered through observation and imitation of male and female models. Other influences come through textbooks and other books describing and depicting differences in roles for boys and girls. See Chapter 10 for more detailed discussion.

In a study related to sex-role stereotyping, Looft (1971) asked 33 second-grade boys and girls what they would like to be when they grew up. His major purpose was to analyze responses in terms of what second-grade boys and girls perceived as appropriate work behavior for their sex. Their responses are summarized as follows:

33 boys
9—football player
4—policeman
Less frequent responses were doctor, dentist, priest, pilot, and astronaut.

33 girls
14—nurse
11—teacher
Less frequent responses were mother, stewardess, and salesgirl. One chose
   doctor.

Biehler (1979) repeated the Looft survey but extended the sample to children from the first through sixth grades in California elementary schools. Because of the differences in sample size and possible bias of the sample, conclusions comparing these two studies can only be considered tentative and not representative of the total population. However, the comparisons do reveal some interesting trends:

1. "Teacher" and "nurse" were popular choices for girls in both studies.
2. In the 1979 study, girls both expressed an interest in a wider range of occupations and selected more nontraditional occupations.
3. "Professional athlete" was a strong choice for boys in both studies.
4. Boys in both studies responded strongly to traditional male roles.

It appears that elementary school girls surveyed in the late 1970s had somewhat changed their attitude about appropriate career roles for their sex. Even though the traditional roles of teachers and nurses were still the most popular, more nontraditional roles were being considered. One possible explanation for the popular choice of professional athletes for boys is the popularity of professional sports on television.

In a related study of the occupational plans of female high school students in the 1980s, Gerstein, Lichtman, and Barokas (1988) found many women planned to enter fields traditionally dominated by women. Although census data in 1985 revealed that women attained higher representation in most occupations, many occupational categories remain dominated by men.

National Study of Career-Development Needs of Nine-Year-Olds

In 1977, a national study of 28,000 nine-year-olds was conducted to determine their career-development needs in terms of knowledge of occupations, perceptions of abilities and interests, attitudes toward work, and knowledge of their abilities and other variables (Miller, 1977). Selected findings are summarized as follows:

1. Self-perception of abilities and limitations
   a. Most 9-year-olds could state two things they could do well (strengths) and two things they could not do well (limitations). Limitations were more difficult for them to talk about than strengths.
   b. More males than females were able to list their strengths.
   c. More Caucasians than African Americans were able to list both strengths and limitations.
2. Methods of evaluating abilities and limitations
   a. Most 9-year-olds had limited methods of evaluating their own abilities, and many were unable to do this at all.
   b. Females tended to judge their abilities and limitations by tests or by what others said, while males more often used personal comparison.
3. Self-perceptions of interest
   a. Nine-year-olds were able to state strong and weak interests, though they had more difficulty stating weak ones.
   b. More males than females were able to state weak interests.
4. Knowledge of the characteristics and requirements of different occupations
   a. Nine-year-olds generally had a high knowledge level of the duties of visible occupations. There was some evidence that sex difference was a variable in knowing about specific occupations.
   b. When identifying occupations, there was some evidence to support sex stereotyping of occupations as an influence on how much was known about specific occupations.
   c. African Americans and students whose parents did not go to high school scored consistently lower on occupational knowledge than the total group.
5. Visits to community places of interest
   a. Most of the 9-year-olds had visited at least four places, but students whose parents did not go to high school indicated they had visited fewer than four places.
6. Interpersonal skills
   a. Most 9-year-olds were able to give acceptable responses to interpersonal skills exercises that measured their ability to work effectively with peers, co-workers, and others.
   b. Students from families whose parents had attended college had a higher percentage of acceptable responses than the total group.
7. Attitudes toward work
   a. Only 40% of the 9-year-olds felt it was their responsibility to select what work they would do for a living. Most felt that this decision would be made by someone else, such as their parents. Some had no idea of whose decision it would be. African Americans and students whose parents did not go to high school were less apt to see their future work as resulting from their own decisions.

8. Assumed responsibility for own behavior
   a. Most 9-year-olds did not perceive themselves as being responsible for their behavior.

The National Occupational Information Coordinating Committee (NOICC, 1992) outlines three areas of career development for students in elementary school as follows:

1. Self-knowledge
   a. Knowledge of the importance of self-concept
   b. Skills to interact with others
   c. Awareness of the importance of growth and change
2. Educational and occupational exploration
   a. Awareness of the benefits of educational achievement
   b. Awareness of the relationship between work and learning
   c. Skills to understand and use career information
   d. Awareness of the importance of personal responsibility and good work habits
   e. Awareness of how work relates to the needs and functions of society
3. Career planning
   a. Understanding of how to make decisions
   b. Awareness of the interrelationship of life roles
   c. Awareness of different occupations and changing male/female roles
   d. Awareness of the career-planning process

Implications for Career Guidance at the Elementary School Level

The results of the 1977 national study of career-development needs of 9-year-olds, combined with other research reported in this section, suggest many ideas that can be applied to career-guidance programs in elementary schools. Following is a representative list. Related career-guidance techniques will be reported in Chapter 10.

1. Self-concepts begin to form in early childhood. Because of the influence of self-concept formation on career development, there is strong evidence of the importance of directed experiences in enhancing self-concept in the elementary school.
2. An important aspect of career development is to build an understanding of strengths and limitations. Learning to identify and express strengths and limitations is a good way to build a foundation for self-understanding.
3. Elementary school children imitate role models in the home and school. Both parents and teachers can provide children with positive role models through precept and example.

4. Children learn to associate work roles by sexual stereotyping at an early age. Exposure to career information that discourages sex-role stereotyping will broaden the range of occupations considered available by children.

5. Community resources provide a rich source of career information, role models, and exposure to a wide range of careers. Students from families whose parents did not attend high school have a special need for community opportunities.

6. Self-awareness counseling is a major goal of the growth stage in elementary schools. Methods used to enhance self-awareness encourage development of the ability to process and interpret information about self and others and about differences among people.

7. Learning to assume responsibility for decisions and actions has major implications for future career decisions. Some beginning steps include skills development that enables children to analyze situations, to identify people who can help them, and to seek assistance when needed.

8. Understanding the relationship between education and work is a key concept for enhancing career development. Skills learned in school and during out-of-school activities should be linked to work-related activities.

9. The idea that all work is important builds an understanding of why parents and others work. Reflection on the reasons for working fosters an awareness that any productive worker should be respected.

10. Learning about occupations and about people who are actually involved in occupations builds an awareness of differences among people and occupations.

STAGES OF DEVELOPMENT AND DEVELOPMENTAL TASKS FOR JUNIOR AND SENIOR HIGH SCHOOL STUDENTS

Adolescence has been described as a period of turmoil resulting in a transition from childhood. Continuity of development is, for some, sporadic and chaotic. The key characteristic of this stage of development, according to Erikson, is the search for identity as one subordinates childhood identifications and reaches for a different identity in a more complex set of conditions and circumstances. The major danger of this period is role confusion; thus, this stage is often designated "Identity vs. Confusion."

In Erikson's (1963) view, this is a critical period of development. As he put it, "These new identifications are no longer characterized by the playfulness of childhood and the experimental zest of youth: with dire urgency they force the young individual into choices and decisions which will, with increasing immediacy, lead to commitments for life" (p. 155).

According to Erikson, the choice of career and commitment to a career has a significant impact on identity. Because of the current difficulty surrounding occupational choice in terms of rapidly changing job markets and impersonal organizations, Erikson suggested that many careers pose a threat to personal identity; subsequently, some individuals avoid a firm career choice. Many adolescents delay commitment or place a psychological moratorium on the decision until further options are explored. Excerpts from an interview with Ted illustrate this point.

Ted: My parents want me here so that I can choose a career. They don't like it that I haven't picked one.

Counselor: As I said, we should be able to help you, Ted, but first, tell me more about jobs or careers you have considered.

Ted: I thought about a few, like photography, but I really don't know what I want.

Counselor: Tell me more about your thoughts on photography.

Ted: A photographer like Mr. Brown is not what I want to be. I guess I'd like to work for a magazine.

Counselor: You mentioned Mr. Brown. What don't you like about his job?

Ted: I don't want to take pictures of weddings and things like that. To tell the truth, I don't really know much about what a photographer or any other worker does. I just wish my parents would leave me alone until I have more time. I'm going to community college next fall and I want to decide while I'm there.

A young person unable to avoid role confusion may adopt what is referred to as a "negative identity," assuming forms of behavior that are in direct conflict with family and society. Those who soon develop a more appropriate sense of direction may find this experience positive, but for others, the negative identity is maintained throughout adulthood. Identity diffusion, according to Erikson, often results in lack of commitment to a set of values and, subsequently, to occupations.

Likewise, Super (1990) and Crites (1973) suggested strong relationships between identity and career commitment as variables of career maturity. Career maturity implies a stabilized identity that provides individuals with a framework for making career choices, a crystallized formation of self-perceptions, and developed skills. Career maturity is a continuous developmental process and presents specific identifiable characteristics and traits essential to career development. Characteristic of career maturity are the traits of decisiveness and independence, knowledge of occupational information, and skills in planning and decision making. Chapter 7 reviews career-maturity inventories that provide specific information about other dimensions of career maturity.

Finally, defining appropriate sexual roles and achieving relationships with peers are crucial developmental tasks for adolescents (Havighurst, 1972). Success in accomplishing these tasks is essential to social adjustment at this stage of life. Socially responsible behavior implies that the first steps have been taken in achieving emotional independence from parents and other adults. According to Havighurst, social relationship patterns learned during adolescence greatly affect an individual's adjustment to the rules and life roles, including the work role, of the dominant society.

Cognitive Development During Junior and Senior High School

Following Piaget's (1969) cognitive developmental stages, as shown in Table 9-2, the transition from concrete operational thinking to formal thought is a gradual process beginning at approximately 12 years of age. During early adolescence, patterns of problem solving and planning are quite unsystematic. Near the end of high school, however, the adolescent has the ability to deal with abstractions, form hypotheses in problem solving, and sort out problems through mental manipulations. Linking observations and emotional responses with a recently developed systematic thinking process, the adolescent reacts to events and experiences with a newly found power of thought. In formal thought, the adolescent can direct emotional responses to abstract ideals as well as to people. Introspective thinking leads to analysis of self in situations, including projection of the self into the adult world of work (Piaget, 1969; Elkind, 1968; Keating, 1980).

The cognitive development of formal thought introduces sets of ambiguities. On one hand, the adolescent is developing a systematized thinking process to solve problems appropriately. On the other hand, there is unrestrained theorizing, extreme self-analysis, and more-than-usual concern about the reactions of others. By virtue of concern for others, the peer group influence is particularly strong during adolescence. Self-analysis can lead to what Tiedeman and Miller-Tiedeman (1990) refer to as "I-power" as a means of self-development. Increased self-awareness is an essential part of the adolescent's development, particularly in clarifying self-status and individualized belief systems in the career decision-making process.

In the development of formalized thinking, adolescents do not simply respond to stimuli but also interpret what they observe (Bandura, 1977). In this connection, they will perceive stimuli in the environment as having positive and negative associations. An example of a negative association is a junior high student who believes that lawyers "rip you off because they are all crooks." In this sense, perceptions and values associated with occupations are developed through generalizations formed by experience and observations. In terms of persons who have the greatest influence or impact on adolescent values, Larsen (1972) found that parents have the greatest influence on the long-range plans of high school students, while peers were more likely to influence immediate identity or status. Occupational stereotypes as perceived in career decision making may be generalized from interactions with both parents and peers, as well as gained through other stimuli such as films and books.

Physiological Development of Adolescents in Junior and Senior High School

A dramatic physiological change, sexual maturity, takes place for most boys and girls during junior and senior high school. Accompanying or preceding sexual maturity are dramatic bodily changes, such as increased muscle tissue and body stature, which permit the adolescent to perform adult physical tasks for the first time. Of particular importance to the adolescent is physical appearance. In junior high school, concern for appearance reaches its peak as girls compare themselves to movie and television stars, females appearing in commercials, and professional models. Boys use the standards of strength and facial and bodily hair for judging early maturity (Biehler & Hudson, 1986). Feeling comfortable within the dominant peer group is highly related to being judged "grown-up" or mature.

Reflecting on sexual maturity, Cal related the following incident:

> I wanted to do everything I could to be grown up, but I was just a little twerp. I even tried to imitate how men walked. I guess I was 12 or 13 when I lit my first cigarette. Even though I coughed until I almost choked, I kept on smoking that cigarette! Yes sir, I wanted to be one of those "cool cats" with all the know-how.
>
> But the worst of it was P.E. I didn't want to undress in front of anybody. I made up all kinds of excuses until the locker room was clear, and then I went home and showered.
>
> You know, it was important then to be accepted by my friends. I guess I ended up being liked by most of them. Now when I look back, it seems we were all trying to fool each other.

Betty, an early-maturing junior high school student, reflected on her experiences:

> All of a sudden it seemed I had outgrown everyone—especially the boys. Some of the girls seemed as physically mature as I was, but they usually acted uneasy around me, and I certainly felt awkward around them. It was during this time that I made friends with some older girls. As far as the boys were concerned, there were mixed feelings. The older boys didn't accept me because I was "too young," while the younger ones were too little for me. I just felt out of place for a few years until everybody caught up.

After reviewing several longitudinal research projects to determine immediate effects of early and late maturity, Livson and Peskin (1980) reached the following conclusions:

1. Early-maturing males were most likely to be viewed more favorably by adults, thus leading to a greater sense of confidence and poise.
2. Late-maturing males exhibited attention-seeking behavior to compensate for feelings of inferiority.
3. Early-maturing girls were psychologically and socially out of sync with their peers.
4. Late-maturing girls who went through less abrupt physical changes were viewed as more petite and feminine and enjoyed popularity and leadership privileges.

The effects of early and late sexual maturity provide a frame of reference for counseling intervention. There is evidence that early maturity for males holds certain benefits in terms of appropriateness among male peer groups and adults. Late-maturing girls also enjoy acceptance and popularity (Livson & Peskin, 1980). Differences in physical development at the junior high school level are quite apparent (Kindred, 1968):

> As an example of spread of development, a typical group of 40 sixth-graders would show two fully adolescent, eight prepubescent, and ten childish girls, with four prepubescent and 16 childish boys. By the time this group becomes eighth-graders, one could expect to find over one-half of the girls fully adolescent, the remainder prepubescent, and none classified as childish. Among the boys, six would be found mature, five prepubescent, and nine still children (p. 41).

Sexual maturity may be one basis for differentiating career-guidance activities. Late-maturing males and early-maturing girls may experience a greater need for counseling intervention than their peers. Thomas (1973) suggests that junior high school students benefit from guidance programs that inform students of the extent, type, and variation of physiological changes in early adolescence. Specifically addressed are anxieties related to bodily changes.

In a related study of guidance needs expressed by 1,518 preadolescent and early adolescent students, Kesner (1977) reports the five most prominent needs: academic skill development, educational and vocational development, interpersonal relationships, intrapersonal understanding, and career development. These findings support the need for diversified guidance strategies in junior high school, including self-concept development for personal and career development.

National Study of Career-Development Needs of Thirteen-Year-Olds

In 1977, a national study of 30,000 thirteen-year-olds was conducted to determine their career-development needs in terms of knowledge of occupations, ability to recognize strengths and limitations, knowledge of the relationships between work and school, and other variables (Aubrey, 1977). Following are selected findings from this study.

1. Most 13-year-olds could state two things they could do well and two things they could not do well. Males and females were practically equal in their ability to list their strengths. More Caucasians than African Americans were able to list both strengths and limitations.

2. Although almost all 13-year-olds could identify something they would like to do better, only about 75% of them had actually tried to find out how to do it better.

3. African American students and students whose parents had not gone to high school indicated an extremely high interest in school and academic areas and a desire to improve in these areas. Caucasian students and students whose parents had gone to college expressed very little interest in this area. Instead

they were interested in group and individual sports, while African Americans had a low interest for improvement in this area.

4. Males indicated that they could perform an activity better than others, while females indicated they did it more poorly. Males judged their performance by personal comparison when performing an activity, while females tended to judge themselves by what others said. African Americans judged more often by test scores and grades, while Caucasians judged more by personal comparison.

5. In terms of learning about ways to improve abilities and decrease limitations, only about 75% had tried to learn how to better perform their preferred activity.

6. Student interests clustered in the areas of group sports and academics. More males responded to group sports than any other single category, and more females responded to the school and academic area.

7. Interests were analyzed in terms of narrow categories in contrast to total life experiences.

8. In assessing the students' knowledge of characteristics and requirements of different occupations, the study found that they knew more about the duties and physical characteristics of jobs than the specifics of earning power and detailed work.

9. The students had general information about occupations but insufficient knowledge concerning specific tasks, duties, and benefits of occupations.

10. About 70% of the students were interested in a current hobby, sport, game, or activity that they felt would be useful for obtaining a job. Males tended to see themselves doing the same thing in a future job that they were doing in their game, hobby, or activity. Females tended to see themselves in a teaching role.

11. In responding to the relationship between school and work, the vast majority stated that at least one school subject had taught them something of use for a job. Mathematics was given as the most probable course in linking school subjects to job requirements.

12. When asked to list ten factors to be considered in choosing a job or career, most could list two, but fewer than half could list more than five.

13. When asked how they could get more information about an occupation, an extremely low percentage stated they would go to their counselor or teacher.

14. A larger percentage of females and Caucasians than of males and African Americans thought about a future job.

15. The first choice for future jobs tended to be occupations generally requiring college degrees or lengthy training periods beyond high school.

16. When the students were asked if they had visited 11 selected places of interest in their community, the vast majority stated they had visited only about half of these places.

17. In identifying skills that are generally useful in the world of work, the study found that 13-year-olds had difficulty with exercises involving numerical skills.

18. In assessing interpersonal skills on three exercises, the study found that a high percentage gave acceptable responses.

19. In assessing employment-seeking skills, the study found that a high percentage were able to list at least three ways people their age could earn money.

20. In terms of assuming responsibility for their own behavior, the students did not see themselves as ultimately responsible for their own behavior.

21. Over 94% could give two or more acceptable reasons why people who wish to work cannot find a job. Over half could give five or more reasons.

22. About 75% felt that they eventually should make the final decision as to how they would earn a living.

The National Occupational Information Coordinating Committee (NOICC, 1992) outlines three areas of career development for students in middle/junior high school as follows:

1. Self-knowledge

    a. Knowledge of the influence of a positive self-concept
    b. Skills to interact with others
    c. Knowledge of the importance of growth and change

2. Educational and occupational exploration

    a. Knowledge of the benefits of educational achievement to career opportunities
    b. Knowledge of the relationship between work and learning
    c. Skills to locate, understand, and use career information
    d. Knowledge of skills necessary to seek and obtain jobs
    e. Understanding of how work relates to the needs and functions of the economy and society

3. Career planning

    a. Skills to make decisions
    b. Knowledge of the interrelationship of life roles
    c. Knowledge of different occupations and changing male/female roles
    d. Understanding of the process of career planning

Implications for Career Guidance in Junior High School

Results from the 1977 national study discussed in the previous section combined with other research yield numerous implications for career-guidance programs in junior high school.

1. In many respects, junior high school is an educational transition from structural classroom settings to more specialized educational programs. Learning to relate acquired skills to educational/occupational goals promotes exploratory reflection and activities.

2. There appears to be a strong need to increase the ability of junior high school students to realistically appraise their own abilities, achievements, and interests. Minority students and students from homes where parents' education level is low need special assistance in understanding their strengths and limitations.

3. Students in junior high school have difficulty in identifying and evaluating their interests in relation to total life experiences.

4. A limited knowledge of occupations makes it difficult for junior high school students to relate in- and out-of-school activities to future jobs. Exposure to jobs and career fields should be expanded to provide a basis for linking various activities to work.

5. The naiveté and limited knowledge of the factors necessary in evaluating future work roles suggest the desirability of introducing informational resources and teaching the necessary skills for their use. Learning about career options, for example, increases awareness of exploration opportunities.

6. Physiological development and sexual maturity during junior high school involve individual changes in self-perceptions and social interactions. Opportunities to explore, evaluate, and reflect on values seem to be very desirable activities for promoting a better understanding of self during this stage.

7. Junior high school students will greatly benefit from hands-on experience with skill activities associated with occupations. Basic and concrete experiences provide a means of learning skills utilized in work.

8. Because junior high school students should begin to assume responsibility for their own behavior, they would greatly benefit from improved knowledge of planning, decision-making, and problem-solving skills.

9. Increased awareness of sexual differences among junior high school students suggests that emphasis be placed on learning how sex-role stereotyping, bias, and discrimination limit occupational and educational choices.

10. Students in junior high school who continue the process of awareness initiated in elementary school will recognize the changing nature of career commitment. The skills and knowledge learned to evaluate initial career choices will be used to evaluate others over the life span.

CAREER-DEVELOPMENT CONCERNS OF SENIOR HIGH SCHOOL STUDENTS

The exploratory stage (ages 15 to 24) as defined by Super (1990) is the time when choices are narrowed but not finalized, and a time of readiness to involve oneself in processing choices. Commitment to a type of training or employment education program underscores the importance of the level of career development attained during the exploratory stage. Research designed to assess career-development needs of senior high school students provides relevant information for building career-guidance programs.

A career pattern study by Super, Starishesky, Matlin, and Jordaan (1963) was designed to assess exploratory steps in career development. The subjects were 342 boys from Middletown, New York, who were surveyed in the 8th, 9th, and 12th grades and responded to a questionnaire two years after high school graduation. Limited progress was noted regarding the career maturity of 9th and 12th graders. Moreover, two out of three 12th-grade boys had done little to implement their vocational preferences (Jordaan & Heyde, 1979).

In another well-known longitudinal study of career development by Gribbons and Lohnes (1968, 1982), 57 boys and 54 girls from five eastern Massachusetts communities were studied until they were 34 or 35 years of age. Specifically, eighth-graders were interviewed prior to being exposed to a guidance program based on *You: Today and Tomorrow* (Katz, 1958) and were interviewed again in the 10th and 12th grades and two years after high school graduation. In addition, they were questioned through correspondence and by telephone when they were 34 or 35 years of age. Among the most significant findings were (1) as adolescents, they were poorly oriented to requirements of career-development tasks, (2) knowledge of careers varied greatly among all subjects, and (3) sex-role stereotypes presented special career-development difficulties for women.

In a search to inventory the talents of youth in the United States, Flanagan and colleagues (1966, 1971) launched Project Talent in 1960. The project began with two days of extensive testing (aptitudes, abilities, interests, a demographic questionnaire, open-ended essays, and questions on guidance services) of more than 400,000 students in grades 9 through 12 from 1,000 high schools. Subsequent follow-up studies were done one, five, and ten years later. Relevant findings included: (1) career plans of 12th-graders were more realistic than those of 9th-graders, (2) there were more realistic career choices among 11th-graders in 1970 than 11th-graders in 1960, (3) girls in 1970 selected a broader range of occupations than in 1960, (4) the majority of students did not make appropriate career choices in high school, and (5) almost half of the students changed their occupational goals within a year of leaving high school.

A summary of selected career-development studies of senior high school students supports the need for comprehensive career guidance at the senior high school level. Crites (1969) suggested that about 30% of students in high school and college are undecided about a career. A study of a sample of high school seniors in Alabama revealed that 18% were undecided (Fottler & Bain, 1980). A 1973 ten-year nationwide follow-up study of the career development of students in grades 8, 10, and 12 revealed that 71% of senior high students continued to express a need for help with career planning (Prediger & Sawyer, 1985).

These data indicate a variety of career-development concerns for seniors in high school. Gribbons and Lohnes (1968) provide some guidelines for career-guidance programs in senior high school: (1) awareness of curriculum choices in terms of abilities, interests, and values; (2) awareness of occupational choices in terms of abilities, interests, values, and requirements; (3) awareness of personal strengths and weaknesses as they relate to educational and occupational requirements; (4) accuracy and evidence of self-ratings in terms of relevant abilities for educational and occupational requirements; (5) accuracy of a description of occupation; and (6) willingness of individuals to take responsibility for their choices. A more comprehensive national study of career development (summarized as follows) provides further guidelines for career-counseling programs for senior high school students.

National Study of Career-Development Needs of Seventeen-Year-Olds

In 1977, a national study of 37,500 17-year-olds was conducted to determine their career-development needs in terms of knowledge of occupations, ability to recognize strengths and limitations, knowledge of the relationship between school and work, and other variables (Mitchell, 1977). The study found the following:

1. Most 17-year-olds have spoken seriously to someone about their future plans, usually to parents, but also to counselors, advisers, or peers. However, only two-thirds of the respondents felt that their abilities were understood by the person(s) with whom they talked.

2. Questions that examined self-perception of abilities indicated that males felt they could do best in group sports, hobbies, and crafts, whereas females named musical or artistic activities and household skills.

3. Males tended to have more confidence in their ability to perform tasks well than did females. Comparison with others was the most frequently used criterion for judging how well they could perform an activity.

4. In matching occupations with physical characteristics and skills, most 17-year-olds were able to match at least five of the nine occupations listed with physical characteristics and skills, but fewer than 10% matched all nine correctly. There were some differences among groups; for example, African Americans scored significantly lower than other populations on this item.

5. When asked about their reasons for accepting or not accepting a promotion on a job, the students cited prestige and status more than twice as often as challenge and responsibility, personal satisfaction, opportunity, and advancement. More males than females named "working conditions" and "benefits" as reasons for accepting promotion. Caucasians were almost twice as likely as African Americans to consider challenge and responsibility as a factor in this decision.

6. In evaluating the ability of 17-year-olds to link leisure activities with possible jobs, the researchers found that more males than females were able to name an activity in which they were interested that might be useful for a job. Five times as many males as females named group sports as job-related activities. More females than males regarded music, art, or artistic activities as useful for a job.

7. Responses relating school subjects to jobs indicated that most 17-year-olds had taken a subject in school that might be useful for a job. Named most frequently and in the following order were business education, mathematics, vocational education, science, English, and industrial arts. More males saw

industrial arts and vocational education as useful for a job, and more females than males similarly named business education.

8. The principal resource for finding out about requirements of a job was direct observation in the job field. Reading about a job and contacting a personnel officer also were frequent responses. Only about one-fourth of the respondents considered their counselor among the top five sources for job requirement information.

9. In terms of linking interests and abilities to jobs, nearly all 17-year-olds had thought about the kinds of jobs they would like to have in the future. More than two-thirds had considered professional jobs, with more males than females aspiring to be professionals. More females considered clerical, homemaker, and service jobs, while more males than females considered craftsperson, farmer, laborer, manager or administrator, operator, proprietor/owner, and the protective services. The reasons given for job choices indicated that females were more interested than males in helping people and in interpersonal relations, and males were more interested than females in mechanical aspects. Only one-third of the respondents were able to name appropriate skills or abilities needed to do the jobs.

10. Most 17-year-olds had worked at a part-time or summer job, mainly for economic independence. Males were somewhat more concerned about this factor than females.

11. Nearly one-half of the respondents reported that they took lessons, training, or courses outside of school in musical or artistic activities, and more than one-fourth had training in individual sports. Caucasians exceeded African Americans in musical, artistic, and sports training, whereas African Americans exceeded Caucasians in training in school or academic areas and in household skills.

12. In evaluating a variety of skills, the study found that fewer than one-half of the respondents were able to compute the area of a room correctly, and only slightly over two-thirds were able to convert inches to feet. Most 17-year-olds could make correct entries of date, name, and address on a shipping order, but few were able to enter correctly the total amount for an order and the shipping and handling charges. Over three-fourths of the students reported that they had been involved in communication skills training through participation in organized group discussions, but fewer than 50% had led such discussions.

The National Occupational Information Coordinating Committee (NOICC, 1992) outlines three areas of career development for students in high school as follows:

1. Self-knowledge
   a. Understanding the influence of a positive self-concept
   b. Skills to interact positively with others
   c. Understanding the impact of growth and development

2. Educational and occupational exploration
   a. Understanding the relationship between educational achievement and career planning

    b. Understanding the need for positive attitudes toward work and learning

    c. Skills to locate, evaluate, and interpret career information

    d. Skills to prepare to seek, obtain, maintain, and change jobs

    e. Understanding how societal needs and functions influence the nature and structure of work

3. Career planning

    a. Skills to make decisions

    b. Understanding the interrelationship of life roles

    c. Understanding the continuous changes in male/female roles

    d. Skills in career planning

Implications for Career-Guidance Programs in Senior High Schools

The findings from the national study of 17-year-olds, combined with related research reported in this section, provide an abundance of implications for career-guidance programs in senior high school:

1. Career guidance at the senior high school level must provide programs designed to meet the needs of students at various stages of career development. Establishing the career-development needs of entry-level high school students and a means of monitoring their progress are relevant goals.

2. According to Super (1990), the exploratory age is characterized by a tentative phase in which choices are narrowed but not finalized. Therefore, it is important for individuals to analyze their own characteristics in terms of career decisions.

3. Senior high school students should benefit from information, activities, and modules that call for matching occupations with physical characteristics and skills. Programs designed to assist senior high school students entering the labor market for the first time are of particular importance.

4. Senior high school students should understand the relationship of career choices and educational requirements. Educational awareness implies a working knowledge of educational opportunities available at specific institutions.

5. Teaching decision-making and planning skills involves guiding students through a series of steps as they formulate career goals. Refined self-knowledge, including interests, abilities, values, and occupational knowledge, is prerequisite to effective career decision making and planning.

6. Work-experience counseling provides individuals with insight into the work setting and prepares them to identify effective models. Work values, work environments, work habits, and other issues associated with work are of particular value to the novice.

7. Many senior high school students also need assistance in choosing an institution of higher learning. Knowledge of how to evaluate the advantages and disadvantages of these institutions is essential.

8. Community visits and interviews with individuals in different occupations are relevant activities for helping senior high school students relate their own personal characteristics to occupational requirements. Relating school subjects to jobs and describing sources of job information are pertinent goals for career development.

9. Students should be guided in creating a set of specific preferences and plans to implement after graduation.

10. Services to help prepare for the job search are offered through placement officers. Related activities may include resume preparation, interview-skills training, preparation for employment tests, job testing, and listing of employment opportunities.

SUMMARY

1. Research suggests that *all* stages of human development are important. Infancy should be viewed as an extremely important and sensitive period in human development, but one not necessarily having a permanent impact on later behavior.

2. Directed experiences in elementary school promote physical and academic growth, interpersonal relationships with members of both sexes, and self-concept development—all important components of career development. Students who fail to accomplish developmental tasks may require special attention and direction.

3. Erikson suggested that the stage of development between ages 6 and 11 emphasizes industriousness; that is, children learn that productivity brings recognition and reward.

4. Piaget described early cognitive development in children as cultivating "schemes" through motor activities and their senses. During the ages of 2 to 5, children begin developing conceptual skills but have not yet developed the abilities to think logically or abstractly.

5. Children are particularly prone to adopting the behavior of models they observe. Parents, teachers, teacher's aides, and classmates are potential models that elementary school children will imitate. Other models may come from television, movies, and books.

6. In elementary school, children experience many aspects of existence in an adult world for the first time, such as competition with others and expectations of productive performance. Differences in growth and psychological changes between girls and boys greatly influence social relationships and emerging self-perceptions. Sex-role stereotyping is quite evident in elementary school. A national study of 9-year-olds focused on career-development needs in terms of knowledge of occupations, perceptions of abilities and interests, attitudes toward work, and other variables.

7. Implications of career guidance for elementary school children include the importance of self-concept development, building an understanding of strengths and limitations, providing appropriate role models, visiting community resources

for career information and role models, developing self-awareness, learning to assume responsibility for decisions and actions, understanding the relationship between education and work, learning that all work is important, and learning about work environments and the people involved in occupations.

8. Adolescence has been described as a period of turmoil resulting in a transition from childhood. According to Erikson, adolescents search intensely for identity as they subordinate childhood identifications. The major danger is role confusion; thus, this stage is designated as "Identity versus Confusion." The choice of career and commitment to a career have a significant impact on identity.

9. According to Piaget, the transition from concrete operational thinking to formal thought is a gradual process beginning at approximately 12 years of age. During early adolescence, patterns of problem solving or planning are quite unsystematic, but near the end of high school the adolescent has the ability to deal with distractions and sort out problems through mental manipulations.

10. Parents have the greatest influence on long-range plans of high school students, while peers are more likely to influence current identity and status.

11. A dramatic physiological change, sexual maturity, takes place for the majority of boys and girls during junior and senior high school.

12. According to Havighurst, defining appropriate sexual roles and achieving relationships with peers are among the major developmental tasks of adolescents.

13. The effects of early and late sexual maturity provide a frame of reference for counseling intervention. The evidence suggests that early maturity for males has certain benefits in terms of appropriateness among male peer groups and adults. Late-maturing girls also enjoy acceptance and popularity. Late-maturing males and early-maturing females may experience a greater need for counseling intervention than do their peers.

14. A national study of 13-year-olds was conducted to determine career-development needs in terms of knowledge of occupation, ability to recognize strengths and limitations, knowledge of relations between work and school, and other variables.

15. Implications for career guidance in junior high school includes the importance of learning to relate acquired skills to educational/occupational goals. These students have a strong need to appraise their own abilities, achievements, and interests accurately. They should be given the opportunity to identify relationships between interests and total life experiences. Exposure to jobs and career fields should be expanded to provide a basis for linking various activities to work. Learning about career options increases awareness of exploration opportunities. Basic and concrete experiences provide a means of learning the skills utilized in work. Skills in planning, decision making, and problem solving are important for junior high school students. Finally, these students should understand that sex-role stereotyping, bias, and discrimination limit occupational choices.

16. Several research projects indicated that senior high school students are limited in career maturity and do little to implement vocational choices. Also,

adolescents have limited awareness of requirements of career development and a wide variation of knowledge of careers. Girls selected a broader range of occupations in 1970 than in 1960, but the majority of students in the 1960s and 1970s did not make appropriate career choices in high school.

17. The need for career guidance at the senior high school level is supported by the fact that 30% to 47% of students expressed a need for help with career planning.

18. A 1977 national study of 17-year-olds was conducted to determine their career-development needs in terms of knowledge of occupations, abilities to recognize strengths and limitations, knowledge of relationships between school and work, and other variables.

19. Implications for career-guidance programs in senior high school are numerous, and they indicate that programs should be designed to meet the needs of students at various stages of career development. Programs designed to assist senior high school students entering the labor market for the first time are of particular importance. Senior high school students should understand the relationships between career choices and educational requirements. Learning decision-making and planning skills is essential. Learning more about work and what is required at work can help senior high school students identify effective role models. Many senior high students need assistance in choosing an institution of higher education.

SUPPLEMENTARY LEARNING EXERCISES

1. Defend the following statement with examples to prove your point: "Individuals have a profound adaptive capacity at various stages of development."
2. Construct at least two activities/strategies in which concrete experiences promote abstract conceptual operations.
3. Construct at least two activities/strategies of observational learning that would promote career development of elementary school-age children.
4. Survey a sample of elementary, junior, and senior high school students to determine their perception of appropriate career roles for their sex.
5. Develop a list of behavioral characteristics of an adolescent experiencing role confusion. Develop counseling strategies designed to overcome identified characteristics.
6. Identify standardized assessment instruments that measure self-concept development. Explain how you would use the results in career counseling.
7. Identify and interview a late- and an early-maturing adolescent. Present your findings to the class.
8. Describe your development from childhood. Identify significant transitions and their influences on your career.
9. Identify at least ten reasons why such a significant number of senior high school students express a need for career guidance. Discuss these issues in class.
10. Using one or more of the implications for career guidance for the elementary, junior, and senior high school levels, identify specific career-guidance needs and develop activities/strategies to meet them.

Chapter Ten

Career Guidance in Schools

This chapter covers samples of selected strategies for career guidance in elementary, junior, and senior high school. The first part of the chapter presents career-education concepts developed in the 1970s. The goals and objectives of career education illustrate a major effort to focus on preparation for the world of work as an integral component of the school curriculum.

The second part of this chapter introduces the competencies and indicators developed by the National Occupational Information Coordinating Committee (NOICC) for elementary, junior/middle, and high school students. The next sections outline strategies for implementing these guidelines and present a comprehensive school guidance program. Changes in vocational education are then discussed, followed by an exploration of other significant government-sponsored programs. Finally, the roles of the school placement office and state placement agencies are discussed.

Before focusing on career education in the past and the rapid changes that are currently taking place, some significant future educational trends should help us establish a perspective of what to expect by the year 2000.

FUTURE TRENDS IN EDUCATION

Cetron & Gayle (1991) have compiled predictions of changes and trends for our educational needs by the year 2000. The following predictions are representative of their findings:

1. The focus on thinking globally will make foreign languages—particularly French, German, Spanish, Russian, and Japanese—a requirement for all students entering college (p. 266).
2. Secondary students will come to value vocational education more highly as reform efforts bring about a restructuring of schools, especially an integration of academic and technical skills (p. 228).
3. Lifetime employment in the same job or company is a thing of the past. Workers will change jobs or careers five or more times; this will require lifelong training and learning (p. 230).

4. The emerging service economy will provide jobs for 85% of the work force by the year 2000 (p. 231).
5. Small businesses (fewer than 100 employees) will employ most of the labor force by the year 2000 (p. 234).
6. Both partners in most family units (married and unmarried) will work; this figure could rise to 75% by 2000 (p. 236).

A Definition of Career Education

In recognition of documented dissatisfaction with educational and vocational training practices, a new concept of education emerged in the 1970s that specifically addressed career development, attitudes, and values in addition to traditional learning (Hoyt, 1972). This comprehensive career-education concept focuses on relationships between traditional educational programs and the world of work. The major purpose of career education is to prepare each individual for living and working in our society. As defined by a national task force (Jesser, 1976), career education is

> essentially an instructional strategy aimed at improving educational outcomes by relating teaching and learning activities to the concept of career development. Career education extends the academic world to the world of work. In scope, career education encompasses educational experiences beginning with early childhood and continuing throughout the individual's productive life. A complete program of career education includes awareness of the world of work, broad orientation to occupations (professional and nonprofessional), in-depth exploration of selected clusters, career preparation and understanding of the economic system of which jobs are a part, and placement for all students (p. 20).

After conducting a comprehensive examination of the definitions and concepts of career education, Hansen (1977) suggested an expanded definition of career education as follows:

> *Career education* is a person-centered developmental, deliberate and collaborative effort by educators, parent-business-industry-labor-government personnel to systematically promote the career development of all persons by creating experiences to help them learn academic, vocational, and basic skills, achieve a sense of agency in making informed career decisions, and master the developmental tasks facing them at various life stages through curriculum, counseling, and community (p. 39).

Thus, career education was considered integral to the educational process, from kindergarten through adulthood. The integration of career-education programs into existing educational curricula had been considered the most feasible method of accomplishing the objectives and goals. Career-education programs were not simply additional courses to be added to traditional curricula but were actually infused into existing curricula. In this section, we concentrate on career-collaboration and infusion models and then present both criticism and defense of the career-education concept.

Career-Education Collaboration and Infusion

In the career-education framework, *collaboration* is the cooperative effort of educators, the family, the work force of the community, and governmental agencies that implement career-education programs. Increased cooperation between school and community enhances and increases opportunities of work-experience programs and on-site visits as well as promoting the mutual advantages of job-placement arrangements. Furthermore, family members and individuals from the business community are very valuable as career role models who can participate in classroom activities. Community representatives are also a valuable resource to school personnel; the importance of community cooperative effort and involvement in the development and operation of career-education programs cannot be overstated.

Career education is not considered simply an extra course in the curriculum but an instructional strategy that relates established subject matter to career-development concepts. The idea of integrating career-development concepts into existing curricula is referred to as *career-education infusion*. Career-education infusion requires teachers to expand their current educational objectives to include career-related activities and subjects. For example, the teaching of decision-making skills can be infused with traditional academic courses. Planning a term project in a history class involves certain decisions, such as specifying the goals of the project, determining the possible approaches to the project and selecting the best one, and actually following through. Decision-making and planning skills are applicable to many—if not all—subjects and should be consciously taught as skills to be developed and refined. The proponents of career-education infusion contend that formal attention should be given to career-related skills and tasks. Examples of infusion models for elementary, junior/middle, and high schools are presented in the following pages.

Elementary School
Career counselors may find that the purposes of career-education infusion need careful delineation to teaching and administrative staffs. Assisting elementary school teachers to conceptualize the role of career-education infusion is a fundamental task for the career counselor. Career counselors advocate career-education concepts by emphasizing that learning modules infused in formalized instruction foster greater self-awareness, knowledge of occupational roles, and an understanding of the purpose of work in our society. Examples of career-education infusion modules are an effective means of illustrating the important role teachers play in career-guidance programs.

The following career-education infusion module is designed to improve career awareness. This module provides rationale, objectives, description, place of activity, personnel required, cost, time, resources, and evaluation measures.

Subject: Math, reading, language
Concept: Career awareness

Answering a Job Advertisement

Rationale
Students should have an understanding of the jobs described in want ads in order to develop an awareness of various occupations. Students should also learn about the requirements of various occupations and draw conclusions of whether they would like to work in the environment described by a want ad and during follow-up.

Objective
Students will describe in writing how different occupations are described in terms of salary, hours of work, training, and educational requirements.

Description

1. Discuss the various ways people find out about openings in the job market.
2. Present a page from the local newspaper with want ads listed.
3. Have students select three careers in which they are interested and research the requirements, salary, training, and education necessary for the job being advertised.
4. Have the students write a description of the job that appeals to them the most and explain their choices.
5. Have students share their findings with classmates in a 3–5 minute report.

Where activity occurs: classroom
Personnel required: teacher
Cost: cost of newspaper
Time: discussion, one-quarter period; research and select careers, one and one-quarter periods; share with classmates, one-quarter period
Resources: newspaper
Evaluation measures: oral and written report[1]

Junior High School

Many of the goals of career education in elementary school are relevant for junior high school students. However, there is a shift of emphasis from general knowledge of work roles to more specific learning activities. Learning to differentiate individual characteristics and to identify broad occupational areas of interest are goals to foster. Awareness of self in relation to personal interests, values, abilities, and personal characteristics is an important objective during this developmental period.

Planning and decision-making skills are emphasized in junior high school. The following career-infusion module for a geography class is designed to include planning, decision making, and awareness of career opportunities in geography.

Subject: Social studies, geography
Concept: Planning and decision making
　　　　　Career awareness

Chamber of Commerce Exercise

Rationale
Students should be exposed to different ways in which different groups make decisions, in order to improve their own decision making.

[1] From *Project Cadre: A Cadre Approach to Career Education Infusion,* by Healy, C. C., and Quinn, O. H., 1977, unpublished manuscript. Reprinted by permission.

Objectives

1. Students will be able to describe their part in the project to accord with teacher observation.
2. Students will list all the Republics of South America and at least one feature from the tourist bulletin for each.
3. Students will identify at least two ways in which their project activity corresponds to duties in two specific occupations.

Description
During a unit on South America, divide the class into six groups. Each group will be a Chamber of Commerce for a Republic of South America. Each group can plan a tourist bulletin with articles and drawings.

1. Students will tell how their group decided who would research information, write articles, draw pictures, etc.
2. Students will describe their responsibilities in preparing the tourist bulletin and tell how they think those responsibilities were like some they might have on a job.
3. Students will answer the question, "Can you see how assuming responsibility for something in this project might help you assume responsibilities in an adult occupation?"

Personnel required: teacher
Cost: none
Time: 3 or 4 periods estimated
Resources: maps and information on South America
Impact on regular offering/curriculum goals: complement regular unit on South America; help students remember important information about the area
Evaluation measures: paper/pencil test[2]

High School
The career-preparation stage in high school requires intensive self-awareness exploration. An important goal is to help students crystallize self-concepts; career-education infusion modules are designed to help students become more aware of their aptitudes, interests, values, and lifestyle preferences. The development of planning skills for future educational and vocational choices also involves a multitude of learning activities and guidance programs. Decision-making skills and knowledge of occupations and job placement are key factors to emphasize in career-education infusion. The following career-education infusion module for a high school English class should help students become more aware of the importance of decision making.

Subject: English
Concept: Planning and decision making
Self-awareness

Decision Making Exemplified in Literature

Rationale
Students should become more aware of the importance of decision making.

[2] From *Project Cadre: A Cadre Approach to Career Education Infusion,* by Healy, C. C., and Quinn, O. H., 1977, unpublished manuscript. Reprinted by permission.

Objectives

1. Students will arrange in order the steps in the systematic decision-making model discussed in class.
2. Students will analyze either a personal decision or a decision made by a literary character by listing the steps taken in making the decision; students will write in one page how that decision followed the steps in the model, or if it didn't how it could.

Description

Read and hold a class discussion on Robert Frost's poem, "The Road Not Taken," having students express their thoughts about the importance of decision making and talk about experiences that led them to make an important decision or to change their minds after making one. Bring out the following points in the discussion:

1. It is important that the student make a decision systematically and participate in its formulation.
2. Before making a decision, one must examine the consequences of the decision, both pro and con.
3. To do this, one must try to get accurate information about each decision.
4. Decision making can be thought of as a series of steps: (a) set the goal; (b) figure out alternative ways of reaching the goal; (c) get accurate information to determine which alternative is best; (d) decide on an alternative and carry it out; (e) figure out if the choice was correct and why; and (f) if you did not reach the goal, try another alternative or start the process over again.

Personnel required: teacher
Cost: none
Time: one period
Resources: Robert Frost's poem, "The Road Not Taken"[3]

Criticism and Defense of Career Education

Career education has not escaped various critics' skepticism. One major criticism is that career education will detract from the basic skills and traditional subject matter taught in schools. Many teachers of basic academic subjects strongly object to vocationally oriented educational programs because they consider other nonvocational values and learning to be of equal or more import. Some critics have argued that instituting career education in elementary school will actually tend to reduce career options, since many students will feel pressured to make career decisions earlier in their school careers. Another major criticism is that the experiential learning activities are overemphasized (Shertzer & Stone, 1976). Grubb and Lazerson (1975) expressed the concern that the benefits derived from work assumed in career-education programs are unrealistic and do not prepare individuals to face the realities of work per se.

[3] From *Project Cadre: A Cadre Approach to Career Education Infusion,* by Healy, C. C. and Quinn, O. H. 1977, unpublished manuscript. Reprinted by permission.

Hoyt (1976) argued that the rationale behind career education has been ignored by its opponents. He implied that basic disagreement with career education is the result of a lack of understanding about the career-education concept. For example, he contended that the concept of work in career education has been misunderstood; there is no attempt to "brainwash" individuals but rather to improve their readiness for work through a realistic and systematic method of evaluating work. No doubt the debate concerning the benefits of career education will continue as long as there is polarization between teachers of academic subjects who stress social values learned through liberal arts programs and those who contend that career-education concepts should be infused in all subjects, from kindergarten through college.

CURRENT SCHOOL CAREER-GUIDANCE PROGRAMS

Hansen's (1977) definition of school career guidance is most appropriate for current school programs:

> a systematic program involving counselors and teachers, which is part of career education, that is, designed to increase one's knowledge of self, of occupations, training paths, and lifestyles, of labor market trends and employability skills, and of the career decision-making process, and which helps the individual gain self-direction through purposefully and consciously integrating work, family, leisure, and community roles. (p. 39)

This comprehensive definition points out the pervasive nature of the career counselor's role in schools.

This section presents competencies and indicators developed by the National Occupational Information Coordinating Committee (NOICC, 1992) for elementary, junior/middle, and high school students along with some guidance strategies. Many of the strategies were borrowed from the career-education movement, specifically from *A Framework for Developing Career Education* (Corpus Christi Independent School District, 1976). The strategies suggested should be considered as examples that will enhance some of the competencies and indicators and as examples of activities and formats that school counselors can use in the career-guidance program.

Elementary School Student: Competencies and Indicators

Self-Knowledge

Competency I: Knowledge of the importance of self-concept

- Describe positive characteristics about self as seen by self and others.
- Identify how behaviors affect school and family situations.
- Describe how behavior influences the feelings and actions of others.
- Demonstrate a positive attitude about self.

- Identify personal interests, abilities, strengths, and weaknesses.
- Describe ways to meet personal needs through work.

Competency II: Skills to interact with others

- Identify how people are unique.
- Demonstrate effective skills for interacting with others.
- Demonstrate skills in resolving conflicts with peers and adults.
- Demonstrate group membership skills.
- Identify sources and effects of peer pressure.
- Demonstrate appropriate behaviors when peer pressures are contrary to one's beliefs.
- Demonstrate awareness of different cultures, lifestyles, attitudes, and abilities.

Strategies

1. In a group discussion, ask students to use open-ended sentences, such as:
   I'm happy when _____.
   I'm sad when _____.
   I'm afraid when _____.
2. Have students compile a list or draw pictures of people they talked to during the week. In groups, discuss types of relationships they have with them.
3. Ask students to describe a friend and then themselves. Discuss and describe individual differences.
4. Play "Who Am I?" with one student playing a role and others trying to guess the role.
5. Have students select magazine pictures of events, places, and persons that interest them. Share interests.
6. Ask students to summarize ways in which individuals may be described. Then, ask students to select descriptions of themselves.
7. Ask students to answer the following questions in writing or orally: What do I do well? What goals do I have? What do I do poorly? Who am I like? What makes me different from others?
8. Have students make lists of "Things I like" and "Things I don't like." Compile the lists and discuss the variety of interests.
9. Form a "Who Am I?" group and meet once a week, during which each person is to describe a personal characteristic of an individual who performs a specific job. Compile list for future discussions.
10. Ask students to list several interests and to describe how they became interested in an activity.

Educational and Occupational Exploration

Competency III: Awareness of the importance of growth and change

- Identify personal feelings.

- Identify ways to express feelings.
- Describe causes of stress.
- Identify and select appropriate behaviors to deal with specific emotional situations.
- Demonstrate healthy ways of dealing with conflicts, stress, and emotions in self and others.
- Demonstrate knowledge of good health habits.

Competency IV: Awareness of the benefits of educational achievement

- Describe how academic skills can be used in the home and community.
- Identify personal strengths and weaknesses in subject areas.
- Identify academic skills needed in several occupational groups.
- Describe relationships among ability, effort, and achievement.
- Implement a plan of action for improving academic skills.
- Describe school tasks that are similar to skills essential for job success.
- Describe how the amount of education needed for different occupational levels varies.

Competency V: Awareness of the relationship between work and learning

- Identify different types of work, both paid and unpaid.
- Describe the importance of preparing for occupations.
- Demonstrate effective study and information-seeking habits.
- Demonstrate an understanding of the importance of practice, effort, and learning.
- Describe how current learning relates to work.
- Describe how one's role as a student is like that of an adult worker.

Competency VI: Skills to understand and use career information

- Describe work of family members, school personnel, and community workers.
- Identify occupations according to data, people, and things.
- Identify work activities of interest to the student.
- Describe the relationship of beliefs, attitudes, interests, and abilities to occupations.
- Describe jobs that are present in the local community.
- Identify the working conditions of occupations (for example, inside/ outside, hazardous).
- Describe way in which self-employment differs from working for others.
- Describe how parents, relatives, adult friends, and neighbors can provide career information.

Competency VII: Awareness of the importance of personal responsibility and good work habits

- Describe the importance of personal qualities (for example, dependability, promptness, getting along with others) to getting and keeping jobs.
- Demonstrate positive ways of performing working activities.

- Describe the importance of cooperation among workers to accomplish a task.
- Demonstrate the ability to work with people who are different from oneself (for example, race, age, gender).

Competency VIII: Awareness of how work relates to the needs and functions of society

- Describe how work can satisfy personal needs.
- Describe the products and services of local employers.
- Describe ways in which work can help overcome social and economic problems.

Strategies

1. Arrange a display of workers' hats that represent jobs in the community. Have each student select a hat that indicates a job he or she would like to do someday and explain why the job is appealing.
2. Assign students to develop a list of skills for their favorite jobs and describe how these skills are learned.
3. Ask each student to pretend that a friend wants a certain job, and ask each to describe the kinds of skills the friend would need.
4. Have students make a list of activities their parents do at home and have them identify the ones that require math, reading, and writing.
5. Have students make a list of school subjects and identify jobs in which the skills learned in the subjects are used.
6. Referring to a list of occupations, have students describe what kind of person may like a particular occupation.
7. Have students make a list of occupations that are involved in producing a loaf of bread.
8. Ask students to find a picture from a magazine or newspaper that depicts a female and male in a nontraditional job.
9. Have students interview their parents about their work roles and discuss these roles with the group.
10. Ask each student to adopt the identity of a worker and list work roles. Discuss how work has a personal meaning for every individual.

Career Planning

Competency IX: Understanding how to make decisions

- Describe how choices are made.
- Describe what can be learned from making mistakes.
- Identify and assess problems that interfere with attaining goals.
- Identify strategies used in solving problems.
- Identify alternatives in decision-making situations.
- Describe how personal beliefs and attitudes affect decision making.
- Describe how decisions affect self and others.

Competency X: Awareness of the interrelationship of life roles

- Describe the various roles an individual may have (for example, friend, student, worker, family member).
- Describe work-related activities in the home, community, and school.
- Describe how family members depend on one another, work together, and share responsibilities.
- Describe how work roles complement family roles.

Competency XI: Awareness of different occupations and changing male/ female roles

- Describe how work is important to all people.
- Describe the changing life roles of men and women in work and family.
- Describe how contributions of individuals both inside and outside the home are important.

Competency XII: Awareness of the career-planning process

- Describe the importance of planning.
- Describe skills needed in a variety of occupational groups.
- Develop an individual career plan for the elementary school level.

Strategies

1. Ask students to make a list of jobs/occupations they would use to describe their neighbors and/or acquaintances. Share with others.
2. Have students identify the kinds of people who work in a selected list of occupations. Emphasize likenesses and differences.
3. In a self-discovery group, discuss how people have different interests and enjoy different/similar activities.
4. Have students describe how workers in different activities are affected by weather.
5. Ask students to collect newspaper and magazine photos of different people and describe likenesses and differences.
6. Have students identify workers that visit their home. Identify differences of work and occupations.
7. Assign students to write a short paragraph answering the question "If you could be anyone in the world, whom would you be?" Follow with a discussion.
8. Divide the class into groups of boys and girls and ask each group to make a list of jobs girls can and cannot do. Compare lists and discuss how women are capable of performing most jobs.
9. Have students describe in writing and/or orally "someone I would like to work with." Make a list of positive characteristics that each student describes.
10. Discuss how people work together and demonstrate with an example of three people building a doghouse together. What would each person do?

Middle/Junior High School Student: Competencies and Indicators

Self-Knowledge

Competency I: Knowledge of the influence of a positive self-concept

- Describe personal likes and dislikes.
- Describe individual skills required to fulfill different life roles.
- Describe how one's behavior influences the feelings and actions of others.
- Identify environmental influences on attitudes, behaviors, and aptitudes.

Competency II: Skills to interact with others

- Demonstrate respect for the feelings and beliefs of others.
- Demonstrate an appreciation for the similarities and differences among people.
- Demonstrate tolerance and flexibility in interpersonal and group situations.
- Demonstrate skills in responding to criticism.
- Demonstrate effective group membership skills.
- Demonstrate effective social skills.
- Demonstrate understanding of different cultures, lifestyles, attitudes, and abilities.

Competency III: Knowledge of the importance of growth and change

- Identify feelings associated with significant experiences.
- Identify internal and external sources of stress.
- Demonstrate ways of responding to others when under stress.
- Describe changes that occur in the physical, psychological, social, and emotional development of an individual.
- Describe physiological and psychological factors as they relate to career development.
- Describe the importance of career, family, and leisure activities to mental, emotional, physical, and economic well-being.

Strategies

1. Introduce the concepts of self-image, self-worth, and self-esteem. Assign small groups to discuss the relationship of these concepts to educational and occupational planning. Compile a list from these groups.
2. Ask students to complete a standardized or original personality inventory. Using Holland's (1985) classification system, have students relate personality characteristics to work environments.
3. Have students list courses in which they have excelled and those in which they have not. Ask students to relate skills learned to their personality characteristics and traits and interests.

4. Assign students to construct a lifeline in which they designate places lived in and visited, experiences in school and with peer groups, and major events. Have them project the lifeline into the future by identifying goals.
5. Have students discuss how different traits are more important for some goals than for others. Compile a list of jobs and corresponding traits.

Educational and Occupational Exploration

Competency IV: Knowledge of the benefits of educational achievement to career opportunities

- Describe the importance of academic and occupational skills in the work world.
- Identify how the skills taught in school subjects are used in various occupations.
- Describe individual strengths and weaknesses in school subjects.
- Describe a plan of action for increasing basic educational skills.
- Describe the skills needed to adjust to changing occupational requirements.
- Describe how continued learning enhances the ability to achieve goals.
- Describe how skills relate to the selection of high school courses of study.
- Describe how aptitudes and abilities relate to broad occupational groups.

Competency V: Understanding the relationship between work and learning

- Demonstrate effective learning habits and skills.
- Demonstrate an understanding of the importance of personal skills and attitudes to job success.
- Describe the relationship of personal attitudes, beliefs, abilities, and skills to occupations.

Competency VI: Skills to locate, understand, and use career information

- Identify various ways that occupations can be classified.
- Identify a number of occupational groups for exploration.
- Demonstrate skills in using school and community resources to learn about occupational groups.
- Identify sources to obtain information about occupational groups including self-employment.
- Identify skills that are transferable from one occupation to another.
- Identify sources of employment in the community.

Competency VII: Knowledge of skills necessary to seek and obtain jobs

- Demonstrate personal qualities (for example, dependability, punctuality, getting along with others) that are needed to get and keep jobs.
- Describe terms and concepts used in describing employment opportunities and conditions.
- Demonstrate skills to complete a job application.

• Demonstrate skills and attitudes essential for a job interview.

Competency VIII: Understanding how work relates to the needs and functions of the economy and society

• Describe the importance of work to society.
• Describe the relationship between work and economic and societal needs.
• Describe the economic contributions workers make to society.
• Describe the effects that societal, economic, and technological change have on occupations.

Strategies

1. Ask students to write a description of the type of person they think they are, their preferences for activities (work and leisure), their strengths and weaknesses, and their desires for a career someday. Discuss.
2. Have students list several occupations that are related to their own interests and abilities. Discuss.
3. Lead a class discussion by identifying relationships of interest and abilities to various occupations. Each student should explore one occupation in depth, including reading a biography, writing a letter to someone, or conducting interviews. The student should research training requirements, working conditions, and personal attributes necessary for the job.
4. Ask each student to visit a place in the community where he/she can observe someone involved in a career of interest. Have students demonstrate their observations, such as type of work, working conditions, or tools of the trade.
5. Have the students make a list of the school subjects that are necessary to the success of persons whose careers are being investigated. Discuss.
6. Ask students to research preparation requirements for several selected occupations. Have them identify one similarity and one difference in preparation requirements for each of the occupations listed. Discuss.
7. Assign students to write short narratives explaining why certain jobs have endured and others have disappeared. Discuss.
8. Have students classify ten occupations by abilities needed, such as physical, mental, mechanical, creative, social, and other. Have students select three occupations that match their abilities and interests.
9. Have students do a mini-internship program where they shadow a worker. Discuss and share with other students.
10. Have students write a story about the many jobs involved in producing a hamburger. Discuss.

Career Planning

Competency IX: Skills to make decisions

• Describe personal beliefs and attitudes

- Describe how career development is a continuous process with series of choices.
- Identify possible outcomes of decisions.
- Describe school courses related to personal, educational, and occupational interests.
- Describe how the expectations of others affect career planning.
- Identify ways in which decisions about education and work relate to other major life decisions.
- Identify advantages and disadvantages of various secondary and post-secondary programs for the attainment of career goals.
- Identify the requirements for secondary and post-secondary programs.

Competency X: Knowledge of the interrelationship of life roles

- Identify how different work and family patterns require varying kinds and amounts of energy, participation, motivation, and talent.
- Identify how work roles at home satisfy needs of the family.
- Identify personal goals that may be satisfied through a combination of work, community, social, and family roles.
- Identify personal leisure choices in relation to lifestyle and the attainment of future goals.
- Describe advantages and disadvantages of various life role options.
- Describe the interrelationships between family, occupational, and leisure decisions.

Competency XI: Knowledge of different occupations and changing male/ female roles

- Describe advantages and problems of entering nontraditional occupations.
- Describe the advantages of taking courses related to personal interest, even if they are most often taken by members of the opposite gender.
- Describe stereotypes, biases, and discriminatory behaviors that may limit opportunities for women and men in certain occupations.

Competency XII: Understanding the process of career planning

- Demonstrate knowledge of exploratory processes and programs.
- Identify school courses that meet tentative career goals.
- Demonstrate knowledge of academic and vocational programs offered at the high school level.
- Describe skills needed in a variety of occupations, including self-employment.
- Identify strategies for managing personal resources (for example, talents, time, money) to achieve tentative career goals.
- Develop an individual career plan, updating information from the elementary-level plan and including tentative decisions to be implemented in high school.

Strategies

1. Present steps in a decision-making model and discuss the importance of each step. Ask students to identify a problem and solve it by applying steps in the model.
2. Organize students into groups and have them construct a list of resources and resource people who could help solve a particular problem.
3. In a group discussion, compare a horoscope from a daily newspaper with other ways of solving problems and making decisions.
4. Assign students to select three occupations and then to choose one using a decision model. Share and discuss in groups.
5. Have students prepare an educational plan for high school. Share and discuss in groups.

High School Student: Competencies and Indicators

Self-Knowledge

Competency I: Understanding the influence of a positive self-concept

- Identify and appreciate personal interests, abilities, and skills.
- Demonstrate the ability to use peer feedback.
- Demonstrate an understanding of how individual characteristics relate to achieving personal, social, educational, and career goals.
- Demonstrate an understanding of environmental influences on one's behavior.
- Demonstrate an understanding of the relationship between personal behavior and self-concept.

Competency II: Skills to interact positively with others

- Demonstrate effective interpersonal skills.
- Demonstrate interpersonal skills required for working with and for others.
- Describe appropriate employer and employee interactions in various situations.
- Demonstrate how to express feelings, reactions, and ideas in an appropriate manner.

Competency III: Understanding the impact of growth and development

- Describe how developmental changes affect physical and mental health.
- Describe the effect of emotional and physical health on career decisions.
- Describe healthy ways of dealing with stress.
- Demonstrate behaviors that maintain physical and mental health.

Strategies

1. Have students list five roles they currently fill. Discuss in small groups and identify future roles, such as spouse, parent, and citizen. Discuss.

2. Discuss or show films on sex-role stereotyping. Have students identify how sex-role stereotyping prohibits many individuals from becoming involved in certain events, including work roles.
3. Assign students to select newspaper and magazine pictures and articles that illustrate societal perceptions of appropriate behavior and dress. Discuss.
4. Have students discuss physical differences among their peers. Emphasize how differences may affect individuals.
5. Discuss the value of cooperative efforts in the work environment. Have students develop a project in which cooperation is essential. Discuss.
6. Have students observe workers performing specific tasks and make notes of skills and time required to complete tasks. Discuss.
7. Have students discuss employer expectations as compared to their own. Develop a consensus about how both are justified and can be attained.
8. Have students role-play a supervisor reacting to an employee's work performance. Discuss reactions of supervisors in a variety of situations.
9. Have students research the various causes of tardiness and absenteeism among workers. Discuss.
10. Ask students to interview at least three workers and three supervisors of workers on the subject of good work habits. Discuss.

Educational and Occupational Exploration

Competency IV: Understanding the relationship between educational achievement and career planning

- Demonstrate how to apply academic and vocational skills to achieve personal goals.
- Describe the relationship of academic and vocational skills to personal interests.
- Describe how skills developed in academic and vocational programs relate to career goals.
- Describe how education relates to the selection of college majors, further training, and/or entry into the job market.
- Demonstrate transferable skills that can apply to a variety of occupations and changing occupational requirements.
- Describe how learning skills are required in the workplace.

Competency V: Understanding the need for positive attitudes toward work and learning

- Identify the positive contributions workers make to society.
- Demonstrate knowledge of the social significance of various occupations.
- Demonstrate a positive attitude toward work.
- Demonstrate learning habits and skills that can be used in various educational situations.

- Demonstrate positive work attitudes and behaviors.

Competency VI: Skills to locate, evaluate, and interpret career information

- Describe the educational requirements of various occupations.
- Demonstrate use of a range of resources (for example, handbooks, career materials, labor-market information, and computerized career-information delivery systems).
- Demonstrate knowledge of various classification systems that categorize occupations and industries (for example, *Dictionary of Occupational Titles*).
- Describe the concept of career ladders.
- Describe the advantages and disadvantages of self-employment as a career option.
- Identify individuals in selected occupations as possible information resources, role models, or mentors.
- Describe the influence of change in supply and demand for workers in different occupations.
- Identify how employment trends relate to education and training.
- Describe the impact of factors such as population, climate, and geographic location on occupational opportunities.

Competency VII: Skills to prepare to seek, obtain, maintain, and change jobs

- Demonstrate skills to locate, interpret, and use information about job openings and opportunities.
- Demonstrate academic or vocational skills required for a full or part-time job.
- Demonstrate skills and behaviors necessary for a successful job interview.
- Demonstrate skills in preparing a résumé and completing job applications.
- Identify specific job openings.
- Demonstrate employability skills necessary to obtain and maintain jobs.
- Demonstrate skills to assess occupational opportunities (for example, working conditions, benefits, and opportunities for change).
- Describe placement services available to make the transition from high school to civilian employment, the armed services, or post-secondary education/training.
- Demonstrate an understanding that job opportunities often require relocation.
- Demonstrate skills necessary to function as a consumer and manage financial resources.

Competency VIII: Understanding how societal needs and functions influence the nature and structure of work

- Describe the effect of work on lifestyles.
- Describe how society's needs and functions affect the supply of goods and services.

- Describe how occupational and industrial trends relate to training and employment.
- Demonstrate an understanding of the global economy and how it affects each individual.

Strategies

1. *To identify geographical factors that can affect choice of a career* (Geary, 1972). Obtain newspapers from urban and rural areas. Compare employment opportunities and contrast differences.
2. *To identify high school courses required for entry into trade schools, colleges, or jobs* (Walz, 1972). Discuss elements of required courses and develop brochures that list jobs and corresponding high school courses required.
3. *To understand how human values are significant in career decision making* (Bottoms et al., 1972). Develop a list of values that may influence selection of a career. Each student selects two values of importance and locates a career that would be congruent with values. Discuss.
4. *To understand the principles and techniques of life planning* (Brown, 1980). In small groups, in eight 1-hour meetings, six components are presented and discussed: "Why People Behave the Way They Do," "Winners and Losers," "Your Fantasy Life," "Your Real Life," "Setting Goals," and "Short- and Long-term Planning."
5. *To prepare for entrance into college* (Hansen, 1970). A college-bound club discusses in weekly meetings such topics as how to read a college catalog, how to visit a college campus, and college study.
6. Discuss the value of leisure activities. Have students report on the benefits involved in five leisure activities of their choice. Discuss.
7. Have students develop a list of leisure activities they enjoy and estimate the amount of time necessary to participate in each. Form groups to decide which occupations would most likely provide the necessary time and which ones would not.
8. Ask students to debate the pros and cons of selected leisure activities.
9. Assign students to develop a list of leisure activities they enjoy now and project which of these can be enjoyed over the life span. Have students collect and discuss brochures from travel agencies and parks.
10. Have students discuss the concept of lifestyle in terms of work commitment, leisure activities, family involvement, and responsibilities and share their projections of future life roles and lifestyle.

Career Planning

Competency IX: Skills to make decisions

- Demonstrate responsibility for making tentative educational and occupational choices.
- Identify alternatives in given decision-making situations.

- Describe personal strengths and weaknesses in relationship to post-secondary education/training requirements.
- Identify appropriate choices during high school that will lead to marketable skills for entry-level employment or advanced training.
- Identify and complete required steps toward transition from high school to entry into post-secondary education/training programs or work.
- Identify steps to apply for and secure financial assistance for post-secondary education and training.

Competency X: Understanding the interrelationship of life roles

- Demonstrate knowledge of life stages.
- Describe factors that determine lifestyles (for example, socioeconomic status, culture, values, occupational choices, work habits).
- Describe ways in which occupational choices may affect lifestyle.
- Describe the contribution of work to a balanced and productive life.
- Describe ways in which work, family, and leisure roles are interrelated.
- Describe different career patterns and their potential effect on family patterns and lifestyle.
- Describe the importance of leisure activities.
- Demonstrate ways that occupational skills and knowledge can be acquired through leisure.

Competency XI: Understanding the continuous changes in male/female roles

- Identify factors that have influenced the changing career patterns of women and men.
- Identify evidence of gender stereotyping and bias in educational programs and occupational settings.
- Demonstrate attitudes, behaviors, and skills that contribute to eliminating gender bias and stereotyping.
- Identify courses appropriate to tentative occupational choices.
- Describe the advantages and problems of nontraditional occupations.

Competency XII: Skills in career planning

- Describe career plans that reflect the importance of lifelong learning.
- Demonstrate knowledge of post-secondary vocational and academic programs.
- Demonstrate knowledge that changes may require retraining and upgrading of employees' skills.
- Describe school and community resources to explore educational and occupational choices.
- Describe the costs and benefits of self-employment.
- Demonstrate occupational skills developed through volunteer experiences, part-time employment, or cooperative education programs.
- Demonstrate skills necessary to compare education and job opportunities.

• Develop an individual career plan, updating information from earlier plans and including tentative decisions to be implemented after high school.

Strategies

1. Ask students to review several job-search manuals. Discuss the steps suggested in the manuals and develop strategies for taking these steps.
2. Assign students to visit a state employment agency and describe its functions. Discuss.
3. Have students research newspaper want-ads and select several of interest. Discuss and identify appropriate occupational information resources.
4. Have students demonstrate the steps involved in identifying an appropriate job, filling out an application, and writing a résumé. Discuss.
5. Have students participate in a mock interview. Critique and discuss appropriate dress and grooming.
6. Help students develop planning skills (Hansen, 1970). A one-year course, taught as an elective, covers six major areas of study: (a) relating one's characteristics to occupations; (b) exploring manual and mechanical occupations; (c) exploring professional, technical, and managerial occupations; (d) relating the economic system to occupations and people; (e) exploring roles, clerical, and service occupations; and (f) evaluating and planning ahead.
7. Help students evaluate careers in terms of standards of living and lifestyle (Steidl, 1972; Sorapuru, Theodore, & Young, 1972a). Students project themselves 10 to 15 years in the future and identify the kind of lifestyle they would like to have. Each student selects four careers and conducts research to determine if the projected lifestyle can be met through these careers.
8. Provide good job-search procedures (Sorapuru, Theodore, & Young, 1972b). Students who have had part-time jobs explain how they got them. Groups investigate local organizations that help people find jobs. Students investigate telephone directories, school placement center files, and state employment agencies for leads to jobs. Students write résumés and "walk through" steps for applying and interviewing.
9. Help students understand the stressors of work responsibility (Bottoms et al., 1972). Students identify individuals who recently attained a position of prominence and compare changes in lifestyle (work, leisure, and family).
10. Involve parents in career planning and decision making in high school (Amatea & Cross, 1980). Students and parents attend six 2-hour sessions per week and discuss the following at school and at home: self-management and goal setting, elements in career planning and decision making, comparing self with occupational data, information gathering skills, and training paths.

Understanding Sex-Role Stereotyping

All children need to be prepared for self-sufficiency in the future. One of the major challenges is to assist both boys and girls in overcoming the problems associated with sex-role stereotyping. Counseling-component modules for the classroom present one method of accomplishing this objective. The following case study uses a counseling module for junior high school.

> Jane, Sarah, Bart, and John are in a junior high school self-discovery counseling group. The counselor asks each member to study an advertisement that uses a man and a woman on television and also to locate one in a magazine. Each will record the product being advertised and describe the individual in the ad.
>
> Sarah and John recorded the information for two ads, which were discussed in the next group session. Sarah's notes included the following: "This woman was beautiful on television, in a long flowing dress with gorgeous hair blowing in the wind. She was advertising a soap to be used for the face and hands for keeping them soft and pretty."
>
> John's notes were taken on a magazine ad: "This ad was on a full page in a magazine. It showed a man advertising cigarettes who had a tatoo on his hand. He looked like a cowboy with a weather-beaten face."
>
> The counselor asked the group to discuss the characteristics of each character in the two ads. The adjectives used to describe each character were recorded. On the woman in the ad, the list included beautiful, graceful, clean, dainty, and sexy. The list for the man included macho, handsome, outdoorsman, self-assured, and rugged.
>
> The counselor asked the group to discuss the appropriate roles in life for men and women implied by these advertisements. The apparent differences in roles were then extended to typical sex-role stereotypes such as women are to be pampered, dependent, and pretty, while men are strong, free to do as they please, and independent. The group discussed how these ads and other types of sex-role stereotyping have influenced their own perceptions of lifestyles for men and women and subsequently the careers they find appropriate for men and women. The counselor summarized the influence of sex-role stereotyping found in advertising and elsewhere in society. Finally, the changing role of women in general and specifically in the work force was emphasized.

Role models may also be used as a counseling component that can effectively emphasize the occupational potential of girls. Examples of women who have enjoyed successful careers provide girls with concrete evidence that women do have opportunities to develop careers in a working world thought to be dominated by men. Numerous techniques are applicable to such a component. One method is to have students interview working women and write a summary of their work-related experience. Biographies of women may also be reviewed and discussed (*Vocational Biographies,* 1985). These examples should emphasize how women can overcome sex-role stereotyping and find equal opportunity in the job market. They also illustrate that women can effectively assume leadership roles in the world of work. Finally, role models provide support for girls seriously considering a career-oriented lifestyle and may also provide some potential mentors.

Locating a mentor from whom one can directly learn the skills of a given career is usually highly productive. Therefore, career education and career-counseling programs that instruct girls on the values of mentor relationships are very useful. A mentor is usually an older person who is admired and respected and has tremendous influence on the young. Levinson (1980) suggested that women who aspire to professional careers have fewer opportunities to find a mentor than do males, primarily because there are fewer female mentors available. There is some evidence that cross-gender mentoring can be of value, but because there is the tendency by men to not take career women seriously, there is the danger of increasing the chances of sex-role stereotyping.

STRATEGIES FOR IMPLEMENTING CAREER-DEVELOPMENT GUIDELINES

Splete and Stewart (1990) reviewed the career-development abstracts included in the ERIC database between 1980 and 1990. On completing their review, they made the following recommendations for how competencies could be achieved at various levels.

Elementary school level

- More parents and community persons should be involved in presenting career information.
- Increased attention should be given to self-knowledge activities, especially as they relate to the development of a positive self-concept.
- Use of media (computer programs, videos, films) should be increased.

Middle/junior high school level

- Place more emphasis on self-knowledge competencies.
- Get business persons involved with students to help them with educational and occupational exploration and career planning.
- Increase attention to the benefits of educational achievement as the amount of education for different occupations varies.
- Emphasize on skills necessary to seek and obtain jobs.

High school level

- Emphasize activities related to awareness of interrelationship of life roles.
- Increased emphasis on understanding the relationship of work to the economy and how work influences lifestyles.
- Find opportunities for students to improve skills to interact with others, a needed workplace characteristic. (Splete & Stewart, 1990)

The strength of the NOICC competency-based program models is that they describe goals and objectives in terms of specific tasks. These competencies also lend themselves quite readily to task statements and activities in order to develop the skills necessary to complete each task. And perhaps even most important, criteria for successful task performance can be specifically defined.

NOICC established the National Career Development Training Institute (CDTI) in 1992. The CDTI's major responsibility has been to design career-development training programs for states to use in training the personnel who help students and adults acquire career-planning skills and make career decisions. The focus has been on in-service training for professional counselors and other advisers and preservice training through counselor-education programs at universities and other institutions. The CDTI also designs and develops training models and reviews the certification and credentials required of career-development personnel. Competencies for staff who deliver career-guidance and counseling programs have been defined by NOICC and are included in the appendix.

The next sections introduce a comprehensive school-guidance program, present recent changes in vocational education, and summarize the impact of other significant government-sponsored programs.

COMPREHENSIVE SCHOOL-GUIDANCE PROGRAMS

Gysbers and Henderson (1988) have developed detailed plans for developing, designing, implementing, and evaluating a comprehensive school-guidance program. In an earlier conceptual treatise on comprehensive guidance programs, Gysbers and Moore (1987) pointed out that a comprehensive guidance model is not an ancillary guidance service, but one in which all staff are involved, including administrators, members of the community, and parents. Furthermore, they are involved in a common objective whose goal is the total integrated development of individual students. According to Gysbers and Henderson (1988), guidance programs should be viewed as developmental and comprehensive in that regularly scheduled activities are planned, conducted, and evaluated, and comprehensive guidance programs feature a team approach. In essence, it is a full commitment to surveying current guidance programs within a district; establishing students' needs; establishing plans, activities, and staff to meet those needs; and recognizing that a comprehensive guidance program is an equal partner with other educational programs.

Human growth and development are the foundation upon which comprehensive guidance programs are built, especially within the domain of lifetime career development. The focus is the interrelationship of all aspects of life. For instance, the family role is not treated separately from other life roles. The life-career developmental domains are characterized as follows: (1) self-knowledge and interpersonal skills (self-understanding and recognizing the uniqueness of others); (2) life roles, settings, and events (roles such as learner, citizen, and worker; settings such as community, home, and work environment; events such as beginning the work role, marriage, and retirement); (3) life career planning (decision making and planning); and (4) basic studies and occupational preparation (knowledge and skills found in various subjects typically offered in school curricula).

Counselor involvement and commitment in this approach is extensive. They are involved in teaching, team teaching, and supporting teachers. A major innovation in this program is the development of student competencies and the methods used to evaluate them. For example, at the perceptual level, the acquisition of knowledge and skills related to selected aspects of community and self are evaluated as environmental orientation and self-orientation. The conceptual level emphasizes directional tendencies (movement toward socially desirable goals) and adaptive and adjustive behavior. The generalization level is the level of functioning students exhibit throughout the mastery of specific tasks. Each of these competencies is broken down into specific goals with identified competencies; student outcomes are specified by grade level and activity objectives.

Monitoring is accomplished using an individualized advisory system; each adviser has 15 to 20 students. The allocation of the counselor's time during the school day is suggested in percentages for participation in curriculum, individual planning, responsive services (recurring topics such as academic failure, peer problems, and family situations), and system support (consulting with parents, staff development, and compensatory programs).

The comprehensive school-guidance program is a means of systematically implementing a program concept for guidance activities in kindergarten through grade 12. The value of this model is its comprehensive nature and the involvement of school professionals, selected members of the community, and parents. The program's flexibility allows for local development of needs. Another major advantage is the evaluation of student outcomes, professional effectiveness, and program design. The program's foundation centers around a life-career development theme. The recognition of the importance of the interrelatedness of all life roles is a profound message to the career-counseling profession.

INTEGRATING ACADEMIC AND VOCATIONAL EDUCATION

Vocational educators have developed a vocational reform strategy that provides a system in which students achieve both academic and occupational competencies. The major goal is to improve the educational and employment opportunities of students who face new technologies and business-management systems that require high-level worker skills. Models for integrating academic and vocational education have been described by Grubb and peers (1991) as follows:

1. Incorporate more academic content in vocational courses (vocational teachers modify vocational courses to include more academic content).

2. Combine vocational and academic teachers to enhance academic competencies in vocational programs (a cooperative effort involves more academic content in vocational courses).
3. Make academic courses more vocationally relevant (academic teachers modify courses or adopt new courses to include more vocational content).
4. Modify both vocational and academic courses (change content of both vocational and academic courses).
5. Use the senior project as a form of integration (teachers collaborate in developing new courses around student projects).
6. Implement the Academy model (use team teaching of math, English, science, and vocational subjects for two or three years and then require other subjects in regular high school).
7. Develop occupational high schools and magnet schools (occupational schools have been more successful in integrating vocational and academic education than the magnet schools).
8. Implement occupational clusters, "career paths," and occupational majors (students are encouraged to think about occupations early in high school).

The interest in integrating academic and vocational education has primarily evolved from a need to encourage vocational-education students to take more rigorous academic courses. A strong academic background is essential for continuing education, which is a growing trend among vocational schools (Cetron & Gayle, 1991). The models described by Grubb and colleagues (1991) underscore the interest in making significant changes in vocational education.

Tech-Prep Programs

Tech-prep is a national strategy that is designed to have students exit high school or a community/technology college with marketable skills for job placement, have academic credentials to pursue higher education, or have both of these options. In this context *tech-prep* means integrated academics and technical training for secondary, postsecondary, and apprenticeship students, plus curriculum development to meet the skills requirements of advanced-technology jobs. Also included is an innovative, up-to-date career counseling program about high-demand occupations, a comprehensive assessment program for students in middle/junior high school, and individualized high school graduation plans.

To accomplish the goals of tech-prep programs, school systems and cooperating colleges and universities have formed consortiums with industry. Through such organizations, education and industry can coordinate work-site-based training. Additionally, graduates' follow-up assessment is enhanced.

Encouraging vocational-education students to take more advanced academic courses is the major goal of tech-prep models. Typically, schools devise a variety of two-year technical curricula that include such subjects as applied mathematics, applied biology/chemistry, and principles of technology. There is often a working relationship with cooperating colleges that have agreed, by prior arrangement, to accept these courses for college credit or as entrance requirements.

Operationally, students concentrate on basic concepts their first year and learn more about applications of the concepts during the second year. In principles of technology, for example, first-year students examine principles of force, work, energy, and power; in the second year, they apply these concepts in optical systems, radiation, and transducers. Many of the colleges that accept the principles of technology course usually count it as a laboratory-science requirement (Cetron & Gayle, 1991). The National Career Development Training Institute plans to incorporate in its training programs the counselor's role in tech-prep programs. We should hear a great deal more about these programs in the near future.

GOVERNMENT-SPONSORED PROGRAMS: PLANNING FOR THE FUTURE

In the late 1980s, the Department of Labor formed the Secretary's Commission on Achieving Necessary Skills (SCANS) to determine the level of skills required to enter employment. Specifically, SCANS was to define the skills needed for employment, propose acceptable levels of proficiency, suggest effective ways to assess proficiency, and develop a dissemination strategy for the nation's schools, businesses, and homes.

After lengthy interviews with workers in a wide range of jobs and discussions and meetings with business owners, public employers, unions, workers, and supervisors in shops, plants, and stores, the prevailing message was that good jobs increasingly depend on people who can put knowledge to work. The Commission concluded that young people in general leave school without the knowledge or foundation required to find and hold jobs. In labeling job performance as *workplace know-how*, SCANS suggested that know-how has two elements: competencies and a foundation. The five identified competencies are found in Box 10-1, and the three-part foundation of skills and personal qualities is reported in Box 10-2.

The five competencies are applicable to practically all jobs and reflect the attributes the employer seeks in tomorrow's employee. A large portion of these competencies involve human resources and interpersonal skills mixed with technological skills and knowledge. The elements of the three-part foundation emphasize basic skills but also place extreme importance on thinking skills and personal qualities. In this respect, the basic skills take on a new meaning in the workplace; now, not only is an employee expected to read well, but even more important, he or she must also understand and interpret information. Further-

Box 10-1
Five Competencies for AMERICA 2000

Resources

Identifies, organizes, plans, and allocates resources

A. *Time*—selects goal-relevant activities, ranks them, allocates time, and prepares and follows schedules
B. *Money*—uses or prepares budgets, makes forecasts, keeps records, and makes adjustments to meet objectives
C. *Material and facilities*—acquires, stores, allocates, and uses materials or space efficiently
D. *Human resources*—assesses skills and distributes work accordingly, evaluates performance, and provides feedback

Interpersonal

Works with others

A. *Participates as member of a team*—contributes to group effort
B. *Teaches others new skills*
C. *Serves clients/customers*—works to satisfy customers' expectations
D. *Exercises leadership*—communicates ideas to justify position, persuades and convinces others, responsibly challenges existing procedures and policies
E. *Negotiates*—works toward agreements involving exchange of resources, resolves divergent interests
F. *Works with diversity*—works well with men and women from diverse backgrounds

Information

Acquires and uses information

A. *Acquires and evaluates information*
B. *Organizes and maintains information*
C. *Interprets and communicates information*
D. *Uses computers to process information*

Systems

Understands complex inter-relationships

A. *Understands systems*—knows how social, organizational, and technological systems work and operates effectively with them
B. *Monitors and corrects performance*—distinguishes trends, predicts impacts on system operations, diagnoses systems' performance, and corrects malfunctions
C. *Improves or designs systems*—suggests modifications to existing systems and develops new or alternative systems to improve performance

Technology

Works with a variety of technologies

A. *Selects technology*—chooses procedures, tools, or equipment including computers and related technologies
B. *Applies technology to task*—understands overall intent and proper procedures for setup and operation of equipment
C. *Maintains and troubleshoots equipment*—prevents, identifies, or solves problems with equipment, including computers and other technologies

SOURCE: U.S. Department of Labor. (1991). What work requires of schools: A SCANS report for AMERICA 2000. Washington, DC: U.S. Government Printing Office.

Box 10-2
A Three-Part Foundation for AMERICA 2000

Basic Skills

Reads, writes, performs arithmetic and mathematical operations, listens, and speaks

A. *Reading*—locates, understands, and interprets written information in prose and in documents such as manuals, graphs, and schedules
B. *Writing*—communicates thoughts, ideas, information, and messages in writing; and creates documents such as letters, directions, manuals, reports, graphs, and flow charts
C. *Arithmetic/mathematics*—performs basic computations and approaches practical problems by choosing appropriately from a variety of mathematical techniques
D. *Listening*—receives, attends to, interprets, and responds to verbal messages and other cues
E. *Speaking*—organizes ideas and communicates orally

Thinking Skills

Thinks creatively makes decisions, solves problems, visualizes, knows how to learn, and reasons

A. *Creative thinking*—generates new ideas
B. *Decision making*—specifies goals and constraints, generates alternatives, considers risks, and evaluates and chooses best alternative

C. *Problem solving*—recognizes problems and devises and implements plan of action
D. *Seeing things in the mind's eye*—organizes, and processes symbols, pictures, graphs, objects, and other information
E. *Knowing how to learn*—uses efficient learning techniques to acquire and apply new knowledge and skills
F. *Reasoning*—discovers a rule or principle underlying the relationship between two or more objects and applies it when solving a problem

Personal Qualities

Displays responsibility, self-esteem, sociability, self-management, and integrity and honesty

A. *Responsibility*—exerts a high level of effort and perseveres toward goal attainment
B. *Self-esteem*—believes in own self-worth and maintains a positive view of self
C. *Sociability*—demonstrates understanding, friendliness, adaptability, empathy, and politeness in group settings
D. *Self-management*—assesses self accurately, sets personal goals, monitors progress, and exhibits self-control
E. *Integrity/honesty*—chooses ethical courses of action

SOURCE: U.S. Department of Labor. (1991). What work requires of schools: A SCANS report for AMERICA 2000. Washington, DC: U.S. Government Printing Office.

more, tomorrow's workers must be prepared to communicate with others, work in teams, and describe complex systems and procedures. What we must communicate to future workers is that proficiency in each competency requires proficiency in the foundation. The report ends with the pronouncement that what America 2000 will need from our schools is progress in teaching skills (the competencies and academic foundations needed by students in the year 2000).

Apprenticeship and the Future of the Work Force

In recognition of the changing needs of the work force, especially the need for technical skills, the U.S. Department of Labor has established a Committee on Apprenticeship. Like other work-based learning, training under the supervision of a master worker is a desirable learning experience. Building technical skills and observing how technical tasks relate to theoretical knowledge and interpretation is a major advantage of apprenticeship.

The Federal Committee on Apprenticeship suggests training strategies with eight essential components as follows:

- Apprenticeship is sponsored by employers and others who can actually hire and train individuals in the workplace, and it combines hands-on training on the job with related theoretical instruction.
- Workplace and industry needs dictate key details of apprenticeship programs—training content, length of training, and actual employment settings.
- Apprenticeship has a specific legal status and is regulated by federal and state laws and regulations.
- Apprenticeship leads to formal, official credentials—a Certificate of Completion and journeyperson status.
- Apprenticeship generally requires a significant investment of time and money on the part of employers or other sponsors.
- Apprenticeship provides wages to apprentices during training according to predefined wage scales.
- Apprentices learn by working directly under master workers in their occupations.
- Apprenticeship involves both written agreements and implicit expectations. Written agreements specify the roles and responsibilities of each party; implicit expectations include the right of program sponsors to employ the apprentice, recouping their sizable investment in training, and the right of apprentices to obtain such employment. (Grossman & Drier, 1988)

Apprenticeships are independent of vocational-technical education programs, tech-prep programs, and cooperative education. This distinction is made because only apprenticeship produces fully trained journeypersons with the skills needed to perform effectively in the workplace. The concept of apprenticeships is important in meeting the ever- and fast-changing technical needs of the workplace.

PLACEMENT AS PART OF CAREER PLANNING

This section covers the role of placement officers in secondary schools and also the role of the state employment agency.

The Role of Placement in Senior High School

A major component of the placement part of career planning involves job listings from local, state, regional, national, and international sources. The numerous federal and state programs that provide job placement for high school graduates and dropouts are valuable referral sources for secondary schools. A cooperative venture between the school, the business community, and federal and state agencies is essential in developing local sources of job listings. One of the most effective approaches is through a community advisory committee (Tolbert, 1974). Local service clubs, chambers of commerce, federal and state agencies, and professional and personnel organizations are excellent resources for developing a local career-advisory committee. As demand for hands-on experience increases, local career opportunities will be essential to the success of these programs. A viable listing of local part-time and full-time jobs will also enhance the popularity of the career-planning and placement office.

Programs that enhance the transition from school to work should also be offered in senior high schools. In this respect, placement should be viewed as a vital function of, and a continuation of, career-guidance programs (Herr & Cramer, 1992). Some suggested program topics include how to prepare for an interview, write a résumé, locate job information, apply for a job, know if you are qualified for a job, and find the right job.

Finally, computer-assisted career-guidance programs (discussed in Chapter 6) provide vital, up-to-date information on the current job market. The ability to generate local job information on available computer programs is extremely helpful to the job seeker. In fact, the fast-changing job market may very well require computer capabilities to keep up-to-date.

Placement services can also provide the vital link between academics and the working world. Career-planning and placement services offered early in secondary programs should provide the student with knowledge of career skills to be developed in secondary education. Such programs should not be established to discourage future formal academic training but should provide relevance and added motivation for learning per se. Career planning and placement in this sense should be an ongoing program for students in various levels of secondary education, with the placement function playing a vital role in student services.

PLACEMENT BY STATE EMPLOYMENT AGENCIES

State employment agencies consist of a network of local offices in cities and rural areas across the nation. This network is based on federal and state partnerships with the U.S. Employment Service, providing broad national guidelines for operational procedures in state and local employment offices. One of the principal sources of job information has been compiled into what is referred to as a *job bank*. The job bank is a listing of all job orders compiled daily within each state. Microfiche copies are distributed daily to authorized users and all state employment offices. Those offices with computer terminals have direct access to the job bank. This up-to-the minute job information is available to all job seekers, who are required to fill out an application and be interviewed before they are given access to the job bank.

The functions of state employment agencies, which have very active placement programs, are to help the unemployed find work and to provide employers with qualified applicants for job orders. Many state agencies divide their services into two categories: (1) placement for job seekers and (2) services to employers. For job seekers, state agencies offer the following services:

1. Job listings in professional, clerical, skilled, technical, sales, managerial, semiskilled, service, and labor occupations
2. Personal interviews with professional interviewers
3. Assistance with improving qualifications
4. Referral to training
5. Testing
6. Counseling
7. Service to veterans
8. Unemployment benefits (for those who qualify while they are looking for work).

Services offered to employers are as follows:

1. Screening for qualified applicants
2. Professional interviews
3. On-site recruitment and application taking
4. Computerized job listing in most areas of the state
5. Aptitude and proficiency testing
6. Labor-market information on technical assistance
7. Technical assistance with job descriptions, master orders, and turnover studies
8. Unemployment insurance tax information.

Job placement is the focus of state employment agencies, but career counseling is available when requested. State employment agencies also administer assessment instruments that are typically used in career counseling, such as aptitude and achievement tests. Individuals are regularly referred to state employment agencies by other state agencies. For example, rehabilitation agencies refer clients who have had extensive career counseling and are in need of job listings. The placement function is enhanced by computerized job banks and lists of qualified job applicants that provide a readily accessible matching system. Employment opportunities are quickly available to job seekers who need immediate placement.

SUMMARY

1. Career education is a comprehensive educational program that should be infused with educational programs at all levels.

2. Career-education infusion is a strategy that requires teachers to expand their current educational objectives to include instruction on career-related activities and subjects in addition to traditional academic subjects.

3. Career-education collaboration is a cooperative effort among educators, family, the total community work force, and government agencies.

4. The NOICC competency-based program models lend themselves readily to task statements and activities. The CDTI conducts training programs to facilitate the proper use of competencies and indicators.

5. Comprehensive school-guidance programs require a complete commitment from school systems. One of the most important domains in these programs is life career development.

6. Other government-sponsored programs address changes in vocational education in order to place a greater emphasis on technology. Work-based programs are being stressed.

7. Secondary placement offers a variety of programs to assist high school students in transition to work and entering college.

SUPPLEMENTARY LEARNING EXERCISES

1. Develop objectives for a career-education program for one or more of the following: (a) primary school, (b) elementary school, (c) middle school, (d) high school, or (e) four-year college.
2. Develop a career-infusion module for career awareness, to be infused into an elementary school history unit.
3. Develop a career-infusion module for planning and decision making for a high school geography class.
4. Interview a representative from the business community for suggestions on how to establish collaborative efforts to meet career-education objectives of the local school system. Summarize your recommendations.
5. Interview at least two parents of school-age children who are willing to participate in career-education programs as career models. Develop a format for presenting the career to a class or an assembly.
6. Develop course objectives and goals for a minicourse on decision making for junior and senior high school students.
7. Visit a local industry to determine the kinds of on-site job experiences available. Write a description of at least five possible on-site jobs.
8. Develop at least five counseling strategies for junior high school students to promote opportunities for reflecting on self-in-situation.
9. Develop at least five counseling strategies for senior high school students designed to help them choose a training program or a college.
10. Visit a senior high school placement office. Report your findings to the class.

Chapter Eleven

Career Guidance in Institutions of Higher Learning

This chapter begins with a discussion of the psychosocial development of college students and is followed by a review of selected research studies of these students in relation to career planning. The chapter also explores representative models of innovative career-counseling programs in postsecondary institutions, including curriculum module, cognitive-developmental, paraprofessional, metroplex, decision-making, and experience models. Finally, the chapter covers the role and function of college placement services.

The *module model* emphasizes an instructional approach to career-counseling strategy. The *cognitive-developmental model* focuses on career development and cognitive processes students use in decision making. The *paraprofessional model* provides examples of the selection and use of paraprofessionals in career-counseling programs. The *metroplex model* considers a wide range of career-related services for students, alumni, and adults in a large metropolitan area. The *decision-making model* provides examples of a decision-making system. Finally, the *experience model* is an example of an extern program that provides college students with "hands-on" work experiences.

THE PSYCHOSOCIAL DEVELOPMENT OF COLLEGE STUDENTS

Sometimes an enigma, always interesting and controversial, the college student has become the focus of increasing research during the last four decades. One of the primary interpreters of the psychosocial development of college students is Keniston (1971), who considered the college years a unique stage of development during which identity tasks shift from a preoccupation with self to a resolution of self within society. According to Keniston, this stage of development has certain "tensions," as students reflect on differences between their own desires and the demands of society. The developmental tasks of this psychosocial stage are experienced by a large proportion of young people: in 1985 to 1986, over 12 million Americans were enrolled in postsecondary institutions (Herr & Cramer, 1992).

Erikson's concept of ego identity versus role confusion, an ongoing conflict for college students, is similar to Keniston's concept of "managing tensions." These two theorists also agreed that this stage of development is crucial in terms of role identity and commitment to future roles, including a career role.

Tiedeman and O'Hara (1963) also suggested that identifying roles in society is closely related to career development. When describing aspects of integration, for example, they contended that society and the individual continually strive toward a common goal, that is, to establish what meaning each has for the other. Career identity is a major goal of this transition. Successfully establishing role identities during the college years is one of society's rites of passage.

Some Research Studies of College Students

In a study of 800 college students over a ten-year period, Marcia (1967) described college students in terms of identity statuses: the "foreclosed student," the "identity-diffused student," the "moratorium student," and the "achieved-identity student." These statuses were determined by the students' capacity for intimacy, moral awareness, respect for individual rights, and reliance on a universal principle of justice. The statuses also represent styles of coping with identity developmental tasks. For example, foreclosed students are closed off from self-exploration and limit their contacts and challenges. Identity-diffused students have few commitments to the future and are less mature than achieved-identity and moratorium students. Moratorium students (described by Erikson as "delaying commitments") are able to effectively use the college experience in coming to terms with their quest for identity. Achieved-identity students have successfully resolved ego identity, as evidenced by firmer commitments to future goals.

The diverse levels of development among college students, as revealed by Marcia's work, are not unexpected but do point out a wide range of career-guidance needs. Walters and Saddlemire (1979) found several of these needs when they surveyed freshmen at Bowling Green State University. Eighty-five percent of the students expressed a need for (1) information on occupations for which their majors were preparing them; (2) knowledge of places and people on campus that could help them in career planning; (3) more direct experiences, such as part-time work or job visits, in occupations that they were considering; (4) better self-understanding so they could choose occupations that closely fit their values, goals, and lifestyle preferences; (5) knowledge of the job market; and (6) help to plan college courses that would give them more flexibility in choosing among different occupations (pp. 227–228).

In related research, Kramer, Berger, and Miller (1974) found that the most relevant problems for graduate and undergraduate students at Cornell University were vocational choice and career planning, as expressed by 48% of the men and 61% of the women surveyed. At the University of Georgia, when 1,624 students filled out a survey of needs, 80% wanted to explore job opportunities related to their major, 77% expressed a need to develop job-seeking skills, and 72% expressed the desire to learn how to prepare for their careers. When compared to other needs surveyed, such as study skills, test anxiety, speech anxiety, writing skills, and time management, for example, career-guidance needs were expressed more often (Weissberg et al., 1982).

Recent evidence overwhelmingly supports career-guidance programs in institutions of higher learning. When over 830,000 high school students responded to an American College Testing Program questionnaire during the 1991–1992 academic year, 42% indicated that they needed help with educational and vocational plans (American College Testing Program, 1992). Accomplishing the tasks required of the transition from Super's (1990) exploration stage to his establishment stage is not easy, as Healy (1982) observed. Almost half of college students change majors and even more change career goals while in college.

A Cognitive-Developmental Model of Career Development

Focusing on the career-development and cognitive processes that college students use in decision making, Knefelkamp and Slepitza (1976) have proposed a stage model to identify developmental patterns of career choice. Students' cognitive processing involves movement from a simplistic view of a career to a more complex pluralistic view. The purpose of identifying and describing stages of cognitive growth is to demonstrate that students develop understandings of the relationships between numerous variables, such as personal identity, values, and interests, in the career decision-making process. These stages are described as follows:

1. *Dualism*—In this stage, the student thinks that there is only one right career; the thinking pattern is simplistic and dichotomous. The student turns to counselors, teachers, parents, and such devices as interest inventories for answers and direction. He or she is externally oriented with little in the way of self-processing.

2. *Multiplicity*—In this stage, the student recognizes more possibilities in making career decisions. However, he or she has not integrated important variables in the decision-making process.

3. *Relativism*—In this stage, the student shifts from an external control point of view to an internal one. The student now sees that he or she is the prime focus in decision making. Recognizing the diverse and complex components involved in decision making, the student assumes more responsibility but is not yet ready to make a commitment.

4. *Commitment with relativism*—In this stage, the student assumes a greater responsibility for the career decision-making process. The student now faces the challenge of a commitment in terms of clarifying and affirming his or her values, purpose, goals, and identity.

The variables that affect students' qualitative changes in this model of developmental sequences are

1. *Focus of control*—a control point of view; that is, students progress from external control to internal reference points.
2. *Analysis*—an ability to process component parts of variables in decision making.
3. *Synthesis*—the ability to integrate diverse perspectives in career decision making.
4. *Semantic structure*—an ability to use more alternatives, qualifiers, and modifiers in written and spoken expression.
5. *Self-processing*—the ability to self-analyze and learn more about self from the experience.
6. *Openness to alternative perspectives*—a willingness to accept other points of view and process different perspectives.
7. *Ability to assume responsibility*—the willingness to assume responsibility for the consequences of decisions.
8. *Ability to take new roles*—the willingness to assume more and different roles as activity demands.
9. *Ability to take risks with self*—the willingness to risk self-esteem through new experiences, actions, and learning.

This comprehensive view of career development offers some interesting areas for research: (1) the model needs to be tested on a wide variety of populations with longitudinal studies; (2) the variables of qualitative change need further specification and validation; (3) a reliable, valid, and efficient instrument should be developed that will enable practitioners to place students along the developmental continuum; (4) staff development and counselor education programs should enable the counselor to work within the concepts of the model to promote developmental growth (Knefelkamp & Slepitza, p. 57).

How College Affects Students' Career Choice and Development

Over a 20-year-period, Pascarel and Terenzi (1991) conducted a comprehensive study of research findings on how college affects students. The following conclusions were selected and paraphrased from the chapter on career choice and development.

1. Students frequently change their career plans.
2. Significant occupational status differences between high school and college graduates are sustained over the life span.
3. Individuals with a bachelor's degree are more likely to obtain high-status managerial, technical, and professional jobs.
4. College graduates are less likely to be unemployed than high school graduates.

5. College graduates are less likely to suffer the effects of prolonged periods of unemployment.
6. College graduates are seen by employers as possessing requisite skills and values that make them more desirable for employment and advancement.
7. College graduates enjoy significantly higher levels of career mobility and advancement.
8. College experiences tend to produce conflicting influences on satisfaction with one's work. College tends to develop a capacity for critical judgment and evaluation that in turn provides sensitivity to shortcomings of jobs.
9. Maturity of career thinking and planning can be modestly improved through various career-development courses.
10. Socialization in college increases student occupational aspirations.
11. College may enhance occupational success by facilitating development of traits that describe a psychologically mature person such as symbolization (reflective intelligence), allocentrism (empathy and altruism), integration (ability to combine a variety of views), and stability and autonomy.
12. In terms of reducing unemployment, a college education was more important for minorities than Caucasians.

The results of this study suggested that the benefits of a college education are quite significant in the world of work. This conclusion came as no surprise but does give credence to recommendations counselors have made for years about the influence of higher education on lifestyle and future opportunities for career development. Not only does the college experience provide for career mobility and advancement, but it also increases occupational aspirations. In essence, the benefits of higher education improve the quality of life and the capacity to make appropriate judgments over the life span.

NOICC GOALS FOR A COLLEGE CAREER-GUIDANCE PROGRAM

We include the NOICC's 1992 competencies and indicators for adults to underscore the necessity of preparing students for the work world and integrating life roles into a future lifestyle. These competencies and indicators present a significant challenge to institutions of higher learning and point out the importance of and need for an effective career-guidance program. Not only is the importance of educational and occupational exploration suggested by these competencies and indicators, but also the importance of work as it affects values and lifestyle. The far-reaching influences on college students suggested by these guidelines are quite apparent. To accomplish these goals will require a comprehensive program and commitment on the part of the college and/or university.

Adult: Competencies and Indicators

Self-Knowledge

Competency I: Skills to maintain a positive self concept

- Demonstrate a positive self-concept.
- Identify skills, abilities, interests, experiences, values, and personality traits and their influence on career decisions.
- Identify achievements related to work, learning, and leisure and their influence on self-perception.
- Demonstrate a realistic understanding of self.

Competency II: Skills to maintain effective behaviors

- Demonstrate appropriate interpersonal skills in expressing feelings and ideas.
- Identify symptoms of stress.
- Demonstrate skills to overcome self-defeating behaviors.
- Demonstrate skills in identifying support and networking arrangements (including role models).
- Demonstrate skills to manage financial resources.

Competency III: Understanding developmental changes and transitions

- Describe how personal motivations and aspirations may change over time.
- Describe physical changes that occur with age and adapt work performance to accommodate these.
- Identify external events (for example, job loss, job transfer) that require life changes.

Educational and Occupational Exploration

Competency IV: Skills to enter and participate in education and training

- Describe short- and long-range plans to achieve career goals through appropriate educational paths.
- Identify information that describes educational opportunities (for example, job training programs, employer-sponsored training, graduate and professional study).
- Describe community resources to support education and training (for example, child care, public transportation, public health services, mental health services, welfare benefits).
- Identify strategies to overcome personal barriers to education and training.

Competency V: Skills to participate in work and lifelong learning

- Demonstrate confidence in the ability to achieve learning activities (for example, studying, taking tests).
- Describe how educational achievements and life experiences relate to occupational opportunities.

- Describe organizational resources to support education and training (for example, remedial classes, counseling, tuition support).

Competency VI: Skills to locate, evaluate, and interpret information

- Identify and use current career information resources (e.g., computerized career-information systems, print and media materials, mentors).
- Describe information related to self-assessment, career planning, occupations, prospective employers, organizational structures, and employer expectations.
- Describe the uses and limitations of occupational outlook information.
- Identify the diverse job opportunities available to an individual with a given set of occupational skills.
- Identify opportunities available through self-employment.
- Identify factors that contribute to misinformation about occupations.
- Describe information about specific employers and hiring practices.

Competency VII: Skills to prepare to seek, obtain, maintain, and change jobs

- Identify specific employment situations that match desired career objectives.
- Demonstrate skills to identify job openings.
- Demonstrate skills to establish a job-search network through colleagues, friends, and family.
- Demonstrate skills in preparing a résumé and completing job applications.
- Demonstrate skills and attitudes essential to prepare for and participate in a successful job interview.
- Demonstrate effective work attitudes and behaviors.
- Describe changes (e.g., personal growth, technological developments, changes in demand for products or services) that influence the knowledge, skills, and attitudes required for job success.
- Demonstrate strategies to support occupational change (e.g., on-the-job training, career ladders, mentors, performance ratings, networking, continuing education).
- Describe career planning and placement services available through organizations (e.g., educational institutions, business/industry, labor, and community agencies).
- Identify skills that are transferable from one job to another.

Competency VIII: Understanding how the needs and functions of society influence the nature and structure of work

- Describe the importance of work as it affects values and lifestyle.
- Describe how society's needs and functions affect occupational supply and demand.
- Describe occupational, industrial, and technological trends as they relate to training programs and employment opportunities.
- Demonstrate an understanding of the global economy and how it affects the individual.

Career Planning

Competency IX: Skills to make decisions

- Describe personal criteria for making decisions about education, training, and career goals.
- Demonstrate skills to assess occupational opportunities in terms of advancement, management styles, work environment, benefits, and other conditions of employment.
- Describe the effects of education, work, and family decisions on individual career decisions.
- Identify personal and environmental conditions that affect decision making.
- Demonstrate effective career decision-making skills.
- Describe potential consequences of decisions.

Competency X: Understanding the impact of work on individual and family life

- Describe how family and leisure functions affect occupational roles and decisions.
- Determine effects of individual and family developmental stages on one's career.
- Describe how work, family, and leisure activities interrelate.
- Describe strategies for negotiating work, family, and leisure demands with family members (e.g., assertiveness and time management skills).

Competency XI: Understanding the continuing changes in male/female roles

- Describe recent changes in gender norms and attitudes.
- Describe trends in the gender composition of the labor force and assess implications for one's own career plans.
- Identify disadvantages of stereotyping occupations.
- Demonstrate behaviors, attitudes, and skills that work to eliminate stereotyping in education, family, and occupational environments.

Competency XII: Skills to make career transitions

- Identify transition activities (e.g., reassessment of current position, occupational changes) as a normal aspect of career development.
- Describe strategies to use during transitions (e.g., networks, stress management).
- Describe skills needed for self-employment (e.g., developing a business plan, determining marketing strategies, developing sources of capital).
- Describe the skills and knowledge needed for preretirement planning.
- Develop an individual career plan, updating information from earlier plans and including short- and long-range career decisions.

Implications for Career-Guidance Programs in Institutions of Higher Learning

Several career-guidance strategies in the senior high school apply to career guidance at postsecondary institutions. For example, career guidance must meet the needs of students at various stages of career development. Understanding the relationships between career choice and educational requirements is essential. College students must learn to relate their personal characteristics to occupational requirements. Career-planning and decision-making skills are essential. College students need assistance in choosing graduate schools.

In general, college students should be assisted in systematically analyzing college and noncollege experiences and in incorporating this information into career-related decisions. In addition, career-guidance services should help students select major fields of study and relate these to career fields. Career life planning that focuses on factors that influence career choices over the life span is a valuable concept to incorporate in career-guidance programs. Placement offices should provide a wide range of services, including projected job markets and overall employment statistics, job-search strategies, interview skills training, and job fairs.

Career-guidance activities in institutions of higher learning must provide assistance in helping each student understand that career development is a lifelong process based on a sequential series of educational and occupational choices. Each student should be given the opportunity to identify and use a wide variety of resources to maximize his or her career-development potential. The following models are examples of strategies designed to meet some of the needs of students in institutions of higher learning.

CURRICULAR CAREER-INFORMATION SERVICE (CCIS): A MODULE MODEL

A very innovative program for delivery of educational and vocational information was initiated at Florida State University in 1975. The program emphasizes an instructional approach to career-planning services. The CCIS is self-help-oriented, utilizes instructional models, and is multimedia-based. The program delivery system is accomplished through paraprofessionals. The CCIS is an outreach program used in residence halls and the university student center. In addition, the modules have been used as the nucleus of a 3-credit course in career planning offered by two academic departments at Florida State University (Reardon & Domkowski, 1977). The instructional modules were conceptualized to meet specific counseling goals and are structured around behavioral objectives. Modules I through V are shown in Table 11-1; modules VI through XII are presented in Table A-1 of the appendix.

After a brief interview, a typical student is directed to the first module, which begins with viewing a 10-minute slide presentation outlining the goals

TABLE 11-1
Curricular Career-Information Service (CCIS) Modules

Module	Title	Objectives	Activities
I	Everything You've Always Wanted to Know About CCIS	1. To introduce you to the CCIS. 2. To help you select the activities in the CCIS that will be most helpful in career and/or academic decision making.	a. View the 10-minute videocassette, "The Vocational Decision-Making Process," which describes the CCIS. b. View a 10-minute slide-tape presentation, "CCIS Introduction," which describes the CCIS. c. Read the script of the "CCIS Introduction" slide-tape, which can be found in the box marked "Module I." d. Ask the proctor to explain the CCIS program to you. e. Browse through the CCIS and examine some of the materials and resources available for your use.
II	What's Involved in Making a Career Decision	1. To help dispel common misconceptions about career planning. 2. To help you to identify many new variables that are important to consider in career development. 3. To help you to establish some guidelines for the process of career decision making.	a. View a 15-minute IIA slide-tape, "Old Wives' Tales and Career Decisions." (You may want to complete a brief preassessment first.) b. Read the script of the slide-tape, "Old Wives' Tales and Career Decisions," located in the box marked "Module II." c. Read a short pamphlet, "Are you an Occupational Ignoramus? Most Students Are . . . and It's a Risky Business." d. View a 15-minute IIB slide-tape, "Dissecting a Career Decision." (A study guide is available with this tape to assist you in career decision making.) e. Read the script of the slide-tape, "Dissecting a Career Decision," located in the box marked "Module II." f. Skim through the more than 30 career-planning books in CCIS catalog DDC 331. g. Review materials in the Module II Supplement folder in the Mobile File.
III	Looking at Your Interests	1. To provide you with the opportunity for self-assessment; that is, to examine some of the values and interests you have.	a. The *Self-Directed Search* (SDS), available in the box marked "Module III," is a self-administered instrument designed for assessing personal interests and values. b. The *Self-Directed Search* does *not* tell you what you should be or

TABLE 11-1
(continued)

Module	Title	Objectives	Activities
		2. To help you identify some occupations or fields of study for further explanation.	predict what you may be successful in but only suggests possible areas you might investigate further. c. The *SDS* is self-explanatory and can be self-scored. d. Several of the *SDS* Summary Codes do not have occupations listed under them. Do not be alarmed if your Summary Code is one of these. Follow the instructions to obtain a list of occupations related to your code. If you would like to talk to someone about this, see the person at the "Help Desk."
IV Information: Where to Find It and How to Use It		1. To help you locate all CCIS information related to the occupations you have identified in Module III and/or any other occupations of interest to you. 2. To help you locate all CCIS information related to your curricular and career-planning needs.	a. Read the section titled "Occupational Information" in *How to Find Information in CCIS* located in the box marked "Module IV." b. View the Module IVA slide-tape, "Occupational Information." c. Read the section titled "Curricular and Career-Planning Information" in *How to Find Information in CCIS*, located in the box marked "Module IV." d. View the Module IVB slide-tape, "Curricular and Career-Planning Information."
V Matching Majors and Jobs		1. List specific job titles related to college majors or fields of study. 2. Identify postgraduate, graduate, or technical training sites for fields of study or specific jobs.	a. Review printed materials in the Module V "Matching Jobs and Majors" folder in the *Mobile File* (1). b. Read sections in these books: DDC/331.702/ME *What Can I Do with a Major In . . . ?* (1) DDC/331.702/03 *The Occupational Thesaurus* (2 vols) (1) DDC/331.7/S73 *Guide to Careers Through College Majors* DDC/378.1552/L5 *What Can I Be? Careers for College Majors* (1)

SOURCE: Curricular Career Information Service, by R. C. Reardon. Unpublished manuscript, Florida State University, 1980. Reprinted by permission.

and purposes of the CCIS. The second module provides an overview of variables considered desirable in career planning using slide-tapes and selected materials. The third module requires self-assessment, primarily accomplished through self-administration and self-interpretation of the SDS (*Self-Directed Search*) interest inventory (Holland, 1987b). The fourth module consists of a slide presentation of career-information resources. The fifth module assists the student in locating careers related to academic majors. Other modules include employment outlooks, leisure planning, career planning for African Americans, career decision making for adult women and students with disabilities, and career-interest exploration through work and occupational skills.

The instructional approach to career planning used in the CCIS has potential application for all career-counseling programs. There is greater opportunity for accountability in the evaluation of career-counseling effectiveness when behavioral objectives are specified as they are in these modules. Major and minor components of the instructional unit can be effectively evaluated through a systematic review process. Effectiveness of materials and of instruction techniques can be measured in relation to specific objectives. Thus, the system provides the opportunity for continuous modification and upgrading of each instructional component. As career-related materials and programs change rapidly in the future, the opportunity to systematically evaluate and subsequently upgrade them will be a major asset.

Additional modules can be developed as needs are identified. As new program needs are identified, such as career assistance for minority groups, an instructional module can be built using materials already at hand and examples of existing modules. Thus, instructional modules are very flexible. Once the system of instructional modules has been established, the building of additional modules can be based on review of needs identified by the professional staff. Inherent in this process is also the identification of additional career materials.

Instructional modules provide the opportunity for more effective choice of entry into career counseling for individuals seeking career-decision assistance. The diversity of the learning activities provided through a series of career-planning modules allows the individual a greater variety of options and a more effective means of choosing a point of entry. The development of modules for specific groups (such as adults, females, minority groups) represents a multi-faceted approach to career counseling that eliminates the necessity of prescribing the same program for everyone. A diversity of programs also provides an attractive means of creating interest in career-exploration activities. Career-counseling programs that provide the opportunity to identify goals and desired outcomes have much greater appeal and assist the individual in identifying expectations of career-planning experiences. (See pages 491–497 for additional modules.)

Library System for the CCIS

The CCIS Library has divided its material into two types: career-planning information and occupational information. The career-planning information is classified according to the Dewey Decimal Classification (DDC). The *Dictionary of Occupational Titles (DOT)* is used to classify all materials related to occupations (Reardon & Domkowski, 1977).

As material reaches the library, it is classified and assigned a DDC or *DOT* number. A cutter number is also assigned to each piece of material to distinguish it from materials with the same DDC or *DOT* number. Since the CCIS uses a large number of materials that have *DOT* numbers printed on them, the classification process is greatly simplified. All material is classified by alphabetical order into one of three catalogs: (1) *DOT* index, (2) *DOT* subject, or (3) DDC subject.

Students are provided with step-by-step instructions in the use of the CCIS Library. For occupational information, the student uses Card Catalog 1 (*DOT* Index) and locates the *DOT* number. The number is used to locate the filed information and may also be used in Catalog 2 (*DOT* Subject Catalog) for information in books and tapes. For curriculum and career-planning information, a student is referred to Catalog 3 (DDC Listing), in which information is filed alphabetically according to subject matter.

The CCIS adopted this system for flexibility of use and for ease of cross-referencing. Many students are interested only in information and want easy access to materials filed by occupations. Cross-referencing is considered very important because each brief, book, chapter, or pamphlet describing a certain occupation is contained in the subject catalog and is available to the student for his or her career search. Students thus have easy access to information from a variety of sources.

The CCIS is an inexpensive system for career-information delivery. The use of paraprofessionals is recommended for on-line supervision and various outreach locations. A relatively small staff commitment is needed for module development and evaluation. The instructional modules developed for the CCIS have a flexible design and can be converted to computer-based career-information systems. The most recent use of the CCIS was described by Peterson, Sampson, and Reardon (1991) and by Sampson, Peterson, Lenz, and Reardon (1992).

A PARAPROFESSIONAL MODEL

In the fall of 1976, a Career Development Resource Center (CDRC) was established at Southwest Texas State University. The center is staffed by trained undergraduate and graduate student paraprofessionals. The CDRC is open daily for walk-in career counseling or academic advising. The center is supervised by a professional staff member from the University Counseling Center.

Career counseling is provided through an established CDRC career-search sequence shown in Table 11-2. The student begins the CDRC career-search sequence by filling out an appointment card for an orientation meeting. Most of the counseling sessions are done on an individual basis, but a paraprofessional may work with several students at any one time. The paraprofessional may have an active case load of 50 students who may be in various stages of the career-search sequence. For some students, several follow-up interviews may

TABLE 11-2
Career-Search Sequence

Program	Sequence
Orientation	1. Review Career Search Program. 2. Review objectives of CDRC. 3. Review the role of the paraprofessional. 4. Review career resources in CDRC. 5. Review materials, inventories, and DISCOVER. 6. Review a typical sequence of activities in Career Search Program. 7. Establish reasons that students come to CDRC. 8. Establish the student's expectations of CDRC. 9. Have student make the decision to participate in CDRC. 10. Fill out commitment card. 11. Set appropriate time for next step.
Assessment	1. Fill out interest inventory. 2. Fill out Dimensions of Lifestyle Orientation Survey. 3. Set up date for interpretation.
Interpretation	1. Summarize interest inventory results. 2. Discuss self-estimates of abilities. 3. Discuss relationship between lifestyle and career choice. 4. Encourage student to clarify values. 5. Encourage student to consider future expectations. 6. Decide on career to review. 7. Explain the purpose of the solo-option form.
Solo search	1. Review the career-classification system. 2. Demonstrate the use of the color-code system. 3. Point out locations of various career-related materials. 4. Reinforce the use of the solo option. 5. Establish time schedule for career review. 6. Set up next appointment.
Review solo option	1. Review each solo option. 2. Establish plan of action. 3. Alternative resources: (a) department chairperson, (b) other campus resources, (c) community resources, (d) further career review.
Follow-up	1. Notify student of appointment by mail. 2. Review plan of action. 3. Continue career search.

be necessary over the academic year. Until a student makes a career choice or drops out of the university, the case folder is kept in the active file.

Orientation sessions can be done individually or in groups, depending on the counseling demand and time of the student's entry into the program. During this session, the paraprofessional makes every attempt to present the CDRC career-search sequence in a realistic manner and points out the necessity of the student's time commitment to the program. The *assessment* period consists of filling out the inventories used in the career-search sequence. The paraprofessional follows certain set guidelines established by the professional counseling center staff to determine which inventories to use for each assigned student. During the *interpretation* phase, the paraprofessional encourages each student to relate career choice and lifestyle orientation to future expectations. This is accomplished by the use of an interest inventory and the Dimensions of Lifestyle Orientation Survey (DLOS) discussed in Chapter 4. Most students are encouraged to spend a minimum of three hours in the career library, reviewing at least three career alternatives using a written research guide called the *solo-option form*. Students are given the opportunity to spend more time, if they desire, before the next appointment for review of their solo-option forms.

The *solo-option review* session is for determining a plan of action that terminates in a career selection, or looking at alternative activities to continue the career search. The *follow-up* session is usually accomplished by mail. At periodic intervals during the semester, the paraprofessionals review their active case load and systematically mail reminders of future counseling appointments to students. A student may terminate counseling by indicating his or her career choice, or may once again return to the career library or other resources for additional information.

After the first nine weeks of the fall and spring semesters, a letter is sent to all students listed as undecided. These students are invited to the CDRC for academic advisement for the next semester. While there, they are encouraged to participate in the career-search program; the main emphasis at this time is on course selection. The student paraprofessionals also staff the "undecided" table during registration.

Organization of Material

The CDRC career materials are organized into three sections: education, career, and job-hunting information. Table 11-3 provides specific information on each section. The career section is organized according to Holland's Occupational Classification (HOC) (Holland, 1985) with one added category for general career information.

Color codes are used to identify specific references, as indicated in the table. Thus, all career materials classified as investigative would be color-coded yellow-brown, government information is green-black, and so forth.

In addition, occupational titles are filed in a card index by alphabetical order and are color-coded according to HOC. The student follows the simple directions, as shown in Table 11-4, to find a desired reference.

The advantage of using HOC is that most materials concerning a particular work environment are placed together, thus simplifying the career search. In addition, new materials can be added with minimal clerical time. Of most significance, however, is the system's popularity with students who often will not take the time to find different resources located in various parts of the career library, a problem typical of other systems of classification.

TABLE 11-3
CDRC Library Organization

	Color Codes
1. *Education Section*	
a. Catalog	red
b. College guides	red-brown
c. Additional educational aids	red-black
d. Graduate and professional education	red-blue
2. *Career Section*	
a. General career information	yellow-black
b. Artistic	yellow-red
c. Enterprising	yellow
d. Investigative	yellow-brown
e. Realistic	yellow-green
f. Social	yellow-blue
g. Conventional	yellow-yellow
3. *Job-Hunting Information Section*	
a. Employment outlook	green-red
b. Job-hunting strategies/general information	green-blue
c. Directories of agencies and organizations	green-brown
d. Government information	green-black

SOURCE: Adapted from the University of Texas at Austin Career Center and modified for CDRC.

Example:

Major Options

● red ___
- brown
B.10

What Can I Do with a Major in
Malning, G. Lawrence, and Sandra Morrow

Gives a student an idea of what job opportunities are available in different areas. Survey of jobs held by alumni of each department.

An example of the grouping of materials is the Management/Marketing section. This particular career field is classified by HOC as "enterprising." It is color-coded yellow and is contained in a notebook binder. Some of the materials collected for management are (1) "Catalyst on Business Administration," (2) a master of public administration degree outline, (3) a publication titled "Invitation to Achievement; Your Career in Management" by Division of American Management Associates, (4) a chronicle guidance brief on job analysts, (5) a chronicle guidance reprint on management, and (6) reprints from a sales magazine.

The advantage of the notebook binder is that it can periodically accommodate new and updated materials with minimal clerical effort. The student is also given the advantage of being able to choose among several articles. Student interest levels are maintained by ease of access to a variety of materials.

TABLE 11-4
How to Use the CDRC Library

1. Look for topic in the card index (Rolodex).
2. Make note of the color code, letter, and number below the colors.
3. Go to the section of the library whose first color matches the one for which you are looking.
4. Now look for the section of books that have both the first and second colors. Note also the letter and number for which you are looking and find the appropriate resource.

NOTE: The sources that have a single number after the letter are the black notebooks. The sources that have a number and a lower-case letter after the number are books.

Selection of Paraprofessionals

Student paraprofessionals are carefully selected, using the criteria shown in Table 11-5. It is important that they be good students. Aptitude-test scores are primarily used to determine potential for meeting academic requirements while taking on the added workload and responsibilities of providing career guidance.

The chosen major field of study is another good criterion in the selection of paraprofessionals. Students majoring in counseling and school psychology are especially motivated to gain the practical experience of working in a career center. Past academic performance is used in the selection process as an indicator of future academic performance. Faculty and staff evaluations are used to assess the individual's leadership ability and communication skills. Staff evaluations coming from resident assistants and dormitory directors (when applicable) are especially helpful. Faculty recommendations are heavily weighed in selecting graduate students. Work-related experiences are assessed on the basis of leadership roles, people-contact, and responsibility of position.

Training of the student paraprofessional is of major importance. A 55-hour training program is used for the student paraprofessional who assumes career-counseling responsibilities in this highly structured program. The sequence is outlined in Table 11-6. Fifty hours of training are accomplished during the spring semester, followed by five hours at the beginning of the fall semester, which consists mainly of reviewing programs. A counseling center professional staff member supervises the training program. Experienced student paraprofessionals are used to demonstrate the use of materials and the career library resources.

As the number of students seeking career counseling grows, innovative ways of delivering career guidance are being devised. Collegiate counseling centers have thus increasingly used paraprofessionals to complement ongoing counseling services (Zunker, 1975a). Zunker and Brown (1966) found that student-to-student counseling can be as effective as professional counselors in academic adjustment guidance. Paraprofessionals are used in a number of institutions: child-guidance clinics (Stollak, 1969), juvenile homes, and a variety of mental-health settings (Gruver, 1971). Significantly, more four-year institutions of higher learning sampled in 1974 were using student paraprofessionals in

TABLE 11-5
Selection Criteria for Student Paraprofessionals

Criteria	Preference
I. Undergraduate's ACT composite score and/or CEEB-SAT score	One-half standard deviation above the mean
Graduate's GRE-SAT score	Minimum combined score of 1000
II. Major field of study	Counseling, Guidance Associate, School Psychologist
III. Grade-point average	B average for high school and college
IV. Faculty or staff recommendations	Positive evaluations, particularly for communication skills
V. Work experience	Previous people-oriented work experience
VI. Interview	Positive evaluation for communication skills

career guidance and educational planning than were using them in a 1963 study (Zunker, 1975b). The case for using student paraprofessionals in well-structured and professionally supervised guidance programs seems fairly well established.

CAREER COUNSELING AT A LARGE UNIVERSITY: A METROPLEX MODEL

A large university located in a metropolitan area may have the added responsibility of satisfying heavy alumni demand for career guidance. Not only is the career center faced with a large volume of currently enrolled students choosing from a diversity of academic programs, but it must also respond to a wide variety of alumni requests for career guidance. Alumni contemplating career changes with subsequent reentry into the work force represent a dimension of career counseling uniquely encountered by a university located in a metropolitan area. The following examples of unique client needs exemplify the complexity of programs needed in such a career center: (1) individuals (young adults through middle age) anticipating a change of career direction; (2) individuals seeking relocation within their career field; (3) individuals desiring mobility within their career field through further educational training; (4) individuals seeking information about specific, current job-market trends; (5) individuals seeking college reentry planning; and (6) individuals seeking second careers after early retirement from a primary career. In addition, many adults residing in the metropolitan area will seek assistance for career-education planning prior to university enrollment. Thus, a career-center metroplex model must be able to provide a wide range of services not only for currently enrolled students but also for alumni and others in the community seeking assistance or career redirection.

TABLE 11-6
Student Paraprofessional Training Program

Meeting	Time (hours)	Activity
	SPRING SEMESTER	
1. Lecture #1	2	1. Purpose of CDRC 2. Its background development 3. The case for the student paraprofessional 4. Objectives and method of operation
2. Lecture #2	2	Introduction to CDRC resources: library, forms, inventories, and computer-assisted career-guidance program, DISCOVER.
3. Lecture #3	2	Career counseling in perspective: overview of theories of guidance with emphasis on Holland's theoretical orientation
4. Lecture #4	2	Career counseling in perspective: career decision-making process, factors affecting decision, and a lifestyle approach
5. Assignment #1	2	Resource material used: all trainees fill out biographical forms and inventories and access DISCOVER
6. Demonstration #1	2	Orientation to CDRC process and initial interview
7. Demonstration #2	2	Interpretation of inventories
8. Assignment #2	2	Resource material; use solo option to preview at least three careers
9. Demonstration #3	2	Simulation of counseling session with solo-option review and follow-up
10. Assignment #3	2	Resource material use: use campus, community, and alumni resources for career-information sequence
11. Lecture #5	2	Academic dean's lecture on advising the undecided student and resource material available, plus review of the college catalog
12. Assignment #4	20	Trainees are assigned to a paraprofessional for observation in CDRC over a two-week period
13. Role Playing #1	2	Orientation and initial interview of counseling sequence followed by critique
14. Evaluation #1	2	Written examination covering resource material, forms, and inventories used in CDRC
15. Evaluation #2	2	Role playing using inventories for mock interpretation
16. Evaluation #3	2	Role playing using solo-option review sequence and follow-up session sequence

TABLE 11-6
(continued)

Meeting	Time (hours)	Activity
		FALL SEMESTER
17. Review #1	1	CDRC objectives, procedures, and materials
18. Review #2	1	Specific procedures for career-search sequence
19. Review #3	1	Specific procedures for academic advising of the undecided major
20. Review #4	2	Covering new materials and resources added to the CDRC

The UCLA Placement and Career-Planning Center is a good example of a metroplex model. Located in its own building, the center offers career planning and placement services to students and alumni from all University of California campuses. Operationally, the center is divided into several units: (1) a career-development unit, (2) a student job-information unit, (3) a campus interview program, and (4) three special units that address the needs of students in the fields of education, management, and engineering. The three special units offer separate, additional programs geared to the unique placement procedures of the respective fields. Of the three, only the education office is housed in the main center, and the others are located in their respective schools. The student job-information unit and campus interview program are traditional services offered on most college and university campuses and for this reason will not be discussed in detail.

The *career-development unit* provides career counseling for students and alumni. Interest inventories, values surveys, personality inventories, specific exercises, and other instruments are used to assist the individual in career planning, decision making, and problem solving. Three specialized programs offer career guidance to minorities, students with disabilities, and foreign students. Several career-exploration seminars offered each quarter provide intensive, in-depth group counseling on such topics as career decision making and problem solving, life/work relationships, career-information resources, graduate school selection, and alternative careers for educators.

A special group seminar titled "Career Discussion Group for Freshmen and Sophomores" assists first- and second-year students in understanding the relationship of academic education and career training (Snodgrass, 1979). This program teaches students to take specific career-preparation steps while in college (1) to better understand the relationship of college and careers, (2) to introduce basic concepts in the career-planning process, (3) to increase awareness of the campus resources that may foster specific skill development, and (4) to introduce the center's career-planning services and resources. There are two 2-hour discussion groups.

In the first meeting, students are asked to choose from a group of selected topics concerning college majors and career requirements. An open discussion follows. The focus of the first session is on individual responsibility in career planning. An assignment consists of identifying at least five courses and five extracurricular activities that could assist the student in the career search.

In the second session, discussion centers on the previous assignment—goal-setting techniques—and on identifying career-planning assistance and services offered by the placement and career-planning offices. The major focus of the discussion is to point out what career opportunities are found within traditional college educational programs. The target group—college freshmen and sophomores—is particularly receptive to discussion groups that provide them with career-planning information.

Numerous services are available for students and alumni already involved in the job-search process. A well-monitored, direct job-referral service provides a list of jobs available from local, regional, national, and international organizations. Seminars on job-search strategies are offered biweekly by the career-counseling staff. Assistance with résumé preparation is offered individually or through scheduled workshops. Interview-skills training is offered on an individual or group basis using videotape for critical feedback. A unique program, the "Job Club," is a peer support group for individuals engaging in similar job searches. Members of the group are required to complete a specified number of tasks each week, such as making personal contacts, writing letters, and seeking information. Members discuss their experiences in the group meeting and receive reinforcement for their activity.

The Career Resources Library is located in the main center. Supervised by an occupational librarian, the library material encompasses categories that include the following: (1) general career information; (2) professional directories; (3) educational directories and college catalogs; (4) employer directories; (5) information for minorities, women, and individuals with disabilities; on foreign employment, and so on; (6) alternative or nontraditional forms of employment; and (7) periodicals. Clients are instructed in the use of the library individually or in groups by one of the staff counselors or interns. A variety of publications concerning career, placement, and career-planning information is available to both students and alumni.

The Placement and Career Planning Center also offers outreach programs on a number of subjects. For example, in conjunction with the Alumni Association and various academic departments, the center offers specific career panels on a broad spectrum of career fields such as mental health, allied health, banking and investments, motion pictures, advertising, and marketing and sales. The programs are videotaped and available on request.

A DECISION-MAKING APPROACH

How to make a career decision is a subject with roots that go back to the origin of occupational guidance. Deciding was perceived as a relatively simple task in early vocational-guidance approaches. The trait-and-factor approach measured an individual's aptitudes, interests, and achievements and matched this profile with the traits necessary for certain occupations. As more sophisticated career-counseling approaches evolved, the process of deciding was seen in a broader perspective. Moving away from authoritative procedures, the counselor would often leave the client stranded along the road of career exploration with the statement, "We can't decide for you—you must make up your own mind." The client's alternatives in many instances were not as "cut and dried" as the non-directive counselor implied. However, it was not until the 1960s that career decision-making strategies made a significant impact on the counseling scene (Gelatt, 1962, 1967; Clark, Gelatt, & Levine, 1965).

Decision making is now viewed as a learned skill that should be part of everyone's educational program. The acquisition of decision-making skills is a vital objective of career counseling. Decision making is distinguished from problem solving in that decision making involves examination of a variety of variables to arrive at satisfying solutions, whereas in problem solving there are no clear-cut right-or-wrong solutions.

Decision making is complex in that individuals must apply their own values, interests, aptitudes, and other unique qualities to each decision. Thus, decision making is a learned skill that should lead to more satisfying solutions according to personally held values. Decision making is a relatively easily learned skill that becomes complex when applied to individual lives. Individuals faced with the same decision often take different paths; varying personal values, knowledge, and strategies of action lead to different outcomes.

Krumboltz and Sorenson (1974) have designed a decision-making system for high school students. Its application is extended not only to ongoing decisions but also to those each individual will face in a lifetime. There are eight steps in the decision-making process that can be taught either to groups or individuals. Group discussion appears to have several advantages since it presents opportunities for reinforcement from peers. Therefore the eight steps are described in the context of group counseling. Following this description, the model for decision making and specific objectives and tasks appropriate for each step are outlined.

The first step requires the individual to state the reason or problem that motivated him or her to seek career counseling. When individuals describe their own problems, individual goals can more easily be formulated within a group. Therefore, step 1 is to *formulate individual goals* for each member of the group. Goals should be described in behavioral terms for more effective evaluation of each individual's progress.

The second step is to *commit time*. The counselor should point out the necessary time commitment required of each member to meet his or her individual goals. It is imperative that the counselor be realistic concerning the amount of committed time and receive a firm commitment from each member. Time commitments will be necessary for specific meetings and individual research. Some resistance to time commitment can be expected. The counselor must remain firm in receiving a pledge from each individual to make the necessary time available.

The third step is to *generate activities*. The purpose of this step is to narrow the alternatives in the career search. Students will be required to complete individual projects (such as taking interest inventories, reviewing filmstrips and films, and studying occupational literature) on their own. Individual conferences may be necessary to reinforce this part of decision making.

The fourth step is to *collect information*. The students now return to the group meeting and share the activities that they have completed during the previous step. Peer group interaction will tend to reinforce students in further career exploration. The counselor should be prepared to suggest specific kinds of resources for each individual student. Group discussion should include the nature of career clusters, job-market information, opportunities for advancement, worker associates, preparation time for certain occupations, pay scales, and other information of this type for each career being considered. The information-collection phase could also include job-site visitation in the community. When it is not possible to visit a job site, job-experience kits (Krumboltz, 1980), which contain exercises simulating actual work experiences, are recommended.

The fifth step entails *sharing information* and *estimating consequences*. This step should assist the student in predicting success, based on information collected. The counselor could provide local expectancy tables for predicting success in specific colleges.

The sixth step is entitled *reevaluate* and is usually accomplished through group discussion. The students share the possibilities of success in specific kinds of occupations that they have explored through the previous steps. The objective of this session is to provide the stimulus for firming up a decision on a career or for changing direction and going back to previous steps in the decision-making process. Individual conferences may be necessary, particularly for those students returning to previous steps.

The seventh step is to *decide tentatively*. Here the objective is to have students narrow their choices and eliminate least-desirable possibilities that have been considered up to this point. The elimination process may require students to team up and explore possibilities together or, for certain individuals, to explore the remaining jobs under consideration. The students should be encouraged to recall the skills they have learned up to this point for the consideration of alternatives.

The last step in the career decision-making process is referred to as *recycle*. Each group member is encouraged to view career decision making as an ongoing process that can be used in various situations other than the immediate one in which the group is involved. Ideally, the group should recognize that although decision making should be systematic and will lead most individuals to satisfying solutions, it is also a process that is repeated over and over again as one recycles information, crystallizes career expectations, and learns more about personal values related to the world of work. Zunker, Ash, Evans, Kight, Sunbury, and Walker (1979) developed objectives and tasks for the Krumboltz and Sorenson model of decision making to be covered in five counseling sessions, which are outlined in Table 11-7.

TABLE 11-7
Objectives and Tasks of Krumboltz and Sorenson's Model of Decision Making

---

Session I: Formulate individual goals and commit time

A. Objectives:
   1. Each student will formulate at least one career goal.
   2. Each student will commit herself or himself to six hours of group time and four to six hours of individual research.
B. Tasks:
   1. Members will introduce themselves to the group.
   2. Through brainstorming, some rules and regulations for group time will be established.
   3. The counselor will define behavioral goals and introduce the goal-development process.
   4. The group will divide into pairs and help each member decide on an individual goal.
   5. Goals will be shared with the group, and the counselor will provide reinforcement as discussion progresses.
   6. The counselor will discuss the time commitment necessary for group participation.
   7. Group accomplishments of Session I will be summarized.

Session II: Generate activities

A. Objectives:
   1. To familiarize students with career-information system and assessment instruments that may be used.
   2. To explain the purpose of assessment instruments and the occupational-information system.
B. Tasks:
   1. Group members will be reintroduced to goals established at the last meeting.
   2. The purpose and objectives of Session II will be explained.
   3. The interest inventory will be administered and interpreted.
   4. Through discussion of the interest inventory (with counselor input), each student will select two or more occupations that he or she wishes to explore.
   5. Through visual aids or demonstration, available career-information materials and the system to be used will be introduced.

Session III: Collect information

A. Objectives:
   1. To introduce career-information resources, their purpose, and their use.
   2. To introduce important components of occupational information for career exploration.
B. Tasks:
   1. Individual career exploration and choices will be reviewed.
   2. The format of published occupational information resources will be clarified. Job-site visitation resources will be identified.
   3. The purpose and use of alternatives for previewing occupations, such as a job-experience kit, will be discussed.
   4. The counselor will present a sample module of the format for previewing an occupation.
   5. Each group member will present his or her individual goals and objectives for the career-information search.

TABLE 11-7
(continued)

6. Through group interaction, each member will commit himself or herself to completing job previews in the following two weeks.
7. Accomplishments and commitments will be reviewed, and the time for the next meeting will be set.

Session IV: Share information and estimate consequences

A. Objectives:
   1. Each group member will share compiled information on a chosen career with the group.
   2. Each group member will select a tentative career field for further exploration.
B. Tasks:
   1. The meeting format will be set, and careers to be discussed will be selected.
   2. Through oral presentation, each group member will share compiled information on occupations reviewed with the group.
   3. Each group member will state tentative conclusions, reasons for conclusions, and ideas for further exploration.
   4. The counselor will summarize conclusions for each member and introduce data that will help students estimate their chances of success in an occupation and/ or career.
   5. The counselor will assist each group member with estimating his or her chances of success in a chosen occupation, or suggest the need to recycle within the decision-making process.
   6. The session will conclude after the next session's format is decided on.

Session V: Reevaluate, decide tentatively, or recycle

A. Objectives:
   1. To share the possibilities of success in specific kinds of occupations.
   2. To provide the stimulus for firming up a decision for further exploration on a career, or changing direction and going back to previous steps in the decision-making process.

WORK AND EXPERIENCED-BASED PROGRAMS

There appears to be a growing trend in all levels of education to provide students the opportunity of work experience as a vital part of their educational program. Although student teaching and a variety of intern and extern experiences are not novel ideas in institutions of higher learning, there are some innovations that should be of interest to the career counselor. One such innovation is the extern experience.

The extern model provides the student with an opportunity to observe ongoing activities in his or her major field of study and interact with individuals on the job. Generally, during senior year, students submit a proposal of their career goals on graduation with a statement of how the extern experience would help them meet these goals. Career-planning and placement centers or other administrative entities have agreements with host agencies to offer such experiences. Selected students will spend a specified time with a host agency during midsemester break or during an interim semester.

Intern models, on the other hand, provide students with the opportunity to spend more time in a workplace and are more work-experience-oriented than the extern model. Students actually do the work they are being trained to do. For example, junior-level students planning to become accountants may be chosen by an accounting firm to intern in one of its offices. Actual accounting work will be done under the supervision of a selected employee. The time spent in this experience is usually negotiated so as not to interfere with the student's progress toward a degree.

The practice of providing college students with actual work experience related to their college major should proliferate over the next decade. The length of the experience should also increase; students will find a longer time more beneficial than current extern programs. As colleges attempt to help students make more realistic career choices, more experience-based models will certainly emerge.

COLLEGE PLACEMENT

Our educational institutions have recently placed more emphasis on the placement office, primarily due to the competitive job market. The traditional placement service has evolved into the career-planning center. Current programs may cover a variety of topics, from interview-skills training to working couples' classes.

The typical college placement office has drastically changed its image in the last 20 years. Traditionally, the college-placement director spent the majority of time scheduling visits from recruiters and posting job opportunities. The major thrust was in arranging for interviews and campus visits by recruiters; that is, matching job requirements with qualified students. In many respects, the placement office resembled an employment agency. The job market was such that nearly every college graduate was assured of a job and, in fact, usually had several opportunities for employment. Job-search strategies were not necessary, as most employers actively recruited the college graduate. The student was in the enviable position of deciding on the best offer and in many cases could ignore the college placement office.

The five functions of the college placement office were summarized by Endicott (1975) as (1) receiving and displaying employer information, (2) registering graduating seniors and maintaining their files, (3) scheduling and arranging interviews, (4) maintaining information about job opportunities for graduating seniors and other students, and (5) maintaining a list of part-time and summer jobs. The intensification of the job search has, however, brought about major changes in the college placement office. In many four-year institutions, the placement office is now referred to as the Career Planning and Placement Office. In recent years, placement and career-planning centers have actively engaged in "selling" their graduates and alumni to prospective employers. Placement office personnel visit prospective employers and mail out information listing qualifications of students. In many instances, the placement office recruits alumni in selected geographical locations to provide information about career opportunities. Another major task of today's career-planning and placement centers is to give prospective graduates the projected job markets and the overall employment picture. In contrast to the placement functions summarized by Endicott, the following programs may be found at typical career-planning and placement offices:

1. Full-time employment listings
2. Temporary-work file
3. Full-time vacation jobs
4. Job-search strategy meetings
5. Résumé-preparation workshops
6. Interview-practice sessions
7. Career-interest testing
8. Career-exploration workshops
9. Individual and group counseling for career search
10. Special programs such as minority recruiting opportunities for employers
11. Follow-up studies of previous graduates

As the demand for services from the placement office increased, the more fortunate centers were given adequate facilities. The University of California at Los Angeles has designed and built a modern facility for its placement and career-planning functions. A floor plan for this building is shown in Figure 11–1. The commitment at UCLA to career planning and placement exemplifies the changing placement role and the emerging services of a university placement office.

The conference room next to the Career Resource Library provides the space needed for orientations that acquaint the student with the services and use of the center. A separate educational career-services unit provides room for storage and study space for individuals searching for graduate and professional school information. Audiovisual equipment is available for teaching interview techniques and other job-search strategies. A secretarial pool provides clerical assistance for the entire office.

At Richland College, a Dallas County Community College, the career-planning and placement office is referred to as the Center for Choice (CFC). The CFC includes career counseling, a comprehensive career-information area, financial aid information, a comprehensive test center, a veterans' service center, an alcoholic-education specialist center, and a job-placement program. The CFC is housed in a building adjacent to the counseling center. The floor plan for the CFC is shown in Figure 11-2.

The CFC is informal in nature and is staffed by peer counselors (called student service aides) and professional personnel. The easily identifiable areas of the CFC are separated and delineated by four-foot-high partitions. The resulting atmosphere is informal. This physical setting provides students with the opportunity to easily establish relationships with the center personnel or

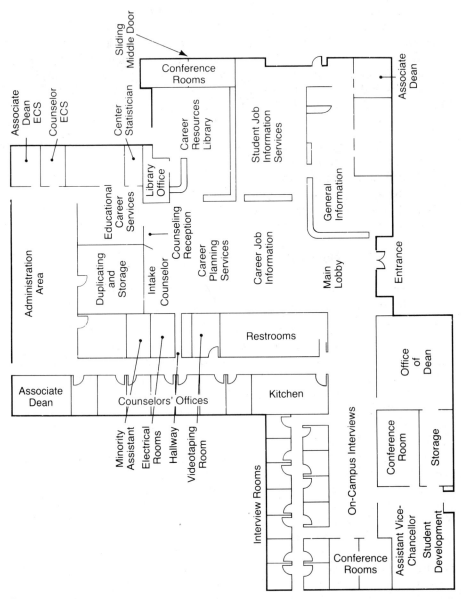

FIGURE 11-1

The UCLA Placement and Career Planning Center. From the University of California, Los Angeles, 1980. Reprinted by permission.

browse through the career-information resources. The CFC offers numerous programs, including a one-hour credit course in human development as well as noncredit classes such as assertiveness training and life-planning seminars. An advisory committee, including faculty representatives, has been established to evaluate and plan for future programs for the CFC.

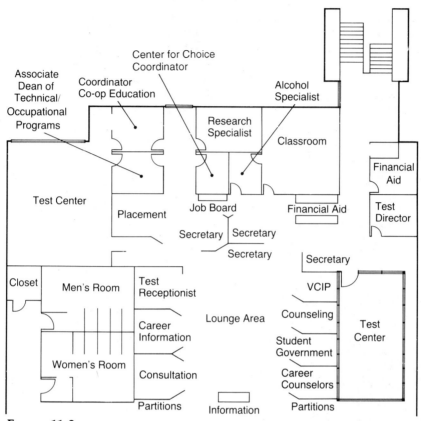

FIGURE 11-2
CFC Floor Plan. From Center for Choice, Richland College, Dallas County Community College District, Dallas, Texas, 1980. Reprinted by permission.

Interview-Skills Training

The importance of training programs designed to improve interview skills is underscored by the fact that employers' decisions are often heavily based on impressions of the interviewee. Also many college students are, at best, only moderately experienced with interview procedures. Instruction has primarily been through role playing, videotape feedback, and mock interviews with personnel directors.

The use of videotape has become a popular method of preparing individuals for an interview. Ehrmann (1977) has developed a videotape that discusses five areas of interview preparation: (1) educational background, (2) experiential background, (3) career goals, (4) skills and abilities, and (5) knowledge of the interviewing organization. Specifically, the videotape illustrates poor interview techniques, followed by suggested changes and demonstrations of interviewee skills. Included in the discussion and demonstration are techniques for maintaining good eye contact, appropriate posture, and voice level and projection;

selecting relevant discussion information; clearly specifying goals; using examples to support statements and demonstrating knowledge of the prospective employer; relating goals to the interviewing organization; and relating personal skills and abilities.

Videotapes can be used for individual training or in a workshop format, and they are also effective for group viewing—with or without discussion. For large groups, Ehrmann suggests that videotapes can be most effective when groups are divided into dyads or triads for practice interviewing. This procedure provides individuals with role-playing opportunities that can be videotaped for immediate feedback.

Snodgrass and Wheeler (1983) suggested that simulated interviews for videotaping could be derived from questions frequently asked during job interviews such as those by Nealer and Papalia (1982). One of the advantages of using videotape is that segments of the interview can be replayed and analyzed to afford greater flexibility of training.

Nealer and Papalia (1982) have developed a list of 55 questions frequently asked by interviewers:

1. What are your short-range objectives?
2. What are your long-range objectives?
3. What do you look for in a job?
4. Why did your business fail?
5. Why are you leaving your present job?
6. What can you do for us that someone else can't?
7. Why should we hire you?
8. How good is your health?
9. Can you work under pressure?
10. What is your philosophy of management?
11. Do you prefer staff or line work? Why?
12. What kind of salary are you worth?
13. What are your five biggest accomplishments in your present or last job?
14. What are your five biggest accomplishments in your career so far?
15. Why didn't you do better in college?
16. What is your biggest strength? Weakness?
17. What business, character, and credit references can you give us?
18. How long would it take you to make a contribution to our firm?
19. How long would you stay with us?
20. How do you feel about people from minority groups?
21. If you could start again, what would you do differently?
22. How do you rate yourself as a professional? As an executive?
23. What new goals or objectives have you established recently?
24. How have you changed the nature of your job?
25. What position do you expect to have in five years?
26. What do you think of your boss?
27. What is your feeling about alcoholism? Divorce? Homosexuals? Women in business? Religion? Abortion?

28. Why haven't you obtained a job so far?
29. What features of your previous jobs have you disliked?
30. Would you describe a few situations in which your work was criticized?
31. Would you object to working for a woman?
32. How would you evaluate your present firm?
33. Do you generally speak to people before they speak to you?
34. How would you describe the essence of success?
35. What was the last book you read? Movie you saw? Sporting event you attended?
36. In your present position, what problems have you identified that had previously been overlooked?
37. What interests you most about the position we have? The least?
38. Don't you feel you might be better off in a different size company? Different type company?
39. Why aren't you earning more at your age?
40. Will you be out to take your boss's job?
41. Are you creative? Give an example.
42. Are you analytic? Give an example.
43. Are you a good manager? Give an example.
44. Are you a good leader? Give an example.
45. How would you describe your own personality?
46. Have you helped increase sales? Profits? How?
47. Have you helped reduce costs? How?
48. What do your subordinates think of you?
49. Have you fired people before?
50. Have you hired people before? What do you look for?
51. Why do you want to work for us?
52. If you had your choice of jobs and companies, where would you go?
53. What other kinds of jobs are you considering? What companies?
54. Why do you feel you have top management potential?
55. Tell us all about yourself.[1]

Résumé Writing

As jobs become more competitive, personnel managers rely more heavily on résumés to select individuals for further evaluation. The résumé is the first criterion of the selection process; its importance cannot be overstressed. The primary purpose of a résumé is to obtain an interview for the desired position. An effective résumé is one that "sells" the candidate's qualifications to the employer and thus provides the candidate the opportunity for an interview. Most effective résumés relate the candidate's skills, experiences, education, and other achievements to the requirements of the job. Résumés are essential for

[1] From *So You Want To Get a Job*, by J. K. Nealer and A. J. Papalia. Moravia, N.Y.: Chronicle Guidance Publications, 1982, p. 21. Copyright 1982 by James K. Nealer and Anthony J. Papalia. Reprinted by permission.

individuals seeking professional, technical, administrative, or managerial jobs and are often needed for clerical and sales positions. Preparation of a good résumé is an essential part of the job-search sequence. The following outline may be used as a guide in preparing a résumé:

I. Personal data

    A. Name, address, and telephone number.

    B. Other personal data are optional, such as date of birth, marital status, citizenship, dependents, height, and weight.

II. Job or career objectives

    A. Prepare a concise statement of job objective and the type of position desired.

III. Educational history (If the previous work experiences are more closely related to the job objective, list them before educational history.)

    A. In reverse chronological order, list the institutions attended for formal education.

    B. High school can be omitted if a higher degree has been awarded.

    C. List dates of graduation and degrees or certificates received or expected.

    D. List major and minor courses related to job objectives.

    E. List scholarships and honors.

IV. Employment history

    A. In reverse chronological order list employment experiences including:

        1. Date of employment

        2. Name and address of employer and nature of firm or business

        3. Position held

        4. Specific job duties

        5. Scope of responsibility

        6. Accomplishments

V. Military experience

    A. List branch and length of service, major duties, assignments, rank, and type of discharge.

VI. Achievements related to job and career objectives (optional)

    A. List other assets, experiences, and skills significant to job objective. For example, knowledge of foreign language, volunteer activities, and special skills.

VII. References

    A. It is often not necessary to list references on the résumé. One may state that references are available on request.

    B. If references are listed, the name, position, and address of at least three persons are usually sufficient.

Here are some additional suggestions:

1. Because of affirmative action laws, many employers prefer that optional personal information (with the exception of citizenship) be deleted from the personal data section (I).

2. The job-objective section (II) is designed to bind the parts of the résumé together into a common theme or direction and should be carefully stated.

3. The educational history section (III) should relate academic skills and achievements to the requirements of the job objective. Specific, relevant courses and experiences as well as degrees and/or specializations of formal education should be recorded.

4. The employment history (IV) should relate previously acquired working skills and accomplishments to the requirements and duties of the job objective. Voluntary as well as paid experiences should be included.

5. The military experience section (V) should relate skills and accomplishments acquired during military duty to the requirements and duties of the job objective.

6. The achievements (VI) listed should relate to the job objective, delineating any relevant special skills or accomplishments that were not recorded previously.

Examples of résumés are an important teaching instrument. The career counselor will want to accumulate copies of résumés from former students who have applied for different types of positions. A good model will make the job of writing a résumé much easier for the novice. There are many formats, and a number of publications on the market today provide examples of them. Such publications should be included in the counseling center's bibliography on job-search strategy.

The following outline may be used as a guide in preparing a functional résumé:

I. List of achievements
   A. Begin with most impressive, relevant achievement.
   B. Disregard chronological sequence.
   C. List your achievements in the order in which you wish to highlight your background.

II. List work experience
   A. Offer an agenda of employers and job titles.
   B. Provide information about your past work experience.

III. List educational background
   A. List schools, colleges, and technical schools with dates of attendance.

IV. References
   A. It is often not necessary to list references on the résumé.
   B. One may state that references are available on request.

The functional résumé is designed to emphasize an individual's qualifications for a specific job. This type of résumé is often used with individuals who have had extensive work experience, particularly if they are applying for a job in the same area in which they have had experience or for a job that is related to their experience. The functional résumé stresses selected skill areas that are marketable, and it allows the applicant to emphasize professional growth.

International Job Market

As more businesses expand their operations globally, placement offices will be required to provide information for individuals interested in the international job market. More multinational corporations, small businesses, and entrepreneurs are expanding internationally. Krannich and Krannich (1990) suggested that the 1990s will be a highly competitive decade for international opportunities for college graduates. They will need the right "mix" of skills and the correct information to know how to find jobs in the international market. Because of the rapid and sometimes chaotic changes in political entities and the international economy, placement offices are faced with a formidable challenge.

Krannich and Krannich (1990) have compiled a list of the major trends in the 1990s that will affect the way individuals approach the international job market:

1. International jobs will be available, but students must learn how to find them. Different approaches are needed, such as making a contact in a foreign country or being willing to take other jobs available in the country of choice.
2. The competition for international jobs will more than likely increase as more individuals pursue them.
3. Most international jobs will require highly specialized, technical skills.
4. Students must prepare early in their academic training for the international job market. Language training, business courses, and technical skills that are marketable in the country of choice are recommended. Internships in foreign countries are also desirable.
5. Corporations based in this country will have few entry-level jobs available. Most will have hired local talent for these jobs.
6. Some ways to break into the international job market are through a volunteer organization working in the country of choice or through educational institutions and the travel industry.
7. Fewer traditional jobs will be available. Engineering, architecture, construction, and public administration will be in demand.
8. Networking skills will be required to locate and develop job information.
9. International career patterns will have a life of their own, as individuals move frequently from job to job and country to country.
10. International jobs could be dangerous, especially in countries with increased political instability and terrorism.

Some of these suggestions for obtaining jobs in the international arena are similar to other job-search strategies. Networking and obtaining internships are good examples. Nevertheless, decentralized and fragmented information makes it difficult to ascertain the overall structure of the international job market. It almost appears to be a closed system to outsiders. Therefore, it is extremely important to begin gathering information and networking early in the college experience, perhaps as early as the freshman or sophomore year. Perhaps the international job market will gain more structure in the near future, particularly when organizations have more experience in this market.

Computer-Assisted Career-Guidance Programs

As discussed in Chapter 6, computer-assisted career-guidance programs provide up-to-date information on the job market. Many of the systems contain local information about jobs. Computer-assisted programs also have components that provide information to students and notify them of other vital information that can be used in the job search. Employers can register job vacancies, salary, interview schedules, and so forth.

Computer-assisted programs also provide a quick method of matching qualified students and requests for job orders from prospective employers. For instance, an employee asks the placement office by phone or through fax printouts for junior-level accounting majors who have at least a 3.00 grade-point average and have plans to graduate in two semesters. Through prearranged agreements with students, the placement office can fax a list of students who meet the requirements. Speed may be of the essence in the competitive job market, and placement offices that are able to quickly provide information to students as well as to prospective employers may have an important advantage. Second, computer-assisted programs place current information at the fingertips of the placement office. The example presented is only one method of assisting students and employers through computer-assisted career-guidance programs, but it points out the potential of these programs.

The Follow-Up

Follow-up information provides a valuable resource for multiple utilization by the college placement office. However, this section covers only the use of follow-up data as an aid in assisting college students in career planning. The overall employment status of graduates paints a realistic picture of the variety of jobs available to graduates from a particular institution. In addition, information on the current employment status of graduates according to majors can be most useful to the prospective graduate. Thus, follow-up is a very important resource that indicates employment trends and employment potential according to specific educational goals offered at the university level.

Follow-up is an important function of the Career Planning and Placement Office, especially in light of the competitiveness of the job market. The information obtained from a follow-up is valuable in helping students plan their education and careers. Even though the labor market may make abrupt changes, the follow-up has many implications for the job-search strategy: (1) this information should aid the student in thinking in terms of the type of organization in which he or she is likely to find employment if holding a particular degree; (2) a realistic salary is usually listed according to field of study; (3) the employment potential is better understood by field of study; and (4) the job satisfaction of working in a particular field is known. In essence, follow-up information should aid the individual in clarifying values and subsequently establishing goals; it also provides practical information concerning initial career-search activities and probable geographical location of prospective jobs.

The UCLA Placement and Career Planning Center conducts an annual follow-up of the most recent graduating class, usually during the first week of September. The survey reports data in seven areas: (1) plans after graduation, (2) job commitment, (3) type of organization, (4) field of employment, (5) job satisfaction, (6) helpfulness of degree in employment, and (7) salary (*Job Market for UCLA 1987 Graduate*, 1988).

Using this data, the placement office can compile information about jobs currently held by graduates, including the graduates' field of study and employer, the nature of the job (part- or full-time), job satisfaction, salaries, plans for the future, and the satisfaction with the university's academic program.

SUMMARY

1. Keniston suggested that the college years are a unique stage of development during which identity tasks shift from a preoccupation with self to a resolution of self within society.

2. Research on college students' expressed needs indicates that a majority desire help with educational and vocational planning.

3. A stage model to identify developmental patterns of career choice among college students has been proposed by Knefelkamp and Slepitza. The stages include (a) dualism, (b) multiplicity, (c) relativism, and (d) commitment with relativism.

4. College affects students' career choices and development by providing career mobility and advancement and by increasing career aspirations. The benefits of higher education can also lead to a fulfilling lifestyle and the capacity to make appropriate judgments over the life span.

5. The NOICC has provided competencies and indicators for self-knowledge, educational and occupational exploration, and career planning for adults. These guidelines can be used to develop career-guidance programs at institutions of higher learning.

6. Implications for career guidance include a wide variety of programs to maximize each student's career-development potential.

7. The CCIS developed at Florida State University utilizes an instructional approach to career planning. The model is self-help-oriented, uses instructional models, and is multimedia-based. A number of modules have been developed to perform a career-search sequence. Several other modules have been developed for special groups such as minorities and blind students. The diversity of learning activities provided through a series of career-planning modules allows the individual a greater variety of options and a more effective means of choosing a point of entry.

8. Student paraprofessionals are used to counsel students in a Career Development Resource Center at Southwest Texas State University. The student paraprofessionals are carefully selected and given extensive training for following a highly structured career-counseling sequence. There is a growing interest in the use of paraprofessionals to complement ongoing counseling services.

9. Career-counseling centers located in metropolitan areas have heavy alumni demands for educational and career planning. The UCLA Placement and Career-Planning Center is a good example of a metroplex model. This center is divided into several units to meet demands of currently enrolled students in undergraduate and graduate programs as well as alumni and others in the community requesting educational and career-planning assistance.

10. Decision making is a learned skill that is vital to educational programs. Decision making is distinguished from problem solving. Decision making is a means of discovering a satisfying solution through the evaluation of options and alternatives; in problem solving, there are no clear-cut, right-or-wrong solutions. Krumboltz and Sorenson designed a decision-making system involving the following steps: (a) formulate individual goals, (b) commit time, (c) generate activities, (d) collect information, (e) estimate consequences, (f) reevaluate, (g) decide tentatively, and (h) recycle.

11. The typical college placement office has drastically changed its image in the last 20 years. The intensification of the job search has led college placement centers to assume a wider scope of responsibilities. The placement office is no longer just an employment agency; it offers a variety of seminars and programs that assist students in planning for careers as well as searching for jobs.

12. Typical programs being offered in career-planning and placement centers in two- and four-year colleges include career-search strategies, interview-skills training, and instructions on writing résumés.

13. The demand for work- and experienced-based programs for college students is increasing. Extern models provide the opportunity to observe ongoing activities in a major field of study. Intern models are more work-oriented and cover a longer time.

14. The international job market is expected to grow. Students will need to plan early in their college career to meet the requirements of jobs in the international marketplace.

15. Computer-assisted career-guidance programs provide the placement office with a wide range of options to react quickly to employers' requests and student needs.

16. Follow-up studies serve as important resources for placement offices when they include (a) types of job opportunities available by geographical areas, (b) general employment patterns and fields of employment of graduates with specific majors and degrees, (c) employment potential within specific industries, and (d) current salary schedules. Follow-up information is being incorporated into career-planning programs.

SUPPLEMENTARY LEARNING EXERCISES

1. Using the CCIS model, develop a module to introduce high school students to career-information resources.
2. Interview a random sample of college students and evaluate their potential as paraprofessional career counselors. Summarize your evaluations and describe your evaluation criteria.
3. Using the paraprofessional model, develop career-counseling components to meet the needs of adults who do not have access to other career-counseling programs. Develop selection criteria and training components for the paraprofessionals you will use as counselors.
4. Write to several large universities located in a metropolitan area and request descriptions of their career-counseling programs. Compare the programs for commonalities and innovative components.
5. Visit an industry to determine potential extern experiences available for college students. Compile the available experiences with recommendations for college majors that could benefit through an extern experience.
6. Survey a community to determine the number and kinds of agencies that are actively involved in career-planning and placement activities. Develop plans to involve all agencies in a cooperative career-planning and placement effort.
7. Develop plans and strategies that would focus on career planning and placement of school dropouts. Include in your plans the strategies you would use for encouraging the dropout to continue in an educational or training program.
8. Defend the statement: Career-planning and placement programs are essential in secondary schools and two- and four-year institutions of higher learning.
9. Compare the decision-making model discussed in this chapter with another. What are the strengths and weaknesses of each?
10. Interview a personnel director in a local firm who is responsible for interviewing prospective employees. Summarize your conclusions of what are considered to be the most important variables in hiring a new employee.

PART THREE

CAREER–GUIDANCE PROGRAMS FOR ADULTS IN TRANSITION

Chapter Twelve
Career Development of Adults in Organizations

Chapter Thirteen
Career Counseling for Adults in Career Transition

Chapter Twelve

Career Development
of Adults in Organizations

Career-counseling programs have grown over the last decade to include a variety of new and different components. However, providing the individual with information about organizations has not been a major counseling effort. The center of attention has been on other occupational-choice variables. Yet, experienced career counselors are well aware that career choices are often directed at organizations as well as at specific career fields. In addition, individuals tend to identify with organizations as well as their occupations. *Work in America* (1973) commented:

> Work is a powerful force in shaping a person's sense of identity. We find that most, if not all, working people tend to describe themselves in terms of work groups or organizations in which they belong. The question, "Who are you?" often solicits an organizationally related response such as " I work for IBM," or "I'm a Stanford professor." . . . In short, people tend to become what they do (p. 6).

Despite the need for information about organizations, career-guidance professionals have documented vast amounts of materials and programs aimed at helping students evaluate occupations, while little attention has been given to helping students evaluate organizations. Moreover, a review of the literature of industrial and management psychology suggests that a number of characteristics of organizations are important considerations in the career-decision process (Schein, 1978; Hall, 1990). Thus, the relevant question for the career counselor is, "How can we make the assumption that individuals are making realistic and effective organizational choices?" Underlying this question is the obvious need for programs, procedures, and materials that build a better understanding of the organizations in which we work. The scope of the issues is indeed complex, but such efforts are greatly needed by the career-counseling profession. Along with the growing list of career-counseling concerns, organizations must also receive our attention.

In the 1990s, often referred to as an age of transition, significant changes are forecast in organizational structure and operational procedures in the work environment. Advances in technology will encourage a greater use of computers and robots in industry. Present work environments will also be significantly changed to accommodate the new technologies. Work itself will be different; many jobs will be created and some will become obsolete. The counseling issues that evolve from these predicted changes must also receive our attention.

This chapter introduces factors to consider in evaluating an organization and discusses how they can be incorporated into the career-counseling process. This information may be used to assist individuals who are choosing an organization and those who are contemplating a career change. Many researchers, including Drucker (1992) and Kanter (1989), predict that the organization of the future will undergo vast changes. Most authorities seem to agree that major changes have begun to occur in management style and structure of the work environment. Middle management has been drastically reduced, and all workers are expected to learn new skills and develop positive attitudes for work in new and changing projects. The implications of these two changes greatly affect the career development of individuals who work in organizations. More specifically, some organizations will not offer predictable career paths and job security as in the past, and most will require continual retraining for development of skills to meet ever-changing demands. Career development in organizations may indeed require greater initiative, interpersonal skills, and the ability to adapt to changing and different work environments.

Because the organizational structure that has been dominant for decades continues to exist, the first section of this chapter provides an overview of pertinent information that remains relevant for understanding the significance of projected changes. More specifically, this section defines (1) the concept of an organization, (2) the organizational structure and its impact on the individual, and (3) leadership styles in organizations.

The second section of the chapter discusses the evolution of career development in organizations, focusing on tasks and transitions of stages of career development.

In the third section, the effects of the projected changes in organizations on career development are discussed. The fourth section outlines the role of career counseling in organizations. The last section covers factors used in evaluating an organization.

THE ORGANIZATION AS IT EXISTS TODAY

Defining the Concept of an Organization

Before we begin to learn about how we as counselors can help individuals develop more realistic perceptions of organizations, we must ask the straightforward question, "What is an organization?" This question is best answered by management experts or industrial psychologists. Throughout this chapter, to a large extent, we follow the research and writings of individuals in these fields because very little has been published by career-guidance professionals about organizations. It seems almost inconceivable that vocational psychologists have practically ignored the dynamics of organizations and their relationship to the individual in the work force, especially in light of the fact that many of our counselees go directly into organizations from our training and educational institutions. Consequently, one of the primary purposes of this chapter is to initiate discussion among career counselors on this very vital subject. Let us now turn to a description of an organization from which we can build a frame of reference. Davis (1967) has described the organization as a social system comprised of technical and human subsystems:

> Organizations are social systems. If one wishes either to work in them or to manage them, it is necessary to understand how they operate. Organizations combine science and people—technology and humanity. Technology is difficult enough by itself, but when you add people you get an immensely complex social system that almost defies understanding. However, society must understand organizations and use them well because they are necessary to reap the cornucopia of goods and services which technology makes possible and they are necessary for world peace, good school systems and other desirable goals which mankind seeks (p. 2).

The first sentence, "Organizations are social systems," should immediately catch the counselor's eye. When we speak of social systems, we are concerning ourselves with human relations—that is, the relationships and interactions between human beings (as the description goes on)—in some type of work environment. The term that is used to describe this human interaction in organizations is often referred to as *organizational behavior.*

Within each formal organization exists a complex system of human interaction referred to as the *informal organization.* This network of personal and social relations has a powerful influence on organizational behavior. Individuals who rise to positions of influence in this system usually earn their position from group members. Of major importance to the individual worker is what the informal group provides: (1) a sense of identity and belongingness, (2) an avenue of peer-group affiliation, and (3) an avenue for job satisfaction as one becomes an accepted member. Understandably, most individuals in a work setting place a high premium on being accepted as a group member.

The informal groups exert control over individuals by a system of rewards and punishments. To be an accepted member, one is expected to conform to the expectations and standards of the group. Learning to conform is often referred to as the *socialization process.* As one is observed and gradually adopts the standards of the group, acknowledgment as a member of the group is usually forthcoming. If an individual is not accepted, he or she is usually socially ostracized.

Of major significance in the context of this chapter are the factors that determine group cohesiveness. Group members tend to be alike in many respects, including background and lifestyle. The individual's lack of homogeneity with the group can hinder acceptance by the group. Further, dissatisfaction with the group modes will make the working environment a very difficult place in which to fulfill personal goals and needs. In effect, the working environment can be greatly affected by the informal organization. Differences with fellow workers about goals, perceptions of work, attitudes, and lifestyle make for a rather uncomfortable existence. No one wants to be considered an outsider, especially in an environment where working hours are spent. The informal organizations found within an organization can have tremendous implications for the individual; first, in choosing an organization, and second, in becoming integrated into the organization.

Organizational Structure—Its Impact on the Individual

What is meant by *organizational structure* may vary, but for most the concept usually includes the design of authority, policies, procedures, job design, and formal control systems (Davis, 1967, pp. 160–166). Of significance is where and by whom decisions are made in the organization. Such factors influence the individual worker's behavior, chances of promotion, creativity, expression of personal goals, and satisfactions associated with individual needs. There are, of course, other interactions within the organization (informal organization, communication, leadership, and so on) that influence the individual worker, but we will primarily consider how the structure of an organization influences the individual's role.

Gray and Starke (1977, pp. 102–115) have classified organizational structures into two categories—mechanistic and organic. *Mechanistic* structures are characterized by rigid rules that are defined in functional specializations; that is, precise definitions of duties and responsibilities including a well-developed hierarchy of reporting lines. *Organic* structures are flexible and adaptable, with less formal definition of functional specializations and lines of authority. Mechanistic structures are more appropriate for environmentally stable organizations; organic structures are more appropriate for organizations that have changing conditions. Representative mechanistic structures include (1) bureaucratic, (2) administrative, and (3) line-staff structure. Representative organic structures include decentralization and matrix-type organization. In comparing organizational structures, remember that pure forms of structures exist only theoretically and are very seldom found in practice. However, these structures provide a good framework for observations of the impact of organizational structures upon the individual.

Mechanistic Structures

The *bureaucratic organizational structure* originally conceptualized by Weber (1974) was primarily designed to provide equality of treatment through a system of policies and procedures. Weber was chiefly concerned with continued involvement of government in organizations and emphasized the need for equalization of treatment for all. The decision-making process in the bureaucratic system minimizes the influence of the individual through explicit rules and procedures. There is a well-defined hierarchy of authority with clearly defined responsibilities. A bureaucratic structure is characterized by being impersonal and having centralized authority. The individual is rule-bound by fairly rigid policies within subunits of the organization. It is most difficult for the individual to relate to the goals of the organization because the major emphasis is directed toward unit goals, which tend to fractionalize the total system. Promotions within the system are primarily based on merit and personally developed qualifications. Individuals who prefer highly structured work roles and wish to specialize their work skills will find congruence with the bureaucratic organization. On the other hand, this structure can be most inhibiting for individuals who prefer more freedom in work environments.

The *administrative-management theorists* tend to view the individual as a resource who must be provided with direction, rules, and policies to achieve organizational goals. This system gives little consideration to human relations and is considered very mechanistic in approach. Of major significance is that economic reward is considered the primary source of motivation. This form of structure operates under well-defined principles of command, span of control, and specialization of labor (Gray & Starke, 1977, p. 102).

The *line-staff structure* is a well-conceived format describing authority relations within an organization. For example, an individual who is responsible for a certain functional area (line) may be required to have support personnel (staff) fulfill the goals of that area. The staff personnel are considered advisers within their fields of expertise. This system provides the line manager with full authority and accountability for the functional area. However, the line-staff structure also has its problems; by its very nature, conflicts over authority between line and staff arise. Individuals who work within this structure may find the working environment in a constant state of confusion concerning jurisdiction of authority. Line managers are often viewed as veterans of practical experience, while staff personnel are often considered too theoretically oriented. Thus, the individual worker may find the lines of authority rather nebulous, and the line manager may feel threatened by the staff personnel. Further, staff personnel may find that their "advice" is often ignored. On the other hand, those individuals who can operate effectively while making use of expert advice may find this system palatable. Those individuals who prefer the role of adviser to manager may also find this type of system rewarding.

Organic Structures

The organic organizational models are considered humanistically oriented, as they are characterized by less central control. In addition, those in authority basically assume that human behavior is not completely influenced by external controls. For example, in the decentralization concept, decision making can conceivably occur in the lowest level of the organization. Leadership is much more consistent with McGregor's (1960) "Theory Y" suggestion that individual workers are intrinsically self-motivated.

In the *decentralization concept of organizational structure,* as its name implies, control and authority are passed down to lower levels in the organization. Employees have increased decision-making responsibility within subunits of the organization. In this system, the individual is considered responsible and capable of making decisions. Furthermore, individuals are not viewed in a mechanistic manner.

The *matrix organizational structure* evolved as a method for focusing on major projects, often resulting in shifts in organizational structure to meet specific goals. Organizations that require rapid changes to mobilize resources in order to concentrate on specific products find this structure essential. Project teams are usually formed in the matrix system to manage specific assignments. In this system, the individual may be called on to use his or her expertise in a variety of circumstances and under differing leadership styles. Individuals who prefer a variety of assignments and definite project life spans will find the matrix organizational structure system rewarding. This system, by its very nature, would be used in organizations involved in the ever-changing technological industries and other industries primarily concerned with product development.

Leadership Styles in Organizations

The leadership style of organizational managers largely determines the condition of the working environment in which the worker will interact. Consequently, leadership may greatly influence the types of worker needs that can be readily fulfilled. For example, the people-oriented leader may consider the satisfaction of intrinsic motivational needs (such as job development, promotion, and job enrichment) on an equal par with extrinsic subsistence needs. On the other hand, the task-oriented leader primarily concerned with efficient task accomplishment may place priority on task analysis and consequently pay less attention to intrinsic worker needs. Therefore, an individual's choice of organization may be determined in part by his or her need priorities and the managerial leadership style most conducive to their fulfillment. In essence, of major consideration is the leader's basic assumption concerning the role of subordinates in an organization. Ultimately, our counselees will have to evaluate their leader's orientation.

Generally, there are two schools of thought concerning leadership styles. One approach is based on the assumption that there is one superior type of leadership style that should be adopted for the organization. In this approach, one prescribed method of leadership is considered effective in all situations. Generally, the leadership style adopted by the top executive in an organization will be followed by other managers and leaders.

The second approach, contingency leadership, is founded on the assumption that the appropriateness of any particular leadership style depends on the nature of the organizational objectives, setting, and individual leadership characteristics. Contingency leadership is used when circumstances are not completely foreseen, and the appropriate management style is adapted to accomplish the goals of certain work assignments. In this approach, the leader's behavior is determined by situational differences; after analyzing those differences, the appropriate leadership style is adopted. Furthermore, there is no particular leader behavior that is appropriate for all situations in the organization (Fielder, 1967).

As mentioned earlier, it is important not to overlook the leader's assumption concerning subordinates. The autocratic leader assumes that subordinates are rather disinterested and irresponsible; therefore, the leader alone makes the decisions (McGregor, 1960; Likert, 1967). On the other end of the scale, the democratic leader makes just the opposite assumption about subordinates and considers their input in decision making very important. Some leaders are "task-oriented" and concentrate their efforts on the performance of workers. Other leaders are "people-oriented" and place importance on the interpersonal relationships in an organization (Blake & Mouton, 1964).

Leadership style does not exist in its purest form in an organization. At one managerial level, a more autocratic approach is used; at another level, the manager is more democratic. Of major concern to the worker is the leader's basic assumption concerning subordinates. The people-oriented manager will usually be more concerned with integrating individual goals with the goals of the organization. McGregor (1960) suggested that an ideal working environment exists when this is accomplished.

Admittedly, the evaluation of leadership style is at best a guessing game, much like trying to evaluate the personality of organizational leaders. Indeed the leader's approach and his or her basic assumption concerning subordinates may reflect personality characteristics. However, some factors that reflect the leader's concern for the individual worker can be evaluated: (1) organizational policy regarding continuing education and training programs, (2) organizational training programs for leadership development, (3) promotion policies, (4) procedures and policies for individual goal development, (5) procedures for organizational policy development, and (6) enhanced opportunities for organizational career development.

EVOLUTION OF CAREER DEVELOPMENT IN ORGANIZATIONS

Just as each developmental stage of career and human development is accompanied by a set of tasks necessary for completing the transition from one stage to another (see Chapters 2 and 9), stages of career development in organizations consist of tasks and transitions. Stages of development in organizations may be referred to as "employee socialization"; new employees are transformed from outsiders to participating, effective corporate members.

Feldman (1988) proposed a three-stage employee socialization process: *getting in* (the individual presents a realistic picture of self to the organization), *breaking in* (the individual is accepted by peer affiliates and supervisor), and *settling in* (the individual resolves conflicts between work life and home life and within the work environment). Kram (1985) suggested four stages based on the personal needs of individuals:

Stage	Needs
Establishment	Support and direction
Advancement	Coaching, exposure, and role models
Maintenance	Making a contribution, sharing with others, serving as a mentor
Withdrawal	Letting go of work identity

Career-stage development may also be viewed as a two-way interactive model; that is, the individual influences the organization while passing through career transitions, and the organization influences the individual's career transitions (Schein, 1971). According to this model, as shown in Table 12-1, organizational socialization is connected to passages through functional boundaries of six basic stages. Individuals exert most influence on organizations by their innovations during the midpoint of stage transitions, and they assume a number of statuses or positions in each stage. A unique feature of this model is the psychological and organizational processes that compare transactions between the individual and the organization.

A three-stage model by Hall (1976, 1986), as shown in Table 12-2, identifies task needs and socioemotional needs for each career stage. According to Hall, the individual needs to develop action skills and apply previous training during the early-career stage. In middle-career, he or she goes through the process of reorganizing various factors about work and self, such as work values and family involvement. The individual may also be involved in mid-career stress. In late-career, the individual begins to make a gradual withdrawal from the organization and learns to accept a decreasing work role.

These models form a frame of reference from which steps in career development can be observed. As individuals progress through stages, they learn new skills, are exposed to previously unknown jobs, become more self-aware, and find more opportunity for self-expression. Within this process, there is an ongoing search for job satisfaction, future career goals, and a direction for lifestyle preferences. Each developmental stage has unique and overlapping needs.

Entry Stage

Organizations and the counseling profession have given little attention to how people choose organizations (Crites, 1969, 1981; Wanous, 1980). Although individual career-choice variables have occupied the attention of many researchers in the counseling profession, organizations have been more interested in selection variables to meet personnel needs. Yet both groups (Crites, 1981; Holland, 1973; Wanous, 1980; Sonnenfeld, 1984; Hall, 1986) have researched the importance of matching individual traits to appropriate work environments. Meanwhile, the individual has little in the way of direction for organizational choice and less in the way of meaningful literature to review.

Work environments researched by Holland (1985), among others, provide individuals with direction in matching their personal styles with occupational environments. Although the attraction of different occupational environments is indeed helpful in career decision making, the task of finding the appropriate work environment has not been fully delineated by organizations or career information materials.

Wanous (1980) has suggested that organizational choice is greatly influenced by an individual's expectations of what the organization is about and what it has to offer. Kotter (1984) compiled a list of these expectations:

TABLE 12-1
Schein's Career Stage Development

Basic Stages and Transitions	Statuses or Positions	Psychological and Organizational Processes: Transactions Between Individual and Organization
1. Pre-entry	Aspirant, applicant, rushee	Preparation, education, anticipatory socialization
Entry (transition)	Entrant, postulant, recruit	Recruitment, rushing, testing, screening, selection, acceptance, passage through external inclusion boundary; rites of entry; induction and orientation
2. Basic training novitiate	Trainee, novice, pledge	Training, indoctrination, socialization, testing of the person by the organization, tentative acceptance into group
Initiation, first vows (transition)	Initiate, graduate	Passage through first inner inclusion boundary, acceptance as member and conferring of organizational status, rite of passage and acceptance
3. First regular assignment	New member	First testing by the person of his own capacity to function; granting of real responsibility ("playing for keeps"); passage through functional boundary with assignment to specific job or department
Substages a. Learning the job b. Maximum performance c. Becoming obsolete d. Learning new skills		Indoctrination and testing of person by immediate work group leading to acceptance or rejection; if accepted, further education and socialization ("learning the ropes"); preparation for higher status through coaching, seeking visibility, finding sponsors, and so on
Promotion or leveling off (transition)		Preparation, testing, passage through hierarchical boundary, rite of passage; may involve passage through functional boundary as well (rotation of job assignments)
4. Second assignment substages	Legitimate member (fully accepted)	Same processes as stage 3
5. Granting of tenure	Permanent member	Passage through another inclusion boundary
Termination and exit (transition)	Old-timer, senior citizen	Preparation for exit, rites of exit (testimonial dinners and so on)
6. Post-exit	Alumnus, emeritus, retired	Granting of peripheral status

SOURCE: "The Individual, the Organization, and the Career: A Conceptual Scheme," by Edgar H. Schein. *Journal of Applied and Behavioral Science*, 1971, 7, p. 405. Reprinted by permission.

TABLE 12-2
Hall's Three-Stage Development

Stage	Task Needs	Socioemotional Needs
Early-career	1. Develop action skills 2. Develop a specialty 3. Develop creativity, innovation	1. Support 2. Autonomy 3. Deal with feelings of rivalry, competition
Middle-career	1. Develop skills in training and coaching others (younger employees) 2. Training for updating and integrating skills 3. Develop broader view of work and organization 4. Job rotation into new job requiring new skills	1. Opportunity to express feelings about midlife (anguish, defeat, limited time, restlessness) 2. Reorganize thinking about self (morality, values, family, work) 3. Reduce self-indulgence and competitiveness 4. Support and mutual problem solving for coping with mid-career stress
Late-career	1. Shift from power role to one of consultation, guidance, wisdom 2. Begin to establish self in activities outside the organization (part-time basis)	1. Support and counseling to help see integrated life experiences as a platform for others 2. Acceptance of one's one-and-only life cycle 3. Gradual detachment from organization

SOURCE: *Careers in Organizations,* by Douglas T. Hall. Goodyear Publishing Company, Inc., Pacific Palisades, CA, 1976, p. 90. Reprinted by permission.

1. A sense of meaning or purpose in the job
2. Personal development opportunities
3. Amount of interesting work
4. The challenge in work
5. Empowered responsibility in the job
6. Recognition and approval for good work
7. The status and prestige in the job
8. The friendliness of people; the congeniality of the work group
9. Salary
10. The amount of structure in the environment
11. The amount of security in the job
12. Advancement opportunities
13. The amount and frequency of feedback and evaluation (p. 501)

These examples of expectations are primarily what make an organization attractive to an individual. The individual's effort in determining the likelihood of a match between an organizational climate and self is a most relevant factor in the selection process. However, final selection is usually based not only on organizational attractiveness but also on the individual's effort to join the organization (Wanous, 1980).

Finally, there is ample evidence that some individuals do little in the way of systematic decision making when choosing an organization (Wanous, 1980). In one study, 47% of the subjects could not specify a set of evaluative criteria to use in judging an organization (Sheridan, Richards, & Slocum, 1975). Clearly, the career-counseling profession needs to place more emphasis on guiding individuals in how to choose an organization. Some suggestions are given later in this chapter.

Early-Career Stage

Early-career experiences provide individuals with opportunities to establish themselves in organizations. For the beginning worker, it is an exciting time of entering the work force. For those who have been in the work force for some time, the content of their experiences may differ from those of the novice, but the developmental process will be very similar.

During early-career, individuals demonstrate their ability to function effectively in organizations. The novice will be naive about the complexities of the work environment and will expend considerable effort in learning how to function within the organizational milieu. Employees who have worked in other organizations will concentrate more on learning the structure of the organization. Some individuals in both groups will move through early-career in a few months, while others will take considerably longer; some may never become fully established.

The major tasks of early-career, compiled by Campbell and Heffernan (1983), are as follows:

1. Become oriented to the organization.
   a. Learn and adhere to regulations and policies.
   b. Learn and display good work habits and attitudes.
   c. Develop harmonious relationships with others in the work environment.
   d. Integrate personal values with organizational values.

2. Learn position responsibilities and demonstrate satisfactory performance.
   a. Acquire new skills as tasks or position change.
   b. Take part in on-the-job training as appropriate.

3. Explore career plans in terms of personal goals and advancement opportunities.
   a. Evaluate current choice of occupation.
   b. Evaluate advancement opportunities.
   c. Develop a plan for advancement or position change.
   d. Consider alternatives in other occupations.

4. Implement plan for advancement or position change (pp. 240–242).

Although the pathway to a successful early-career has pitfalls and stumbling blocks, there is a relatively well defined direction. For example, building harmonious relationships in the work environment, becoming oriented to organizational rules and regulations, and demonstrating satisfactory performance are common concrete tasks of early-career. The individual's personal reaction to advancement opportunities and acceptance of the values associated with organizational goals and peer affiliates are less tangible. Objective indexes (salary, merit pay, regulations, policies, and so on) and subjective indexes (meeting expectations, goal attainment, match between personal needs and organizational needs) are evaluative criteria the individual can use to determine future direction in the organization or change to another work environment.

In the following counseling session, Lil, who has been with an organization for ten months, reflected a need to withdraw and find another work environment.

Counselor: Yes, we do have some information about the organization you asked about. But first I would like to know about the one you are leaving.

Lil: As you know, it's a well-known organization, and I was excited about the opportunity of working there. But I don't seem to fit in.

Counselor: Could you be more specific?

Lil: Well, the job assignment was not what I expected. The recruiter told me I would have a lot of responsibilities and interact with people at high levels, but in actuality there was little of either.

Counselor: So it really wasn't the kind of job you expected?

Lil: No, I was put off in a side office and no one seemed to pay much attention to me. I did have a few assignments that seemed more like busywork than anything else.

Counselor: Could this have been a part of the training program?

Lil: Well, partly, but my supervisor hardly ever came around, and when he did, he seemed preoccupied.

In this case, reality shock and unused potential, as described by Hall (1990), were frustrating experiences for Lil. She had high expectations from what she was told about the job and hoped to be challenged, but experienced far less. There also appeared to be a communication gap between Lil and her supervisor.

Wanous (1980) suggested that reality shock and lack of appraisal and appropriate feedback while in early-career are major causes of withdrawal from an organization. In such cases, the career counselor must focus on the individual's perception of these two conditions and his or her level of sophistication in appraising them. Some early-career individuals will have unrealistically high expectations, while others may indeed find their jobs to be less than challenging and experience poor feedback from their supervisors.

Work environments in organizations also provide a variety of learning experiences that are relevant to career development. For example, exposure to unknown jobs could begin career direction for some members of an organization. In other cases, the individual's work experiences provide a meaningful sense of direction in career development. Developing harmonious relationships, for example, means learning effective communication skills, interpersonal relationships, and general modes of behavior that are easily transferable to other work environments.

Fast-Track Careers

In the 1950s and 1960s, American corporations grew very rapidly, and in the process many organizations experienced a shortage of middle- and upper-level managers (Thompson, Kirkham, & Dixon, 1985). In response to this need, organizations created "fast-track" training programs to fill vacancies. Prospective managers on the fast-track were given rapid transfers and promotions; upward movement was regarded as a sure sign of career success.

However, fast-track programs encouraged work habits that in the long run were not beneficial to the individual or to the organization. Rather than concentrating on building a solid technical foundation and keeping up-to-date on technological changes, fast-track individuals focused their attention on management techniques and skills. As a result, many were unprepared to manage others who had learned technical changes and functions (Louis, 1982). In addition, many in the fast-track program experienced family problems due to numerous transfers and other demands (Feldman, 1988).

To some extent, organizations continue the use of fast-track programs, and more important, some individuals choose to put themselves on a fast-track course. Career counselors can expect to interact with individuals who have been under tremendous pressure to produce results in a short time and who have the perception that they make their mark with programs they initiate. Their success is judged by dramatic results, which in turn increase their visibility as "rising stars." The intensity, pressure, and demands of fast-trackers in early-career often result in the burnout discussed in Chapter 3.

Understanding the hazards of fast-track careers enables career counselors to relate problematic situations to individuals they assist in career development. For example, dual-career couples need to understand the complexities associated with the rigidness of fast-track pathways. Individuals also need to recognize that keeping abreast of technical advances is an essential ingredient for career growth, a sense of accomplishment, and increased self-confidence and self-esteem (Feldman, 1988). Career development viewed as a long-term developmental process encourages the development of a wide range of personal qualities that must be kept in perspective with other aspects of life such as family.

The following dialogue illustrates Jim's frustration with his experiences from a fast-track program.

Jim: I suddenly realized that life should have more to offer than this rat race I'm in. I don't seem to have time for my family or anything else. Over the last eighteen months, I have moved twice and have been working almost constantly. I want to change to something different.

Counselor: Have you discussed this subject with your supervisor?

Jim: Oh yeah, but he tells me that I'll get used to it and to stick with it. Besides, he told me that the company would frown on a move to something different right now. I got the distinct impression that he would not consider a different direction for me.

After the counselor listened to Jim's frustrations about his current situation, he commented:

Counselor: I think it would be wise for us to take the time to fully evaluate your career development up to this point. Before we look at future plans, let's fully assess what factors have made you unhappy with the current situation.

Jim: That sounds like a good idea—I can start the list right now. I want more time with my family and I don't want to move every few months. I'd like to settle into a more stable type of job.

Counselor: Okay, that's a good start. We can also discuss your likes and dislikes about the job itself.

Jim: You're right. Sometimes I'm not sure which has caused me the most problems—my job or the things the job requires of me, such as taking up so much time.

Individuals in fast-track programs are vulnerable to many hazards in the organizational milieu. Careful analysis of factors that lead to frustration allows individuals to evaluate current career-development status realistically. Career life-planning skills and decision-making techniques, discussed in several chapters, are relevant strategies to help individuals fully evaluate future options.

Mid-Career

Mid-career has been identified as the middle phase of an individual's work life, with its own set of tasks and social-emotional needs (Hall, 1986). In terms of Super's vocational developmental stages, mid-career may be thought of as the beginning of the maintenance stage, which is characterized by a continual adjustment process to improve working position and situation. In Tiedeman's model of implementation and adjustment, mid-career is characterized by greater self-understanding and identification within the total system of a career field. Feldman (1988) labeled the mid-career experience as "settling in," characterized by resolution of conflicts and conflicting demands within the organization and in personal life. Mid-career is not necessarily age-related; individuals who make career changes may experience several mid-career stages.

The transitional process from early- to mid-career has residual effects, as individuals establish themselves in an organization. In early-career, the major course of change is the socialization process, but in mid-career, changes are from diversified sources, such as new and different technology, product demand, and changes in the labor market. Developing a perspective of positive growth orientation in organizations and encouraging individuals to adapt to changes is a healthy attitude to promote. Also, finding a meaningful area of contribution is part of the process of establishing an organizational identity. Individuals must distinguish between real barriers (no growth, slow growth, and organizational decline) and perceived barriers (role confusion, poor career identity, nebulous perceptions of career success and direction) that affect their ability to reach personal goals.

In a study of barriers to growth in organizations, referred to as "career plateaus," Ference, Stoner, and Warren (1977) identified organizational and individual factors that cause individuals to become "plateaued performers" (likelihood of promotion is very low). Organizational factors include

1. Fewer positions at the top of the hierarchical organizational structure;
2. More severe competition for promotion;
3. Age (some organizations emphasize promoting younger workers); and
4. Needs of the organization (the individual may be more valuable in the position currently occupied).

Individual factors include

1. Lack of technical skills (due to inadequate development opportunities or the lack of motivation to keep pace with technical change);
2. Uncertainty about future career role in the organization (individual fails to recognize organizational systems for career-pathing); and
3. No strong desire or need to advance (for various reasons, such as geographical location, hours, or other job changes, some individuals simply do not want to be promoted).

The following dialogue demonstrates some sources of organizational and individual plateaus.

Counselor: Tell me how you arrived at the decision to change jobs.
Chuck: Well, you know I've been with the company for twelve years, but I don't have the same enthusiasm for the job. I just can't put my finger on it.
Counselor: Is the company doing well financially?
Chuck: That's a part of it; no promotion to speak of now.
Counselor: Is this a company policy?
Chuck: No, John, a friend of mine, got one the other day. He's a lucky guy. He seems to always be in the right place at the right time.
Counselor: Did you say that John was in your division?
Chuck: Yeah, he's always got something going. I don't understand how he does it. He went to this training program and six weeks later there he goes— up the ladder!
Counselor: Tell me more about the training program.
Chuck: The company sponsored it. I could have gone, but I don't believe I like that kind of extra work. Besides, it would have interfered with the city golf tournament.

It appears from this conversation that Chuck is not willing to be more assertive in his career development. The source of his plateau appears to be primarily a lack of a strong desire to advance. Perhaps Chuck felt that he only needed to put in time for the next advancement. In mid-career, individuals may have difficulty balancing commitment to outside activities with intense competitiveness for promotions.

Ann, also in mid-career, tells how she discovered a career path in an organization:

Ann: I kept looking in the want ads for a career in management after I finished college. I don't know how many times I was turned down. Finally, I took an entry-level job in this company just to tide me over. As I kept looking at the want ads, I also started meeting more people in the company. I began to realize that this wasn't such a bad place after all. But what really did it for me was when I met Linda. When she told what she was doing in the company, I knew

I wanted to know more about it. Well, you know the rest of the story. I found out about several jobs I never knew existed and I landed one I like very much. I guess I'll stick around.

In Ann's case, she was exposed to occupations and career opportunities she had never known before. An entry-level job provided the means to discover unknown opportunities, and after a successful socialization period, she discovered a career path that appealed to her.

In a more preconceived manner, Al began his career in a high-tech organization with the goal of reaching the management level.

Al: I started out as a computer salesman. After a few years, the company offered me a retail store management job in the eastern part of the state. My wife didn't want to move. That was a tough decision; the kids didn't want to leave either. We spent eight years there, but made the best of it. Meanwhile, I took advantage of every career-development opportunity through a variety of training programs. I got good feedback from my supervisor, which really helped. During that process, I became familiar with many aspects of the company. It finally paid off when I was made regional manager a few years ago. It worked out well. I live near a lake now and in a delightful part of the state.

Counselor: What are your future plans?

Al: I like what I'm doing, but I have become more interested in civic organizations and church work.

Counselor: Do you have as strong a commitment to the organization as you once had?

Al: Yes and no. It's different than before. My wife is happy that I devote more time to other things, but I still get excited about the future. I enjoy working with these young kids. They have good management skills and I enjoy helping them.

As shown in this interview, mid-career is a time when individuals develop an increased awareness of the long-term dimensions of a career and shift their focus from the work world to personal roles. Attention is focused not only on career maintenance but also on life issues, such as parenting, joining civic organizations, and caring for aging parents. Priorities between work roles and personal roles fluctuate according to circumstances. A healthy attitude to promote is a balance of roles, as career and life changes become increasingly connected.

Mid-career is also a time when individuals become more aware of life stages in terms of time spans and begin to view career in terms of implementing future opportunities, as shown in Super's (1977) model of vocational maturity in mid-career. Super's concept of vocational maturity defines life stages and tasks as interrelated in career development. His earlier studies of vocational maturity followed the vocational development of secondary students through adulthood (discussed in Chapter 2). More recently, he has been concerned with establishing the criteria of vocational maturity for older adults in mid-career. The developmental tasks associated with mid-career developed by Super (1977) are provided in Table 12-3.

TABLE 12-3
A Theoretical Model of Vocational Maturity in Mid-Career

I. Planfulness or time perspective

  A. Past: Exploration
    1. Crystallizing
    2. Specifying
    3. Implementing
  B. Present and immediate future: Establishment
    4. Stabilizing
    5. Consolidation
    6. Advancement
  C. Intermediate future: Maintenance
    7. Holding one's own
    8. Keeping up with developments
    9. Breaking new ground
  D. Distant future: Decline
    10. Tapering off
    11. Preparing for retirement
    12. Retiring

II. Exploration

  E. Querying
    1. Self
      a. In time perspective
      b. In space (organizational geography)
    2. Situation
      a. In time perspective
      b. In space (organizational geography)
  F. Resources (attitudes toward)
    3. Awareness of
    4. Valuation of
  G. Participation (use of resources)
    5. In-house resources (sponsored)
    6. Community resources (sought out)

III. Information

  H. Life stages
    1. Time spans
    2. Characteristics
    3. Developmental tasks
  I. Coping behaviors: Repertoire
    4. Options in coping with vocational development tasks
    5. Appropriateness of options for self-in-situation
  J. Occupational outlets for self-in-situation
  K. Job outlets for self-in-situation
  L. Implementation: Means of access to opportunities
  M. Outcome probabilities

IV. Decision making

  N. Principles
    1. Knowledge of
    2. Valuation of (utility)
  O. Practice
    3. Use of in past
    4. Use of at present

TABLE 12-3
(continued)

V. Reality orientation
   P. Self-knowledge
       1. Agreement of self-estimated and measured traits
       2. Agreement of self-estimated and other estimated traits
   Q. Realism
       3. Agreement of self- and employer-evaluated proficiency
       4. Agreement of self- and employer-evaluated prospects
   R. Consistency of occupational preferences
       5. Current
       6. Over time
   S. Crystallization
       7. Clarity of vocational self-concept
       8. Certainty of career goals
   T. Work experience
       9. Floundering versus stabilizing in mid-career
      10. Stabilizing or maintaining versus decline in mid-career

SOURCE: "Vocational Maturity in Mid-Career," by D. E. Super. In *Vocational Guidance Quarterly*, June 1977, 25(4), p. 297. Copyright 1977 by American Personnel and Guidance Association. Reprinted by permission.

Super's model for adults has five basic dimensions of developmental tasks, similar to those in his adolescent model. The first dimension, *planfulness* or *time perspective*, focuses on the awareness of life stages and tasks. The second dimension, *exploration*, considers the tasks of exploring both goals and jobs for an eventual established position. *Information*, the third dimension, focuses on tasks dealing with the proper use of occupational sources, options, and outcome probabilities. The fourth dimension, *decision making*, considers skills, principles, and practices in decision making. The final dimension, *reality orientation*, considers the vocationally mature adult as having acquired self-knowledge, consistency, and stabilization in occupational preferences, choices, and work experiences.

The model provides a basis for determining which of the developmental tasks the adult has accomplished. It is useful for counseling because the identified dimensions and substages provide a frame of reference from which counseling procedures can be built. The vocational maturity in the mid-career model should also provide the basis for informative research projects in the future.

Late-Career

In late-career, the major focus of an individual's life is on activities outside the organization. The individual builds outside interests and begins a gradual detachment from the organization. Activities within the organization may also shift from a power role to a minor role. Super refers to this stage as decline characterized by preretirement considerations. Within the organization, the individual is preparing to "let go" of responsibilities and pass them on to others. One of the major adjustments during late-career is learning to accept a reduced work role and changing focus away from a highly involved work identity.

Emotional support in late-career comes primarily from peers and particularly from old acquaintances. Moving away from the stress and turmoil associated with younger workers who are striving to move upward, late-career employees identify with peers and rekindle closer attachments to spouses. Having resolved many of the uncertainties of mid-career, they tend to focus on broader issues, such as the organization as a whole and the future of their profession or work (Kram, 1985).

Work Performance in Late-Career

The relationship between age and job performance is not clear. Rhodes (1983) found that research findings do not show a clear pattern as to whether job performance increases or decreases with age. She suggested that the type of work is the most important variable that determines the answer to this question. In related research, Sonnenfeld (1984) reported that older workers remain successful as salespersons, in creative and scholarly pursuits, and, surprisingly, as manual workers. Manual workers' job performance remains steady until about age 50, with a decline in productivity of less than 10% in later life.

In studying innovations among scientists and engineers in terms of publications and patent production, Dennis (1966) found that two peak periods of productivity for these professions occur between the ages of 40 and 55. In a related study of late-career workers, Rosen and Jerdee (1975) found that older workers were rated lower than younger workers on performance capacity but were seen as more reliable, stable, dependable, and less likely to quit and to be absent from work for personal reasons (Feldman, 1988).

There is strong evidence of discrimination against older workers. Although the Age Discrimination in Employment Act of 1967 was intended to stem discrimination against older workers and a 1979 amendment to this act was passed to raise the mandatory retirement age, discrimination against older employees continues (Feldman, 1988): there was a 76% increase in reported age discrimination cases between 1978 and 1982. Also, a survey conducted by the U.S. House Select Committee on Aging (1982) indicated that over 80% of all American workers felt that employers discriminated against older workers. Bird and Fisher (1986) suggested that supervisors tend to have negative attitudes about older workers. Negative attitudes and discrimination are why late-career presents individual challenges during this developmental stage. However, counseling research places less emphasis on this stage of development than on other stages (Feldman, 1988).

Phasing Out in Late-Career

When to retire is a relevant decision faced by most workers; the ideal time is at least partly a subjective judgment. Factors other than health reasons that influence individuals to retire have been studied by a number of researchers, including Walker and Price (1976). They found that individuals are less likely to retire if they are facing economic hardships or fear inflation, have a strong work ethic and enjoy their work, and view retirement as signaling death and a lower quality of life. Financial security is considered the best single predictor of when to retire (Barfield, 1970) among most workers, with the exception of blue-collar workers who react strongly to job boredom (Pollman & Johnson, 1979). Feldman (1988) suggested that the decision to retire is accomplished in two stages: the evaluation of the financial situation (pensions, savings, projections of inflation), and the evaluation of quality of life while working versus retirement (boredom with work triggers retirement; satisfaction with work increases reluctance to retire). The following counseling session illustrates Joe's gradual detachment from a work role:

Counselor: You say that you planned on retiring five years ago.

Joe: Yeah, you know how people talk. I'm gonna quit as soon as I can. But, when the time came, I wasn't ready to get out. I felt good and I said to myself, "What would I do? Got to have something to do."

Counselor: That was five years ago.

Joe: The biggest thing was the new semiretirement plan the organization offered. Now I can work a little, less than half-time, still make some money, and have time for other things.

Counselor: That sounds great, Joe. You must have a number of things you want to do in retirement.

Joe: Yeah, I take my wife places. We drove to Mexico last week, and I've been fishing with my grandson and all that kind of stuff.

Counselor: You seem happy about your decision.

Joe: I do. My wife told me it's about right. We go places and yet I have something to do that I've always done. I'm getting more used to not being there full-time. One of these days, I'll quit altogether.

Gradual withdrawal from the work world was Joe's way of "letting go." He examined options available to him from the organization and took the first step toward full retirement. A successful change from a lesser work role to more involvement with family satisfies the emotional need of maintaining a sense of integrity.

Implications for Career-Guidance Programs

The stages of career development in organizations provide guidelines for career-guidance needs and program development. The case for the need to assist individuals in organizational choice and the processes involved in organizational choice has not been clearly delineated by the counseling profession or by organizations. However, the need for counselors to encourage careful evaluations of organizations on the basis of individual needs and realistic expectations has been clearly established. Learning to evaluate and to choose an organization and to establish realistic expectations is an important component of counseling.

The stages of entry in early-career are highlighted by the socialization processes that take place in each organization. The individual evaluates self-in-situation by observing the many facets of environmental working conditions, supervisor-worker relations, opportunities for advancement, and congruence with peer affiliates. During the socialization process, the individual needs support in developing a sense of direction in the worker-social milieu where he or she is also being observed and evaluated. Helping individuals assess the complexities associated with organizational life and establish an identity with a new organization are major counseling goals of this stage. For those who decide to withdraw and try again in a different organization, the decision process must include a careful analysis of the reasons for the desired change.

Learning to deal with competition is one of the major social-emotional needs of middle-career, when individuals may need to reevaluate their career direction in organizations. As an individual integrates skills and becomes aware of organizational career paths, help in establishing a set of new goals is a relevant counseling objective. The hazards associated with obsolescence and "career plateaus" suggest that counseling programs encourage continuing education and training.

In late-career, the individual is preparing to "phase out" or "let go" of major work responsibilities. Super (1990) used the term *decline* to indicate that a minor work role is imminent. Many people may be reluctant to accept the fact that their work life is almost over. For others, this stage has been eagerly anticipated as a time of freedom from work and obligations. Counseling strategies that help all workers prepare for this phasing out should include preretirement and retirement programs. More specifically, career programs should be designed to help individuals assess future needs as discussed in Chapter 13.

CHANGING ORGANIZATIONS AND NEW CONCEPTS IN CAREER DEVELOPMENT

In the 1970s and 1980s, career development in organizations was related to upward mobility with predictable promotions and job descriptions. An employee aspired to reach the top of the pyramid in an orderly progression of steps. However, numerous forecasts predict the replacement of the pyramidal organizational structure with a "flat" model, in which workers move laterally and use their skills in different projects. In this environment, workers are expected to learn new skills and adapt to the requirements of working with a team. Workers rotate to different projects and are required to initiate objectives that meet goals through innovation and learning. Management coordinates projects and participates directly in achieving these objectives. There appears to be a partnership between workers and managers and between workers and workers. Greater cooperation—sharing skills and mentoring—is encouraged. In sum, structural changes are already underway, accompanied by closer relationships between employees and employers and the reshaping of careers.

The implications for career development in restructured organizations are quite significant. Kanter (1989) has suggested that organizations will no longer provide highly structured guidelines for careers; the individual must be more assertive in developing his or her destiny. Self-reliance and the ability to adapt to new and different work circumstances are key factors in career development. The new workplace will require greater flexibility from employees and the ability to do several jobs; that is, in some cases, to be more of a generalist than a specialist. Competency in new skills—and, more important, the ability to anticipate future skills—will make individuals more marketable and secure. Although technical competence is extremely important, people skills and the ability to create synergy within a team will also have high priority.

Tomasko (1987) suggested that organizations' structure will have the following components: (1) a lean headquarters (limited staff), (2) networks, not conglomerates (workers can be rotated), (3) vertical disintegration and decentralization (no superstructures), (4) staff services that can be sold to others (once an efficient staff has been assembled they can be marketed to other users), (5) expert systems rather than experts (development of computer-based expert systems), and (6) greater human resource planning (switch from personnel administration).

COUNSELING IN ORGANIZATIONS

The career counselor's role in organizations has not been fully determined or evaluated. However, Osipow (1983) has suggested that career counselors can fulfill definite needs in organizations. Some of his suggestions include programs to help individuals: (1) identify hazards in work, (2) identify work styles that match work sites, (3) deal with work-related stress, (4) deal with problems associated with dual-career roles, (5) deal with the effects of transferring to another job, (6) deal with interpersonal problems on the job, (7) deal with job loss, (8) deal with family problems, (9) deal with healthcare issues, and (10) prepare for retirement. The competencies necessary to meet the counseling needs of individuals in organizations suggest specialized training programs for career counselors.

Hall (1990) has suggested that organizations in general are not fully prepared to manage an individual's career development in terms of resources and information materials. He suggested that individuals should be persuaded to assume responsibility for their own career development and to develop career competencies as opposed to job skills. The key word used by Hall to describe career competencies is *adaptability;* that is, learning to manage changes personally and tolerate the ambiguities of uncertainty. Organizations, on the other hand, should provide a supportive environment for career development by making it possible for individuals to use in-house human-management systems to explore various work roles and to experience various work sites in organizations.

Employee Assistance Programs

Over the last ten years, organizations have been making greater use of employee assistance programs (EAPs). Recognizing the variety of counseling needs of their employees, especially on such problems as alcoholism and alcohol abuse, organizations are providing at least minimal services. The reasons for the growing popularity of EAPs have been identified by McGowan (1984): (1) increased public sophistication about the interaction of psychological stress, work, and health; (2) limited availability of low-cost community mental health and family services; (3) increased concern about worker productivity and morale; (4) increased labor and management recognition of the value of maintaining a stable work force; and (5) repeated research findings that indicate that 15% to 20% of the working population have personal problems that may interfere with job performance.

Although the functions of EAPs may vary significantly in different organizations, they usually perform one or more of the following functions: (1) identification of employees with problems or potential problems, (2) intake and assessment counseling, (3) case coordination, (4) monitoring, information, and referral to other agencies, and (5) follow-up (Myers, 1984).

Some EAPs are part of the organization's personnel offices and human resources offices and are used primarily as a referral service. Organizations also contract with EAP consortiums for services. There is a wide range of program service arrangements, and many have specified numbers of visits for counseling assistance. For example, some organizations pay for intake and diagnosis and the employee pays the charges for treatment services. Other organizations may pay for five or six counseling sessions. EAPs are found in every type of organization and are staffed by social workers, psychologists, personnel administrators, educational counselors, alcohol counselors, and occupational-program consultants (McGowan, 1984).

In a study of personal problems presented by employees to EAPs, Myers (1984) found the following problems to be most prevalent: (1) alcoholism and alcohol abuse, (2) compulsive gambling, (3) drug abuse, (4) employee theft, (5) family and marital problems, (6) personal finances, (7) legal problems, and (8) mental health problems and stress.

Career counselors should be aware of services available to employees and the specific services offered through EAPs. The evidence suggests that such programs will move increasingly toward comprehensive services while developing new types of programs to meet the special needs of a variety of groups. For example, childcare planning, healthcare planning for elderly relatives, preretirement counseling, and single-parent groups may be future EAP services.

The Emergence of Outplacement Counseling

The relatively new term *outplacement counseling* is used to define counseling services offered to employees terminated from industrial and governmental organizations and educational institutions. Outplacement counseling grew out of a need to help terminated employees assess individual strengths, evaluate career options, and learn effective job-search strategies. The costs of outplacement counseling are absorbed by the terminating employer. There is little reference in the literature to outplacement counseling prior to the mid-1970s. This counseling service is expected to grow rapidly in the next decade.

Knowdell, McDaniels, and Walz (1983) have studied the contributing factors that led to the emergence of outplacement counseling:

1. *Technical change*—The increased use of computers and other technological changes have made many traditional employees obsolete. Robot systems are expected to replace many assembly-line positions in the near future.

2. *Corporate reorganization*—Rapidly growing corporations will have periodic reorganizations and power struggles. Many corporate executives will be terminated.

3. *Economic downturns*—Some organizations will find it necessary to periodically reduce staff because of changing economic conditions.

4. *Takeovers, mergers, and divestitures*—During the 1970s and 1980s, many corporations were merged, and as a result, executive officers were displaced.

5. *Stagnation and burnout*—Organizations have discovered that many executives have become ineffective due to various factors, including burnout, divorce, and identity crisis. These managers have difficulty focusing their energies on a job that they have had for a significant time.

6. *Obsolescence and overspecialization*—Many career specialists have difficulty finding use for their highly specialized skills when they are displaced from some organizations. For example, the space industry drew many workers into engineering positions that were highly specialized. As the aerospace industry declined, many of these individuals were displaced.

7. *Promotion to a level of incompetence*—It has been the practice to promote technically competent workers to managerial positions, but many have not had the necessary managerial skills and competencies. The result has been that many of these individuals are ineffective managers and need to be displaced.

8. *Changing value systems in society*—The stigma of being terminated by an organization is not as great as it once was. Tomasko (1987) suggests that downsizing organizations will result in more terminations of staff and executives.

Organizations have discovered that outplacement counseling provides them with many benefits. For example, most organizations wish to keep a good public and community image, and they have resorted to outplacement counseling to help preserve this image. Also, organizations want to minimize lawsuits and grievance procedures (Drucker, 1992).

Counseling Strategies for Outplacement Counseling

Outplacement counseling is primarily designed to assist adults in career transition; therefore, most of the counseling components discussed in this chapter are relevant strategies for outplacement counseling. For example, the terminated employee will be encouraged to identify experiences and skills that are marketable in other organizations. Interest identification and value clarification are major counseling efforts. Decision-making exercises are relevant learning experiences for employees.

Among the special needs of displaced employees are strategies designed to help them deal with their anger and frustration. One useful strategy is helping displaced employees accept their anger as a normal reaction. Providing opportunities to express anger and frustration, individually or in groups, is considered helpful for adults in career transition. Résumé writing and interview-skills development are other needs to be addressed by the career counselor in outplacement counseling (Knowdell, McDaniels, & Walz, 1983).

Retirement Counseling

Throughout this book, career development has been presented as a continuous process over the life span. It is influenced by many variables; some are externally generated (for example, economic crisis and job loss) and others are internally generated (for example, perceptions of retirement), but all are integrated into the continuous career-development process. Nevertheless, retirement counseling may often be overlooked as part of the career-development process and as a career-counseling objective. As we prepare to meet the needs of individuals in the 21st century, the evidence suggests that retirement counseling will be a major component of the career-development process. For example, Sheppard and Rix (1977) pointed out that 31 million Americans will be 65 or older by the year 2000 and 52 million will be that age by the year 2030, clearly indicating that over the next decades, there will be significantly more retirees.

To meet this increasing need, organizations have developed preretirement programs (Morrow, 1985). These programs offer assistance in projecting pensions and other future benefits when the individual reaches retirement age. This type of preretirement program has often been referred to as a "probable inflation" model from which the individual can project his or her financial status at retirement. Other topics often addressed in organizational preretirement programs are optional retirement plans (such as partial retirement, which allows the individual to work part-time), time management, financial planning, leisure alternatives, and marital and social relationships (Feldman, 1988).

Some organizations also offer planning services to individuals near retirement age. There are two types: limited and comprehensive. Limited retirement programs typically provide guidance in pension planning, social security and Medicare information, health insurance options, and information on retirement benefits at various ages of retirement. Areas included in comprehensive programs commonly include those covered in the limited programs plus the following: maintaining good health, marital/emotional aspects of retirement, leisure activities, relocation advantages and disadvantages, legal concerns (wills, estate planning, inheritance laws), family relations, employment possibilities, and lifestyle change.

Other topics that career counselors can use in retirement planning have been suggested by Sinick (1977):

1. *Facing another phase in life*—Individuals are instructed to view retirement as another stage in life with its own tasks and transitions.

2. *Adjusting attitudes and roles*—Individuals realistically look for options in lifestyle according to their own needs.

3. *Working part-time for pay or working part-time as a volunteer*—Some individuals find that a different work environment can be rewarding and can offer opportunities to continue a work identity or help others.

4. *Using free time creatively or following avocation interests*—During the work years, many individuals have limited time to do creative work, such as arts and crafts or writing. Retirement offers opportunities to learn and participate with groups or to pursue interests individually.

5. *Health and nutrition*—Participation in wellness or other health-related programs provides a sense of security that one is doing the best he or she can to prolong a healthy life span.

EVALUATING THE ORGANIZATION

This chapter has presented several suggestions on how we might help others evaluate an organization. These suggestions were offered in different contexts. You will recall that the purpose of this chapter is to build a frame of reference on organizational structure, leadership styles, motivation studies, and other factors that would help us evaluate an organization. We will, therefore, develop a number of key questions to help us in our evaluation. The questions that follow are, in most cases, very general and will be difficult to answer. They are only representative samples and are not inclusive of all that should be learned about organizations during the career search.

Our first question is, Can we evaluate an organization effectively enough to justify including organization evaluations as another step in the career-exploration process? Lawler (1973) pointed out that gathering information about organizations would be very time-consuming, of questionable value, and may even produce an information overload. Following this logic, one could present the same argument about collecting information concerning an occupation. Certainly, there are many ramifications in evaluating an occupational choice—this is the major concern of this text and many others. Many of the questions we may pose concerning organizations are similar to those we attempt to answer about occupations. Admittedly, the evaluation of organizations will be difficult and time-consuming, but this is an important challenge; similar problems were faced by the early pioneers in vocational counseling in their quest for occupational information.

At this point, we have little research that might give us guidelines on how to effectively choose an organization (Hall, 1990). Therefore, our attempt here to develop a format and guidelines for evaluating an organization will have to be considered exploratory and tentative. For the individuals who will work in organizations, the question of whether we can effectively evaluate them is academic—for, after all, they must do it.

Let us begin by reviewing the major components of this chapter in order to generate questions that may be used as an evaluation format. (The sequence of the major components addressed in an evaluation format need not be the same as that presented in the chapter.) One of our major concerns was organizational structure. This immediately led to a consideration of the authority relationships in the organization. Thus, we will first ask questions concerning the form of structure, policies, and formal control systems, as these appear to be relevant to our observations. We will primarily want to consider how the structure of the organization influences the individual's role. Questions to be answered include the following:

- What is the pattern of the formal organizational structure?
- Where and by whom are organizational decisions made?
- What are the requirements for promotion in the organizational structure?
- What kinds of "movement" are available in the organizational structure?
- How would you characterize the organizational structure?
- Are the social systems compatible with my lifestyle?
- Will the entry point in the organization provide opportunities to meet goals and needs?

Our next major component for consideration is that of leadership style found in the organization. As you will recall, leadership style is a very important determinant of the role of subordinates. Another important point to remember is that some organizations take a contingency approach and determine a leadership style for each situational difference within the organization. In these organizations, there may be combinations of differing approaches to leadership. Questions in this part of the evaluation include the following:

- Do the leaders appear to be task-oriented or people-oriented?
- What is the organization's philosophy or procedure for developing leaders?
- Do the leaders appear to be autocratic or democratic?
- What interaction, if any, takes place between leader and subordinate in the decision-making process?
- How are the goals and needs of the individual considered by the leaders?
- To what degree do leaders involve subordinates in sharing organizational goals?

Our third and final major component is our concern for work motivation in the organization. The evaluation of this component, like others, should be very individualized. Identifying individually developed goals and needs may be considered a prerequisite to evaluating this aspect of the organization. Of major consideration are opportunities for satisfying needs for affiliation, achievement, power, status, recognition, actualization, and so on. In Chapter 2, we discussed Tiedeman and O'Hara's (1963) paradigm of decision making within which goals can be categorized as crystallized, reaffirmed, and integrated. Tiedeman postulated that an individual modifies goals or realigns them to find consistency in the working environment. Thus, the organizational work environment does provide a frame of reference within which certain individual considerations can be made. It is important to find congruency with as many organizational variables as possible to ensure a satisfactory work environment. Even though we may modify personally held goals, we should not be expected to change them completely. Finding a satisfactory work environment, like making an occupational choice, is an individual matter; both choices may be painstakingly difficult to make but are essential in satisfying individually developed goals and needs. Key questions about motivation include the following:

- Will the working environment provide a means of satisfying immediate goals?
- What are the job satisfactions that can be realized in the organizational work environment? Do these opportunities satisfy my goals and needs?
- Will the social interaction satisfy my needs for affiliation?
- Will there be a fulfillment of need for recognition and status with this organization?
- Will my need for achievement be met now and in the future?
- Are there adequate reinforcers provided by the organization and in what form?
- Can I find consistency between the organizational goals and my own values, beliefs, and attitudes?
- Do all persons have equal opportunities for achieving their individual goals?

Now that the questions have been generated, we must turn our attention to how they may be answered. Our first approach is to investigate published materials that may provide us with pertinent information. Two publications that have received considerable attention and are good references for the evaluation of corporations are *The 100 Best Companies to Work for in America* (Levering, Moskowitz, & Katz, 1984) and *In Search of Excellence* (Thomas & Waterman, 1982). Both books describe organizational structure, working atmosphere, benefits, and projections of organizational growth.

Other publications that may be helpful are as follows: *Manufacturers and Thomas Register Catalog* (1988), *Predicasts Funk and Scott Index of Corporations and Industries* (1989), *World Guide to Trade Associations*, (1985), and *Handbook of Corporate Social Responsibility* (1975). These publications can only partially help us evaluate an organization from the frame of reference we have established. They are generally designed to provide only a broad exposure to corporations and organizations, reporting some operational aspects, management procedures, and institutional structures. Individual publications developed by organizations provide the same type of information but are published mainly for public relations use. In essence, we cannot expect to fulfill our quest for evaluating organizations using only published materials.

The suggested alternatives are visitation and interview. Career-counseling programs have long suggested on-site job visits as valuable experiences during career exploration. From our frame of reference, assessment of occupational climate and other organizational variables are of equal importance. On-site visits may also present the opportunity to interview a variety of individuals within the organization.

When visitations are not practical, the interview becomes our primary method of evaluating an organization. In this context, the interview becomes a "mutual interview" in which the individual not only provides information but also receives information from organizational representatives. Both this method of evaluating an organization and the on-site visit method have obvious limitations. Organizational representatives are hired to project a "good image" of their organizations and may present a biased appraisal of organizational climate. On-site visits may often do the same. Nevertheless, the individual with a good understanding of organizational structure, leadership styles, and organizational behavior will be in a much better position to evaluate an occupation within an organization during the career decision-making process. In the meantime, research is needed to develop more effective methods of evaluating organizational climate.

Summary

1. Organizations are social systems combining people and technology in a working environment.

2. Individuals tend to identify with organizations as well as occupations. Evaluating organizations is important in the career-decision process.

3. The informal organization is the network of personal and social relationships that has a powerful influence on organizational behavior.

4. Organizational structure may have a significant impact on the individual's role in an organization. Mechanistic environments include bureaucratic, administrative, and line-staff structures. Organic organizational systems include decentralization and the matrix organizational structure.

5. Organizational leadership styles largely determine the conditions of the working environment. Leadership styles do not exist in their purest form in an organization. Nevertheless, the leader's basic assumption about subordinates greatly influences the working climate.

6. Models of career-development stages in organizations offer a frame of reference for observing the steps in career development. Each developmental stage has similar yet unique needs.

7. The major tasks of early-career include becoming oriented to the organization, learning position responsibilities and demonstrating satisfactory performance, and implementing plans for advancement or position change.

8. Fast-track programs typically offer prospective managers rapid promotions, but they may encourage work habits that in the long run are not beneficial to the individual or the organization.

9. Mid-career is a "settling-in" process characterized by resolutions of conflicts and conflicting demands within the organization and in personal life.

10. In late-career, the individual turns his or her attention to activities outside the organization. One of the major adjustments is learning to accept a reduced work role and work identity.

11. Although the relationship between age and job performance is not clear, the type of work seems to be the most important variable.

12. The changing organization will bring about new concepts in career development. The individual must be more assertive in developing his or her destiny. Learning new skills and adapting to new and different work environments are key factors to success.

13. Organizations are using EAPs to meet the personal counseling needs of their employees. The primary functions of EAPs are identifying employees with problems or potential problems, intake and assessment counseling, and referring employees to other agencies for counseling.

14. Outplacement counseling is offered to employees terminated from industrial and governmental organizations and educational institutions. Outplacement counseling evolved from the need to assist terminated employees in assessing individual strengths, evaluating career options, and learning effective job-search strategies.

15. Retirement counseling is also being offered by organizations. Some organizations provide comprehensive programs, including information concerning leisure activities, legal concerns, and lifestyle change.

16. Procedures for evaluating an organization have not been fully developed. Important considerations include authority relationships in the organizations, leadership style found in the organization, and potential opportunities for satisfying individual needs. Publications, visitations, and interviews provide some means for evaluating organizations.

SUPPLEMENTARY LEARNING EXERCISES

1. Using the references listed in this chapter and others, develop strategies for evaluating an organization from published material. Explain how these evaluations could be incorporated into career-counseling programs.
2. Develop a counseling component that gives an orientation to the realities of working in an organization.
3. Compare a bureaucratic organizational structure with a matrix structure. Describe personal characteristics of individuals who would function effectively within each structure.
4. What kind of leader would you prefer in an organization? Describe the leader's characteristics and basic assumptions about the role of subordinates. List the reasons you consider leadership an important element to be considered in career-counseling programs.
5. Interview an individual who has a leadership position in an organization. Focus your questions on relationships with subordinates. Develop a set of questions that could be used by your counselees to assess leader-subordinate relationships.

6. Interview an individual who has worked in an organization for several years to determine how that individual would evaluate an organization, based on past experience. Compare this evaluation with the questions listed in this chapter for evaluating an organization. What are your conclusions?
7. Develop at least five counseling strategies to meet the needs of individuals in early-career. Discuss.
8. Compare the career development of an individual who works for an organization with someone who owns his or her own business. Discuss similarities and differences.
9. Develop a counseling component for individuals who are planning to retire.
10. Project what you consider to be an organization of the future. Focus on the roles of the worker, management, and the work force.

Chapter Thirteen

Career Counseling for Adults in Career Transition

This chapter concentrates on the growing need for programs and strategies to assist adults in career transition. Traditionally, career-counseling programs have focused on strategies for initial career choices, while giving only limited help to adults who change careers. However, in the last decade, greater attention has been focused on the development of counseling programs for individuals who choose to make a career change and for those who are forced into it. In the 1970s, Arbeiter and colleagues (1978) found that 40 million American adults were in some phase of career transition. Many were victims of an economic slowdown, which triggered the downsizing of organizations as discussed in the preceding chapter. More recently, the changing workplace has become somewhat dismal, with the decline of manufacturing, downscaling of jobs, and high unemployment (McDaniels, 1990). However, Waterman (1992) argued that change is to be expected, especially in an environment where advanced technology makes some jobs obsolete while creating new ones. Change is a way of life and can provide exciting new challenges. An individual's response to change should be the counseling focus for those who work with adults in career transition. The NOICC (1991) emphasized this point when developing the national guidelines for career-guidance programs, in particular the competencies for adults making career transitions. Two other important facts should also be understood: society's needs and functions affect occupational supply and demand, and a global economy can directly affect the career development of many individuals.

Because individuals in any generation differ from each other and from one generation to the next, counseling programs cannot be expected to meet everyone's needs. However, components of existing programs may be effectively combined and used in counseling a broad spectrum of adults. As we learn more about various aspects of the life span, stages of development, vocational maturity, motivation, and specific tasks related to life and work, better guidelines for developing programs will become available. Meanwhile, the development of counseling components that meet specific needs should provide for flexibility in program structure. Specific components can then be combined to meet the general needs of a particular population. In addition, interchangeable techniques and alternative procedures are needed to provide flexible strategies.

Finally, specific counseling objectives need to be developed as guidelines for accomplishing various parts of specific counseling programs. These factors have been considered in developing the counseling program discussed in the second section of this chapter.

This chapter first covers the issues facing adults in career transition. This discussion is followed by a brief review of midlife crisis and basic coping skills for managing transitions. Then, several approaches to developmental stages and tasks are reviewed, followed by implications for career-guidance programs for adults in career transition. Finally, seven counseling components for adults in career transition are explored.

ISSUES FACING ADULTS IN CAREER TRANSITION

The first issue is a practical one: the unavailability of career-counseling programs for adults. Adults are generally unaware of available jobs and lack direction in making satisfactory career changes. Furthermore, many adults have not developed career-exploration skills such as decision making and do not know about resources that give job descriptions, requirements, and so forth (Brown & Minor, 1989). In essence, many adults are generally confused about future directions and where to find assistance. However, counseling should do more than just supply exploration skills. The important components of career counseling not addressed in original career decisions (such as values, needs, goals, and developed skills) are major targets of career counseling for adults. The issue here involves helping individuals reassess the contributing factors that led to the desire for a career change. The complex nature of arriving at a career decision underscores the need for career-counseling programs that meet individual needs at all age levels and in a variety of settings.

One of the problems many adults face in their development is that they have not kept pace with changing job technologies, procedures, and practices that characterize their occupational field. When an individual does not stay abreast of changing demands, he or she becomes obsolescent. Closely related to the studies of life-span development are concerns about job obsolescence. In the last decade, a variety of changes in technology, occupational structure, organizational format, and management techniques have focused greater attention on this subject. The relationship of obsolescence to career crisis has been a major concern in recent research. Kaufman (1974) developed a synthesized definition of obsolescence as follows: "Obsolescence is the degree to which organizational professionals lack up-to-date knowledge of skills necessary to maintain effective performance in either their current or future work roles" (p. 23). This definition has been drawn primarily from his work with obsolescence among professionals who work in organizations, but it seems acceptable for general purposes.

Keeping this definition in mind, let us explore some of the reasons for obsolescence. Industrial organizations have experienced almost revolutionary changes in the last 20 years through technical advancement and subsequent changes in production. An almost immediate result has been a vast change in the technical skills needed to complement technological advances.

The changes in training needed for certain occupations, particularly in the sciences, have been so accelerated that even individuals who have just completed professional training find they are not up-to-date with recent advances in their field. Of major significance is that age is not necessarily the contributing factor. Thus, obsolescence of professionals is not necessarily related to midlife or aging but may be more related to professional training demands. The same demands for retraining and upgrading of skills are also prevalent for many lower-level occupations. In many instances, certain jobs have been completely eliminated because they are no longer required for an organization to meet its goals. Thus, job obsolescence is possible at all levels of work and may occur at any time during the worker's life span.

Potential causes for obsolescence cannot be generalized but seem to be more related to individual factors such as ability and motivation. For example, ability to acquire new knowledge may be one limiting factor in learning new job requirements, particularly in the demanding, higher-level occupations. However, lack of motivation has been identified as the greatest single factor contributing to obsolescence (Kaufman, 1974). Individuals who have strong needs for achievement tend to be motivated to remain up-to-date in their field (McClelland et al., 1953). Likewise, those individuals who are motivated by higher-order needs of personal growth will tend to attain self-development (Herzberg, Mausner, & Snyderman, 1959). According to Kaufman (1974), motivational drives are not necessarily age-related, but as individuals grow older there may be differences in the desire to work on projects requiring new learning. Older, more established workers tend to be more oriented toward maintaining stability and security. Thus, obsolescence is not necessarily related to age, although energy and initiative levels may diminish somewhat with age. Individual factors such as needs, goals, personality, ability, experiences, and life events are major considerations in evaluating causes for obsolescence.

Downsizing organizations is another issue facing adults in the workplace. This term is used to describe the removal of significant numbers of managers, professionals, and blue-collar workers from organizations. Since 1979, 1 million managers and professionals have been laid off by organizations that have "downsized" (Tomasko, 1987). Massive layoffs are a trend that has affected the career plans of the middle-level work force. However, widespread cutbacks have affected most departments in large organizations; for example, Kodak recently eliminated 13,000 employees from all levels of its worldwide organization (Tomasko, 1987). There are many reasons for the continuing retrenchment of organizations, such as strong overseas competition, declining manufacturing, declining energy and commodity prices, and deregulation. The globalization of American companies, due to satellite-linked computer networks that make it feasible for companies to become multinational, has also contributed to the weakening U.S. job market.

Reich (1991) presents an example of how products are produced and marketed internationally: "Precision ice hockey equipment was designed in Sweden, financed in Canada, and assembled in Cleveland and Denmark for distribution in North America and Europe, respectively, out of alloys whose molecular structure was researched and patented in Delaware and fabricated in Japan" (p. 112). This example illustrates the mode of operation of multinational corporations, underscoring the fact that many organizations will lose their national identity.

These events have triggered a rethinking of bureaucratic assumptions about long-term employment commitments. As Kanter (1989) put it, "Climbing the career ladder is being replaced by hopping from job to job" (p. 299). The lack of certainty and clear direction for the future work role has generated many personal dilemmas. Adults who find themselves in career transition as a result of downsizing need career-intervention strategies that focus on establishing a career direction in the ever-changing workplace.

Along with evolving organizational structure changes will come a work force that is more diverse in terms of culture and gender. By the year 2000, White males will no longer dominate the work force as the number of women, minorities, and immigrants significantly increase (U.S. Department of Labor, 1992–1993). These new demographics offer challenges to supervisors and fellow workers as well as to the career-development specialist. A greater sensitivity to such diverse populations in the workplace will become increasingly important. Evolving organizational settings will reflect the new demographics, and effective team members will have to be able to function well with all groups of people. Career counselors must be able to offer professional leadership to help individuals develop these skills. (In this section, we will focus on cultural diversity; for more information on women, see Chapter 14.)

Organizations will also become more globally oriented, which translates into a greater potential for working with people from many cultures (Kanter, 1989). A multiethnic work force may include natives of Mexico, Japan, Germany, and France, for example, and American team members will have to understand the basic differences in cultural perceptions of work, in processing information, and in responding to tasks and fellow workers (Wigglesworth, 1992). Here are some examples of differences between cultures, as compiled by Harris and Moran (1991):

Nonverbal signals—the "A-OK" gesture

- In America, it means everything is fine.
- In Germany and Brazil, it is interpreted as obscene.
- The Japanese interpret it as money.
- To the French, it means "zilch" or zero.

Eye contact

- In America, poor eye contact translates into a "shifty" character.
- In Japan, children are taught to look at the tie knot or Adam's apple.
- In Latin America, prolonged eye contact can be considered disrespectful.
- Arabs look at each other squarely in the eye.

- The widening of the eyes in China is a danger signal and may indicate suppressed anger.

These few examples are indicative of the vast array of differences among cultures and underscore the increasing need to become more culturally aware. Other differences include time factors, body language, physical distance, and what gives rise to conflict (Wigglesworth, 1992). The acquisition of skills to be an effective worker in a diverse work force is long overdue and should be a high-priority focus for career counselors. For more information on ethnic groups, see Chapter 16.

We must also recognize the issues involved with the unfulfilled worker who is generally dissatisfied with work because his or her needs have not been met. Where do I go from here? What is it that I am doing? What is the purpose of my life and work? These questions are typical of the unfulfilled worker who looks for a link between purpose of work and existence. A major concern is for some tangible evidence that what has been or is currently being accomplished serves a social purpose. The social worth of work has been recognized as a prime consideration among professional workers (Sarason, Sarason, & Cowden, 1977). However, a need to recognize work and its relationship to societal needs has also become a growing concern for many others in the work force. O'Toole (1977) pointed out that the "working class" is also concerned with challenge and the intrinsic value of work. Thus, the disenchantment with work is not necessarily job related or a social class issue, but is prevalent throughout our entire work force.

In summary, the unfulfilled worker is searching for autonomy, challenge, and meaning in work. The motivational drives of the search may be centered on combinations of the following: (1) a change in needs (to higher-order needs) and subsequent restructuring of goals from the time of the original career commitment, (2) a recognized disparity between current work content and reformulated goals, (3) a lack of conformity between personal goals and organizational or employer policies and goals, (4) a recognized disparity between self-perceived abilities and the utilization of these abilities in the current work environment, (5) a feeling of isolation resulting from a lack of conformity with goals and values of peer affiliates or the informal organization, and (6) a feeling of a lack of accomplishment from what has been achieved in the past and the potential for the future.

Finally, we must deal with the variety of expectations individuals have concerning their career choice. Many have enthusiastically entered a career with the expectation of a continuous, challenging, intrinsically rewarding work environment only to experience something quite different. For these individuals, the realities of working somehow have been misinterpreted. Many may see this as a broken promise of what they were led to expect from their careers and react as if in a "crisis," ultimately seeking changes in their lifestyles. The conflicts between career and expectations are characteristically intense, leading many toward a search for a second career. Their message is quite clear—help us find fulfillment from life and work.

MIDLIFE CRISIS AND CAREER DEVELOPMENT

Recently, the influence of midlife crisis on career change has received consider-able attention. Many have speculated about the adversities of the so-called midlife crisis, but with little agreement on why and when it happens (Zimbardo, 1978). For some people, this period of life may have a profound impact, while for others, there are only subtle, almost unnoticed differences in lifestyles. Profound changes may take the form of job change, expansive think-ing and behavior, alienation of family, depression, and many acting-out behav-iors. For others, there may be noticeable physiological change with few, if any, accompanying psychological disturbances.

Menopause is often associated with changes of behavior in many middle-aged women. Men generally experience a decline in muscular coordination and sexual activity. This is accompanied by a decrease in muscle tone and energy. For both sexes, the awareness of aging and passage of time may be the most difficult adjustment of this period in the life span. The emphasis on youth and youthful appearance in our society may have devastating effects on some indi-viduals. Learning to accept the physiological process of aging can be considered a major objective of counseling programs.

The "empty-nest syndrome" may be another contributing factor to a potential midlife crisis situation (Sheehy, 1976). As the name implies, this period of life is associated with the last child leaving the home. For many individuals, particularly women, one of the major purposes of life has ended. For some, there may be a feeling of freedom to experience a different lifestyle and/or begin a new career. The difficulty of this adjustment for both parents is highly related to the roles established in the marriage and whether they have the flexibility required for finding new meaning and purpose in the marital relationship. A lack of sense of purpose at home may very well be reflected in one's work and, in fact, the total lifestyle.

There is considerable disagreement on the impact of midlife on human behavior. One stereotype is that of a disenchanted, depressed individual who feels useless and unwanted. Almost the opposite impression of midlife is held by others. For certain, there are confusing and differing perceptions of midlife, as expressed by Zimbardo (1978):

> According to another stereotype, a major crisis occurs in middle age, the "mid-life crisis." However, psychologists have not been able to agree when it occurs, some arguing for the twenties, some for the sixties, and others about the nature of the crisis. One might suspect, then, that the concept lacks a firm basis of facts. Supporting this suspicion, a recent study showed that middle age is actually the best period of adulthood. Feelings of alienation, powerlessness, meaninglessness, and disengagement were most prevalent in young adulthood and least prevalent in middle age (p. 266).

Potential midlife crisis situations demand the concern of developers of adult career-counseling programs. Thus, career counseling must consider the needs of adults in the entire life span—young, middle-aged, and elderly adults.

The following issues are representative examples of potential career-crisis situations over the entire spectrum of adulthood. Therefore, the term *adult* will be used in the following discussions to represent all ages of full-time working adults.

BASIC COPING SKILLS FOR MANAGING TRANSITIONS

Brammer and Abrego (1981) have developed a model for basic coping skills that assist adults in managing transitions (see Table 13-1). The first set of coping skills relates to perceiving and responding to transitions, such as developing self-control and a style for responding to change. The second set of skills relates to assessing, developing, and utilizing external support systems. By developing a personal support system network, the individual can use friends and professionals in crisis situations. The third set is related to assessing, developing, and utilizing an internal support system, such as assessing positive and negative attitudes and personal strengths and activating these strengths when needed. The fourth set involves reducing emotional and physiological distress through relaxation exercises and the verbal expression of feelings associated with distress. The fifth set, which involves planning and implementing change, promotes planning various courses of action and formulating strategies for implementing them.

One example of applying these skills might be a man who is given the news that his job is to be terminated because of economic conditions. He can use self-control skills to perceive the current situation realistically. By recognizing he has time to make future plans before the termination turns into a financial crisis, he can call on friends for emotional support and for suggestions on how to conduct a job search. He can rely on skills used to develop inner strength to help him evaluate the current job market and make plans for the future.

Brammer and Abrego (1981) suggested that people often feel powerless to respond to change. Coping skills help adults in transition react more rationally when responding to changing conditions over the life span. Coping skills are often best taught in seminars or in small groups.

CAREER-COUNSELING IMPLICATIONS IN ADULT DEVELOPMENTAL MODELS

The demonstrated need for programs that focus on career change has created concern about adult development over the entire life span. The significant pattern of change that characterizes adult career histories indicates that the need for career counseling goes beyond the point of choice. Further assistance may be needed to accomplish career-developmental tasks and to solve related developmental problems encountered throughout life.

TABLE 13-1
Basic Coping Skills for Managing Transitions

1 *Skills in perceiving and responding to transitions*

  1.1 The person mobilizes a personal style of responding to change. He or she

    1.11 Accepts the proposition that problematic situations constitute a normal part of life and that it is possible to cope with most of these situations effectively (perceived control over one's life).

    1.12 Recognizes the importance of describing problematic situations accurately (problem definition).

    1.13 Recognizes the values and limitations of feelings as cues to evaluate a transition (feelings description).

    1.14 Inhibits the tendency either to act impulsively or to do nothing when confronted with a problematic situation (self-control).

  1.2 The person identifies his or her current coping style (style of responding to change).

2 *Skills for assessing, developing, and utilizing external support systems*

  2.1 The person can assess an external support system. He or she can

    2.11 Identify his or her emotional needs during times of transition.

    2.12 Identify people in his or her life who provide for personal needs.

    2.13 Describe a personal support network in terms of physical and emotional proximity.

  2.2 The person can develop a personal network based on data from 2.1 or he or she can

    2.21 Seek sources (groups, organizations, locales) of potential support persons.

    2.22 Apply social skills to cultivate persons to meet identified needs.

  2.3 The person can utilize an established support network. He or she can

    2.31 Develop strategies for spending time with persons considered most helpful.

    2.32 Apply skills for utilizing persons in his or her network when a transition is anticipated or arrives.

3 *Skills for assessing, developing, and utilizing internal support systems*

  3.1 The person can assess the nature and strength of positive and negative self-regarding attitudes. He or she can

    3.11 Identify personal strengths.

    3.12 Identify negative self-descriptive statements, as well as the assumptions and contextual cues that arouse such statements.

  3.2 The person can develop positive self-regard attitudes. He or she can

    3.21 Affirm personal strengths.

    3.22 Convert negative self-descriptions into positive descriptive statements when the data and criteria so warrant.

  3.3 The person can utilize his or her internal support system in a transition. He or she can

    3.31 Construe life transitions as personal growth opportunities.

    3.32 Identify tendencies to attribute personal deficiencies as causative factors in distressful transitions.

4 *Skills for reducing emotional and physiological distress*

  He or she can

  4.1 Practice self-relaxation responses.

  4.2 Apply strategies to control over-stimulation/under-stimulation.

  4.3 Express verbally feelings associated with his or her experience of transition.

TABLE 13-1
(continued)

5 *Skills for planning and implementing change*

  5.1 The person can analyze discrepancies between existing and desired conditions.
  5.2 The person exercises positive planning for new options. To the best of his or her abilities, the person can
    5.21 Thoroughly canvass a wide range of alternative courses of action.
    5.22 Survey the full range of objectives to be fulfilled and the values implied by the choice.
    5.23 Carefully weigh whatever he or she knows about the cost and risk of negative consequences that could flow from each alternative.
    5.24 Search intensely for information relevant to further evaluation of the alternatives.
    5.25 Utilize feedback to reassess his or her preferred course of action.
    5.26 Reexamine the positive and negative consequences of all known alternatives.
    5.27 Make detailed provisions for implementing or executing the chosen course of action including contingency plans.
  5.3 The person successfully implements his or her plans. He or she can
    5.31 Identify stressful situations related to implementing goals.
    5.32 Identify negative self-statements that interfere with implementing plans.
    5.33 Utilize self-relaxation routines while anticipating the stressful implementation of plans.
    5.34 Utilize self-rewards in goal attainment.
    5.35 Identify additional skills needed to implement goals (for example, anxiety management, training in assertiveness, overcoming shyness).

SOURCE: "Intervention Strategies for Coping with Transitions," by L.M. Brammer and P.J. Abrego, *The Counseling Psychologist*, 1981, 9, 27. Reprinted by permission.

Three major kinds of models that describe adult development dominate professional literature: (1) developmental-stages models; (2) experiential models; (3) and biosocial, career, and family dimensions models.

Developmental-Stages Models

In the developmental-stages approach, significant life-span changes and events are seen as occurring in a fixed sequence and are roughly related to chronological age. Stage theorists assume that similar challenges and problems are confronted at nearly the same period of life span. For example, Erikson (1950) postulated that there are eight stages in the life span that present challenges and turning points faced by individuals at particular age periods. Troll (1975, pp. 6–7) used Erikson's eight stages as redefined by Gruen (1964) to illustrate how these stages fit adult behavior (see Table 13-2).

These stages focus on successful resolutions of periodic crisis. Although the research founded upon these theories has not produced concrete results (Troll, 1975, p. 7), Gruen (1964) reported evidence supporting Erikson's assumption that adult development has sequential stages. These stages at least define guidelines in terms of adult progress in development from which counseling strategies may be developed. The stages may be considered separately or in combination. Since the eight stages are perceived to occur in sequence, the counselor may consider the resolutions to specific problems of each stage as potential career-counseling objectives. For example, Stage 7, Generativity Versus Stagnation, provides a resolution applicable to work-related tasks and problems. Counseling strategies can be developed to aid the adult in the resolution process. The individual who has difficulty resolving the feelings of stagnation from work may be helped by a search for a means of renewing interest in the current work environment or by developing new methods of utilizing skills and abilities in a different work environment.

Havighurst (1953) proposed a series of developmental tasks similar to those within Erikson's and Gruen's stages. He postulated that there are sets of tasks that when accomplished provide satisfactory life-span development. For example, during early adulthood, these tasks include finding a spouse and successfully adjusting to married life, rearing children, beginning a career, participating in civic affairs, and establishing social relationships. In middle age, the tasks include establishment of an economic standard of living, a satisfactory relationship with a spouse, preparing teenage children for adulthood, adjusting to physiological changes, and the development of leisure-time activities. These model developmental tasks also suggest potential crisis situations and, consequently, objectives for adult career-counseling programs. For example, adult tasks include establishing social relationships and adjusting to physiological changes. Both are important objectives for career-counseling strategies in that social relationships at work and personal adjustment will have an important influence on the efficacy and overall satisfaction of the individual worker. The worker plagued by concerns about conflicting or dissatisfying relationships and physical changes is unable to devote full energy to work tasks. Reduced efficiency may then result in further dissatisfaction and lowered self-esteem.

Vaillant (1977) supported Erikson's and Havighurst's assumptions that adult development has sequential stages. In a longitudinal study of almost 300 Harvard graduates, he concluded that adults do indeed change dynamically as they pass through stages of life. "Although one stage of life is not superior to another, the given stage of development could rarely be achieved until the previous one was mastered" (p. 207).

Vaillant contended that long-term relationships and recurrent events in adult development are of greater importance than isolated traumatic events. Although the death of a loved one could severely affect an individual, the cumulative effect of the relationship is of greater significance. The results drawn from the 300 Harvard graduates studied indicated that among this group no single event greatly influenced the process of midlife adjustment. Vaillant suggested that unique long-term relationships and occurrences are major points of reference in adult development. The important finding is that cumulative effects of events and relationships are most important in determining an individual's adaptive ability to deal with current and future issues. The

TABLE 13-2
Erikson's Eight Stages of the Life Span

Stage 1. Basic trust versus basic mistrust

Successful resolution: the person likes or trusts work associates, friends, relatives; feels essentially optimistic about people and their motives; has confidence in self and in the world in general.

Unsuccessful resolution: the person distrusts people; prefers to be alone because friends "get into trouble"; dislikes confiding in anyone; distrusts both self and the world in general.

Stage 2. Autonomy versus shame and doubt

Successful resolution: attitudes and ways of doing things are his or her own and are not followed because others expect them; is not afraid to hold own opinions or do what he or she likes.

Unsuccessful resolution: is self-conscious about own ideas and ways of doing things and prefers to stay within tried and trusted ways; avoids asserting self against group; emphasizes how much like others he or she acts and feels.

Stage 3. Initiative versus guilt

Successful resolution: takes pleasure in planning and initiating action; plans ahead and designs own schedule.

Unsuccessful resolution: lets others initiate action; plays down success or accomplishment.

Stage 4. Industry versus inferiority

Successful resolution: likes to make things and carry them to completion; strives for skill mastery; has pride in production.

Unsuccessful resolution: is passive; leaves things undone; feels inadequate about ability to do things or to produce work.

Stage 5. Ego identity versus role diffusion

Successful resolution: has strongly defined social roles; feels at home in work, family, affiliations, sex role; enjoys carrying out role behavior; has sense of belonging; takes comfort in style of life and daily activities; is definite about self and who he or she is; feels continuity with past and present.

Unsuccessful resolution: is ill at ease in roles; lost in groups and affiliations; does not enter into required role behavior with much conviction; may have radical switches in work or residence without meaning or purpose.

Stage 6. Intimacy versus isolation

Successful resolution: has close, intimate relationship with spouse and friends, sharing thoughts, spending time with them, and expressing warm feelings for them.

Unsuccessful resolution: lives relatively isolated from friends, spouse, children; avoids contact with others on an intimate basis; is either absorbed in self or indiscriminately sociable; relations with people are stereotyped or formalized.

Stage 7. Generativity versus stagnation

Successful resolution: has plans for future that require sustained application and utilization of skills and abilities; invests energy and ideas into something new; has sense of continuity with future generations.

TABLE 13-2
(continued)

Unsuccessful resolution: seems to be vegetating; does nothing more than routines of work and necessary daily activities; is preoccupied with self.

Stage 8. Integrity versus despair

Successful resolution: feels satisfied and happy with life, work, accomplishments; accepts responsibility for life; maximizes successes.

Unsuccessful resolution: feels depressed and unhappy about life, emphasizing failures; would change life or career if had another chance; does not accept present age and mode of life, emphasizing past; fears getting older; fears death.

SOURCE: *Early and Middle Adulthood*, 2nd ed., by L. E. Troll. Copyright 1985, 1975 by Wadsworth, Inc. Reprinted by permission of the publisher, Brooks/Cole Publishing Company, Pacific Grove, CA, and of Dr. Walter Gruen.

total lifestyle is of major consideration when helping adults develop life-planning strategies.

Growth, the theme of Gould's (1978) approach to adult development, is a process of freeing oneself from childhood restraints and ties. As individuals develop adult consciousness, freed from false childhood assumptions, they create their own lives. Steps of adult growth include getting married, working, buying a home, and having a first child. Each step progressively provides a more meaningful adult life; adulthood is not the plateau of growth but merely a period of change and evolution.

The stages of growth are thwarted by major and component false assumptions. For example, the period from ages 16 to 22, referred to as Leaving Our Parents' World, has the major false assumption, "I'll always belong to my parents and believe in their world." A component assumption is, "If I get any more independent, it will be a disaster" (Gould, 1978, p. 4).

As individuals come to recognize that false childhood assumptions restrict self-development, they take steps to break away from these ties. The following transformations are usually discomforting and painful throughout the life cycle: (1) I'm Nobody's Baby Now (age 22–28), (2) Opening Up to What's Inside (age 28–34), (3) Midlife Decade (age 35–44), and (4) The End of an Era (beyond midlife).

Gould painted adulthood with an aura of excitement—a period full of exciting challenges. Adults rediscover vital talents, and maturity brings a clearer vision of self in the developmental process. The positive elements of adulthood give growth a true sense of meaning, geared for managing age-related changes. An integral view of total lifestyle development provides purpose and a sense of meaning for transformations in adult life.

Levinson and associates (1978) used the term *life cycle* to emphasize that the course of life has distinct character and follows a basic sequence. Although each life cycle has individual variations, there is a general pattern that Levinson saw as a journey from birth to death. The life cycle has four eras referred to as *seasons* or *times of life*: (1) childhood and adolescence (age 0–20), (2) early adulthood (age 17–45), (3) middle adulthood (age 40–65), and (4) late adulthood (age 60–?). The sequence of the life cycle has overlapping periods, providing for individual variation of development. Transition from one stage to another takes four to five years.

The transitional periods are considered milestones along the adult life course. In the transitional process, one era is brought to gradual closure as the initiating process for the future one is begun. The transitional process can be accomplished with only minor problems or it can lead to turmoil. For example, one individual may react to a 40th birthday as a rather minor event while for another this is a period of personal decline in general and work in particular. The important message here is that individualized self-evaluations are important determinants of the individual's ability to successfully and satisfactorily proceed through transitional periods.

The role of self-esteem in transitional processes throughout the life cycle is an important career-counseling consideration. Super (1957), among others, has emphasized the importance of self-concept in career development. Individual judgments of and similarities between self and peer affiliates in work environments is crucial to career establishment. The vocational self-concept is the driving force, establishing a career pattern one will follow throughout life.

Sheehy (1976) identified life stages as Pulling Up Roots (18–22), the Trying Twenties (22–29), Catching Thirty (approaching 30), Rooting and Extending (early 30s), the Deadline Decade (35–45), and Renewal and Resignation (mid-40s). Passages are the transitional periods between life stages and are difficult for most adults. However, she pointed out that transitions also provide opportunities for growth; we live more abundantly as we give up the securities and familiarities of one life stage and move to another. The willingness to change is a positive approach to making the critical transition between stages and providing opportunities for a more profound understanding of self. Growth, as seen by Sheehy, is a part of the crisis one faces in making constructive changes between life stages.

According to Aslanian and Brickell (1980), Sheehy emphasized the biological and psychological or internal changes that determine the smoothness of transition from one life stage to another. Neugarten (1968), on the other hand, supported social and cultural issues as major determinants influencing adult behavior; biological changes are important, but insufficient for explaining life-stage transitions. Schlossberg (1984) also suggested that transitions from one life stage to another involve a broad range of events, aspirations, and expectations. For example, job entry, marriage, birth of the first child, and bereavement are significant life events that influence the process of life-stage transitions. Loss of career aspirations and the promise of promotions that never occur are examples of subtle factors in the transitional process. Using a more inclusive and integrative approach to life-stage development, Schlossberg's view includes (1) the transitional process itself (role change, timing, onset, duration, and stress), (2) pretransition and posttransition (interpersonal support systems, institutional support, and physical environment), and (3) the individual (sex, age, state of health, race, ethnic background, socioeconomic status, value orientation, psychological competence, and previous transitional experiences).

Another stage theorist, Kohlberg (1973), concentrated on the development of moral judgment and behavior. He suggested that the development of morality occurs through a sequence of stages, each successive stage representing a more mature form of moral reasoning. For example, although the young child may make decisions about right and wrong to avoid punishment or censure, the adult's moral decisions are influenced more by conscience and established personal values.

The work role can involve a complexity of moral decisions that may delineate conflicts between the personal values of an individual worker and those of the employing organization. Choosing an employer requires much critical thought, because an adult with established values can be uncomfortable with the products or services offered by some organizations. In essence, because most relevant decisions have a moral basis, there is a need for values clarification in adult career-counseling programs.

In sum, the life-stage approach to adult development suggests that adult life consists of ordered stages having fixed times. The transitional process from one stage to another is challenging and stressful, providing growth opportunities. Most researchers agree that stages of life are determined by the biological, psychological, and social nature of human beings.

Those adults who make successful transitions are able to cope with biological and psychological changes and with major social and economic life-cycle events. Unsuccessful transitions are related to major events that do not occur on schedule, such as an accident restricting one physically or the loss of a career because of severe economic change. Untimely or profoundly unusual events can change the pattern and complexity of movement from one life stage to another.

References for career-counseling components are the biological and psychological issues associated with the life cycle, the transitional process of passing from one stage to another, and social and economic conditions. Stage theorists provide reference points for potential age-related problems. Finally, cumulative lifestyle experiences provide a relevant perspective for adult development.

Experiential Models

Adult development over the life span may also be considered from an experiential or learning approach. Here the emphasis is on the significant experiences or events in life that provide stimulus for psychological development in adulthood. Moreover, psychological development is not considered closely related to chronological age as emphasized in the developmental-stage approach (Troll, 1975, p. 3). Brim (1966) and Neugarten (1968) stressed that life events and experiences provide cues that are relevant in the developmental process. Troll (1975) suggested that psychological development is not highly contingent on significant physiological changes in the adult, such as menopause or climacteric.

Within this frame of reference, the counselor would evaluate the adult's development from an experiential point of view rather than from a life-stage or tasks-accomplishment perspective. Of major importance are the long-term social influences. Following this model, experiences such as being married for 10 years, rearing a child to adulthood, or working in a career field for 20 years are significant life events to be taken into consideration in career counseling. Experiences and skills derived from various life events are currently being given more emphasis in adult career decision making (Bolles, 1993). Likewise, the skills developed from serving in the armed service for several years may be considered relevant to certain jobs or for the general career decision-making process.

Biosocial, Career, and Family-Dimension Models

An integrative approach to adult development gives credence to both the stage theorists and the experiential point of view. Although the following example is based primarily on research of male adult development, it illustrates career development from a combination of three dimensions: stages, tasks, and experiences. Schein (1978) has specified the three dimensions of his integrative approach as life cycles: biosocial, career, and family.

The *biosocial dimension* combines the age-related biological changes with social and personal tasks that are generally confronted by males in certain age ranges. For example, the period from late adolescence to the late 20s is one in which an individual is commonly confronted with the tasks of establishing a home and a career. Other transitions are seen as closely related to age ranges. During the 30s, reappraisal of values is generally accomplished, while during the late 30s and early 40s, midlife transitions become prominent. In the 50s, one becomes more concerned with broader issues of society, and during the 60s, one copes with retirement and prepares for death. Schein suggests that these tasks are most effectively accomplished by learning from a mentor who has experienced similar patterns of development.

The *career dimension* is closely related to the biosocial dimension but is conceptualized as being more externally influenced than the biosocial dimension. For example, technological and economic changes and external incentives may have more influence on career transitions. However, the career dimension includes both external and internal factors that influence career development. Schein (1978, p. 46) viewed entry into an occupation as being "like growing up"; although skills have been developed and the individual shows initiative and assertiveness, at the same time he or she may be required to be somewhat subordinate. The tasks required for entry into a work organization include becoming a member of the organization, finding a mentor or a sponsor, moving within the organization, and later becoming a mentor. According to Schein's model, career development occurs through a series of age-related stages similar to those defined by Super (1990). Each stage contains specified tasks for accomplishment.

The traditional stereotyped family model is used as the basis of tasks for the *family dimension*. In this dimension, the interrelationship of family members and career is stressed. For example, the tasks of providing financial support, maintaining an intimate relationship with the spouse, and rearing children interject profound influences on career development. Schein contended that the commitment to family members imposes significant constraints, often leading to conflicts that affect self-development.

Schein postulated that these three simultaneous dimensions of development have stages and contain general issues to be confronted and specific tasks to be accomplished. Human development involves the integration of all three dimensions. As the individual progresses through life, new skills and value systems are developed in meeting the specific tasks of each stage. Schein suggested that objectives of counseling programs for adults should include task accomplishment in all three dimensions.

In sum, many adults in career transition could benefit from programs that help them evaluate and specify reasons for a desired career change. Changes within the individual and the work environment are factors to consider when job change specifics are delineated.

Adults appear to have a strong need to learn the purpose and techniques of using sources of educational and training information and to combat obsolescence through continuing training.

Methods of evaluating career-path plans and identifying methods of advancement in current career fields are relevant counseling components for adults. Some adults have difficulty evaluating their current situation and develop erroneous assumptions about their future.

Career counselors should help adults in career transition relate lifestyle preferences to career goals and promote introspective evaluations that can be integrated into future goals. Many important lifestyle factors—such as leisure time, geographical location of job, financial needs, and community involvement opportunities—are often overlooked.

Constant components for clarifying short-term and long-term goals for personal and family needs should be designed to provide career/life direction. Planning that integrates family needs provides for a broader perspective of satisfaction variables to be considered in the future.

CAREER-COUNSELING COMPONENTS FOR ADULTS IN CAREER TRANSITION

Career-counseling programs for adults in career transition have many elements in common with programs designed for initial career choice. However, there are enough different and distinct factors involved in career transition to merit the development of specific programs for adults considering career change. Of major consideration are the individual adult experiences associated with work, leisure, family, and individualized lifestyle. Life's experiences provide both the counselor and the individual with a rich source of information from which to launch a career exploration. Identifying developed skills, interests, work experiences, and reformulated goals are examples of program strategies for the adult in career transition.

A counseling program for adults in career transition is outlined in Table 13-3. This program consists of seven components referred to as *strategies*. Each

TABLE 13-3
Counseling Program for Adults in Career Transition

Strategy Component	Technique Option	Specific Tasks
I. Experience identification	1. Interview 2. Autobiography 3. Background information format and guide 4. Work- and leisure-experience analysis	1. Identify and evaluate previous work experience 2. Identify and evaluate life experiences 3. Identify desired work tasks and leisure experiences 4. Assess familial relationships 5. Identify reasons for job change 6. Identify career-satisfaction variables 7. Identify factors that contributed to job changes 8. Identify reasons for current interest in career change
II. Interest identification	1. Interest inventories	1. Identify and evaluate occupational interests 2. Identify specific interest patterns 3. Relate interest to past experience 4. Compare interest with identified skills 5. Relate interest to potential occupational requirements 6. Relate interests to avocational needs
III. Skills identification	1. Self-analysis of developed skills 2. Self-estimates of developed skills 3. Standardized measures of developed skills	1. Identify and evaluate developed skills from previous work tasks 2. Identify and evaluate developed skills from leisure-learning experiences 3. Identify and evaluate developed skills from formal-learning experiences 4. Identify and evaluate developed functional, technical, and adaptive skills
IV. Value and needs clarification	1. Value and needs assessment through standardized inventories 2. Values-clarification exercises	1. Clarify values in relation to life and work 2. Determine level and order of needs in relation to life and work 3. Identify satisfaction and dissatisfaction variables associated with work

TABLE 13-3
(continued)

Strategy Component	Technique Option	Specific Tasks
		4. Identify satisfaction and dissatisfaction
		5. Identify expectations of future work and lifestyle
		6. Identify desirable work environments, organizations, and peer affiliates
		7. Realistically assess potential future achievements
		8. Assess potential movement within current work environment
		9. Identify work roles and leisure roles and how they interrelate with lifestyle
		10. Relate values to factors that contribute to obsolescence
		11. Identify personal factors associated with career decision
V. Education/training planning	1. Published materials	1. Identify sources of educational/training information
	2. Locally compiled information resources	2. Identify continuing-education programs
	3. Microfiche system	3. Identify admission requirements to educational/training programs
	4. Computerized system	4. Investigate potential credit for past work experience and previously completed training programs
		5. Evaluate accessibility and feasibility of educational/training programs
		6. Identify and assess financial assistance and other personal assistance programs
		7. Relate identified skills to educational/training programs for further development

TABLE 13-3
(continued)

Strategy Component	Technique Option	Specific Tasks
VI. Occupational planning	1. Published printed materials 2. Microfiche system 3. Computer information systems 4. Visit files	1. Identify sources of occupational information 2. Identify and assess occupational opportunities 3. Relate identified skills and work experience to specific occupational requirements 4. Evaluate occupations from a need-fulfilling potential 5. Relate identified goals to occupational choice 6. Relate family needs to occupational benefits 7. Identify educational/training needs for specific occupations
VII. Toward a life learning plan	1. Decision-making exercises 2. Life-planning exercises	1. Learn decision-making techniques 2. Clarify short-term and long-term goals 3. Identify original and reformulated career goals 4. Contrast differences between original and reformulated goals 5. Identify alternative goals 6. Clarify goals in relation to family expectations 7. Develop a flexibility plan for life learning 8. Develop life-planning skills 9. Identify lifestyle preferences

component has suggested technique options and specific tasks. The technique options suggested do not rule out other methods of accomplishing the specific tasks. In many instances, reference will be made to other chapters in this text and other publications for program considerations. Following are brief explanations of each component.

Component I—Experience Identification

Valuable assets often overlooked in career counseling are work and life experiences. One of the main purposes of this component is to carefully evaluate past experiences in relation to potential use in career selection. Typically, the adult overlooks the value of developed skills or only casually considers them in career exploration. This component emphasizes providing the structure from which counselor and counselee can effectively evaluate an individual's background of experiences and relate them to interests, work requirements, and other variables associated with occupations.

The technique options suggested for Component I provide the counselor with alternatives to meet individual needs. In most instances, combinations of suggested options may be used. For example, after an individual writes an autobiography, the counselor can follow with an interview or work-experience analysis or both. In other instances, it may be feasible to use only one of the options. This decision may often be based on time availability and the educational level of the counselee.

The first of the technique options is the interview. The primary purpose of the interview is to assist the counselee in evaluating work and leisure experiences, training, and education in relation to potential occupational choices. The focus of the interview should include (1) specific work experiences, (2) specific educational/training experiences, (3) specific leisure experiences and preferences, (4) specific likes and dislikes of former jobs, and (5) special recognitions. In general, the interview should provide the basis from which the next step in the counseling program is determined. (See chapter 18.)

The format for the autobiography can be either structured or unstructured. In the latter approach, the individual is instructed to write an autobiography without being given any specific guidelines. In the structured approach, the individual may be instructed to follow an outline or answer specific questions or both. The structured approach has obvious advantages for our purposes in that we are attempting to identify and evaluate specific information.

An autobiographical sketch can be used to identify developed skills (Radin, 1983). First, the individual is instructed to describe a significant accomplishment, such as starring in a dramatic production, being a leader in a scout group, or teaching photography. Descriptions of the accomplishment are analyzed to determine the use of functional, adaptive, and technical skills. Each autobiographical sentence is analyzed and later compiled and related to Holland's six modal personal styles. The following sentence is taken from a description of teaching photography and is analyzed for functional, adaptive, and technical skills.

"I started each class by demonstrating the proper use of a number of different cameras."

Functional	Adaptive	Technical
teaching	leadership	knowledge of cameras
communication	articulate	
	orderly	

Skills that are easily identifiable are those that are explicitly stated, whereas other skills are only implied, such as those needed to accomplish the task. In this case, teaching, communication, and camera knowledge are fairly explicit, while being articulate, orderly, and showing leadership are only implied.

The next option, background information, requires the individual to fill out a specified form. The information requested includes demographic data, marital status and family size, a list of jobs held and duties, education and training completed, armed-service experiences, honors and awards, leisure preferences, hobbies, and other related information. A variety of approaches may be used to identify satisfaction and dissatisfaction variables associated with work and other experiences. One technique is to request the individual to rank-order or to list likes and dislikes of each past job held. Another option is to provide spaces for free-response reactions to work and other experiences.

Following the examples of Lathrop (1977), Bolles (1993), and Crystal and Bolles (1974), a work and leisure experience analysis form was designed (Figures 13-1 and 13-2). The formats require the individual to recall and list specific work (Part I) and leisure experiences (Part II). In addition, the individual indicates likes and dislikes of the experiences listed. The objective is to identify tasks and experiences that may be considered in future career choices.

A review of the tasks for Component I suggests that the major objective is to identify specific desired work tasks, leisure experiences, family concerns associated with work, lifestyle, and potential reasons for job change. Using this information, the counselor and counselee should be able to identify a partial list of career-satisfaction variables. The tentative conclusions and outcomes of this component will usually provide information for Component III, Skills Identification, but will also be integrated into other components of the program.

Component II—Interest Identification

Career counseling and interest identification have had a close association in their respective developments. Measured interests have been primarily used in predicting job satisfaction in career-counseling programs. In our efforts to assist the adult in career transition, we must also be concerned with interests and their relationship to potential occupational choices. Conceptually, it is thought that interest identification can broaden and stimulate the exploratory career

Part I

Work experience	General duties	Specific tasks
		O over number if liked
		X over number if not liked
Bank teller	*Customer accounts*	① Record + deposit receipts
	Transactions	② Pay out withdrawals
		✗ Cash checks
		✗ Record transactions
		✗ Exchange money

FIGURE 13-1
Work Experience Analysis Form

Part II

Leisure experience	Specific tasks
	O over number if liked
	X over number if not liked
PTA Secretary	① Record minutes
	✗ Call roll
	③ Read minutes

FIGURE 13-2
Leisure Experience Analysis Form

options of adults. The adult should be in a relatively better position to identify individual interests, primarily due to past experiences. However, there are instances when the adult is able to identify uninteresting tasks and jobs but unable to identify positive interests. For these individuals, interest identification is most essential.

The suggested technique option for this component consists of the use of interest inventories. Careful consideration should be given to the selection of the inventory; it should assess the counselee's educational level, expectations of the future, reading level, and educational and training potentials among other factors. A number of inventories are available for nonreaders. A list of inventories is provided in Chapter 7.

The task for this component requires the individual to identify interest clusters or patterns as well as specific interest indicators. A major task is to relate identified interests to occupational variables and education/training opportunities in the following components to ensure that all components are well integrated.

Component III—Skills Identification

In recently developed career-counseling programs, skills identification has received special attention (Bolles, 1993; Holland, 1985). The focus is on identifying skills developed from previous experiences in work, hobbies, social activities, community volunteer work, and other leisure experiences. (See examples of skills in Figures 13-3 and 13-4.) The rationale for this objective is that people, in general, fail to recognize developed skills and also do not know how to relate them to occupational requirements.

Skills-identification techniques have been used by Bolles (1993), Holland (1985), and Burton and Wedemeyer (1991). Bolles suggested that functional/transferable skills can best be identified by using a "quick job-hunting map." Holland provided a method to identify developed skills through self-estimates of ability. These methods concentrate on self-estimates of developed skills. Traditional standardized measures of skills and aptitudes may also be used.

The first technique option, self-analysis of developed skills, can be accomplished through the use of the work- and leisure-experience analysis forms used in Component I. For example, the compiled specific tasks on this form provide sources for identifying developed skills. Following are some examples of this process.

Three steps are necessary to identify skills from the work and leisure analysis form: (1) list specific work tasks; (2) identify functional, adaptive, and technical skills for each work task; and (3) relate each functional, adaptive, and technical skill to one or more of Holland's six modal personal styles. For those skills that are difficult to identify with Holland's six modal personal styles, the *Occupations Finder* (Holland, 1987c) will be most helpful.

The second technique option, self-estimates of developed skills, can be accomplished by having the individual rate each functional, adaptive, and

Skills used in tasks

a. Functional
1. *Clerical*
2. *Communication*
3. *Editing*
4. *Organizational*

b. Adaptive
1. *Articulate*
2. *Leadership*
3. *Diplomatic*
4. *Courteous*

c. Technical
1. *Accounting*
2. *Knowledge of foreign money exchange*

FIGURE 13-3
Skills Identification Form

Classification:
Conventional
1. *Clerical*
2. *Bookkeeping*
3. *Teller*

Rate yourself as:
Good   Average   Poor
✓ (Average)
✓ (Good)
✓ (Good)

FIGURE 13-4
Lifestyle Identification Form

technical skill as good, average, or poor as illustrated in the above example. These rankings provide self-estimates of skills within Holland's (1985) modal personal styles and corresponding work-environments model.

A more traditional method of evaluating skills is through standardized testing, which is our third technique option. A variety of aptitude tests on the market today provide methods of evaluating skills based on normative data. A number of aptitude tests have been identified in Chapter 7.

The importance of specific skills identification is to encourage the counselee to consider skills developed from a variety of experiences as important factors in career exploration. By requiring the individual to identify skills in terms of adaptive, functional, and technical groups, a more precise relationship to occupational requirements is understood, thus promoting a more realistic evaluation for future goals. This component stresses the identification of skills from the individual's total lifestyle experiences.

Component IV—Lifestyle Identification

The emphasis thus far has been on considering the "whole person" when counseling adults. This component correspondingly includes the adult's total lifestyle. Component IV focuses on the individual adult's values and needs. More specifically, these individualized values and needs are considered in relation to work, leisure, peer affiliates, and family. Each value and need must be considered in relation to the others. For example, work values are only one part of the value system that must be considered in career-counseling programs for adults. Individuals who are unable to clarify or satisfy their goals and needs concerning family may express dissatisfaction with work-associated tasks when in reality the source of difficulty is unrelated to the work environment itself. Hence, the need for the lifestyle-identification approach used in this component is established.

The first of the technique options is the assessment of values and needs through standardized inventories. A number of inventories on the market today can be used for this purpose. Most inventories provide complete instructions for interpretation and counseling use. (See Chapter 7 for available inventories.)

Values-clarification exercises are suggested as a second technique option. Values clarification may be accomplished in groups as well as in individual counseling programs. It is most important to select strategies that emphasize skills that assist individuals in identifying and developing their value systems. *Value Clarification* by Simon, Howe, and Kirschenbaum (1972) provides 79 values-clarification strategies.

The lifestyle component is indeed a broad, rather all-encompassing concept of career counseling. In this context, we consider the individual's entire system of values and needs associated with lifestyle. Individually developed values and needs may be considered an integrated system that determines satisfaction with life. We may dichotomize value systems for clarification, but eventually we must address the entire system of values. Our goal is to communicate to the adult in career transition that life is indeed multifaceted and that satisfactory solutions cannot be oversimplified. We must consider what we are, where we have been, and that our future is relatively unpredictable. A change in career may reflect a desire to change lifestyle.

Component V—Education and Training

Education/training information was ranked as a high-priority interest among adults in career transition (Burton & Wedemeyer, 1991). The major purpose of Component V is to assist adults in identifying sources of educational/training information and making the most effective use of it. As community colleges and four-year institutions offer a greater variety of continuing-education programs, the working adult will be in a much better position to upgrade and improve occupational skills. Exposure to educational/training opportunities should enhance the career decision-making process.

There are four technique options for this component. As with most components and particularly with this component, the use of all or combinations of the options is recommended. The first option suggests the use of published materials. As illustrated in Chapter 8, there are a variety of publications from which education/training program information may be obtained. One of the most important sources for working adults is locally compiled information resources, suggested as the second technique option. Educational/training programs within reasonable commuting distances provide opportunities for training while maintaining occupational and family obligations.

Microfiche systems, the third technique option, provide another resource for educational/training information delivery. First, an advantage of a microfiche system is that it requires a relatively small storage area. Second, updating the system can be accomplished easily and regularly to assure accurate information delivery. Third, accessing and refiling is very quick and systematic. Of major importance to the working adult is the accessibility of information provided by microfiche systems.

The fourth technique option for this component is the computerized career-information system. A number of interactive and information-oriented computer-assisted guidance programs are available today (as discussed in Chapter 6). Generally, two types of educational/training information files are available by computer: files containing programs for all states, and files containing program information on a regional basis within states. The latter has the advantage of providing current localized programs.

The specific tasks for this component encourage a systematic approach to using educational/training information. Exposure to educational-training opportunities will no doubt encourage many adults to consider methods of upgrading their skills for higher-level job opportunities. Second, many adults will be encouraged to consider educational/training programs to keep from becoming obsolescent. Possible educational credit from past work experiences should also provide the incentive to enter continuing educational/training programs. Finally, we must encourage the fullest development of identified skills through educational/training opportunities delivered in this component.

Component VI—Occupational Planning

Occupational planning and the previously discussed educational/training component have many commonalities. Both focus on providing information to assist the adult in making the most effective use of occupational information. In fact, these two components are so closely related that they are often accessed at the same time (since occupational planning must take into account educational/training requirements). Therefore, many of the published materials combine educational/training requirements with occupational information.

Three of the technique options for this component suggest the use of published materials, microfiche, and computer-assisted programs. Representative samples of published materials that provide occupational information are provided in Chapter 8. Microfiche systems, discussed for the educational/training component, provide occupational information, as do computer-assisted programs. Most computer-assisted programs contain national occupational-information files, but many provide occupational information on a local and/or regional basis within states. Many state and federal agencies provide labor forecasts and occupational information that should be incorporated into this component.

The fourth technique option, visit files, can be a most important segment for delivering relevant occupational information. This file provides the names of individuals or organizations who agree to visits and interviews by people interested in obtaining firsthand information about certain occupations. This file is usually compiled locally through personal contacts and in some cases may be available through purchased programs. Many of the computer-assisted programs that provide localized and regional data contain visit files.

The tasks for this component suggest that occupational information is more than just information about a job. Indeed, occupational information should enable individuals to evaluate the variables that will influence their lifestyles. For example, personal goal satisfaction, family/financial needs, and use of identified skills are just some of the variables to consider when accessing occupational information. Of major importance are the potential need-fulfilling opportunities available in each occupation under consideration.

In 1987, the National Career Development Association (NCDA) commissioned the Gallup Organization to survey a sample of adults about their career-planning processes and workplace. One major finding suggested that 6 out of 10 adults would request more information if they were to begin another career search. Another 1 out of 2 adults did not know how to interpret and use career information (Brown & Minor, 1989). These findings suggest that a greater effort should be made to introduce adults to career decision-making techniques, with thorough instruction in how to interpret occupational information.

Component VII—Toward a Life Learning Plan

This component assists in the development of a life learning plan. The intro-duction of decision-making techniques and life-planning exercises provides two methods of developing effective planning. The rationale for life learning is based on a continuing need to develop planning strategies to (1) meet techno-logical changes, (2) stay abreast of the information explosion, (3) upgrade skills, and (4) reduce the chances of become obsolete. In addition, and perhaps more important, changing individual needs and reformulated goals also create a demand for effective planning. The techniques and skills developed in this component enhance decision-making techniques for meeting both occupational changes and changing individual needs associated with work, leisure, and life-style. Furthermore, these skills not only provide methods for formulating cur-rent plans but also provide strategies for continued life learning–planning in the future.

The first technique option, decision-making exercises, helps individuals effectively decide on options related to their future. As adults are faced with more options for continuing education/training and career choices, learning how to decide becomes a most relevant skill. In addition to the decision-making techniques suggested by Krumboltz and Sorenson (1974) (discussed in Chapter 11), there are a number of decision-making programs available. Representative examples are also listed in Chapter 11.

The second technique option promotes life-planning strategies. The specific task of establishing alternative plans for the future should be emphasized in this component. Skills-identification and personal-lifestyle preferences are inte-grated to provide the basis for alternative plans to meet future goals. Clarifying differences between original goals and reformulated goals is one way to show how changes in an individual's priorities change lifestyle patterns. Effective life-planning strategies help individuals in developing options and making effective decisions (as discussed in Chapter 4).

The tasks for this component may suggest to the adult in career transition that the career-counseling program has ended. On the contrary, a life learning plan should be viewed as cyclic; individual changes and external conditions may require the individual to recycle through one or more of the counseling components. A life learning plan should be viewed as continuous, with inter-mittent pauses. The important message is that the skills learned through these components will provide effective methods of finding and using resource infor-mation, clarifying individual needs, making decisions, and planning for the future.

SUMMARY

1. Current issues related to career problems among adults are (a) the lack of available career-counseling programs, (b) the relationship of obsolescence to career crisis, (c) the downsizing of organizations, (d) a multicultural work force,

(e) general dissatisfaction with work resulting from unmet needs, (f) a strong desire to realize the social worth of one's work, and (g) misinterpretation of the realities of work.

2. Midlife has a profound impact on some individuals, while for others there are subtle, almost unnoticed differences in lifestyle. Factors associated with mid-life crisis are menopause, decline in muscular coordination and sexual activity, the empty-nest syndrome, and awareness of aging and the passage of time.

3. More attention is being directed toward adult stages of development and developmental tasks related to career satisfaction. Life-span and vocational-maturity models both outline stages associated with aging as well as general patterns of human development. The developmental-stage approach provides us with an overview of tasks to be accomplished over a life span, reference points from which to build sequential counseling strategies, a continuum from which to base vocational maturity, and points of reference that provide clues for potential crisis situations.

4. Erikson's eight stages of development as redefined by Gruen provide guidelines from which counseling strategies may be developed by considering the stages either separately or in combination. Counseling objectives are designed to aid the adult in the resolution process.

5. Havighurst postulated sets of tasks that, when accomplished, provide satisfactory life-span development. Inherent in these sets of tasks are potential crisis situations that merit consideration for adult career-counseling programs.

6. Vaillant supported Erikson's and Havighurst's assumptions that adult development has sequential stages. He concluded that cumulative events and relationships are most important in determining an individual's adaptive process in dealing with current and future issues.

7. Levinson emphasized that the course of life has a distinct character and follows a basic sequence. Transitional periods are considered milestones along the adult life course; one era is brought to closure while the process for a future one is initiated.

8. Gould's approach to adult development is growth in the fullest sense; adulthood is not the plateau of growth but a period of change and evolution of self.

9. Sheehy labeled transitional periods between life stages as passages. Transitions between stages are opportunities for growth and lead to a more profound understanding of self.

10. Schlossberg suggested that transition from one life stage to another involves a broad range of events, aspirations, and expectations. Major and subtle events influence the process of life-stage transitions.

11. Kohlberg concentrated on the development of moral judgment and behavior. The moral basis from which relevant decisions are made suggests the need for values clarification in adult counseling programs.

12. In the experiential or learning approach to adult development, the emphasis is on significant experiences or events in life that provide stimulus for psychological development. Of major importance are the long-term social influences rather than the chronologically related stages of development.

13. An integrative approach to adult development, developed by Schein, specifies three dimensions in life cycles: biosocial, career, and family. These three simultaneous dimensions of development have stages, general issues to be confronted, and specific tasks to be accomplished. Human development involves the integration of all three dimensions.

14. Career-counseling programs for adults in career transition have many elements in common with programs designed for initial career choice. However, there are enough different and distinct factors to merit the development of specific programs for adults considering career change. Counseling components that meet specific needs of adults include (a) experience identification, (b) interest identification, (c) skills identification, (d) values and needs clarification, (e) educational/training planning, (f) occupational planning, and (g) life learning plan.

SUPPLEMENTARY LEARNING EXERCISES

1. Develop a list of the ten most dominant needs in your life at the present time. Share these with a colleague and project how these needs may change over a life span. Identify major sources of satisfaction and dissatisfaction and how these factors may cause you to become an unfulfilled individual.

2. Develop a counseling component to help individuals overcome their single-career orientation. Provide strategies and specific tasks to be accomplished.

3. What is meant by the term *unfulfilled worker?* Describe the characteristics.

4. What are your suggestions for counseling programs that would meaningfully interpret the realities of working? Obtain your suggestions by interviewing workers and by observing working climates.

5. Develop an outline for writing a work autobiography. Using the outline, write your own work autobiography.

6. Using the experience-identification component strategy, develop a counseling program to accomplish two or more of the specific tasks.

7. Compile a list of your own skills developed through previous work, leisure, and learning experiences. Relate these skills to specific kinds of occupations. Why is skills identification important for adults in career transition?

8. Develop a set of counseling strategies to clarify values and needs associated with expectations of future work and lifestyle. Why is it important to clarify values and needs for the adult in career transition?

9. Review several community college and four-year college catalogs' financial-aid information. Compile this information and specify how you would use it in counseling adults in career transition.

10. Identify and list your personal goals and relate these to your career choice. Why is it important for adults to identify personal goals for career exploration?

PART FOUR

CAREER–GUIDANCE PROGRAMS FOR SPECIAL POPULATIONS

Chapter Fourteen
Special Issues in Career Counseling for Women

Chapter Fifteen
Special Issues in Career Counseling for Men

Chapter Sixteen
Career Counseling for Various Ethnic Groups

Chapter Seventeen
Career Counseling for Individuals with Disabilities

Chapter Fourteen

Special Issues in Career Counseling for Women

A few short years ago, career-counseling programs for women consisted of an exploration of the traditionally held working roles. The choices were narrowed to such occupations as clerk, teacher, or nurse. One of the first questions asked was, "How will this job fit into your husband's occupational goal?" The message to women was quite clear: you have but a few jobs to choose from, and your career is secondary to your husband's or other family obligations. Currently, career counselors find that women are rearranging their career priorities—planning for a lifelong career in a wide range of occupations has become the highest priority. A career first and marriage maybe or later is the new order of preference for many.

Moreover, women are looking beyond the traditional feminine working roles. The women who have charted this career course will find a variety of barriers. First, the bias associated with sex-role stereotypes in the working world still exists (Fairley, 1980; McBride, 1990; Wentling, 1992). Second, the woman who gives her career development equal status with her husband's will find acceptance of her role personally challenging, with little support from many men and women (Betz & Fitzgerald, 1987). There may also be resistance by male and female counselors in accepting the changing career priorities of women (Kahn & Schroeder, 1980; Harway, 1980). In essence, there is resistance in our society to the changing role of women in the working world from men and women at all levels of the work force, from managers and professionals to blue-collar workers. A number of professional counselors and organized groups have recommended the development of counseling programs to assist women who are strongly committed to pursuing a full-time career. However, for many other women who are unable to perceive themselves as career-oriented and who wish to break away from traditional feminine roles, the need for counseling programs may be even greater. For these women, the consideration of a lifelong career is entirely new and conflicts with concepts developed in early socialization; that is, women were primarily "socialized" to see themselves as homemakers while men pursued careers (Smith et al., 1982). America's rapidly changing values regarding traditional sex roles suggest that a number of additional factors influence the type and magnitude of critical career decisions currently being made by women. For example, the decline of motherhood as a full-time occupation is becoming increasingly prevalent in our society (Hansen, 1978a; *Nations Business Magazine,* 1991), and consequently, women feel freer to consider full-time careers outside the home. In addition, current financial needs of families have made it necessary for both husband and wife to work. Also, jobs traditionally allocated to men are now available to women (U.S. Department of Labor 1978b, 1980). Finally, research shows that we have not adequately addressed the role of women in our work force or the special needs of women who work (Wedenoja, 1981; Gianakos & Subick, 1986).

In this chapter, we discuss special career-counseling needs of women and describe several career-counseling components. The chapter is divided into six sections: the first part reviews the career-development patterns of women; the second part identifies and discusses special career-counseling needs; career counseling and career-counseling programs for girls and women are discussed in the third part; the fourth part describes some career-counseling components that meet the special needs identified in part two; counseling bias is discussed in the fifth part; and finally, issues of gender bias and gender fairness in interest assessment are reviewed.

The term *gender role* will be used from here on instead of the more familiar *sex role.* Although many researchers have used these terms synonymously, Money (1982) pointed out that an individual's sex role is a component of his or her gender role; the sex roles are physiological components of sex-determining role sets for men and women. The more inclusive term, *gender role,* is composed of nonphysiological components of sex, including behaviors, expectations, and roles defined by society as masculine, feminine, or androgynous (Unger, 1979).

CAREER-DEVELOPMENT THEORIES AND WOMEN

The career development of women has received only cursory attention by career-development theorists (Osipow, 1983). The need for career-development theories free of gender-role stereotyping has been suggested by Betz & Fitzgerald (1987). Super (1990) is one of the major career-development theorists (discussed in Chapter 2) who addressed career-development patterns of women, which he classified into seven categories: stable homemaking, conventional, stable working, double track, interrupted, unstable, and multiple trial. Still significant today is Super's double-track career pattern, which establishes homemaking as a second career. Conflicts between homemaking and career remain a concern that must be addressed in career-counseling programs (Wilcox-Matthew & Minor, 1989).

Ginzberg (1966) considered three lifestyle dimensions for women that may be used in career-counseling approaches: (1) *traditional* (homemaker-oriented), (2) *transitional* (more emphasis on home than job), and (3) *innovative* (giving equal emphasis to job and home). These dimensions seem to represent realistic lifestyles found among today's working women, with the addition of a *career-oriented* dimension; that is, one in which the highest priority is given to the development of a career. It is difficult for many women to move toward the innovative dimension, primarily because of psychological barriers; some women may be reluctant to become more career-oriented for fear of losing the stereotypical female identity so readily accepted by our society. For many, the loss of this identity is indeed threatening and deters a serious focus on career development.

According to Betz & Fitzgerald (1987), occupational choices for women are greatly influenced by home and family responsibilities. They suggested that social class, plus attitudes generated by marriage, financial resources, educational level, and general cultural values of past and immediate families, are major determinants influencing occupational choice. Furthermore, women's occupational choices are not made independently of other variables in our society. Women do indeed have special needs that must be addressed in career-counseling programs.

Zytowski (1969) denoted the vocational development patterns of women as (1) mild vocational, (2) moderate vocational, and (3) unusual vocational. These patterns closely follow the lifestyle dimensions developed by Ginzberg in that each category is progressively more occupationally oriented. According to Zytowski, the modal life role for women in our society is that of homemaker. Through vocational participation, a woman may change her modal lifestyle. Patterns of vocational participation for women are determined by age at entry, the length of time the woman works, and the type of work undertaken. Further determinants of vocational patterns for women are individual motivation, ability, and environmental circumstances such as financial needs (Wolfson, 1972). Of significance to our considerations is that women do differ and have special needs to be included in career-development programs.

Sanguiliano (1978) emphasized the theme of different and special needs of women. Although she agreed that women do follow a serial life pattern, there are unique times of hibernation, renewal, postponement, and actualization. She contended that life-stage theorists such as Erikson (1950), Havighurst (1953), Kohlberg (1973), and Levinson (1980) reveal significant shortcomings in describing the development of women. Stage theorists do not account for the unexpected, critical events and the myriad of unusual influences that shape feminine life patterns. Sanguiliano suggested that a woman's life cycle does not follow a rigid progression of developmental tasks but is similar to a sine curve representing the impact of unique experiences and critical events.

According to Sanguiliano, the formulation of self-identity is one of the fundamental differences between the developmental patterns of men and women. Women's self-identification is significantly delayed because of the conflicting expectations ascribed to feminine identity. Men learn their masculinity early and are better prepared to adapt to changes, but women do not have comparable, clearly defined boundaries and images of appropriate gender-linked roles. Men are reinforced in their efforts to attain clearly defined masculine roles; women depend on loosely defined feminine roles and have few support systems.

Sanguiliano's principal argument is that women's individual life patterns require special consideration. Attention should focus on unique paths women take to break away from gender-role stereotyping. Individual progress toward self-identity is germane to Sanguiliano's approach to determining counseling components for women.

Spencer (1982) supported Sanguiliano's denial that women's development follows the rigid progression suggested by life-stage theorists. She contended that feminine developmental tasks are unlike masculine tasks and that women follow unique patterns of development. Using Levinson's life-cycle sequence and transitional periods of men discussed in Chapter 15, Spencer compared women's development to the men's model: early transitions (age 17–28), age-30 transitions (age 28–39), midlife transitions (age 39–45), and late-adult transitions (age 65–?).

The early transitional period, the time when one reappraises existing structures, begins the search for personal identity (Erikson, 1950; Levinson, 1978). Spencer contended that separating from the parental home is more difficult for the young woman than for the young man; women receive less encouragement and experience less social pressure to become independent. Furthermore, women do not have adequate support systems to encourage self-expression in a society that presents conflicting messages. In essence, women have a more difficult time developing self-identity.

During the age-30 transitions, marital conflicts are prevalent in women who look for new directions. For example, women who want to spend time in career development often find difficulty forming egalitarian marital relationships. The frustrations women face in dual family/career commitment are often misunderstood. On one hand, women are socialized to think of themselves only as homemakers, but on the other hand, they have a strong need to express themselves in a career. Women have to struggle to realize that greater freedom and satisfaction are options.

Midlife transitions are periods of reappraising the past and of continuing the search for meaning in life. This period is marked by an increased awareness that some long-held beliefs may not be valid. For women, successful appraisal of life accomplishments is usually reflected in what others (husband and children) have done (Troll, Israel, & Israel, 1977). Therefore, when their children leave home, women have difficulty creating a new identity and a new life purpose.

The late-adult transition is a continued reappraisal of self in society. According to Spencer, the primary task of this period is to gain a sense of integrity in one's life. Spencer (1982) concluded that women rarely achieve the developmental goal of ego autonomy—"They are doomed from the start" (p. 87).

Spencer and Sanguiliano suggested that women have different developmental patterns than men: (1) women experience intense role confusion early in their development; (2) women are more inhibited in their self-expression; (3) women tend to delay their career aspirations in lieu of family responsibilities; and (4) women's developmental patterns are more individualized. These unique and individualized developmental patterns may present significant problems in career decision making. Career counselors should carefully consider self-concept development and value assessment in career decision-making programs for women.

Chusmir (1983) identified characteristics and background traits of women in nontraditional vocations (construction trades, skilled crafts, technical fields, science, law, engineering, and medicine). He suggested that women who choose nontraditional occupations have personality characteristics usually attributed to men. For example, they tend to be more autonomous, active, dominant, individualistic, intellectual, and psychologically male-identified than women who choose traditional careers (social work, nursing, teaching, and office work). Motivational characteristics of women who choose nontraditional occupations are also similar to those attributed to men: achievement orientation, status seeking, and strong need for self-regard and recognition. Examples of background traits of women in nontraditional occupations are better education, better mental health, fewer or no children, eldest or only child, postponed marriages, fathers who were younger and in management roles, well-educated fathers, and enrollment in women's-studies courses.

Chusmir suggested that personality and motivational traits of women who choose nontraditional occupations are formed by the time they are teenagers. Clearly, the research focuses on the importance of feminine early developmental patterns. Intervention strategies designed to expand occupational choice for girls should be introduced during elementary school years.

In each of the career developmental patterns of women briefly reviewed, emphasis was placed on the woman's role as homemaker, and the special needs of women interested in developing careers were stressed. Women who give at least equal emphasis to job and home were considered "innovative" (Ginzberg, 1966) or "unusual" (Zytowski, 1969) because they differed in lifestyle from the "typical" homemaker. However, these terms are very misleading today, as there are increasing numbers of women in the work force and more are expected in the future (U.S. Department of Labor, *The Occupational Outlook Handbook*, 1992–1993). Even more important are the considerations we should give to women as individuals, free of gender-role stereotyping, in an expanding job market.

The general developmental patterns of women suggest that a woman's life cycle does not follow life-stage models developed from the study of men. Compared with men, self-identity is slower to develop, primarily as a result of gender-role stereotyping. Our society accords a secondary priority to career choice as well as career development for women. Women's difficulty with career decision making is closely associated with role confusion and the lack of role models and support systems.

IDENTIFYING SPECIAL NEEDS OF WOMEN

Our society has seen a significant number of women go to work in nontraditional jobs during times of emergency. For example, during World War II, women assumed many jobs that were then considered reserved for men. The concept of the working role of women during this time was well exemplified in the then-popular song, "Rosie the Riveter," as most people saw the situation of women in nontraditional jobs as somewhat humorous and temporary. The trend today is toward equalization of job opportunities, particularly those jobs that were predominantly held by men. That the number of women working in skilled occupations (as defined in the Bureau of Census Classifications) has significantly increased underscores that attitudes toward working women are changing.

The emerging trend toward equalization suggests a number of special needs for women. One need is for information resources about nontraditional occupations for women. To make a wider range of choices available to women, the U. S. Department of Labor (1980) has sponsored programs to inform them of nontraditional jobs. These programs will be expanded into public schools, two- and four-year colleges, and other federal, state, and local community agencies.

One program, Women in Nontraditional Careers (WINC) (Alexander, 1985), is designed to help women consider nontraditional occupations. This model consists of three major components: (1) training of school staff to alert them to the need for broadly based career planning and how occupational choice affects lifetime earnings, (2) classroom instruction that provides students with information about the labor market and other topics that is free of gender bias, and (3) the establishment of nontraditional job exploration in the community. In addition, the program activities include women working with other women who are employed in nontraditional occupations.

Federal Law Requirements

Women need to be made aware of the federal laws under Title VII of the Civil Rights Act of 1964 and Title IX of the Educational Amendments of 1972. These laws prohibit discrimination on the basis of gender in employment, payment received for work, and educational opportunities, and they assist women in attaining equal opportunity in these three important areas. Title VII applies to all employers with 15 or more employees, employment agencies, and labor organizations. Discrimination is prohibited against employees on the basis of race, color, religion, gender, or national origin. Policy on discrimination applies to hiring, upgrading, promotion, salaries, fringe benefits, training, and all other terms and conditions of employment. Title IX refers to all educational agencies and institutions receiving federal assistance. This law prohibits discrimination against students and employees on the basis of gender, including the admission and recruitment of students, the denial or differential provision of any aid, benefit, or service in an academic, extracurricular, research, occupational, or other educational program or activity, as well as in any term, condition, or privilege of employment (including hiring, upgrading, promotion, salaries, fringe benefits, and training).

Career Information

Through affirmative action and other programs, women are more frequently considered for leadership positions previously reserved for men. However, the number of women in doctoral-training programs and in certain scientific fields has remained relatively out of proportion (Betz & Fitzgerald, 1987). Clearly, women are in need of career information that encourages them to consider a wide variety of careers—especially those previously pursued only by men. Women who have the interest and ability to pursue assertive, managerial careers need direction and encouragement, as do women who are interested in skilled labor and technical occupations.

Dual Roles

Economic conditions have greatly contributed to an increase in the number of married women who are employed full time. For many families, it has been essential that both parents work to fulfill financial responsibilities. Today's husband and wife consider their work efforts a joint venture. The family stereotype of homemaking mother and breadwinning father is no longer typical. In greater numbers, women are assuming a dual role of homemaker and worker. Managing both roles has caused conflicts for many women, particularly in meeting their own individual needs (Hansen, 1990). Although the dual role of working women has found greater acceptance, personal contradictions that need clarification persist in the working woman's life (Nadelson & Nadelson, 1982). Today's women need to more fully value an independent lifestyle and clarify their self-concepts. More specifically, counseling should help women identify their abilities and skills and provide them with the same opportunities given to men in making use of their talents in our society.

An Integrative Life Planning (ILP) model by Hansen (1991) incorporates career development, life transitions, gender-role socialization, and social change. This model is designed to expand career options for both men and women because fragmented approaches to development and life roles places limits on decisions clients will make in their lifetime. A more integrative approach to career development recognizes that an individual's total development includes a broad spectrum of domains. The impact of decisions on lifestyle, including relationships, is a major part of a more comprehensive view of development.

As women make a greater commitment to education and training, their willingness to accept full responsibility for household tasks, including childrearing, is decreasing (Benin & Agostinelli, 1988). The increasing pressure for an equitable division of household responsibilities focuses on what men actually do in the home. Coleman (1988) found that men spend over 50% of their time in play with their children, whereas women only spend 10% of their time in this way. However, some evidence suggests that women are frequently reluctant to delegate household tasks to men (Bernardo, Shehan, & Leslie, 1987).

Klinger (1988) has developed a model designed to delegate household tasks based on interests, aptitudes, and time available. This flexible model provides for changes in tasks and in who performs them as the situation or economic factors change. It also addresses the fact that some tasks may be viewed as more desirable than others, so that the most-preferred and least-preferred tasks should be rotated between the spouses. The last part of the model provides for a "recycling" that ensures an equitable division of labor.

Part I Formulate list of household tasks.

Part II Agree on the frequency of the tasks (daily, biweekly, weekly, monthly, annually).

Part III Agree on the person(s) responsible for accomplishing the task (considering each person's available time, interest, abilities). Highly desirable or highly undesirable tasks are rotated.

Part IV Review of the tasks to determine the following:
    a. Did the person(s) designated perform the task?
    b. Was the task viewed as satisfactorily completed?
    c. If "no" responses to questions a or b, what were the obstacles to completing the task?
    d. What additional resources (time, dollars, people, or other factors) are needed to complete the task successfully?

Part V Recycle: Add or delete tasks, change person(s) responsible for completing task if changes are necessary to maintain the perception of both persons that the division of labor is equitable.

The model can also be adapted to include childcare. When the couple begins using the model, they should go through all of the stages on a weekly basis. As they become familiar with the model, and if they are generally satisfied, then they can cycle through less frequently. The main determinant in how frequently the process is reviewed should be the level of dissatisfaction: The greater the level of dissatisfaction, the greater the need for the couple to recycle through the process.

Working Environment

The working environment is relatively unknown to women who have primarily considered themselves housewives. Because a significant number of women will work outside the home (U.S. Department of Labor, 1992–1993), programs that inform women about what typically can be expected in work settings are needed more than ever. Employee expectations, effective communication with peers and supervisors, promotional policies, and authority relationships are examples of items requiring clarification.

Needs of Displaced Homemakers

Attention must also be directed to the needs of displaced homemakers; that is, older women who are former homemakers and whose children are now on their own, and who may be widowed or divorced, require special attention (Langelier & Deckert, 1980; Morgan, 1980). Typically, these women's lives have centered on their husbands' careers and the raising of children. Because of their previous lifestyle, many displaced homemakers lack job-search skills and are completely unprepared for entry into an occupation. Marano (1979) has included the following among career-preparation needs: values clarification, skills identification, stress management, time management, assertiveness training, résumé preparation, and interview-skills training.

Needs of Divorced Women

Similarly, divorced women are often unprepared for self-sufficiency and often have children who depend on them. Not only are many forced to seek employment, but they also have the sole responsibility for rearing their children. This new lifestyle requires balancing the responsibilities of parenthood and home management with the responsibilities of work. In addition to the recommendations for the displaced homemaker, other possible counseling components may cover day-care centers, transportation information, and quick, efficient methods of food preparation. These women must learn to set priorities to effectively meet both home and employment responsibilities.

Internal Restrictions

Of major importance are the internal restrictions women experience when considering full-time careers and/or nontraditional roles. To project oneself into an occupational environment dominated by men may indeed be a difficult task for many women who grew up under the influence of traditional gender stereotyping of occupations. Women who have only considered traditional jobs such as teacher, nurse, or clerical worker find the contemplation of many other careers foreign to them. On one hand, early socialization has instilled identification with certain society-sanctioned gender roles; on the other hand, women are being told to break away from the traditional gender role. Indeed, many find this dichotomy too great to bear. In general, some women lack confidence and self-esteem, which tends to limit their career choices. There is also evidence that gender-role orientation adversely affects achievement motivation (Frenza, 1982; Eccles, 1987).

Need for Leadership Roles

Other inhibiting barriers prevent women from reaching their full potential in the world of work. Epstein (1980) suggested that our cultural heritage does not encourage women to excel in business-related occupations. In our culture, the model for a business manager is typically masculine (Lindsey, 1990). Through social conditioning, men are perceived as leaders and better able to carry out demanding tasks. Women who have taken on leadership roles are often regarded merely as tokens, and their abilities and skills are questioned, even by their colleagues. Women are often made to feel like outsiders in organizations and are ostracized by the existing formal and informal structures. Epstein contended that women need more experience (access to formal and informal structure) and exposure to feminine-leadership role models to encourage a greater degree of motivation to attain leadership positions.

The Glass Ceiling

The so-called glass ceiling is an invisible barrier that consists of subtle attitudes and prejudices that have blocked women and minorities from ascending the corporate ladder. For example, one method used to block women and minorities from top-level corporate jobs is to insist that senior executives have 25 years' experience. Another method used to exclude women is to groom them for either lower-level positions or those positions not on track for senior-level positions. Garland (1991) reported that White males most often prefer mentoring other White males. *Nations Business Magazine* (1991) pointed out that although women and minorities account for 50% of the nation's work force, only 5% hold senior-level management positions. According to this same source, women are chipping away at the glass ceiling and will have more success in industries where the customer base is women. Through affirmative action policies, the government is also attempting to break the glass ceiling.

The Trials and Tribulations of Women Who Want to Climb to the Top

Wentling (1992) suggested that the following actions are necessary for women to attain senior-level management positions:

1. *Educational credentials*—have at least an MBA or equivalent
2. *Hard work*—be ready and willing to work at least 54 hours per week at the office and take work home
3. *Mentors*—find and network with the most qualified mentor
4. *Interpersonal/people skills*—female executives have several common characteristics, including the ability to manage people
5. *Demonstrate competency on the job*—expect to be more thoroughly evaluated and screened than men
6. *Willingness to take risks*—be innovative and initiate projects

Childcare

Although this topic is considered relevant for both parents, research has shown that mothers shoulder the greater burden with regard to childcare problems (Fernandez, 1986). The enormity of childcare problems is evidenced by the fact that over 33 million children have mothers who work full time (U. S. Department of Labor, 1983), and about 5 million children under the age of ten come home from school to an empty household (Williams, 1984). Childcare providers include caretakers in the home, day-care centers, adult members of the household, older siblings, and no provider at all—children are left to look after themselves (Fernandez, 1986).

Many work, family, and personal difficulties for women evolve from childcare problems. Examples of work-related problems are arriving late for work, leaving early from work, scheduling problems, missing work, and having difficulty in concentrating on work tasks. Family-related problems primarily focus on family conflicts over childcare arrangements. Personal problems usually involve stress and the conflict that results between the need to achieve in a work situation and the need to be a responsible parent. Some women may decide not to take a promotion because the new position may interfere with childcare. Others may decide not to return to work after childbirth because childcare problems cannot be resolved to their satisfaction. The problems of childcare are exacerbated for workers who have less money to budget for it.

Some solutions to these problems are flexible work options, such as job-sharing (two individuals responsible for one job) or flexible hours (work schedule is adjusted to meet individual needs). Some evidence suggests that more corporations may in the future subsidize existing off-site day-care centers or provide them on- or near-site (Fernandez, 1986).

Lesbian Women

There appears to be a growing trend for more open discussion about the effects of sexual orientation on career development. Kronenberger (1991) reported that more lesbian women and gay men are coming out of the closet and discussing issues they face, especially in the workplace. In fact, gay men and lesbian women are creating support networks, educating co-workers and pushing for reforms for benefits and freedom to move up the career ladder. However, there are many homosexuals who don't identify with being gay and find it easier to assimilate into a heterosexual workplace. There is evidence to suggest that more companies are supporting gay associations and networks, including Xerox, AT&T, Lockheed, RAND Corporation, Hewlett Packard, Sun Microsystems, U.S. West Communications, and Levi Strauss. Many of these organizations have looked on gay men and lesbian women as another diverse group in the work force and are dealing with this group just as they do multiethnic groups; they have added a sexual-orientation component to diversity training programs.

However, the negative bias against homosexuals can be very intense (Goleman, 1992). For example, anti-gay legislation was introduced in two states in the fall of 1992 and passed in one of them. On the other hand, it appears that gay men and lesbian women will no longer be excluded from the armed services (Barry & Glick, 1992). The issues surrounding homosexuality in general and its effect on career development and bias in the workplace are far from being settled.

In the meantime, there is some evidence that lesbian women are more satisfied with their career choices than gay men and heterosexual men and women (Hetherington & Orzek, 1989). Nevertheless, research is so meager that most conclusions about adaptability in the workplace, self-efficacy, career choice, and career development are only tentative at best. (Further discussion on this subject can be found in Chapter 15.)

IMPLICATIONS FOR CAREER COUNSELING

Thus far, we have identified or implied several career-counseling needs for women. More specifically, these needs include (1) job-search skills, (2) occupational information, (3) self-concept clarification, (4) strategies and role models for managing dual roles—homemaker and worker, (5) assertiveness training, (6) information on a variety of working environments, (7) lifestyle clarification, and (8) development toward a value of independence. These needs suggest specially designed programs for women in terms of program content, techniques, and subject matter. For example, many job-search skills are universal for all job seekers, but women have a special need to develop strategies for negating employer discrimination. Other examples of specific programming needs include providing a more complete understanding of job-search techniques, teaching women to use occupational information, encouraging women to evaluate a wide range of careers, and alerting them to the stereotyping of female workers. Programs designed to assist women with managing dual roles, childcare, and lifestyle skills may be accomplished in a variety of counseling settings, including groups of women or with their spouses.

COMPONENTS FOR COUNSELING WOMEN

In the next section of this chapter, four counseling components that partially meet these needs are presented. These components can also be combined with the counseling components of the previous chapter to provide more options for meeting women's special needs. For example, occupational information on nontraditional jobs can be obtained through the occupational-information component of the previous chapter and combined with suggested technique options and specific tasks developed here (as shown in Table 14-1). The suggested technique options do not exhaust all possible methods of accomplishing the specific tasks. Following is a brief explanation of each component.

Component I—Job-Search Skills

A specially designed job-search skills component is recommended to help women deal with potentially discriminatory practices. The primary purpose of this component is to prepare women to apply for nontraditional jobs, although

TABLE 14-1
Components for Counseling Women

Strategy Component	Technique Options	Specific Tasks
I. Job-search skills	1. Workshop 2. Group and/or individual counseling 3. Resource exploration	1. Evaluate and clarify purpose of the interview. 2. Require each counselee to demonstrate interview skills. 3. Evaluate and clarify purpose of résumé. 4. Require each counselee to demonstrate résumé-preparation skills. 5. Clarify potential discriminatory employment practices. 6. Clarify federal laws that prohibit discrimination on the basis of gender in employment, pay, and education. 7. Clarify possible strategies for combating employer discrimination.
II. Working climate	1. Workshop 2. Group and/or individual counseling 3. Role-clarification exercises	1. Identify typical stereotyping of female workers by peer affiliates. 2. Clarify competitive nature of working environment. 3. Identify and clarify interpersonal skills associated with peer affiliates. 4. Identify and clarify interpersonal skills associated with supervisors. 5. Increase understanding of work setting.
III. Lifestyle skills	1. Workshop 2. Group and/or individual counseling 3. Role-clarification exercises	1. Clarify goals and specific needs associated with potential career. 2. Identify methods of jointly meeting family and personal needs. 3. Identify and require each counselee to demonstrate an understanding of the dynamics associated with dual careers. 4. Identify and require each counselee to demonstrate assertiveness skills. 5. Identify and clarify the implications of early socialization and needs for establishing a value of independence. 6. Clarify the concept of implementing one's self-concept into a career.
IV. Support and follow-up	1. Group and/or individual counseling support 2. Follow-up visits	1. Identify and clarify problems associated with working environment. 2. Identify and clarify problems associated with family. 3. Identify and clarify problems associated with personal goals.

the skills learned may be applied to any job search. The point is that women need special assistance with preparing applications for jobs that are primarily reserved for men. Displaced homemakers especially need this component because most have little experience in applying for a job. To be effective, women must not only learn the general skills needed for interviewing and résumé writing, they must also be prepared to deal with discriminatory practices associated with gender-role stereotyping. For example, in typical gender-role stereotyping, the woman is considered best suited as a homemaker and mother. When women work, it is assumed to be a necessity, as the man is perceived to be the primary breadwinner. Thus, men are typified as leaders who make decisions; women are seen as passive, cooperative, and unable to rise to leadership positions in the world of work. In essence, traditional gender-role stereotyping implies that women are generally inferior in marital roles and work roles (Reschke & Knierim, 1987).

The technique options suggested to accomplish this component are workshops, group and/or individual counseling, and resource exploration. As with other components, combinations of the technique options are recommended. Examples of materials that may be used to develop this component are found in Chapter 11. Three representative resources that may be used to build resource exploration and other parts of the program are *Exercises for the Résumé Workshop: A Program for Women, Résumé Preparation Manual—A Step-by-Step Guide for Women,* and *Launching Your Career* (all available from Catalyst, 14 East 60th Street, New York, NY 10022).

Component II—Working Climate

The purpose of this component is to prepare women for typical gender-role stereotyping found in many working environments. Unfortunately, gender-role stereotyping has been prevalent in many sectors of our society. For example, advertising portrays women as being very dependent and almost helpless (Schaffer, 1980). There is also evidence of gender stereotyping in textbooks and in teachers' interactions with students (Schaffer, 1980). One of the most serious problems facing working women is the large gap in earning power between men and women. Fundamental to this problem are sex-based wage discrimination and occupational sex segregation (Ferraro, 1984). It appears that women continue to select occupations from a more restricted range of options and continue to see fewer suitable occupations (Poole & Clooney, 1985). Women need special assistance to cope with typical stereotyping of women workers.

A combination of role-playing, discussion groups, and effective use of audiovisual material is recommended for accomplishing the specific tasks of this component. A speaker who is willing to share experiences can also be effective. "How to listen" exercises and clarification of differences among assertiveness, nonassertiveness, and aggressive behavior are important segments of this component. Other learning outcomes include (1) effective methods of communicating in a working environment, (2) identifying and understanding authority lines in typical organizations, (3) effective group decision-making techniques, (4) factors contributing to good worker-supervisor relationships, (5) understanding the role of the informal group in a typical organization, and (6) effective methods of establishing rapport with peer affiliates.

Some representative resource materials that may be used for this component follow:

Conversations: Working Women Talk About Doing a Man's Job
Terry Wetherby, Ed.
Les Femmes Publishing
231 Adrian Road
Millbrae, CA 94030

Nontraditional Careers for Women
Sarah Splaver, Ph.D., and Julian Messner
Simon and Schuster
1 West 39th Street
New York, NY 10018

The Educated Women: Prospects and Problems
Committee on the College Student
Group for the Advancement of Psychiatry
419 Park Avenue, South
New York, NY 10016

Career Guidance for Young Women: Considerations in Planning Professional Careers
John G. Cull and Richard E. Hardy, Eds.
Charles C Thomas
Bannerstone House
301–327 East Lawrence Avenue
Springfield, IL 62717

You Pack Your Own Chute
(16mm 30-min. color film)
Ramic Productions
58 West 58th Street
New York, NY 10019

Component III—Lifestyle Skills

To learn that every person is unique and should be considered as an individual who has certain aptitudes, interests, and aspirations is the primary purpose of this component. Women especially have more control over their lives than ever before. We have not yet reached the ultimate androgynous society, but we have taken giant steps away from gender-role stereotypes. The time has come for all women to consider their individual needs in determining their lifestyle. What should be communicated is that every woman is an individual who has certain strengths and weaknesses and, like everyone else, is unique. The challenge is to clarify the uniqueness (self-image, skills, and aspirations) and to project those characteristics into work, family, and life planning.

In this component, special attention is directed toward goal setting from an individualized frame of reference. Identifying and clarifying individual strengths and weaknesses through self-concept exercises is recommended. Assertiveness training with emphasis on interpersonal work relationships is another technique for accomplishing the tasks of this component. Individual personality development could be explored through discussion of background experiences, including those involving family, peers, school, and other life events.

Special consideration should be given to the task of identifying and clarifying dual-career family problems (Pleck, 1985). Rapoport and Rapoport (1978) identified five areas of stress common to couples who are both pursuing full-time careers and have at least one child: (1) *overload dilemmas* (the management of household and child-rearing activities), (2) *personal norm dilemmas* (conflicts arising from what parents consider proper lifestyle and what other individuals consider proper), (3) *dilemmas of identity* (intrinsic conflicts associated with life roles), (4) *social network dilemmas* (conflicts associated with relatives, friends, and other associates), and (5) *role cycle dilemmas* (conflicts associated with family life cycles such as birth of a child, child leaving home, and other domestic issues that produce stress on career development). Suggested solutions include shared responsibility exercises, time-management techniques, and effective planning between parents who have discussed and established individual and family priorities.

The following representative materials may be used for this component.

Planning for Work (especially Chapter 9, "How Can You Manage Home and Job?")
Catalyst
14 East 60th Street
New York, NY 10022

Sex, Career and Family
Michael P. Fogarty, Rhona Rapoport, and Robert N. Rapoport
Sage Publications, Inc.
2111 West Hillcrest Drive
Newbury Park, CA 91320

American Lifestyles
Vocational Biographies, Inc.
Sauk Centre, MN 56378

Counseling Girls and Women: A Guide for Jewish and Other Minority Women
Kenneth Wolkon
B'nai B'rith Career and Counseling Services
1640 Rhode Island Avenue, N.W.
Washington, DC 20036

Component IV—Support and Follow-Up

A follow-up component provides support through either group participation or individual visits. The primary purpose of this component is to reinforce those skills learned from other components. The need for this component is underscored by research that suggests that women have difficulty finding acceptance of their ability to contribute significantly in a working environment. In fact, more than likely they will experience rejection and isolation, which often leads to withdrawal and the subsequent assumption of a more passive position (Wilcox-Matthew & Minor, 1989). In addition, women who are actively expressing their needs through a career may also receive negative reactions from spouse, family members, relatives, and friends (Gilbert, 1981). Research indicates that the chances are high that a woman may experience difficulty in attaining fulfillment in a career because many of her associates will strongly suggest that she change her position. Because of the potential negative feedback from associates, friends, relatives, and spouse, reinforcement is considered an essential component in counseling women.

The specific task suggests that problems that may be encountered ought to be identified and clarified. In the process of clarification, a recycling through one or more of the components may prove valuable. For example, more effective methods of home management may be needed, or a reformulation of goals may be required. The follow-up component provides support as well as problem identification associated with work, family, and personal goals. Exercises that promote problem identification and provide subsequent alternative solutions are recommended.

COUNSELOR BIAS

During the 1970s, there was an explosion of research concerning counselor bias; more specifically, that is, gender bias that frequently occurs in career counseling by both male and female counselors. The problem centered around the charge that counselors of both sexes may dissuade women from choosing a traditionally masculine role. Betz and Fitzgerald (1987) conducted an excellent review of the literature from the 1970s through the mid-1980s and concluded that the methodology and other factors make the results less than definite. The authors suggest that some sex-role bias among counselors did exist during this time, but the research results do not necessarily substantiate this conclusion.

Although all research findings do not point to gender discrimination among counselors, there appears to be sufficient evidence that counselors need to give more consideration to an androgynous model (counseling free of gender roles) in their career-counseling approaches. More specifically, all career options in educational programs should be made available as a viable part of career exploration for all individuals, regardless of their gender. Counselors should be challenged to evaluate their personal views of the world of work and to understand that others may have legitimately different views.

The federal law requirements in Titles VII and IX, identified earlier in this chapter, should be carefully reviewed by career counselors for their counseling implications. A major implication is that women must be informed about the equal opportunities provided by these acts. More explicitly, women are not to be dissuaded by counselors from considering any career for which they are qualified. In addition, women should be encouraged to feel free to pursue jobs that may traditionally be reserved for men only. Finally, women should be encouraged to seek admission to educational or training programs for which they qualify. Clearly, counselors should be supportive of women and foster equal opportunities in employment, wages, and educational/training programs.

GENDER BIAS AND GENDER FAIRNESS OF INTEREST ASSESSMENT

In recent years, a considerable body of literature has been published on issues of gender bias and unfairness in career-interest measurement. Under the sponsorship of the National Institute of Education (NIE), Diamond (1975) compiled a number of the most relevant articles. The NIE published guidelines that identify gender bias as "any factor that might influence a person to limit—or might cause others to limit—his or her consideration of a career solely on the basis of gender" (Diamond, 1975, p. xxiii). Prediger and Hanson (1975) offered an alternate interpretation of gender bias:

> An interest inventory is sex-restrictive to the degree that the distribution of career options suggested to males and females as a result of the application of scoring or interpretation procedures used or advocated by the publisher is not equivalent for the two sexes. Conversely, an interest inventory is not sex-restrictive if each career option covered by the inventory is suggested to similar proportions of males and females. A sex-restrictive inventory can be considered to be sex-biased unless the publisher demonstrates that sex-restrictiveness is a necessary concomitant of validity (p. xxviii).

The issues of gender bias and gender fairness are indeed complex and will no doubt be researched over the next decades. One of the major objectives in evaluating interest inventories for their gender bias and gender fairness is to provide equal options to both men and women in career counseling. In response to this basic objective, Harmon (1975) suggested that gender bias is prevalent in most current interest inventories primarily because they are constructed with the assumption that work is dichotomized into man's work and woman's work. This position restricts women from exploring certain career options that are presented as reserved for men only. For example, inventories containing items (statements, questions, or names of occupations) such as salesman rather than salesperson or statements such as "He likes auto mechanics" encourage role stereotyping. As a result, women may be discouraged from responding positively to occupations for which they have an interest just because the phrasing implies that the occupation is "off limits" to women (Harmon, 1975).

Another issue involves the norm reference groups used for interpreting completed interest inventories. More explicitly, the prevailing question is whether gender bias in interest inventories can be most effectively overcome through the use of separate norms (reference group by gender) or combined-gender norms (reference groups combining males and females). According to Prediger and Johnson (1979), one way of reducing gender bias in interest inventories is by using gender-balanced scales as found in the Unisex edition of the *American College Test Interest Inventory*. In this inventory, items are sex-balanced; that is, "they capture the essence of a work-related activity preference while minimizing sex role connotations" (p. 11). The rationale is that gender-balanced items will elicit similar responses from men and women, thereby eliminating different sets of scales. They argued that different sets of occupational scales for men and women perpetuate gender-role stereotyping because such tests inherently suggest that some work is typically male-oriented and other work is typically female-oriented.

In contrast to the combined-gender-norm approach, separate gender norms for men and women have been developed for the *Strong Interest Inventory (SII)* and the *Kuder Occupational Interest Survey*. Apparently, both inventories plan to expand the number of feminine occupational scales as more data become available about women in different occupational roles. Johansson (1975) also suggested the use of separate gender norms for interpretive purposes until more research is done on gender bias in our society. These contrasting approaches underscore the current dilemmas associated with interest measurement of women and point to the need for counselors to be cautious when using interest inventories in career-counseling programs for women. Clearly, there is a need for more research on career-development patterns of women so that a better understanding of their patterns of interests will be revealed.

Holland (1975) suggested that vocational aspirations of women and men differ primarily because of their life histories. As women's lives are changed when society is freed of gender-role stereotyping or by counseling programs that minimize the effects of gender-role stereotyping, different patterns of interest will emerge. Holland argued that greater emphasis should be put on achieving an androgynous society as opposed to attacking interest inventories that reflect early socialization and conditioning.

Conversely, Cole and Hansen (1975) suggested that we do not have to wait for a society free of gender-role stereotyping to evolve in order to broaden women's interest patterns. They contended that expanded career options for women, specially presented in interest inventories, will encourage exploration in a wider range of careers and, thus, provide greater opportunities for satisfaction. Within this frame of reference, interest inventories should indeed be attacked if they do not provide equal career options for both men and women.

Because counselors may have to rely heavily on information contained in test manuals, Birk (1975) recommended that interest-inventory manuals delineate information concerning problems of occupational stereotyping and other issues of gender bias and gender fairness. For example, the counselor should be informed that (1) all jobs are available to any individual of any gender, (2) the purpose of interest inventories is to generate career options for both men and women, and (3) false notions or myths concerning gender-role stereotyping of women should be discussed and clarified. Furthermore, a summary of Title IX of the 1972 Educational Amendment of Higher Education should be provided. In essence, Birk suggested that the interest-inventory manuals should provide some solutions to their gender-stereotyping limitations.

Interpretation formats and materials should include guidelines for using score results to counsel women (Birk, 1975). Case studies for men and women in a variety of occupations are recommended to provide the counselor with representative examples of both in the work force. In addition, the same interpretation format should be used for both men and women. In summary, interest-inventory manuals and interpretive materials should clearly establish that both men and women are to be encouraged to consider all occupations and college majors.

As Diamond (1975) pointed out, changes in interest-inventory approaches may be very slow in coming. Although guidelines have been developed for assessing gender bias and gender fairness in interest inventories, more research is needed. In the meantime, the career counselor will have to rely heavily on manuals and research reports that describe the limitations and uses of the interest-inventory scores for women. As more research becomes available, better guidelines for gender-fair interest inventories will be developed.

One promising method for exploring females' interests is the *Non-Sexist Vocational Card Sort (NSVCS)* developed by Dewey (1974). This instrument was derived from a modified version of Dolliver's (1967) *Tyler Vocational Card Sort (VCS)*. The *NSVCS* is nonsexist in that the same occupational options are presented to both men and women, occupational titles have been neutralized (salesman to salesperson), and the gender-role biases are confronted and discussed.

The *NSVCS* consists of 76 3×5-inch cards containing occupational titles derived from the forms for men and women of the *Strong Vocational Interest Blank* and the *Kuder Occupational Interest Survey* (Form DD). Each occupation is coded according to Holland's classification system (discussed in Chapter 2). In addition, there are 4×6-inch cards that serve the following categories: "Would not choose," "In question," or "Might choose."

Step 1 of the *NSVCS* requires the individual to sort the cards according to these categories. Step 2 involves a discussion of the occupations in the category "Would not choose." The individual cites the reasons for placing occupations in this category, and some of the remarks are recorded by the counselor. Likewise, the individual cites reasons for placing occupations in the other two categories. In Step 3, the individual selects and rank orders ten occupations. The counselor encourages the individual to consider such factors as values, abilities, and lifestyle when ranking the occupations. Step 4 involves the discussion of recorded remarks made in earlier sessions and provides the opportunity for individuals to describe their perceptions of certain occupations. During this time, women are encouraged to discuss gender-role biases associated with occupations and clarify their own position in regard to gender-role stereotyping.

Dewey suggested that the *NSVCS* encourages women to form new self-perceptions and attitudes. Although she did not claim that these procedures and techniques will completely solve the effects of gender-role stereotyping, she believed women are provided opportunities to enhance their career potentials. In addition, the *NSVCS* process actively involves women in confronting the issues of gender-role stereotyping in career decision making.

The *NSVCS* and other card-sort programs may be alternatives to standardized interest inventories for women. After comparing the impact of the *Strong Interest Inventory* and the *VCS* on career salience and career exploration of women, Cooper (1976) concluded that the *VCS* is more effective than the *SII* for encouraging career exploration among women. Dolliver (1967) also suggested a major advantage of the card sort is that client attitudes and self-perceptions are elicited during the sorting process. This process encourages women to confront the issues of gender bias and gender-role stereotyping in the career-decision process.

SUMMARY

1. Women are rearranging their career priorities and are looking beyond the traditional feminine working roles. However, even though they are being given greater opportunities to expand their career choices, barriers to the changing role of women in the working world still exist.

2. Super was one of the major career-development theorists who addressed career-development patterns of women. Ginzberg denoted three lifestyle dimensions—traditional, transitional, and innovative—in career-counseling approaches for women. Zytowski labeled vocational developmental patterns of women as *mild vocational, moderate vocational,* and *unusual vocational.* Sanguiliano suggested that a woman's life cycle does not follow a rigid progression of developmental tasks and that attention should focus on unique paths women take to break away from gender-role stereotyping. Spencer supported Sanguiliano's denial that women's development follows the rigid progression suggested by life-stage theorists. She contended that feminine developmental tasks are unlike masculine tasks and that women follow a unique pattern of development. Chusmir suggested that personality and motivational traits of women who choose nontraditional occupations are formed by the time they are teenagers.

3. The emerging trend toward equalization suggests specially designed career-counseling programs for women. Special career-counseling needs for women are job-search skills, occupational information, self-concept clarification, managing dual roles, assertiveness training, information on a variety of working environments, lifestyle clarification, and development toward a value of independence.

4. The family stereotype of a homemaking mother and a breadwinning father is no longer typical. In greater numbers, women are assuming a dual role of homemaker and worker. Managing both roles has created conflicts for women, especially in meeting their own individual needs.

5. Career-counseling approaches should be androgynous; that is, free of gender-role stereotyping. Counseling strategy components include job-search skills, working climate, lifestyle skills, and support and follow-up.

6. Developmental components for girls prepare them for career-related events that are highly probable during their life spans. Counseling components can assist girls in overcoming gender-role stereotyping, and may include identifying successful career women as role models and mentors.

7. Issues of gender bias and gender fairness of interest assessment are indeed complex and involve numerous technical problems such as test item development and norm references as well as issues concerning societal changes. Guidelines developed for assessment of gender bias and gender fairness in career-interest inventories primarily encourage both males and females to consider all career and educational opportunities.

8. One promising method of exploring interests for women is the *Non-Sexist Vocational Card Sort*.

SUPPLEMENTARY LEARNING EXERCISES

1. Support or disagree with Spencer's contention that feminine developmental tasks are unlike masculine tasks. Back up your arguments through interviews with at least two females.
2. Interview a woman who has had a successful career. Identify her reactions to the gender-role stereotyping of women and to the barriers that still exist for the woman in the working world. If she is married, ask her how she has managed the dual career of homemaker and career woman.
3. Write to the Women's Bureau (Employment Standards Administration, U.S. Department of Labor, Washington, DC 20402) and request materials developed to promote equalization for women in the work force. Indicate how several examples of materials may be used in career-counseling programs for women.
4. Divide the class into three groups and identify and clarify dual-career family problems. One group considers problems associated with the husband, another group considers problems associated with the wife, and the third group considers problems associated with other family members. Build counseling components for solving the identified problems.
5. Visit a women's center and obtain descriptions of career-related counseling programs. Summarize your findings and point out the potential use of the women's center as a referral source.
6. Develop a list jointly and/or independently of the early socialization processes that promote gender-role stereotyping. Explain how this information can be used in career-counseling programs for women.
7. Develop a scenario to be used for emphasizing gender-role stereotyping in a work setting. Present it to the class for critiquing.
8. Develop a list of questions that women are typically asked in a job interview. Provide guidelines for answering these questions.
9. Interview at least two women who are currently holding nontraditional jobs. Summarize the problems they have faced and their recommendations to other women.
10. Using the counseling components developed for women in this chapter, develop strategies for one or more components designed to accomplish the specific tasks.

Chapter Fifteen

Special Issues in Career Counseling for Men

In the previous chapter, the recent changes in working roles for women were identified and discussed. It stands to reason that when there are role changes for one sex, pressure develops toward changes for the other. Recently, men have reexamined their roles, beliefs, and values regarding their relationships with women. Marciano (1981) suggested that men do not have an easy time adjusting to the egalitarian movement toward equal rights for women in the workplace and other areas in our society. To change their perspective of what is an appropriate masculine role, men will have to modify their belief that they are supposed to dominate women. Moreover, the change in lifestyle for men will be difficult because they are the products of a socialization process that mandates that men should be aggressive and competitive, acting as protectors and providers. It is no surprise, then, that men are confused when faced with a new set of values suggesting that the traditional masculine role should be significantly modified.

In this chapter, we examine the socialization process that has shaped men's lives and influenced their perspective on an appropriate masculine role. We attempt to understand why men have adopted stereotyped behavioral roles that are not conducive to equality and cooperation in the working environment. We attempt to analyze why men behave so aggressively in their attempts to gain career achievement and success. All of the answers to these questions are related to career-counseling procedures designed to help men meet the demands of their career and their life roles in a changing society.

This chapter begins with a discussion of the influence of parents, school, and media on gender-role development. Next, the special needs of men are identified and discussed. In the final part, four counseling components are presented and analyzed.

INFLUENCES ON GENDER-ROLE DEVELOPMENT

This section examines three sets of influences on gender-role development: parents, the schools, and the media.

Parental Influence

The purpose of this section is to determine whether parents treat boys and girls differently and the effects, if any, that parents' reactions to children have on gender-role stereotyping. An introduction to research studies that attempt to answer these questions is a good starting point for understanding the socialization process children experience from interaction with important adults in their environment. Insights into potential reasons that individuals behave the way they do is relevant information for career counselors.

According to Schaffer (1980), a strong preference for boys is found in many studies of pregnant women, indicating that higher value is given to boys than to girls. Rubin, Provenzano, and Luria (1974) suggested that parental attitudes toward newborn infants vary at the time of birth; baby girls are regarded as softer, smaller, and finer-featured than boys. Review of relevant research by Lindsey (1990) supports the concept of differential parental attitudes toward infants, in that parents were found to regard boys as sturdier than girls and tended to play more roughly with baby boys. Evidence supports the contention that parents expect sons to be more active and aggressive and daughters to be passive and nonassertive.

Solomon (1982) contended that the growing boy is surrounded by a multiplicity of social influences, including parental attitudes, that facilitate his internalization of the masculine role. For example, parents tend to choose different types of toys for boys and girls. Although this method of gender typing has decreased in recent years, there is evidence that parental choice of toys continues to be based on perceived appropriate gender-roles (Rosenwasser, 1982).

In a provocative nationwide study, Hoffman (1977) asked parents what they expected their sons or daughters to be when they grew up. Characteristics such as hardworking, intelligent, honest, ambitious, aggressive, independent, and successful were given for boys. Parents of girls responded that they wanted them to be good mothers, to make good marriages, and to be kind, loving, and attractive. Different parental expectations of boys and girls may, to some extent, influence career and other roles children envision for themselves (Rosenwasser, 1982).

According to Schaffer (1980), men are more likely to perceive children in a stereotypical manner, attributing independence and aggressiveness to boys and passivity and dependence to girls. Hantover (1980) suggested that gender-appropriate activities are more strongly encouraged for sons than for daughters by both parents. There is some evidence that parents' treatment and expectations of children in early childhood can foster developmental patterns that may determine future role behavior.

According to cognitive-development theory, once gender identity is developed much behavior is organized around it (Lindsey, 1990). Parents who have been gender-role socialized provide models for their children, who actively seek identification with the same-sex parent. As boys learn gender concepts, there is an increasing agreement with adult stereotypes (Leahy & Shirk, 1984). Thus, home tasks that parents consider appropriate for boys and girls reinforces learned gender-role concepts. Rosenwasser (1982) suggested that although there are changes in mothers' perceptions of appropriate tasks for girls and boys, tasks still tend to be gender-typed.

School Influence

The process of formal education further reinforces expectations learned in the home. Elementary school is often described as being very feminine in that the vast majority of teachers are women, providing feminine models for children (Rosenwasser, 1982; Tracy, 1990). Moreover, there is evidence to suggest that teachers in elementary school treat boys and girls differently. After reviewing research on this subject, Doyle (1983) found that boys were encouraged to be more aggressive than girls, whereas girls were more likely to be noticed for dependent, clinging behaviors. Boys are portrayed as being resourceful, brave, and creative, while girls are portrayed as passive, helpless, and dull (Scott, 1981).

According to Etaugh and Liss (1992), there is a significant influence from our educational system on the development of gender-stereotyped work roles. "Feminine-appropriate" courses are language, home economics, and typing; boys are encouraged to take math and science courses. Sadker and Sadker (1980) argued that teachers respond differently to boys and girls in all grade levels, K–12, partly because teacher-education training books are gender-biased.

The appropriate future work role is made clear by educators and counselors, who further socialize boys and girls to conform to the established norms society has fostered. Teachers and counselors who endorse traditional gender-role behavior directly influence the choice of career options, and the message is clear to the boy that much more is expected of him in the way of career achievement.

Media Influence

Television.   Programs on television have a tremendous potential for shaping children's values and gender role. Rosenwasser (1982) suggested that masculine and feminine roles children observe on television programs may affect their perception of reality and of what is appropriate for adults to do in the real world. In a summary of studies analyzing prime-time programs between 1969 and 1972, McGhee (1975) discovered that women were given the role of leading characters in only 25% of television productions. Furthermore, women portrayed more light and comedic characters than men did, two-thirds of the women were unemployed, one-third of the men were unemployed, and women were likely to play roles of married women. Dominick (1979), who analyzed prime-time shows from 1953 to 1977, also discovered that the majority of women featured were in situational comedies. However, there appears to be some evidence that starring roles for women have changed since the 1960s, with a trend toward fewer starring in comedies. Nevertheless, there have been protests by women in the 1990s concerning the roles women are given in television programs and movies. The protests have centered around roles that require them to portray simple sex objects or extremely violent characters.

A study reported by *U.S. News and World Report* (1981) estimated that approximately three-quarters of a million young children are watching television between midnight and 2 A.M. According to Doyle (1983), on television males are usually presented as aggressive and dominant while females are deferential. Barcus (1983) contends that children see more males in significant roles, whereas females are usually relegated to minor roles with little responsibility concerning the outcome of a story.

Television commercials may also contribute to children's perception of appropriate gender-role stereotypes (Jones, 1991). Products advertised by men represent a broad variety of uses and depict men in more dominant roles or as tough and rugged as in the Marlboro man. On the other hand, women have been used to advertise products used in kitchens or bathrooms.

Books.   There appears to be substantial evidence that boys and girls are highly stereotyped in children's books as well (Nelson, 1990). S. St. Peter (1979) reviewed 206 children's books and grouped them into the following three categories: books published before the women's movement, books published since the women's movement, and books selected from nonstereotyped lists (*Little Miss Muffett Fights Back*) of books about girls. Her results revealed that boys were the central character twice as often as girls in the first two categories of children's books. Furthermore, boys were pictured more often, a 3:2 ratio, on the covers of the books reviewed. The titles of books in the first two categories used boys more often than girls by more than 2:1. Interestingly, she found that, with the exception of books from nonstereotyped lists, the proportion of boys to girls on the covers of children's books has increased since the women's movement. An examination of the character roles portrayed in children's books indicated that girls were more expressive than boys, whereas boys were more likely to be portrayed as fulfilling goals.

Although comic books and comic strips have included heroines like Wonder Woman, they continue to portray the roles of masculinity in our culture. Kirschner (1981) concluded that comic superheroes have remained virtually the same since the time of Superman, Batman, Spiderman, Captain Marvel, and other extraordinary, superior males. One of the primary lessons learned from these characters and scripts is the continued existence of the traditional masculine role of protector and the companion feminine role of the protected one. Solomon (1982) suggested that these images of males and the romantic versions of great adventurers in our past history encourage the adoption of the masculine role.

IDENTIFYING SPECIAL NEEDS OF MEN

The emerging trend toward androgyny will create a need for counseling programs to help men reevaluate their roles, beliefs, and values in all areas of their lifestyle, including their relationships with women in the home and workplace. Boles and Tatro (1982) pointed out that the idea of androgyny has freed both men and women to consider alternative lifestyle behaviors and gives both the opportunity to acknowledge their masculine/feminine qualities. Career counselors are to be especially concerned with social changes that affect career development and interpersonal relationships in the home and at work.

Fear of Femininity

Researchers seem to agree that men's fear of being perceived as feminine has been indoctrinated through gender-role socialization (O'Neil, 1982; Solomon, 1982). A group of investigators led by Levinson (Levinson et al., 1978) proposed that gender-role socialization has created a masculine/feminine polarity. O'Neil (1982) summarized the roles associated with masculine/feminine polarity:

Masculinity is associated with:
1. Power, exercising control over others; (and being recognized as) a person of strong will, a leader who "gets things done";
2. Strength, bodily prowess, toughness, and stamina to undertake long, grueling work and endure severe bodily stress without quitting;
3. Logical and analytical thought, intellectual competence, understanding of how things work;
4. Achievement, ambition, success at work, getting ahead, earning one's fortune for the sake of self and family.

Femininity is associated with:
1. Weak, frail, submissive, and unassertive behavior; victimized by others who have more power and are ready to use it exploitatively; limited bodily resources to sustain a persistent effort toward valued goals;
2. Emotions, intuition; likelihood of making decisions on the basis of feelings rather than careful analysis;
3. Building a nest, taking care of needs of husband and children;
4. Homosexuality (pp. 21–22).

According to the Levinson research team (1978), the integration of masculine/feminine polarity is usually achieved during midlife, because younger men tend to identify strongly with stereotypic masculine characteristics and are reinforced by cultural conditions. The Levinson group suggested that evolving tasks in early adulthood make it difficult for men to deviate from learned masculine roles.

Other investigators have concentrated on problems associated with fear of femininity (O'Neil, 1982; Stokes, Fuehrer, & Child, 1980). O'Neil (1982) suggested that the fear of femininity among men contributes to their obsession with achievement and success and is associated with (1) restrictive self-disclosure (fear their thoughts and actions will be associated with femininity), (2) health problems arising from conflicts, and (3) stress and strain.

Stokes, Fuehrer, and Child (1980), who researched gender differences in self-disclosure, concluded that there is a tendency for men to avoid emotional intimacy with one another. Furthermore, they suggested that women were more willing than men to disclose to intimates. Another of these conclusions suggests that fear of femininity is one of the major factors that contributes to men's avoidance of emotional intimacy. Clearly, the fear of femininity is a most appropriate topic to address in helping men understand the effects of their gender-role socialization.

Placing Achievement and Success in Perspective

According to O'Neil (1982) and Russo, Kelly, and Deacon (1991), men are conditioned to perceive career success and achievement as primary measurements of manhood and masculinity. These researchers suggested that a man's work represents his status in society and is the primary base for measuring success over the life span. O'Neil (1982) pointed out that men are conditioned to be overly competitive, ambitious, and status seeking because these are the qualities associated with a successful man. Furthermore, a man's obsessive work behavior stimulates him to seek power and control and to become overly aggressive. Men who exhibit obsessive patterns of work behavior clearly need counseling assistance to help them place achievement and success in perspective.

Learning to Relax

Highly valued masculine traits (such as competitiveness, independence, and self-reliance) make it difficult for men to learn to relax (Solomon, 1982). Masculinity is associated with work that consumes energy and imposes stress. Being passive is considered feminine and drives men to constant activity. Solomon (1982) suggested that men's leisure activities are not always conducive to relaxation. For example, a "friendly" game of tennis or golf often turns into a highly competitive activity that is not compatible with relaxation.

Learning to relax during leisure time appears to be an important need for men who are overly ambitious and competitive. Leclair (1982) suggested that when there is a balance between work and leisure, leisure is a definite source of need satisfaction. Herr and Cramer (1992) contended that choice and control of leisure is important to self-esteem and holistic health. Edward (1980) suggested that counselors provide a valuable service when they assist individuals in determining sources of leisure that are practical, satisfying, and relaxing. Leisure counseling, as suggested by Leclair (1982) and McDaniels (1990), is a productive activity for professional counselors. Leisure-counseling activities include (1) value clarification of work and leisure, (2) interest and attitude clarification, (3) identification of leisure opportunities, and (4) application of decision-making skills.

Restrictive Emotionality

As a result of research in the 1970s, Skovholt (1978) suggested that emotional expression and self-disclosure are serious problems for men. Lindsey (1990), while concentrating on the social perspective of gender-role development, contended that expression of grief, pain, or weakness is perceived to be unmanly. The fear of being perceived as unmanly makes many men resist being open, honest, and expressive, for such expressions are considered an open admission of vulnerability and loss of control so important to the masculine role. O'Neil (1982) believed that restrictive emotionality is one of the leading causes of poor interpersonal relationships between men, men and women, and men and children. These authors suggested that men and women have developed two different styles and levels of communication: men deemphasize interpersonal relationships in communication, whereas women tend to be more expressive and more concerned with interpersonal processes. Different levels and styles of communication can lead to misunderstandings and conflicts in many social situations, including interactions in the home and the workplace.

Dealing with Competition

Some men have been socialized to be highly competitive; winning is perceived as important to maintaining the masculine role. In other words, men validate their masculinity through competition at work. The effects of intense competition among men in the workplace may result in some men being very reluctant to be honest with their peers and having difficulties in developing interpersonal relationships. That is, intense competition among men may be highly related to stressful work environments and work anxiety (O'Neil, 1982).

As discussed in Chapter 3, Yankelovich (1981a) believed that work environments in America will change dramatically in the near future. Highly competitive environments will become ones in which honesty, openness, and sharing will be practiced. Future organizations will require more cooperation among their workers, and workers will be required to deal with a wider variety of assignments and other workers (Bennis, 1981). In such work environments, openness and honesty with peer affiliates are important qualities to foster.

Learning to Recognize Self-Destructive Behavior

A number of researchers have suggested that behaviors that lead to healthcare problems should be a major consideration for the counseling profession (Harrison, 1978; Fasteau, 1974; Goldberg, 1977, 1979; Mayer, 1978). Waldron (1978) suggested that significant differences in life expectancy between men and women can, at least in part, be attributed to gender-role-related behaviors. The relationship between values associated with masculinity and poor health is supported by a number of researchers (Harrison, 1978; Olson, 1978; Nichols, 1975; Mayer, 1978).

Friedman and Rosenman (1974) conceptualized a model of how men function and behave in the workplace and designated the two masculine styles of functioning as Type A and Type B. Type A persons have an accelerated overall lifestyle with involvement in multiple functions. They are overcommitted to their vocation and/or profession, with an intense drive for achievement, and they develop feelings of guilt when relaxing. Other characteristics include excessive drive, impatience, competitiveness, restlessness, abrupt speech, nervous gestures, and rapid walking, eating, and moving. Type B persons are the opposite. They are characterized by serenity, an ability to relax, and a lack of time urgency.

According to Goldfried and Friedman (1982), Type A behavior is more characteristic of men than women. However, women employed outside the home tend to develop Type A characteristics more often than women not employed outside the home (Waldron, 1978). Several investigations have concluded that Type A behavior contributes to a higher rate of heart disease and mortality than Type B behavior (Jenkins, 1976; Suinn, 1975; Rosenman, Friedman, & Straus, 1964).

In the workplace, Type A individuals have an intense sense of time urgency and attempt to participate in most tasks, job assignments, and events that are ongoing in the workplace. Type A individuals give the impression that they can meet all challenges and successfully cope with any challenge, especially at work. Goldfried and Friedman (1982) suggested a program of cognitive restructuring as an effective intervention to modify Type A behavior. In cognitive restructuring, individuals learn to recognize behaviors that are self-destructive by acknowledging unrealistic and irrational beliefs that have reinforced their Type A behavior patterns. Counseling sessions, designed to promote cognitive restructuring, help them identify anxiety-arousing situations and take steps to modify their behavior (Doyle, 1992). Relaxation training, developed by Wolpe (1958), is another method of helping Type A individuals deal with anxieties.

Changing Male Roles in Dual-Career Homes

In homes where both husband and wife are actively involved in their careers, household roles are changing. According to Beckett and Smith (1981), men with employed wives are participating in more household tasks than men with unemployed wives. However, Hoffman (1983) contended that women continue to shoulder the major burden of childcare/household responsibilities. Hoffman's position suggests that men are expressing difficulty in perceiving housework as their responsibility and role. Her position is supported by Lein (1979) and Model (1981). In a study based on 25 interviews with Boston-area families, Lein (1979) concluded that husbands were ridiculed by their peers for helping their wives with childcare/household tasks and subsequently were reluctant to help with housework. In another research project based on the study of 650 women in the Detroit metropolitan area, Model (1981) found that the greater the difference in wages between husband and wife—that is, when the husband's wages were significantly higher—the less likely it was that the husband would participate in household work. In review of these studies, Rosenwasser and Patterson (1984) suggested that a husband's reluctance to help with household tasks is at least partially a function of what men consider to be their familial role of provider; the greatest determinant of a husband's household/childcare activities is gender-role ideology. In essence, if men perceive their primary familial role as that of provider, they are less likely to participate in housework.

In a provocative study of dual-career couples, Wilcox-Matthew & Minor (1989) pointed out some concerns, benefits, and counseling implications. Because men have been socialized to play the role of "king of the hill," they may have difficulty sharing family roles and feeling comfortable in a nurturing role. One of the major issues is the management of household tasks. Counselors need to encourage men to share household duties, particularly in dual-career homes. The concept of shared responsibility is a step toward accepting new learning patterns that may require shifting roles for both husbands and wives in dual-career homes.

Needs of Househusbands

In the 40-year span from 1940 to 1980, the percentage of employed mothers with children under 18 rose from 8.6% to 56.6% (Hoffman, 1983). These figures underscore the possibility of more involvement among men in primary and shared household/childcare activities. A significant question involves how men react to the role of househusband. In the scanty literature that exists, there is evidence of resentment among fathers involved in paternal caretaking (Lamb et al., 1982). Russell (1982) reported that fathers involved in shared care-giving were bored with their role, desired adult interaction, and were pressured by male peers. On the other hand, Russell (1982), Radin (1983), and Sagi (1982) found that shared care-giving fathers experienced an enhanced father-child relationship.

Perhaps men need to be made aware of the benefits of primary and shared responsibility for household/childcare activities. In a study of 16 fathers who had assumed 50% or more of the responsibility of childcare and household tasks, Rosenwasser and Patterson (1984) found that all but one indicated that they would recommend their lifestyle to other men. The results of this study provide some encouragement for men who assume the role of househusband.

When we learn more about the problems men face with childcare and household tasks, appropriate guidelines for counseling consideration may emerge. In the meantime, counseling considerations for househusbands may include methods for dealing with ridiculing peers, boredom, household management, role conflict, and balancing household tasks with career.

Needs of Divorced Men

In the preceding chapter, the needs of divorced women were identified and discussed. Divorced men have similar needs. In particular, men who have dependent children will find that balancing the responsibilities of parenthood and managing a home with the responsibilities of work is a definite need. Halle (1982) studied 26 men whose wives filed for divorce and identified the following problems experienced by these men: depression, self-blame, suicidal ideation, rage, jealousy, stress of new demands, vulnerability, being judged less of a man, and needing help with child-rearing. As with divorced women, men must learn to cultivate composure to effectively meet both home and employment responsibilities.

Men in Nontraditional Careers

Nontraditional occupations, as identified by Chusmir (1990), are those that have less than 30% of the same-sex workers. For example, four careers that are female-dominated (57% women) are social work, nursing, elementary school teaching, and office work. Although there is greater acceptance of men in nontraditional careers, there continues to be prejudice, ridicule, and negative perceptions of the men who choose them. It appears that gender-typing of careers is still prevalent in our society and those who deviate experience the scorn of those whose thinking is dominated by gender-role stereotyping.

The career counselor should make it clear that all careers are to be considered in the decision-making process. Both negative and positive aspects of choosing an atypical career should be discussed. The negative aspects have been mentioned; the positive ones include faster opportunities for promotion, upward mobility, and increased compensation (Chusmir, 1990).

Gay Men

As discussed in the preceding chapter, more gays are making their sexual orientation known. Two major objectives are to find acceptance in the workplace and remove barriers that discriminate and inhibit their career development. Gay men appeared to have less certainty about their career choice and less job satisfaction with their career than gay women and heterosexual men and women (Hetherington, Hillerbrand, & Etringer, 1989). Furthermore, these researchers suggested that gay men are sensitive to negative stereotyping (such as assuming certain occupations are mainly for them), employment discrimination, and limited role models.

Hudson (1992) suggested that counselors should prepare for counseling gays by building an extensive body of resources including specific information on those organizations and companies that support gay employees and a list of gay professionals who would provide support and information. Eldridge (1987) provides the following recommendations for counselors: (1) keep in mind the subtle, insidious nature of heterosexual bias and use this knowledge as a reminder for reflection; (2) use gender-free language; (3) become familiar with models of gay identity formation; (4) identify a consultant who can provide helpful information or feedback on working with gay clients; and (5) become familiar with local support networks for gays.

IMPLICATIONS FOR CAREER COUNSELING OF MEN

The preceding sections identified some effects of gender-role conflicts in men. These conflicts are important considerations in counseling men on career development, maintenance, and lifestyle orientation. Of particular value are programs that foster the idea that both men and women are gender-role socialized. Generally speaking, men are more resistant to self-disclosure than women, suggesting a greater need for men to understand socialization processes. The importance of learning about leisure and relaxation techniques suggests programs designed to assist men in identifying and planning for appropriate leisure activities. The problem many men have with putting work achievement in proper prospective and learning to deal with competition suggests programs that delineate differences between aggressiveness and assertiveness. Finally, the concept of dual-career roles needs clarification.

COMPONENTS FOR COUNSELING MEN

The four counseling components that follow (outlined in Table 15-1) address general as well as specific career issues that arise from gender-role conflicts in men. Within each component there are specific tasks that can be selected as counseling objectives to meet specific needs or interests of groups and/or individuals. Likewise, each counseling component may be selected for its special appeal to specific individuals or groups; the components need not be offered in any particular sequence. The technique options do not exhaust all possible methods of accomplishing the specific task.

Component I—Expressiveness Training

The two goals of this component are to help individuals identify situations in which it is appropriate to express their emotions and learn that it is acceptable to freely express emotions in those situations. Dosser (1982) reported that men have a more difficult time experiencing their emotional feelings than do women. Specifically, they have more difficulty expressing emotions of happiness, sorrow, tenderness, delight, sadness, and elation. Jourard (1964), who initiated studies of self-disclosure, suggested that men reveal less information about themselves than do women. Research has shown that there is a high correlation between self-disclosure/self-awareness and interpersonal functioning (Dosser, 1982). In general, men devalue what they perceive as feminine traits of gentleness, expressiveness, and responsiveness (Solomon, 1982; O'Neil, 1982). In the work environment, men tend to be much more guarded

TABLE 15-1
Components for Counseling Men

Strategy Component	Technique Options	Specific Tasks
I. Expressiveness training	1. Workshop 2. Group and/or individual counseling 3. Role-clarification exercises 4. Videotaped feedback 5. Homework assignments	1. Clarify how men's behavior has been shaped through socialization. 2. Identify and clarify inexpressive behavior. 3. Require each counselee to demonstrate an inexpressive behavior. 4. Clarify the advantages of expressive behavior and disadvantages of inexpressive behavior. 5. Clarify the advantages of a less rigid masculine role. 6. Clarify potential problems of inexpressive behavior in the working environment. 7. Clarify potential problems of inexpressive behavior in the home, with colleagues, and with friends. 8. Identify and discuss factors that prohibit expressive behavior. 9. Clarify strategies for becoming more expressive. 10. Demonstrate consequences of inexpressive and expressive behaviors in the work environment. 11. Clarify the differences between self-control and inexpressive behavior. 12. Role play/rehearse expressive behavior.
II. Assertiveness training	1. Workshop 2. Group and/or individual counseling 3. Role-clarification exercises 4. Videotaped feedback 5. Homework assignments	1. Clarify the differences between assertive, aggressive, and unassertive behavior. 2. Develop a philosophy of assertiveness (i.e., one's assertive bill of rights). 3. Identify behavioral expressions that are assertive. 4. Identify behavioral expressions that are aggressive. 5. Identify positive assertive responses to interpersonal situations with friends, fellow employees, and strangers. 6. Identify positive responses that are assertive.

TABLE 15-1
(continued)

Strategy Component	Technique Options	Specific Tasks
		7. Identify the differences between aggressive and passive behaviors.
		8. Clarify factors of socialization that inhibit assertiveness.
		9. Identify and clarify the concept of self-disclosure.
III. Dual-career roles	1. Workshop 2. Group and/or individual counseling 3. Role-clarification exercises 4. Videotaped presentations 5. Homework assignments	1. Clarify the concept of dual careers.
		2. Clarify reasons women have the same rights as men in developing a career.
		3. Clarify reasons men have the same rights as women in nurturing their families.
		4. Clarify how socialization has determined gender roles in our society.
		5. Clarify the concept of an egalitarian marriage.
		6. Identify and discuss methods of sharing household management and tasks.
		7. Clarify how husband and wife can look on their dual career and work roles as a joint venture.
		8. Clarify the role of a "liberated" husband in a dual-career marriage.
		9. Identify and clarify fears about possible loss of status or self-esteem among men when adjusting to changing roles in dual-career families.
		10. Identify and clarify changing styles of interaction between spouses who both support dual-career concepts.
		11. Identify changing attitudes in relation to work and responsibilities in dual-career families.
		12. Clarify the family-nurturing role for men in dual-career marriages.

TABLE 15-1
(continued)

Strategy Component	Technique Options	Specific Tasks
IV. Support groups	1. Group and/or individual counseling 2. Role-clarification exercises 3. Videotaped presentations 4. Homework assignments	1. Identify the concept of androgyny. 2. Identify and clarify problems associated with the modification of masculine roles. 3. Identify and clarify problems associated with reactions to the women's movement. 4. Increase understanding of the masculine socialization process. 5. Increase understanding of the feminine socialization process. 6. Identify stereotyped work roles for men and women. 7. Identify and clarify problems men will encounter when they adopt a more androgynous role. 8. Identify and clarify problems associated with maintaining modified behaviors of expressiveness, sharing in dual-career homes, and assertiveness. 9. Identify and clarify the purpose of men's consciousness-raising groups.

than women against revealing weaknesses to fellow workers and may resist certain cooperative tasks that could expose their vulnerability (Lindsey, 1990). Inexpressiveness can become highly dysfunctional in many relationships, including those with peer affiliates in the working environment, children, spouse, and friends.

The workshop described for this component should incorporate all or most of the other technique options. For example, inexpressive behavior can be succinctly illustrated through videotaped presentations or other video media. Role-clarification exercises can be used to demonstrate the impact of inexpressive behavior on interpersonal relationships. Videotaped feedback is a good procedure to help individuals perceive how others may see them. Homework assignments can be quite varied and inclusive and may include an assignment of recording one's behavior for a week and reporting back to a group, or keeping records of the behavior of others. Individual goals and strategies should be identified, and group counseling may be used to provide the counselee with feedback from his peers regarding his progress toward accomplishing established goals. Peer-group interaction is also a valuable means of support for individual and group efforts.

The specific tasks for this component can be sequenced to meet the needs of individuals or groups. The tasks of identifying and clarifying inexpressive behaviors are especially important for men, because they have been socialized to regard their inexpressiveness as an appropriate masculine trait. Indeed, these tasks may be used at various times to provide the framework from which men can learn to identify the differences between inexpressiveness and expressive behavior and to judge their progress toward becoming more expressive.

Other tasks to be emphasized by the career counselor are those that direct attention to behaviors that interfere with establishing appropriate interpersonal relationships with fellow workers, family, and friends; expressiveness is an important characteristic for establishment of relationships at work, in the home, and during leisure time.

Component II—Assertiveness Training

Assertiveness training has become immensely popular during the last 20 years, providing a basis for research in the scientific community and training programs for the general public. Programs for women have included assertiveness training to help them achieve individual goals for improving interpersonal relationships. Recognition of the need for special programs for men has led to a reexamination of several existing programs for women—including assertiveness training. There is evidence from research that men also benefit from programs designed to help them become more assertive (Dosser, 1982; Goldberg, 1983). Wolpe's (1973) discussion of assertive behavior suggested that men generally need to be more assertive when expressing affection, admiration, and praise. Wolpe also suggested that differences between hostile/aggressive behaviors and assertive behaviors need to be delineated. Wolpe pointed out that some individuals might experience embarrassment when expressing affection, admiration, and praise. Goldberg (1983) suggested that men need to learn how to become less competitive and aggressive when interacting with colleagues and spouses.

The specific tasks of this component are primarily designed to assist men in clarifying the differences between aggression and assertiveness. The technique options provide several strategies to help them recognize the benefits of appropriately expressing their emotions, thoughts, and beliefs in a direct and honest manner. Assertiveness training can provide behavioral guidelines for men to use in modifying their aggression when interacting with peer affiliates on the job and with their families at home. Examples of appropriate verbal and non-verbal behaviors help men target specific situations in the process of modifying their behaviors. Dosser (1982) suggested that it is advantageous to concentrate on the expression of positive feelings in assertiveness training. Rich and Schroeder (1976) compiled a list of suggested techniques and procedures for assertiveness training, including developing a philosophy of assertiveness, role playing, role reversal, response practice, constructive criticism, modeling, relaxation, exaggerated role taking, postural and vocal analysis training, and homework assignments. Most of these suggested procedures can be accomplished with the technique options recommended for this component.

Component III—Dual-Career Roles

In Chapter 14, we learned that an increasing number of women are planning lifelong careers in a wide range of occupations. In their life plans, women are giving career development a higher priority or at least a status equal to other priorities, such as marriage and family. Dual-career families are becoming less of a novelty in the 1980s, but the increased prevalence of this lifestyle has not been accompanied by changes in the values, beliefs, or behavior of many of the men or women in these marriages. Men may have difficulty making the transition from traditional attitudes of man-at-work/woman-at-home to that of negotiating dual-career and family roles. These entrenched attitudes and perceptions of appropriate masculine roles will die slowly because of the long-standing socialization process that has stereotyped gender-role models. The process of change requires the recognition of deeply rooted patterns of masculine-role behavior and attitudes toward women in general. However, there is recent evidence that when men are challenged to modify their behavior in dual-career families they change their attitudes and actions (Wilcox-Matthew & Minor, 1989). The recent shift of roles in dual-career families gives this counseling component credibility for helping husbands make adjustments in their attitudes toward their wives' career aspirations, demonstrating advantages of fathers' being able to participate in their children's lives more directly, and encouraging men to assume a greater role in household-management responsibilities.

The specific tasks in this component are designed to clarify the concept of dual-career families and to introduce changes in male role models. Special attention should be given to identifying and clarifying dual-career family problems as discussed in Component III—Lifestyle Skills for Women in Chapter 14. Other suggested solutions contained in this component for women, such as shared responsibility and role-coping exercises, can also be used in this component for men.

Component IV—Support Groups

Other counseling considerations may evolve as men begin to reexamine their roles as males. During the process of reexamination, some men may experience a sense of loss of status and self-esteem when confronted with the prospect of egalitarianism. At the beginning of the transition process, husbands may make pseudo attempts at conforming to newly established goals of sharing, but they may continue to consider their wives as being primarily responsible for fulfilling household and family needs. A combination of role playing and discussion groups is recommended for encouraging men to share these responsibilities. Other special issues that may be addressed include the following: (1) men may place more importance on their careers because they have considered themselves the primary breadwinners, (2) men may react negatively toward women who are successful and strong, (3) men may experience difficulty in changing and modifying the nature of adult relationships, and (4) men may have difficulty adopting a different male role in work and recreation (Stein, 1982). These issues clearly indicate the need for career counselors to provide support groups for men to express their needs in career-related issues and lifestyle concerns. Stein (1982) suggested that support groups for men provide an effective environment for addressing gender-role and career-related issues.

The technique options and specific tasks for this component provide the opportunity for men to freely express their emotions. Men should be encouraged to recognize and express emotions and behaviors that are usually associated with the feminine role, such as gentleness, sadness, caretaking, and nurturing. Conversely, they should also be encouraged to express typical masculine-role traits of assertiveness, dominance, and competitiveness when appropriate. Both activities provide a rich source of learning how men react and relate to each other when assuming feminine and masculine role models. These experiences should be designed to help men establish caring and empathic interpersonal relationships in the work environment. In essence, men should be encouraged to modify traditional, stereotyped patterns of behavior in order to build personal relationships that do not require them to resort to rigid, masculine role models.

A men's support group also provides the opportunity to introduce specific topics of interest, such as difficulties in parenting, excessive need to achieve, expressing emotions, sharing household tasks, and competitiveness in the work place. The group can be divided into dyads and triads to discuss specific topics of interest.

The general goal of a men's support group is to change rigid, gender-role masculine behavior in order to build better relationships with women and other men. The peer interaction in men's groups should lead to greater flexibility in all interpersonal relationships.

SUMMARY

1. Recently, men have begun reexamining their roles, beliefs, and values regarding their relationships with women. Boys exhibit gender-role-appropriate behavior at a very early age. The learned framework of societal expectations intensifies in early childhood through social learning from parents, the schools, and the media.

2. Parents expect sons to be more active and aggressive and daughters to be passive and nonassertive. Parents' treatment and expectations of children in early childhood foster developmental patterns that may determine future role behavior.

3. The process of formal education further reinforces expectations of gender-role behavior learned in the home. Our educational system fosters the development of gender-typed work roles.

4. Television programs and commercials, children's books, and comic strips foster the development of gender-typed roles.

5. Special career-counseling needs of men include fear of femininity, placing achievement and success in perspective, learning to relax, restrictive emotionality, dealing with competition, learning to recognize self-destructive behaviors, changing roles in dual-career homes, support for househusbands and divorced men, difficulties in nontraditional careers, and workplace acceptance of gay men.

6. Career-counseling approaches should be free of gender-role typing. Counseling-strategy components include expressiveness training, assertiveness training, dual-career families, and support groups.

SUPPLEMENTARY LEARNING EXERCISES

1. Develop a counseling component to help individuals identify typical masculine aggressive responses.
2. Review several history textbooks and identify descriptions of strong, masculine characters.
3. Develop a script that demonstrates the "Sturdy Oak" gender role.
4. Develop a list of masculine roles that interfere with cooperative efforts in the work environment.
5. Interview a husband and wife of a dual-career family to determine the extent of sharing of household planning and duties.
6. Using the dimension of the masculine role descriptions, develop a list of behaviors that are detrimental to career fulfillment.

7. While observing several television programs, develop a list of characters that represents the dimensions of the role-appropriate behavior.
8. List your experiences in school that influenced gender-role appropriate behavior.
9. Develop a counseling component that is designed to help men modify their masculine role behavior in the work environment.
10. Meet with an individual of the opposite sex and develop a list of ideas that could be used to encourage sharing of responsibilities in a dual-career family.

Chapter Sixteen

Career Counseling for Various Ethnic Groups

The challenge of counseling various ethnic groups has received renewed impetus with recent changes in educational and employment opportunities. Legislation requiring that ethnic groups have equal access to training and employment has generated career-counseling programs that aid the "culturally different." Career counselors are intent on developing career-counseling objectives and strategies that will assist individuals of various ethnic groups in overcoming a multitude of barriers including prejudice, language differences, cultural isolation, and culture-related differences. Because this group is composed of persons from a wide variety of ethnic backgrounds, counselors are being challenged to become culturally aware, evaluate their personal views, and understand that other people's perspectives may be as legitimate as their own (Sue & Sue, 1990).

The need to develop career-guidance strategies for ethnic minorities will increase in the next century. An article (*San Antonio Express-News*, 1993b) based on a report from the Population Reference Bureau of the U.S. Census Bureau suggested that by the middle of the next century, the United States will no longer be a predominately Anglo society. The more appropriate reference will be "a global society," in which half of all Americans will be from four ethnic groups: Asian Americans, African Americans, Hispanic Americans, and Native Americans. As more ethnic minority groups gain access to opportunities for education and higher-status jobs, the career-guidance profession should be prepared to assist them. These projected demographics of diversity will present a significant challenge to all of the helping professions.

OPINIONS OF ETHNICS ABOUT PREPARING FOR WORK

In 1989, the National Career Development Association (NCDA) commissioned the Gallup Organization to survey the opinions of some ethnic minority groups (African Americans, Hispanics, and Asian Pacific Islanders) about their own career-planning processes and workplaces. African Americans strongly expressed a need for career planning and access to appropriate occupational information. They also expressed problems of discrimination in the workplace. The Asian Pacific Islander group reported that their skills were not fully used on the job. They also experienced more job-related stress than other ethnic minority groups surveyed. Hispanics indicated that pay was the greatest incentive to motivate them to do more on a job (Brown, Minor, & Jepsen, 1991).

Although these findings are helpful in determining career-guidance programs for ethnic minorities, the limitations of the study should be carefully scrutinized. For example, a telephone survey was used, thus limiting the subgroups studied to those who have telephones; the sample size was relatively small, and Native Americans were excluded. As a result of these limitations, the results should be used with caution. However, the need for career planning and access to appropriate occupational information found in this study is not surprising and was also expressed as a need in a similar research project reported in 1989 (Brown & Minor, 1989).

ASIAN AMERICANS

Asian Americans represent a culturally diverse group that includes Cambodians, Chinese, Filipinos, Indians, Japanese, Pakistanis, Thai, and Vietnamese (Sue & Abe, 1988). Many Asian American groups place a high value on education. Sue and Okazaki (1990) suggested that Asian Americans perceive education as a means of upward mobility and are highly motivated to remove barriers that may limit them. However, Cabezas and Yee (1977) contended that Asian Americans are often victimized by discriminatory employment practices. Asian women are given especially low status and are exploited in the working world (Chu, 1981; Kumata & Murata, 1980). Hsia (1981) argued that Asian Americans are hindered in the job market because of poor communication skills, which accounts for their tendency to choose jobs such as engineering, computer science, and economics.

In evaluating counseling processes as a source of conflict for Chinese Americans, Sue and Sue (1990) made several pertinent observations: (1) Chinese American students inhibit emotional expression and do not actively participate in the counseling process, (2) Chinese Americans are discouraged from revealing emotional problems by their cultural conditioning, and (3) Chinese American students react more favorably to well-structured counseling models. Sue's conclusions emphasize the importance of understanding cultural influences when counseling Chinese Americans.

Fernandez (1988) argued that Southeast Asian students should be counseled using behavioral approaches. She considered it inappropriate to use counseling techniques that require clients to verbalize excessively. Evanoski and Tse (1989) have successfully used bilingual materials and role models in workshops directed toward parents of Chinese and Korean children that exposed them to methods of accessing a variety of occupations. The basic assumption was that these parents have a tremendous influence on their children.

Special needs and problems associated with Asian Americans in counseling are summarized from Kaneshige (1979): (1) Asian Americans are very sensitive about verbalizing psychological problems, especially in group encounters;

(2) Asian Americans tend to be inexpressive when asked to discuss personal achievements and limitations; (3) Asian Americans tend to misinterpret the role of counseling in general and the benefits that may be derived from it; (4) Asian Americans may be perceived as very passive and nonassertive with authority figures, but in reality they are reacting to cultural inhibitions that discourage them from being perceived as aggressive; and (5) Asian Americans may strongly resist suggestions to modify behavior that is unassuming and nonassertive.

In recent years, Vietnamese have presented particular problems to career counselors who have assisted them in relocating in this country. The needs and problems of this adult ethnic group are good examples for illustrating limitations of employment for first-generation Asian Americans. In addition to the need to learn English, other problems and difficulties are (1) recognizing the importance of transferable skills, (2) considering past work history as relevant, (3) understanding the concept of career ladders, (4) locating information about unemployment, and (5) recognizing the importance of résumé preparation and interview-skills training.

As a group, Asian Americans have the lowest rate of unemployment (Smith, 1983). In general, Asian Americans are very industrious workers, seem to value education, and have taken advantage of higher education to enhance their career development. They are also known to do well in business administration, engineering, and sciences. However, the stereotype of the Asian American as being good in sciences but lacking in verbal skills may limit their access to careers that require communication skills.

Suggested Developmental Strategies for Asian Americans

Although the following strategies meet the specific needs of Asian Americans, they can probably be generalized to other groups discussed in this chapter. In fact, many of the counseling strategies, models, and components discussed in other chapters are relevant for all groups discussed in this chapter, so that the strategies suggested here should not be considered exhaustive of all pertinent counseling strategies.

Components of counseling for Asian Americans include the following:

1. *Learning self-assertion skills*—This component should be designed to help Asian Americans overcome the stereotype of being passive and noncommunicative.
2. *Learning to understand organization systems and bureaucracies*—This component should be especially useful for first-generation Asian Americans.
3. *Improving communication skills*—Many Asian Americans may be hampered in their career development and career options because of poor communication skills.
4. *Improving interpersonal skills*—Learning how to establish satisfying and productive relationships with others should help Asian Americans meet social-emotional needs.

5. *Learning to understand work environments*—Forming relationships with supervisors and peers should help Asian Americans adjust to work roles and work environments.

AFRICAN AMERICANS

The largest racial minority in this country is African Americans. Most African Americans live in urban areas and have assumed a moderate position in our society. For the most part, they have been wage earners as opposed to being self-employed. In essence, they have been blue-collar workers rather than managers or proprietors. African American men have achieved greater career mobility than African American women. Although some of both sexes have managed to achieve upward mobility to professional occupations, the overall success of upward movement of African Americans is minimal. Those who have attained middle-class status are also in the position to take advantage of educational opportunities and career mobility. Others, particularly those classified as under-class, primarily from three-generation families on welfare, are without job skills and lack motivation to change their status (Smith, 1983; Axelson, 1993).

According to Jackson (1975), African Americans have a unique psychological development. He has devised four developmental stages that depict the psychological development:

1. *Passive acceptance*—in this stage, African Americans imitate Caucasians as a way of coping with them.
2. *Active resistance*—in this stage, African Americans reject Caucasian cultural patterns and become active in militant groups.
3. *Redirection*—in this stage, African Americans give less attention to the cultural mores of Caucasians and focus on their own identity.
4. *Internalization*—in this stage, cultural and self-identity are achieved.

In all stages of a developmental approach, counselors must be aware of their counselees' current stage and the tasks associated with transitions and moving from one stage to another. In this model, for example, an individual in stage 2 may have difficulty relating to a Caucasian counselor.

African American College Students

Although African American college students experience many of the same adjustment problems encountered in the transition from high school to college as their White counterparts, Vontress (1971) believed their special problems and needs warrant consideration. He outlined their problems as (1) *impaired self-concept* (influenced primarily by social interaction, segregated schools, and poor opportunities); (2) *parental disassociation* (they are often estranged from parents); (3) *drug use* (poor self-concept and socialization often lead to this); (4) *loneliness* (fewer social opportunities); (5) *academic frustration* (they often have difficulty meeting academic demands); (6) *student-faculty relations* (difficulty approaching faculty members); (7) *identity crisis* (loss of cultural heritage); (8) *compulsive behavior* (they may turn to this behavior to counteract the stereotyped image of lethargy and poor aspirations); and (9) *ambivalence toward Whites*. These characteristics may greatly inhibit the development of positive motivation and constructive action toward the career-decision process.

Achievement and motivation among African Americans in college have been found to be equally high for both men and women. This finding suggests that African American women have high expectations for work and a sense of responsibility to contribute to family income. However, they tend to choose the more traditional feminine professional occupations at about the same rate as White women (Woody, 1992). The message to the counselor is twofold: encourage and enhance the high level of achievement motivation of African American women; and encourage more to consider nontraditional, professional occupations.

The National Science Foundation (1989) gathered statistics on the number of African Americans enrolled in graduate courses in doctorate-granting institutions as a percentage of total graduate enrollment: 1.7% in both computer sciences and life sciences, 1.3% in physical sciences, and 1.4% in mathematical sciences. The number of doctoral degrees awarded to African Americans from 1975 to 1989 in physical sciences, life sciences, and engineering ranged from a low of 101 in 1980 to a high of 133 in 1978 (Vetter, 1989). Malcolm (1990) suggested that we must encourage more African Americans to major in mathematics and the sciences by engaging the children in these subjects early in their educational experience and by encouraging parents to influence their children in this direction. In essence, we must encourage African Americans to choose majors in a wider variety of career fields.

Vontress (1979) suggested that African Americans are made to feel as outsiders in public schools. Even after 25 years of integration, they are treated differently than Caucasians. More important, they continue to receive inferior educational opportunities compared to Caucasians. Vontress implied that African Americans have reached or soon should reach the point of not being considered so unlike Caucasians; thus, special expertise to counsel or teach them may not be warranted. In the meantime, they remain socially isolated in church, school, and at work.

African American Workers

Taylor (1990) suggested that the major reasons for fewer job prospects for African Americans are related to industrial decentralization and shifts from manufacturing to service industries. These events have significantly reduced job prospects for unskilled and semiskilled workers and have had devastating effects on the poorly educated. However, Johnson (1990) reported that underemployed and underpaid African Americans have developed coping strategies to maintain self-worth and self-esteem through personal and familial achievements. Mogull (1978) postulated that the causes for discontentment among African American workers are psychological, social, cultural, and economic in origin. According to Mogull, some of the underlying causes include:

1. *Class values*—Social position tends to inhibit aspirations and probability of success in certain occupations.
2. *Family stability*—The prevalence of family instability among African Americans contributes to dissatisfaction at work.
3. *Motivational aspirations*—A number of causes for poor motivation and low aspirations include differences in cultural values among racial and ethnic groups, fear of failure, limited job opportunities, and low expectations from educational and training experiences.
4. *Dignity*—This cause is mainly psychological in that African American males retain their dignity by refusing to accept Caucasian middle-class work values.
5. *Dead-end jobs*—The level of work open to African Americans is low-grade and provides little security (p. 569).

Woody (1992) researched work patterns of African American women and found that many lack requisite skills to compete for technical work and will fail to qualify for higher-level jobs. She argued that African American women have severe job limitations and many are restricted to low-end jobs because of discrimination. She suggested that there is a "women's work subculture" that may only be alleviated through an improved national employment policy.

Suggested Developmental Strategies for African Americans

Selected developmental strategies to help African Americans include assisting self-concept development, developing more internally directed behavior, becoming more aware of job opportunities, clarifying motivational aspirations, and dealing with ambivalence toward Caucasians.

1. *Developing self-concept*—Many African Americans can benefit from being made keenly aware of how feelings of personal inadequacies affect their perception of current and future work roles.
2. *Learning to be more internally directed*—Programs designed to help African Americans take control of their career direction and break away from old patterns of life will help them toward self-improvement.
3. *Learning about job opportunities*—Career information that delineates trends in the labor force and explains equal opportunity laws will alert African Americans to job opportunities. Careful attention should be directed toward the effective use of materials and the steps involved in a job search.
4. *Clarifying motivational aspirations*—This module should include causes of low expectations and fear of failure and methods of improving motivation.

5. *Learning to cope with the Caucasian society*—This component should include interrelationships in work environments and the development of
sense of identity.

HISPANIC AMERICANS

Hispanic Americans compose the second largest minority group in the country.
The largest subgroup of Hispanics are Mexican Americans, followed by Cubans
and Puerto Ricans. The states with the largest Hispanic populations are California, Texas, New York, and Florida. Most Hispanics live in metropolitan areas
(Smith, 1983; Axelson, 1993). Pollack and Menacker (1971, p. 12) suggested
that minority students such as Puerto Ricans and Mexican Americans have
needs that may be classified into three categories: *administration needs* (students
should be made to feel a part of a school community), *maturation needs* (students need to be encouraged to become self-reliant), and *mastery needs* (mastery
skills are needed for work and to improve self-image). They suggested the
"caring" relationship as a most effective counseling approach for bilingual
minority groups.

Although Ponterotto (1987) reported that Hispanics underutilize counseling services in both mental health and academic settings, there is good evidence
that they could benefit from these services, especially when intervention strategies meet special needs. Rodriguez and Blocher (1988) found that interventions
with academically and economically disadvantaged Puerto Rican women produced positive results by raising their level of career maturity and developing
beliefs that they can control their own destiny.

Social factors such as social-class membership, environment of the home
and school, and the community in which the individual resides significantly
influence career perspectives and attitudes toward work (Osipow, 1983; Pietrofesa & Splete, 1975). Arbona (1989) supported this conclusion by debunking
the idea that cultural traits have restricted Hispanics in career choices. Instead,
socioeconomic status and lack of opportunity have restricted Hispanics from
access to higher education and subsequently to their occupational aspirations.
However, Hispanics are not a homogeneous group; there are important differences between subgroups and between Hispanics from different socioeconomic
backgrounds (Arbona, 1989). Career counselors should attempt to assess levels
of acculturation before developing intervention strategies. Ponterotto (1987)
recommended the following information be obtained as a measure of acculturation: socioeconomic status, place of birth, language preference, generation
level, preferred ethnic identity, and ethnic group social contacts.

It is not a good idea, however, to overgeneralize about the Hispanic
students in our schools today; many are acculturated and fit well into the
mainstream of society. One can expect, for example, to find diverse value systems among Hispanics. There are, however, those Hispanics who cling to their
traditional heritage and consequently may have difficulty in adjusting to an
Anglo-dominant school and culture. Caught between conflicting cultures, the

adolescent Hispanic seeks out the support of peers who are experiencing similar conflicts. As a result, there is usually less interaction with other groups of students and, typically, school becomes a low priority.

The Mexican American family, in particular, has been characterized as a closely knit group that greatly influences the values of its members. For example, Axelson (1993) suggested that Spanish-speaking children are generally taught to value and respect family, church, and school as well as masculinity and honor. Families are primarily patriarchal (as far as the center of authority is concerned) with a distinct division of duties; that is, the father is the breadwinner, and the mother is the homemaker. Spanish is the primary language spoken in the home and the barrio.

Suggested Developmental Strategies for Hispanic Americans

The vast differences in origins and diversity of Hispanics make it difficult to generalize counseling needs and subsequent career-counseling strategies. The suggested developmental strategies for other groups are particularly relevant for first-generation Hispanic Americans. For example, learning about effective communication skills, work environments and organizations, the use of career information, job-search strategies, and interpersonal relationships are viable components of counseling. Other suggestions include the following:

1. *Learning goal-setting and problem-solving skills*—The major goal of this component is to help Hispanics set goals and priorities, analyze situations, and apply realistic and productive techniques in planning.
2. *Developing working-parent skills*—The purpose of this component is to help Hispanics develop more awareness of the need to effectively balance parenting responsibilities with work responsibilities.
3. *Improving financial management of resources*—The goal of this component is to help Hispanics effectively utilize anticipated monetary resources from employment. The focus should be on principles of budgeting.

NATIVE AMERICANS

More than 1.5 million Native Americans live in the United States. Approximately half of them live on Native American lands and some 275 reservations. Of those Native Americans who live outside the reservations, the largest concentrations are in Los Angeles, San Francisco, and Chicago, but Minneapolis, Denver, Tulsa, Phoenix, and Milwaukee also contain significant numbers.

On the reservations, many are involved in farming, ranching, fishing, and lumber production. Off the reservations they work in factories, on farms, and as skilled craftsworkers. Some tribes are engaged in various enterprises, such as motel management, while others offer bingo and lottery games to the general public (Axelson, 1993).

According to Bryde (1971), Native American values have developed primarily from their religious beliefs, their traditional view of self and others, and their conceptual view of the universe. From their spiritual God, they have been given wisdom, which has been transmitted from one generation to another. Their tradition encourages them to help others, live in harmony with others, and respect the natural world. In Native American culture, self has a viable connection with nature, and one learns about self from nature.

One of the most influential factors in the career development of Native Americans is their preference not to adopt the dominant cultural values. As Bryde (1971) pointed out, many counselors falsely assume that Native Americans accept the values of the dominant society. Parrillo (1985) suggested that we may never fully understand the Native American social system. Native Americans may be thought of as being caught between two cultures. Thus, the early stages of career development we would normally expect may be inhibited by strong ties to the Native American social-cultural milieu. While most White Americans view industrial development as superior to agrarian, many Native Americans disagree.

In general, Native Americans have resisted assimilation into mainstream American society. Feeling misunderstood, isolated, and resistant to cultural assimilation, Native American youths have difficulty identifying with career roles in the dominant society. In addition, about 50% to 60% of all Native American children drop out of the educational system before they finish high school (Parrillo, 1985).

Behavior, customs, and interests of Native Americans have often been misunderstood, and their tribal lifestyle and value systems have been grossly misrepresented (Heinrich, Corbine, & Thomas, 1990). Forbes (1973) suggested that native societies have culturally conditioned Native Americans to view life from a different perspective and to behave differently from many people in the dominant society. For example, they are generally not motivated to achieve status through the accumulation of wealth; many Native Americans attach little value to the possession of material goods or to the success status of those who achieve wealth. Native Americans are usually not concerned with the acquisition of power over others; their lifestyle is extremely democratic, and their culture promotes egalitarianism. As with other ethnic minority groups, cultural heritage is an important consideration in counseling Native Americans.

Henderson (1979) suggested that Native American cultural conditioning is a good means of determining specific counseling needs: (1) Native Americans tend to live in the present and are not future-oriented, (2) they are not conditioned to be punctual and have little concept of time, (3) saving and providing for the future are not encouraged; (4) there are few leadership positions for the young provided in the society; and (5) individual initiative or aggressive action to accomplish personal occupational goals is not encouraged (Native Americans value shared working conditions).

Another variable to be considered in counseling approaches is that tribes do differ in value orientations and individuals differ within tribes. Thus, as in all minority groups, general recommendations for counseling have to be modified to meet individual needs. Thomason (1991) pointed out that a major consideration is the degree of acculturation in the dominant society. Furthermore, he suggested that the client's set of beliefs as to how changes occur is an important consideration for developing intervention strategies for Native Americans.

Perhaps one of the greatest problems Native Americans have in the context of career counseling is their attitude toward work. According to Bryde (1971), Native Americans are perceived as being undependable and not very industrious. They are known to work hard for periods and then suddenly quit their jobs. This behavior is also rooted in their cultural heritage in that they consider work a necessity to satisfy immediate needs. The tendency to live in the present is not conducive to career life planning.

However, Herring (1990) argued that there are many career myths about Native Americans; he believes that we simply do not have the necessary research results to draw many conclusions about their career development. Like other minority groups, Native Americans have not been exposed to a wide range of careers and have limited opportunities to attend college because of high unemployment rates. He suggested that Native Americans be introduced to more nontraditional occupations and be provided with career information using Native American role models to expand their career considerations.

Native Americans have a strong desire to retain the symbolic aspects of their heritage, much of which is different from the dominant culture. The challenge for counselors is to assist them in preserving the positive aspects of their heritage while encouraging them to modify some behaviors. For example, the ability to enjoy the present should be combined with planning skills, and the ability to share with others should be combined with assertive behavior. The value orientation of Native Americans is a sensitive issue for career counselors.

Native American resistance to counseling in general is exemplified by the group's underuse of existing mental health services. Manson (1982) suggested that Native Americans are the most neglected group in the mental health field. Miller (1982) suggested that more Native Americans would take advantage of counseling relationships if appropriate counseling strategies were used. Trimble and Lafromboise (1985) summarized Miller's strategies as follows:

1. Personal ethnic identity in itself is hardly sufficient for understanding the influence of culture on the client.
2. The client's history contains a number of strengths that can promote and facilitate the counseling process.
3. The counselor should be aware of his or her own biases about cultural pluralism—they might interfere with the counseling relationship.
4. The counselor should encourage the client to become more active in the process of identifying and learning the various elements associated with positive growth and development.

5. Most important are empathy, caring, and a sense of the importance of the human potential (p. 131).

Developmental Strategies for Native Americans

The following strategies are designed to help Native Americans maintain their cultural heritage and at the same time introduce concepts of career development of the dominant society.

1. *Using parents and relatives as counseling facilitators*—The rationale for this approach is embedded in the strong family ties of Native Americans.
2. *Using Native American role models*—They should assist in helping to break down resistance to counseling objectives. Native Americans should react more favorably to other Native Americans.
3. *Emphasizing individual potential in the context of future goals*—Identity conflicts make it difficult for Native Americans to project themselves into other environments, including work environments.

THE POOR

This section focuses on the career-counseling needs of the urban and rural poor.

Urban Poor

The urban poor are identified as mostly African Americans, with significant numbers of Puerto Ricans and Mexican Americans, some Native Americans, and children of first- and second-generation Europeans. Their vocational perspectives are considered to be severely restricted; that is, they are primarily exposed to substandard jobs with limited occupational advancement opportunities and little chance for job tenure. The urban poor also have limited opportunities to interact with workers who are successful and employed in rewarding career fields. Because of poor reading skills, they are unable to take advantage of the abundance of available printed materials that describe jobs and job opportunities. Parents of the urban poor have generally been reared in similar restrictive environmental conditions and may perpetuate exiguity of occupational perspective and low career aspirations. Finally, the norms and values of the urban poor tend to inhibit academic achievement.

Feck (1971) argued that to be effective, teachers and counselors must have knowledge of the characteristics and environmental backgrounds of urban-poor students. He implied that learning attitudes and motivation to achieve are often adversely affected by home and other environmental factors. Feck (1971) described the social, socioeconomic, health, and educational environment of the urban poor as follows:

1. Most of the urban disadvantaged live in ghettos or barrios.
2. Minority groups such as African Americans, Puerto Ricans, Mexican Americans, Appalachian Whites, and first- and second-generation Europeans make up the population group.
3. Families are large and are often without a father.
4. The disadvantaged typically live in substandard housing in older sections of cities.
5. Crime and unemployment rates among the urban poor are relatively high.
6. Many families rely on welfare programs.
7. Many have problems caused by poor management of financial resources.
8. Malnutrition is prevalent due to inadequate diets.
9. There are high rates of physical and mental disorders.
10. There is usually a high rate of drug addiction.
11. Many of the residents have a meager educational background (pp. 5–13).

Beliefs, values, and attitudes that develop from these environmental conditions are often counterproductive to career development. Generally, educational achievement is not encouraged, and dependence on crime or welfare is considered essential for survival. As family members experience constant discrimination and financial failure, they are likely to develop poor self-images.

Rural Poor

The rural disadvantaged as defined by Sweeney (1971) are those living on farms and rural nonfarms such as small towns, villages, and other open territory. Included as rural poor are many low-income ethnic families. Sweeney summarized their more common problems as limited social and recreational activities, poor health services, limited educational experiences, and limited exposure to vocational role models.

Poor Appalachian Whites reside in the rural areas of Pennsylvania, Kentucky, West Virginia, Virginia, and Tennessee. They are characterized as holding on to past traditions, being highly individualistic and action-oriented, and avoiding long-term commitments. Families are very mobile, marriage occurs at an early age, and there is little emphasis on education. There is a strong affiliation with the Appalachian "folk culture" and little motivation to upgrade vocational skills or to change their way of life (Axelson, 1993).

The guidance needs of Appalachian Whites do not differ substantially from those of other ethnic groups. Hansen and Stevic (1971) suggested that longitudinal studies are needed to provide a better understanding of the unique characteristics of Appalachian Whites. Moreover, stronger community involvement in rural areas is needed to provide more facilities and services. More specifically, a coordinated community effort to provide counseling services is needed in Appalachia. Agencies providing services for rehabilitation, mental health, and social welfare can most effectively meet the apparent diversity of needs in this region by coordinating their efforts with those of schools and service clubs.

Courtland (1984) studied the work values of rural African American, White, and Native American high school students. The results of his research suggest that among the group studied, general salary and steady work were more important than values of an intrinsic nature. Because intrinsic work values provide excellent sources of satisfaction, contemporary rural school counselors should design programs to enhance such values as altruism, aesthetics, creativity, and value of relationship with associates. Career choice and maintenance include the consideration of all values including intrinsic ones.

BARRIERS TO EMPLOYMENT

From a survey of 409 economically disadvantaged individuals in the Denver metropolitan area, Miller and Oetting (1977) developed a list of barriers to employment commonly faced by various ethnic groups. These barriers were clustered into four groups: poor job qualifications, social and interpersonal conflicts, legal and financial problems, and emotional problems. Individual barriers include inability to manage family responsibilities, lack of transportation, excessive alcohol consumption, drug abuse, and health-related problems. Programs and services suggested to help remove the barriers are as follows:

1. A Head Start parental-advisory council or other community programs to assist with childcare;
2. Information on how to use transportation systems available in the community;
3. Programs that teach techniques for presenting job qualifications to prospective employers and provide interview-skills training;
4. Assertiveness training with emphasis on differences between aggression and assertion;
5. Program components that help people resolve legal and financial problems;
6. Programs that help people overcome emotional/personal problems (such as stress reduction and support systems);
7. Drug abuse and problem-drinking programs;
8. Healthcare programs; and
9. Language usage and communication training.

The variety and complexity of problems and needs of different ethnic groups truly challenge career counseling. Although there is a diversity of needs among minority racial, urban, and rural groups, the following statements attempt to summarize common problems of the various ethnic groups.

1. Many ethnic groups experience cultural isolation and lack exposure to different elements of society, which tends to limit their educational and employment opportunities.

2. The minority ethnic groups usually experience prejudice, language barriers, and cultural differences that limit their educational and employment opportunities.

3. There is a general need among ethnic groups for exposure to role models that might enhance relationships to work, family, and social responsibilities. Because of this lack of exposure, it is difficult for ethnic groups to envision a different kind of future with any feeling of certainty or security.

4. Many members of ethnic groups are not aware of agencies established to provide a variety of social assistance, including career counseling. Also, some may be reluctant to use social agencies because of a lack of understanding of their purpose.

5. Developing a sense of trust is a basic need of many disadvantaged. The culturally different are often characterized as suspicious of authority and viewing the entire world with distrust and suspicion (Amos, 1968).

6. There is a general need for academic abilities such as study habits and reading, writing, and arithmetic skills. Programs that upgrade these skills and give G.E.D. training are viable considerations.

7. Members of ethnic groups generally lack the social skills and ability to communicate effectively outside their social groups, which has a limiting effect on their career mobility.

8. Many ethnic group members may lack knowledge of appropriate job-maintenance behaviors. In particular, they may experience difficulty in coordinating personal problems and responsibilities with the demands of a job, such as being on time for work, arranging for family needs, and managing their personal finances.

9. Recently, the glass ceiling has been defined as an invisible barrier that consist of subtle attitudes and prejudices that have blocked minorities from climbing the corporate ladder. Although there is some evidence that the glass ceiling is cracking, it still is a barrier that inhibits minorities from reaching senior-level positions in some organizations.

COUNSELING STRATEGIES FOR ETHNIC GROUPS

The personal and environmental characteristics described above serve as barriers to the career development of the culturally different in the dominant culture and establish the need for specific counseling strategies that help overcome these barriers. Feck (1971) noted that essential counseling strategies for the culturally different generally include frequent rewards and reinforcements of positive behaviors. It is important in the planning process to relate ongoing activities with long-term goals. Operationally, the counselor presents short-term plans and gradually introduces plans for the future. Exposure to success models, particularly from the individual's ethnic community and cultural background, is highly recommended as a means for developing positive self-concepts.

Vontress (1971) encouraged counselors of African Americans to have a good background in sociology and the psychology of race and race relations. It is essential that counselors be well-versed on the effects of discrimination and segregation on the personality development of African Americans. Of a more practical nature, Caucasian counselors should not attempt to become overly friendly or demonstrative with African Americans, as they may very well misinterpret the counselor's intention. According to Vontress, African Americans in general tend to have serious doubts about the intentions of Caucasians, particularly when in a helping role.

African American children from middle-class families generally accept Caucasians and want to be accepted by them. Middle-class African Americans are highly sensitive to educational attainment and encourage their children accordingly. Caucasian counselors will have little difficulty in establishing rapport with these children. African American females generally tend to react more favorably to counseling and Caucasian counselors than do African American males (Vontress, 1971).

Menacker (1971) suggested that the role of the school counselor for the urban poor should be that of an ombudsman; that is, an advocacy role to assist students with any problems that might prevent them from matriculating in school. In this role, the counselor should be quite familiar with environmental factors that could be damaging to students as well as with resources that could be used to aid them. The counselor would solicit the help of teachers, administrators, and other school personnel and community leaders to assist the urban poor with educational and environmental problems. To better establish the advocacy role, the counselor's office should be located in the community rather than in the school.

Sue and Sue (1990) suggested that current mental-health practices cannot be applied universally to culturally different populations without recognition of those differences. They implied that counselors who are unaware of different world views (psychological orientation, manners of thinking, ways of behaving and interpreting events) are essentially ineffective. In effect, counselors must learn to accept the world views of others. The following characteristics are necessary to be a culturally effective counselor (Sue, 1978):

1. An ability to recognize which values and assumptions the counselor holds regarding the desirability or undesirability of human behavior;
2. Awareness of the generic characteristics of counseling that cut across many schools of counseling theory;
3. Understanding of the sociopolitical forces (oppression and racism) that have served to influence the identity and perspective of the culturally different;
4. An ability to share the world view of his or her clients without negating its legitimacy; and
5. True eclecticism in his or her counseling (p. 451).

Sue implied that counselors may use their entire repertoire of counseling skills as long as they are accepting of different views and are cognizant of the experiences and lifestyle of the culturally different. He emphasized that counselors must be alert to the influences of different views and environmental factors. Finally, counselors must be cautious not to impose their values on others.

Sue (1981) also developed a minority identity model that describes the psychosocial development of minority group members. Stages of development and transitions between stages are expressed in terms of the minority members' attitude toward self, others of the same minority, others of a different minority, and the dominant society or groups.

Stage 1. *Conformity*—the individual is self-deprecating and prefers to be identified with dominant cultural values.

Stage 2. *Dissonance*—the individual develops conflicts about the dominant system and is in a state of cultural confusion.

Stage 3. *Resistance and immersion*—the individual is more self-appreciating and rejects the dominant society.

Stage 4. *Introspection*—the individual carefully evaluates his or her attitude toward self and the dominant society.

Stage 5. *Synergetic articulation and awareness*—the individual accepts his or her cultural identity and develops selective appreciations of the dominant culture.

In addition to providing guidelines for career-guidance activities, this model also provides counselors with a greater understanding of the stress and adjustment problems of minorities and the role of environment and culture in minority identity development.

Axelson (1993) suggested basic points of awareness for improving counseling in a multicultural society, including cultural-total awareness, self-awareness, client awareness, and counseling procedure awareness. These basic points of awareness lead to focusing on the client's needs. Needs are most appropriately conceptualized from a broad base of human experiences to more discrete distinctions. The broad base of human experiences includes common human experiences, specific cultural experiences, individual experiences, and the unique individual. This approach to counseling in a multicultural society consists of four steps:

1. Recognize the fact that all human beings possess the like capacity for thought, feeling, and behavior.
2. Be knowledgeable in several cultures; study differences and similarities among people of different groups and their special needs and problems.
3. Gain an understanding of how the individual relates to important objects of motivation, what his or her personal constructs are, and how they form his or her world view.

4. Blend steps 1, 2, and 3 into an integrated picture of the distinctive person as experienced during the counseling process. (p. 18)

The counseling procedures outlined by Sue and Sue (1990) and Axelson (1993) suggest an awareness of the fact that when we counsel in a multicultural society, we are likely to have clients who have a distinctively different cultural background and thus different world views. A most important step is to recognize other world views and discover what those views might be in order to eventually arrive at a point where the uniqueness of the individual dictates the counseling-intervention strategies. In the next section, relational counseling focuses on realistic self-appraisals.

Relational Counseling

The major goal of relational counseling is to assist individuals in developing realistic self-images by focusing on positive aspects of self and relating these images to existing opportunities. Axelson (1993) suggested that individuals with self-doubts have difficulty projecting into a work environment with any degree of expectation for success. On the surface, such individuals may appear lazy or lacking ambition or motivation, but in reality, they are reacting to pessimistic expectations. Counseling can help these individuals alter their poor self-perceptions by emphasizing individual strengths and resources, highlighting resources in the community, and providing a positive approach to what can be accomplished within the boundaries of existing conditions, including labor trends and economic realities.

The focus of relational counseling is on *realistic* opportunities and conditions. Economic conditions, for example, should help shape the individual's perception of what can realistically be achieved in the working world. Specific techniques of relational counseling follow.

1. Identify and reinforce self-perceived qualities and accomplishments. Identify areas of desired improvement with accompanying short-term goals.
2. Point out that negative feelings are related to low expectations and may be a negative factor throughout a lifetime.
3. Practice positive visual imagery, such as imagining oneself in a successful job interview.
4. Validate self through identification with others, using role models from everyday life rather than celebrities. Emphasize characteristics such as honesty, forthrightness, and persistence.
5. Learn self-assertion skills, which increase self-respect.
6. Understand and use services and resources. Many minority group members are not aware of or question the credibility of these resources.
7. Disseminate knowledge and information through career guidance and education. Career guidance with a life-centered focus in the social context of "individual, family, culture, national, and international" should be available at all levels (p. 256).

Relational counseling focuses on the development of realistic self-appraisals, developing personal strengths, and expanding perceptions of occupational choices. Removing self-doubts that interfere with personal expectations is a major goal, accomplished through the identification and strengthening of personal abilities. The individuals' perception of life must be evaluated from environmental experiences, and negative factors are balanced by positive ones. Emphasizing positive experiences is an important method to reduce negative perceptions in mind-sets. Finally, social factors that influence values and attitudes, economic factors that impact an individual's career opportunities, political factors that impact special interests, and chance factors of events that are beyond one's control are to be emphasized in career-development counseling.

A Sample Counseling Component for Ethnic Groups

In considering the special problems and needs of ethnic groups, countless options for program objectives come to mind. Therefore, the following counseling component should not be considered a comprehensive counseling program that resolves all needs and special problems of ethnic groups but rather just one example of a counseling component that accomplishes only one of many possible objectives. This component illustrates how a counselor can assist members of various ethnic groups to take charge of their lives.

Rotter's (1966) concept of *locus of control* suggests that there are internal and external personality types. The locus of control for internal people is contingent on their behavior and their own characteristics; external people consider rewards and outcomes as independent of their actions and behavior. Putting it another way, internal people feel they can control their lives through their actions and behavior, whereas external people feel they have little control over their lives. Powell and Vega (1972) suggested that internal people generally have a good self-concept, are more independent and self-reliant, and show more initiative and effort in controlling their environment than do external people. Rotter postulated that a person's locus of control is highly related to the events in life and subsequent positive and negative reinforcements received. The following individual counseling sessions illustrate techniques to assist the culturally different individual in establishing greater feelings of control of life.

Rosalita, a 17-year-old Mexican American girl and a junior in high school, was referred to the counseling office when she indicated she planned to drop out of school to get a job. During the course of the interview, Rosalita indicated that she really felt powerless to change the direction of her life. She expressed despair when thinking in terms of her family situation because most of her older brothers and sisters had taken menial jobs and lived in the "barrio." Her feeling was that this was a matter of fate and there was little she could do about it. After looking over Rosalita's academic record, the counselor discovered that her grades were average and above. There were also indications from previous test data that Rosalita had the aptitude to continue with academic training beyond the high school level.

Counselor: Well, let's state it in more specific terms. How high do you think you could raise your grade?

Rosalita: I might be able to raise it to a B on my next paper.

Counselor: Okay, let's set that as a goal.

The day following Rosalita's meeting with her English teacher, she returned to the counselor's office very enthusiastic about the conference. She stated that the teacher was very cordial and had offered constructive criticism and encouragement. The counselor quickly made the point that this is one example of how individuals can control the outcomes of their lives if they are willing to take initiative to effect change.

The importance of this approach in counseling disadvantaged individuals is that it can provide them with concrete evidence that some control over their lives can be effected through their own actions. By arranging learning situations that prove individuals can gain control through appropriate action, specific behavior and subsequent outcomes are reinforced. As the individual recognizes alternatives to past unsuccessful behaviors, more internally oriented behavior can evolve.

PREVOCATIONAL TRAINING PROGRAM FOR ETHNIC GROUPS

A prevocational training program for adults of ethnic groups was launched at Southwest Texas State University. The program was designed to provide prevocational training to adults residing in small towns and rural areas within a 50-mile radius of the university. The major purpose of the program was to assist these adults to prepare for employment. The classes were held four hours each day, five days a week for six weeks. The class size ranged from 10 to 15 students.

The major components of the prevocational training program were adapted from two manuals, *Prevocational Training Manual* (1980) and *Career Orientation Manual* (1985), developed by the Texas Rehabilitation Commission and used for similar training programs within the state. The instruction involves lecture, group discussion, role playing, individual instruction, homework assignments, visitation, and audiovisual presentations. Table 16-1 delineates several of the components.

Orientation Component

The instructor is required to make advance preparations before each group of students enters the program. Most class members are individually interviewed and cumulative files are reviewed. This phase of the program is crucial in that the ground rules for class have to be firmly established. The important objec-

TABLE 16-1
Prevocational Training Program

Components	Class Periods	Activities
Orientation	2	Sharing of individual family history; setting goals and objectives; reinforcement of individual and group involvement
Exploring	5	Group discussion of self-image, self-worth, self-esteem, and locus of control; administer attitude scale; group discussions on self-assessments; role playing using stereotyped models; discussion groups relating self-concept to work
Communication skill and relationships	3	Role playing various situations using assertiveness training; role playing using listening skills with group discussion; reinforcement of appropriate behavior; client involvement in self-exploration of values toward others and work
Goal setting and problem solving	4	Discussion of time-management principles; self-exploration of goals; reinforcement of appropriate behavior; advising on individual goals and problems
Working parents' skills	1	Problem solving using daily chore schedule
Occupational information	5	Administer interest inventory; group discussion of results; field trip to university Career Development Resource Center; individual and group career exploration
Job interview skills	5	Role playing an interview; filling out job-application forms; advising on individual basis
Expectations in the world of work	4	Group discussion of employer expectations, employee expectations, and peer group affiliation
Consumer information	1	Discussion of budgeting principles; presentation of sample budget; review of wise use of credit and filling out a sample credit application form

tive here is to emphasize class attendance and participation in class projects. The students are encouraged to view the classes as if they were working at a job and were expected to be on time; that is, they are expected to attend regularly and to put forth a maximum effort.

Exploring Component

The exploring component is considered of major importance primarily because it is designed to improve the student's self-image. Many participants will have had very few positive experiences in their lives, particularly in work-related activities. This component is structured to promote a more positive attitude regarding their future work expectations. Group discussion is the major delivery system for accomplishing the learning and action objectives outlined for each student (*Prevocational Training Manual*, 1980):

1. Every person is unique and worthwhile and has important contributions to make to others.
2. How you feel about yourself determines to a large extent how you act and what you do.
3. Identify at least five things about yourself that you like and that will be helpful to you on a job.
4. Identify some things in yourself that you don't particularly like and would like to change.
5. Learn to use what you know about yourself to your best advantage. To do this, choose activities and goals in which the strengths you have are important and can be used well. Accept some of your weaknesses and choose activities in which those weaknesses are not very important. Decide to change some of your weaknesses (p. 15).

Other components provide students with the opportunity to identify their strengths and weaknesses as related to successful employment. Throughout the entire program, the students are encouraged to focus on effective behavior patterns necessary in maintaining employment and a productive lifestyle. The program focuses on future expectations. Many students may express that they feel powerless to change the direction of their lives and, in fact, feel they have very little control over their own lives. In an attempt to change these perceptions, modules were structured to emphasize that students should (1) accept more responsibility for their behavior, (2) become less dependent on others, (3) be more willing to correct their weaknesses, (4) be willing to experiment with new behaviors, (5) improve decision-making skills, (6) become more realistic in their aspirations, and (7) show more initiative and effort in controlling their environment.

The evaluation of the prevocational training program was accomplished through comparisons of pretest and posttest scores on an attitude scale developed by the TRC from *The Career Maturity Inventory* (Crites, 1978a), *The Locus of Control* (Rotter, 1966), and a follow-up of the graduates. The results of the pretest and posttest scores suggest that there was a significant change in the graduates' attitude toward making a career choice and entering the world of work. There was significant improvement in orientation toward work, independence in career decision-making tasks, and involvement in the career-decision process. A follow-up of the graduates of the program revealed that 78% were either attending other training programs or were actively seeking employment.

Group-Counseling Procedures: Communication Skills

The communication skills component has been selected to illustrate the group-counseling procedures and techniques used in this program. In this component, each counselee should be able to demonstrate (1) effective listening skills and the ability to express thoughts clearly and precisely, (2) effective methods of communicating in working situations, and (3) effective methods of communicating as a working parent. The following scenario demonstrates the techniques used to accomplish the first two objectives.

There are six participants: Sam, a 34-year-old African American male; Yolanda, a 27-year-old Mexican American female; Carla, a 24-year-old Mexican American female; Jane, a 30-year-old Caucasian female; Rod, a 32-year-old African American male; and Georgia, a 32-year-old African American female.

Session 1:

Objective: Each group member will be able to demonstrate effective listening skills.

Counselor: Carla, I would like you and Georgia to move to the center of the room. Now, Carla, you tell Georgia about two people you know, including their ages, how you met them, where they work, and anything else you can think of that would be of interest about the individuals. Georgia, I would like you to listen carefully to Carla's description of those individuals and try to remember as much as you can. The rest of the group is to observe both Carla and Georgia.

The counselor gave the group members a handout outlining listening skills to sharpen their observations. After Carla had described two individuals, the following exchange took place.

Sam: Hey, Georgia, why can't you look people in the eye when they are talking to you? That turns me off!
Yolanda: I agree! I don't like talking to people who don't pay attention.
Rod: Well, maybe she was listening—you know—but it was hard to tell.
Counselor: Carla, tell us how you felt.
Carla: I thought she was listening, but I wasn't sure. But anyway, I didn't think she was interested.
Georgia: I thought I was listening too! But maybe I didn't get that message across.

The counselor then asked the group to review what had been said. The following points were made and listed on the chalkboard: (1) Georgia did not maintain eye contact; (2) she tended to lean away from Carla; and (3) she seemed uninterested. The counselor had two other group members repeat the same procedure, which was followed by a more positive reaction from the group members.

Counselor: Now, let's think of some other listening skills that are important. Jane, can you give us another skill that you think is important?
Jane: Well, some people interrupt you too much. They just can't shut up.
Georgia: They just jump in and talk before thinking—like they don't understand you or have no feeling for you.
Sam: You can say that again—they judge before you can say much.
Counselor: That's good. Now, let's list some listening skills on the board.

Session 2:

Objective: Each group member will be able to demonstrate effective methods of listening and communicating in a working environment. This scenario includes the same group members.

Counselor:	Let's all pretend we are working in a factory where car radios are made. Our supervisor tells Yolanda that we are going to have to work all day next Saturday, which happens to be Thanksgiving weekend. Yolanda goes to Sam and tells him that the supervisor said we have to work next Saturday because the plant boss wants to show more profit. How would you respond, Sam?
Sam:	Man, I'd say they're off their rocker. I'd probably plan to call in sick because I'm going to see that football game on TV. More profit, what are they thinking about?
Carla:	We got our rights—they ought to remember that!
Yolanda:	Hey, and what about our families? Just to make more money isn't worth it!
Counselor:	Now, let's go back to the conversation between Jane and Yolanda. Remember the reason for working on Saturday was to make more profit. Did anyone think to check out this statement with the supervisor? Let's pretend that Yolanda checked out the story with the supervisor before she talked to Sam and found that the real reason for working on Saturday was that the major contractor with the factory had put in a special order. Now, Sam, how would you react?
Sam:	[after a brief pause] Well, I wouldn't like working on a Saturday, but this reason makes it easier.
Rod:	Those guys (major contractors) give us the bread—you know—we don't want to lose them.

The counselor then made the point that communication and listening skills were important factors for motivation and maintenance in the working environment.

Counselor:	All of you experienced a change of mind when the reason for working was properly communicated. Perhaps the supervisor did not make it clear to Yolanda, or maybe Yolanda wasn't listening.
Georgia:	Man, when you get things mixed up you sure can cause unnecessary trouble.
Jane:	I guess you have to listen to get it straight.
Sam:	Yeah, and you better talk straight too!

The counselor followed this exercise by having group members pretend they were a supervisor delivering a message to the group concerning change of policies, announcement of new regulations, and other relevant topics. The group members were required to repeat the most important parts of the announcement. Each member was provided with reinforcement of his or her listening and communicating skills by the group and the counselor.

ASSESSMENT OF ETHNIC GROUPS

The controversy surrounding the use of standardized tests to evaluate ethnic groups has intensified in recent years. One of the major arguments is that most standardized assessment instruments are discriminatory because they have been developed from data based on White male middle-class values, beliefs, attitudes, and experiences. Norms for tests based on these data do not account for the cultural distinctions of ethnic groups. More recently, the use of intelligence tests in evaluating and classifying ethnic groups has been attacked. Some educators claim that African Americans and other members of ethnic groups are frequently mislabeled by intelligence tests and are placed in classes for slow learners (Samuda, 1975, p. 13).

The Association of Black Psychologists, at its annual meeting in 1969, charged that tests (1) label African American children as uneducable, (2) place them in special classes, (3) potentiate inferior education, (4) assign African American children to lower educational tracks than Caucasians, (5) deny African Americans higher educational opportunities, and (6) destroy positive intellectual growth in their development (Williams, 1971).

There is considerable disagreement as to the cause of intelligence-test score deficits. The hereditarian argues that genes are the cause, whereas the environmentalist argues that cultural isolation is a primary reason (Samuda, 1975, p. 45). This ongoing debate has directed attention to the use of all standardized tests and assessment inventories used for ethnic groups. Some of the most common concerns are discussed in the following paragraphs. This discussion will be followed by a brief review of several selected tests and inventories that have been developed for certain racial groups and minorities.

Pollack and Menacker (1971) suggested that test results can be useful for Puerto Rican students in terms of measuring their rate of progress rather than comparing the scores to data in the test manual. They suggested that local norms should be developed in schools where there are large numbers of Spanish-speaking students. Of particular significance is the counselor's responsibility to make certain that Spanish-speaking students are familiar with test-taking requirements such as time limits, how to record answers, and how to follow other essential directions. The reading level of all tests and inventories should be checked carefully to make certain that Spanish-speaking individuals are able to comprehend the questions.

Vontress (1971) suggested that the usefulness of test results for African Americans is circumscribed by the limiting effects of cultural isolation; that is, they tend to be less verbal, have fewer educational opportunities, be less motivated to do well on tests, and be generally less conforming to middle-class standards. He warned that counselors should be very alert to the reading level of tests or inventories used for African Americans because a common problem is reading proficiency. He also suggested that counseling programs be established to encourage African Americans to do well on tests.

Feck (1971) recommended that if standardized tests are to be used, considerable effort should be spent on familiarizing culturally different students with test format and test-taking procedures. A partial list of his overall recommendations for using test results for the disadvantaged follows.

1. Tests might be used as standardized instruments to observe and record behavior related to processes involved in responding to items.
2. Paper-and-pencil tests that require interpretation of writing in order to respond seem unsuited for the socially disadvantaged.
3. The nature and norms of personality inventories seem to render them of little value with youngsters who are predominantly from lower classes.
4. Use of performance tests whenever possible is best, since these appear to be less affected by the vocabulary of the disadvantaged students.
5. Perhaps fewer tests, selected for specific purposes and used analytically in individual sessions with students, would be more helpful (p. 20).

Test publishers of certain standardized tests that predict future performance are now required to make public their studies on validity, release test questions and correct answers to students who have taken a test, and provide information concerning the meaning of test scores and how the results will be reported. These issues point out the growing concern for the use of standardized tests in general and focus greater attention on the issues surrounding the use of standardized tests with various ethnic groups.

The solutions to these issues will no doubt occupy the research efforts of numerous individuals in the counseling profession in the future. In the meantime, counselors have the option of using tests and inventories designed for certain racial and ethnic groups; representative examples of these instruments are provided in the following section.

U.S. Employment Service (USES) Tests for the Culturally Different

Since the mid-1930s, USES and the training administration of the U.S. Department of Labor have been involved in test development and research. Since the mid-1960s, the major emphasis has been toward developing tests for the culturally different. One of their major goals was to develop a nonreaders' edition of the *General Aptitude Test Battery (GATB)*. In the early 1970s, research priorities were directed toward developing specific aptitude tests and pretesting orientation techniques for the culturally different (Division of Testing Staff, USES, 1978).

After ten years of research, USES produced several aptitude tests and related publications designed to expand occupational and educational training programs for the educationally deficient. Research efforts attempted to assure test fairness; that is, the aim was to provide illiterate, bilingual, or educationally deficient individuals with an equal opportunity to demonstrate their abilities. Of these tests, the *Nonverbal Aptitude Test Battery (NATB)* is a measure of aptitudes of individuals unable to take the *GATB* because of an inability to read. This test measures the same aptitudes as the *GATB* (intelligence, verbal, numerical, spatial, form perception, clerical perception, motor coordination, finger dexterity, and manual dexterity).

Another test developed by USES, the *Specific Aptitude Test Batteries*, measures an individual's potential to acquire skills needed in specific occupations. Separate norms for minority groups have been developed for more effective use of these tests.

A *Basic Occupational Literacy Test (BOLT)* is a measure of achievement for reading and arithmetic. The four parts of this test (reading vocabulary, reading comprehension, arithmetic computation, and arithmetic reasoning) are easily related to general educational development requirements of jobs. The four levels of the test measure achievement for grades 1 through 11.

A Spanish edition of the *GATB, Bateria de Examenes de Aptitud General (BEAG)*, has also been published. This edition may be used for all Spanish-speaking individuals.

USES has developed several publications designed to orient the culturally different to test-taking techniques, among them: *Doing Your Best on Aptitude Tests* (Spanish and English), *Group Pretesting Orientation on the Purpose of Testing* (Spanish and English), *Doing Your Best on Reading and Arithmetic Tests*, and *Pretesting Orientation Exercises*.

Although the USES tests were developed primarily for public employment-service systems, they are available for release to some agencies. Counselors may develop cooperative arrangements with state employment systems for the purpose of referring clients for testing. Tests are also released to agencies for use in counseling and research. The following are examples of other tests and inventories that may be used to assist the culturally different in career exploration.

The Adult Basic Learning Examination (ABLE)
The Psychological Corporation
555 Academic Court
San Antonio, TX 78204-2498

ABLE was designed to measure the general educational level of adults who have not completed high school. Three levels of the test measure achievement in vocabulary, reading, spelling, and arithmetic. Norms are available for job-corps trainees and adults enrolled in basic-education courses.

Escala de Inteligencia Wechsler para Niños
The Psychological Corporation
555 Academic Court
San Antonio, TX 78204-2498

A Spanish-American translation of the *Wechsler Intelligence Scale for Children*, developed in Puerto Rico, yields three IQ scores—verbal, performance, and full-scale. Norms are available for several Puerto Rican groups.

Tests of General Ability
Science Research Associates
155 Wacker Drive
Chicago, IL 60606

These tests are appropriate for students from culturally deprived backgrounds as a measure of general intelligence and basic learning ability. All items are pictorial, and the examiners' manual has been translated into Spanish. One part of the test measures the individual's ability to recognize relationships and understand meanings and basic concepts. The second part of the test measures reasoning ability.

> *Chicago Nonverbal Examination*
> The Psychological Corporation
> 555 Academic Court
> San Antonio, TX 78204-2498

This is an intelligence test designed specifically for individuals with reading difficulties or those who have been reared in a foreign language environment. The test is administered with either verbal directions or pantomime directions. Standardization sample includes 70% White and 30% foreign-born students.

> *Test de Aptitud Diferencial*
> The Psychological Corporation
> 555 Academic Court
> San Antonio, TX 78204-2498

This is an authorized translation of the *Differential Aptitude Test* for use with Latin Americans. Its coverage includes verbal reasoning, numerical ability, abstract reasoning, space relations, mechanical reasoning, clerical speed and accuracy, and language usage.

> *California Occupational Preference Survey*
> Educational and Industrial Testing Service
> P.O. Box 7234
> San Diego, CA 92107

This test has been translated into Spanish and is primarily designed to assist individuals in defining broad areas of interest.

> *Geist Picture Interest Inventory for Men, Spanish Edition*
> Western Psychological Services
> 12031 Wilshire Boulevard
> Los Angeles, CA 90025

An interest inventory for Spanish-speaking and bilingual males. The interest areas are depicted by occupational activities. The general interest areas assessed are persuasive, clerical, mechanical, musical, scientific, outdoors, literary, computational, artistic, social service, and dramatic.

SUMMARY

1. Many Asian American ethnic groups place a high value on education. Asian Americans tend to inhibit emotional expression; many do not actively participate in counseling programs. In general, Asian Americans are reluctant to

admit personal problems because of their cultural conditioning. Asian Americans tend to misinterpret the role of counseling and its potential benefits.

2. The largest racial minority in this country is African Americans. Culturally different African Americans tend to remain social isolates in church, school, and employment.

3. The second largest minority group in this country is Hispanic Americans. General cultural characteristics of Hispanic Americans appear to distinguish them as the least Americanized of the ethnic groups. The Hispanic American family is typically a closely knit group that greatly influences the value systems of its members.

4. Native Americans are culturally conditioned to view life from a different perspective. Native Americans are generally not motivated to achieve status through the accumulation of wealth. The lifestyle of most Native Americans is extremely democratic, and their culture promotes egalitarianism.

5. The vocational perspectives of the urban poor are considered to be severely restricted. Learning attitudes and motivation to achieve are often adversely affected by home and other environmental factors. Beliefs, values, and attitudes that develop from poor environmental situations are often counterproductive.

6. The rural culturally different have limited resources in social and recreational activities and health services, and limited educational experiences and exposure to vocational role models.

7. Essential counseling components for various ethnic groups include frequent rewards and reinforcements of positive behavior. Operationally, the counselor presents short-term plans and gradually introduces plans for the future.

8. Effective counselors have knowledge of and are sensitive to different cultural orientations when establishing rapport in counseling relationships. To be effective with culturally different populations, counselors must be aware of different world views (the psychological orientation of thinking, behavior, and interpretation of events). Counselors must be cautious not to impose their values on others.

9. An effective model of minority development provides guidelines for career-guidance activities designed to meet the needs of the culturally different in terms of their adjustment to the dominant culture. The model should also provide counselors with a greater understanding of adjustment problems of minorities.

10. Relational counseling focuses on developing realistic self-appraisals, personal strengths, and perceptions of occupational choices. The individual's perception of life must be evaluated from environmental experiences, and negative factors are balanced by positive ones.

11. Prevocational training programs for adults include components designed to develop and improve self-image, communication skills, goal-setting and problem-solving techniques, working-parent skills, job-interview skills, and expectations of the world of work.

12. Interpretation and use of assessment inventories for the culturally different remains a controversial issue. One of the major arguments is that most

standardized assessment instruments are discriminatory, primarily because they have been developed from data based on White male middle-class values, beliefs, attitudes, and experiences. Recent controversies concerning the use of standardized tests have focused on the use of standardized tests with the culturally different.

13. The descriptive characteristics relative to the culturally different cannot be generalized to all members of any group. However, homogeneity is greater within groups than among them.

SUPPLEMENTARY LEARNING EXERCISES

1. Develop profiles for culturally different urban and rural teenagers. Compare differences and similarities of needs.
2. By interview and visitation, two or more class members may develop a description of the environmental conditions and home atmosphere of an individual living in a barrio or poor urban neighborhood.
3. Using the description in the chapter, describe how the environmental conditions of the urban poor discourage positive motivation and constructive actions.
4. Develop a scenario and script depicting a family in a poor urban area having a conversation about their work experience for the day and/or week. Have your classmates take notes on how such conversation influences children's perception of work.
5. Using the barriers to employment listed on p. 394, develop two or more counseling strategies to help members of various ethnic groups remove barriers.
6. Describe how you would help a culturally different individual overcome distrust and suspicion of counselors and authority figures.
7. Develop counseling strategies for two or more of the components of the prevocational training program for adults described in this chapter.
8. Write a review of two or more of the tests or inventories listed in the "Assessment of Ethnic Groups" section of this chapter.
9. In the following reference, read Chapter 2, "The Culture of the Counselor," and summarize the major points made about the ethics, training, and professional dimensions of the professional counselor.

   Axelson, John A. (1993). *Counseling and development in a multicultural society* (2nd ed.). Pacific Grove, CA: Brooks/Cole.

10. In the following reference, read pages 567–584 on the subject of other approaches to testing minority-group members. Summarize your findings.

    Kaplan, Robert M., & Saccuzzo, Dennis P. (1993). *Psychological testing: Principles, applications, and issues* (3rd ed.). Pacific Grove, CA: Brooks/Cole.

Chapter 17

Career Counseling for Individuals with Disabilities

Rehabilitation services and special-education programs on career counseling for persons with disabilities have recently received considerable attention. Innovative career-related educational programs and counseling strategies have been developed to assist disabled individuals in making the best possible life/work adjustment. The major emphasis in these programs is to maximize each individual's potential for employment. Career-counseling programs for individuals with disabilities have elements in common with traditional career-counseling programs. However, the diversity of needs requires specially designed assessment instruments, career-counseling techniques, materials, and career-related educational-training programs.

The terms used to describe people with disabilities have been changed to negate stereotypes and false ideas. The major objection was the labeling of individuals with demeaning names. For example, a spastic does not describe a person but refers to a muscle with sudden involuntary spasms. It is much more acceptable to think of a disability as a condition that interferes with an individual's ability to do something independent such as walk, see, hear, or learn. Thus, it is preferable to say "people with disabilities" rather than "the disabled"; "Joe is a wheelchair user," not "confined to a wheelchair"; "hearing impaired" rather than "deaf-mute"; and "persons with mental retardation" rather than "the mentally retarded." The focus should be on the unique identity of a person as opposed to a label that implies that everyone with that particular label is alike and has a separate status. A person's identity should be an individual matter that focuses on a unique condition, and the words we use should convey this message.

The first section of this chapter focuses on the Americans with Disabilities Act (ADA). The second section describes special problems and needs of individuals with disabilities. Implications for career guidance and the role of state rehabilitation agencies are then discussed. An actual counseling case of an individual with a disability who sought services from a state rehabilitation agency is described in the next section. A career education program for students with disabilities is covered in the next section, followed by a description of a group-counseling program for individuals with disabilities who have been hospitalized. Finally, assessment instruments for individuals with disabilities are discussed.

THE AMERICANS WITH DISABILITIES ACT

The Americans with Disabilities Act (ADA), signed into law on July 26, 1990, is a comprehensive law. For example, Title III regulations require public accommodations (including private entities that own, operate, or lease to places of public accommodation), commercial facilities, and private entities to make reasonable modifications of policies, practices, and procedures that deny equal access to individuals with disabilities. Table 17-1 provides an overview of requirements in public accomodations.

The ADA identifies individuals with disabilities as follows:

- An individual with a disability is a person who
  has a physical or mental impairment that substantially limits one or more "major life activities," or
  has a record of such an impairment, or
  is regarded as having such an impairment.

TABLE 17-1
Americans with Disabilities Act
Requirements in Public Accommodations Fact Sheet

General
- Public accommodations such as restaurants, hotels, theaters, doctors' offices, pharmacies, retail stores, museums, libraries, parks, private schools, and day-care centers may not discriminate on the basis of disability. Private clubs and religious organizations are exempt.
- Reasonable changes in policies, practices, and procedures must be made to avoid discrimination.

Auxiliary aids
- Auxiliary aids and services must be provided to individuals with vision or hearing impairments or other individuals with disabilities, unless an undue burden would result.

Physical barriers
- Physical barriers in existing facilities must be removed, if removal is readily achievable. If not, alternative methods of providing the services must be offered, if they are readily achievable.
- All new construction in public accommodations, as well as in "commercial facilities" such as office buildings, must be accessible. Elevators are generally not required in buildings under three stories or with fewer than 3,000 square feet per floor, unless the building is a shopping center, mall, or a professional office of a health care provider.
- Alterations must be accessible. When alterations to primary function areas are made, an accessible path of travel to the altered area (and the bathrooms, telephones, and drinking fountains serving that area) must be provided to the extent that the added accessibility costs are not disproportionate to the overall cost of the alterations. Elevators are required as described above.

SOURCE: U.S. Department of Justice, Civil Rights Division, *Coordination and Review Section*, 1991.

- Examples of physical or mental impairments include, but are not limited to, such contagious and noncontagious diseases and conditions as orthopedic, visual, speech, and hearing impairments; cerebral palsy, epilepsy, muscular dystrophy, multiple sclerosis, cancer, heart disease, diabetes, mental retardation, emotional illness, specific learning disabilities, HIV disease (whether symptomatic or asymptomatic), tuberculosis, drug addiction, and alcoholism. Homosexuality and bisexuality are not physical or mental impairments under the ADA.
- "Major life activities" include functions such as caring for oneself, performing manual tasks, walking, seeing, hearing, speaking, breathing, learning, and working.
- Individuals who currently engage in the illegal use of drugs are not protected by the ADA when an action is taken on the basis of their current illegal use of drugs. (*Americans with Disabilities Act Handbook*, 1991, pp. 3–4)

Of interest to the career counselor are the ADA's requirements concerning employment of individuals with disabilities and transportation accessibility. Table 17-2 includes a fact sheet prepared by the U.S. Department of Justice on employment and transportation requirements and the dates on which these requirements are effective.

One of the major issues covered in this act is employment discrimination. The ADA prohibits discrimination in all employment practices including job application, hiring, firing, advancement, compensation, training, and other terms and conditions of employment. Also included are advertising for employment, fringe benefits, and tenure. However, employers are free to select the most-qualified applicant available and to make decisions based on reasons unrelated to a disability. For example, two individuals may apply for a typist job and one is able to accurately type more words per minute. Thus, the employer can hire the better typist even though that particular person does not have a disability and the other does. The key to such decisions appears to center around job-performance needs, and in this case, typing speed is needed for successful performance of the job.

Other subjects covered in the ADA that may be of interest to the career counselor are job descriptions, job-application forms, job-application process, interviews, testing and medical examinations, hiring decisions, benefits, working conditions, raises and promotions, and reasonable accommodations. More information about the ADA can be obtained at the following address:

Office on the Americans with Disabilities Act
Civil Rights Division
U.S. Department of Justice
P.O. Box 66118
Washington, DC 20035-6118

TABLE 17-2
Americans with Disabilities Act Requirements Fact Sheet

Employment

- Employers may not discriminate against an individual with a disability in hiring or promotion if the person is otherwise qualified for the job.

- Employers can ask about one's ability to perform a job, but cannot inquire if someone has a disability or subject a person to tests that tend to screen out people with disabilities.

- Employers will need to provide "reasonable accommodation" to individuals with disabilities.This includes steps such as job restructuring and modification of equipment.

- Employers do not need to provide accommodations that impose an "undue hardship" on business operations.

Who needs to comply:

- All employers with 25 or more employees must comply, effective July 26, 1992.

- All employers with 15–24 employees must comply, effective July 26, 1994.

Transportation

- New public transit buses ordered after August 26, 1990, must be accessible to individuals with disabilities.

- Transit authorities must provide comparable paratransit or other special transportation services to individuals with disabilities who cannot use fixed route bus services, unless an undue burden would result.

- Existing rail systems must have one accessible car per train by July 26, 1995.

- New rail cars ordered after August 26, 1990, must be accessible.

- New bus and train stations must be accessible.

- Key stations in rapid, light, and commuter rail systems must be made accessible by July 26, 1993, with extensions up to 20 years for commuter rail (30 years for rapid and light rail).

- All existing Amtrak stations must be accessible by July 26, 2010.

SOURCE: U.S. Department of Justice, Civil Rights Division, *Coordination and Review Section*, 1991.

SPECIAL PROBLEMS AND NEEDS OF INDIVIDUALS WITH DISABILITIES

The problems and needs associated with disability are inclusive and pervasive. Career counselors address adjustment problems associated with disability as well as career choice and career-development factors. The severity of functional limitations and the individual's adjustment to his or her limitations are the most important factors to consider in career counseling. The special problems and needs of disabled individuals discussed in this section should be considered as representative examples from a diverse population.

Adjustment

Individuals whose disabilities result from physical trauma may have difficulty adjusting to and accepting disability, which may interfere with motivation to seek retraining and employment. Cook (1981) postulated that individuals may experience shock, depression, and denial before accepting and adjusting to a disability. Psychological denial of a disability is discussed frequently in rehabilitation literature. Failure to accept its limitations can impede counseling assistance; the individual will not be open to retraining or experiences provided by rehabilitation agencies or educational institutions.

Wright (1983) contended that individuals with physical disabilities are given an inferior status position in our society. The frustrations produced from a physical disability can be accompanied by shame and feelings of inferiority. The acceptance of one's physical condition is often linked with one's total self-esteem. Careful consideration is to be given to the sources of poor self-concept, ways of reacting to physical disability, and ways of adjusting to it.

Attitudinal Barriers

Individuals who are labeled *handicapped* or *disabled* face attitudinal barriers to employment. Employers are reluctant to hire individuals with disabilities because of erroneous assumptions: more sick leave will be required, insurance rates will be affected, safety on the job will be endangered, and plant modifications will be mandatory. The mentally retarded are especially considered to need constant supervision and are perceived as incapable of learning. In general, employers have stereotyped views of individuals with disabilities, resulting in discrimination (Daniels, 1981).

Wright (1980) suggested that one of the most successful methods of improving employers' hiring attitudes is through placement of individuals with disabilities who turn out to be successful workers. An advocacy role through personal contact with potential employers is also an effective method for building positive attitudes. The importance of the advocacy role in career counseling is underscored by Neff (1985), who contended that individuals with disabilities face an impressive array of negative social attitudes, prejudice, and other social barriers.

Generalizations Formed as a Result of Being Labeled Disabled or Handicapped

Being identified as disabled or handicapped may limit access to the job market. For example, the label *amputee* may conjure up an image of someone who has lost a leg because of amputation and is severely restricted. Another individual who has had successful open heart surgery may be perceived as sickly and weak. Such generalizations inhibit opportunities for employment, especially in the case of individuals who have minor functional limitations because of an amputation and/or illness. The career counselor should emphasize that each individual is to be judged on his or her own merits; a disability is only one individual characteristic to be considered in the employment process.

Lack of Models and Norm Groups

The current lack of visibility of individuals with physical disabilities working successfully in a broad spectrum of career fields may reinforce low self-esteem and negative attitudes about labor-market potential. Standardized tests and inventories are not always normed for the physically disabled, resulting in conflicting or misleading assumptions concerning employment potential.

Kriegel (1982) addressed problems of societal acceptance of individuals with disabilities. He suggested that they are often perceived as second-class citizens, and he contended that society ignores the reality of the disabled: "The terms of our visibility have been created not by us but by those who see what they want to see rather than what is there" (p. 55). Kriegel also appealed to individuals with disabilities to learn to accept their disability and to make the most of their assets. Those who have accomplished these goals are good role models.

Onset of Disability

The age at which a disability occurs is a relevant factor to be considered in career counseling. Stone and Gregg (1981) suggested that the effects of a child-hood disability can result in parental and/or community overprotection. In early onset of a disability, an individual's exposure to occupations is limited and career development is usually delayed. The type of disability is also a factor for consideration; for example, Bolton (1973) reported that deaf adolescents are more limited in career development than hearing adolescents.

Early onset of disability may greatly influence career choice. For example, juvenile diabetes may later result in heart disease or visual impairment that could limit an individual's ability to function in occupations requiring keen vision and/or physical exertion (Stone & Gregg, 1981). Finally, Smith and Chemers (1981) suggested that individuals may be deficient in assertiveness and in independence if they have experienced early onset of a disability.

Onset of disability in adulthood often requires career counselors to introduce the process of career redevelopment. By assessing the realities of their functional limitations, individuals may be required to change career direction. In sum, later onset of disability may (1) have disturbing effects on personal adjustment (Joiner & Fisher, 1977), (2) be related to lower levels of educational or vocational aspirations (Thurer, 1980), and (3) be related to indecisiveness in career choice, especially with individuals whose medical conditions will be improved or stabilized in the future (Roessler & Rubin, 1982).

Social/Interpersonal Skills

Persons with disabilities have special needs, including a restrictive view of career opportunities. Misconceptions about disabilities have limited intervention strategies that would usually be considered in career-development theories (Curnow, 1989) such as social skills training. Fine and Asch (1988) suggested that social and psychological problems for persons with disabilities should receive greater or at least equal attention as the disability itself.

Individuals with disabilities tend to limit their social lives to interactions with other persons with disabilities. She suggested that they are reluctant to develop friendships outside the disabled community. Positive reinforcement received from peer groups is especially important. Strategies to assist these individuals to develop more inclusive interpersonal relationships is an important counseling component.

Self-Concept

Roessler and Bolton (1978) contended that disability conditions have the potential of creating a poor self-concept. Individuals with disabilities tend to report lower self-esteem. A life associated with constant rejection and being labeled as different can potentially create a poor self-image. "Who am I?" may indeed be a difficult question to answer positively. Our goal in this context is to assist individuals in accurately assessing strengths and weaknesses in order to help them modify their self-perceptions. Programs that include components to help develop positive self-images are of critical importance in meeting the needs of these individuals.

Skills for Independent Living

Individuals with disabilities need special help in developing skills for independent living. For some, the greatest problem is learning to accept limitations that may restrict their ability to become fully independent. For others, increasing their desire to be independent may be the counseling challenge. In essence, some individuals may be unrealistic about their ability to be fully independent, while others may lack the motivation to become independent, preferring to maintain their dependence on others.

The following special problems and needs were compiled from *Barriers and Bridges* (California Advisory Council on Vocational Education, 1977):

1. Architectural barriers place limits on the mobility of the orthopedically disabled. Inaccessible transportation, training, and workplaces will eventually be overcome by legislation, but progress is slow.

2. Employers' bias and reluctance to hire the disabled limit placement opportunities.

3. There is a lack of trained personnel in vocational education to deal effectively with special problems of the disabled.

4. The general public's lack of knowledge concerning the needs and problems of the disabled creates barriers for employment.

5. Families of the disabled, who are often the main source of physical and psychological support, often fail to understand the problems and needs of the

physically disabled. Without professional training, family members may find it difficult to determine whether to foster acceptance of limitations or motivation for independence.

IMPLICATIONS FOR CAREER GUIDANCE

The problems associated with the career development of individuals with disabilities exemplifies the need for career counselors to adopt advocacy roles. In addition to directly assisting the client with physical disabilities, career counselors should support community education and training programs to foster acceptance in the work world. Programs that assist educators, families, and employees in working with individuals with disabilities can be invaluable in reducing the physical and psychological barriers that currently exist. People with disabilities face negative attitudes, prejudice, discrimination, and other social barriers. As a consequence, counseling programs should provide more positive roles and role models. Developing positive self-images and interpersonal relationship skills are important counseling components. Finally, the role of an advocate implies considerable dedication to removing social barriers and to providing supportive counseling.

REHABILITATION PROGRAMS

This section focuses on programs for individuals with disabilities sponsored by state rehabilitation agencies and on rehabilitation centers sponsored by the private sector.

State Rehabilitation Agencies

State rehabilitation agencies provide career counseling and other services to individuals who meet two eligibility requirements: (1) the person must have a disability that results in a substantial handicap to employment, and (2) vocational rehabilitation services must reasonably be expected to benefit the person in terms of employability (Texas Rehabilitation Commission, 1984). The disabling conditions among populations served by state agencies are extensive and inclusive. Rehabilitation services have been extended to individuals with mental illness, orthopedic problems, mental retardation, visual and hearing problems, circulatory problems, amputation of limbs, and other disabling conditions, such as alcoholism, cancer, epilepsy, kidney disease, multiple sclerosis, muscular dystrophy, and cerebral palsy (Porter, 1981).

   To meet the needs of such a diverse group of individuals, state rehabilitation agencies have developed numerous and varied programs designed to assist individuals reentering the work force and/or maintaining their chosen occupation. Parker and Hansen (1981) have compiled a list of services provided by state rehabilitation agencies: (1) counseling and guidance; (2) medical and psychological evaluation; (3) physical and mental restoration services; (4) prevocational evaluation and retraining; (5) vocational and other training services; (6) expense allowances; (7) transportation; (8) interpretive services for the deaf; (9) reader, orientation, and mobility services for the blind; (10) prostheses and other technical aids and devices; (11) work adjustment and placement counseling, (12) job-placement services; (13) occupational license, tools, equipment, and so forth; and (14) other goods and services to benefit the client in achieving employability.

Privately Supported Rehabilitation Agencies

Among the most widely known, privately sponsored, nonprofit rehabilitation agencies are Goodwill Industries, Salvation Army, Jewish Vocational Services, St. Vincent De Paul Society, National Society for Crippled Children and Adults, United Cerebral Palsy Association, Volunteers of America, and Deseret Industries. Although there are a diversity of programs sponsored by these organizations and other national, state, and local private rehabilitation agencies, Goodwill Industries of America serves as a good example of a national network of programs for individuals with disabilities. Lewis (1977) suggested that Goodwill Industries of America is generally recognized as the world's leading privately sponsored agency for training individuals and with facilities for individuals with disabilities.

Local Goodwill Industries are autonomous, having their own board of directors, and are affiliated with the national organization, Goodwill Industries of America of Bethesda, Maryland. A wide range of activities are conducted by Goodwill Industries, including classroom instruction, sheltered workshops, encounter sessions, therapy (physical, occupational, or speech), counseling, and placement. Many of the Goodwill Industries collect donated clothing, furniture, household goods and appliances, books, art objects, radios, and televisions for repairing, refurbishing, and rebuilding by individuals with disabilities. These items are sold in a network of bargain retail outlets. Subcontracting with private industries and with state and federal governmental agencies for assembling and manufacturing of goods, janitorial, grounds maintenance, and other services is another method used by Goodwill Industries to provide jobs.

Goodwill Industries also provide educational skills-training programs. For example, Goodwill Industry of San Antonio provides the following services: psychological testing, vocational evaluation, personal and social adjustment, work adjustment, prevocational training, special academic instruction, therapeutic recreation, skills training, and job placement. The individualized services offered by this agency are funded from service fees charged to referring agencies such as the Texas Rehabilitation Commission, the Commission for the Blind, local independent school districts, the City of San Antonio Manpower Consortium, the Veteran's Administration, and private insurance firms.

Most age groups can be served by privately supported, nonprofit rehabilitation agencies. Services include provisions for assistive devices such as artificial limbs, braces, wheelchairs, glasses, and hearing aids. Assistance is also given to help individuals develop independent living skills through programs in which individuals share supervised apartments. The Salvation Army and Volunteers of America have emphasized programs for homeless individuals with alcohol or psychological problems (Nelson, 1971).

Career counselors need to be aware of the goals, objectives, and services of private rehabilitation agencies in their community or local area. Programs that help prepare individuals with disabilities for employment (such as work-adjustment seminars, prevocational classes, personal counseling, medical management, and mobility training) are valuable referral resources for career counselors. Sheltered workshops, supported by a number of private rehabilitation agencies, provide a workplace for individuals who are unable to meet work requirements in the competitive job market. Career counseling for disabled individuals is greatly enhanced through a wide variety of programs offered by rehabilitation programs supported by the private sector.

COUNSELING PROGRAM: A CASE STUDY

The following is an actual case of an individual who received rehabilitation services from a state agency. Names, dates, and other information have been changed to protect client confidentiality. This example illustrates rehabilitation services provided by a state agency in a small town of about 25,000 people. The following steps in the rehabilitation process are covered in this case: (1) initial contact, (2) diagnostic workup, (3) evaluation and certification, (4) vocational assessment, (5) service planning, (6) placement, and (7) postemployment services.

Initial Contact

The purposes of the initial contact are to establish a counseling relationship, provide the client with information about the state agency, and obtain information from the client to determine eligibility for rehabilitation services. In this case, Sam, the rehabilitation counselor, interviewed the client to obtain personal/social information, educational background, past work experiences, physical limitations, and financial needs. Excerpts from the case file are used to illustrate examples of information recorded from the initial contact.

Dora was a self-referred high school graduate and had never received rehabilitation services. She was 40 years old, divorced for approximately three years, and had two children. Her older child was married and living nearby, but the younger had chosen to live with her. Dora had married at age 18 and had lived in several cities and states with her salesman husband. Sam noted in his report that her mood was very flat and that she seemed remorseful and lethargic. She became extremely emotional when she referred to her marriage, stating, "I resent that my husband left me because of my arthritis."

Dora reported that she had suffered serious problems with arthritis for the past ten years, requiring five surgical procedures on her hands. During the interview, she demonstrated lack of finger flexibility and restricted hand mobility. She was taking two prescribed medications.

Dora's only source of income was $600 monthly child support, and she had no savings. She was unable to insure her 5-year-old automobile, and her current rent and utility bills totaled $310. Dora's work experience was very limited; she had worked as a teacher's aide for approximately nine months but was unemployed at the present time.

Sam decided that Dora was a good candidate for rehabilitation services and had her fill out an official request form. She was then scheduled for a medical and psychological evaluation. Sam had to verify reported physical problems, and he wanted a full report on potential psychological disturbances associated with the emotional instability he had observed. Sam also requested reports of previous medical diagnosis and treatment.

Diagnostic Workup

The orthopedist's report indicated that Dora had a severe case of rheumatoid arthritis. After carefully studying the medical report, Sam arrived at the following functional limitations and vocational handicaps.

1. Can stand for short periods of time only	1. Orthopedic report from Dr. Bone
2. Unable to lift anything over 10 lbs. on a repetitive basis	2. Orthopedic report from Dr. Bone
3. Unable to push or pull	3. Client's statement
4. Cannot bend for prolonged periods	4. Client's statement
5. Has limited finger dexterity	5. Orthopedic report from Dr. Bone

The psychological report discussed results of intelligence, achievement, personality, and several aptitude tests. Sam summarized Dora's assets from the psychological evaluations as follows:

1. Normal intelligence
2. Good clerical skills
3. Ability to learn and retain new information
4. Good reading skills
5. Good oral expressive skills
6. Average academic achievement for her educational level
7. Potential for college-level training

In addition, Sam summarized Dora's limitations as follows:

1. Diagnosed as depressive reaction
2. Poor self-concept
3. Lacks confidence
4. Subject to mood swings
5. Limited work history

6. Poor manual dexterity
7. Easily fatigued

Evaluation and Certification

After reviewing medical and psychological reports, Sam approved Dora's request for rehabilitative services. The results of her disability as well as the degree of her handicap were evaluated. In this case, her physical disability was considered severe enough to merit services. Psychological problems associated with the depressive reaction would also be considered in planning services for her. In developing a rehabilitation plan, Sam was required to address all services that would help Dora reach her rehabilitation goal. Dora was notified of her acceptance, and an appointment was set for the following day.

In preparation for the next counseling appointment, Sam carefully reviewed the material that had accumulated in Dora's file. He paid particular attention to medical problems resulting in functional limitations. The psychological report clearly indicated that Dora would need supportive counseling. However, he decided that his first goal was to establish a vocational objective.

Vocational Assessment

In the counseling sessions that followed, limitations and assets were thoroughly discussed. Although Dora had strongly considered teaching as a vocational objective, she agreed that an interest inventory would help verify her interests and introduce other career considerations. Dora was given a computer-scored inventory, and a date was set for the next counseling session.

The vocational assessment phase of the rehabilitation process continued with an interpretation and discussion of interest inventory results and the test data contained in the psychological report. Dora decided that she would like to explore a career in either elementary school teaching or social work. With these two careers in mind, Sam directed her to references describing these occupations in detail. Dora spent considerable time reviewing job descriptions and requirements. At Sam's suggestion, she made on-site visits to a school and a social welfare agency. Shortly after these visits, Dora decided that she would prefer a career as an elementary-education teacher.

Service Planning

Sam developed a comprehensive vocational plan for Dora. This plan, known as the Individualized Written Rehabilitation Program (IWRP), contains the following aspects of action:

1. The rehabilitation goal and immediate rehabilitation objectives
2. Vocational rehabilitation services
3. The projected date of initiating services and the anticipated duration of services.

4. Objective criteria, evaluation procedures, and schedules for determining whether the rehabilitation goal and intermediate objectives are being achieved
5. Explanation of availability of a client assistance program (Roessler & Rubin, 1982, p. 132)

Sam postulated that Dora would need assistance with medical and emotional problems during the course of her college training. He also recognized that he would have to assist Dora in obtaining grants and other benefits that might be available to her. Excerpts from Sam's service plan suggestions follow: (1) enrollment in a local college with financial assistance for tuition, fees, and transportation; (2) other financial assistance through grants and Social Security benefits; (3) physical treatment to be continued as necessary; and (4) regular counseling sessions necessary to address reported psychological problems. Sam decided to provide supportive counseling and, if necessary, refer Dora to a college counseling center or local mental-health unit.

Thomas and Butler (1981) suggested that rehabilitation clients often need extensive personal counseling designed to assist them in accepting their disability, adjusting to reactions of others to their disability, reintegrating their self-concepts, and adjusting to changes in relationships with family and others in their lives. Career counselors are to evaluate different counseling theories and techniques in meeting the needs of different types of clients. In essence, individuals with disabilities may require extensive personal-adjustment counseling.

During the course of the next four years, Dora made remarkable academic progress in spite of recurring physical and psychological problems. She had three operations on her hands to improve flexibility, and the regular supportive counseling provided by Sam helped her overcome the depressive reaction. Financial assistance provided by the state and other agencies helped Dora maintain subsistence. During her final year in college, Sam directed Dora to attend seminars on résumé preparation and job-interview skills.

Placement

In a conference with Sam, Dora decided that she wanted to remain in the area. Sam evaluated the local job market for teachers and found it to be keenly competitive for elementary school teachers. However, he decided that he could improve Dora's chances of obtaining a position by assisting her in job-interview preparation. Sam also helped Dora develop a list of alternate school systems to which she could apply.

Postemployment Services

Sam plans to follow Dora's work for at least 60 postemployment days. He will focus on her adjustment to the new job and adaptations she must make in her daily schedule. Finally, Dora will be notified that if services are needed in the future, he can reopen her case.

This case illustrates the comprehensive nature of rehabilitation counseling for individuals with disabilities. The services offered involved considerable client contact and coordination of functions provided through training programs, financial assistance resources, and medical treatment. Although state rehabilitation programs follow a general pattern, there are variations in services given. Nevertheless, it is clear that rehabilitation counselors must possess numerous skills and considerable knowledge to foster client career development.

CAREER EDUCATION
FOR STUDENTS WITH DISABILITIES

Brolin and Gysbers (1989) have developed the Life-Centered Career Education Curriculum (LCCE) for individuals with disabilities. This program has been widely adopted in school systems in several states and in some foreign countries. This curriculum focuses on 22 major competencies that students need to succeed in daily living, personal-social, and occupational areas after leaving school. For daily living, competencies include buying and preparing food, managing finances, and caring for personal needs. For personal-social skills, competencies include achieving self-awareness, achieving independence, and making adequate decisions. Finally, for occupational preparation, competencies include selecting and planning occupational choices and obtaining a specific occupational skill. This model is competency based and specifies counselor time for carrying out guidance activities in each component.

Counselors are provided with a trainer/implementation manual, activity books, and an inventory to assess competency levels. The suggested competencies for this model are infused into the kindergarten through grade 12 curriculum. Some school systems have used this model to facilitate and improve community awareness of students' needs and increase parent participation in learning activities. It has also been used for staff in-service training to make them aware of the structure and purpose of the model.

Brolin and Gysbers (1989) suggested that career awareness, career exploration, and preparation are major benefits of this model. The career-awareness phase is very important during the elementary years. Programs that focus on helping students with disabilities should emphasize developing self-worth, socially desirable behaviors, communication skills, positive attitudes toward work, and desirable work habits.

The career-exploration phase includes guidance activities that explore abilities, needs, and interests. The use of work samples, simulated job tasks, and community jobs are important hands-on experiences. In addition, this phase includes experiences with the work roles of homemaker, family member, volunteer, and individuals engaged in productive avocational/leisure activities.

The preparation phase includes guidance activities that help clarify personal-social and occupational competencies. Interests, aptitudes, and skills are further clarified. Lifestyle and career choices are more clearly delineated.

This phase emphasizes that many students with disabilities require more than the usual amount of time to prepare for an occupation.

One issue that needs to be addressed in the 1990s is the place of proficiency tests required for graduation in many states. Should all students with disabilities be required to take and make acceptable scores on these tests? Perhaps more important, what kind of criteria should be used for students with disabilities to determine high school graduation? Finally, can the stereotypes and negative attitudes toward individuals with disabilities be erased from many professionals, including some members of the counseling profession? No doubt, some students with disabilities need individual attention, but counselors need to view these students' needs in perspective rather than in a stereotypic manner. As with other special populations, students with disabilities should receive career counseling first by identifying their individual needs and second by building programs to meet them (Brolin & Gysbers, 1989).

A GROUP COUNSELING PROGRAM FOR INDIVIDUALS WITH DISABILITIES

The following counseling program illustrates a group-counseling procedure for individuals with disabilities. The descriptions include excerpts that illustrate relevant counseling techniques. The counseling activity sequence consisted of four highly structured meetings, shown in Table 17-3. The counselees were hospitalized male patients who were accepted as clients for a vocational rehabilitation project.

John had been injured in a car accident and was almost totally paralyzed. The other counselees had been injured in industrial accidents. Rex's right leg

TABLE 17-3
Vocational Rehabilitation-Counseling Activity Sequence

Title	Activity
Personal/social-adjustment counseling	Briefing on the purpose of counseling session; discussion of problems of workers with disabilities, personal/social-adjustment problems, and factors influencing work performance
Peer-group affiliation	Counseling session on the importance of good peer relations, factors influencing peer-group affiliation, the give-and-take of working with others, and the influence of the working environment on job satisfaction
Worker-supervisor affiliation	Counseling session on the factors determining good relations with a supervisor, the role of the supervisor, and the influence of good worker-supervisor relations on work proficiency and job satisfaction
Job attitude	Counseling session on factors determining vocational success, factors influencing attitudinal development, and the influence of job attitude on work proficiency and job satisfaction

was amputated below the knee. Roberto had lost three fingers. Harold's injury prevented him from bending his left leg.

Several days before the first counseling meeting, each counselee completed a vocational-counseling inventory. The inventory was to be used as a counseling tool for each of the group meetings.

Session I: Personal/Social-Adjustment Counseling

The counselor began the first session by introducing himself and having each member introduce himself. The counselor briefed the counselees on the purpose of the counseling session.

Counselor: We're going to have four meetings to talk about some problems that you may experience when you return to the work force. Today we're going to cover some personal problems that you might experience in readjusting to a work role and general factors that influence the performance of workers who have similar problems.

The next excerpt illustrates the use of the previously completed vocational-counseling inventory and the importance of group interaction. The counselor selected items to stimulate discussion. For example, the item, "Now that I have a disability, life is going to be difficult," generated considerable discussion.

Harold: I've thought about this a lot since I've been in the hospital, and things are really going to be different when I get out.

Roberto: Well, I've been here for almost eight months, and I've learned to accept the fact that I probably will be doing a different kind of work than I did before. By the way, what kind of work did you do? (*looking at Harold*)

Harold: I was a foreman on a construction job, and I had to go around the different jobs for this contractor I worked for.

Roberto: Well, you might be able to do the same kind of thing.

During this meeting, it was difficult for John to enter into the discussion, for he had been recently injured and was almost completely paralyzed. However, toward the end of the session he spoke.

John: I used to play in a band before I had this car accident, but I don't know what I am going to be able to do now. Anyway, I'm going to this Warm Springs Foundation, and I hope I will get some feeling back in my body and I will find out something.

John's response had a great impact on the entire group because his message was quite clear; here was someone who still had hope even though his injury had the potential of being much more restrictive than those of the other members of the group.

Session II: Peer-Group Affiliation

The next excerpt illustrates how group interaction enhanced Session II. This meeting began with the counselor's question, "What kind of people did you like to work with on previous jobs?" During the course of exchanging ideas, several opinions were expressed. It became apparent to the counselor that all but one member of the group seemed to have a fairly healthy attitude toward peer workers. The counselor used several key questions and phrases to stimulate discussion: "Are most people you work with easy to talk to during breaks?" "Some people feel like an outsider on the job." "A friend of mine prefers working alone." "Are most of the people you have worked with friendly?"

Through group interaction, the point was made that good peer relations are most important for the worker with disabilities. Examples of statements from group members follow:

John: Some people are going to try to pity me because I've got a disability, while some are going to be very uncomfortable when I'm around.
Rex: To have a friend, you have to be a friend, and you can also do that as a disabled person.
Harold: Not everybody you work with is going to be friendly, but it sure helps if *you* try.

Session III: Worker-Supervisor Affiliation

The excerpts from this session illustrate how the counselor took advantage of the experiences of one group member to enhance the discussion. Harold had been employed in a supervisory position before his accident but was rather hesitant in communicating his viewpoint as a supervisor. The counselor began this session by having each member of the group discuss his relationships with a past supervisor or a boss. Each counselee stated that he had very little difficulty in worker-supervisor relationships. However, the counselor suspected that the relationships between employee and supervisor were not as appropriate as expressed by the counselees. Therefore, the counselor introduced several topics, hoping to elicit further responses from the group. An example of the exchange among group members follows:

Counselor: I've had some bosses that I would have worked harder for had they been a little more friendly. How about the rest of you?
Roberto: I remember a few guys like that, and we used to really chew them up during our bull sessions.
John: Yeah, sometimes bosses give too many orders and are not really interested in you.
Harold: (*finally responding*) Well, when I was the boss, sometimes I had to get on people to make them work. Look at it this way, bosses have bosses, and they also have pressure to get the job done.
Rex: I never thought of it that way!
John: Yeah, I guess everybody has to answer to someone.

The discussion continued, centering on how one's perception of a supervisor influences personal reactions to the work environment.

Session IV: Job Attitude

The following excerpt illustrates how the counselor continued with the very productive previous counseling session and related the previous topic of discussion to the purpose of this final meeting.

Counselor: Well, last time we raked bosses over the coals, but we finally agreed that bosses and supervisors do have a pretty tough job and they are generally good guys if you act like you want to work with them and do a good job. This will be especially important as a worker with disabilities.

The counselor then asked each group member to restate what he had learned from the previous meeting.

Counselor: Each of you has illustrated how your attitudes about a supervisor influence your perception of the work environment. Now, let's direct our attention to how your attitudes will affect your return to the work force as a worker with disabilities.

Roberto: If you have a good attitude about your boss and people you work with, you will probably like your job too.

John: We have gotta think positive or we'll lose hope.

Harold: Sometimes it's going to be hard to have the right attitude—but you only hurt yourself.

This group-counseling program encouraged group interaction by sharing concerns about new and different lifestyles as persons with disabilities. The program emphasized (1) personal/social-adjustment problems that might be encountered by each member of the group when he or she returned to the workforce, (2) retraining that may be necessary for a different occupation, (3) peer affiliation and supervisor relationships as a person with disabilities, and (4) the influence of one's attitudes on work proficiency and job satisfaction.

ASSESSMENT INSTRUMENTS FOR INDIVIDUALS WITH DISABILITIES

Micro-Tower—A Group Vocational Evaluation System

The *Micro-Tower* system of vocational evaluation was developed by ICD Rehabilitation and Research Center of New York City. The original instrument *Tower* is an acronym for Testing, Orientation, and Work Evaluation in Rehabilitation. *Tower* is an evaluation system consisting of 94 work samples that are individually administered. The *Micro-Tower* system is a group of 13 work samples that can be administered in a group session lasting three to five days. The *Micro-Tower* work samples are objectively scored and are considered to be performance tests. Work samples are measures of aptitude for a number of unskilled and skilled occupations grouped according to five broad areas of aptitude:[1]

[1] *Micro-Tower: The Group Vocational and Research Center*, ICD Rehabilitation and Research Center, 1977. Reprinted by permission.

Primary Aptitude	*Work Sample Tests*
Motor	Electronic connector assembly; bottling, capping, and packing; lamp assembly
Clerical Perception	Zip coding; record checking; filing; mail sorting
Spatial	Blueprint reading; graphics illustration
Numerical	Making change; payroll computation
Verbal	Want-ads comprehension; message taking

A third- to fourth-grade reading level is required to take the *Micro-Tower* system test. Work samples can be administered to an individual who is seated but do require the use of at least one hand. The individual must understand spoken English.

A unique feature of the *Micro-Tower* system is the involvement of the clients in group discussions that explore their interests, values, lifestyles, and so on. A separate manual is provided, which has specific procedures and variations for the discussion groups. One of the major objectives of the discussion group is to improve the client's motivation for job placement. Discussion groups are also used as an entrée for the testing period in an effort to make the testing situation as nonthreatening as possible.

There are several sets of normative data available, including sets for groups that are in general rehabilitation, Spanish-speaking, left-handed, physically disabled, psychiatrically disturbed, brain-damaged, cerebral palsied, in special education, culturally different, ex-drug abusers, ex-alcoholics, and adult offenders. Interpretive materials for the *Micro-Tower* system are elaborate and thorough. The results are plotted on a graph from weak to strong for the skill area and specific work samples. Additional reports for the counselor include (1) behavioral observations made during testing, (2) a summary of the client's interest and perceived performance, (3) a client data sheet, (4) a summary report that includes a narrative of the test results, (5) a recommendation summary sheet that covers such areas as special training recommended, (6) referral recommendations, and (7) vocational recommendations (*Micro-Tower*, 1977).

The *Micro-Tower* system grew out of a need for a work-evaluation instrument that could be administered to a group in a relatively short period. The evaluation system may also be used as a screening device to determine which clients would benefit from a more extensive evaluation of specific aptitudes. A manual is provided to convert *Micro-Tower* scores into estimates of *DOT* aptitude levels. The variety of norms available for interpretation increases the usefulness of the instrument.

Valpar Component Work Sample System

The *Valpar Component Work Sample System* (*VALPAR*) (Peterson, 1982) was developed by the Valpar Corporation of Tuscon, Arizona, for disabled and nondisabled in all age groups. Its purpose is to assess vocational and functional skills through a series of 16 work samples. Each work sample measures a certain universal worker characteristic. The work samples involve hands-on tasks;

some focus on general work characteristics, and others are related to specific job requirements. The following is a brief description of each of the work samples.

1. *Small tools*—measures the ability to work with small hand tools, including screwdrivers and small wrenches.
2. *Size discrimination*—measures visual discrimination by requiring the individual to screw correct-sized nuts onto threads mounted in a box.
3. *Numerical sorting*—measures the ability to sort, file, and categorize by number code.
4. *Upper extremity range of motion*—measures the range of motion of upper extremities and fatigue factors, finger dexterity, and sense of touch.
5. *Clerical comprehension and aptitude*—measures the ability to perform certain clerical tasks and aptitude for typing.
6. *Independent problem solving*—measures the ability to perform work that requires detailed visual comparisons of colored shapes.
7. *Multilevel sorting*—measures the ability to sort according to number, letter, and color.
8. *Simulated assembly*—measures the ability to do repetitive assembly tasks.
9. *Whole-body range of motion*—measures gross motor abilities and fatigue factors.
10. *Tri-level measurement*—measures the ability to perform precise measurements.
11. *Eye-hand-foot coordination*—measures the ability to use eyes, hands, and feet simultaneously in a coordinated manner.
12. *Soldering and inspection*—measures the ability to solder.
13. *Money handling*—measures skills that are necessary in dealing with money and making change.
14. *Integrated peer performance*—measures work behavior in interaction in small-group assemblies.
15. *Electrical circuitry and print reading*—measures the ability to understand and apply principles of electric circuits.
16. *Drafting*—measures basic drafting skills and ability to learn drafting.

Each of the *VALPAR* work samples can be used as a separate evaluation or integrated with a combination of other work samples or other testing instruments. The administrator gives the directions verbally, and each work sample can be completed in one or two hours. Modifications of the work samples are available for visually disabled and deaf persons. Norm groups include institutionally retarded, culturally disadvantaged, U.S. Air Force recruits, San Diego employed workers, low-income unemployed, hearing impaired, and what is described as employer workers that were unselected.

VALPAR is well designed and easy to administer and score. The value of work-sample testing is the ease of associating the results with requirements of a particular job. Counselors who need work-sample evaluations should carefully consider the content of each work sample in the *VALPAR* system. The focus of this system is on physical skills and the ability to use eyes, hands, and feet in a coordinated manner (Peterson, 1982).

Other work-sample tests include the following:

Jewish Employment Vocational Service Work Sample System—JEVS
Vocational Research Institute
Jewish Employment and Vocational Service
1700 Sansom St.
Philadelphia, PA 19103

SINGER Vocational Evaluation System
SINGER Career Systems
80 Commerce Drive
Rochester, NY 14623

Vocational Information and Evaluation Work Samples—VIEWS
Vocational Research Institute
Jewish Employment and Vocational Service
1700 Sansom St.
Philadelphia, PA 19103

Social and Prevocational Information Battery (SPIB)

The *SPIB* (Halpern et al., 1975) was designed for use with educable mentally retarded (EMR) students in junior and senior high schools. The *SPIB* is useful for EMR program identification, individual evaluation for placement in EMR programs, and monitoring progress and outcomes of EMR programs. There are nine tests that can be used to assess students' needs for social and vocational skills. The tests measure nine domains identified by the authors as part of five long-range goals for the EMR that should be achieved in secondary schools. These five goals are (1) employability, (2) economic self-sufficiency, (3) family living, (4) personal habits, and (5) communication skills. Tests have been developed to measure the objectives of each goal. The nine tests consist of 277 mostly true-or-false items that are administered orally. The authors identify the goal of economic self-sufficiency as one of the major objectives necessary to postsecondary adaptation. The three domains set for this particular goal are (1) purchasing habits, (2) budgeting, and (3) banking. Test items were subsequently developed to measure self-sufficiency in these three domains. For example, in measuring purchasing habits, test items include measures of knowledge of sales tax, knowledge of types of stores, and effectiveness in using newspaper ads for best buys.

The *SPIB* can be compared with three reference groups. A junior high school–level conversion table permits comparisons from the derived raw scores with equivalent percentage correct scores and percentile ranks with junior high school–level students on each *SPIB* test. Likewise, a senior high school–level conversion provides comparisons with high school–level students on each *SPIB* test. The third conversion table is a combination of junior and senior high school–level normative samples.

The authors suggest a "task analysis" method of evaluating specific competencies within each domain *SPIB* measures. To accomplish this, each content area is divided into subcontent areas. For example, see how the domain of job-related behavior is divided into content and subcontent areas in Table 17.4. Each subcontent area defined provides the basis for developing instructional activities and measuring of outcomes for each domain. In this way, the *SPIB* provides the foundation for establishing instructional programs for the EMR as well as being a tool for measuring the outcomes of the instructional activities. The *SPIB* is a well-devised test battery for assessing and evaluating programs and provides the framework from which to build instructional programs for the EMR.

TABLE 17-4
Content and Subcontent Areas for the Domain of Job-Related Behavior

Domain	Content Areas	Subcontent Areas
Job-related behavior	1. Knowledge of role and duties of a supervisor	a. Instruction b. Criticism c. Praise d. Hiring and firing e. Inspection of work f. Promotion g. Task assignment
	2. Knowledge of appropriate job-related communications	a. Job progress reports b. Relaying messages c. Reporting serious errors d. Requesting supplies e. Asking for help when needed f. Knowing whom to ask for help g. Asking for clarification
	3. Knowledge of what constitutes job completion	a. Importance of finishing a job b. Factors affecting job completion c. The effect of mistakes on job completion
	4. Recognition and knowledge of appropriate work relations with fellow employees	a. Compromising b. Cooperation c. Friendliness d. Showing appreciation e. Controlling temper f. Responsibility to others

American Association of Mental Deficiency's (AAMD) Adaptive Behavior Scale

The *AAMD Adaptive Behavior Scale* (Nihira et al., 1975) is designed to replace the IQ test as a means of identifying mentally retarded individuals. It is primarily a rating scale for identifying adaptive behavior of mentally retarded and other individuals who have special needs. The American Association of Mental Deficiency has endorsed this effort of using descriptions for identifying an individual's adaptive behavior as opposed to the use of a single intelligence quotient (Nihira et al., 1975).

Of major importance in this approach is that adaptive behavior can be described from a developmental frame of reference. Thus, an individual is observed from an established standard that provides certain descriptive information as to the individual's functioning. Using this technique, a more comprehensive and informative description in terms of skills, habits, social expectations, and personal independence is provided.

The *AAMD Adaptive Behavior Scale* (Nihira et al., 1975) has two parts. Part I is a measure of 10 behavioral domains and 21 subdomains. The examiner is required to react to statements descriptive of behavior in certain identified situations. The examiner may circle a number representative of the individual being observed or may be required to check all statements that apply to the individual being observed. For example, in evaluating independence functioning, the examiner is required to rate individuals according to which statements may apply to them, such as "drops food on the table or floor" or "talks with mouth full" or "chews food with an open mouth." Behavioral domains that are evaluated include economic activity, language development, domestic activities, vocational activities, self-direction, responsibility, and socialization.

Part II is a measure of social expectations in 14 domains related to personality and behavioral disorders. The examiner is required to rate whether the individual occasionally or frequently is involved in a particular behavior. For example, in rating violent and destructive behavior, the examiner may be required to evaluate whether the individual occasionally or frequently "tears up magazines or books" or "rips or tears clothing." Other domains measured include antisocial and rebellious behaviors and unacceptable and eccentric behaviors.

The *AAMD Adaptive Behavior Scale* is designed to provide information that can be used to determine classroom instructional programs. A profile summary is provided for all adaptive behavioral domains measured by the rating scale. The scores are interpreted in terms of percentiles and deciles. Percentiles are arranged according to age groups. Comprehensive information received from the scale should assist teachers in planning specific programs for individuals and groups according to behavioral domains. Thus, the behavioral domains can be used to formulate objectives to be achieved. Systematic evaluation of the objectives can be provided by periodic retesting. The adaptive behavior scale is an instrument that can serve many purposes: it can be used to identify students for placement in certain programs, provide evaluation of ongoing special programs, assist in administrative decisions for students with special needs, and provide specific objectives for instructional planning.

SUMMARY

1. The terms used to describe people with disabilities have changed to negate stereotypes and false ideas.

2. The passage of the Americans with Disabilities Act (ADA) has focused more attention on career-counseling programs especially designed to meet the needs of individuals with disabilities. The ADA is a comprehensive document that covers a number of subjects significant to the rights of individuals with disabilities, including fair employment practices and access to public accommodations and transportation.

3. Special problems and needs of persons with disabilities include difficulty adjusting to and accepting physical disabilities, attitudinal barriers, being labeled disabled, lack of role models, onset of disability, social/interpersonal skills, self-concept, skills for independence living, and architectural barriers. Educational programs that develop a better understanding of the special problems are needed by both employers and families.

4. State rehabilitation agencies provide numerous and varied programs for persons with disabilities. An actual case of an individual who received rehabilitation services from a state agency included the following steps: initial contact, diagnostic workup, evaluation and certification, vocational assessment, service planning, placement, and postemployment services.

5. Privately supported rehabilitation agencies provide educational, work, and counseling programs. Among services offered are psychological testing, vocational evaluation, personal/social-adjustment counseling, work adjustment, prevocational training, special academic instruction, skills training, job placement, and sheltered workshops.

6. A career education program for students with disabilities uses a Life-Centered Career Education Curriculum. Included are a career-awareness phase, a career-exploration phase, and a preparation phase.

7. A group-counseling program that promotes the vocational rehabilitation of disabled individuals included activities in (a) personal/social adjustment, (b) peer-group affiliation, (c) worker-supervisor affiliation, and (d) job-attitude counseling.

8. The *Micro-Tower* system of vocational evaluation consists of a group of 13 work samples and is used as a screening device to determine which individuals would benefit from more extensive evaluation of specific aptitudes.

9. The *Valpar Component Work Sample System* consists of 16 work samples used to measure certain universal worker characteristics. The focus of this system is on physical skills and the ability to use eyes, hands, and feet in a coordinated manner.

10. The *SPIB* was designed for use with educable mentally retarded (EMR) students in junior and senior high schools. Nine tests are used to assess students' needs for social and vocational skills.

11. The *AAMD Adaptive Behavior Scale* provides a means of identifying mentally retarded individuals. It is primarily a rating scale for identifying adaptive behavior of mentally retarded and other individuals who have special needs.

SUPPLEMENTARY LEARNING EXERCISES

1. Interview a rehabilitation counselor and obtain program descriptions for individuals with disabilities.
2. Make several observations of a special-education class. Compile a list of common problems based on your observations. Relate these problems to job placement.
3. Develop a list of rehabilitation journals that publish articles of interest concerning career-counseling programs for individuals with disabilities.
4. Visit an industry that employs individuals with disabilities. Compile a list of jobs performed and worker-function activities.
5. Survey your campus to find physical barriers that restrict individuals with disabilities. Discuss how these barriers and others contribute to psychological barriers.
6. Using the *SPIB* goals and domains, develop a rationale for using assessment results of this type in career-counseling programs.
7. Compile a list of audiovisual materials that can be incorporated in career-counseling programs for individuals with disabilities. Review and report on at least two.
8. Develop counseling components designed to meet two or more special problems and needs.
9. Survey a community to determine programs available for individuals with disabilities. Using the survey results, develop plans for utilizing these programs in a high school and/or community-college counseling program.
10. Interview a personnel director of an industry that employs individuals with disabilities to determine common problems experienced by these workers. Develop counseling components to help individuals overcome the common problems reported.

TECHNIQUES FOR THE CAREER-COUNSELING INTERVIEW

Chapter Eighteen
Career-Counseling Interview and Assessment Techniques

Chapter Nineteen
Career-Counseling Interviews

Chapter Eighteen

Career-Counseling Interview and Assessment Techniques

The preceding chapters contained examples of the growing knowledge of the foundations for career guidance, different perspectives of career development, and strategies for career intervention. The wide range of content in these chapters provides background information for developing techniques that assist individuals in making career decisions. Recently, more attention has been directed toward personal problems such as faulty cognitions that can adversely affect career decision making and behavioral problems that inhibit career development. For example, Brown and Brooks (1990) suggested that deficits in cognitive clarity require intervention other than career guidance for individuals who cannot objectively assess their own strengths and weaknesses and relate them to environmental situations. Gysbers and Moore (1987) pointed out that individuals who have been found to have irrational beliefs more than likely have distorted views of self and the career decision-making process. Spokane (1991) suggested that an increasing proportion of career-counseling clients have a combination of career and personal problems. Furthermore, because career problems are often an integral part of personal problems, treatment requires intervention strategies to deal with them simultaneously. In other words, one affects the other to the point that it is less productive to separate them in treatment. Finally, Krumboltz (1983) argued that certain faulty cognitions lead to serious problems in career decision making such as, "I can do anything if I work hard enough for it," or "There is only one career for me." Career counselors should make every attempt to identify problems that would impede career development and/or the ability to adequately process information in career decision making. One way to accomplish this goal is through an assessment interview.

THE ASSESSMENT INTERVIEW

The assessment interview has different meanings and purposes for mental-health professionals. In counseling, the interview assists clients in developing self-understanding, forming conclusions, looking at alternative actions, and so forth; it is viewed as a "helping interview." As a key tool for establishing objectives and goals, the interview is used by social workers to build a social history. Psychiatrists and clinical psychologists use the interview as a diagnostic tool to help form treatment considerations. For career counselors, the proposed purposes of the assessment interview borrow from each of these functions. As a diagnostic tool, the interview should help uncover behavioral problems that can lead to work maladjustment and faulty cognitions, which may in turn interfere with the client's ability to make career decisions. In a helping role, the interview assists clients in understanding the integral relationship of all life roles. Finally, all parts of the interview (including historical and demographic data) are used to help develop goals.

This chapter focuses on accomplishing the objectives of an assessment interview by providing some techniques for conducting the interview, a suggested sequence for interviewing, and a brief discussion of selected life roles with suggested topics for discussion. In addition, there is a supplement to the interview that will assist in discovering problems that interfere with career development, such as problems in living, work maladjustment, faulty cognitions, and memory and persistence. Depending on the needs of the client, the interview may take several sessions. In Chapter 19, the interview process is illustrated using case studies.

A SUGGESTED SEQUENCE FOR AN INTERVIEW

The following interview sequence is designed to provide career counselors with structured guidelines for observing their clientele while in dialogue with them. Most of the topics, such as demographic information and educational history, are typically found in career-counseling programs. However, the discussion of selected life roles significantly increases the options for obtaining pertinent information. For example, work history and preference for a future career are discussed as a part of the work role and in association with other life roles. Individual client needs will directly determine the major focus of the interview and the sequence to be followed. For instance, an interview may be terminated during the discussion of life roles if it is determined that the individual is unable to effectively communicate with a counselor because of major clinical depression. In another case, the interview may focus on only selected life roles. Yet, in another case, the counselor may need to evaluate memory and persistence. The flexibility suggested for using the interview provides the opportunity for meeting the needs of a wide range of clients. The suggested sequence is as follows:

I. Current status information

   A. General appearance

   B. Attitude and behavior

   C. Affect and mood

   D. Demographic information

   E. Work experience

    F. Medical history
    G. Educational history
    H. Family history

II. Discovering the significance of life roles and potential conflict

    A. Worker role
        1. Work history
    B. Homemaker
        1. Spouse
        2. Parent
    C. Leisure role
    D. Citizen role

III. Developing goals and objectives (see Chapter 19)

    A. Identifying client goals
    B. Determining the feasibility of goals
    C. Establishing subgoals
    D. Assessing commitment to goals (Brown, Brooks, and associates, 1990)

IV. Supplement to the interview: Discovering problems that interfere with career development

    A. Problems in living
    B. Behaviors that may lead to work maladjustment
    C. Faulty cognitions
    D. Memory and persistence

TECHNIQUES FOR INTERVIEWING

The techniques for interviewing discussed in the following paragraphs are used within a counselor-client dyadic relationship. The objectives focus on techniques and strategies that foster productive dialogue and focus on potential deficits in career decision making and other career-development concerns. The major purpose for the interview, in this context, is to determine client needs and the subsequent direction intervention strategies will take. In some instances, the following techniques are illustrated by counselor-client dialogue: (1) rapport, (2) observation, (3) self-disclosure, (4) open- and close-ended questions, (5) echoing, restatement, or paraphrasing, (6) continuation, and (7) staying on track.

Techniques for Establishing Rapport

Jan, a 28-year-old woman, was considering a return to graduate school at a local university. She asked for an appointment at the career-counseling center.

On the morning Jan reported for the appointment, she was frowning noticeably and moved around the waiting room picking up one magazine and then another. She constantly looked at her watch, sighing aloud as if impatient.

Al, the counselor assigned to Jan, observed this behavior while finishing with another client. A few minutes before the time for the appointment, Al greeted Jan with enthusiasm.

Counselor: Jan, my name is Al, and I'm here to help you.
Client: Yes, I'm Jan.
Counselor: This is Rita, our secretary, and she will help also, especially for appointments, just call either one of us for anything you need.
Client: (*Nodding*) Okay, thanks.
Counselor: Let me show you around. Here is our career library. There is one of my clients reading about careers. Notice another person is using the computer program to find information. To our left is a room used for taking tests, as you see two people are currently taking an interest inventory. Now here is my office.

As they entered Al's office, he made the following comments:

Counselor: I'm pleased that we've been able to help most everyone who comes to us either directly through one or more of our programs or by referring people to proper sources.

Thus far, Al had responded to his client's signs of tension and continued to establish rapport. However, some clients do not exhibit signs of tension or apprehension as clearly as Jan did, so it is important to communicate to each client an expression of sincerity and competence. After a short period of explanation of ethical issues and confidentiality rules, Al asks the following question.

Counselor: How may we help you?
Jan: My parents want me to choose another job, so I promised them I'd come here. I'm really upset and mad about this whole idea!
Counselor: You do seem upset, particularly with your parents.

By responding with empathy, the counselor continues to build rapport. Also, Al used the client's terms for expressing an emotion rather than a psychological one. Paraphrasing responses using the client's wording communicates understanding to the client (Othmer & Othmer, 1989). He also helped to improve rapport by expressing an interest in the anxiety that he observed through Jan's body language and verbal expressions. Al had learned that he must be genuine and resist using psychological jargon or the client might withdraw. For example, the conversation may have gone as follows:

Counselor: You were apprehensive and overwrought when I met you, you must really be somewhat unstable.
Jan: Oh really! Do you honestly think you know me that well? I've heard that psychological claptrap before.

Counselors must communicate to their counselees an understanding of their emotional status and empathetically appreciate the frustrations they are experiencing. Instead of using technical language, clear behavioral descriptions are suggested (Hersen & Turner, 1985). The use of more technical terms may be appropriate in sessions that follow the establishment of rapport and trust.

Techniques for Observation

Mental-health workers have a long history of using observation as a tool to provide insights into their client's behavior. Psychiatrists, psychologists, clinical social workers, and counselors have refined systematic procedures for observation. Then they use the information gained, along with other data, to determine intervention strategies.

Throughout the interview, the effective interviewer is alert to any clues that provide insights into the client's personality, mood, social functioning, and other characteristics. General appearance, behavior, affect, nutritional status, hygiene and dress, eye contact, psychomotor activity, speech, attitude, and other characteristics provide important information for the assessment interview.

A career-counseling assessment interview may be conducted in a number of different types of settings such as a high school, college or university, private practice, mental health center, rehabilitation and employment agency, or other agency. Physical appearance may then be judged from the perspective of what is considered appropriate to the environment and to the purpose for which the interview is conducted. Appropriate physical appearance in this context is relative, but in all instances, it can provide important information. The following examples illustrate this point.

> Charles, a 17-year-old high school student, made an appointment with the school counselor for the stated purpose of "I want help in choosing a future job." He reported promptly for the interview. The counselor made the following notes: Charles was neatly dressed in freshly pressed trousers, a clean shirt, and shined shoes. He was of average weight, clean-shaven, with combed, short hair. There were no unusual movements and he made eye contact throughout the interview. Charles expressed himself well and had an impressive vocabulary. There were no indications of depression.

At first glance, one may conclude that little was revealed about Charles other than his physical appearance was unremarkable—that is, nothing negative. However, the observer could conclude that his dress was appropriate and that he was aware of social convention and had insights into how to function adequately during the interview. His appearance gave an initial impression that he was indeed serious and highly motivated to initiate a counseling relationship.

The next example takes place in a state employment agency:

> Fred was age 33 and had had several different jobs during the last ten years. The reason he gave for coming for counseling was that he was out of work and looking for a job. The counselor made the following notes: Fred was

a disheveled-looking man whose clothes were unpressed and soiled. He seemed to have very poor personal hygiene; he had not shaved for several days and had very strong body odor. Fred appeared to be anxious during the interview, as observed by his behavior. First of all, he spoke at times with a differently pitched voice, particularly when past work experiences were discussed. He also seemed to be very guarded about his reasons for leaving certain jobs. He was quite fidgety, moving around in his chair and clenching his fists. There was a strong smell of alcohol on his breath.

From just these few notes, the client's problems with getting and keeping employment were rather clear. At least two needs were obvious: personal hygiene and substance abuse. Other information obtained from Fred in the interview reinforced these conclusions.

In these two cases, the counselor jotted down first impressions. Careful scrutiny of these impressions, along with other data, may reinforce or justify modification of them. Without spending more time with a client and looking beyond surface information, recommending appropriate programming may be questionable. The skilled counselor is willing to modify early conclusions when it is justifiable.

Other descriptions of behavior include:

Rapport was difficult to establish and maintain.
Appeared to be nervous.
Seemed to tire easily.
Gave up on tasks easily.
Did not appear to be well.
A speech-articulation disorder was noted.
Seldom initiated conversation.
Responded impulsively to many questions.
Talked in a loud voice.
Talked in a low voice and was hard to understand.
Easily distracted.
Has short attention span.
Daydreams.
Has nervous tics.
Expresses negative view of self.
Lacks interest in personal appearance.
Expresses feelings of sadness, cries readily.

Techniques for Using Self-Disclosure

At certain times during the interview, counselors may find it advantageous to convey information about themselves to their clients. This technique is known as self-disclosure and may be positive or negative in nature. Successful personal experiences, such as "I'm known as a task-oriented person and my persistence has paid off for me," convey successful positive experiences, while "I lacked self-confidence on my first job" conveys a negative type of experience. Both types of self-disclosure may be used effectively for establishing rapport, communicating empathy, and facilitating dialogue during the interview.

Self-disclosure by counselors can also facilitate self-disclosure from clients (Cozby, 1973). However, counselors should be very selective when using self-disclosure and should only use this technique sparingly. The following example illustrates the effective use of self-disclosure.

Jan: My father has always wanted me to follow in his footsteps like owning your own business. But I have no interest in business and especially in · retail—I just wish they would leave me alone.

Counselor: This sounds so familiar! My parents wanted me to become an architect and applied plenty of pressure before I went to college. I thought they would never get off my back.

Jan: I can't believe it. We had similar experiences—wow! Let me tell you more about my dad ———.

By sharing common experiences, the counselor attempts to increase the client's disclosure level and foster discussion of unresolved relationship issues. The counselor's responses to Jan's problems through self-disclosure influenced, structured, and directed the discussion topic during the interview. Immediate feedback through self-disclosure about a client's personal problems usually enhances the client's willingness to discuss them in greater depth (Halpern, 1977; Thase & Page, 1977; Cormier & Cormier, 1991).

Techniques for Using Open- and Close-Ended Questions

The types of questions used during an interview are usually selected to obtain specific information or encourage clients to express themselves more fully by elaborating on certain subjects, emotions, or events. The two options discussed here are the use of open- and close-ended questions. Research on the use of these two types of questions suggested that open-ended questions facilitate emotional expression (Hopkinson, Cox, & Rutter, 1981), while close-ended questions have higher reliability and narrow the focus of the interview (Othmer & Othmer, 1989). Open-ended questions usually are formed with the words *tell me, explain more fully, what, how, when,* or *where.* For instance, "Tell me more about your work experiences" gives the client the opportunity to select the direction and subject of his or her response within the broad category of work experiences. Close-ended questions request more specific information; for example, "Have you served in the armed services?" Both types of questions are useful during an interview as illustrated below:

Counselor: How far did you go in school?
Ben: I quit in the tenth grade.
Counselor: Why did you quit?
Ben: I don't know. I didn't like it.

Now the counselor turns to more open-ended questions in the interview.

Counselor: What kind of problems did you have at school?
Ben: I couldn't get along with the teachers and the principal didn't like me, so I just quit.
Counselor: Can you tell me more about your problems?
Ben: Well, I was absent a lot, and they must have known I was doing drugs and selling them, because they were always watching me. Man, I didn't do anything in school—I just quit.

In this case, the counselor quickly realized that there was more to the story about quitting school than Ben had suggested earlier. He shifted from questions used to get specific information to a free-response type and Ben responded with pertinent information. Inconsistencies suggested by clients' statements or "mixed messages" can be clarified through the use of both open-ended and close-ended questions.

Techniques for Using Echoing, Restatement, or Paraphrasing

To focus attention on the cognitive and/or affective content of a client's statement, the counselor can use the techniques of echoing, restatement, or paraphrasing. One purpose of these techniques is to focus attention on the situation, object, person, or general idea of a statement. Paraphrasing or echoing the cognitive portion of a statement provides greater chances for obtaining a measure of the emotional tone associated with its content. Client affect may be expressed through nonverbal communication (gestures, facial expressions) or through descriptive words such as *sad, angry,* and *depressed* or *happy, affectionate,* and *supportive.* The degree to which affect is associated with the content of a client's statement provides counselors with important evaluative information. The following case illustrates this point.

Kay: My father thinks I should plan my life around a typical stereotyped role like homemaker, but—well, I've already told you that my father and I don't agree. He is just impossible!
Counselor: You obviously do not agree with your father about future life roles.
Kay: On some things I guess I do, but most of the time no.
Counselor: You mentioned the role of homemaker.
Kay: I really don't know at this time. Most of my friends are going after a career and not worrying about marriage and kids. I guess I'd like to get married someday, but I'm not sure. Honestly, it depresses me to even think about it.

In this case, the counselor wanted to find out more about Kay's feelings about her father and particularly her feeling about the role of homemaker. The counselor was interested in determining if there were perceived role conflicts that might influence career development. Kay seemed to be struggling with the message of her father's view of the appropriate role for women and with what friends were projecting as a role model. Such conflicts may inhibit ongoing career decision making well into the future.

Techniques for Using Continuation

Continuation is one of the so-called steering techniques used to encourage clients to go on with a topic and provide reinforcement that he or she is on the right course. Techniques used include nonverbal gestures such as keeping eye contact, nodding, staying silent, and using hand movements that invite the client to continue. Typical statements include "Go on," "Tell me more," "Hmm," and "What happened after that?" (Othmer & Othmer, 1989). An example follows:

Counselor: What do you consider to be your major problem in selecting a career?
Abe: I don't know very much about different kinds of jobs.
Counselor: Go on.
Abe: What's the future look like? What are the possibilities? I'm not sure what I like, but I know what I don't like.
Counselor: Hmm. Tell me more.
Abe: How can you find out about all these things? Sometimes I feel like giving up and just taking any old job. But, then I may not be happy with it and have to start all over again. How does anyone really decide what to do?

In this case, the counselor steered Abe to elaborate on his lack of career information, interests, and decision-making procedures. Armed with such information as "What's the future look like" and "I'm not sure about what I like," the counselor is in a good position to obtain client agreement for specific career-counseling goals.

Techniques for Staying on Track

Maintaining content focus is an effective technique for gainful productivity in a dyadic relationship. The counselor may have clients who are rather nonverbal, whose responses are short and abrupt, or clients who enjoy verbalizing. In both cases, keeping the conversation within the interview guidelines is one way of avoiding the possibility of wasting time with irrelevant information.

Some clients have difficulty maintaining focus on a subject for a variety of reasons, including the defense mechanism of denial, lack of motivation to persist, and conflicting thoughts that make staying on track difficult. When clients have consistent patterns of difficulty maintaining focus on the subject of discussion, referral for an in-depth analysis of the problem may be warranted. In those cases where clients deviate from the subject with unessential circumstantial information, abrupt and assertive action by the counselor may be necessary. The following case illustrates this point:

Counselor: Tell me more about your interest in working with people.

Joan: I think I like people. My friend Julie was working in a day-care center and the children there were okay. She got married and is taking a trip to the Bahamas. She and her husband like to swim and sail, they will probably go there every vacation and ——

Counselor: (*interrupts*) Joan, let's continue talking about *your* interests.

The process of interviewing clients for career counseling is a dynamic one and requires the skillful use of the techniques discussed in this section. Assessing and generating hypotheses about clients involves the possibility of a profound number of career-related problems. In the next sections, each part of the interview is discussed.

CURRENT STATUS INFORMATION
General Appearance

General appearance is a generalized observation of the client's personal grooming, posture, facial expressions, and mannerisms. Forming a visual perception of the client's general appearance provides a reference point as the interview progresses. For example, appearance may provide some important clues about personality, awareness of social conventions, and ability to function in current life roles.

Attitude and Behavior

Attitude and behavior are also obtained through observation and, more specifically, through the quality of the interaction with the counselor. One client may relate easily and be cooperative while another may be suspicious and guarded, requiring the counselor to offer reassurance and frequently refer to the confidentiality of the interview. Specific examples of clients' attitude and behavior should be recorded for later review. Some descriptive examples follow: articulate, avoids eye contact, shy, elated, depressed, relaxed, aggressive, anxious, tense, overbearing, alert, oppositional, self-righteous, sullen, insubordinate.

Affect and Mood

Affect is evaluated through observation of the client's emotional tone during the interview, whereas mood is the client's current reported status. Affect is a momentary reaction to a current situation or conversation and may change as stimuli change. Mood, on the other hand, is self-reported for a specified period. Affect and mood can differ; for example, a client may appear happy (affect) when meeting the counselor but later report depression and despair (mood).

Inappropriate affect refers to clients who demonstrate incongruence with the content of conversation, such as laughing inappropriately when a sad topic is discussed.

Demographic Information

Demographic information should include sex, ethnicity, age, and marital status. This information may be obtained by direct questioning or by self-report to questions on a structured form.

Work Experiences

Past work experience may also be recorded by the client or obtained through questioning. Report forms usually require listing both part- and full-time jobs. Other information commonly required on report forms includes likes and dislikes about jobs, career successes and failures, and jobs that may be considered for the future. Work roles are further discussed in the next section.

Medical and Educational History

Likewise, medical and educational history may also be obtained by direct questioning or by self-report. Both topics may have a significant effect on life roles. For example, physical and academic limitations are important factors to be considered in educational and career planning.

Family History

Family roles may be obtained by various methods, such as through career genograms. Gysbers and Moore (1987) describe these methods in detail. Another method referred to as an occupational family tree requires clients to list the occupations of grandparents, parents, aunts and uncles, and brothers and sisters. The respondent is questioned about his or her reactions to relatives' occupations in terms of pride or embarrassment. Other questions probe such subjects as family satisfaction with occupations and the benefits the family has received from specific occupations. The client is also asked to identify with any of the family members (Dickson & Parmerlee, 1980).

Direct questioning has the important advantage of observing client behaviors and emotional reactions. It is therefore suggested that even if a written self-report is used to obtain demographic data and work, medical, educational, and family history, a discussion of this information should be included in the interview.

DISCOVERING THE SIGNIFICANCE OF LIFE ROLES AND POTENTIAL CONFLICTS

There is an abundance of evidence, as suggested in Chapter 2, that career counseling not only is concerned with strategies for selecting a career but is much broader in scope and content. Among others, Super (1990) has suggested an integrative approach to career counseling that focuses on the development of life roles over the life span with emphasis on interrole congruence. The key to this concept is the effect of the development of one role on others. For instance, has the homemaker role inhibited career development or does the work role leave ample time for fulfillment of the citizen role? As Super (1980) pointed out, "Success in one facilitates success in others, and difficulties in one role are likely to lead to difficulties in another" (p. 287).

Hansen's (1991) Integrative Life Planning (ILP) model incorporates career development, life transitions, gender-role socialization, and social change. This model involves a "lifelong process of identifying our primary needs, roles, and goals and the consequent integration of these within ourselves, our work, and our family" (Hansen, 1990, p. 10).

The ILP model evolved from Hansen's (1987b) *BORN FREE* project, which was designed to expand career options for both men and women. She suggested that fragmented approaches to development place limits on decisions clients will make in their lifetime. A more integrative approach recognizes that an individual's total development includes the broad spectrum of domains: social-emotional, physical, sexual, intellectual, vocational, and spiritual. Finally, in the context of our discussion, this model suggests that life roles are to be integrated in our planning and not isolated from the career decision-making process. The impact of decisions on lifestyle, including relationships, is a major part of a more comprehensive view of development.

The life roles to be evaluated in the interview include worker, homemaker, leisure, and citizen. Included in the work role is work history and in the homemaker role, spouse and parent. Life roles increase and decrease in importance according to the individual's current status. For example, the student role is much more dominant in early life, even though career development is continuous and requires a lifetime learning involvement. The potential complexity and variety of life roles over the life span may include a multitude of possible scenarios that warrant exploration. In the following paragraphs, each role is identified and examples of topics to be covered in the interview are presented.

Worker Role

Over time, the term *work* has generated many definitions and has meant different things to the individuals who do it. Also the objectives people have for work may be quite different and may change as they pass through stages of career development. For example, some individuals may work for the intrinsic enjoyment of it; for others, the primary objective may be a narrowly concerned way of making a living, and yet others work for social status or for self-identity. For many, a combination of objectives and other factors are of equal importance. Super (1984) suggested an inclusive perspective of the work role that covers most segments of lifestyle as follows:

> The approach of recent years has shifted from a focus on work alone as a central life concern to an interest in the quality of life, life in which work is one central concern in a constellation of roles such as homemaking, citizenship, and leisure that interact to make for life satisfaction. The terms work motivation and job satisfaction are now perhaps not displaced by, certainly incorporated into, the terms quality of life and life satisfactions. (p. 29)

The different purposes individuals have for the work role are central to our concerns in the interview. Herr and Cramer (1992) suggested that the purposes of work can be classified as economic, social, and psychological. For example, a major economic purpose is to provide the individual with assets to satisfy current and future basic needs. In the social realm, friendships and social status are established through peer-group affiliations where mutual goals are achieved. A work identity, self-efficacy, and a sense of accomplishment are examples of the psychological purposes of work.

The purposes and meanings of work are uniquely individualized. For example, a family-oriented individual who has strong needs to spend ample time with his or her children may be somewhat unhappy in a work role that limits family activities. A strong orientation for work-leadership roles may inhibit an individual's needs associated with the life roles of citizen and leisurite. Although it may be difficult to satisfy the needs of all life roles, a greater balance of roles may enhance some people's quality of life. The following list of topics for discourse and samples of content for work-role interviewing represent only a few of the possibilities that can be discussed. Client needs should dictate the selection of subjects.

For a client making an initial choice of work role, the counselor should assess the following:

- Knowledge of life role concepts
- Acceptance of the idea of different life roles
- Ability to evaluate how work roles affect other life roles
- Ability to project an ideal work role
- Ability to identify purpose of the work role
- Ability to project self into work roles
- Ability to identify future work roles
- Knowledge of personal characteristics
- Level of skill development

Although many of the variables considered in the initial choice may need to be reevaluated with individuals who wish to change careers, the degree to which the individual is able to do the following should also be explored:

- Adapt to changes
- Learn new and different skills
- Function under different management styles
- Assess reasons for career changes and work commitments
- Assess his or her abilities, limitations, interests, and values to adapt to work-environment changes
- Use decision-making procedures
- Identify career resources and how to use them
- Identify sources of stress
- Apply methods of modifying behavior
- Identify educational and training programs

Homemaker Role

The role of homemaker has a wide spectrum of possibilities. For example, a 35-year-old single person may not consider this role a very important one, whereas a married 35-year-old who has children may consider the role of homemaker a major role. A high school student may consider this role as something to be dealt with in the future, whereas a 50-year-old who has reared several children will place less emphasis on this role when planning a career change. The more recent phenomenon of the househusband and more emphasis on the male role as a homemaker adds to the diversity of possible interrole conflicts (see Chapters 14 and 15).

The number of working mothers is expected to increase by 1995, when 7 of every 10 mothers with infants and young children will be employed (Hoffreth & Phillips, 1987). A major concern for maternal employment is its effect on children, the family, and the working women themselves. In a comprehensive review of the literature concerning the effects of maternal employment on children, Herr and Cramer (1992) concluded that in general it does no harm to children (infants, preschoolers, and adolescents). Working mothers also seem to fare well according to Ferree (1984), who conducted a national research study concerning satisfaction variables. She concluded that there were no significant differences of life satisfaction between working mothers and those who did not work outside the home. In a related study, results indicated that stress experienced by working women can be offset by spousal approval, dependable child care, and shared family responsibilities (Suchet & Barling, 1985; Scarr, Phillips, & McCartney, 1989).

The issues surrounding the homemaker role in families where both husband and wife work outside the home (dual-earner and dual-career) have major significance as a result of the expected growing number of working mothers. In dual-earner and dual-career families, both husband and wife work outside the home, but dual-career families are characterized as more career-oriented and committed to career development on a continuous basis. Both types of families share some common goals as well as sources of stress such as role conflict, role overloads, and decreased opportunity for leisure. The following is a list of subjects for general discourse.

- Degree of commitment to the role of homemaker
- Career now and homemaker later
- The woman as a homemaker and the husband as a breadwinner
- The reason both spouses may have to work
- The homemaker-worker connection
- Family life versus career commitment
- The significance of integrated life roles

Potential conflict issues such as the following should also be assessed:

- Decreased leisure
- Share of homemaker responsibilities
- View of traditional gender-based roles
- Stress from physical and emotional demands
- Multiple role demands
- Commitment to household chores
- Commitment to sharing childcare responsibilities
- Commitment to development of spouse's career
- Nonsupport of spouse's career development
- Dissimilar levels of involvement in both work and family needs
- Decision-making procedures for such family matters as when to have children

Leisure Role

There are a number of clichés about the relationship of work and leisure that have endured for generations. The primary message has been that a quality lifestyle is one in which there is a balance between time spent at work and time devoted to leisure activities. This message still prevails and has received renewed recognition as a means of fostering need satisfaction (Leclair, 1982). Within this frame of reference, quality of life is attained through a more holistic viewpoint of human and career development. Simply stated, individuals are to recognize that quality of life is associated with all life roles. Central to our concerns as career counselors is a balance of life roles that gives clients the freedom for self-expression to meet their needs. Moreover, when interrole conflicts are discovered, we have at our disposal a menu of suggestions designed to enhance all life roles.

The complementary role that leisure has to the work role is expressed by Kando and Summers (1971) as two-dimensional; that is, it reinforces positive associations that are also expressed in the work role (supplemental compensation) and provides activities to reduce stress associated with unpleasant work experiences (reactive compensation). Following this logic but with a somewhat different twist, Jackson (1988) suggested that individuals can receive psychological benefits from leisure, but only if they learn how to use the time spent in leisure in a purposeful manner. Remember that sources of stress found in work, such as competition, can also become sources of stress in leisure activities.

The availability of time that can be devoted to leisure for any one individual is situational. However, McDaniels (1990) advocated planning for different types of leisure as a part of a counseling model. He also suggested that counselors act in an advocacy role to promote leisure activities in schools, workplace, homes, and community.

In sum, the leisure role should be assessed as a prolific means of complementing other life roles. The proportion of time a person allocates to leisure should be judged from the perspective of lifestyle. For example, the ambitious accountant may consider leisure activities as a luxury that has little current relevance, while the individual who is working full-time as a bus driver and part-time on two other jobs may view leisure as something other, more fortunate people do. The *involvement* in leisure may simply be haphazard and left to chance. Although there is not a plethora of research suggesting the benefits of leisure activities, there are research conclusions that strongly suggest effective participation in leisure can be therapeutic (Ragheb & Griffith, 1982) and can compensate for dissatisfaction found in work (Bloland & Edwards, 1981). Suggested subjects for discourse are as follows:

- Benefits of leisure activities
- Purpose for planning activities
- Types of leisure, including intellectual, creative, social, and physical activities
- Resources for information on leisure activities
- How to become involved in a leisure/work model
- Perspectives of a holistic lifestyle
- Recognition of conflicts with other life roles
- The role of leisure and career development
- The advantages of balancing life roles with leisure
- Identification of needs and values associated with the leisure role
- Psychological needs satisfied through leisure activities
- The work/leisure connection
- Developmental tasks related to leisure development
- Development of a greater level of interest in leisure activities

Citizen Role

Similar to the leisure role's link to quality of life, the citizen role may serve as an additional or compensating source of satisfaction. Also this role provides opportunities for fulfillment of individual needs in a wide variety of activities found in most communities. Local civic organizations offer an abundance of opportunities to express civic responsibility as a way of responding to community needs. Involvement in volunteerism is on the increase for community, state, national, and international projects (McDaniel, 1990). A growing number of Americans seem to be making serious commitments to civic and service activities.

Perhaps Yankelovich (1981a) is correct in his observation that American values have shifted from duty-to-self to a more balanced lifestyle involving a greater concern for improving community and country. The way we judge success and fulfill our personal needs may have shifted to noneconomic issues that lead to a more agreeable lifestyle (Yankelovich & Lefkowitz, 1982). In essence, the citizen role provides opportunities for all social groups to experience satisfaction; we can all participate in building playgrounds, cleaning neighborhoods, raising funds for worthy projects, working with children, and providing assistance to the elderly.

The concept of balanced life roles implies that there are numerous opportunities to build a quality lifestyle. Individual work situations may not provide outlets to meet client needs associated with, for example, reading to blind students or being a tutor or hospital aide. Productive opportunities outside the work role are means of satisfaction that enhance interrole activities. That is, some needs that might otherwise be left to go to seed or produce stress can be satisfied through civic activities.

Among others, Bolles (1991) has suggested that skills learned and developed through participation in civic organizations and activities may be used in career decision making. These skills can be matched with work requirements in career exploration (see Chapter 13). Also, volunteer experiences, along with education and other experiences, are considered in job placement (McDaniels, 1990).

In the interview, the counselor should assess the client in terms of

- perception of the citizen's role;
- knowledge of civic organizations;
- knowledge of benefits from participating in civic activities;
- knowledge of benefits from participating in volunteerism;
- evaluation of skills learned through participation in civic activities;
- knowledge of how skills can be transferred to work roles;
- degree of participation in civic organizations;
- desire to participate in civic organizations;
- reasons for lack of participation in community activities;
- likes and dislikes of civic activities; and
- family involvement in civic activities.

INTERVIEWING ETHNIC MINORITIES

Developing a greater sensitivity to culturally diverse clients has become increasingly important for career counselors; we must foster specific counseling techniques to accommodate the human diversity that exists in our society. The core dimension of interviewing is effective communication between clients and counselors. Also, during the course of the interview, counselors form opinions and assumptions about clients from both verbal and nonverbal communications. Because of cultural and ethnic differences between counselor and client, the counselor must be alert to a wide spectrum of ethnic and cultural characteristics that influence behavior. For example, some ethnic groups may conceptualize their problems differently from those of the dominant White culture and seek solutions based on these assumptions. For instance, a client who views his problem as being ostracized because of race may be much more interested in finding immediate employment than pursuing a program for identifying a long-term career goal. Another client may be reluctant to share her personal problems with someone outside the family circle, and in fact, direct questioning can be interpreted as an infringement on privacy.

Although it is difficult to generalize techniques suggested for ethnic minorities, it seems feasible to first determine the level of acculturation by socioeconomic status, language preference, place of birth, generation level, preferred ethnic identity, and ethnic group social contacts (Ponterotto, 1987). Questions must be carefully selected and presented so as not to offend the client. For example, directness may be judged as demanding, intrusive, or abrupt by some ethnic minority groups. Furthermore, an open person may be seen by some cultures as weak, untrustworthy, and incapable of appropriate restraint (Copeland & Griggs, 1985).

Some other points to remember when interviewing ethnic minorities include the following:

- General appearance may be quite distinctive for some subcultures and should be accepted on that basis.
- Attitude and behavior are considered difficult to ascertain. Major belief themes of ethnic minorities influence their attitudes about themselves and others. Their perceptions of the world may be quite different from those of the counselor.
- Affect and mood are also related to cultural beliefs and to what is considered appropriate within a culture. The meaning given to gestures often differs by culture. Work experience may be quite limited because of lack of opportunity. Also in some cultures, it is considered very immodest to speak highly of yourself and the skills you have mastered.
- Life roles, and particularly relationships, are unique to cultural socialization. In some cultures, females are considered equal to males, while in others they are expected to be subservient.

These examples illustrate the necessity of building an extensive body of resources for interviewing ethnic minorities. Other general recommendations include (1) use straightforward, slang-free language, (2) become familiar with minority life-role models, (3) identify an ethnic-minority consultant who can provide helpful information, and (4) become familiar with support networks for ethnic minorities. Finally, Chapter 16 provides suggestions and strategies for career development for some ethnic groups.

SUPPLEMENT TO THE INTERVIEW: DISCOVERING PROBLEMS THAT INTERFERE WITH CAREER DEVELOPMENT

The focus of this part of the interview is on behavioral patterns of maladjustment. The identification of specific behavior domains that may contribute to conflicts in the work environment provides a practical and workable system for the career counselor to identify goals and objectives for counseling intervention. For instance, individuals whose basic behavior style has been identified as overtly hostile and aggressive may respond to programs designed to manage anger and reduce aggression.

"Problems in living" and methods of coping with these problems need to be identified. This approach does not rule out psychiatric etiology as a source of work maladjustment but focuses more on the individual's ability to cope with work demands. Perhaps more important, mental disorders may or may not affect work behavior. Neff (1985) pointed out that the ability to function on a job is related to the nature of both an individual's mental health and mental illness. However, more research is needed to establish the relationship between work maladaption and mental disorders.

Some research has suggested that career competence is not grossly affected by mental illness (character and affective disorders, severe psychoneurosis, and functional psychosis) when the mental illness subsides (Huffine & Clausen, 1979). The findings of this longitudinal research project suggested that developed competencies and socialization into the work world were not necessarily affected by the mental illness of the men studied.

The 1987 third edition of the *Diagnostic and Statistical Manual of Mental Disorders* (DSM-III-R) has several categories of mental, social, and behavioral disorders. Although all of these disorders can appear in the workplace, references to work impairment are very generalized. The following quote is a guideline for how we must individualize our interpretation of mental disorders and the subsequent behavior associated with a disorder.

> Another misconception is that all people described as having the same mental disorder are alike in all important ways. Although all the people described as having the same mental disorder have at least the defining features of the disorder, they may well differ in other important respects that may affect clinical management and outcome. (p. xxiii)

Behaviors that May Lead to Work Maladjustment

One of our objectives in the assessment interview is to identify individualized behavior patterns that impair the work role. Table 18-1 presents symptoms of behavior and faulty cognitive functioning that can lead to work impairment. These symptoms were adapted from personality disorders and descriptions of depression found in DSM-III-R (1987). The information can be used as guide-

TABLE 18-1
Work-Role Projections

Identification	Behaviors, Beliefs, Traits	Work Impairment	Other Work-Role Observations
Cluster A[1] Paranoid career client	Suspicious of others, especially authority figures Avoids participation in group activities Reluctant to self-disclose Hostile and defensive Strong need to be self-sufficient	Poor interpersonal relationships with boss and peer group.	May meet demands of work role because of high ambition, especially in work environments that are highly structured and nonthreatening.
Schizoid career client	Very indecisive Vague about goals Does not desire or enjoy close relationships Prefers solitary activities Often aloof	Work involving interpersonal interactions is difficult.	May work well in an environment that provides social isolation.
Cluster B[1] Antisocial career client	Truancy, vandalism, stealing Nonconformity to social norms Very aggressive Inconsistent work behavior Poor emotional control	Difficulty in sustaining productive work.	Clients who are identified as having only several characteristics of this disorder may be able to function successfully in a work role. However, full-blown antisocial career clients have considerable interference with work roles.
Borderline career client	Poor self-concept Difficulty in establishing long-term goals Difficulty with career choice Difficulty with identifying preferred values Impulsive Unstable interpersonal relations Uncertainty about life roles	Impulsive behavior interferes with work-role functioning; poor commitment to work.	The instability and impulsive nature of borderline career clients presents considerable interference with most life roles, including the work role.

[1] Not all personality disorders are included in Clusters A, B, and C.

TABLE 18-1
(continued)

Identification	Behaviors, Beliefs, Traits	Work Impairment	Other Work-Role Observations
Narcissistic career client	Exploits others Shows little concern for others Expects favorable treatment Excessive feelings of self-importance Constantly seeks attention	Poor interpersonal relationships; may pursue unrealistic goals while exploiting co-workers.	Because of a strong need for success and power, these clients are able to meet requirements and sometimes excel in work-role functioning.
Cluster C[1] Obsessive-compulsive career client	Preoccupied with trivial details Seeks perfection in work tasks to the point that task completion is constantly delayed Has strong need for inflexible routines Avoids decision making Unnecessarily devoted to organizing tasks	Poor task completion. Poor productivity. Subject to stress because of indecision.	Because of excessive conscientiousness and extreme attention to detail, these clients are able to function in work roles that require highly organized procedures.
Passive-aggressive career client	Makes excessive excuses for poor productivity Passively resists demands of work role Excessive procrastination Deliberately works at a slow pace Usually covertly defiant of authority	Work role is greatly affected by intentional inefficiency.	Some clients with this disorder are able to maintain enough efficiency to function in a work role.
Depressed[2] career client	Lacks interest and pleasure in most activities Has difficulty in concentrating on tasks Behavior is typically lethargic and shows loss of energy Has difficulty sleeping or sleeps excessively Expresses negative feelings toward and about self Dejected mood Low self-evaluations	In severe cases, clients are not able to function in work role.	In mild to moderate cases of depression, some interference can be expected, but not all clients are totally inefficient.

[1]Not all personality disorders are included in Clusters A, B, and C.
[2]The depressed career client is not considered a personality disorder.
SOURCE: Adapted from *Diagnostic and Statistical Manual of Mental Disorders* (1987).

lines for identifying similar patterns of behavior in clients being interviewed. The purpose of this table is not to classify clients according to any particular disorder, but more important, to serve as a guide to identify behavioral contingencies and faulty assumptions that may lead to work impairment. A client who may be identified as having poor social interaction skills, for instance, may also have difficulty relating to work affiliates and thus develop negative meanings associated with work.

Table 18-1 identifies disorders by behaviors, beliefs, and traits. The column "Potential Work Impairments" suggests that some clients may have difficulty in the workplace when the behaviors, beliefs, or traits listed in the column are dominant and extreme. On the other hand, behaviors, beliefs, and traits associated with disorders may not necessarily lead to work impairment as suggested in the column "Other Work-Role Observations." Using this logic, the interviewer attempts to determine the degree to which an identified behavior or trait affects the work role. For example, work involving interpersonal interactions may be difficult for some clients, but these clients have managed to become productive workers. Perhaps they could improve their potential with counseling designed to help them overcome this problem in all life roles, but their needs are not as obvious as someone who simply cannot function effectively with others. In sum, the severity of the identified needs determines the course and extent of intervention strategies.

In the DSM-III-R (1987), personality disorders are grouped into three clusters—A, B, and C—to accommodate the commonalities found among them. For example, career clients who resemble the characteristics, traits, and behaviors found in the Cluster A group may appear strange, peculiar, and bizarre. Likewise, those career clients who resemble the characteristics associated with the Cluster B group may appear highly emotional and dramatic. Those identified with Cluster C may appear anxious and fearful. The commonalities and overlap of symptoms found in personality disorders suggest to the interviewer that clients may demonstrate behaviors, beliefs, and traits of more than one personality disorder.

In an attempt to organize qualities of work behavior that lead to failure in work, Neff (1985) identified five types or patterns of work psychopathology using classifications ranging from Type I to Type V, as shown in Table 18-2. Individuals can be "typed" only when the characteristics listed predominate work behavior. Neff warns that not all clients will fit into these categories; some may have characteristics of several.

The guidelines for identifying characteristics that could lead to work impairment must be used with caution. Identified characteristics must predominate to be significant. Moreover, work behavior is considered to be a semiautonomous area of personality and as such may not be affected by personality disorders. On the other hand, work maladaption may be linked to personality disorders. In sum, these guidelines present examples of potential work behavior problems and should be used as such. In the next chapter, examples of methods of identifying potential work behavior problems are illustrated.

TABLE 18-2
Neff's Patterns of Work Psychopathology

Type	Characteristics
I—Individuals who lack motivation to work	• Have a negative concept of the work role. • Are indifferent to productive work. • Will work if coerced. • Meet minimum standards of work tasks. • Resist work commitment. • Require close supervision. • Lack need or desire to work.
II—Individuals who experience fear and anxiety in response to being productive	• Feel incapable of being productive. • Feel too inept to meet work demands. • Have low self-esteem. • Competition at work is extremely threatening. • Cooperative work efforts are difficult. • Lack self-confidence. • May retreat from work environment if severely threatened.
III—Individuals who are hostile and aggressive	• Underlying hostility is easily aroused. • Peer affiliation is viewed as potentially dangerous. • Are quick to quarrel with others. • Relation with supervisory personnel is precarious and threatening. • Work roles are often viewed as too demanding and restrictive. • Have very poor interpersonal relationships.
IV—Individuals who are very dependent on others	• Early socialization convinces them that the way to self-preservation is to please others. • Believe that the key to work success is pleasing authority figures. • Have a strong need for constant approval, particularly from supervisors.
V—Individuals who display a marked degree of social naivete	• Have very little knowledge of work environment and demands of work role. • Lack simple understanding of work-role involvement. • Have no perception of self as a successful worker to meet even minimal standards. • Unable to project self into work role.

Faulty Cognitions

We are challenged to give more attention to cognitive processes in career counseling from the social-learning theory approaches to career development discussed in Chapter 2 (Mitchell & Krumboltz, 1990). Somewhat similar approaches to cognitive functioning are irrational beliefs (Ellis, 1962) and faulty reasoning (Beck, 1985). More specifically, the individual's perceptions of self and of people, events, experiences, and environment are seen as potential sources of mistaken and troublesome beliefs. Inaccurate information, faulty alternatives, and negative constructs derived from life experiences are sources of faulty cognitions.

Faulty cognitions inhibit systematic, logical thinking and as such can be self-defeating. For example, a client's expectations and assumptions can cause distorted perceptions and unrealistic thinking such as "There is only one career for me." Doyle (1992) presented other examples of faulty cognition that he suggested can lead to false conclusions and negative feelings:

1. *Self-deprecating statements*—These expressions reveal poor self-worth, for example, "I'm not a good student" or "No one really likes me."

2. *Absolute or perfectionist terms*—When an individual sets up overly stringent guidelines for his or her behavior, the individual sets himself or herself up for self-criticism and a negative self-image. Conclusions that are absolute or perfectionistic often include the words *must, ought, should, unless,* or *until.* For example, "I should have been the one promoted" or "Unless I get an 'A,' I can't go home."

3. *Overgeneralization of negative experiences*—These are deductions based on too few examples of situations. Frequently, they are based on negative experiences that make clients think there are many obstacles making the future hopeless and bleak. For example, "Since I failed the first exam, I will fail the course" or "All the children in school hate me."

4. *Negative exaggerations*—These statements greatly magnify the true meaning of an event or reality. For example, "All professional athletes are greedy" or "You insulted my mother—you hate my family!"

5. *Factually inaccurate statements*—These remarks are based on inadequate or incorrect information. These erroneous data distort the client's perceptions of reality. For example, "You need an 'A' average to get into college" or "Autistic children are lazy."

6. *Ignorance of the effects of time*—These assertions ignore growth, maturation, and the effect that the passage of time can have on experience or events. For example, "He was a very poor student last year—he will surely fail this year" or "I have to go back to the lake and relive my vacation there." (p. 85).

Although faulty cognitions can lead to a multitude of personal problems, Mitchell and Krumboltz (1990) argued that the career decision-making process is most affected. Looking at it from a positive viewpoint, individuals with accurate, constructive beliefs will have fewer problems reaching their career goals. Moreover, realistic expectations foster positive emotional reactions to self and others.

In sum, this portion of the interview requires an assessment of the client's beliefs, generalities that cause a belief, other bases for a belief, and the actions that are a result of a belief (Mitchell & Krumboltz, 1987). Chapter 19 provides other criteria for evaluating faulty cognitions and also presents counseling-intervention strategies designed to introduce more rational, productive ways of thinking.

Memory and Persistence

A prerequisite to more complex capabilities is the client's ability to concentrate on tasks without being distracted by other stimuli (Schwartz, 1989). In the context of career counseling, clients must be able to process information about work environments and themselves in order to make decisions in their best interests. The ability to attend selectively and to concentrate over time is a vital part of cognitive functioning necessary in the career decision-making process.

Some of the specific tasks for evaluating memory and concentration are reported in Hersen and Turner (1985), Craig (1989), and Othmer and Othmer (1989). Techniques suggested are straightforward, informal, and designed to screen clients for gross deficits in memory and concentration.

Memory is usually classified into three types: immediate (the client's ability to recall information he or she has just been told), recent (the client's ability to recall events that took place in the last several days, weeks, or months), and remote (the client's ability to recall events that happened several years in the past). Assessment for each type of memory provides important insights into each client's current cognitive-functioning capabilities. Impairment of memory may indicate the client is easily distracted, preoccupied, confused, anxious, or depressed and/or may have psychiatric disorders. The important point for the counselor to ascertain is the degree of severity of impairment in memory and concentration. The counselor will want to find out if the client is capable of adequately attending to the tasks of a selected career-counseling program. The rule of thumb here is, when in doubt, seek assistance from other professionals. A client with significant deficits in concentration and/or memory should be referred for a formal inquiry (Rosenthal & Akiskal, 1985).

Memory can be evaluated during the course of the interview in an informal manner. For example, one way to check immediate recall is to spell your name or the name of the school or a city and ask the client to repeat the spelling. To check recent memory, ask the client to give directions to a well-known location or to your office. Remote memory can be evaluated during a discussion of past events (Othmer & Othmer, 1989). A more formalized method of evaluating memory is described in Hersen and Turner (1985).

Assessing immediate recall.   To assess immediate recall, the client is asked to remember three things that are presented verbally; for example, pen, blue, and the number 14. After the client successfully repeats the items, he or she is instructed to keep remembering them, because the counselor will ask for a repetition in approximately 5 minutes.

In another assessment technique, the client is instructed to listen carefully to a series of numbers; he or she will be asked to repeat them immediately after the presentation. For example, "Listen carefully and repeat these numbers after I'm finished." (Present them at the rate of one each second.) "2-7-9." After each successful answer, the number of digits is increased, 1-5-4-7, and so forth. When the client is no longer able to recall the digits in proper sequence, the process is repeated with the instructions to recall the digits in backward order, starting with two numbers and increasing the number of digits each time. Individuals with normal intelligence and without any organic impairment can usually repeat six digits forward and five in reverse (Hersen & Turner, 1985).

Assessing for recent memory. A measure of recent memory can be accomplished by asking clients about verifiable information that has transpired within a few days. Some example questions are as follows:

What did you eat for lunch yesterday?
Who was the presidential candidate who spoke at the municipal auditorium this week?
Tell me what you saw on TV news last night.
What national holiday did we celebrate on Wednesday?

Assessing remote memory. Remote memory can be evaluated by asking clients to assess recollections of significant historical events. The ability to cognitively select and recall significant events in the past is a measure of remote memory. Some examples follow:

Where were you born?
Where did you go to high school?
What was the Great Depression?
What was your first job outside the home?
What was Watergate?
What was Desert Storm?

Assessing concentration and task persistence. Concentration and task persistence refer to the ability to sustain focused attention sufficiently to permit the completion of tasks commonly found in career-counseling programs. For example, is the client able to sustain focused attention to permit the completion of such tasks as gathering information; generating, evaluating, and selecting alternatives; and formulating plans to implement decisions? According to Hersen and Turner (1985), deficiencies in concentration and memory can be observed through serial subtraction.

For assessment of concentration, the client is asked to subtract 3 from 100, then 3 from that number, then 3 again, and so forth. If this task is done correctly for five or six subtractions, then the client is asked to subtract 7 from 100, and so forth. The counselor will need to determine whether an inability to perform these calculations is primarily due to educational level and calculating ability or to the inability to concentrate. For example, if a client has a college degree and is unable to calculate beyond one subtraction, the counselor could probably conclude that the ability to concentrate has been adversely affected.

SUMMARY

1. Recently, more attention has been directed to personal problems and faulty cognitions that can adversely affect career decision making.

2. Deficits in cognitive clarity require intervention other than career guidance. Because career problems are often an integral part of personal problems, intervention strategies deal with both simultaneously.

3. The assessment interview is designed to identify client needs for career counseling and/or other career needs that could interfere with career development and life-role functioning.

4. The assessment interview includes gathering current status information, discovering problems that interfere with career development, discovering the significance of life roles and potential conflicts, and developing goals and objectives.

5. Techniques for interviewing include establishing rapport, observation, self-disclosure, open- and close-ended questions, echoing, continuation, and staying on track.

6. General appearance is a generalized observation of the client's personal grooming, posture, facial expressions, and mannerisms.

7. Attitude and behavior are observed through the quality of the interaction with the counselor.

8. Affect and mood are evaluated by the client's emotional tone and reported status.

9. Demographic information and work, medical, educational, and family history are obtained by self-report and/or through direct questioning.

10. Life roles selected for interviewing include worker, homemaker, citizen, and leisurite. Life roles are considered an integral part of each individual's development. Success in one life role enhances success in another.

11. Behavior patterns that impair the work role are identified in the assessment interview as needs that determine intervention strategies.

12. Faulty cognitions inhibit systematic, logical thinking and can be self-defeating. Sources of faulty cognitions are primarily from life experiences.

13. Memory is classified as immediate, recent, and remote. Memory can be evaluated during the course of the interview through informal questioning and by more formalized procedures.

SUPPLEMENTARY LEARNING EXERCISES

1. Develop a list of reasons to support assessment interviewing for career counseling. Give specific examples to support your reasons.
2. Present two examples of irrational beliefs that could interfere with career decision making.
3. Develop interview objectives for a specific ethnic client. Justify your rationale.
4. Discuss how work history can identify work maladjustment. Build two cases to illustrate.

5. Defend and/or criticize the following statement: Life roles are to be considered as a significant part of career development.

6. Develop two examples to illustrate how self-disclosure can or cannot be effective in the interview.

7. Present several examples of dialogue to illustrate the effective use of open- and close-ended questions.

8. Have the benefits of leisure activities been overemphasized? Defend your arguments to classmates.

9. Develop a list of intervention strategies that could be used to encourage shared responsibilities in the home for two-earner families.

10. Give several examples of behavior that could be identified with career client personality disorders in Table 18-1. Explain how these identified behavior patterns would or would not interfere with the work role.

Chapter Nineteen
Career-Counseling Interviews

In the preceding chapter, the rationale for interviewing clients for career counseling pointed out the need for developing an assessment interview to determine appropriate intervention strategies. Embedded in this rationale is the recognition that some career clients may not fully benefit from career decision-making procedures for a variety of reasons including illogical thinking, irrational beliefs, other faulty cognitions, and/or severe psychological problems. What is needed are methods of identifying potential problems that inhibit clients from making decisions in their best interests. For example, those clients who cannot reason in a rational manner, have erroneous perceptions of work roles, and are unable to accurately process career information because of false beliefs would best be served by intervention programs to correct these problems before continuing in career decision making.

We cannot, of course, deal only with factors that inhibit career decision making. We must also deal with contingencies that contribute to work-role maladjustment and potential problems associated with family, homemaker, citizen, and leisure roles. The assumption that life-role development is the outcome of the long process of personal and interpersonal development gives credence to the position of focusing attention on each client's perception of the interrelationship of these roles. For example, poor interpersonal skills found as limiting factors in the work role may also impair the development of the citizen role (interpersonal relations in civic clubs) and the leisure role (activities involving others). Although life roles are discussed as separate entities, problems in one life role may affect development in another. In essence, the career counselor's ability to effectively tease out problems that inhibit positive growth must be recognized as a necessary skill for using the assessment interview.

In the first section of this chapter, an assessment interview closely follows the sequence for interviewing suggested in Chapter 18, starting with current status information. The second section contains a discussion of problems that interfere with career development; identification of these problems is illustrated with case studies. Part three covers life roles and potential conflicts. Finally, the development of goals and objectives is discussed.

CURRENT STATUS INFORMATION

Techniques for observing clients were illustrated in Chapter 18; therefore, in this section, more emphasis will be devoted to the value of demographic information and work, medical, and educational histories.

The Case of What Was Left Unsaid

Ida, a 36-year-old woman, was referred by a mental health agency to a state-supported agency that provided career counseling. The information that was sent with the referral contained demographic data, a sparse educational history, a diagnosis of clinical depression, and prescribed medication. The following notes were made by the career counselor as she interviewed Ida:

A. General appearance
  - Client was appropriately dressed.
  - Hair had not been recently washed.
  - Wore little or no makeup.
  - Wore glasses.
  - Gait was normal.
  - Movements were without tremor.
  - Carried envelope and placed it on desk.
B. Attitude and behavior
  - Introduced herself.
  - Eye contact was appropriate.
  - Showed no evidence of unusual behavior.
C. Affect and mood
  - Said she was depressed but did not look it.
  - Appeared rather lifeless.
  - Stated that she was somewhat nervous about being interviewed.
  - Stated she "felt good" especially when she was alone.
  - Said she didn't like "being around a lot of people."
  - Was vague when expressing herself.
D. Demographic information
  - Said she was married four times, but could not remember the sequence of birth of four children or which marriage they were from.
  - High-pitched voice used during discussion of marriages.
  - Currently living with a cousin who helps care for her children.
E. Work experiences
  - Difficulty in recalling work experiences.
  - Held part-time job in fast-food restaurant during senior year in high school.
  - Held part- and full-time jobs in fast foods for several months after graduation.
  - Waitressed in different local restaurants.
  - Was a receptionist in accounting firm for about four months.
  - Disliked restaurant work.

- Enjoyed work as a receptionist; claims she left because she was hospitalized.
F. Medical history
  - Stated that she was in good health until age 29 when she was hospitalized for depression. Stayed in a psychiatric hospital for five days. Has been treated as an outpatient with medication for several years but was unable to specify exactly how long.
  - Felt that failure in marriage was a major cause of depression.
  - Reported problems with sleeping.
  - Reported no other significant illnesses.
G. Educational history
  - Finished high school with average grades.
  - Did not finish a course in computer programming. Said she had a strange feeling "that she should not finish this course."

During the interview the counselor became concerned about vague references to past history. Even with further questioning, she could not get appropriate feedback:

Counselor: Ida, could you tell me more about the feeling you experienced that convinced you not to finish the computer programming course?
Ida: I don't know how to explain it—it was just like something told me not to finish.
Counselor: Something told you not to finish?
Ida: Yeah, I can't explain it.

Another example was expressions about work experiences.

Ida: I quit working with them because my uncle told me to.
Counselor: Does your uncle often give you advice?
Ida: He helps me a lot—he just seems to know what's best.

The counselor decided to end the interview and get more information about Ida's past history. Another appointment was set to continue the interview. In the meantime, a complete report was received from a mental health agency, which contained a signed release, a social history, and psychological workup. Ida had been diagnosed as a schizophrenic, undifferentiated type, and had been hospitalized on three occasions in the last five years.

When Ida was asked why she didn't mention the hospitalization, she responded with a shrug. The counselor also discovered that the uncle who was currently advising Ida had died ten years earlier.

In the case of severe psychiatric problems, there is usually evidence of marked impairment of life-role functioning, particularly in the work role and homemaker role. The client's suggestion of a "sixth sense" telling her to abruptly quit an educational program and the fact that she felt controlled by someone else was enough evidence to request more in-depth information. Since the psychiatric and psychological evaluation was three years old, the counselor requested a complete update.

One of the major learning outcomes of this case is the importance of obtaining all available client information. The documented history of severe psychological problems does not always translate into suspending career counseling but may require an up-to-date evaluation of current psychological status.

DISCOVERING PROBLEMS THAT INTERFERE WITH CAREER DEVELOPMENT
Faulty cognitions

Examples of faulty cognitions from Doyle (1992) in Chapter 18 offer a sound basis for assessing a faulty deductive-thinking process. Doyle's (1992) six examples are ways of thinking that reflect negative feelings about oneself. Irrational expectations of career counseling, as suggested by Nevo (1987), are examples of faulty cognitions and irrational thoughts often found in prospective clients.

1. There is only one vocation in the world that is right for me.
2. Until I find my perfect vocational choice, I will not be satisfied.
3. Someone else can discover the vocation suitable for me.
4. Intelligence tests would tell me how much I am worth.
5. I must be an expert or very successful in the field of my work.
6. I can do anything if I try hard, or I can't do anything that doesn't fit my talents.
7. My vocation should satisfy the important people in my life.
8. Entering a vocation will solve all my problems.
9. I must sense intuitively that the vocation is right for me.
10. Choosing a vocation is a one-time act.

The goal for the interviewer is to help clients identify maladaptive thinking. Using "choosing a vocation is a one-time act" as an example, the counselor asked the client to explain this expressed belief.

The Case of Faulty Assumptions

Client: I want to find my lifetime job now and get it over with so I can go on to other things.

Counselor: What kind of job did you have in mind?

Client: I thought that's what you're supposed to help me with. . . . anyway, I want a job that I can start in when I graduate.

The counselor then asked the client to describe the basis for his belief.

Counselor: Do you think you will stay with the job you choose now for the rest of your life?

Client: Well, I guess so. My father has worked as a bookkeeper as long as I can remember.

Counselor: Was he always a bookkeeper?

Client: Umm, come to think of it, he did work somewhere else.
Counselor: Do you think you might also have other job opportunities in the future?
Client: I never thought of that, but I guess I will.

The counselor was now in a position to explain the idea of career development over the life span and the importance of learning career decision-making techniques. In addition, he could help the client analyze faulty reasoning and false assumptions. The path to a more logical approach to career decision making had been established.

Doyle (1992) suggested a technique for helping this client work through faulty reasoning. The client writes out beliefs and conclusions and the assumptions on which they are based. For example:

All bankers are rich.
Once you are a banker, you drive a big car.
The only way for me to get rich is to become a banker.

The rationale for this exercise is based on the premise that faulty reasoning and faulty logic usually have underlying faulty assumptions. Having clients write out their assumptions in this manner assists them in recognizing that their beliefs may be inaccurate.

Yet another way of helping clients identify faulty cognitions is through the use of the *Career Beliefs Inventory* (*CBI*) (Krumboltz, 1991) discussed in Chapter 7. If a counselor strongly suspects that a client has developed faulty assumptions, which are measurable with the *CBI*, this instrument could prove to be a valuable counseling tool. Career counselors should be familiar with such inventories, particularly those that help clients expose false beliefs that interfere with wise decision making.

Another technique used to help clients recognize that they have some control of their destiny is illustrated in Chapter 18. This technique is based upon Rotter's (1966) concept of locus of control. In sum, counselors arrange learning situations that prove clients can gain control of their lives through appropriate actions.

Behaviors That May Lead to Work Maladjustment

Observing current behavior and recording behavioral patterns from past events is a means of studying life experiences and their relationship to how clients have learned to behave. In this part of the interview, the focal point is on clients who manifest maladaptive behavior and methods to teach them appropriate ways to behave. Two case summaries are used to illustrate how behaviors may lead to work maladjustment.

The Case of the Confused Decision Maker
Maria, a 17-year-old high school student, asked for help in choosing a career. She reported to the counselor's office with one of her older brothers. She stated, "I cannot decide what to major in at college."

Maria was neatly dressed and well groomed. Her speech was fluent and of normal rate and rhythm. She tended to speak very softly. She seemed to be somewhat anxious about making a career decision. She did not appear to be depressed. She constantly looked to her brother for approval.

In the top 10% of her class, Maria had a record of being a very capable student. She had good rapport with teachers as well as with her peer group. She strongly identified with several girls her age at the high school.

Maria had five brothers and her father was a meat inspector in a local plant. He worked hard to maintain the family. Her mother had never worked outside the home.

When the counselor asked Maria to come into his office alone, she seemed very uncomfortable and asked if her brother could attend the session with her. The counselor reassured her that they would have ample time to talk with her brother later. She reluctantly agreed to begin the interview.

From the description Maria gave of her home environment, the counselor assumed it was very traditional. Moreover, the chores assigned to the children were typically based on what the parents considered appropriate work for boys and for girls. There seemed to be strict stereotypical roles embedded in Maria's perception of traditional work roles for women. She appeared to be very passive and gave the impression that she expected someone else to make decisions for her.

When discussing future objectives, Maria seemed quite confused when the counselor suggested she consider all careers including nontraditional ones. At one time she had expressed an interest in architecture but considered it to be for men only and therefore decided against it as a possible choice.

Maria's behavior pattern reflected little confidence in her own abilities and deference to others for decision making. She appeared to be quite uneasy when she was asked to leave her brother and constantly referred to him as giving her good advice and reassuring her of what was best for her. The following dialogue demonstrates her dependency needs.

Maria: My parents will help me choose the right kind of work.
Counselor: Could you tell me more about your parents' choosing the right kind of work for you?
Maria: My mother and father usually help me with most of the things that I decide on, and if they don't, my older brothers do.

From these excerpts, it seemed clear that Maria was quite dependent on others for decision making. Maria's background and behavior patterns closely matched Neff's (1985) Type IV pattern of individuals who are very dependent on others. The counselor feared that Maria might make career decisions based on what her family considered best for her rather than on her interests, values, and abilities. Also, the counselor suspected that if Maria's current behavior patterns continued as is, she would suffer the consequences of a Type IV worker.

The counselor's strategy consisted of building greater rapport with Maria and establishing a basic trust as follows:

1. Be respectful and genuine.
2. Focus on developing self-awareness by using reflective procedures.
3. Assist her in understanding how environmental circumstances influenced her behavior.
4. Help her establish alternative ways of thinking and behaving.
5. Assist her in recognizing how she can control her own destiny by illustrating the concept of locus of control; that is, how external and internal people think.
6. Help her recognize the relevance of her values and interests in a career decision-making mode.
7. Introduce career decision-making steps as discussed in Chapter 14.

To promote more realistic goals for career decision making, especially toward self-direction, the counselor chose a cognitive behavioral-intervention strategy (Ellis, 1971; Corey, 1991). The first step included techniques to help Maria separate rational beliefs from irrational ones. Second, the counselor assisted Maria in modifying her thinking, especially the thoughts associated with stereotypical gender-role development. Third, the counselor challenged Maria to develop a greater self-awareness and a more realistic philosophy of integrated life-role development. To help her reduce stereotyping in career options, Maria was also scheduled to view the *BORN FREE* series (Hansen, 1978).

The Case of the Anxious Computer Technician

A 28-year-old male computer technician named John sought out the services of a career counselor in private practice. His major complaint was a recent upsurge in anxiety when a new group of workers was assigned to his department. He felt threatened by them and, as he saw it, was treated as an outsider and definitely not a part of their group. He feared that he would be fired and considered resigning and finding a different job or asking for reassignment to another department.

John appeared to be anxious; he moved around in his chair and the pitch of his voice changed, particularly when talking about this new group of people. He constantly moved his arms and hands and clenched his fists. He did not appear to be depressed and stated that he felt very anxious.

John had never seriously considered marriage; he saw himself as a "loner." Furthermore, he had few friends and spoke of himself as being shy with limited social contacts.

John evaluated his educational background as average or above in academics. He had received computer training from a local community college. He was currently taking more courses. John characterized his student life in much the same way as his current situation, that is, few social activities and a feeling of isolation.

The role of citizen was interpreted as voting in most elections; he did not participate in any civic activities. He expressed a feeling of rejection by the individuals in organizations he had met. John collected musical records from the Big Band era and enjoyed listening to them when he was alone. He occasionally attended movies, visited his parents, and watched TV.

When expressing work-role experiences, his anxiety seemed to peak, as observed by increased motor activities. Earlier trends of isolating himself from contact with others continued in the current work environment; he ate by himself in the cafeteria and did not join bull sessions during breaks. He did not have a "good" friend among the peer group. He characterized his work role as quietly getting the job done.

John's symptoms of anxiety seemed to be related to a long-standing pattern of difficulty with social interactions. Low self-esteem, feelings of rejection, and avoidance of social activities were embedded in most of his statements. These characteristics are found in Neff's (1985) Type II work psychopathology and in Cluster A personality disorders (see Chapter 18). However, John does not exhibit all of the Type II characteristics; likewise he cannot be identified with any one personality disorder but has characteristics of two or more. This example could be quite typical of many career clients and supports the assumption that identified behaviors, actions, beliefs, and thinking can be generically evaluated as contingencies that could lead to work maladjustment. In sum, John had a history of being an acceptable worker. His life roles could be enhanced with better social skills and more positive self-concepts as a worker and social being. John wanted to change jobs for the wrong reasons. The counselor suggested that he could explore other career opportunities and simultaneously participate in a counseling program designed to help him recognize sources of stress. Other intervention strategies selected were anxiety-management training, social skills and assertiveness training, and relaxation training. In addition, thought-stopping techniques (Cautela & Wisock, 1977; Doyle, 1992) were used to eliminate inappropriate thinking, negative self-concepts, and worry-oriented thinking.

The counseling intervention strategies proposed for John were based on the following premise: emotions are often the result of how we think, and a change in John's thinking process could reduce or eliminate emotional disorders and dysfunctional behaviors (Trower, Casey, & Dryden, 1988; Ellis & Grieger, 1977; Lazarus, 1989).

There are many sources of stress in the work environment, as discussed in Chapter 3, including poor communications between management and workers and between peer groups. Techniques for group-counseling procedures designed to improve communication skills are illustrated in Chapter 16.

Memory and Persistence

This part of the interview is used when there is sufficient evidence to suspect problems with immediate, recent, and/or remote memory. Typical examples of memory loss include forgetting names, telephone numbers, directions, and so forth. In more severe cases, memory loss may interfere with social and occupational functioning. Excerpts from a case history are used to illustrate the identification of memory loss and persistence.

The Case of the Forgotten Work Address

A 52-year-old man named Jack was accompanied by his wife to see a career counselor in private practice. She stated that she wanted her husband to get a steady job with a guaranteed salary.

Jack was neatly dressed and groomed. He had short combed hair and was freshly shaven. He appeared confused and was somewhat bewildered as to why he was there and what he was to do. His speech patterns suggested he had difficulty in recalling words to complete sentences. He stated that he felt well and was looking forward to being "talked to." There had been no indications of depression. Jack had been married on two occasions. His first marriage lasted only about 18 months because, as he put it, "I was very young." He has two children from his current marriage of 20 years. He lives with his wife in a home they own. One child is currently attending college.

For over 20 years, Jack's main occupation was cafeteria manager in a small town. Approximately a year ago, he was fired from his job and was currently selling cosmetics as a door-to-door salesman. When asked why he was fired, Jack stated that they told him he was not capable of doing the work anymore. When asked what he would like to do in the future, he replied "I like to read a lot and wouldn't mind working in a bookstore."

Jack appeared to be in good health and was of medium build and weight. He stated that he did have hypertension, which was controlled by medication.

Jack had gone to the local high school and received a B.S. degree from the state university. He had above-average grades in high school and college. When asked why he had planned to change jobs, Jack responded by asking that his wife be allowed to come in and describe his current condition. Jack's wife mentioned that he had been an effective cafeteria manager until about 18 months ago, when he started having difficulty remembering chores that he'd done automatically in the past. He misplaced cash receipts, forgot to make assignments of the personnel (causing chaos in the cafeteria), and forgot the address of the cafeteria. Jack was given a second chance but was not able to improve his work efficiency. He had now taken a sales job selling cosmetics and had not been too successful. His wife also pointed out that he had difficulty coordinating his clothing; he selected conflicting color combinations and at times put his T-shirt on backward. He also stumbled frequently, and when he mowed the yard, he made criss-cross patterns, leaving part of the lawn unmowed. At night when he got up to go to the bathroom, he would return to the wrong room. At this point, the counselor got agreement from the couple to evaluate Jack's memory. When Jack was asked to repeat the spelling of the city in which he lived, he was only able to spell it with prompting. He also failed to repeat other spellings that were presented. When asked, Jack was unable to give directions to several well-known locations within the city. The counselor then asked Jack to listen carefully to a series of numbers and repeat them immediately after presentation. He was unable to respond correctly after two trials with only three digits. He was not able to recall any digits backward.

The procedure used for assessing recent memory was as follows: When Jack was asked what he had for lunch yesterday, he responded with a typical luncheon menu, but his wife stated that this was not the food that she served him. When he was asked what he saw on the TV news the night before, he simply responded by saying "the same old thing."

The assessment of remote memory was more encouraging. Jack was able to state his birthdate, where he went to high school, and where he obtained his first job outside his home. The counselor concluded that he had poor immediate and recent recall, but his remote memory was fairly well intact.

Jack's wife verified that he had difficulty concentrating and following tasks through to completion. She gave several examples in which he had difficulty maintaining focus on a particular task like mowing the yard or going to a local store to purchase a single item. It seemed that Jack would easily leave a task without giving much thought to the consequences of his actions.

The counselor referred Jack to a neurologist, who discovered Jack had a brain tumor. An operation followed shortly thereafter, and the tumor turned out to be benign. Several months after rehabilitation, Jack returned to the counselor's office ready to search for a new occupation. He had decided during his recovery time that he wished to follow his desire of working in a bookstore. The counselor began the assessment interview once again.

DISCOVERING THE SIGNIFICANCE OF LIFE ROLES AND POTENTIAL CONFLICTS

Life roles are considered significant determinants of an individual's lifestyle (Super, 1990) and as such constitute a formidable influence on career development. Assessment interviews also help discover if clients have significant role conflicts and the degree to which such conflicts inhibit career development. However, the evaluation of life roles for this interview should be based on individual needs and interests. For example, not everyone needs or wants to participate in a civic organization. What is profound, however, is to identify a need that can be fulfilled in civic activities. Life roles should be viewed as having individualized meanings and purposes and as developmentally linked to career development; conflicts in one role can hamper the development and satisfaction of other roles. The following excerpts from interviews illustrate the significance of life-role evaluations.

The Case of the Fired Plumber
Jim, a 40-year-old plumber, requested career counseling to change jobs. "I don't like this plumbing work anymore," he said. He was dressed in soiled work clothes and hadn't shaved for several days. Jim appeared to be anxious; he constantly moved in his chair, raised his arms, and clenched his fists. He

was grossly overweight and requested that he be given permission to smoke. His speech was fluent and of normal rate and rhythm.

Jim completed high school but had no other formal training. He claimed to be an average student and never failed a grade. During on-the-job training, he learned the skills to become a licensed plumber.

Starting at the lowest level in plumbing, he had advanced to the master plumber status and had been employed as a plumber for 12 years. He was recently fired for disruptive behavior and fighting with two fellow workers.

Jim reported no serious medical problems and had no history of psychiatric treatment. He had been a tobacco smoker for 15 years and occasionally drank alcohol.

For leisure, Jim watched sports on TV and enjoyed renting movies for home viewing. He also enjoyed watching his son play Little League baseball and regularly practiced with him. Short family vacations consisted of visiting relatives and camping.

Jim was not active in civic affairs, other than annually helping organize the local Little League. He claimed that he had such little time off from his work that it would be difficult for him to actively participate in civic organizations.

Evidently Jim felt that household duties were "woman's work," and even though his wife worked full-time outside the home, he did not help with such tasks as cooking, shopping, washing, or housecleaning. He did mow the yard and water the grass. Jim complained that his wife had recently demanded his help with household chores, which resulted in several major arguments that lasted for days. It was obvious that Jim and his wife were not on very good terms and had seriously considered divorce. Shortly after his wife chose to spend several days with her mother to "sort things out," Jim was fired for fighting on the job.

The fact that Jim had worked for the same plumbing company and with most of the same peer affiliates for 15 years indicated that he had the skills necessary to interact appropriately within the work environment. It was also clear that Jim's relations with his wife were in turmoil. Although it was difficult for the counselor to determine at this time if serious marital problems had existed for a long time, it was clear that Jim's refusal to help with household chores precipitated the most recent problems. Jim admitted that he enjoyed working as a plumber, but the stress associated with dual-earner problems had probably influenced how he felt about his current work environment.

This case is a good example of how one life role affects another. The major problem was conflict between husband and wife who both worked full-time outside the home, not wanting a job change. The counselor's plan was to have Jim and his wife commit to counseling with emphasis on sharing responsibilities and household tasks.

The techniques suggested were based on Hansen's (1991) Integrative Life Planning Model, which encourages couples to move away from dominate-subordinate relationships to equal partners. Among other changes suggested in this model are movement from the position of "job to life roles, and from achievement only to achievement and relationships for both women and men"

(Hansen, 1991, p. 84). Career decision making for a different job would be deferred for the time being. Jim agreed to relocate with a different company as a plumber.

Work and family are not separate worlds, and the case of the fired plumber illustrates how conflict in the homemaker role influenced Jim's behavior in the work role. Other problem areas that may contribute to conflicts include the following:

Shift work
Separation and travel
Relocation
Work spillover (preoccupation with work role)
Relationships with supervisors
Relationships with co-workers

The Case of the Unfulfilled Worker

Karen, a 42-year-old married woman, was self-referred to a career counselor in private practice because, as she put it, "I really don't know what's wrong with me. I like my job and I'm happy with my marriage and my family, but something is missing in my life." Karen was very attractive and neatly and appropriately dressed. She had a new hairdo and made an outstanding appearance. She was very fluent and her speech was of normal rate and rhythm. Although Karen had a positive attitude about her work and many other factors of her life, she still felt that she could improve her lifestyle. She expressed dismay at not being able to be more specific about what was troubling her. She seemed to be somewhat depressed but stated that she was feeling well.

Karen had been married on two different occasions. Her first marriage lasted only a short period, and as she put it, she married when she was very young and made a mistake. She'd been married the second time for over 20 years and had one child from this marriage. Her child was now attending college. Her husband was a professional engineer and had a good income.

Karen had several odd jobs while in high school and college working in fast-food places and dress shops. She was currently managing a local dress shop and had had this job for at least six years. She felt very comfortable in this work and enjoyed meeting people and doing the usual tasks that were involved in running and managing the shop. She expressed no particular desire to get another job but would be willing to if she were able to fulfill her needs better.

Karen stated that she was in excellent health and had never had significant problems with bad health. She was of medium height and weight.

Karen had received an A.A. degree at a local community college and was currently taking courses at a nearby college. She hoped to receive a degree in business management in the near future.

Karen and her husband, a dual-career couple, seemed to have worked out a very satisfactory relationship in their homemaker roles. Her husband participated in household tasks and assumed responsibilities that gave Karen more time to take care of her work and attend classes at college. She expressed no problems with her marital life and stated that her husband also seemed to be very happy.

As stated earlier, Karen felt that her work role was satisfactory. She had dreamed of managing a dress shop while she was an employee several years ago and now the opportunity had been given to her. The dress shop she currently managed had been very successful, and she had received several awards from the parent company for exceptional sales. She claimed to relate well to both employees and customers. She was taking a business management course to improve her skills in management

Because of the strong commitment to upgrade their careers, both Karen and her husband devoted little time to leisure activities. They exercised together in the morning by jogging and/or walking and attended various events in the community such as theater, movies, and art exhibits. Karen stated that they took the usual vacations, had taken their son to national parks, and had visited historical places.

When asked about participation in civic activities, Karen seemed somewhat bewildered and stated that she simply wouldn't have time to participate in these activities because of her full schedule. She was not aware of activities in local civic organizations and had not considered volunteerism.

The counselor returned to Karen's statement, "Something's missing in my life." The counselor asked her to express this feeling more fully:

Karen:	I don't know how to really explain it, and I feel guilty about even talking to someone about this. For gosh sakes, I have a great husband and a marvelous child and a very good job. I can't put a finger on what's wrong with me, but I seem to have a feeling that I want to do other things that I'm not doing at this time.
Counselor:	Tell me more about the feeling that you want to do "other things."
Karen:	Well, I have to give that some thought, but I guess what I really mean is I have a lot of interests and I haven't been able to fulfill many of them.
Counselor:	Tell me more about your interests.
Karen:	The first one that strikes my fancy is that I had dreams of being an artist, but when I took art classes and started painting, I quickly realized that I didn't have the talent to go on. But, I'm still interested in art and miss being around arts-and-crafts people.
Counselor:	Have you ever thought of taking an art class in college?
Karen:	Yes, I've had several of those, but I don't want to continue taking art classes.

As the conversation continued, the counselor felt that a values inventory might help Karen clarify needs she could not identify. The counselor recalled that values tend to remain fairly stable and endure over the life span. She felt that this might be an area that would help Karen come to some realization of what she would like to do in the future.

The counselor decided to use the Five-Step Process for Using Assessment Results developed by Zunker (1994). The steps are paraphrased as follows:

Step 1: Analyzing needs. In this step, the counselor ascertains the client's perception of her needs for information in order to foster self-knowledge. In evaluating Karen's lifestyle, she decided that work climate, family responsibilities, and leisure time had been committed, but rewarding activities in the community had been given little attention.

Counselor: Karen, you've expressed a very positive viewpoint of your work, family, and leisure activities. In fact, you had no negative thoughts concerning these life roles. It seems to be that other areas of your lifestyle may be lacking—what do you think?

Karen: You're probably right, but the only thing that you've mentioned so far has been civic activities, and as I told you, I know very little about them.

Counselor: Okay, well, I can give you more information about them, but at the same time I would like to know more about your needs and how you might fulfill them. Since we cannot identify specific needs at this time, let's agree that we want to identify some unknown need that gives you the feeling that something is "missing in your life."

Step 2: Establishing a purpose. Following the needs analysis, the counselor and the counselee decide on the purpose of testing. Both should recognize that testing cannot be expected to meet all identified needs. In Karen's case, however, the counselor was thinking of only one or two tests to foster self-knowledge. The purpose of each test and inventory should be explained in terms that the counselee can understand. In the following dialogue, the counselor attempts to link the purpose of the test to Karen's needs:

Counselor: As you recall, we've been talking about a number of needs that you feel have not been satisfied or, as you put it, fulfilled. Would you agree that an exploration of your values would be helpful?

Karen: Yes, I do, but what kind of test do you have in mind?

Counselor: Well, I was thinking of a values inventory that would help us establish priorities of values and also introduce sets of values for dialogue.

Step 3: Determining the instrument. The client and the counselor agree on the type of assessment instrument to be administered. The counselor relates the characteristics of the test and the kinds of information that it will provide.

Karen: Well, I think it would be great to take a values inventory, but I don't quite understand how it's going to help.

Counselor: You expressed a need to fill a gap in your life, and I think a values inventory that provides such measures as ability utilization, aesthetics, altruism, creativity, and lifestyle would be helpful.

Karen: Oh, that sounds great! Maybe they will tell me just what I need to know.

Counselor: A word of caution, Karen. These tests will help us discover some life-career values, but they are not designed to tell you what to do in the future. They will provide us with some information to discuss.

Step 4: Utilizing the results. The counselor interprets the test scores in a manner that the client can understand and relates the results to the established purpose of testing.

Counselor: Karen, here is a profile of your scores. You will notice that you have high scores in aesthetics, creativity, and social interaction. A high score in aesthetics means ——————

As the counselor went through an explanation of scores, she made certain that Karen understood that test scores from a values inventory are not necessarily more valid or accurate than her own perceptions of her problems. However, the results do provide new ideas and opportunities for specificity in the counseling dialogue. In Karen's case, this was important because she had been very vague about what she felt were her unfulfilled needs. As they discussed the results of the test, Karen agreed with the results from the standpoint that she did have a very high value in aesthetics; perhaps this was one area that was lacking in her life. It could provide other opportunities and interesting social interactions and creative endeavors.

Step 5: Making a decision. The final step is to make a decision based on the assessment's results. Karen decided that she would set aside more time to become involved as a volunteer at the local art museum. She also felt that it would be a good idea to eventually become a docent. She would seek agreement for her plans from her husband and son. The counselor was to see Karen after she had established herself at the art museum to continue dialogue and evaluate her progress.

DEVELOPING GOALS AND OBJECTIVES

The unique and distinct information obtained from an assessment interview is used to generate individualized goals for career-intervention counseling. The information that emerges about how clients interact in their environment and function in a diversity of life roles provides a clearer understanding of needs and subsequent counseling strategies and interventions. In an informative discussion of the goals of career intervention, Spokane (1991) suggests that clients are to become more positive about their ability to obtain major life goals as follows: "The goal of career intervention is to enhance the mobilization of persistently constructive attitudes, emotions, and behaviors that will improve the client's career attainment" (p. 56).

As part of a strategic planning model for practitioners and human service organizations, Kurpius, Burrello, and Rozecki (1990) recommend systematic planning as a necessary element to improve effectiveness. Part of this model includes a section that addresses the formulation of goals and objectives as follows:

1. Specify objectives.
2. Generate strategies.
3. Implement action plans.
4. Recycle (p. 5).

Brown and Brooks (1991) recommend the following sequence for goal setting:

1. Identify client goals.
2. Determine the feasibility of goals.
3. Establish subgoals.
4. Assess commitment to goals.

Using the case of the unfulfilled worker, we will apply the sequence for goal setting recommended by Brown and Brooks (1991).

Karen's identified goals were as follows:

1. to identify sources of anxiety;
2. to identify resources for a more balanced lifestyle; and
3. to identify values and their application to unmet needs.

The feasibility of these goals was established as being realistic.

1. The client was highly motivated to explore and discuss solutions.
2. There was mutual agreement on the overall goal of lifestyle direction.
3. There was mutual agreement on subgoals such as assessing values.

Subgoals were established as follows:

1. Assess values.
2. Visit the local art museum.
3. Share plans with family.

The commitment to goals was established by a mutually agreed-on systematic plan that the counselor carefully and fully explained. Her systematic approach enhanced Karen's willingness to participate. The key ingredients were the identification of needs and mutually agreed-on goals with systematic plans for action.

SUMMARY

1. Specially designed intervention programs are most useful for identifying clients who cannot reason in a rational manner, have erroneous perceptions of work roles, or have false beliefs.

2. Work-role maladjustment behaviors are also identified and modified through intervention programs. Attention should be focused on life-role development and the interrelationships of these roles.

3. The "Case of What Was Left Unsaid" points out the importance of obtaining all client background information available.

4. The "Case of Faulty Assumptions" illustrates the rationale that faulty reasoning and faulty logic are based on false assumptions.

5. The "Case of the Confused Decision Maker" illustrates how sex-role stereotyping can influence behavior and career decision-making.

6. The "Case of the Anxious Computer Technician" illustrates how fear and anxiety can interfere with work behavior and other life roles. Counseling-intervention strategies focused on helping the client recognize the sources of stress.

7. The "Case of the Forgotten Work Address" illustrates how memory can be evaluated with clients who demonstrate the inability to do routine work tasks.

8. The "Case of the Fired Plumber" illustrates how one life role can influence behavior in another role.

9. The "Case of the Unfulfilled Worker" is an example of how an unidentified need can be clarified through a five-step interpretation procedure using a values inventory.

SUPPLEMENTARY LEARNING EXERCISES

1. Using the "Case of What Was Left Unsaid," specify how the interviewer could have probed for more background information. Identify clues to the client's problems.
2. Suggest intervention strategies to deal with the following beliefs: "Psychological tests can tell me what to do in the future" and "I am destined to have only one vocation."
3. How can the concept of locus of control be effectively used to assist clients in controlling their future? Identify symptoms of behavior that would support the use of this procedure.
4. Develop a profile of behaviors that indicate stereotyped gender roles. Suggest intervention strategies.
5. What are the major symptoms of interpersonal relationship problems? Develop goals and objectives for modifying behavior.
6. Develop a supportive argument for the idea that life roles have individualized meanings.
7. Present examples of how one life role affects another. Give suggestions for identifying such problems in the interview.
8. Develop a case that illustrates how a narcissistic career client may behave in the workplace.
9. Illustrate the five steps for using assessment results with an interest inventory and an abilities test.
10. Present suggestions for detecting serious psychological problems in the interview. Illustrate with examples.

Appendix

EXPLANATION OF RELATIONSHIPS
WITHIN DATA, PEOPLE, AND THINGS HIERARCHIES

DATA: Information, knowledge, and conceptions related to data, people, or things, obtained by observation, investigation, interpretation, visualization, and/or mental creation; incapable of being touched; written data take the form of numbers, words, and symbols; other data are ideas, concepts, and oral verbalization.

0. *Synthesizing*—Integrating analyses of data to discover facts and/or develop knowledge concepts or interpretations.
1. *Coordinating*—Determining time, place, and sequence of operations or action to be taken on the basis of analysis of data; executing determinations and/or reporting on events.
2. *Analyzing*—Examining and evaluating data. Presenting alternative actions in relation to the evaluation is frequently involved.
3. *Compiling*—Gathering, collating, or classifying information about data, people, or things. Reporting and/or carrying out a prescribed action in relation to the information is frequently involved.
4. *Computing*—Performing arithmetic operations and reporting on and/or carrying out a prescribed action in relation to them. Does not include counting.
5. *Copying*—Transcribing, entering, or posting data.
6. *Comparing*—Judging the readily observable functional, structural, or compositional characteristics (whether similar to or divergent from obvious standards) of data, people, or things.

PEOPLE: Human beings; also animals dealt with on an individual basis as if they were human.

0. *Mentoring*—Dealing with individuals in terms of their total personality to advise, counsel, and/or guide them with regard to problems that may

be resolved by legal, scientific, clinical, spiritual, and/or other professional principles.

1. *Negotiating*—Exchanging ideas, information, and opinions with others to formulate policies and programs and/or arrive jointly at decisions, conclusions, or solutions.

2. *Instructing*—Teaching subject matter to others, or training others (including animals) through explanation, demonstration, and supervised practice; or making recommendations on the basis of technical disciplines.

3. *Supervising*—Determining or interpreting work procedures for a group of workers, assigning specific duties to them, maintaining harmonious relations among them, and promoting efficiency.

4. *Diverting*—Amusing others.

5. *Persuading*—Influencing others in favor of a product, service, or point of view.

6. *Speaking-Signaling*—Talking with and/or signaling people to convey or exchange information. Includes giving assignments and/or directions to helpers or assistants.

7. *Serving*—Attending to the needs or requests of people or animals or the expressed or implicit wishes of the people.

THINGS: Inanimate objects as distinguished from human beings; substances or materials; machines, tools, equipment; products. A thing is tangible and has shape, form, and other physical characteristics.

0. *Setting Up*—Adjusting machines or equipment by replacing or altering tools, jigs, fixtures, and attachments to prepare them to perform their functions, change their performance, or restore their proper functioning if they break down. Workers who set up one or a number of machines for other workers or who set up and personally operate a variety of machines are included here.

1. *Precision Working*—Using body members and/or tools or work aids to work, move, guide, or place objects or materials in situations where ultimate responsibility for the attainment of standards occurs and selection of appropriate tools, objects, or materials and the adjustment of the tool to the task require exercise of considerable judgment.

2. *Operating-Controlling*—Starting, stopping, controlling, and adjusting the progress of machines or equipment designed to fabricate and/or process objects or materials. Operating machines involves setting up the machine and adjusting the machine or material as the work progresses. Controlling equipment involves observing gauges, dials, and so on, and turning valves and other devices to control such factors as temperature, pressure, flow of liquids, speed of pumps, and reactions of materials. Setup involves several variables and adjustment is more frequent than in tending.

3. *Driving-Operating*—Starting, stopping, and controlling the actions of machines or equipment for which a course must be steered, or which must be guided, in order to fabricate, process, and/or move things or people. Involves such activities as observing gauges and dials; estimat-

ing distances and determining speed and direction of other objects; turning cranks and wheels; pushing clutches or brakes; and pushing or pulling gear lifts or levers. Includes such machines as cranes, conveyor systems, tractors, furnace charging machines, paving machines and hoisting machines. Excludes manually powered machines, such as hand trucks and dollies, and power-assisted machines, such as electric wheelbarrows and hand trucks.

4. *Manipulating*—Using body members, tools, or special devices to work, move, guide, or place objects or materials. Involves some latitude for judgment with regard to precision attained and selecting appropriate tool, object, or materials, although this is readily manifest.

5. *Tending*—Starting, stopping, and observing the functioning of machines and equipment. Involves adjusting materials or controls of the machine, such as changing guides, adjusting timers and temperature gauges, turning valves to allow flow of materials, and flipping switches in response to lights. Little judgment is involved in making these adjustments.

6. *Feeding-Offbearing*—Inserting, throwing, dumping, or placing materials in or removing them from machines or equipment which are automatic or tended or operated by other workers.

7. *Handling*—Using body members, hand tools, and/or special devices to work, move, or carry objects or materials. Involves little or no latitude for judgment with regard to attainment of standards or in selecting appropriate tool, object, or material.

NOTE: Included in the concept of Feeding-Offbearing, Tending, Operating-Controlling, and Setting Up is the situation in which the worker is actually part of the setup of the machine, either as the holder and guider of the material or holder and guider of the tool (U.S. Department of Labor, 1977, pp. 1369–1371).

The Standard Occupational Classification Manual

For a number of years, occupational analysts have expressed a need for an occupational classification system that could combine occupational data into one system. Traditionally, occupational data have been gathered from a variety of sources and compiled under different classification systems. Combining the data has been a growing problem. In 1940 only two major classification systems, the Census Classification System and the *DOT* system, existed. The problem of combining occupational data was compounded in the 1960s when several other classification systems evolved. It was during this period that the first steps were taken toward developing a classification system that standardized occupational data collection. For over ten years the interagency Occupational Classification Committee met; it eventually published the first edition of the *Standard Occupational Classification Manual* in 1977 (U.S. Executive Office of the President [USEOP], 1977).

Format and Structure of the SOC **Manual**

The *SOC Manual* format is divided into four levels of successively greater detail as follows: (1) division, (2) major group, (3) minor group, and (4) unit group. The first level of the format, *division*, is broad in scope, providing a general description of an occupational field.

There are 21 divisions of occupational groups included in the 1977 *SOC* as follows:

Executive, Administrative, and Managerial Groups
Engineers and Architects
Natural Scientists and Mathematicians
Social Scientists, Social Workers, Religious Workers, and Lawyers
Teachers, Librarians, and Counselors
Health Diagnosing and Treating Practitioners
Nurses, Pharmacists, Dietitians, Therapists, and Physicians Assistants
Writers, Artists, Entertainers, and Athletes
Health Technologists and Technicians
Technologists and Technicians, except Health
Marketing and Sales Occupations
Clerical Occupations
Service Occupations
Agriculture and Forestry Occupations, Fishers, and Hunters
Construction and Extractive Occupations
Transportation and Material Moving Occupations
Mechanics and Repairers
Production Working Occupations
Material Handlers, Equipment Cleaners, and Laborers
Military Occupations
Miscellaneous Occupations

Each division is further subdivided into *major groups*. The following examples of two division groups followed by major groups illustrate this part of the format and structure of the *SOC* system (USEOP, 1977, pp. 35–59).

(Divisions)	
Executive, Administrative, and Managerial Occupations	Engineers and Architects
(Major Groups)	
11 Officials and Administrators; Public Administration	14 Management-Related Occupations
12–13 Officials and Administrators, other	15 Architects
	16 Engineers and Surveyors

The two-digit numbers adjacent to the major groups in the preceding example are the actual numbers assigned to those major groups in the *SOC* system. All major groups are assigned two-digit numbers; minor groups three-digit numbers; and unit groups four-digit numbers. All minor groups and unit groups begin with the first two digits of their major group. Likewise, the third digit of the unit group corresponds to the third digit of its minor group. The following example illustrates the numerical scheme used in the *SOC* system (USEOP, 1977, p. 166).

Major Group	55	Farm Operator and Manager
Minor Group	551	Farmer (Working Proprietors)
Unit Groups	5512	General Farmer
	5513	Crop, Vegetable, Fruit, and Tree Nut Farmer
	5514	Livestock, Dairy, and Poultry Farmer
	5515	Horticultural Specialty Farmer

A *minor group* of the major group 14, management-related occupations, is illustrated in the following box (USEOP, 1977, p. 49).

The following illustration is typical of minor group levels found in the *SOC*. The 705 digits are *DOT* industry designations that identify the industry in which the occupation is most commonly found. In this illustration, the industrial designation is professional and kindred. The nine-digit numbers assigned to each occupation are the fourth edition *DOT* codes.

A *unit group* is provided when it is necessary to further break down a minor group. For example, in the case of a Natural Resource Program Administrator, other occupations involving administration of related programs are listed in the unit group, as illustrated on page 490 (USEOP, 1977, p. 37).

The *SOC* is designed for conversion of *DOT* data, thus making it possible to use data collected by *DOT* codes or by the broader *SOC* for analysis. The system is flexible in that unit groups can be analyzed for specific information. For example, sales supervisors are classified according to products sold, which allows for combining one unit group with another sales group for supplemental analysis according to products or other combinations. Governmental agencies will be encouraged to use *SOC* for collecting occupational data as well as for research and planning occupational, educational-training programs.

The *SOC*'s four levels of detail seem to provide the flexibility needed for the ever-changing world of work. New and unique occupations can be classified according to similar minor or unit groups within the system. The grouping of classifications is designed to allow for additional breakdown into units when necessary. To move from the currently diverse occupational classification systems, each with its own uses, to a national standard is a technically demanding process. The Office of Federal Statistical Policy and Standards, which is responsible for the continued development of *SOC*, has emphasized its flexibility and the need to adapt it to various analytical situations (USEOP, 1977, p. 9). The

---

142 Management Analysis

This minor group includes occupations concerned with reviewing, analyzing, and improving business and organizational systems to assist management in operating with greater efficiency and effectiveness. Activities such as conducting organizational studies and evaluations, designing systems and procedures for new work processes, conducting work simplification and measurement studies, and preparing and maintaining systems and procedures manuals are performed in these occupations.

Director, records management	705	161117014
Management analyst	705	161167010
Manager, farm analysis	705	161167014
Manager, records analysis	705	161167018
Manager, reports analysis	705	161167022
Clerical methods analyst	705	161267010
Records-management analyst	705	161267022
Reports analyst	705	161267026

1133 Natural Resource Program Administrator

This unit group includes occupations involving administering programs related to preservation, management, and restoration of natural or manmade environments within the public domain.

Chief, fishery division	425	188117018
Commissioner, conservation of resources	425	188117026
Federal Aid Coordinator	425	188167054
Park superintendent	425	188167062
Wildlife agent, regional	425	379127018

---

first use of *SOC*, and its first revision, was made for the 1980 Census of Population. The numerous revisions to the 1977 edition reflect the needs of the Census Bureau. No doubt *SOC* will be closely scrutinized in the years ahead by the many agencies that collect occupational data and are charged with the responsibility of projecting labor-market trends.

CURRICULAR CAREER-INFORMATION SERVICE (CCIS) MODULES

The Curricular Career-Information (CCIS) program for delivery of educational and vocational information emphasizes an instructional approach to career-planning services. The program consists of 12 modules. The first 5 modules were discussed in Chapter 11. The remaining 7 modules are discribed in Table A-1.

TABLE A-1
Curricular Career-Information Service (CCIS)

Module	Title	Objectives	Activities

VI	Employment, Outlooks	1. To describe the present distribution of workers in different job areas; e.g., sex, race
		2. To describe the projected employment trends in various career fields
		3. To understand the complexity and accuracy of employment forecasting
		4. To identify the lowest and highest employment demand areas
			a. Read the materials in the Module VI folders in the mobile file. "Employment Outlooks" contains information regarding forecasts nationwide, while "Florida Outlooks" contains projections for the various geographic sections of Florida.
			b. View the slidetape "Looking Ahead to a Career."
			c. View the slides "Supply and Demand of the College Graduates in the South, 1980, by Field of Study" reading the accompanying script (DDC 331.126 S6).
			d. View the slidetape "Increasing Job Options for Women" (DDC 331.4 C4).
			e. Scan books such as the following:
			  DDC 331.06 U5 *Handbook of Labor Statistics*
			  DDC 331.1 U5 *Occupation Manpower and Training Needs*
			  DDC 331.12 015 *Occupational Outlook Handbook*
			  DDC 331.126 SREB series on outlook for college students in the south
			  DDC 331.4 U53 *Chapter 5, Handbook on Women Workers*
			  DDC 331.4 L4 *New Job Opportunities for Women*
			f. Review occupational information materials located in the lateral or vertical CCIS files.
			g. Consult with staff in Career Placement Services (234 Bryan Hall) or Cooperative Education Services (228 Bryan Hall).
			h. Scan bulletin boards in Career Placement Services and CCIS.

TABLE A-1
(continued)

Module	Title	Objectives	Activities
VII	Leisure Planning	1. To understand the role of leisure in your life 2. To introduce you to a leisure planning process that you can use to plan your discretionary time	a. Complete the module "Lifestyle: The Leisure Complement." Start with the notebook; view the slidetape, and complete the task sheet as directed. b. Read appropriate sections of the following books: DDC 371 K7 *The Nature of Work: Readings for College Students* DDC 331 T4 *Tempo—Life, Work, and Leisure* DDC 331.702 *Career Perspective: Your Choice of Work* DDC 331.7 C *If You Don't Know Where You're Going, You'll Probably End Up Somewhere Else* DDC 331.4 K *Catalyst. Planning for Career Options* c. Read the poster "Leisure Activities and Careers" hanging in the leisure carrel. d. Visit the Leisure Program Office in the University Union, Room 238, for current events and ideas on other leisure activities.
VIII	Career Planning for African American College Students	1. To help you examine how nearly your personality and/or interest pattern match those of people in various careers 2. To assist you in locating sources of career planning information of special interest to African American students	a. Complete Module III in CCIS on self-assessment. b. Review materials in the "Career Planning for African Americans" folder in the mobile file (take a copy of the resources list). c. View videotapes featuring prominent African Americans in careers. d. Read occupational files for current information on opportunities for African Americans in various fields. e. Skim through current minority student magazines that feature career planning articles. f. Listen to the audiotape "Career Planning for African American College Students" featuring Mr.

TABLE A-1
(continued)

Module	Title	Objectives	Activities
			g. Listen to the audiotape "Affirmative Action: Implications for Career Planning" featuring Dr. Freddie Groomes, Assistant to the President, FSU.
			C. C. Cunningham, Placement Director, FAMU, and Mr. Robert Shoemaker, Placement Director, FSU.
			h. Consult with Placement and Cooperative Education staff members at FSU.
IX	Career Decision Making for Adult Women	1. To provide you with the opportunity for self-assessment; to examine your strengths, interests, accomplishments, experiences, and motivations 2. To help you examine how nearly your interests match those of persons employed in various fields 3. To assist you in locating sources of information that will help you shape a tentative educational and/or career plan for yourself	a. Complete the Catalyst "Planning for Work" self-guidance booklet, which can be obtained from the proctor at the Help Desk. b. Complete the *Strong-Campbell Interest Inventory (SCII)* which can be obtained from the proctor at the Help Desk. c. Read any of the materials identified in the "Third Step," a bibliography attached to this sheet. By selecting the question which is most similar to what you have been asking, you can be directed to the appropriate information available in CCIS. d. View the videotape "Life Career Patterns of Women" in which several adult women discuss their different lifestyles. e. View the slidetape "Increasing Job Options for Women." f. Read the material in the "Women's Folder" in the mobile file. g. Read the magazines located in the magazine rack relating to women and work.

TABLE A-1
(*continued*)

Module	Title	Objectives	Activities
X	Career Planning for Disabled Students	1. To assist you in locating sources of career planning information of special interest to disabled students	a. Review current articles and pamphlets in the Module X folder in the mobile file. b. Read sections in the following books: DDC 362 S6 *Your Handicap: Don't Let It Handicap You*; DDC 362 U5 *Selected Career Education Programs for the Handicapped: The College Guide for Students with Disabilities* c. Read the abbreviated versions of Sections 503 and 504 of the Rehabilitation Act of 1973 located in the Module X folder in the mobile file . . . or listen to the taped version in Study Carrel #1. d. Listen to the audiotape "Affirmative Action: Implications for Career Planning" featuring Dr. Freddie Groomes. e. Consult with Placement and Cooperative Education staff members at FSU. f. Consult with Ms. Darlene Stutts, Disabled Students Services Coordinator, 101 Bryan Hall, or Mr. Paul Nolting, Division of Blind Services, 120 Bryan Hall.
XI	Exploring Career Interest Through Work	1. To assist you in identifying resources that will help you obtain experience relevant to your area of career interest	a. Read sections in these books: DDC 331.128 B4 *Career Through Cooperative Work Experience*; DDC 331.2 L5 *On the Job Training and Where to Get It*; DDC 331.702 L6 *Exploring Careers through Volunteerism*

TABLE A-1
(continued)

Module	Title	Objectives	Activities
			DDC 378 S6 *Nontraditional College Routes to Careers*
			DDC 378.3 I5 *International Directory of Youth Internships*
			DDC 378.3 H4 *Where to Look*
			DDC 378.3 D55 *Director of Washington Internships*
			DDC 378.3 D5 *A Directory of Public Service Internships*
			DDC 378.3 D5 *Directory of Undergraduate Internship Programs*
			DDC 378.169 K4 *Stepping Out*
			DOT 07 N3 *A Directory of Preceptorship Programs in the Health Professions*
			b. View the videotape "Cooperative Education." The Office of Cooperative Education, 116 Bryan Hall, has paid and nonpaid placements available with over 450 employers in Florida and throughout the Southeast. Information on special federal and state internships is available as well as resources identifying summer job opportunities.
			c. The Student Community Interaction (SCI) offers volunteer work opportunities. Their office is located in 338 Union. Phone: 644-6410.
			d. The voluntary action center, 488 West Brevard Street, offers opportunities for volunteer work experience with agencies in the Tallahassee area. Call 224-0581 for an appointment.
			e. Research your area of career interest by using the CCIS vertical file(s) pertaining to areas you would like to pursue. Work experience ideas can often be found in these files.

TABLE A-1
(continued)

Module	Title	Objectives	Activities
			f. Check the *FSU CATALOG* for internship requirements in your major.
			g. Refer to Module XI of the mobile file for current articles.
			h. Ask your academic advisor or a faculty member in your academic area for suggestions.
XII	Employability Skills	1. To help you start your job hunt	a. Attend a "How to Start Your Job Hunt" clinic in CCIS.
			b. Review current articles in the "Looking for a Job" file located in the Module XII Section of the mobile file.
			c. Review sections in the many CCIS resource books catalogued DDC 331.128.
			d. Register for Unit III of the Career Planning Course, MAN 3935r. A course syllabus is available for you to review in the Module XIII section of the mobile file.
		2. To write a résumé appropriate for your job objective	a. Obtain a copy of the *Résumé Writing Guide* from the Module XII section of the mobile file.
			b. Attend a résumé writing clinic in CCIS.
			c. Review current articles in the "Looking For a Job" file located in the Module XII section of the mobile file.
			d. Review sections in the many CCIS resource books catalogued DDC 331.128.
		3. To write an appropriate letter pertaining to your job campaign	a. Obtain a copy of the *Letter Writing Guide* from the Module XII section of the mobile file.

TABLE A-1
(continued)

Module	Title	Objectives	Activities
			b. Review current articles in the "Looking for a Job" file located in the Module XII section of the mobile file.
			c. Review sections in the many CCIS resource books catalogued DDC 331.128.
		4. To become informed about services available to you from the FSU Career Placement Services Center	a. View the videotape describing FSU Career Placement Services.
			b. Obtain a copy of the *Placement Manual* from the Career Placement Services Library for your reference. (Room 225—Bryan).
			c. Visit the Career Placement Services Center for special questions and information (Room 228—Bryan).
		5. To prepare yourself for your job interview	a. Obtain a copy of the *Interview Preparation Guide* from the Module XII section of the mobile file.
			b. Attend an interview preparation clinic in CCIS.
			c. Review current articles in the "Looking for a Job" file located in the Module XII section of the mobile file.
			d. Review sections in the many CCIS resource books catalogued DDC 331.128.

SOURCE: Curricular Career Information Service, by R. C. Reardon. Unpublished manuscript, Florida State University, 1980. Reprinted by permission.

A High School Student's Experience in a Cooperative Education Program

The following account of a student's participation in a high school cooperative education program points out the values of work experiences.[1] Experiential activities involved money management, cooperative work activities with regular work staff, coping with work-related stress, and responsibility for work tasks. This student credits the cooperative education program as the single most influential aspect of her career education.

During my high school years, I was enrolled in a cooperative education program—I was a co-op student. As many people know, a co-op program is where a high school or college student earns academic credit and sometimes wages by working in the "real world" as part of a specified vocational curriculum. For example, a student in a retail merchandise program can earn credit and money through working in a department store. A food services student can work in a restaurant, a welding student can work for a sheet metal company, and so on.

I attended a high school that contained an areawide vocational skill center. Because I planned to attend college, I enrolled in the typical college prep courses, but I was also able to combine a college prep track with a vocational course (two hours a day for two years) that led to vocational certification by the State of Michigan. Early in my high school career, I had chosen elective courses from business: typing, shorthand, general business. I did quite well in these courses, and although I had no aspirations of becoming a business tycoon, I thought that having a background in business could prove helpful in the future, so I planned to take the Stenographer/Secretarial vocational program in my junior and senior years.

Immediately after finishing my sophomore year I was told of a co-op job working in the County Treasurer's Office, which sounded more interesting than cleaning motel rooms (which I had done the previous summer). So I interviewed for, and subsequently landed, the position of clerk/"go-fer"/secretary in the Office of the County Treasurer of Chippewa County.

It was then that my real education began. As a 16-year-old, my work experience consisted of being a paper girl for two years, extensive babysitting, and cleaning motel rooms. I was now in an "adult" job, one full of responsibility and of learning a tremendous amount of information. During the two-and-a-half years I worked in that office, I learned more about the world of work than I did in any class I have ever taken—in high school, college, or graduate school.

The first major concept I learned was responsibility. I was required to be on time, day-in, day-out, even if I did not feel like going to work. However, my responsibility did not end with punctuality. I also had to *perform,* usually in pressure situations, under legal deadlines imposed by the State. I was responsible for accepting delinquent taxes and penalties and had to figure out the charges. At certain times of the year the office would become extremely hectic,

[1] Wiinamaki, M. K. (1988). My Vocational Experience. Unpublished manuscript, Southwest Texas State University. Reprinted by permission.

but I was still expected to be accurate. After all, I was dealing with public funds.

Another area of my on-the-job education involved money management. For the first time in my life I was receiving a substantial amount of money in the form of a regular paycheck. Granted, it was only minimum wage, but working 20 hours per week during the school semester and 40 hours per week during summer, even minimum wage looked good to a high school girl with few expenses. I began to buy all my own clothes, my own gas, and was responsible for all of my entertainment expenses. Looking back, I believe both my parents and I appreciated this step of "economic independence."

Another crucial concept learned through my co-op experience was decision making, particularly the idea that decisions do have consequences and should be weighed before plunging head-first into one. I learned this in a variety of ways: first, by watching the adults with whom I worked, and second, by becoming aware of the political process around me. Decisions I made during those years still affect my life today.

The most generalizable skills I learned through co-op were interpersonal skills. I worked in an office with three women; though all of us had vastly different personalities, we had to cooperate and learn to co-exist peacefully, even when we did not agree. I also dealt with the public, people who were often paying delinquent land taxes, plus penalties, and who were generally unhappy about having to do so. I learned to be tactful, diplomatic, patient, and above all, to have a sense of humor about myself and about people. Working in such a stressful environment also taught me the importance of dealing with stress in a productive manner.

Time management was another skill I learned in my co-op job. When I began working regular hours, I was forced to use free time in a more productive manner—suddenly I had less time to goof off, do homework, and participate in household chores. I gained respect for adults who dealt with their job, spouse, children, and home. Life was more complicated than it had previously seemed.

In my position in the County Treasurer's Office, I had many occasions to talk to and become acquainted with a variety of people who held various city and county positions, such as county clerk, registrar of deeds, district attorneys, judges, and county commissioners. While students my age were learning about local politics in government class, I knew the officials by name and discovered what they actually did in their respective positions.

Also significant was the fact that I had greatly increased my job experience during the time I worked as a co-op student. Many of the skills, such as typing, interpersonal skills, and problem-solving proved invaluable in subsequent positions.

While all these skills and concepts were worthwhile, I think the most valuable benefit was a very positive increase in my self-esteem. I was now capable of working in the real world, of earning a living, of sticking with something that was not always pleasant. And that is a tremendous benefit.

So what happened after I left the County Treasurer's Office? During the time I worked there, I discovered some things about myself and the kind of environment I wanted to work in, and office work as a career was not what I envisioned. I learned that I did not enjoy the rigid structure, the routine, the repetition, but I did like working with people rather than with things. I entered college as a psychology major and thoroughly enjoyed the world of concepts, ideas, theories, and speculation. Throughout my years in college, I worked as a typist, a secretary in the Admissions Office, and as a word processor. Upon receiving a B.A. in psychology and realizing that graduate school was a necessity, I moved to Texas and promptly got a job as a word processor in a large law firm in Austin. Once again I was using the skills learned first in my co-op job as a high school student. In fact, that word-processing job supported me throughout graduate school, and also confirmed my decision to work in the field of counseling. I am glad to say that I am now working as a counselor, and I think I appreciate it more due to the years I spent in various secretarial jobs.

In summary, I learned a great deal about working, life, and myself through my experiences in cooperative education, experiences that continue to influence my life. For me, being a co-op student was the single most influential aspect of any career education I received. It was valuable not because it showed me what I wanted to do with my life, but rather what I did *not* want to do—at a time when I was not forced to make irrevocable decisions on majors, careers, and locations. It provided me with the opportunity to navigate the transition from adolescence to adulthood gradually, and it is an experience I will never forget.

NATIONAL CAREER-DEVELOPMENT GUIDELINES FOR COUNSELORS

TABLE A-2
National Career-Development Guidelines for Counselors

Area	Characteristics
Counseling	Knowledge of developmental issues individuals address throughout the life span.
	Knowledge of counseling and career-development theories and techniques.
	Knowledge of decision-making and transition models.
	Knowledge of role relationships to facilitate personal, family, and career development.
	Knowledge of different cultures to interact effectively with all populations.
	Skills to build productive relationships with counselees.
	Skills to use appropriate individual- and group-counseling techniques to assist individuals with career decisions and career-development concerns.
	Skills to assist individuals in identifying influencing factors in career decision making, such as family, friends, educational opportunities, and finances.
	Skills to assist individuals in changing biased attitudes that stereotype others by gender, race, age, and culture.
	Skills to assist individuals in understanding the relationship between interpersonal skills and success in the workplace.
	Skills to assist individuals in setting goals and identifying strategies for reaching goals.

TABLE A-2
(continued)

Area	Characteristics
	Skills to assist individuals in continually reassessing their goals, values, interests, and career decisions. Skills to assist individuals in preparing for multiple roles throughout their lives.
Information	Knowledge of changes taking place in the economy, society, and job market. Knowledge of education, training, employment trends, labor market, and career resources. Knowledge of basic concepts related to career counseling such as career development, career progression, and career patterns. Knowledge of the changing gender roles and how these affect work, family, and leisure. Knowledge of employment-information and career-planning materials. Knowledge of employment-related requirements such as labor laws, licensing, credentialing, and certification. Knowledge of state and local referral services or agencies for job, financial, social, and personal service. Knowledge of federal and state legislation that may influence career development programs. Skills to use career-development resources and techniques designed for specific groups. Skills to use computer-based career-information systems.
Individual and group assessment	Knowledge of assessment techniques and measures of skills, abilities, aptitudes, interests, values, and personalities. Skills to identify assessment resources appropriate for specific situations and populations. Skills to evaluate assessment resources and techniques related so that their validity, reliability, and relationships to race, gender, age, and ethnicity can be determined. Skills to administer, interpret, and personalize assessment data in relation to the career-development needs of the individual.
Management and administration	Knowledge of program designs that can be used in organizing career-development programs. Knowledge of needs-assessment techniques and practices. Knowledge of management concepts, leadership styles, and techniques to implement change. Skills to assess the effectiveness of career-development programs. Skills to identify staff competencies for effective career-development programs. Skills to prepare proposals, budgets, and timelines for career-development programs. Skills to identify, develop, annd use record-keeping methods. Skills to design, conduct, analyze, and report the assessment of individual and program outcomes.

TABLE A-2
(continued)

Area	Characteristics
Implementation	Knowledge of program-adoption and planned-change strategies. Knowledge of barriers affecting the implementation of career-development programs. Skills to implement individual and group programs in a variety of areas such as assessment, decision making, job seeking, career information, and career counseling. Skills to implement public relations efforts that promote career-development activities and services. Skills to establish linkages with community-based organizations.
Consultation	Knowledge of consulting strategies and consulting models. Skills to assist staff in understanding how to incorporate career-development concepts into their offerings to program participants. Skills to consult with influential parties such as employers, community groups, and the general public. Skills to convey program goals and achievements to legislators, professional groups, and other key leaders.
Specific populations	Knowledge of differing cultural values and their relationship to work values. Knowledge of unique career-planning needs of minorities, women, the handicapped, and older persons. Knowledge of alternative approaches to career-planning needs for individuals with specific needs. Skills to identify community resources and establish linkages to assist adults with specific needs. Skills to find appropriate methods or resources to communicate with limited English-proficient individuals.

SOURCE: National Occupational Information Coordinating Committee, 1989.

References

Adkins, D. C. (1947). *Construction and analysis of achievement tests.* Washington, DC: U.S. Government Printing Office.

Adler, A. (1929). *The practice and theory of individual psychology.* New York: Harcourt, Brace & World.

Aigaki, D. A. (1970). *Life planning for low-income youth.* Unpublished master's thesis, Colorado State University, Fort Collins.

Alexander, L. C. (1985). *Women in nontraditional careers: A training program manual.* Washington, DC: Women's Bureau, U.S. Government Printing Office.

Alper, T. (1974). Achievement motivation in college women: A now-you-see-it-now-you-don't phenomenon. *American Psychologist, 29,* 194–203.

Amatea, E. S., & Cross, E. G. (1980). Going places: A career guidance program for high school students and their parents. *Vocational Guidance Quarterly, 28*(3), 274–282.

American College Testing Program. (1978–1979). *Using ACT on campus.* Iowa City, IA: American College Testing Program (ACT).

——— (1979). Unisex edition of *The American college testing program interest inventory.* Iowa City, IA: ACT.

——— (1984). *Career planning and placement program.* Iowa City, IA: ACT.

——— (1987). DISCOVER. Iowa City, IA: ACT.

——— (1992). *High school profile report, normative data for high school class of 1992.* Iowa City, IA: ACT.

Americans with disabilities act handbook. (1991). Washington, DC: U.S. Government Printing Office.

Amos, W. E. (1968). The nature of disadvantaged youth. In W. E. Amos & J. D. Grambs (Eds.), *Counseling the disadvantaged youth.* Englewood Cliffs, NJ: Prentice-Hall.

Anastasi, A. (1954). *Psychological testing.* New York: Macmillan.

——— (1988). *Psychological testing* (6th ed.). New York: Macmillan.

Anderson, B. E. (1981). Minorities in work: The decade ahead. In J. O'Toole, J. L. Schieber, & L. C. Wood (Eds.), *Working changes and choices.* Sacramento: Regents of the University of California.

Anderson, T. B., & Olsen, L. C. (1965). Congruence of self and ideal self and occupational choices. *Personnel and Guidance Journal, 44,* 171–176.

Arbeiter, S. (1979). Mid-life career change: A concept in search of reality. *American Association for Higher Education Bulletin, 32,* 1.

Arbeiter, S., Aslanian, C. B., Schmerbeck, F. A., & Brickell, H. M. (1978). *40 million Americans in career transition: The need for information.* New York: College Entrance Examination Board.

Arbona, C. (1989). Hispanic employment and the Holland typology of work. *Career Development Quarterly, 37,* 257–268.

Argeropoulous, J. (1981). *Burnout, stress management, and wellness.* Moravia, NY: Chronicle Guidance.

Aslanian, C. B., & Brickell, H. M. (1980). *Americans in transition: Life changes and reasons for adult learning.* New York: College Entrance Examination Board.

Assouline, M., & Meir, E. I. (1987). Meta-analysis of the relationship between congruence and well-being measures. *Journal of Vocational Behavior, 31,* 319–332.

Astin, A. W. (1984). Student values: Knowing more about where we are today. *Bulletin of the American Association of Higher Education, 36*(9), 10–13.

Astin, H. S. (1976). Continuing education and the development of adult women. *The Consulting Psychologist, 6,* 55–60.

Astin, H. S., & Myint, T. (1978). Career development of young women during the post-high school years. In H. L. Sunny & R. S. Rapoza (Eds.), *Career development and counseling of women.* Springfield, IL: Charles C Thomas.

Aubrey, R. G. (1977). *Career development needs of thirteen-year-olds: How to improve career development programs.* Washington, DC: National Advisory Council for Career Education.

Axelson, J. A. (1993). *Counseling and development in a multicultural society* (2nd ed.). Pacific Grove, CA: Brooks/Cole.

Bailey, L. J., & Stadt, R. W. (1973). *Career education: New approaches to human development.* Bloomington, IL: McKnight Publishing Company.

Baird, L. L. (1969). The prediction of accomplishment in college: An exploration of the process of achievement. *Journal of Counseling Psychology, 16,* 246–254.

Banathy, B. H. (1973). Employer-based career education. In J. H. Magisos (Ed.), *Career education.* Washington, DC: American Vocational Association.

Bandura, A. (1977). *Social learning theory.* Englewood Cliffs, NJ: Prentice-Hall.

Barcus, F. E. (1983). *Images of life on children's television: Sex roles, minorities, and families.* New York: Praeger.

Barfield, R. E. (1970). *The automobile worker and retirement: A second look.* Ann Arbor: University of Michigan, Institute of Social Research.

Barkhaus, R. S., & Crandall, R. (1976). Computer placement at a commuter campus. *Journal of College Placement, 36,* 40–43.

Barry, J., & Glick, D. (1992). Crossing the gay minefield. *Newsweek,* Nov. 23, 26.

Bawid, L., & Kram, K. (1984). Career dynamics managing the superior/subordinate relationship. In J. A. Sonnenfeld (Ed.), *Managing career systems,* pp. 540–557. Homewood, IL: Richard D. Irwin.

Beck, A. T. (1985). Cognitive therapy. In H. J. Kaplan & B. J. Sadock (Eds.), *Comprehensive textbook of psychiatry,* pp. 1432–1438. Baltimore: Williams & Wilkins.

Beckett, J. O., & Smith, A. D. (1981). Work and family roles: Egalitarian marriage in black and white families. *Social Service Review, 55,* 314–326.

Beckman, L. J., & Houser, B. B. (1979). The more you have, the more you do: The relationship between wife's employment, sex-role attitudes, and household behavior. *Psychology of Women Quarterly, 4,* 160–174.

Benin, M. H., & Agostinelli, J. (1988). Husbands' and wives' satisfaction with the division of labor. *Journal of Marriage and the Family, 50,* 349–361.

Bennett, G. K., Seashore, H. G., & Wesman, A. G. (1981). *Differential aptitude test.* New York: The Psychological Corporation.

Bennis, W. (1981). Beyond bureaucracy: Organizations of the future. In J. O'Toole, J. L.

Schieber, & L. C. Wood (Eds.), *Working changes and choices*. Sacramento: Regents of the University of California.

Bergin, A. E. (1971). The evaluation of therapeutic outcomes. In A. E. Bergin & S. L. Garfield (Eds.), *Handbook of psychotherapy and behavior change*. New York: Wiley.

Bergland, B. (1974). Career planning: The use of sequential evaluated experience. In E. L. Herr (Ed.), *Vocational guidance and human development*. Boston: Houghton Mifflin.

Bernard, H. W., & Fullmer, D. W. (1977). *Principles of guidance* (2nd ed.). New York: Thomas Y. Crowell.

Bernardo, D. H., Shehan, C. L., & Leslie, G. R. (1987). A residue of tradition: Jobs, careers, and spouses' time in housework. *Journal of Marriage and the Family, 49*, 381–390.

Betz, N. E. (1992). Counseling uses of career self-efficacy theory. *The Career Development Quarterly, 41*, 22–26.

Betz, N. E., & Fitzgerald, L. F. (1987). *The career psychology of women*. Orlando, FL: Academic Press.

Biehler, R. F. (1979). [A repeat of the Looft survey.] Unpublished study. California State University, Chico.

Biehler, R. F., & Hudson, L. M. (1986). *Developmental psychology*. Boston: Allyn & Bacon.

Binder, D. M., Jones, J. C., & Strowig, R. W. (1970). Non-intellective self-report variables as predictors of scholastic achievement. *Journal of Educational Research, 63*, 364–366.

Bird, C. P., & Fisher, T. D. (1986). Thirty years later: Attitudes toward the employment of older workers. *Journal of Applied Psychology, 71*, 515–517.

Birk, J. M. (1975). Reducing sex bias: Factors affecting the client's view of the use of career interest inventories. In E. Diamond (Ed.), *Issues of sex bias and sex fairness in career interest measurement*, pp. 101–122. Washington, DC: National Institute of Education.

Birney, D., Thomas, L. E., & Hinkle, J. E. (1970–1971). Life planning workshops: Discussion and evaluation. *Student Development Report, 8*, 2. Colorado State University.

Blake, R., & Mouton, J. (1964). *The managerial grid*. Houston: Gulf.

Blau, P. M., & Duncan, O. D. (1965). *The American occupational structure*. New York: Wiley.

Blau, P. M., Gustad, J. W., Jessor, R., Parnes, H. S., & Wilcox, R. S. (1956). Occupational choices: A conceptual framework. *Industrial Labor Relations Review, 9*, 531–543.

Blauner, R. (1964). *Alienation and freedom: The factory worker and his industry*. Chicago: University of Chicago Press.

Bloland, P. A., & Edwards, P. B. (1981). Work and leisure: A counseling synthesis. *Vocational Guidance Quarterly, 30*(2), 101–108.

Boles, J., & Tatro, C. (1982). In K. Solomon & N. B. Levy (Eds.), *Men in transition*. New York: Plenum.

Bolles, R. N. (1993). *A practical manual for job-hunters and career changers: What color is your parachute?* (9th ed.). Berkeley, CA: Ten Speed Press.

———— (1982). *The three boxes of life and how to get out of them*. Berkeley, CA: Ten Speed Press.

Bolton, B. (1973). *Introduction to rehabilitation of deaf clients*. Fayetteville: University of Arkansas.

Bordin, E. S., Nachmann, B., & Segal, S. J. (1963). An articulated framework for vocational development. *Journal of Counseling Psychology, 10*, 107–116.

Borow, H. (Ed.). (1964). *Man in the world at work.* Boston: Houghton Mifflin.

Bottoms, G., & Metheny, K. B. (1969). *A guide for the development, implementation, and administration of exemplary program and projects in vocational education.* Atlanta: Georgia State Department of Education, and Division of Vocational Education.

Bottoms, J. E., Evans, R. N., Hoyt, K. B., & Willers, J. C. (Eds.). (1972). *Career education resource guide.* Morristown, NJ: General Learning Corporation.

Bowen, C. W. (1968). The use of self-estimates of ability and measures of ability in the prediction of academic performance. Unpublished doctoral dissertation, Oklahoma State University, Stillwater.

Bradfield, J. M., & Moredock, H. S. (1957). *Measurement and evaluation in education.* New York: Macmillan.

Brammer, L. M., & Abrego, P. J. (1981). Intervention strategies for coping with transitions. *The Counseling Psychologist, 9,* 27.

Brewer, J. M. (1918). *The vocational guidance movement.* New York: Macmillan.

Brim, O. G. (1966). Socialization through the life cycle. In O. G. Brim & S. Wheeler (Eds.), *Socialization after childhood,* pp. 1–49. New York: Wiley.

Brolin, D. E., & Gysbers, N. C. (1989). Career education for students with disabilities. *Journal of Counseling and Development, 68,* 155–159.

Bross, I. D. (1953). *Design for decisions.* New York: Macmillan.

Brown, D. (1984). Trait and factor theory. In D. Brown & L. Brooks (Eds.), *Career choice and development,* pp. 8–31. San Francisco: Jossey-Bass.

———— (1990). Trait and factor theory. In D. Brown and L. Brooks, *Career choice and development* (2nd ed.), pp 13–37. San Francisco: Jossey-Bass.

Brown, D., & Brooks, L. (1991). *Career counseling techniques.* Boston: Allyn & Bacon.

Brown, D., Brooks, L., & Associates. (1990). *Career choice and development* (2nd ed.). San Francisco: Jossey-Bass.

Brown, D., & Minor, C. W. (1989). *Working in America: A status report on planning and problems.* Alexandria, VA: National Career Development Association.

Brown, D., Minor, C. W., & Jepsen, D. A. (1991). The opinions of minorities about preparing for work: Report of the second NCDA national survey. *The Career Development Quarterly, 40,* 5–19.

Brown, D. A. (1980). Life-planning workshop for high school students. *The School Counselor, 29*(1), 77–83.

Brownstein, R., & Nairn, A. (1979). Are truth-in-testing laws a fraud? No! *Phi Delta Kappa, 61,* 189–191.

Bryde, J. F. (1971). *Indian students and guidance.* Boston: Houghton Mifflin.

Bucher, G. R. (1976). *Straight, white, male.* Philadelphia: Fortress.

Burnett, F. E. (1977). *Guidelines for establishing a career information center.* Washington, DC: American Personnel and Guidance Press.

Burow, H. (1984). The way we were: Reflections on the history of vocational guidance. *Vocational Guidance Quarterly, 33*(1), 5–14.

Burton, M., & Wedemeyer, R. (1991). *In transition.* New York: Harper Business Publications.

Byrne, E. (1983). Robots and the future of work. In H. F. Didsbury, Jr. (Ed.), *The world of work.* Bethesda, MD: World Future Society.

Cabezas, A. Y., & Yee, H. I. (1977). Discriminatory employment of Asian-Americans: Private Industry in the San Francisco-Oakland area. Paper presented to management in San Francisco-Oakland area, San Francisco.

California Advisory Council on Vocational Education. (1977). *Barriers and bridges.* Sacramento: California State Department of General Services.

Callard, E. (1964). Achievement motive in the four-year-old and its relationship to achievement expectancies of the mother. Unpublished doctoral dissertation, University of Michigan, Ann Arbor.

Campbell, D. P. (1974). *Manual for the Strong-Campbell interest inventory.* Palo Alto, CA: Stanford University Press.

Campbell, R. E., & Cellini, J. V. (1981). A diagnostic taxonomy of adult career problems. *Journal of Vocational Behavior, 19*(2), 175–190.

Campbell, R. E., & Heffernan, J. M. (1983). Adult vocational behavior. In W. B. Walsh & S. H. Osipow (Eds.), *Handbook of vocational psychology* (Vol. 1, 223–262): Hillsdale, NJ: Lawrence Erlbaum Associates.

Campbell, R. E., Walz, G. R., Miller, J. V., & Kriger, S. F. (1973). *Career guidance: A handbook of methods.* Columbus, OH: Charles E. Merrill.

Caplow, T. (1954). *The sociology of work.* Minneapolis: University of Minnesota Press.

Career education for the handicapped. (1978). Downey: Los Angeles County Superintendent of Schools.

Career information center. (1979). Austin, TX: Austin Independent School District.

Career information system. (1974). Eugene, OR: University of Oregon.

—— (1979). Eugene, OR: University of Oregon

Career monograph. (1977). San Jose, CA: Career Planning and Placement, San Jose State University.

Career opportunity index. (1979). Huntington Beach, CA: Career Research System, Inc.

Career orientation manual. (1985). Austin, TX: Texas Rehabilitation Commission.

Career patterns of the Illinois graduate class of 1970—Urbana five years later. (1975). Urbana-Champaign: University of Illinois.

Cattell, R. B., Eber, H. W., & Tatsuoka, M. M. (1970). *Handbook for the sixteen personality factor questionnaire (16PF).* Champaign, IL: Institute for Personality and Ability Testing.

Cautela, J. & Wisock, P. (1977). The thought-stopping procedure: Description, application and learning theory interpretations. *The Psychological Record, 2,* 264–266.

Center for choice. (1980). Dallas: Richland College, Dallas County Community College.

Centra, J. A. (1974). *Women, men and the doctorate.* Princeton, NJ: Educational Testing Service.

Cetron, M., & Davies, O. (1988). *The great job shake-out.* New York: Simon & Schuster.

Cetron, M., & Gayle, M. (1991). *Educational renaissance.* New York: St. Martin's Press.

Cetron, M. J. (1983). Jobs with a future. In H. F. Didsbury, Jr. (Ed.), *The world of work.* Bethesda, MD: World Future Society.

CHEMICALWEEK. (1992). ISO 9000: Providing the basis for quality, April 29, 30–41.

Cherniss, C. (1980). *Staff burnout: Job stress in the human services.* Beverly Hills, CA: Sage Publications.

Chick, J. M. (1970). *Innovations in the use of career information.* Boston: Houghton Mifflin.

Chu, L. (1981, April). Asian-American women in educational research. Paper presented at annual conference of the American Educational Research Association, Los Angeles.

Chusmir, L. H. (1983). Characteristics and predictive dimensions of women who make nontraditional vocational choices. *Personnel and Guidance Journal, 62*(1), 43–48.

—— (1990). Men who make nontraditional career choices. *Journal of Counseling and Development, 69,* 11–16.

Clark, R., Gelatt, H. B., & Levine, L. (1965). A decision-making paradigm for local guidance research. *Personnel and Guidance Journal, 44,* 40–51.

Clements, I. (1977). *Career education and vocational education.* Washington, DC: National Education Association.

Cline-Nalzinger, C. A. (1971). Survey of counselors' and other professionals' attitudes toward women's roles. (Doctoral dissertation, University of Oregon, 1971.) *Dissertation Abstracts International, 32,* 3021A. (University Microfilms No. 72-955).

Clowers, M. R., & Fraser, R. T. (1977). Employment interview literature: A perspective for the counselor. *Vocational Guidance Quarterly, 26,* 13–26.

Coats, J. F. (1983). The changing nature of work. In J. G. Didsbury, Jr. (Ed.). *The world of work.* Bethesda, MD: World Future Society.

Cohen, A. R., & Gadon, H. (1981). Flexible working hours. In J. O'Toole, J. L. Scheiber, & L. C. Wood (Eds.), *Working changes and choices.* Sacramento: Regents of University of California.

Cohen, B. N., & Ethredge, J. M. (1975). Recruiting's main ingredient. *Journal of College Placement, 35,* 75–77.

Cole, M. L. (1963, Sept.). Our Lutheran heritage. Address to faculty of Texas Lutheran College, Seguin.

Cole, N. S., & Hansen, G. R. (1975). Impact of interest inventories on career choice. In E. E. Diamond (Ed.), *Issues of sex bias and sex fairness in career interest measurement,* pp. 1–17. Washington, DC: National Institute of Education.

Coleman, M. T. (1988). The division of household labor. *Journal of Family Issues, 9(1),* 132–148.

College placement annual. (1980). Bethelehem, PA: College Placement Council, Inc.

Colorado career information system handbook. (1975). Longmont: Colorado State Department of Education.

Computer-Based Education Research Laboratory. (1977). *The Plato system.* Urbana-Champaign: University of Illinois.

Computerized vocational information system catalog. (1977). Westminster: Western Maryland College.

Cook, D. W. (1981). Impact of disability on the individual. In R. M. Parker & C. E. Hansen (Eds.), *Rehabilitation counseling.* Boston: Allyn & Bacon.

Cooper, B. S. (1977). Occupational help for the severely disabled: A public school model. *Rehabilitation Literature, 38,* 67–74.

Cooper, J. F. (1976). Comparative impact of the SCII and the vocational card sort on career salience and career exploration of women. *Journal of Counseling Psychology, 23,* 348–352.

Copeland, L., & Griggs, L. (1985). *Going international.* New York: Random House.

Corey, G. (1991). *Theory and practice of counseling and psychotherapy.* Pacific Grove, CA: Brooks/Cole.

Cormier, W., & Cormier, L. S. (1991). *Interviewing strategies for helpers: Fundamental skills and cognitive behavioral interventions* (3rd ed.). Pacific Grove, CA: Brooks/Cole.

Corpus Christi Independent School District. (1976). *A framework for developing career education.* Corpus Christi, TX: Corpus Christi I.S.D.

Costrich, N., Feintein, J., Kidder, L., Maracek, J., & Pascale, L. (1975). When stereotypes hurt: Three studies of penalties for sex-role reversals. *Journal of Experimental Social Psychology, 11,* 520–530.

Courtland, L. (1984). Work values of rural Black, White, and Native American adolescents: Implications for contemporary rural school counselors. *Counseling and Values, 28(2),* 63–71.

Courtney, A. E., & Whipple. T. W. (1974). Women in t.v. commercials. *Journal of Communication, 24,* 110–118.

Cozby, P. C. (1973). Self-disclosure: A literature review. *Psychological Bulletin, 79,* 73–91.

Craig, R. J. (1989). *Clinical and diagnostic interviewing.* Northvale, NJ: Jason Aronson, Inc.

Crites, J. O. (1969). *Vocational psychology.* New York: McGraw-Hill

——— (1973). *Theory and research handbook: Career maturity inventory.* Monterey, CA: CTB-MacMillan-McGraw-Hill.

Crites, J. O. (1978a). *Theory and research handbook: Career maturity inventory.* Monterey, CA: CTB-MacMillan-McGraw-Hill.

——— (1978b). *Career maturity inventory.* Monterey, CA: CTB-MacMillan-McGraw-Hill.

——— (1981). *Career counseling: Models, methods, and materials.* New York: McGraw-Hill.

Crites, J. O., & Fitzgerald, L. F. (1978). The competent male. *Counseling Psychology, 7,* 10–14.

Cronbach, L. J. (1949). *Essentials of psychological testing.* New York: Harper & Brothers.

——— (1984). *Essentials of psychological testing* (4th ed.). New York: Harper & Row.

Crystal, J. C., & Bolles, R.N. (1974). *Where do I go from here with my life?* New York: Seabury Press.

Curnow, T. C. (1989). Vocational development of persons with disability. *The Career Development Quarterly, 37,* 269–277.

D'Costa, A. G., Winefordner, D. W., Odgers, J. G., & Koons, P. B. (1981). *Ohio vocational interest survey.* New York: The Psychological Corporation.

Daniels, J. L. (1981). World of work in disabling conditions. In R. M. Parker & C. E. Hansen (Eds.), *Rehabilitation counseling,* pp. 169–199. Boston: Allyn & Bacon.

Danish, S. J. (1977). Human development and human services: A marriage proposal. In I. Iscoe, B. L. Bloom, & C. D. Spielberger (Eds.), *Community psychology in transition.* New York: Halsted Press.

Danish, S. J., & D'Augelli, A. R. (1983). *Helping skills II: Life-development intervention.* New York: Human Sciences Press.

Davidson, P. E., & Anderson, H. D. (1937). *Occupational mobility in an American community.* Palo Alto, CA: Stanford University Press.

Davis, D. A., Hagan, N., & Strouf, J. (1962). Occupational choice of twelve-year-olds. *Personnel and Guidance Journal, 40,* 628–629.

Davis, F. B. (1947). *Utilizing human talent.* Washington, DC: American Council on Education.

Davis, K. (1967). *The dynamics of organizational behavior.* New York: McGraw-Hill.

Dawis, R. B., & Lofquist, L. (1984). *A psychological theory of work adjustment: An individual differences model and its application.* Minneapolis: University of Minnesota.

Delworth, U. (1972, Sept.). The life planning workshop: Program evaluation. In D. Aigaki (Chair), *Career development symposium.* Symposium presented at the meeting of the American Psychological Association, Honolulu.

Dennis, W. (1966). Creative productivity between the ages of 20 and 80 years. *Journal of Gerontology, 21,* 1–8.

Dewey, C. R. (1974). Exploring interests: A non-sexist method. *Personnel and Guidance Journal, 52,* 311–315.

Diagnostic and statistical manual of mental disorders. (1987). (3rd ed., rev.). Washington, DC: American Psychiatric Association.

Diamond, E. E. (1975). Overview. In E. E. Diamond (Ed.), *Issues of sex bias and sex fairness in career interest measurement.* Washington, DC: U.S. Government Printing Office.

Dickson, G. L. & Parmerlee, J. R. (1980). The occupational family tree: A career counseling technique, *The School Counselor, 28* (2).

DiSabatino, M. (1976). Psychological factors inhibiting women's occupational aspirations and vocational choices: Implications for counseling. *The Vocational Quarterly, 25,* 43–49.

DISCOVER: A computer-based career development and counselor support system. (1984). Iowa City, IA: American College Testing Foundation.

Dittenhafer, C. A., & Lewis, J. P. (1973). *Guidelines for establishing career resource centers.* Harrisburg: Pennsylvania Department of Education.

Division of Testing Staff, U.S. Employment Service. (1978). Ten years of USES test research on the disadvantaged. *Vocational Guidance Quarterly, 26,* 334–341.

Djeddah, E. (1978). *Moving up.* Berkeley, CA: Ten Speed Press.

Dolliver, R. H. (1967). An adaptation of the Tyler Vocational Card Sort. *Personnel and Guidance Journal, 45,* 916–920.

——— (1982). Card sorts: In J. T. Kapes & M. Mastie (Eds.), *A counselor's guide to vocational guidance instruments.* Falls Church, VA: American Personnel and Guidance Association.

Dominick, J. R. (1979). The portrayal of women in prime time, 1953–1977. *Sex Roles, 5,* 405–411.

Dosser, D. A. (1982). Male inexpressiveness: Behavioral interventions. In K. Solomon & N. B. Levy (Eds.), *Men in Transition,* pp. 343–432. New York: Plenum.

Doyle, J. A. (1983). *The male experience.* Dubuque, IA: Wm. D. Brown.

Doyle, R. E. (1992). *Essential skills and strategies in the helping process.* Pacific Grove, CA: Brooks/Cole.

Drake, L. R., Kaplan, H. R., & Sonte, R. A. (1972). How do employers value the interview? *Journal of College Placement, 32,* 47–51.

Driscoll, J. B., & Hess, H. R. (1974). The recruiter: Woman's friend or foe? *Journal of College Placement, 34,* 42–48.

Drucker, P. F. (1992). *Managing for the future.* New York: Truman Talley Brooks/Dutton.

DuBrin, A. J. (1978). *Fundamentals of organizational behavior.* New York: Pergamon Press.

Dudley, G. A., & Tiedeman, D. V. (1977). *Career development: Exploration and commitment.* Muncie, IN: Accelerated Development.

Duncan, D., Schuman, H., & Duncan, B. (1973). *Social change in a metropolitan community.* New York: Russell Sage Foundation.

Dunnette, M. D., Campbell, J. P., & Hakel, M. D. (1967), Factors contributing to job satisfaction and job dissatisfaction in six occupational groups. *Organizational Behavior and Human Performance, 2,* 143–174.

Eccles, J. S. (1987). Gender roles and women's achievement-related decisions. *Psychology of Women Quarterly, 11,* 135–172.

Edelwich, J., & Brodsky, A. (1980). *Burnout: Stages of disillusionment in the helping professionals.* New York: Human Sciences Press.

Edward, P. B. (1980). *Leisure counseling techniques, individual and group counseling step by step.* Los Angeles: Constructive Leisure.

Ehrmann, R. (1977). *Effective interviewing techniques.* Topanga, CA: Robert Ehrmann Productions.

Eldridge, N. S. (1987). Gender issues in counseling same-sex couples. *Professional Psychology: Research and Practice, 18*(6), 567–572.

Elkind, D. (1968). Cognitive development in adolescence. In J. F. Adams (Ed.), *Understanding adolescence.* Boston: Allyn & Bacon.

—— (1971). *A sympathetic understanding of the child from six to sixteen.* Boston: Allyn & Bacon.

Ellis, A. (1962). *Reason and emotion in psychotherapy.* Secaucus, NJ: Lyle Stuart.

—— (1971). *Growth through reason.* Hollywood, CA: Wilshire Books.

Ellis, A., & Grieger, R. (1977). *Handbook of rational-emotive therapy.* New York: Springer.

Emener, W. G., & Rubin, S. E. (1980). Rehabilitation counselor roles and functions and sources of role strain. *Journal of Applied Rehabilitation Counseling, 11*(2), 57–69.

Endicott, F. S. (1975). *The Endicott report.* Evanston, IL: Northwestern University.

Englander, M. E. (1960). A psychological analysis of a vocational choice: Teaching. *Journal of Counseling Psychology, 7,* 257–264.

Epstein, C. F. (1980). Institutional barriers: What keeps women out of the executive suite? In M. O. Morgan (Ed.), *Managing career development.* New York: Van Nostrand.

Erikson, E. H. (1950). *Childhood and society.* New York: Norton.

—— (1963). *Childhood and society* (2nd ed.). New York: Norton.

Erwin, T. D. (1982). The predictive validity of Holland's construct of consistency. *Journal of Vocational Behavior, 20,* 180–182.

Etaugh, C., & Liss, M. B. (1992). Home, school, and playroom: Training grounds for adult gender roles. *Sex-Roles: A Journal of Research, 26,* 129–147.

Ettinger, J. M. (Ed.). (1991). *Improved career decision making in a changing world.* Garrett Park, MD: Garrett Park Press.

Evanoski, P. O., & Tse, F. W. (1989). Career awareness program for Chinese and Korean American parents. *Journal of Counseling and Development, 67,* 472–474.

Exton, W. (1983). The future of management. In H. F. Didsbury, Jr. (Ed.), *The world of work.* Bethesda, MD: World Future Society.

Fagot, B. I. (1974). Sex differences in toddlers' behavior and parental reaction. *Developmental Psychology, 10,* 554–558.

Fairley, L. (1980). *Sexual shakedown: The sexual harassment of women on the job.* New York: Warner Books.

Farber, B. A., & Heifetz, L. J. (1981). The satisfaction and stresses of psychotherapeutic work: A factor analytic study. *Professional Psychology, 12*(5), 621–630.

Farmer, H. S. (1971). Helping women to resolve the home-career conflict. *Personnel and Guidance Journal, 49,* 795–801.

—— (1978a). Why women choose careers below their potential. (In H. L. Sunny & R. S. Rapoza (Eds.), *Career development and counseling of women.* Springfield, IL: Charles C Thomas.

—— (1978b). Career counseling implications for lower social classes and women. *Personnel and Guidance Journal, 56,* 467–471.

Farmer, H. S., & Bohn, M. J., Jr. (1970). Home-career conflict reduction and the level of career interest in women. *Journal of Counseling Psychology, 17,* 218–232.

Fasteau, M. F. (1974). *The male machine.* New York: McGraw-Hill.

Feck, V. (1971). *What vocational education teachers and counselors should know about urban disadvantaged youth.* Columbus: Ohio State University, Center for Vocational Technical Education (Information Series #46, ERIC Clearing House).

Fein, G., Johnson, D., Kosson, N., Strok, L., & Wassman, L. (1975). Sex stereotypes and preferences in the toy choices of 20-month-old boys and girls. *Developmental Psychology, 11,* 527–528.

Feldman, D. C. (1988). *Managing careers in organizations.* Glenview, IL: Scott, Foresman.

Ference, T. P., Stoner, J. A. F., & Warren, E. K. (1977). Managing the career plateau. *Academy of Management Review, 2,* 606–612.

Fernandez, J. P. (1986). *Child care and corporate productivity*. Lexington, MA: Lexington Books.

Fernandez, M. S. (1988). Issues in counseling Southeast Asian students. *Journal of Multicultural Counseling and Development, 16*, 157–166.

Ferraro, G. A. (1984). Bridging the wide gap: Pay equity and job evaluations. *American Psychologist, 39*, 1166–1170.

Ferree, M. M. (1984). Class, housework, and happiness: Women's work and life satisfaction. *Sex Roles, 11* 1057–1074.

Festinger, L. (1957). *A theory of cognitive dissonance*. Evanston, IL: Row, Peterson.

Fielder, F. E. (1967). *A theory of leadership effectiveness*. New York: McGraw-Hill.

Figler, H. E. (1975). *PATH: A career workbook for liberal arts students*. Cranston, RI: Carroll Press.

Fine, M., & Asch, A. (1988). Disability beyond stigma: Social interactions, discrimination, and activism. *Journal of Social Issues, 44*(1), 3–21.

Finkelman, J. (1969). [A study of individuals with high self-esteem.] Unpublished paper. New York University.

Flanagan, J. C., & Cooley, W. W. (1966). *Project talent: One-year follow-up studies*. Pittsburgh, PA: University of Pittsburgh Press.

Flanagan, J. C., Shaycroft, J. F., Richard, J., & Claudy, J. G. (1971). *Project talent: Five years after high school*. Pittsburgh, PA: American Institute for Research.

Flanagan, J. C., Tiedeman, D. V., Willis, M. B., & McLaughlin, D. H. (1973). *The career data book*. Palo Alto, CA: American Institute for Research.

Flanders, R. B. (1979). Foreword. In National Occupational Information Coordinating Committee, *Vocational preparation and occupations: Vol. 1. Occupational and educational code crosswalk*. Washington, DC: U.S. Government Printing Office.

———— (1980). NOICC: A coordinator for occupational information. *Occupational Outlook Quarterly, 24*(4), 22–28.

Florida Occupational Information Coordinating Committee (1979). *Choices evaluation*. Tallahassee: Florida Research Center.

Forbes, J. D. (1973). Teaching Native American values and cultures. In J. A. Banks (ed.), *Teaching ethnic studies: Concepts and strategies 43rd yearbook*. Washington, DC: National Council for the Social Studies.

Forney, D. S., Wallace-Schultzman, F., & Wiggens, T. T. (1982). Burnout among career development professionals: Preliminary findings and implications. *Personnel and Guidance Journal, 60*, 435–439.

Forrest, D. V., & Baumgarten, L. (1975). An hour for job interviewing skills. *Journal of College Placement, 36*, 77–78.

Fottler, M. D., & Bain, T. (1980). Sex differences in occupational aspirations. *Academy of Management Journal, 23*(1), 144–149.

Frederickson, R. H., Macy, F. U., & Victers, D. (1978). Barriers to adult change. *Personnel and Guidance Journal, 57*, 166–169.

Frenza, M. (1982). *Counseling women for life decisions*. Ann Arbor: ERIC Counseling and Personnel Services Clearing House, University of Michigan.

Freud, S. (1953). *The standard edition of the complete psychological works* (J. Strachey, Trans.). London: Hograth.

Freudenberger, H. J. (1974). Staff burnout. *Journal of Social Issues, 30*(1), 159–165.

Freudenberger, H. J., & Richelson, G. (1980). *Burnout: The high cost of high achievement*. Garden City, NY: Anchor Press.

Friedman, M., & Rosenman, R. (1974). *Type A behavior and your heart*. Greenwich, CT: Fawcett.

Fulmer, R. M. (1983). Nine paradoxes for the 1990's. In H. F. Didsbury, Jr. (Ed.), *The world of work*. Bethesda, MD: World Future Society.

Galassi, J. P., & Galassi, M. D. (1978). Preparing individuals for job interviews: Suggestions from 60 years of research. *Personnel and Guidance Journal, 57,* 188–191.

Gallagher, J. J. (1979). What do you owe the executive you fire? *Dun's Review, 113*(6), 109–111.

Garland, S. B. (1991). Throwing stones at the glass ceiling. *Business Week,* Aug. 19, 29.

Garte, S. H., & Rosenblum, M. L. (1978). Lighting fires in burned-out counselors. *Personnel and Guidance Journal, 57*(3), 158–160.

Geary, J. (1972a). Forty newspapers forty. In J. E. Bottoms, R. N. Evans, K. B. Hoyt, & J. C. Willers (Eds.), *Career education resource guide,* Morristown, NJ: General Learning Corporation.

———— (1972b). The me nobody knows. In J. E. Bottoms, R. N. Evans, K. B. Hoyt, & J. C. Willers (Eds.), *Career education resource guide.* Morristown, NJ: General Learning Corporation.

Gelatt, H. B. (1962). Information and decision theories applied to college choice and planning. In *Preparing school counselors in educational guidance,* pp. 101–114. New York: College Entrance Examination Board.

———— (1967). Information and decision theories applied to college choice and planning. In *Preparing school counselors in educational guidance.* New York: College Entrance Examination Board.

———— (1989). Positive uncertainty: A new decision-making framework for counseling. *Journal of Counseling Psychology, 36*(2), 252–256.

George B. (1972). Mississippi. In J. E. Bottoms, R. N. Evans, K. B. Hoyt, & J. C. Willers (Eds.), *Career education resource guide.* Morristown, NJ: General Learning Corporation.

Gerstein, M., Lichtman, M., & Barokas, J. (1988). Occupational plans of adolescent women compared to men: A cross-sectional examination, *The Career Development Quarterly, 35–36,* 222–231.

Ghiselli, E. (1966). *The validity of occupational aptitude tests.* New York: Wiley.

Gianakos, I., & Subick, L. M. (1986). The relationship of gender and sex-role orientation to vocational undecidedness. *Journal of Vocational Behavior, 29,* 42–51.

Gibson, R. L., Mitchell, M. H., & Basile, S. K. (1993). *Counseling in the elementary school: A comprehensive approach.* Boston: Allyn & Bacon.

Gilbert, L. A. (1981). Coping with conflict between professional and maternal roles. *Family Relations, 30,* 419–426.

Ginzberg, E. (1966). *Life-styles of educated American women.* New York: Columbia University Press.

———— (1971). *Career guidance: Who needs it, who provides it, who can improve it.* New York: McGraw-Hill.

———— (1972). Toward a theory of occupational choice: A restatement. *The Vocational Guidance Quarterly, 20,* 169–176.

———— (1984). Career development. In D. Brown & L. Brooks (Eds.), *Career choice and development.* San Francisco: Jossey-Bass.

Ginzberg, E., Ginsburg, S. W., Axelrad, S., & Herma, J. L. (1951). *Occupational choice: An approach to general theory.* New York: Columbia University Press.

Gold, D., & Andres, D. (1980). Maternal employment and development of ten-year-old Canadian Francophone children. *Canadian Journal of Behaviorial Science, 12,* 233–240.

Goldberg, H. (1977). *The hazards of being male.* New York: New American Library.

———— (1979). *The new male: From self-destruction to self-care.* New York: Morrow.

———— (1983). *The new male-female relationship.* New York: Morrow.

Goldfried, M. R., & Friedman, J. M. (1982). Clinical behavior therapy and the male sex role. In K. Solomon and N. B. Levy (Eds.), *Men in transition*. New York: Plenum.

Goleman, D. (1990, July 10). Homophobia: Scientists find clues to its roots. *The New York Times*, C1, C11.

Goodenough, F. L. (1949). *Mental testing*. New York: Rinehart.

Gordon, L. V. (1967). *Survey of personal values*. Chicago: Science Research Associates.

Gottfredson, L. S. (1981). Circumscription and compromise: A developmental theory of occupational aspirations. *Journal of Counseling Psychology, 28*(6), 545–579.

Gould, R. (1978). *Transformations*. New York: Simon & Schuster.

Gray, J. L., & Starke, F. A. (1977). *Organizational behavior: Concepts and applications*. Columbus, OH: Charles E. Merrill.

Green, L. B., & Parker, H. J. (1965). Parental influence upon adolescents' occupational choice: A test of an aspect of Roe's theory. *Journal of Counseling Psychology, 12*, 379–383.

Greenberg, R. M., & Tully, R. B. (1976, Feb.). *Employability of college graduates in Indiana business and industry* (Indiana College Level Manpower Study, Report No. 5). Indianapolis: Indiana Commission on Higher Education.

Gribbons, W. D., & Lohnes, P. R. (1969). *Career development from age 13 to 25*. (Final Report, Project No. 6-2151) Washington, DC: U.S. Department of Health, Education, and Welfare.

——— (1982). *Careers in theory and experience: A twenty-year longitudinal study*. Albany: State University of New York Press.

Grossman, G. M., & Drier, H. N. (1988). *Apprenticeship 2000: The status of and recommendations for improved counseling, guidance, and information processes*. Columbus: National Center for Research in Vocational Education, Ohio State University (ED 298 356).

Grubb, W. M., & Lazerson, M. (1975). Rally round the workplace: Continuities and fallacies in career education. *Harvard Educational Review, 45*, 451–474.

Grubb, W. N., Davis, G., Lum, J., Plihal, J., & Mograine, C. (1991). *The cunning hand, the cultured mind: Models for integrating vocational and academic education*. Berkeley, CA: National Center for Research in Vocational Education (ED 334 421).

Gruen, W. (1964). Adult personality: An empirical study of Erikson's theory of ego development. In B. Neugarten (Ed.), *Personality in middle and late life: Empirical studies*. New York: Atherton.

Gruver, C. G. (1971). College students as therapeutic agents. *Psychological Bulletin, 76*, 111–127.

Guidance information system guide, The. (1977). West Hartford, CT: Time Share Corporation.

——— (1978). West Hartford, CT: Time Share Corporation.

Gulliksen, H. (1950). *Theory of mental tests*. New York: Wiley.

Gump, J., & Rivers, L. (1975). The consideration of race in efforts to end sex bias. In E. E. Diamond (Ed.), *Issues of sex bias in interest measurement*. Washington, DC: U.S. Government Printing Office.

Gysbers, N. C., & Henderson, P. (1988). *Developing and managing your school guidance program*. Alexandria, VA: American Association for Counseling and Development.

Gysbers, N. C., & Moore, E. J. (1987). *Career counseling, skills and techniques for practitioners*. Englewood Cliffs, NJ: Prentice-Hall.

Hackett, R. D., & Betz, N. E. (1981). A self-efficacy approach to the career development of women. *Journal of Vocational Behavior, 18*, 326–329.

Hackman, J. R., & Oldham, G. R. (1981). Work redesigned: People and their work. In

J. O'Toole, J. L. Scheiber, & L. C. Woods (Eds.), *Working changes and choices.* Sacramento: Regents of the University of California.

Hall, D. T. (1976). *Careers in organizations.* Pacific Palisades, CA: Goodyear.

—————— (Ed.). (1986). *Career development in organizations.* San Francisco: Jossey-Bass.

—————— (1990). Career development theory in organizations. In D. Brown & L. Brooks, (Eds.), *Career choice and development* (2nd ed.) (pp. 422–455). San Francisco: Jossey-Bass.

Hall, F. S., & Hall, T. (1979). *The two-career couple.* Reading, MA: Addison-Wesley.

Hall, R. H. (1975). *Occupations and the social structure* (2nd ed.). Englewood Cliffs, NJ: Prentice-Hall.

—————— (1983). Theoretical trends in the sociology of occupations. *Sociological Quarterly, 24,* 5–23.

Halle, E. (1982). The abandoned husband: When wives leave. In K. Solomon & N. B. Levy (Eds.), *Men in transition.* New York: Plenum.

Halloran, W. E., Hull, M. E., Charles, F. H., Lampe, A., & Morgan, C. A. (1978, June). *The Vermont guide for teaching adolescents with special needs* (Project No. 5-0125). Washington, DC: U.S. Office of Education, U.S. Government Printing Office.

Halpern, A., Raffeld, P., Irvin, L. D., & Link, R. (1975). *Social and prevocational information battery.* Monterey, CA: CTB-MacMillan-McGraw-Hill.

Halpern, T. P. O. (1977). Degree of client disclosure as a function of past disclosure, counselor disclosure, and counselor facilitativeness. *Journal of Counseling Psychology, 24,* 42–47.

Halverson, C. F., & Shore, R. E. (1969). Self-disclosure and interpersonal functioning. *Journal of Counseling Clinical Psychology, 33,* 213–219.

Handbook of corporate social responsibility. (1975). Radnor, PA: Chilton Book Company.

Hansen, J. C., & Stevic, R. R. (1971). *Appalachian students and guidance.* Boston: Houghton Mifflin.

Hansen, L. S. (1968). Editorial: The placement function. *The School Counselor, 15,* 166.

—————— (1970). *Career guidance practices in school and community.* Washington, DC: National Vocational Guidance Association.

—————— (1977). *An examination of the definitions and concepts of career education.* Washington, DC: National Advisory Council for Career Education.

—————— (1978a). Promoting female growth through a career development curriculum. In L. S. Hansen & R. S. Rapoza (Eds.), *Career development and counseling of women.* Springfield, IL: Charles C Thomas.

—————— (1978b). *BORN FREE: Training packets to reduce stereotyping in career options.* Minneapolis: University of Minnesota.

—————— (1990). Integrative life planning: Work, family and community. Paper presented at International Round Table for the Advancement of Counseling, July 1990. Helsinki, Finland.

—————— (1991). Integrative life planning: Work, family, community. *Futurics, 15* (3 & 4), 80–86. (Special Issue from World Future Society Conference on "Creating the Future: Individual Responsibility," Minneapolis, MN, July 25).

Hansen, L. S., & Tennyson, W. W. (1975). A career management model for counselor involvement. *Personnel and Guidance Journal, 53*(9), 638–645.

Hantover, J. P. (1980). The social construction of masculine anxiety. In R. A. Lewis (Ed.), *Men in difficult times,* pp. 87–98. Englewood Cliffs, NJ: Prentice-Hall.

Hariton, R. (1970). *Interview! The executive's guide to selecting the right personnel.* New York: Hastings House.

Harmon, L. W. (1975). Technical aspects: Problems of scale development, norms, item differences by sex, and the rate of change in occupational group characteristics—I. In E. E. Diamond (Ed.), *Issues of sex bias and sex fairness in career interest measurement.* Washington, DC: National Institute of Education.

———— (1978). Career counseling for women. In L. S. Hansen & R. S. Rapoza (Eds.), *Career development and counseling of women.* Springfield, IL: Charles C Thomas.

Harris, N. C., & Grede, J. F. (1977). *Career education in colleges.* San Francisco: Jossey-Bass.

Harris, P. R., & Moran, R. T. (1991). *Managing cultural differences* (3rd ed.). Houston: Gulf.

Harris-Bowlsbey, J. (1984). The computer and career development. *Journal of Counseling and Development, 63*(3), 145–149.

Harris-Bowlsbey, J., & Rabush, C. M. (1984). *DISCOVER for adult learners: Professional manual.* Hunt Valley, MD: American College Testing Program.

Harrison, J. (1978). *The male mid-life crisis: Fresh start after 40.* New York: New American Library.

Harway, M. (1980). Sex bias in educational-vocational counseling. *Psychology of Women Quarterly, 4,* 212–214.

Havighurst, R. J. (1953). *Human development and education.* New York: Longman.

Havighurst, R. (1972). *Developmental tasks and education* (3rd ed.). New York: Longman.

Healy, C. C. (1974a). *Career counseling in the community college.* Springfield, IL: Charles C Thomas.

———— (1974b). Toward a replicable method of group career counseling. *Vocational Guidance Quarterly, 23,* 34–41.

———— (1982). *Career development: Counseling through life stages.* Boston: Allyn & Bacon.

———— (1990). Reforming career appraisals to meet the needs of clients in the 1990s. *The Counseling Psychologist, 18,* 214–226.

Hedges, J. N., & Bemis, S. E. (1978). Sex stereotyping: Its decline in the skilled trades. In L. S. Hansen & R. S. Rapoza (Eds.), *Career development and counseling of women.* Springfield, IL: Charles C Thomas.

Heinrich, R. K., Corbine, J. L., & Thomas, K. R. (1990). Counseling Native Americans. *Journal of Counseling & Development, 69,* 128–133.

Heller, C. S. (1963). Ambitions of Mexican-American youth—goals and means of mobility of high school seniors. Unpublished doctoral dissertation. Columbia University, New York.

Henderson, G. (1979). American Indians: Introduction. In G. Henderson (Ed.), *Understanding and counseling ethnic minorities.* Springfield, IL: Charles C Thomas.

Hennessy, M. (1972). Career Corners. In J. E. Bottoms, R. N. Evans, K. B. Hoyt, and J. C. Willers (Eds.), *Career education resource guide.* Morristown, NJ: General Learning Corporation.

Heppner, P. P., & Krauskopf, C. J. (1987). An information processing approach to problem solving. *The Counseling Psychologist, 15,* 371–447.

Herr, E. L. (1989). Career development and mental health. *Journal of Career Development, 16*(1), 5–18.

Herr, E. L., & Cramer, S. H. (1972). *Vocational guidance and career development in the schools: Toward a systems approach.* Boston: Houghton Mifflin.

———— (1992). *Career guidance through the life span.* (4th ed.). Boston: Little, Brown.

Herring, R. D. (1990). Attacking career myths among Native Americans: Implications for counseling. *The School Counselor, 38,* 13–18.

Hersen, M., & Turner, S. M. (1985). *Diagnostic interviewing.* New York: Plenum Press.

Herzberg, F. (1966). *Work and the nature of man.* Cleveland, OH: World Book Company.

Herzberg, F., Mausner, B., & Snyderman, B. (1959). *The motivation to work.* New York: Wiley.

Hesketh, B., Elmslie, S., & Kaldor, W. (1990). Career compromise: An alternative account to Gottfredson's theory. *Journal of Counseling Psychology, 37*(1), 49–56.

Hetherington, C., Hillerbrand, E., & Etringer, B. (1989). Career counseling with gay men: Issues and recommendations for research. *Journal of Counseling and Development, 67,* 452–454.

Hetherington, C., & Orzek, A. (1989). Career counseling and life planning with lesbian women. *Journal of Counseling and Development, 68,* 52–57.

Hill, R. E., & Miller, E. L. (1982). Career change: Implications and suggested response strategies for the individual and the organization. In G. R. Walz (Ed.), *Career development in organizations,* pp. 21–47. Ann Arbor: ERIC Counseling and Personnel Services Clearinghouse, University of Michigan.

Hoffman, L. W. (1963). Parental power relations and the division of household tasks. In F. I. Nye & L. W. Hoffman (Eds.), *The employed mother in America.* Chicago: Rand McNally.

———— (1972). Early childhood experiences and women's achievement motives. *Journal of Social Issues, 28,* 129–155.

———— (1977). Changes in family roles, socialization, and sex differences. *American Psychologist, 32,* 644–657.

———— (1983). Increased fathering: Effects on the mother. In M. E. Lamb & A. Sagi (Eds.), *Fatherhood and family policy.* Hillsdale, NJ: Lawrence Erlbaum.

Hoffreth, S. L., & Phillips, D. A. (1987). Child care in the United States: 1970 to 1985. *Journal of Marriage and the Family, 49,* 559–571.

Holland, J. L. (1966). *The psychology of vocational choice.* Waltham, MA: Blaisdell.

———— (1974). *Self-directed search.* Palo Alto, CA: Consulting Psychologists Press.

———— (1975). The use and evaluation of interest inventories and simulations. In E. E. Diamond (Ed.), *Issues of sex bias and sex fairness in career interest measurement.* Washington, DC: National Institute of Education.

———— (1985). *Making vocational choices: A theory of careers* (2nd ed.). Englewood Cliffs, NJ: Prentice-Hall.

———— (1987a). Current status of Holland's theory of careers: Another perspective. *The Career Development Quarterly, 36,* 31–34.

———— (1987b). *The self-directed search professional manual.* Odessa, FL: Psychological Assessment Resources.

———— (1987c). *The occupations finder.* Odessa, FL: Psychological Assessment Resources.

Holland, J. L., & Astin, A. W. (1962). The prediction of academic, artistic, scientific and social achievement. *Journal of Educational Psychology, 53,* 132–143.

Hollandsworth, J. G., Jr., Dressel, M. E., & Stevens, J. (1977). Use of behavioral versus traditional procedures for increasing job interview skills. *Journal of Counseling Psychology, 24,* 503–510.

Hollender, J. (1967). Development of a realistic vocational choice. *Journal of Counseling Psychology, 14,* 314–318.

Hopkinson, K., Cox, A., & Rutter, M. (1981). Psychiatric interviewing techniques III: Naturalistic study: Eliciting feelings. *British Journal of Psychiatry, 138*: 406–415.

Hoppock, R. (1976). *Occupational information* (4th ed.). New York: McGraw-Hill.

Howard, J. H. (1975). Management productivity, rushing out of burning out. *The Business Quarterly, 40,* 44–49.

Hoyt, K. B. (1972). *Career education: What it is and how to do it.* Salt Lake City: Olympus.

———— (1976). *Refining the career education concept.* Washington, DC: U.S. Government Printing Office.

———— (1977). *The school counselor and career education.* Washington, DC: U.S. Government Printing Office.

Hsia, J. (1981, April). Testing and Asian and Pacific Americans. Paper presented at the National Association for Asian and Pacific American Education, Honolulu.

Hudson, J. S. (1992). Vocational counseling with dual-career same-sex couples. Unpublished manuscript, Southwest Texas State University.

Huffine, C. L., & Clausen, J. A. (1979). Madness and work: Short and long-term effects of mental illness on occupational careers. *Social Forces. 57*(4), 1049–1062.

Iowa State University. (1977). *Extern program.* Ames: University Counseling Center.

Issacson, L. E. (1985). *Basics of career counseling.* Boston: Allyn & Bacon.

Ivancevich, J. J., & Matteson, M. T. (1980). *Stress and work, a managerial perspective.* Dallas: Scott Foresman.

Jackson, B. (1975). Black identity development. *Meforum: Journal of educational diversity and innovation, 2,* 19–25.

Jackson, E. L. (1988). Leisure constraints: A survey of past research. *Leisure Sciences, 10,* 203–215.

Jacobson, T. J. (1972). Career guidance center. *Personnel and Guidance Journal, 50,* 599–604.

Jenkins, C. O. (1976). Recent evidence supporting ecologic and social risk factors for coronary disease. *New England Journal of Medicine, 294,* 987–994.

Jesser, D. L. (1976). *Career education: A priority of the chief state school officers.* Salt Lake City: Olympus.

Job market for UCLA 1987 graduates. (1988). Los Angeles: University of California at Los Angeles.

Johansson, C. B. (1975). Technical aspects: Problems of scale development, norms, item differences by sex, and the rate of change in occupational group characteristics—II. In E. E. Diamond (Ed.), *Issues of sex bias and sex fairness in career interest measurement.* Washington, DC: National Institute of Education.

Johnson, G. J. (1990). Underemployment, underpayment, and self-esteem among Black men. *Journal of Black Psychology, 16*(2), 23–44.

Johnson, R. B. (1977). Life planning and life planning workshops. *Personnel and Guidance Journal, 55,* 546–549.

Johnson, R. H., & Myrick, R. D. (1971). MOLD: A new approach to career decision making. *Vocational Guidance Quarterly, 21*(1), 48–53.

Joiner, J., & Fisher, J. (1977). Post-mastectomy counseling. *Journal of Applied Rehabilitation Counseling, 8,* 99–106.

Jones, L. K. (1981). *Occ-U-Sort Professional manual.* Monterey, CA: Publishers Test Service of CTB-MacMillan-McGraw-Hill.

Jones, M. (1991). Gender stereotyping in advertisements. *Teaching of Psychology, 18,* 231–233.

Jordaan, J. P., & Heyde, M. (1979). *Vocational maturity during the high school years.* New York: Teachers College Press.

Jordaan, J. P., & Super, D. E. (1974). The prediction of early adult vocational behavior. In D. F. Ricks, A. Thomas, & M. Roff (Eds.), *Life history research in psychopathology* (vol. 3). Minneapolis: University of Minnesota Press.

Jourard, S. M. (1964). *The transparent self.* Princeton, NJ: Van Nostrand.

Juhasz, A. M. (1974). The teacher and sex-role stereotyping. *School Health Review, 5,* 17–22.

Kagan, J., & Moss, H. A. (1962). *Birth to maturity: A study in psychological development.* New York: Wiley.

Kahn, S. E., & Schroeder, A. S. (1980). Counselor bias and occupational choice for female students. *Canadian Counselor, 21,* 156–159.

Kando, T. M., & Summers, W. C. (1971). The impact of work on leisure: Toward a paradigm and research strategy. *Pacific Sociological Review, 14,* 310–327.

Kaneshige, E. (1979). Cultural factors in group counseling and interaction. In G. Henderson (Ed.), *Understanding and counseling ethnic minorities,* 457–467. Springfield, IL: Charles C Thomas.

Kanter, M. (1989). *When giants learn to dance.* New York: Simon & Schuster.

Kapes, J. T., Borman, C. A., Garcia, G., Jr., & Compton, J. W. (1985, April). Evaluation of microcomputer based career guidance systems with college students: SIGI and DIS-COVER. Paper presented at the annual meeting of the American Educational Research Association, Chicago.

Kaplan, H. H. (1970). A case for better training in pre-college guidance: Counselors speak out. In S. H. Cramer (Ed.), *Pre-service and in-service preparation of school counselors for educational guidance.* Washington, DC: American Personnel and Guidance Association.

Karasek, R. & Theorell, T. (1990). *Healthy work: Stress, productivity, and the reconstruction of working life.* New York: Basic Books, Inc.

Kasl, S. V. (1978). Epidemiological contributions to the study of work stress. In C. L. Cooper & R. Payne (Eds.), *Stress at work.* New York: Wiley.

Katz, M. (1958). *You: Today and tomorrow.* Princeton, NJ: Educational Testing Service.

Katz, M. R. (1975). *SIGI: A computer-based system of interactive guidance and information.* Princeton, NJ: Educational Testing Service.

Kaufman, H. G. (1974). *Obsolescence and professional career development.* New York: American Management Association.

Kavruck, S. (1956). Thirty-three years of test research: A short history of test development in the U.S. Civil Service Commission. *American Psychologist, 11,* 329–333.

Keating, D. P. (1980). Thinking processes in adolescence. In J. Adelson (Ed.), *Handbook of adolescent psychology.* New York: Wiley.

Kelly, J. R. (1981). Leisure interaction and the social dialectic. *Social Forces, 60*(2), 304 322.

Kenniston, K. (1971). *Youth and dissent: The rise of the new opposition.* New York: Harcourt Brace Jovanovich.

Kesner, P. M. (1977). *A comparison of guidance needs expressed by preadolescent and early adolescent students.* E.D. dissertation, DeKalb: Northern Illinois University.

Kibrick, A. K., & Tiedeman, D. V. (1961). Conception of self and perception of role in schools of nursing. *Journal of Counseling Psychology, 8,* 26–29.

Kindred, L. W. (1968). *The intermediate schools.* Englewood Cliffs, NJ: Prentice-Hall.

Kingston, J. (1983). Telecommuting: Its impact on the home. In H. F. Didsbury, Jr. (Ed.), *The world of work.* Bethesda, MD. World Future Society.

Kirschner, A. M. (1981). Masculinity in American cities. In R. A. Lewis (Ed.), *Men in difficult times.* Englewood Cliffs, NJ: Prentice-Hall.

Klinger, G. (1988). Dual-role model. Unpublished manuscript, Southwest Texas State University, San Marcos.

Knapp, R. R., & Knapp, L. (1977). Interest changes and the classification of occupations. Unpublished manuscript, EDITS, San Diego, CA.

Knefelkamp, L. L., & Slepitza, R. (1976). A cognitive developmental model of career development—an adaptation of the Perry scheme. *Counseling Psychologist, 6*(3), 53–58.

Knowdell, R. L., McDaniels, C., & Walz, G. R. (1983). *Outplacement counseling.* Ann Arbor: ERIC Counseling and Personnel Service Clearinghouse, University of Michigan.

Kohlberg, L. (1973). Continuities in childhood and adult moral development revisited. In P. B. Baltes and K. W. Schase (Eds.), *Lifespan developmental psychology: Personality and socialization.* New York: Academic Press.

Korman, A. K. (1967). Self-esteem as a moderator of the relationship between self-perceived abilities and vocational choice. *Journal of Applied Psychology, 51,* 65–67.

—— (1977). *Organizational behavior.* Englewood Cliffs, NJ: Prentice-Hall.

Kotter, J. P. (1984). The psychological contract: Managing the joining-up process. In J. A. Sonnenfeld (Ed.), *Managing career systems,* pp. 499–509. Homewood, IL: Richard D. Irwin.

Kram, K. E. (1985). Improving the mentoring process. *Training and Development Journal, 39*(4), 40–43.

Kramer, H. C., Berger, F., & Miller G. (1974). Student concerns and sources of assistance. *Journal of College Student Personnel, 15*(5), 389–393.

Krannich, R. L., & Krannich, C. R. (1990). *The complete guide to international jobs and careers.* Woodridge, VA: Impact Publishers.

Krause, E. A. (1971). *The sociology of occupations.* Boston: Little, Brown.

Kriegel, L. (1982). Claiming the self: The cripple as American male. In M. G. Eisenberg, D. Kriggins, & R. J. Duval (Eds.), *Disabled people as second class citizens.* New York: Springer.

Kronenberger, G. K. (1991). Out of the closet. *Personnel Journal,* June, 40–44.

Krumboltz, J. D. (1979). A social learning theory of career decision making. In A. M. Mitchell, G. G. Jame, & J. D. Krumboltz (Eds.), *Social learning and career decision making,* pp. 19–49. Cranston, RI: Carrole Press.

—— (1980). *Job experience kits.* Chicago: Science Research Associates.

—— (1983). *Private rules in career decision making.* Columbus, OH: National Center for Research in Vocational Education.

—— (1991). *Career beliefs inventory.* Palo Alto, CA: Consulting Psychologists Press, Inc.

Krumboltz, J. D., Mitchell, A., & Gelatt, H. G. (1975). Applications of social learning theory of career selection. *Focus on Guidance, 8,* 1–16.

Krumboltz, J. D., & Sorenson, D. L. (1974). *Career decision making.* Madison, WI: Counseling Films, Inc.

Kuder, G. F. (1963). A rationale for evaluating interests. *Educational and Psychological Measurement, 23,* 3–10.

—— (1964). *Kuder general interest survey: Manual.* Chicago: Science Research Associates.

—— (1966). *Kuder occupational interest survey: General manual.* Chicago: Science Research Associates.

—— (1977). *Kuder general interest survey.* Chicago: Science Research Associates.

Kumata, R., & Murata, A. (1980, March). *Employment of Asian/Pacific American women in Chicago.* Report of conference sponsored by the Women's Bureau, U.S. Department of Labor, Chicago.

Kurpius, D., Burello, L., & Rozecki, T. (1990). Strategic planning in human service organizations. *Counseling and Human Development, 22*(9), 1–12.

Lamb, M. E., Frodi, A. M., Hwang, C., & Frodi, M. (1982). Varying degrees of paternal involvement in infant care: Attitudinal and behavioral correlates. In M. E. Lamb (Ed.), *Nontraditional families: Parenting and child development*. Hillsdale, NJ: Lawrence Erlbaum.

Lange, A. J., & Jakubowski, P. (1976). *Responsible assertive behavior: Cognitive/behavioral procedures for trainers*. Champaign, IL: Research Press.

Langelier, R., & Deckert, P. (1980). Divorce counseling guidelines for the late divorced female. *Journal of Divorce, 3,* 403–411.

Larsen, L. F. (1972). The influence of parents and peers during adolescence: The situation hypothesis revisited. *Journal of Marriage and the Family, 34,* 67–74.

Lathrop, R. (1977). *Who's hiring who?* Berkeley, CA: Ten Speed Press.

Latona, J. R. (1989). Consistence of Holland code and its relation to persistence in a college major. *Journal of Vocational Behavior, 34,* 253–265.

Lawler, E. E., III. (1973). *Motivation in work organizations*. Pacific Grove, CA: Brooks/Cole.

Lazarus, A. A. (1973). On assertive behavior: A brief note. *Behavioral Therapy, 4,* 697.

—— (1989). *The practice of multimodal therapy*. Baltimore: Johns Hopkins University Press.

Lazarus, R. S. (1980). The stress and coping paradigm. In L. A. Bond & J. C. Rosen (Eds.), *Primary prevention of psychopathology* (Vol. 4). Hanover, NH: University Press of New England.

Leahy, R. L., & Shirk, S. R. (1984). The development of classificatory skills; and sex-trait stereotypes in children. *Sex-Roles, 10,* 281–292.

Leclair, S. W. (1982). The dignity of leisure. *The School Counselor, 29*(4), 289–296.

Lein, L. (1979). Male participation in home life: Impact of social supports and breadwinner responsibility on the allocation of tasks. *The Family Coordinator, 28,* 489–495.

Levering, R., Moskowitz, M., & Katz, M. (1984). *The 100 best companies to work for in America*. Reading, MA: Addison-Wesley.

Levi, L. (1984). *Preventing work stress*. Reading, MA: Addison-Wesley.

Levinson, D. J. (1980). The mentor relationship. In M. A. Morgan (Ed.), *Managing career development*. New York: Van Nostrand.

Levinson, D. J., Darrow, C. N., Klein, E. B., Levinson, M. H., & McKee, B. (1978). *The seasons of a man's life*. New York: Knopf.

Lewin, K. (1951). *Field theory in social science*. New York: Harper & Row.

Lewis, J. F. (1977). *Goodwill: For the love of people*. Bethesda, MD: Goodwill Industries of America.

Lewis, M., & Freedle, R. (1973). Mother-infant dyad: The cradle of meaning. In P. Pliner, L. Krame, & T. Alloway (Eds.), *Communication and affect: Language and thought*. New York: Academic Press.

Likert, R. (1967). *The human organization: Its management and value*. New York: McGraw-Hill.

Lindquist, E. F. (1951). *Educational measurement*. Washington, DC: American Council on Education.

Lindsey, L. L. (1990). *Gender roles: A sociological perspective*. Englewood Cliffs, NJ: Prentice-Hall.

Livson, N., & Peskin, H. (1980). Perspectives on adolescence from longitudinal research. In J. Adelson (Ed.), *Handbook of adolescent psychology*. New York: Wiley.

Lofquist, L. H., & Dawis, R. V. (1984). Research on work adjustment and satisfaction: Implications for career counseling. In S. Brown and R. Lent (Eds.), *Handbook of counseling psychology*, pp. 216–237. New York: Wiley.

Looft, W. R. (1971). Sex differences in the expression of vocational aspirations by elementary school children. *Developmental Psychology, 5,* 366.

Loring, R., & Wells, T. (1978). Our sex-role culture. In L. Hansen and R. S. Rapoza (Eds.), *Career development and counseling of women,* pp. 184–199. Springfield, IL: Charles C Thomas.

Louis, M. R. (1982). Managing career transitions: A missing link in career development. *Organizational Dynamics, 10,* 68–77.

Lunneborg, P. W. (1981). *The vocational interest inventory (VIII) manual.* Los Angeles: Western Psychological Services.

—— (1984). Practical application of Roe's theory of career development. In D. Brown and L. Brooks (Eds.), *Career choice and development,* pp. 54–61. San Francisco: Jossey-Bass.

Lyle, J. (1972). Television in daily life: Patterns of use. In E. A. Rubinstein, G. A. Comstock, & J. P. Murray (Eds.), *Television and social behavior* (Vol. 4). Washington, DC: U.S. Government Printing Office.

Maccoby, M., & Terzi, K. A. (1981). What happened to the work ethic? In J. O'Toole, J. L. Scheiber, & L. C. Wood (Eds.), *Working changes and choices.* Sacramento: Regents of the University of California.

Magnuson, J. (1990). Stress Management. *Journal of Property Management, 55,* 24–28.

Magoon, T. M. (1969). *Effective problem solving.* College Park: University of Maryland.

Malcolm, S. M. (1990). Reclaiming our past. *Journal of Negro Education, 59*(3), 246–259.

Maley, D. (1975). *Cluster concept in vocational education.* Chicago: American Technical Society.

Mamarchev, H. L. (1982). *Career management and career pathing in organizations.* Ann Arbor: ERIC Counseling and Personnel Services Clearinghouse, University of Michigan.

Manson, N. M. (Ed.). (1982). *Topics in American Indian mental health prevention.* Portland: Oregon Health Sciences University Press.

Manufacturers and Thomas register and catalog. (1988). New York: Thomas.

Marano, C. (1979). The displaced homemaker network: Looking ahead. *Journal of Home Economics, 71*(2), 34–35.

Marcia, J. E. (1967). Ego identity status: Relationship to change in self-esteem, "general adjustment," and authoritarianism. *Journal of Personality, 35*(1), 119–133.

Marciano, T. D. (1981). Men in change: Beyond mere anarchy. In R. A. Lewis (Ed.), *Men in difficult times.* Englewood Cliffs, NJ: Prentice-Hall.

Marland, S. P., Jr. (1974). *Career education: A proposal for reform.* New York: McGraw-Hill.

Martin, G. M. (1979). Getting chosen: The job interview and before. *Occupational Outlook Quarterly, 23*(1), 2–9.

Maslach, C. (1976). Burned out. *Human Behavior, 5*(9), 16–22.

—— (1981). Burnout: A social psychological analysis. In J. W. Jones (Ed.), *The burnout syndrome: Current research, theory, interventions.* Park Ridge, IL: London House Press.

Maslach, C., & Jackson, J. E. (1981). The measurement of experienced burnout. *Journal of Occupational Behavior, 2,* 99–113.

Maslow, A. A. (1943). A theory of human motivation. *Psychological Review, 50,* 379–393.

Matthews, E., & Tiedeman, D. (1964). Attitudes toward career and marriage and the development of life-style in young women. *Journal of Counseling Psychology, 11,* 375–384.

Mayer, H. (1978). *The male mid-life crisis: Fresh start after 40.* New York: New American Library.

Maze, M. (1984). How to select a computerized guidance system. *Journal of Counseling and Development, 63*(3), 158–162.

————— (1985). How much should a computerized guidance program cost? *Journal of Career Development, 12*(2), 157–164.

Maze, M., & Cummings, R. (1982). Analysis of DISCOVER. In M. Maze and R. Cummings, *How to select a computer-assisted guidance system,* pp. 97–107. Madison: University of Wisconsin, Wisconsin Vocational Studies Center.

McBride, A. B. (1990). Mental health effects of women's multiple roles. *American Psychologist, 45,* 381–384.

McBride, M. C. (1990). Autonomy and the struggle for female identity: Implications for counseling women. *Journal of Counseling and Development, 69,* 22–26.

McClelland, D. C. (1961). *The achieving society.* Princeton, NJ: Van Nostrand.

McClelland, D. C., Atkinson, J., Clark, R., & Lowell, E. L. (1953). *The achievement motive.* New York: Appleton-Century-Crofts.

McCormac, M. E. (1988). Information sources and resources. *Journal of Career Development, 16,* 129–138.

McDaniels, C. (1984). Work and leisure in the career span. In N. C. Gysbers & associates (Eds.), *Designing careers, counseling to enhance education, work and leisure* (Chap. 21). San Francisco: Jossey-Bass.

————— (1990). *The changing workplace: Career counseling strategies for the 1990s and beyond.* San Francisco: Jossey-Bass.

McGhee, P. E. (1975). Television as a source of learning sex-role stereotypes. Paper presented at the meeting for the Society for Research in Child Development, Denver.

McGovern, T. V., Tinsley, D. J., Liss-Levinson, N., Laventure, R. O., & Britton, G. (1975). Assertion training for job interviews. *The Counseling Psychologist, 5,* 65–68.

McGowan, B. G. (1984). *Trends in employee counseling programs.* New York: Pergamon Press.

McGregor, D. (1960). *The human side of enterprise.* New York: McGraw-Hill.

McIlroy, J. H. (1979). Career as lifestyle: An existential view. *Personnel and Guidance Journal, 57,* 351–354.

Menacker, J. (1971). *Urban poor students and guidance.* Boston: Houghton Mifflin.

Micro-tower: The group vocational and research center. (1977). New York: ICD Rehabilitation and Research Center.

Military Career Guide (1989). North Chicago, IL: U.S. Military Processing Command.

Miller, A. W. (1968). Learning theory and vocational decisions. *Personnel and Guidance Journal, 47,* 18–23.

Miller, C., & Oetting, E. (1977). Barriers to employment and the disadvantaged. *Personnel and Guidance Journal, 56,* 89–93.

Miller, D. C., & Form, W. H. (1951). *Industrial sociology.* New York: Harper & Row.

Miller, J. (1977). *Career development needs of nine-year-olds: How to improve career development programs.* Washington, DC: National Advisory Council for Career Education.

Miller, J. M., & Springer, T. P. (1986). Perceived satisfaction of a computerized vocational counseling system as a function of monetary investment. *Journal of College Student Personnel, 27,* 142–146.

Miller, M. F. (1974). Relationship of vocational maturity to work values. *Journal of Vocational Behavior, 5,* 367–371.

Miller, N. B. (1982). Social work services to urban Indians. In J. W. Green (Ed.), *Cultural awareness in the human services.* Englewood Cliffs, NJ: Prentice-Hall.

Miller-Tiedeman, A. (1987). *How to not make it and succeed.* Vista, CA: LIFECAREER Foundation.

————— (1988). *Lifecareer: The quantum leap into a process theory of career.* Vista, CA: LIFECAREER Foundation.

Miller-Tiedeman, A. L., & Tiedeman, D. V. (1982). *Career development: Journey into personal power.* Schenectady, NY: Character Research Press.

——— (1990). Career decision making: An individualistic perspective. In D. Brown, L. Brooks, & associates (Eds.), *Career choice and development: Applying contemporary theories to practice* (2nd ed.), pp. 308–337. San Francisco: Jossey-Bass.

Minor, F. J., Myers, R. A., & Super, D. E. (1972). An experimental computer-based educational and career exploration system. In J. M. Whiteley & A. Resnikoff (Eds.), *Perspectives on vocational development.* Washington, DC: American Personnel and Guidance Association.

Mischel, W. (1970). Sex typing and socialization. In P. H. Mussen (Ed.), *Carmichael's manual of child psychology* (3rd ed.) (Vol. 2). New York: Wiley.

Mitchell, A. M. (1977). *Career development needs of seventeen year olds: How to improve career development programs.* Washington, DC: National Advisory Committee for Career Education.

Mitchell, L. K., & Krumboltz, J. D. (1984). Social learning approach to career decision making: Krumboltz's theory. In D. Brown & L. Brooks (Eds.), *Career choice and development.* San Francisco: Jossey-Bass.

——— (1987). Cognitive restructuring and decision-making training on career indecision. *Journal of Counseling and Development, 66,* 171–174.

——— (1990). Social learning approach to career decision making: Krumboltz's Theory. In D. Brown & L. Brooks (Eds.), *Career choice and development. Applying contemporary theories to practice,* (2nd Ed.), pp. 145–196. San Francisco: Jossey-Bass.

Model, S. (1981). Housework by husbands: Determinants and implications. *Journal of Family Issues, 2,* 225–237.

Mogull, R. (1978). Dissatisfaction and habits of black workers. *Personnel and Guidance Journal, 56,* 567–570.

Moir, E. (1981). Career resource center in business and industry. *Training and Development Journal, 35*(2), 54–62.

Money, J. (1982). Introduction. In K. Solomon & N. B. Levy (Eds.), *Men in transition.* New York: Plenum.

Montana, P. J., & Higgenson, M. V. (1978). *Career life planning for Americans.* New York: AMACOM.

Morgan, L. A. (1980). Work in widowhood, a viable option? *Gerontologist, 20,* 581–587.

Morrow, P. C. (1985). Retirement planning: Rounding out the career process. In D. W. Myers, *Employee problem prevention and counseling.* Westport, CT: Quorum Books.

Mosher, E. H. (1976). Portrayal of women in drug advertising: A medical betrayal. *Journal of Drug Issues, 6,* 72–78.

Moss, H. A. (1967). Sex, age, and state as determinants of mother-infant interaction. *Merrill-Palmer Quarterly, 13,* 19–36.

Myers, D. W. (1984). *Establishing and building employee assistance programs.* Westport, CT: Quorum Books.

Nadelson, T., & Nadelson, C. (1982). Dual careers and changing role models. In K. Solomon & N. B. Levy (Eds.), *Men in transition.* New York: Plenum.

Naisbitt, J. (1982). *Megatrends.* New York: Warner Books.

National Occupational Information Coordinating Committee, U. S. Department of Labor. (1979). *Vocational preparation and occupations, Vol. 1. Occupational and educational code crosswalk.* Washington, DC: U.S. Government Printing Office.

——— (1992). *The national career development guidelines project.* Washington, DC: U.S. Department of Labor.

National Science Foundation. (1989). *Science and engineering indicators—1989*. Washington, DC: National Science Foundation.

Nations Business. (1991, May). Chipping away at the glass ceiling. 20–21.

Nealer, J. K., & Papalia, A. J. (1982). *So you want to get a job: A manual for the job seeker and vocational counselor*. Moravia, NY: Chronicle Guidance.

Neff, W. S. (1985). *Work and human behavior* (2nd ed.). Chicago: Aldine.

Nelson, C. (1990, March). The beast within Winnie-the Pooh reassessed. *Children's Literature in Education*, V21, 17–22.

Nelson, N. (1971). *Workshops for those handicapped in the United States*. Springfield, IL: Charles C Thomas.

Neugarten, B. (Ed.). (1968). *Middle age and aging*. Chicago: University of Chicago Press.

Nevo, O. (1987). Irrational expectations in career counseling and their confronting arguments. *Career Development Quarterly, 35*, 239–250.

Newman, R. R. (1980). Southwest Texas State University Career Development Resource Center. Unpublished manuscript. Southwest Texas State University, San Marcos.

Nichols, J. (1975). *Men's liberation: A new definition of masculinity*. New York: Penguin.

Nihira, K., Foster, R., Shellhaas, M., & Leland, H. (1975). *AAMD adaptive behavior scale*. Washington, DC: American Association on Mental Deficiency.

Norrell, G., & Grater, H. (1960). Interest awareness as an aspect of self-awareness. *Journal of Counseling Psychology, 7*, 289–292.

Odgers, J. G. (1968). Placement: A counselor's job. *The School Counselor, 15*, 343–349.

Ogden, R. F. (1982). Environment for managing human resources. Address to faculty of Southwest Texas State University, San Marcos.

O'Hara, R. P. (1968). A theoretical foundation for the use of occupational information in guidance. *Personnel and Guidance Journal, 46*, 636–640.

O'Hara, R. P., & Tiedeman, D. V. (1959). Vocational self-concept in adolescence. *Journal of Counseling Psychology, 6*, 292–301.

Olmsted, B. (1981). Job sharing—a new way to work. In J. O'Toole, J. L. Scheiber, & L. C. Wood (Eds.), *Working changes and choices*. Sacramento: Regents of the University of California.

Olson, K. (1978). *Hey man! Open up and live*. New York: Fawcett.

O'Neil, J. M. (1982). Gender role conflict and strain in men's lives: Implications for psychiatrists, psychologists, and other human-services providers. In K. Solomon & N. B. Levy (Eds.), *Men in transition*. New York: Plenum.

Osipow, S. H. (1983). *Theories of career development* (3rd ed.). New York: Appleton-Century-Crofts.

Othmer, E., & Othmer, S. (1989). *The clinical interview*. Washington, DC: American Psychiatric Press.

O'Toole, J. (1977). *Work, learning, and the American future*. San Francisco: Jossey-Bass.

———— (1981). *Making America work*. New York: Continuum.

Papke, D. R. (1976). Doubleknit showmanship—the new look in college placement. *Change Magazine, 8*, 15–18.

Pardine, P., Higgins, R., Szeglin, A., Beres, J., Kravitz, R., & Fotis, J. (1981). Job-stress, worker-strain relationship moderated by off-the-job experience. *Psychological Reports, 48*, 963–970.

Parker, R. M., & Hansen, C. E. (1981). *Rehabilitation counseling*. Boston: Allyn & Bacon.

Parrillo, V. N. (1985). *Stranger to these shoes*. (2nd ed.) New York: Wiley.

Parsons, F. (1909). *Choosing a vocation*. Boston: Houghton Mifflin.

Pascarel, E. T., & Terenzi, P. T. (1991). *How college affects students: Findings and insights from twenty years of research*. San Francisco: Jossey-Bass.

Payne, D. A. (1962). The concurrent and predictive validity of an objective measure of academic self-concept. *Educational and Psychological Measurement, 22,* 773–780.

Peatling, J. H., & Tiedeman, D. V. (1977). *Career development: Designing self.* Muncie, IN: Accelerated Development.

Peterson, G. W., Ryan-Jones, R. E., Sampson, J. P., Jr., Reardon, R. C., & Shahnasarian, M. (1987). *A comparison of the effectiveness of three computer-assisted career guidance systems on college students' career decision making processes* (Technical Report No. 6). Tallahassee: Florida State University, Center for the Study of Technology in Counseling and Career Development, Tallahassee.

Peterson, G. W., Sampson, J. P., & Reardon, R. C. (1991). *Career development and services: A cognitive approach.* Pacific Grove, CA: Brooks/Cole.

Peterson, M. (1982). VALPAR component work sample system. In J. T. Kapes & M. M. Mastie (Eds.), *A counselor's guide to vocational guidance instruments.* Falls Church, VA: The National Vocational Guidance Association.

Piaget, J. (1929). *The child's conception of the world.* New York: Harcourt Brace.

Piaget, J., & Inhelder, B. (1969). *The psychology of the child.* New York: Basic Books.

Picchioni, A. P., & Bonk, E. C. (1983). *A comprehensive history of guidance in the United States.* Austin: Texas Personnel and Guidance Association.

Pietrofesa, J. J., & Splete, H. (1975). *Career development: Theory and research.* New York: Grune & Stratton.

Pines, A., & Aronson, E. (1988). *Career burnout causes and cures.* New York: Free Press.

Pines, A., & Maslach, C. (1979). Characteristics of staff burnout. *Psychiatry, 29,* 233–237.

Pine, G. J., & Innis, G. (1987). Cultural and individual work values. *Career Development Quarterly, 35*(4), 279–287.

Placement and career planning center. (1979). *Career guide.* Salt Lake City: University of Utah.

Plato System, The. (1977). Urbana-Champaign: University of Illinois.

Pleck, J. H. (1979). Men's family work: Three perspectives and some new data. *The Family Coordinator, 28,* 481–488.

———— (1985). *Working wives/working husbands.* Newbury Park, CA: Sage.

Pollack, E. W., & Menacker, J. (1971). *Spanish-speaking students and guidance.* Boston: Houghton Mifflin.

Pollman, A. W., & Johnson, A. C. (1979). Resistance to change, early retirement, and managerial decisions. *Industrial Gerontology, 1,* 33–41.

Ponterotto, J. G. (1987). Counseling Mexican Americans: A multimodal approach. *Journal of Counseling and Development, 65,* 308–311.

Poole, M. E., & Clooney, G. H. (1985). Careers: Adolescent awareness and exploration of possibilities for self. *Journal of Vocational Behavior, 26,* 251–263.

Porter, T. L. (1981). Extent of disabling conditions. In R. M. Parker & C. E. Hansen (Eds.), *Rehabilitation counseling.* Boston: Allyn & Bacon.

Powell, A., & Vega, M. (1972). Correlates of adult locus of control. *Psychological Reports, 30,* 455–460.

Powell, D. H. (1957). Careers and family atmosphere: An empirical test of Roe's theory. *Journal of Counseling Psychology, 4,* 212–217.

Prazak, J. A. (1969). Learning job seeking interview skills. In J. D. Krumboltz & C. E. Thoresen (Eds.), *Behavioral counseling: Cases and techniques.* New York: Holt, Rinehart & Winston.

Predicasts Funk and Scott index of corporations and industries. (1989). Cleveland, OH: Predicasts.

Prediger, D. J. (1974). The role of assessment in career guidance. In E. L. Herr (Ed.), *Vocational guidance and human development*. Boston: Houghton Mifflin.

Prediger, D. J., & Hanson, G. (1975). Guidelines for assessment of sex bias and sex fairness in career interest inventories. In E. E. Diamond (Ed.), *Issues of sex bias and sex fairness in career interest measurement*. Washington, DC: National Institute of Education.

Prediger, D. J., & Johnson, R. W. (1979). *Alternatives to sex-restrictive vocational interest assessment* (ACT Research Report No. 79). Iowa City, IA: American College Testing Program.

Prediger, D. J., & Sawyer, R. L. (1985). Ten years of career development: A nationwide study of high school students. *Journal of Counseling and Development, 65*(1), 45–49.

Prevocational training manual. (1980). Austin: Texas Rehabilitation Commission.

Products lists, Skyline High School. (1979). Dallas: Dallas Independent School District.

Psathas, G. (1968). Toward a theory of occupational choice for women. *Sociology and Social Research, 52*, 253–268.

Raanan, S. J., & Lynch, T. H. (1974). Approaches to job hunting workshops. *Journal of College Placement, 34*, 67–74.

Radin, N. (1983). Primary caregiving and role-sharing fathers. In M. E. Lamb (Ed.), *Nontraditional families: Parenting and child development*. Hillsdale, NJ: Lawrence Erlbaum.

Ragheb, M. B., & Griffith, C. A. (1982). The contribution of leisure participation and leisure satisfaction to life satisfaction of older persons. *Journal of Leisure Research, 14*, 295–306.

Rapoport, R., & Rapoport, R. (1978). The dual career family. In L. S. Hansen & R. S. Rapoza (Eds.), *Career development and the counseling of women*. Springfield, IL: Charles C Thomas.

Reardon, R. C. (1980). Curricular career information service. Unpublished manuscript, Florida State University, Tallahassee.

Reardon, R. C., & Domkowski, D. (1977). Building instruction into a career information center. *Vocational Guidance Quarterly, 25*, 274–278.

Reardon, R. C., & Minor, C. W. (1975). Revitalizing the career information service. *Personnel and Guidance Journal, 54*, 169–171.

Reardon, R. C., Zunker, V. G., & Dyal, M. S. (1979). The status of career planning programs and career centers in colleges and universities. *Vocational Guidance Quarterly, 28*, 154–159.

Redmond, R. E. (1972). Increasing vocational information seeking behavior of high school students. Unpublished doctoral dissertation, University of Maryland, University Park.

Regehr, C. N., & Herman, A. (1981). Developing the skills of career decision making and self assessment in ninth grade students. *Vocational Guidance Quarterly, 28*(5), 335–342.

Reich, R. B. (1991). *The work of nations*. New York: Knopf.

Reschke, W., & Knierim, K. H. (1987). How parents influence career choice. *Journal of Career Planning and Employment*, Spring, 54–60.

Rhodes, S. R. (1983). Age-related differences in work attitudes and behavior: A review and conceptual analysis. *Psychological Bulletin, 93*, 328–367.

Rich, A. R., & Schroeder, H. E. (1976). Research issues in assertiveness training. *Psychological Bulletin, 83*, 1081–1096.

Rodriguez, M., & Blocher, D. (1988). A comparison of two approaches to enhancing career maturity in Puerto Rican college women. *Journal of Counseling Psychology, 35,* 275–280.

Roe, A. (1956). *The psychology of occupations.* New York: Wiley.

———— (1972). Perspectives on vocational development. In J. M. Whiteley and A. Resnikoff (Eds.), *Perspectives on vocational development.* Washington, DC: American Personnel and Guidance Association.

Roe, A., & Lunneborg, P. W. (1990). Personality Development and Career Choice. In D. Brown & L. Brooks (Eds.), *Career choice and development. Applying contemporary theories to practice* (pp. 68–101). San Francisco: Jossey-Bass.

Roessler, R., & Bolton, B. (1978). *Psychological adjustment to disability.* Baltimore: University Park Press.

Roessler, R., & Rubin, E. (1982). *Case management and rehabilitation counseling: Procedures and techniques.* Baltimore: University Park Press.

Rogers, C. R. (1942). *Counseling and psychotherapy.* Boston: Houghton Mifflin.

———— (1961). *On becoming a person.* Boston: Houghton Mifflin.

Roselle, B., & Hummel, T. (1988). Intellectual development and interaction effectiveness with DISCOVER, *The Career Development Journal, 35–36,* 241–251.

Rosen, B., & Jerdee, T. H. (1975). The corporate double standard. *Human Behavior, 4,* 47–48.

———— (1976). The nature of job-related age stereotypes. *Journal of Applied Psychology, 61,* 180–183.

Rosenberg, M. (1957). *Occupations and values.* Glencoe, IL: Free Press.

Rosenman, R. H., Friedman, M., & Straus, R. (1964). A predictive study of coronary heart disease. *Journal of the American Medical Association, 189,* 103–110.

Rosenthal, R. H., & Akiskal, H. S. (1985). Mental status examination. In M. Hersen & S. M. Turner (Eds.), *Diagnostic interviewing.* New York: Plenum Press.

Rosenwasser, S. M. (1982, April). Differential socialization processes of males and females. Paper presented to the Texas Personnel and Guidance Association, Houston.

Rosenwasser, S. M., & Patterson, W. (1984, April). Nontraditional males: Men with primary childcare/household responsibilities. Paper presented to the Southwestern Psychological Association, New Orleans.

Ross, C. C., & Stanley, J. C. (1954). *Measurement in today's schools* (2nd ed.). New York: Prentice-Hall.

Rotter, J. B. (1966). Generalized expectancies for internal versus external control of reinforcement. *Psychological Monographs, 80* (1 Whole No. 609).

Rubin, J. A., Provenzano, F. J., & Luria, A. (1974). The eye of the beholder: Parents' views on sex of newborns. *American Journal of Orthopsychiatry, 44,* 512–519.

Russell, G. (1982). Shared-caregiving families: An Australian study. In M. E. Lamb (Ed.), *Nontraditional families: Parenting and child development.* Hillsdale, NJ: Erlbaum.

Russo, N. F., Kelly, R. M., & Deacon, M. (1991). Gender and success-related attributions: Beyond individualistic conceptions of achievement. *Sex Roles, 25,* 331–350.

Ryan, C. W., & Drummond, R. J. (1981). University based career education: A model for infusion. *Personnel and Guidance Journal, 60,* 89–92.

Ryan, C. W., Drummond, R. J., & Shannon, M. D. (1980). Guidance information systems: An analysis of impact on school counseling. *The School Counselor, 28*(2), 93–97.

Saario, T. N., Jacklin, C. N., & Tittle, C. K. (1973). Sex role stereotypes in the public schools. *Harvard Educational Review, 43,* 386–416.

Sadker, M. P., & Sadker, D. M. (1980). Sexism in teacher-education texts. *Harvard Educational Review, 50,* 36–46.

Saegert, S., & Hart, R. (1976). The development of sex differences in the environmental competence of children. In P. Burnett (Ed.), *Women in society*. Chicago: Maaroufa Press.

Safilios-Rothchild, C. (1970). *The sociology and social psychology of disability in rehabilitation*. New York: Random House.

Sagi, A. (1982). Antecedents and consequences of various degrees of paternal involvement in child rearing: The Israeli project. In M. E. Lamb (Ed.), *Nontraditional families: Parenting and child development*. Hillsdale, NJ: Erlbaum.

Salomone, P. R., & Slaney, R. B. (1978). The applicability of Holland's theory to professional workers. *Journal of Vocational Behavior, 13*, 63–74.

Sampson, J. P. (1983). Computer-assisted testing and assessment: Current status and implications for the future. *Measurement and Evaluation in Guidance, 15*(3), 293–299.

Sampson, J. P., & Pyle, K. R. (1983). Ethical issues involved with the use of computer-assisted counseling, testing and guidance systems. *Personnel and Guidance Journal, 61*(3), 283–287.

Sampson, J. P., Peterson, G. W., Lenz, J. G., & Reardon, R. C. (1992). *Career Development Quarterly, 41*, 67–73.

Samuda, R. J. (1975). *Psychological testing of American minorities*. New York: Dodd Mead.

San Antonio Express-News. (1993a). *Job stress at work around the world*. March 23, p. 1B. San Antonio, TX: San Antonio Express-News Publisher.

——— (1993b). *Minority numbers expected to grow*. March 25, p. 12A. San Antonio, TX: San Antonio Express-News Publisher.

Sanguiliano, I. (1978). *In her time*. New York: Morrow.

Sarason, S. B., Sarason, E. K., & Cowden, P. (1977). Aging and the nature of work. In H. J. Peters & J. C. Hensen (Eds.), *Vocational guidance and career development*. New York: Macmillan.

Sato, K. (1979). *The Asian-American employment market: The Japanese experience*. Washington, DC: Department of Health, Education, and Welfare, ERIC National Institute of Education (ED175976).

Scarr, S., Phillips, D., & McCartney, K. (1989). Working mothers and their families. *American Psychologist, 44*, 1402–1409.

Schaffer, K. R. (1980). *Sex-role issues in mental health*. Reading, MA: Addison-Wesley.

Scharf, R. S. (1992). *Applying career development theory to counseling*. Pacific Grove, CA: Brooks/Cole.

Schein, E. H. (1971). The individual, the organization, and the career. *Journal of Applied Behavioral Science, 7*, 401–426.

——— (1978). *Career dynamics: Matching individual and organizational needs*. Reading, MA: Addison-Wesley.

Schlossberg, N. K. (1984). *Counseling adults in transition*. New York: Springer.

Schlossberg, N. K., & Pietrofesa, J. J. (1978). Perspectives on counseling bias: Implications for counselor education. In L. S. Hansen & R. S. Rapoza (Eds.), *Career development and counseling of women*. Springfield, IL: Charles C Thomas.

Schnall, M. (1981). *Limits: A search for new values*. New York: Clarkson N. Potter.

Schuetz, J. L. (1974). *Career training center for the handicapped*. Bakersfield, CA: Kern High School District.

Schutz, R. A., & Blocher, D. H. (1961). Self-satisfaction and level of occupational choice. *Personnel and Guidance Journal, 39*, 595–598.

Schwab, R. L. (1981). The relationship of role conflict, role ambiguity, teacher background variables and perceived burnout among teachers. (Doctoral dissertation, University of Connecticut, 1980.) *Dissertation Abstracts International, 41*(9), 3823-A.

Schwartz, E. (1989). The mental status examination. In R. J. Craig (Ed.), *Clinical and diagnostic interviewing.* Northvale, NJ: Aronson.

Scott, K. P. (1981). Whatever happened to Jane and Dick? Sexism in texts re-examined. *Peabody Journal of Education,* April, 135–140.

Seavy, C. A., Katz, P. A., & Zalk, S. R. (1975). Baby X: The effect of gender labels in adult responses to infants. *Sex Roles, 1,* 103–110.

Serbin, L. A., & O'Leary, K. O. (1975). How nursery schools teach girls to shut up. *Psychology Today,* 8.

Sharf, R. S. (1984). Vocational information-seeking behavior: Another view. *Vocational Guidance Quarterly, 33*(2), 120–129.

Shaw, E. A. (1973). Behavior modification and the interview. *Journal of College Placement, 34,* 52–57.

Shaw, M. C. (1968). Underachievement: Useful construct or misleading illusion. *Psychology in the Schools, 5,* 41–46.

Sheehy, G. (1976). *Passages: Predictable crises of adult life.* New York: Dutton.

Shepard, H. A. (1965). Planning for living workshop. Unpublished manuscript. Redondo Beach, CA.

Sheppard, H. L., & Rix, S. E. (1977). *The graying of working America.* New York: Free Press.

Sheridan, J. E., Richards, M. D., & Slocum, J. W. (1975). Comparative analysis of expectance and heuristic models of decision making. *Journal of Applied Psychology, 60,* 311–368.

Shertzer, B., & Stone, S. C. (1976). *Fundamentals of guidance* (3rd ed.). Boston: Houghton Mifflin.

Shirreffs, J. H. (1975). Sex-role stereotyping in elementary school health education textbooks. *Journal of School Health, 45,* 519–523.

Shostak, A. B. (1980). *Blue-collar stress.* Reading, MA: Addison-Wesley.

Simon, S. B., Howe, L. W., & Kirschenbaum, H. (1972). *Value clarification.* New York: Hart.

Sinick, D. (1975). *Counseling older persons: Careers, retirement, dying.* Ann Arbor: ERIC Clearing House on Counseling and Personnel Service, University of Michigan.

———— (1977). *Counseling older persons: Career, retirement, dying.* New York: Human Science Press.

Skovholt, T. M. (1978). Feminism and men's lives. *The Counseling Psychologist, 7*(4), 3–10.

Smith, A., & Chemers, M. (1981). Perception of motivation of economically disadvantaged employees in a work setting. *Journal of Employment Counseling, 18,* 24–33.

Smith, C. K., Smith, W. S., Stroup, K. M., & Ballard, B. W. (1982). *Broadening career options for women.* Ann Arbor: ERIC Counseling and Personnel Services Clearing House, University of Michigan.

Smith, D. (1981, April). The robots (beep, click) are coming. *Pan Am Clipper.* New York: Pan American Airlines.

Smith, E. J. (1983). Issues in racial minorities' career behavior. In W. B. Walsch & J. H. Osipow, *Handbook of vocational psychology* (Vol. 1.) (161–222). Hillsdale, NJ: Erlbaum.

Smith, M. L. (1974). Influence of client sex and ethnic group on counselor judgments. *Journal of Counseling Psychology, 21,* 516–521.

Snodgrass, G. (1975). The individual in the organization and the need for interpersonal competence. Unpublished manuscript, University of California at Los Angeles.

———— (1977). A comparison of student paraprofessional and professional counselor trainees in career counseling with university undergraduate students. Unpublished doctoral dissertation, University of California at Los Angeles.

———— (1979). Relating college to careers: A group for first- and second-year students. *Journal of College Student Personnel, 20,* 278–279.

Snodgrass, G., & Healy, C. C. (1979). Developing a replicable career decision-making counseling procedure. *Journal of Counseling Psychology, 26,* 210–216.

Snodgrass, G., & Wheeler, R. W. (1983). A research-based sequential job interview training model. *Journal of College Student Personnel, 24*(5), 449–454.

Soelberg, P. O. (1967). Unprogrammed decision making. *Industrial Management Review, 8,* 19–29.

Solomon, K. (1982). The masculine gender role: Description. In K. Solomon & N. B. Levy (Eds.), *Men in transition.* New York: Plenum.

Sommers, T., & Shields, L. (1979). The economics of aging homemakers. *Journal of Home Economics, 71*(2), 16–19.

Sonnenfeld, J. A. (Ed.). (1984). *Managing career systems.* Homewood, IL: Richard D. Irwin.

Sorapuru, J., Theodore, R., & Young, W. (1972a). Financial facts of life. In J. E. Bottoms, R. N. Evans, K. B. Hoyt, & J. C. Willers (Eds.), *Career education resource guide.* Morristown, NJ: General Learning Corporation.

———— (1972b). Job hunting. In J. E. Bottoms, R. N. Evans, K. B. Hoyt, and J. C. Willers (Eds.), *Career education resource guide.* Morristown, NJ: General Learning Corporation.

Special Education, Rehabilitation, and Vocational Education. (1970). *Vocational education or special needs.* St. Paul, MN: East Metropolitan Special Education Council (EMSEC).

Spencer, A. L. (1982). *Seasons.* New York: Paulist Press.

Spindler, G. (Ed.). (1955). *Education and culture.* Stanford, CA: Stanford University Press.

Splete, H., & Stewart, A. (1990). *Competency-based career development strategies and the national career development guidelines.* Information Series No. 345. Columbus: ERIC Clearinghouse on Adult, Career, and Vocational Education (ED 327 739).

Splete, H. H., Elliott, B. J., & Borders, L. D. (1985). Computer-assisted career guidance systems and career counseling services. Unpublished manuscript, Oakland University, Adult Career Counseling Center, Rochester, MI.

Spokane, A. (1985). A review of research on person-environment congruence in Holland's theory of careers. *Journal of Vocational Behavior, 26,* 306–343.

Spokane, A. R. (1987). Conceptual and methodological issues on person-environment congruence in Holland's theory of careers. *Journal of Vocational Behavior, 31,* 217–221.

———— (1991). *Career intervention.* Englewood Cliffs, NJ: Prentice-Hall.

Spokane, A. R., & Oliver, L. W. (1983). The outcomes of vocational intervention. In S. H. Osipow & W. B. Walsh (Eds.), *Handbook of Vocational Psychology,* Vol. 2. Hillsdale, NJ: Erlbaum.

St. Peter, S. (1979). Jack went up the hill . . . but where was Jill? *Psychology of Women Quarterly, 4,* 256–260.

Steidl, R. (1972). Financial facts of life. In J. E. Bottoms, R. N. Evans, K. B. Hoyt, & J. C. Willers (Eds.), *Career education resource guide.* Morristown, NJ: General Learning Corporation.

Stein, P. J., & Hoffman, S. (1978). Sports and male role strain. *Journal of Social Issues, 24,* 136–150.

Stein, T. S. (1982). Men's groups. In K. Solomon & N. B. Levy (Eds.), *Men in Transition,* pp. 275–307. New York: Plenum.

Stephens, E. W. (1970). *Career counseling and placement in higher education: A student personnel function.* Bethelehem, PA: The College Placement Council.

Stephenson, R. R. (1961). Occupational choice as a crystallized self-concept. *Journal of Counseling Psychology, 8,* 211–216.

Stephenson, W. (1949). *Testing school children.* New York: Longmans, Green.

Stintzi, V. L., & Hutcheon, W. R. (1972). We have a counseling problem—can you help us? *The School Counselor, 19,* 329–334.

Stokes, J., Fuehrer, A., & Child, L. (1980). Gender differences in self-disclosure to various target persons. *Journal of Counseling Psychology, 27,* 192–198.

Stollak, G. E. (1969). The experimental effects of training college students as play therapists. In B. G. Guerney, Jr. (Ed.), *Psychotherapeutic agents: New roles for nonprofessionals, parents, and teachers.* New York: Holt, Rinehart & Winston.

Stone, J., & Gregg, C. (1981). Juvenile diabetes and rehabilitation counseling. *Rehabilitation Counseling Bulletin, 24,* 283–291.

Strong, E. K. (1983). *Vocational interest blank for men.* Stanford, CA: Stanford University Press.

Strong, E. K., & Campbell, D. P. (1974). *Strong-Campbell interest inventory.* Stanford, CA: Stanford University Press.

Suchet, M., & Barling, J. (1985). Employed mothers: Interrole conflict, spouse support, and marital functioning. *Journal of Occupational Behavior, 7,* 167–178.

Sue, D. W. (1978). Counseling across cultures. *Personnel and Guidance Journal, 56,* 451.

——— (1981). *Counseling the culturally different.* New York: Wiley.

Sue, D. W., & Sue, D. (1990). *Counseling the culturally different: Theory and practice* (2nd ed.). New York: Wiley.

Sue, S., & Abe, J. (1988). *Predictors of academic achievement among Asian American and White students* (Report No. 88-11). New York: College Entrance Examination Board.

Sue, S., & Okazaki, S. (1990). Asian-American educational achievements: A phenomenon in search of an explanation. *American Psychologist, 45,* (8), 913–920.

Suinn, R. M. (1975). The cardiac stress management program for Type A patients. *Cardiac Rehabilitation, 5,* 13–16.

Super, D. E. (1949). *Appraising vocational fitness.* New York: Harper & Brothers.

——— (1957). *The psychology of careers.* New York: Harper & Row.

——— (1970). *Work values inventory.* Boston: Houghton Mifflin.

——— (1972). Vocational development theory: Persons, positions, and processes. In J. M. Whiteley & A. Resnikoff (Eds.), *Perspectives on vocational development.* Washington, DC: American Personnel and Guidance Association.

——— (1974). *Measuring vocational maturity for counseling and evaluation.* Washington, DC: National Vocational Guidance Association.

——— (1977). Vocational maturity in mid-career. *Vocational Guidance Quarterly, 25,* 297.

——— (1980). A life-span, life-space approach to career development. *Journal of Vocational Behavior, 16,* 282–298.

——— (1984). Career and life development. In D. Brown & L. Brooks (Eds.), *Career choice and development.* San Francisco: Jossey-Bass.

——— (1990). A life-span, life-space approach to career development. In D. Brown & L. Brooks (Eds.), *Career choice and development: Applying contemporary theories to practice,* pp. 197–261. San Francisco: Jossey-Bass.

Super, D. E., & Crites, J. O. (1962). *Appraising vocational fitness by means of psychological tests* (Rev. ed.). New York: Harper & Row.

Super, D. E., & Overstreet, P. L. (1960). *The vocational maturity of ninth grade boys.* New York: Teachers College, Columbia University.

Super, D. E., Starishesky, R., Matlin, N., & Jordaan, J. P. (1963). *Career development: Self-concept theory.* New York: College Entrance Examination Board.

Survey finds "male stronghold" persists in schools. (1979, September 5). *New York Times,* p. A16.

Sweeney, T. J. (1971). *Rural poor students and guidance.* Boston: Houghton Mifflin.

Tanner, J. M. (1972). Sequence, tempo, and individual variation in growth and development of boys and girls aged twelve to sixteen. In J. Kagan & R. Coles (Eds.), *Twelve to sixteen: Early adolescence.* New York: Norton.

Tanney, M. F., & Birk, M. J. (1976). Women counselors for women clients? A review of research. *Journal of Counseling Psychology, 6,* 28–32.

Taylor, R. L. (1990). Black youth: The endangered generation. *Youth and Society, 22*(1), 4–11.

Texas Rehabilitation Commission. (1984). *Eligibility requirements of rehabilitation.* Austin: Texas Rehabilitation Commission.

Thase, M., & Page, R. A. (1977). Modeling of self-disclosure in laboratory and nonlaboratory settings. *Journal of Consulting Psychology, 24,* 35–40.

Thelen, M., Frautsch, N., Roberts, M., Kirkland, K., & Dollinger, S. (1981). Being imitated, conformity, and social influence: An integrative review. *Journal of Research in Personality, 15,* 403–426.

Thomas, A. H., & Stewart, N. R. (1971). Counselor response to female clients with deviate and conforming career goals. *Journal of Counseling Psychology, 18,* 352–357.

Thomas, J. K. (1973). Adolescent endocrinology for counselors of adolescents. *Adolescence, 8,* 395–406.

Thomas, K. R., & Butler, A. J. (1981). Counseling for personal adjustment. In R. M. Parker & C. E. Hansen (Eds.), *Rehabilitation Counseling.* Boston: Allyn & Bacon.

Thomas, L. E. (1972, Sept.). Life planning workshops in community colleges and four-year universities. In D. Aigaki (Chair), *Career development symposium.* Symposium presented at the meeting of the American Psychological Association, Honolulu.

Thomas, T. J., & Waterman, R. H. (1982). *In search of excellence.* New York: Warner Communications.

Thomason, T. C. (1991). Counseling Native Americans: An introduction for non-Native American counselors. *Journal of Counseling & Development. 69,* 321–327.

Thompson, P. H., Kirkham, K. L., & Dixon, J. (1985). Warning: The fast track may be hazardous to organizational health. *Organizational Dynamics, 13,* 21–33.

Thorndike, R. L. (1949). *Personnel selection, tests, and measurement techniques.* New York: Wiley.

Thorndike, R. L., & Hagen, E. (1959). *10,000 careers.* New York: Wiley.

Thurer, S. (1980). Vocational rehabilitation following coronary bypass surgery: The need of counseling the newly well. *Journal of Applied Rehabilitation Counseling, 11,* 98–99.

Tiedeman, D. V. (1968). Can a machine develop a career? A statement about the process of exploration and commitment in career development. *Information system for vocational decisions project report no. 16a.* Cambridge, MA: Graduate School of Education, Harvard University.

Tiedeman, D. V., & Miller-Tiedeman, A. (1977). In "I" power primer: Part one; Structure and its enablement of interaction. *Focus on Guidance, 9*(7), 1–16.

————— (1984). Career decision-making: An individualistic perspective. In D. Brown & L. Brooks (Eds.), *Career choice and development*. San Francisco: Jossey-Bass.

Tiedeman, D. V., & O'Hara, R. P. (1963). *Career development: Choice and adjustment*. Princeton, NJ: College Entrance Examination Board.

Tolbert, E. L. (1974). *Counseling for career development*. Boston: Houghton Mifflin.

Tomasko, R. T. (1987). *Downsizing*. New York: American Management Association.

Tracy, D. M. (1990). Toy-playing behavior, sex role orientation, spatial ability, and science achievement. *Journal of Research in Science Teaching, 27*, 637–649.

Trimble, J. E., & Lafromboise, T. (1985). American Indians and the counseling process: Culture, adaptation, and style. In P. Pedersen, *Handbook of cross-cultural counseling and therapy*, (pp. 125–134). Westport, CT: Greenwood Press.

Troll, L. E. (1975). *Early and middle adulthood*. Monterey, CA: Brooks/Cole.

Troll, L., Israel, J., & Israel, K. (1977). *Looking ahead*. Englewood Cliffs, NJ: Prentice-Hall.

Trower, P., Casey, A., & Dryden, W. (1988). *Cognitive-behavioral counseling in action*. Newbury Park, CA: Sage.

Tyler, L. E. (1961). Research explorations in the realm of choice. *Journal of Counseling Psychology, 8*, 195–202.

————— (1972). Counseling girls and women in the year 2000. In E. Matthews (Ed.), *Counseling girls and women over the life span*. Washington, DC: National Vocational Guidance Association.

UCLA Placement and career planning center. (1980). Los Angeles: University of California at Los Angeles.

Unger, R. K. (1979). "Toward a redefinition of sex and gender." *American Psychologist, 34*, 1085–1094.

U.S. Department of Labor. (1970). *Career thresholds*. Washington, DC: U.S. Government Printing Office.

————— Employment Standards Administration, Women's Bureau. (1974). *The myth and reality*. Washington, DC: U.S. Government Printing Office.

————— (1977). *Dictionary of occupational titles* (4th ed.). Washington, DC: U.S. Government Printing Office.

————— (1978a). *U.S. newsletter*. Washington, DC: U.S. Government Printing Office.

————— Office of the Secretary, Women's Bureau. (1978b). *Women in nontraditional jobs: A program model*. Washington, DC: U.S. Government Printing Office.

————— (1979). *Guide for occupational exploration*. Washington, DC: U.S. Government Printing Office.

————— (1980). *Job options for women in the eighties*. Washington, DC: U.S. Government Printing Office.

————— (1983). *Children of working mothers*. Washington, DC: U.S. Government Printing Office, Bulletin 21, pp. 1–2.

————— (1991a). *Dictionary of occupational titles* (4th ed. revised). Washington, DC: U.S. Government Printing Office.

————— (1991b). *What work requires of school: A SCANS report for AMERICA 2000*. Washington, DC: U.S. Department of Labor.

————— (1992–1993). *Occupational outlook handbook*. Washington, DC: U.S. Government Printing Office.

U.S. Executive Office of the President, Office of Management and Budget. (1972). *Standard industrial classification manual*. Washington, DC: U.S. Government Printing Office.

—— Statistical Policy Division. (1977). *Standard occupational classification manual.* Washington, DC: U.S. Government Printing Office.

U.S. Government Printing Office. (1970). *General aptitude test battery.* Washington, DC: U.S. Government Printing Office.

U.S. House Select Committee on Aging. (1982). *Age discrimination in employment: A growing problem in employment.* Washington, DC: U.S. Government Printing Office.

U.S. Military Enlistment Processing Command. (1978). *Armed Services vocational aptitude test battery.* Washington, DC: United States Military Enlistment Processing Command.

U.S. News and World Report. (1981). *TV's disastrous impact on children.* Jan. 19, p. 43.

Vaillant, G. E. (1977). *Adaptation to life.* Boston: Little, Brown.

Vandergoot, D. (1982). Placement and career development counseling in rehabilitation. In R. M. Parker & C. E. Hansen (Eds.), *Rehabilitation counseling.* Boston: Allyn & Bacon.

Velasquez, J. S., & Lynch, M. M. (1981). Computerized information systems: A practice orientation. Administration in Social Work, 5(3/4), 113–127.

Vetter, B. M. (1989). *Professional women and minorities: A manpower data resource service* (8th Ed.). Washington, DC: Commission on Professionals in Science and Technology.

Vetter, L. (1978). Career development of women. In L. S. Hansen & R. S. Rapoza (Eds.), *Career development and counseling of women.* Springfield, IL: Charles C Thomas.

Vocational biographies. (1985). Sauk Centre, MN: Vocational Biographies.

Vontress, C. E. (1971). *Counseling Negroes.* Boston: Houghton Mifflin.

—— (1979). Cross-cultural counseling: An existential approach. *Personnel and Guidance Journal, 58,* 117–121.

Vorland, A. (1972). Obstacle course. In J. E. Bottoms, R. N. Evans, K. B. Hoyt, and J. C. Willers (Eds.), *Career education resource guide.* Morristown, NJ: General Learning Corporation.

Waggoner, C. (1972). At your leisure. In J. E. Bottoms, R. N. Evans, K. B. Hoyt, and J. C. Willers (Eds.), *Career education resource guide.* Morristown, NJ: General Learning Corporation.

Waldron, I. (1978). The coronary-prone behavior pattern, blood pressure, employment and socioeconomic status in women. *Journal of Psychosomatic Research, 22,* 79–87.

Walker, B. J. (1974). Approaches to job hunting workshops. *Journal of College Placement, 34,* 66–71.

Walker, J. W., & Price, K. F. (1976). Retirement policy information: A system perspective. Personnel Review, *15,* 119–154.

Wall, W. (1984, May). Student values in the workplace. *Bulletin of the American Association of Higher Education,* 2–6.

Walters, L., & Saddlemire, G. (1979). Career planning needs of college freshmen and their perceptions of career planning. *Journal of College Student Personnel, 20,* 224–229.

Walth, D. (1972). Who needs it? In J. E. Bottoms, R. N. Evans, K. B. Hoyt, & J. C. Willers (Eds.), *Career education resource guide.* Morristown, NJ: General Learning Corporation.

Walz, A. (1972). Required courses. In J. E. Bottoms, R. N. Evans, K. B. Hoyt, & J. C. Willers (Eds.), *Career education resource guide.* Morristown, NJ: General Learning Corporation.

Walz, G. R. (1982). The career development diamond: Touching all the bases. In G. R. Walz (Ed.), *Career development in organizations.* Ann Arbor: ERIC Counseling and Personnel Services Clearinghouse, University of Michigan.

Wanous, J. P. (1980). *Organizational entry.* Reading, MA: Addison-Wesley.

Waterman, J. A. (1992). Career and life planning: A personal gyroscope. In J. Kummerow (Ed.), *New directions in career planning and the workplace*, pp. 1–33. Palo Alto, CA: Consulting Psychological Press, Inc.

Weber, M. (1958). *The Protestant ethic and the spirit of capitalism.* New York: Scribner.

——— (1974). *The theory of social and economic organization* (A. M. Henderson & T. Parsons, Trans.). Fair Lawn, NJ: Oxford University Press.

Wedenoja, M. (1981). *Sex equity in guidance and counseling.* Ann Arbor: ERIC Counseling and Personnel Services Clearinghouse, University of Michigan.

Weinrach, S. G. (1984). Determinants of vocational choice: Holland's theory. In D. Brown & L. Brooks (Eds.), *Career choice and development.* San Francisco: Jossey-Bass.

Weissberg, M., Berentsen, M., Cote, A., Cravey, B., & Heath, K. (1982). An assessment of the personal career, and academic needs of undergraduate students. *Journal of College Student Personnel, 23,* 115–122.

Wentling, R. M. (1992). Women in middle management: Their career development and aspirations. *Business Horizons,* Jan.–Feb., 48–54.

White, R. W. (1959). Motivation reconsidered: The concept of competence. *Psychological Review, 66,* 297.

Whyte, W. H., Jr. (1956). *Organization man.* New York: Simon & Schuster.

Wigglesworth, D. C. (1992). Meeting the needs of the multicultural work force. In J. Kummerow (Ed.), *New directions in career planning and the workplace,* pp. 155–167. Palo Alto, CA: Consulting Psychological Press, Inc.

Wilcox-Matthew, L., & Minor, C. W. (1989). The dual career couple: Concerns, benefits, and counseling implications. *Journal of Counseling and Development, 68,* 194–198.

Wiley, M. O., & Maggon, T. M. (1982). Holland high point social types: Is consistency related to persistence and achievement? *Journal of Vocational Behaviors, 20,* 14–21.

Williams, D. A. (1984, Sept. 10). What price day care? *Newsweek,* p. 14.

Williams, R. L. (1971). Abuses and misuses in testing Black children. *The Counseling Psychologist, 2,* 62–73.

Williamson, E. G. (1939). *How to counsel students: A manual of techniques for clinical counselors.* New York: McGraw-Hill.

——— (1949). *Counseling adolescents.* New York: McGraw-Hill.

——— (1965). *Vocational counseling: Some historical, philosophical, and theoretical perspectives.* New York: McGraw-Hill.

Wilson, R. N. (1981). The courage to be leisured. *Social Forces, 60*(2), 282–302.

Winter, J., & Schmidt, J. S. (1974). A replicable career program for junior high. *Vocational Guidance Quarterly, 23*(2), 177–180.

Wolfson, K. T. P. (1972). *Career development of college women.* Unpublished doctoral dissertation. University of Minnesota, Minneapolis.

Wolman, C., & Frank, H. (1975). The solo woman in a professional peer group. *American Journal of Orthopsychiatry, 45,* 164–171.

Wolpe, J. (1958). *Psychotherapy by reciprocal inhibition.* Palo Alto, CA: Stanford University Press.

——— (1973). *The practice of behavior therapy.* New York: Pergamon Press.

Woody, Bette. (1992). *Black women in the workplace.* Westport, CT: Greenwood Press.

Work in America. (1973). Report on the Special Task Force for the Secretary of Health, Education, and Welfare. Cambridge: Massachusetts Institute of Technology Press.

World guide to trade associations. (1985). New York: R. R. Bowker.

Worsnop, R. L. (1987). Part-time work. *Editorial Research Reports, 6,* 3–7.

Wrenn, C. G. (1966). What has happened to vocational counseling in our schools? In H. J. Peters & J. C. Hansen (Eds.), *Vocational guidance and career development.* New York: Macmillan.

—— (1988). The person in career counseling. *The Career Development Quarterly, 36*(4), 337–343.

Wright, B. A. (1983). *Physical disability—A psychological approach* (2nd ed.). New York: Harper & Row.

Wright, G. N. (1980). *Total rehabilitation.* Boston: Little, Brown.

Wulfhurst, A. (1972). From craftsman to factory worker. In J. E. Bottoms, fR. N. Evans, K. B. Hoyt, & J. C. Willers (Eds.), *Career education resource guide.* Morristown, NJ: General Learning Corporation.

Wylie, R. C. (1963). Children's estimates of school work ability. *Journal of Personality, 31,* 203–224.

Yankelovich, D. (1979). Work, values and the new breed. In C. Kerr & J. M. Rosow (Eds.), *Work in America: The decade ahead,* pp. 3–26. New York: Van Nostrand Reinhold.

—— (1981a). *New Rules.* New York: Random House.

—— (1981b). The meaning of work. In J. O'Toole, J. L. Scheiber, & L. C. Wood (Eds.), *Working: Changes and choices* (pp. 33–34). New York: Human Sciences Press.

Yankelovich, D., & Lefkowitz, B. (1982). Work and American expectations. *National Forum, 62*(2), 3–5.

You can do it: A guide for effective job search strategy. (1977). Urbana-Champaign: Office of Career Development and Placement, University of Illinois.

Zaccaria, J. (1970). *Theories of occupational choice and vocational development.* Boston: Houghton Mifflin.

Zajonc, E. (1980). Feeling and thinking: Preferences need no influence. *American Psychologist, 35,* 151–175.

Zanna, M. P., & Pack, S. I. (1975). On the self-fulfilling nature of apparent sex differences in behavior. *Journal of Experimental Social Psychology, 11,* 583–591.

Zenur, T. B., & Schnuelle, L. (1972). *An evaluation of the self-directed search.* Baltimore: Center for Social Organization of Schools, Johns Hopkins University.

Zimbardo, P. G. (1978). *Psychology and life.* Glenview, IL: Scott, Foresman.

Zunker, V. G. (1968). A comparison of the effectiveness of group and individual counseling in an experimental guidance program for vocational rehabilitation. Unpublished manuscript. University of Texas Medical School at Galveston.

—— (1975). Students as paraprofessionals in four-year colleges and universities. *Journal of College Student Personnel, 16,* 282–286.

—— (1987). The life-style and career development standard. *Counselor Education and Supervision, 27,* 110–118.

—— (1990). *Using assessment results in career counseling.* Pacific Grove, CA: Brooks/Cole.

—— (1994). *Using assessment results for career development* (4th ed.). Pacific Grove, CA: Brooks/Cole.

Zunker, V. G., Ask, K. A., Evans, D. A., Kight, L. E., Sunbury, R. V., & Walker, A. E. (1979). Counseling objectives and specific tasks for career decision making. Unpublished manuscript, Southwest Texas State University, San Marcos.

Zunker, V. G., & Brown, W. F. (1966). Comparative effectiveness of student and professional counselors. *Personnel and Guidance Journal, 44,* 738–743.

Zytowski, D. G. (1969). Toward a theory of career development for women. *Personnel and Guidance Journal, 47,* 660–664.

Name Index

Abe, J., 383
Abrego, P. J., 316–318
Adkins, D. C., 11
Adler, A., 65
Agostinelli, J., 347
Aigaki, D. A., 96
Akiskal, H. S., 463
Alexander, L. C., 346
Amatea, E. S., 226
Amos, W. E., 395
Anastasi, A., 11, 24, 137
Anderson, B. E., 20
Anderson, H. D., 32
Anderson, T. B., 30
Arbeiter, S., 18, 310
Arbona, C., 388
Argeropoulous, J., 78
Aronson, E., 78–79
Asch, A., 417
Ask, K. A., 261
Aslanian, C. B., 18, 310, 322
Assouline, M., 48
Astin, A. W., 71
Atkinson, J., 67
Aubrey, R. G., 195
Axelrad, S., 27–29, 61, 187
Axelson, J. A., 385, 388, 389, 390, 393,
    397, 398, 399, 410

Bailey, L. J., 34, 44
Bain, T., 199
Ballard, B. W., 341
Bandura, A., 186, 193
Barcus, F. E., 366
Barfield, R. E., 298

Barling, J., 452
Barokas, J., 188
Barry, J., 351
Basile, S. K., 186
Beck, A. T., 461
Beckett, J. O., 370
Benin, M. H., 347
Bennet, G. K., 140
Bennis, W., 369
Berentsen, M., 241
Beres, J., 78
Berger, F., 240
Bernardo, D. H., 347
Betz, N. E., 55, 56, 341, 342, 343,
    347, 357
Biehler, R. F., 182, 188, 194
Binet, A., 4, 6, 23
Bird, C. P., 297
Birk, J. M., 359, 360
Birney, D., 91, 96
Blake, R., 285
Blau, P. M., 57, 58
Blocher, D., 30, 388
Bloland, P. A., 454
Boles, J., 366
Bolles, R. N., 83, 84, 85, 96–98, 137, 155,
    323, 330, 332, 455
Bolton, B., 416, 417
Bonk, E. C., 5, 6, 13, 15
Borders, L. D., 124
Bordin, E. S., 12, 56, 57
Borman, C. A., 124
Borow, H., 4, 24
Bottoms, J. E., 226
Brainard, P. O., 145
Brammer, L. M., 316–318

Brewer, J. M., 5
Brickell, H. M., 18, 310, 322
Brim, O. G., 323
Brodsky, A., 77
Brolin, D. E., 424, 425
Brooks, L., 26, 32, 36, 54, 55, 62, 439, 441, 482
Brown, D., 26, 32, 36, 54, 55, 62, 311, 383, 439, 441, 482
Brown, W. F., 255, 335
Bryde, J. F., 390, 391
Bryne, E., 19, 20
Burello, L., 481
Burnett, F. E., 160
Burow, H., 4, 24
Burton, M., 332, 334
Butler, A. J., 423

Cabezas, A. Y., 383
Campbell, D. P., 146
Campbell, J. P., 67
Campbell, R. E., 289
Casey, A., 474
Cattel, J., 4, 5, 6, 23, 147
Cautela, J., 474
Cellini, J. V., 289
Cetron, M., 18, 19, 85, 88, 206, 232
Chemers, M., 416
Cherniss, C., 77, 78
Child, L., 367
Chu, L., 383
Chusmir, L. H., 345, 361, 372
Clark, R., 67, 260
Claudy, J. G., 140, 199
Clausen, J. A., 457
Clooney, G. H., 354
Coats, J. F., 22
Cohen, A. R., 22
Cole, M. L., 100
Cole, N. S., 359
Coleman, M. T., 347
Compton, J. W., 124
Cook, D. W., 414
Cooley, W. W., 140, 199
Cooper, J. F., 361
Copeland, L., 456
Corbine, J. L., 390
Corey, G., 473
Cormier, L. S., 445

Cormier, W., 445
Cote, A., 241
Courtland, L., 394
Cowden, P., 314
Cox, A., 445
Cozby, P. C., 445
Craig, R. J., 463
Cramer, S. H., 17, 26, 27, 57, 77, 78, 158, 236, 239, 368, 451, 452
Cravey, B., 241
Crites, J. O., 16, 85, 153, 154, 192, 199, 286, 402
Cronbach, L. J., 11, 138
Cross, E. G., 226
Crystal, J. C., 83, 84, 96–98, 330
Cummings, R., 124
Curnow, T. C., 47

Daniels, J. L., 415
Danish, S. J., 87–88
Darrow, C. N., 321, 367
D'Augelli, A. R., 87–88
Davidson, P. E., 32
Davies, O., 18, 19, 88
Davis, D. A., 29
Davis, F. B., 11
Davis, G., 230, 231
Davis, J., 5
Davis, K., 281, 282
Dawis, R. B., 69–71, 82
Deacon, M., 368
Deckert, P., 348
Delworth, U., 96
Dennis, W., 297
Dewey, C. R., 360, 361
Dewey, J., 5, 23
Diamond, E. E., 143, 358–360
Dickinson, G. L., 449
Dittenhafer, C. A., 162
Dixon, J., 291
Dollinger, S., 186
Dolliver, R. H., 155, 360, 361
Dominick, J. R., 365
Domkowski, D., 247, 251
Dosser, D. A., 373, 377, 378
Doyle, J. A., 365, 366, 370
Doyle, R. E., 462, 470, 471, 474
Drier, H. N., 235
Drucker, P. F., 18, 85, 280, 302

Drummond, R. J., 125
Dryden, W., 474
Dudley, G. A., 40
Dunnette, M. D., 67
Dyal, M. S., 158, 163

Eber, H. W., 147
Eccles, J. S., 349
Edelwich, J., 78
Edward, P. B., 368, 454
Ehrmann, R., 266
Eldridge, N. S., 372
Elkind, D., 187, 193
Elliot, B. J., 124
Elliot, C. W., 6
Ellis, A., 461, 473, 474
Elmslie, S., 42
Emener, W. G., 78
Endicott, F. S., 264, 265
Englander, M. E., 30
Epstein, C. F., 349
Erikson, E. H., 37, 182, 184, 185, 191,
    192, 203, 204, 240, 318, 319, 320,
    337, 342, 344
Etaugh, C., 365
Etringer, B., 372
Ettinger, J. M., 103
Evanoski, P. O., 383
Evans, D. A., 226
Evans, R. N., 261

Fairley, L., 341
Farber, B. A., 78
Fasteau, M. F., 369
Feck, V., 392, 393, 395, 405
Feldman, D. C., 285, 291, 292, 297,
    298, 303
Ference, T. P., 78, 292
Fernandez, J. P., 350, 351
Fernandez, M. S., 383
Ferraro, G. A., 354
Ferree, M. M., 452
Festinger, L., 65, 68
Fielder, H. E., 284
Figler, H. E., 155
Fine, M., 417
Finkleman, J., 68
Fisher, J., 416

Fisher, T. D., 297
Fitzgerald, L. F., 55, 341, 342, 343,
    347, 357
Flanagan, J. C., 140, 199
Flanders, R. B., 14
Forbes, J. D., 390
Form, W. H., 32
Forney, D. S., 78
Foster, R., 433
Fotis, J., 78
Fottler, M. D., 199
Frenza, M., 349
Freud, S., 65
Freudenberger, H. J., 77
Friedeman, J. M., 370
Friedman, M., 369, 370
Frodi, A. M., 371
Frodi, M., 371
Fuehrer, A., 367
Frautsch, N., 186

Gadon, H., 22
Galton, F., 4, 6, 23
Garcia, G., 124
Garland, S. B., 350
Garte, S. H., 78
Gayle, M., 85, 206, 232
Geist, H., 145, 408
Gelatt, H. B., 9, 12, 49–52, 62, 85, 260
Gerstein, M., 188
Ghiselli, E., 26
Gianakos, I., 342
Gibson, R. L., 187
Gilbert, L. A., 357
Ginsburg, S. W., 27–29, 61, 187
Ginzberg, E., 9, 27–29, 61, 187, 342, 343,
    345, 361
Glick, D., 351
Goldberg, H., 369, 377, 378
Goldfried, M. R., 370
Goleman, D., 351
Goodenough, F. L., 11
Gordon, L. V., 150
Gottfredson, L. S., 41–42, 61
Gould, R., 321, 337
Grater, H., 30
Gray, J. L., 282, 283
Green, L. B., 43
Gregg, C., 416

Gribbons, W. D., 199
Grieger, R., 474
Griffith, C. A., 454
Griggs, L., 456
Grossman, G. M., 235
Grubb, W. N., 211, 230, 231
Gruen, W., 318–321, 337
Gruver, C. G., 255
Gulliksen, H., 11
Gustad, J. W., 57, 58
Gysbers, N. C., 229, 424, 425, 439, 449

Hackett, R. D., 55, 56
Hackman, J. R., 73–74
Hagan, N., 29
Hagen, E., 26, 137
Hakel, M. D., 67
Hall, D. T., 279, 286, 288, 290, 292, 300, 304
Hall, G. S., 5, 23
Hall, R. H., 58
Halle, E., 372
Halpern, A., 431
Halpern, T., 445
Hansen, C. E., 417
Hansen, G. R., 358
Hansen, J. C., 393
Hansen, L. S., 207, 212, 226, 342, 347, 450, 473, 477, 478
Hanson, G., 358, 359
Hantover, J. P., 364
Harmon, L. W., 358, 359
Harris, P. R., 313
Harris-Bowlsbey, J., 134
Harrison, J., 369
Harway, M., 341
Havighurst, R. J., 182, 183–184, 187, 192, 204, 319, 337, 343
Healy, C. C., 17, 85, 137, 154, 209–211, 241
Heath, K., 241
Hefferman, J. M., 289
Heifetz, L. J., 78
Heinrich, R. K., 390
Henderson, G., 390
Henderson, P., 229–230
Henri, U., 4, 23
Heppner, P. P., 53
Herma, J. L, 27–29, 61, 187

Herr, E. L., 17, 26, 27, 57, 77, 78, 158, 236, 239, 368, 451, 452
Herring, R. D., 391
Hersen, M., 443, 463, 464
Herzberg, F., 65, 66, 67, 81, 82, 312
Hesketh, B., 42
Hetherington, C., 352, 372
Heyde, M., 199
Higgins, R., 78
Hillerbrand, E., 372
Hinkle, J. E., 91, 96
Hoffman, L. W., 364, 370, 371
Hoffreth, S. L., 452
Holland, J. L., 9, 12, 45–49, 61, 63, 118, 119, 121, 137, 143, 144, 145, 146, 250, 359, 286, 332, 333
Hollender, J., 29
Hopkinson, K., 445
Howard, J. H., 78
Howe, L. W., 333
Hoyt, K. B., 207, 212, 226
Hsia, J., 383
Hudson, J. S., 372
Hudson, L. M., 182, 194
Huffine, C. L., 457
Hull, C. L., 8
Hummel, T., 124
Hwang, C., 371

Inhelder, B., 109
Innis, G., 71–72
Irvin, L. D., 431
Israel, J., 344
Israel, K., 344
Issacson, L. E., 30
Ivancevich, J. M., 76

Jackson, B., 385
Jackson, E. L., 453
Jackson, J. E., 78
Jenkins, C. O., 370
Jepsen, D. A., 383
Jerdee, T. H., 297
Jesser, D. L., 207
Jessor, R., 57, 58
Johansson, C. B., 145, 359
Johnson, A. C., 298
Johnson, G. J., 386
Johnson, R. B., 91, 96

Johnson, R. W., 359
Joiner, J., 416
Jones, L. K., 155, 156
Jones, M., 366
Jordaan, J. P., 31, 153, 186, 198, 199
Jourard, S. M., 373

Kagan, J., 184
Kahn, S. E., 341
Kaldor, W., 42
Kando, T. M., 453
Kaneshige, E., 383
Kanter, R. M., 280, 300, 313
Kapes, J. T., 124
Karasek, R., 79–80
Kasl, S. V., 76
Katz, M., 124, 199, 306
Kaufman, H. G., 311, 312
Kavruck, S., 137
Keating, D. P., 193
Kelly, J. R., 86
Kelly, R. M., 368
Keniston, K., 239, 274
Kesner, P. M., 195
Kibrick, A. K., 30
Kight, L. E., 261
Kindred, L. W., 195
Kingston, J., 22
Kirkham, K. L., 291
Kirkland, K., 186
Kirschenbaum, H., 333
Kirschner, A. M., 366
Klien, E. B., 321, 367
Klinger, G., 347
Knapp, L., 44
Knapp, R. R., 44
Knefelkamp, L. L, 241, 242, 274
Knierim, K. H., 354
Knowdell, R. L., 302, 303
Kohlberg, L., 323, 337, 343
Korman, A. K., 64, 66, 67, 68
Kotter, J. P., 286
Kram, K. E., 285, 297
Kramer, H. C., 240
Krannich, C. R., 271, 272
Krannich, R. L., 271, 272
Krause, E. A., 58
Krausekopf, C. J., 53
Kravitz, R., 78

Kriegel, L., 416
Kronenberger, G. K., 351
Krumboltz, J., 12, 49–52, 62, 186, 260,
    261, 262, 275, 336, 439, 461,
    462, 471
Kuder, G. F., 143, 144
Kumata, R., 383
Kurpius, D., 481

Lafromboise, T., 391
Lamb, M. E., 371
Langelier, R., 348
Larsen, L. F., 193
Lathrop, R., 330
Latona, J. R., 48
Lawler, E. E., 304
Lazarus, A. A., 87, 474
Lazerson, M., 211
Leahy, R. L., 364
Leclair, S. W., 368, 453
Lefkowitz, B., 455
Lein, L., 370
Leland, H., 433
Lenz, J. G., 251
Leslie, G. R., 347
Levering, R., 306
Levi, L., 76
Levine, L., 260
Levinson, D. J., 228, 321, 337, 343,
    344, 367
Levinson, M. H., 321, 337, 367
Lewin, K., 65
Lewis, J. F., 419
Lewis, J. P., 162
Lichtman, M., 188
Likert, R., 284
Lindsey, L. L., 349, 364, 368
Link, R., 431
Liss, M. B., 365
Livson, N., 194, 195
Lofquist, L. H., 69–71, 82
Lohnes, P. R., 199
Looft, W. R., 187
Louis, M. R., 291
Lowell, E. L., 67
Lum, J., 230, 231
Lunneborg, P. W., 43, 44
Luria, A., 364
Lynch, M. M., 125

Maccoby, M., 22, 72–73, 74
Magnuson, J., 77
Malcolm, S. M., 386
Maley, D., 116
Manson, N. M., 391
Marano, C., 349
Marcia, J. E., 240
Marciano, T. D., 363
Marland, S. P., 13
Maslach, C., 78
Maslow, A. A., 43, 65, 66, 81, 82
Matlin, N., 31, 186, 198
Matteson, M. T., 76
Mausner, B., 312
Mayer, H., 369
Maze, M., 124, 125, 134, 135
McBride, M. C., 341
McCartney, K., 452
McClelland, D. C., 65, 67, 68, 81, 84, 312
McCormac, M. E., 127, 129
McDaniels, C., 82, 84, 86, 302, 303, 310,
    368, 454, 455
McGhee, P. E., 365
McGowan, B. G., 301
McGregor, D., 283, 284, 285
Menacker, J., 388, 396, 405
Meir, E. I., 48
Merrill, G. A., 5
Miller, A. W., 58, 59
Miller, C., 394
Miller, D. C., 32
Miller, G., 240
Miller, J., 188
Miller, J. M., 124
Miller, N. B., 391
Miller-Tiedeman, A., 40–41, 85, 193
Minor, C. W., 311, 335, 342, 357, 371,
    378, 383
Mitchell, A. M., 200
Mitchell, L. K., 49–52, 62, 186, 461, 462
Mitchell, M. H., 187, 200
Model, S., 370
Mograine, C., 230
Mogull, R., 387
Moir, E., 174, 175
Money, J., 342
Moore, E. J., 229, 439, 449
Moran, R. T., 313
Morgan, L. A., 348
Morrow, P. C., 303

Moskowitz, M., 306
Moss, H. A., 184
Mouton, J., 285
Munsterberg, H., 7
Murata, A., 383
Myers, D. W., 301

Nachmann, B., 56, 57
Nadelson, C., 347
Nadelson, T., 347
Naisbitt, J., 20
Nealer, J. K., 267, 268, 269
Neff, W. S., 415, 457, 460, 461, 472, 474
Nelson, C., 366
Nelson, N., 420
Neugarten, B., 322, 323
Nevo, O., 470
Nichols, J., 369
Nihira, K., 433
Norrell, G., 30

Oetting, E., 394
Ogden, R. F., 19, 20
O'Hara, R. P., 29, 36–41, 58, 59, 85, 146,
    240, 305
Okazaki, S., 383
Oldham, G. R., 73–74
Olmsted, B., 22
Olsen, L. C., 30
Olson, K., 369
O'Neil, J. M., 367, 368, 369, 373
Orzek, A., 352
Osipow, S. H., 27, 29, 34, 44, 48, 56, 57,
    300, 342, 388
Othmer, E., 442, 445, 447, 463
Othmer, S., 442, 445, 447, 463
Otis, A. S., 7
O'Toole, J., 74–75, 84, 314
Overstreet, P. L., 32

Page, R. A., 445
Papalia, A. J., 267–269
Pardine, P., 78
Parker, H. J., 43
Parker, R. M., 418
Parmerlee, J. R., 449
Parnes, H. S., 57, 58
Parrillo, V. N., 390

Parsons, F., 4, 5, 6, 23, 24, 25
Pascarel, E. T., 242
Patterson, W., 370, 371
Peatling, J. H., 40
Peskin, H., 194, 195
Peterson, G. W., 52–55, 124, 251
Peterson, M., 429, 431
Phillips, D. A., 452
Piaget, J., 182, 184, 185, 193, 203, 204
Picchioni, A. P., 5, 6, 13, 15
Pietrofesa, J. J., 388
Pine, G. J., 78–79
Pines, A., 78
Pleck, J. H., 356
Plihal, J., 230, 231
Pollack, E. W., 388, 405
Pollman, A. W., 298
Ponterotto, J. G., 388, 456
Poole, M. E., 354
Porter, T. L., 418
Powell, A., 399
Powell, D. H., 43
Prediger, D. J., 17, 138, 155, 199, 358, 359
Price, K. F., 297
Provenzano, F. J., 364
Pyle, K. R., 125

Quinn, O. H., 209–211

Radin, N., 329, 371
Raffeld, P., 431
Ragheb, M. B., 454
Rapoport, R., 356
Rapoport, R. N., 356
Reardon, R. C., 52–55, 124, 158, 163, 247, 251
Reich, R. B., 312
Reschke, W., 354
Rhodes, S. R., 297
Rich, A. R., 378
Richard, J., 140, 199
Richards, M. D., 289
Richelson, G., 77
Rix, S. E., 303
Roberts, M., 186
Rodriquez, M., 388

Roe, A., 9, 42–45, 56, 61, 62, 119, 121, 146
Roessler, R., 416, 417, 423
Rogers, C. R., 9
Roselle, B., 124
Rosen, B., 297
Rosenberg, M., 71
Rosenblum, M. L., 78
Rosenman, R. H., 369, 370
Rosenthal, R. H., 463
Rosenwasser, S. M., 364, 365, 370, 371
Ross, C. C., 7
Rotter, J. B., 399, 402, 471
Rozecki, T., 481
Rubin, E., 416, 423
Rubin, J. A., 364
Rubin, S. E., 78
Russell, G., 371
Russo, N. F., 368
Rutter, M., 445
Ryan, C. W., 125
Ryan-Jones, R. E., 124

Saddlemire, G., 240
Sadker, D. M., 365
Sadker, M. P., 365
Sagi, A., 371
Salomone, P. R., 49
Sampson, J. P., 52–55, 124, 125, 251
Samuda, R. J., 405
Sanguiliano, I., 343, 344
Sawyer, R. L., 17, 199
Sarason, E. K., 314
Sarason, S. B., 314
Scarr, S., 452
Schaffer, K. R., 354, 364
Schein, E. H., 279, 286, 287, 324, 325, 338
Schertzer, B., 211
Schlossberg, N. K., 322, 337
Schmerbeck, F. A., 18, 310
Schnall, M., 71
Schroeder, A. S., 341
Schroeder, H. E., 378
Schutz, R. A., 30
Schwab, R. L., 78
Schwartz, E., 463
Scott, K. P., 365
Seashore, H. G., 140

Segal, S. J., 56, 57
Shannon, M. D., 125
Sharf, R. S., 26, 159
Shaw, M. C., 68
Shaycroft, J. F., 140, 199
Sheehy, G., 315, 322, 337
Shehan, C. L., 347
Shellhaas, M., 433
Shepard, H. A., 83, 91
Sheppard, H. L., 303
Sheridan, J. E., 289
Shirk, S. R., 364
Shostak, A. B., 76, 77
Simon, S. B., 333
Sinick, D., 304
Skovholt, T. M., 368
Slaney, R. B., 49
Slepitza, R., 241, 242, 274
Slocum, J. W., 289
Smith, A., 416
Smith, A. D., 370
Smith, C. K., 341
Smith, D., 19
Smith, E. J., 384, 385, 388
Smith, W. S., 341
Snodgrass, G., 65, 258, 267
Snyderman, B., 312
Solomon, K., 364, 366, 367, 368, 373
Sonnenfeld, J. A., 286, 297
Sorapuru, J., 226
Sorenson, D. L., 260, 261, 262, 275, 336
Spencer, A. L., 344, 361
Spindler, G., 71
Splete, H. H., 124, 228, 388
Spokane, A. R., 48, 439, 481
Springer, T. P., 124
St. Peter, S., 366
Stadt, R. W., 34, 44
Stanley, J. C., 7
Starishesky, R., 31, 186, 198
Starke, F. A., 282, 283
Steidl, R., 226
Stein, T. S., 379
Stephenson, W., 11, 30
Stevic, R. R., 393
Stewart, A., 228
Stokes, J., 367
Stollak, G. E., 255
Stone, J., 416
Stone, S. C., 211

Stoner, J. A. F., 78, 292
Straus, R., 370
Strong, E. K., 4, 7, 143
Strouf, J., 29
Stroup, K. M., 341
Subick, L. M., 342
Suchet, M., 452
Sue, D. W., 382, 383, 396, 397, 398
Sue, S., 382, 383, 396, 398
Suinn, R. M., 370
Summers, W. C., 453
Sunbury, R. V., 261
Super, D. E., 9, 25, 26, 30–36, 61, 85, 88,
    146, 151, 153, 186, 192, 198, 241,
    342, 361, 294, 295, 296, 299, 322,
    324, 450, 451, 476
Sweeney, T. J., 393
Szeglin, A., 78

Tanner, J. M., 187
Tatro, C., 366
Tatsuoka, M. M., 147
Taylor, R. L., 386
Terenzi, P. T., 242
Termen, L. M., 7
Terzi, K. A., 22, 72–73, 74
Thase, M., 445
Thelen, M., 186
Theordore, R., 226
Theorell, T., 79–80
Thomas, J. K., 195
Thomas, K. R., 390
Thomas, L. E., 91, 96
Thomas, T. J., 306
Thomason, T. C., 391
Thompson, P. H., 291
Thorndike, R. L., 11, 26, 137
Thurer, S., 416
Tiedeman, D. V., 9, 12, 29, 30, 36–41, 61,
    85, 146, 193, 240, 305
Tolbert, E. L., 3, 236
Tomasko, R. T., 300, 302, 312
Tracy, D. M., 365
Trimble, J. E., 391
Troll, L., 344
Troll, L. E., 318, 320, 321, 323
Trower, P., 474
Tse, F. W., 383
Turner, S. M., 443, 463, 464

Tyler, L. E., 155

Unger, R. K., 342

Vaillant, G. E., 319, 337
Vandergoot, D., 158
Vega, M., 399
Velasquez, J. S., 125
Vetter, B. M., 386
Vontress, C. E., 385, 386, 396, 405

Waldron, I., 369, 370
Walker, A. E., 417
Walker, J. W., 261, 297
Wall, W., 71
Wallace-Schultzman, F., 78
Walters, L., 240
Walz, A., 224
Walz, G. R., 302, 303
Wanous, J. P., 286, 289, 290
Warren, E. K., 78, 292
Waterman, J. A., 305, 310
Weber, M., 72, 282
Wedemeyer, R., 332, 334
Wedenoja, M., 342
Weinrach, S. G., 49
Weissberg, M., 241
Wentling, R. M., 341, 350
Wesman, A. G., 140
Wheeler, R. W., 267
White, R. W., 65, 181
Wiggens, T. T., 78

Wigglesworth, D. C., 313, 314
Wiinamaki, M. K., 498
Wilcox, R. S., 57, 58
Wilcox-Matthew, L., 342, 357, 371, 378
Willers, J. C., 226
Williams, D. A., 351
Williams, R. L., 405
Williamson, E. G., 6, 9, 26
Wilson, R. N., 86
Wisock, P., 474
Wolfson, K. T. P., 343
Wolpe, J., 370, 377
Woody, B., 386, 387
Worsnop, R. L., 20
Wrenn, C. G., 41
Wright, B. A., 415
Wright, G. N., 415
Wundt, W., 4, 7, 23

Yankelovich, D., 72, 73, 75–76, 82,
    369, 455
Yee, H. I., 383
Yerkes, R., 4, 7
Young, W., 226

Zaccaria, J., 26, 44
Zajonc, E., 53
Zimbardo, P. G., 315
Zunker, V. G., 12, 89–90, 137, 155, 157,
    158, 163, 255, 256, 479
Zytowski, D. G., 343, 345, 361

Subject Index

AAMD Adaptive Behavior Scale, 433
Adult Basic Learning Examination (ABLE), 407
Adult Career Concerns Inventory, 155
Adults:
  biosocial, career, and family dimensions, 324, 325
  career development, 285–298, 318–323
  career transition, 310–315
  counseling components for, 325–336
  developmental stages, 318–323
  and "empty nest" syndrome, 315
  and experiential view, 323
  and late career, 296–298
  and menopause, 315
  and mid-career change, 292–296
  and obsolescence, 312
  as unfulfilled worker, 314
  and vocational maturity, 295–296
Advisory Committee, 160–161
African Americans, 385–388
African American college students, 385
African American workers, 386
Alternative work patterns, 21, 22
American College Testing Program (ACT), 137
  World-of-Work Map, 120
Americans with Disabilities Act (ADA), 412–414
Apprenticeship, 235
  information, 168
  training, 235
Aptitude tests, 138–141
Armed Forces information, 167
Armed Services Vocational Aptitude Battery (ASVAB), 141

Asian Americans, 383–385
Assessment:
  achievement 141–143
  aptitude, 138–141
  career maturity, 153–155
  interest, 143–146
  personality, 146–150
  role of, 138
  self-assessment, 155–156
  values, 150–153
Audiovisual materials, 172, 173

Barriers to employment (disabled), 415
Basic Occupational Literacy Test, 407
Brainard Occupational Preference Inventory, 145
Bureaucratic organization, 282
Burnout, 77–79

California Occupational Preference Survey, 408
California Test of Personality, 148
Campbell Interest and Skill Survey (CISS), 146
Campbell Organizational Survey, 153
Career, defined, 3
Career Assessment Inventory, 145
Career Beliefs Inventory, 154
Career choice, 85, 86
Career clusters, 115–120
  Holland Occupational Classification System (HOC), 117–118
  ladder approach, 117
  occupations, by products, 116

Career clusters (*continued*)
purpose of, 115
two-dimensional, 119–120
USOE, 117
Career development, 27–42, 285–294,
318–323
guidelines for counselors, 500–502
guidelines, implementation of, 228–229
in organizations, 285–294
stages, 181–190, 191–197
theories, 27–42, 54–56, 342
of women, 342–345
Career Development Inventory, 153
Career education, 13
collaboration, 208
criticism and defense, 211
defined, 207
in elementary school, 208–209
future skills, 232–234
future trends, 206
in high school, 210, 211
infusion, 208
in junior high school, 209, 210
modules, 208–211
in postsecondary schools, 247
Career guidance, defined, 3
Career guidance, for:
adults, 298, 303, 316, 325–328
elementary schools, 190–191, 208–209
ethnic groups, 384–392
junior high schools, 197–198, 209
senior high schools, 202, 203, 210
persons with disabilities, 418, 420–423,
425–428
postsecondary institutions, 244–246,
247
men, 373–380
women, 352–358
Career information, components,
164–170
Career life planning, dimensions of, 84,
86–88, 99
Career maturity, 32–35
Career Maturity Inventory, 154
Career pattern study, 32
Career patterns:
of men, 31
of women, 32
Career-planning resources, 170
Career Resource Centers, 158–176

Career Resource Centers (*continued*)
components of, 163–174
floor plans, 266, 267
in industry, 174–175
objective development, 161, 162
purpose of, 159
Chicago Nonverbal Examination, 408
Classification systems:
cluster, 115–120
by industry, 114, 115
occupational groups, 116, 487–490
two-dimensional, 119–120
Cognitive-developmental model of career
development, 241, 242
Cognitive dissonance theory, 68
Cognitive information processing, 52–54
Cognitive Vocational Maturity Test, 154
College, and career choice and
development, 242, 243
Colleges, sources of information,
127–129, 166
Colorado Career Information System
127, 128
Comprehensive school-guidance
programs, 229, 230
Computer programs, 126–129
Career Information Delivery Systems
(CIDS), 127–129
Colorado Career Information System,
127, 128
DISCOVER, 128–133
Guidance Information System, 129
selection of, 134, 135
Systems of Interactive Guidance and
Information (SIGI), 129
Continuing education, 165, 167, 169
Cooperative education programs,
498–500
Counselor bias, 357, 358
Cultural differences:
of African Americans, 385–388
of Asian Americans, 383–385
assessment of, 405–408
and barriers to employment, 394
counseling strategies for, 395–400
of Hispanic Americans, 388–389
of Native Americans, 389–392
prevocational training program for,
400–402
of rural poor, 393–394

Cultural differences (*continued*)
  of urban poor, 392, 393
Curricular Career Information System
  (CCIS), 247–251, 490–497

Decentralization organizational structure,
  283
Decision making, 171, 259–263
  models, 259
  objectives, 262
  strategies, 259–263
  tasks, 262
Development (*see also* Career
  development theories):
  adult models, 285, 318
  early childhood, 42–44, 181–190
  stages of, 182–185, 285–298,
    318–323
Dictionary of Occupational Titles (DOT),
  102–110
  digit code for revised 4th edition, 106
  editions, 103–104
  4th edition revised, 105–108
  supplement to 4th edition, 110–114
  use of, 108–109
Differential Aptitude Test, 140
Disabilities:
  assessment instruments for, 428–434
  and barriers, 415
  and career education, 424
  case study, 420–424
  defined, 411
  and group counseling sequence,
    425–428
  private rehabilitation agencies for,
    419–420
  special problems and needs, 414–418
  state rehabilitation agencies for, 418,
    419, 420–424
DISCOVER, 128–133
Dual roles, 347-348, 378

Early childhood development, 42–44,
  181–190
Educational information, 165–168
Edwards Personal Preference Schedule
  (EPPS), 148
Employee assistance programs, 301

Employment
  barriers to, 415
  outlook for, 127–129, 165
  skills needed for, 232–234
"Empty nest" syndrome, 315
Endicott Report, 264
Equal Opportunity Employment Act, 346
Escala de Inteligencia Wechsler para Ninos,
  407
Ethnic groups, 383–392
EXTERN program, 263

Federal acts, 8
File, resource-persons, 170
Filing systems:
  CCIS, 250–251
  HOC, 117–118
  DOT, 105–108
Films, 172, 173
Financial aid information, 170
First National Conference on Vocational
  Guidance, 6
Flanagan Aptitude Classification Tests, 140
Follow-up, 273-274
Future jobs, 18–22
Future organizations, 299, 300
Future perspectives of current industries,
  18–23

Geist Picture Interest Inventory, 408
Gender bias, 358–360
Gender-role development, 342, 358,
  363–366
General Aptitude Test Battery, 139, 140,
  406
Girls:
  gender bias of interest inventories,
    358–360
  role models for, 227
Group counseling:
  examples of, 91–96, 260–263, 402–404,
    425–428
Guidance, defined, 3
Guidance Information System, 129
Guide for Occupational Exploration,
  110–114
  description of, 110–111
  use of, 112–114

Guidelines, for counselors, 500–502
Guilford-Zimmerman Temperament Survey, 148

Hispanic Americans, 388–389
Holland Occupational Classification System, 117–118
Horizontal mobility, 323

Industries, future perspectives, 18–23
Information, career, 127–129, 163–174
   films on, 172
   industrial classification, 487–490
   systems of, 115–120
Integration, academic and vocational education, 230
Interests, assessment of, 143–146
International job market, 272–273
Internship, 263
Interviews:
   assessment of, 439, 440
   case studies, 468–482
   for career counseling, 440–441, 468–481
   to establish rapport, 441–443
   and ethnic minorities, 455–456
   and faulty cognitions, 461–463, 470–471
   for life roles, 441, 450–455, 476–478
   and observation, 443–444
   and self-disclosure, 444–445
   skills training, 267–269
   and staying on track, 447, 448
   for work maladjustment, 457–461, 471–473
Inventories (see Assessment)

Jobs:
   defined, 3
   simulation of, 172
Job experience kit, 172
Job-hunting map, quick, 97
Job-hunting skills, 171, 172
Job information (*see* Career information)
Job placement (*see* Placement)

Kuder Occupational Interest Survey, 144

Labor force:
   employment outlook for, 102, 114, 127–129
   statistics on, 114
   women in, 114
Late career, 296–298
Leadership styles in organizations, 284, 285
Learning theory approaches to career development, 58, 59
Leisure counseling, 86, 331
Life planning:
   concepts, 84
   life/work, 86–88
   workshops for, 91
Life roles:
   citizen, 454–455
   homemaker, 452–453
   leisure, 453–454
   worker, 450–452
Life stages, 181–190, 191–197
Lifestyle:
   dimensions of orientation, 88–90
   indentification, 333–334
Line/staff organizational structure, 283

Matrix organizational structure, 283, 284
Maturity, career, 32–35, 154
Measurement movement, 7,8
Mechanistic organizational structure, 282–283
Men:
   and achievement, 368
   and competition, 369
   counseling components for, 373–380
   counseling needs, 366–373
   and divorce, 371
   and dual-careers, 378
   and fear of femininity, 367
   gender-role development, 363–366
   househusbands, 371
   parental influence on, 364
   and restrictive emotionality, 368, 369
   school influence on, 365, 366
   and self-destructive behavior, 369
Mentors, 285, 350
Metroplex model, 256, 258, 259
Micro-Tower, 428, 429
Mid-life crisis, 315, 316

Military Career Guide, 109
Minnesota Counseling Inventory, 149
Minority groups (*see* Cultural differences)
Minority identity model, 397
Modules:
   career education, 208–211
   Curricular Career Information System,
     247–251
Myers-Briggs Type Indicator, 149

National career development guidelines
   for counselors, 500–502
National Career Development Training
   Institute, 229
National Occupational Information
   Coordinating Committee (NOICC),
   14, 15, 127, 188–190, 197, 201,
   212–226, 243–246
Native Americans, 389–392
Need to achieve theory, 67
Needs approach to career development,
   42–45
Needs, hierarchy of, 66
New Mexico Career Education Test, 154
Non-Sexist Vocational Card Sort, 360
Nonverbal Aptitude Test Battery, 406

Obsolescence, 312
Occupational classification systems, 114,
   116, 117, 119
Occupational descriptions, 164, 165
Occupations, defined, 3
Occupational Outlook Handbook (OOH),
   114, 115
OCC-U-SORT, 156
Ohio Vocational Interest Survey, 144
On-the-job training, 168, 235, 263, 264
Organic organizational structures,
   283–284
Organizations:
   defined, 281
   downsizing, 312
   evaluation of, 304–307
   forecast for changes, 299, 300
   informal, 281
   leadership styles of, 284–285
   socialization of, 281
   structure of, 282–284

Outplacement counseling, 301–303

Paraprofessionals, 251–257
Personality assessment, 146–150
Placement:
   center plans, 266, 267
   colleges, 264–266
   computer-assisted, 273
   concept of, 236
   follow-up, 273
   functions of, 236
   for senior high school, 236
   state employment agencies, 236, 237
Prevocational training, 400–402
Professionalism, 15
Psychoanalytical theory of career
   development, 56, 57
Psychometric movement (*see*
   Measurement movement)

Quick job-hunting map, 97

Rehabilitation counseling, 418, 420–423,
   425–428
Relational Counseling, 398, 399
Resource-persons file, 170
Résumé, strategies for, 269–272
Retirement counseling 303, 304
Robots in the work force, 19, 20
Roe's classification system, 119–120
Role models:
   for ethnic groups, 398
   for girls, 227
   for women, 345

Salience Inventory, The, 155
SCANS, 232
Self-concept development, 186, 187, 417
Self-directed search (SDS), 144
Simulation:
   of job, 172
   kit, 172
Sixteen Personality Factor Questionnaire
   (16PF), 149
Skill identification, 332
Social and Prevocational Information
   Battery, 431–432

Socialization process, 281
Social-learning theory, 49–52
Sociological approach to career
    development, 57–58
Special populations (*see* Disabilities,
    Ethnic groups, Men, and Women)
Specific Aptitude Test Batteries, 407
Stages of human development:
    Erikson, 185
    Havighurst, 183–184
    Levinson and associates, 321, 337,
        343, 344
    Piaget, 184
*Standard Occupational Classification
    Manual*, 487–490
Standards of work, 80, 81
Stereotypes:
    of men, 363–366
    of women, 342, 358, 363–366
Strategies, for:
    adults, 325–336
    career-development guidelines,
        228
    decision-making, 259–263
    ethnic groups, 383–392
    men, 373–380
    prevocational program, 400–402
    women, 352–357
Strong Interest Inventory, 145
Survey of Interpersonal Values, 152
Survey of Personal Values, 152
System of Interactive Guidance and
    Information (SIGI), 129

"Tech-Prep" programs, 231, 232
Temperament and Values Inventory,
    149
Test de Aptitud Diferencial, 408
Testing movement, 10–12
Tests of General Ability, 407
Title VII, 346
Title IX, 346
Training:
    on-the-job, 168, 235, 263, 264
    prevocational, 400–402
Trait-and-factor theory, 25–27
Two-dimensional classifications:
    ACT system, 120
    Roe's system, 43

Two-factor theory of work motivation, 66
Typology, 45–49

Universities, sources of information,
    127–129, 163–174
Urban poor, 392, 393
USOE Classification system, 117

VALPAR, 429–431
Values:
    assessment of, 150–153
    DISCOVER, 128–133
    SIGI, 129
    study of, 152
Values Scale, The, 152
Vocation, defined, 3
Vocational education:
    school information, 166, 167
    "Tech-Prep" programs, 231, 232
    trends, 230–231

Wide Range Interest and Opinion Test, 146
Women:
    career development, 342–345
    counseling bias, 357–360
    counseling components, 352–357
    counseling needs, 345–352
    dual roles, 347–348
    gender bias of interest inventories,
        358–360
    and mentors, 350
    role models for, 345
Work:
    adjustment, 69–71
    alternative work patterns, 21, 22
    burnout, 77–79
    commitment to, 73–74
    ethic, 72–76
    in future, 18–22
    healthful, 79–80
    maladjustment to, 457–461, 471–474
    motivation for, 64
    quality of, 80
    standards of, 80–81
    and stress, 76–77
    and values, 71–72
Work Environment Preference Schedule, 151

Work experienced-based programs, 263–264
Work-role projections:
  Antisocial career client, 458
  Borderline career client, 458
  Depressed career client, 459
  Narcissistic career client, 459

Work-role projections (*continued*)
  Obsessive-compulsive career client, 459
  Schizoid career client, 458
Work Values Inventory, 151
Worker functions, 485–487
World-of-Work Map, 120

TO THE OWNER OF THIS BOOK:

I hope that you have enjoyed *Career Counseling: Applied Concepts of Life Planning*, Fourth Edition, as much as I have enjoyed writing it. I'd like to know as much about your experiences with the book as you care to offer. Only through your comments and the comments of others can I learn how to make *Career Counseling* a better book for future readers.

School and address: _____

Department: _____

Instructor's name: _____

1. What did you like most about *Career Counseling*, Fourth Edition? _____

_____

_____

2. What did you like least about the book? _____

_____

_____

3. Were all of the chapters of the book assigned for you to read? _____

   If not, which ones weren't? _____

4. Did you use *Using Assessment Results for Career Development?* _____

5. If so, please tell us what component was most useful: _____

_____

_____

6. In the space below, or on a separate sheet of paper, please let us know any other comments about the book you'd like to make. (For example, were any chapters *or* concepts particularly difficult?) We'd be delighted to hear from you!

_____

_____

_____

_____

_____

_____

Optional:

Your name: _____ Date: _____

May Brooks/Cole quote you either in promotion for *Career Counseling: Applied Concepts of Life Planning*, Fourth Edition, or in future publishing ventures?

Yes: _____ No: _____

Sincerely,

Vernon G. Zunker